Essentials of CASH MANAGEMENT

SEVENTH EDITION

Association for
Financial Professionals

7315 Wisconsin Avenue
Suite 600 West
Bethesda, MD 20814
Phone: 301.907.2862
Fax: 301.907.2864
AFP@AFPonline.org
www.AFPonline.org

Association for Financial Professionals

Essentials of Cash Management, Seventh Edition.
Copyright 2001 by the Association for Financial Professionals (AFP).
ALL RIGHTS RESERVED.

First Printing, September 2001

This publication is designed to provide authoritative information in regard to the subject matter covered. It is not intended to offer accounting, legal or other professional advice. If accounting, legal, or other professional advice is required, or if expert assistance is needed, the services of a competent professional person should be sought.

No part of this book may be reproduced in any form, by photostat, microfilm, xerography, or any other means, or incorporated into any information retrieval system, electronic or mechanical, without prior written permission of the copyright owner when the intent of reproduction is for internal or external distribution to avoid multiple purchases of the document. Each violation of this copyright may result in pursuit by the copyright owners of financial penalties of up to $100,000 per violation.

All inquiries should be addressed to:

Communications Department
Association for Financial Professionals
7315 Wisconsin Avenue, Suite 600 West
Bethesda, MD 20814
Phone: 301.907.2862   Fax: 301.907.2864   E-mail: AFP@AFPonline.org
Web: www.AFPonline.org

ISBN 0-9708725-2-6

Table of Contents

1 The Role of Cash Management in Corporate Finance — 1

Exhibit 1.1	Operating Cycle	3
Exhibit 1.2	General Cash Flow Timeline	4
Exhibit 1.3	A Company's Cash Flow Timeline	6
Exhibit 1.4	Typical Organization of the Financial Function	11

2 Financial Accounting and Related Concepts — 25

Exhibit 2.1	Sample Year-End Income Statement	31
Exhibit 2.2	Sample Balance Sheets (Current and Prior Year)	33
Exhibit 2.3	Sample Statement of Cash Flows	34
Exhibit 2.4	Debt vs. Equity	39
Exhibit 2.5a	Effect of Leverage with 10% Increase in Revenue	40
Exhibit 2.5b	Effect of Leverage with 10% Decrease in Revenue	40
Exhibit 2.6	Use of Financial Ratios and Performance Measurements	49
Exhibit 2.7	Summary of Ratio Analysis	50

3 The U.S. Financial Environment — 53

Exhibit 3.1	Federal Reserve Check Processing Regions	67

4 U.S. Payments System — 83

Exhibit 4.1	Sample Business Check	86
Exhibit 4.2	Steps in Check Clearing System	88
Exhibit 4.3	Example of Ledger and Deposit Deadlines	92
Exhibit 4.4	Sample of Availability Schedule	93
Exhibit 4.5	Application of Availability Schedule	94
Exhibit 4.6	ACH Transaction Participants	97
Exhibit 4.7	An ACH Credit Transaction (Direct Deposit of Payroll)	99
Exhibit 4.8	Mechanics of a Wire Transfer	104

5 Credits and Accounts Receivable Management — 111

Exhibit 5.1	Annualized Cost of Trade Credit	126
Exhibit 5.2	Days' Sales Outstanding (DSO) Calculation	128
Exhibit 5.3	Example of an Aging Schedule	128
Exhibit 5.4	Example of a Receivables Balance Pattern	129

6 Collections — 139

Exhibit 6.1	Components of Collection Flat	142
Exhibit 6.2	Example of Float Measurement	144
Exhibit 6.3	Collection Systems	147
Exhibit 6.4	Example of Wholesale Lockbox Processing	154
Exhibit 6.5	Example of Lockbox Cost/Benefit Analysis	157

7 Cash Concentration — 171

Exhibit 7.1	Example of a Cash Concentration System	175
Exhibit 7.2	Example of EDT Clearing	177

8 Accounts Payable and Disbursements — 187

Exhibit 8.1	Components of Disbursement Float	191

9 Electronic Commerce — 207

Exhibit 9.1	Relationship Between EDI, FEDI and EFT	213
Exhibit 9.2	Steps Performed by EDI Software	221

10 Information Management and Technology — 233

Exhibit 10.1	Treasury Workstation Modules	245

11 Forecasting Cash Flows — 257

Exhibit 11.1	Receipts and Disbursements Forecast	264
Exhibit 11.2	Forecasting Using the Distribution Method	265
Exhibit 11.3	Forecasting with Pro Forma Financial Statements (Percentage-of-Sales Method)	266, 267, 268
Exhibit 11.4	Forecast with Simple Moving Averages and Exponential Smoothing	269

12 Investing — 273

Exhibit 12.1	Short-Term Credit Rating Agencies	281
Exhibit 12.2	Example of Taxable Equivalent Yield Calculation	296
Exhibit 12.3	Summary of Yield-Quoting Conventions	299
Exhibit 12.4	Example of T-Bill Purchase Price Calculation	301
Exhibit 12.5	Example of T-Bill Discount Rate Calculation	301
Exhibit 12.6	Example of Money Market Yield Calculation	302
Exhibit 12.7	Example of Bond Equivalent Yield Calculations	302
Exhibit 12.8	Example of Commercial Paper Nominal Yield Calculation	303
Exhibit 12.9	Summary of Yield Equations	304
Exhibit 12.10	Normal Yield Curve	305
Exhibit 12.11	Inverted Yield Curve	305

13 Borrowing — 309

Exhibit 13.1	Effective Annual Borrowing Rate Calculation Example	318
Exhibit 13.2	Commercial Paper Issuance Process	319
Exhibit 13.3	Effective Cost for Commercial Paper Calculation Example	321

14 Financial Risk Management — 333

Exhibit 14.1a	Forward Contract — Long Position	341
Exhibit 14.1b	Forward Contract — Short Position	341
Exhibit 14.2	A Swap Between X and Y	345
Exhibit 14.3a	Payoff From a Long (Buy) Call	347
Exhibit 14.3b	Payoff From a Long (Buy) Put	347

15 International Treasury Management — 355

Exhibit 15.1	Hierarchy of International Trade Payment Methods	370
Exhibit 15.2	Illustration of a Documentary Collection	373
Exhibit 15.3	Illustration of a Letter of Credit Transaction (Time Draft)	374
Exhibit 15.4	Illustration of Multilateral Netting	379
Exhibit 15.5	Illustration of Re-Invoicing	381

16 Relationship Management — 387

Exhibit 16.1	Earning Credit Average Calculation Example	400
Exhibit 16.2	Collected Balances Required Calculation	401

Glossary — 407

Answers — 495

Index — 547

Editor's Acknowledgments

The planning and writing of this text has been a challenging and rewarding process, and there have been many individuals who contributed their efforts to its completion. This project would not have been possible without the funding and support of the Association for Financial Professionals (AFP), headed by James Kaitz, President and CEO. In particular, I would like to thank Rori Ferensic, AFP's Director of Certification, for selecting, encouraging and managing the *Essentials of Cash Management* Body of Knowledge Committee. I also want to thank Lucretia Boyer, AFP's Director of Publications, who was in charge of the final editing and publication process.

The CCM Body of Knowledge Committee was a group of dedicated volunteers who shared both their experience and insights to ensure that this version of *Essentials* was both up-to-date and easy to understand. As chair of the committee, Mary Adams, CCM, Senior Vice President, JP Morgan Chase, kept us all in line and personally reviewed all the chapters. The other committee members included: Drew Boatner, CCM, Vice President, AmSouth Bank; Barbara Doyne, CCM, Vice President, SEI Investments; Woody Johnson, CCM, Vice President, Firstar Bank; Mark Krawczyk, CCM, Assistant Treasurer, University of Michigan; Terry Maness, Ph.D., CCM, Dean, Hankamer School of Business, Baylor University; James McCoy, CCM, Client Sales Executive, Electronic Data Systems; and Dennis Reedy, CCM, Director, Treasury Operations, Indiana University.

I am also grateful to the AFP CCM Review Course faculty for their valuable comments and suggestions for improving the text. I would especially like to recognize Michele Allman-Ward, CCM, CertCM, President, Allman-Ward Associates, for her comments and review of the International Treasury Management chapter, Gregory V. Kitter, President, VSG Consulting, for his help on the Investments chapter; Joesph Tinucci, CCM, Assistant Director of Asset Management, University of Colorado, for his comments and review of both the Electronic Commerce and Information Systems chapters; and David Wikoff, Ph.D., CCM, CertCM, President, End Results, Inc., for his support and encouragement on this entire project. The other faculty members, who also provided many valuable insights and comments, include: Mark Krawczyk, CCM, Assistant Treasurer, University of Michigan; Jeffrey Lewis, CCM, President, Lewis & Company; George Shilling, CCM, President, Shilling and Associates; James Washam, Ph.D., CCM, Chair, Accounting, Finance and Law, Associate Professor of Finance, Arkansas State University; Peggy Weber, CCM, CPA, University of Texas, Austin; Debra Yaley, CCM, President, LessonWise; and John Zietlow, Ph.D., CCM, Professor of Business, Mount Vernon Nazarene College.

Others who contributed to this text include James Sagner, Principal, Sagner and Marks, who helped in the initial development of the chapter outlines; Ruth Andersen, Partner, EDI Partners, who helped with the E-commerce chapter; the AFP Research department, which verified facts and information sources; Arlene Chapman, CCM, AFP's Vice President of Government Relations and Technical Services, who reviewed materials related to electronic commerce, financial EDI and current legislation and regulations; Amy Prytula, who managed the financial editing; and Ann Williams, who managed the design and layout.

Finally, I would like to thank Betsy and the rest of my family for their understanding and support, especially when this project had me spending many days away from home and many nights in my office rather than being with them.

D.J. Masson, President
The Resource Alliance

About the Editor

DUBOS J. MASSON, Ph.D., CCM, CertCM

D.J. Masson is President of The Resource Alliance, a training/consulting firm specializing in treasury management, electronic commerce, sales management, and business process redesign. He is a frequent worldwide conference speaker on treasury and electronic commerce topics and is author of AFP's ***Treasurer's Handbook of Financial Management*** and co-editor of ***Essentials of Cash Management, 5th Edition.*** Dr. Masson has an M.B.A. and Ph.D. in finance from Indiana University, is a Certified Cash Manager and holds the International Cash Management Certification (CertCM) from the Association of Corporate Treasurers in the United Kingdom.

CHAPTER 1

The Role of Cash Management in Corporate Finance

Overview

This chapter establishes the basis for the development of cash management as a separate discipline within a company's financial organization. It also describes how cash management has evolved as a subset of overall treasury management in response to changes in financial practices and institutional arrangements in the United States. This chapter introduces a number of terms and concepts that will be developed in more detail later in this book.

Learning Objectives

Upon completion of this chapter and the related study questions, the reader should know:

- The objectives of cash management
- How cash management supports major corporate financial objectives
- The major functions of cash management within the treasury function
- The place of cash management in the corporate financial organization
- The historical evolution of cash management in the United States

Key Concepts

- A company's operating cycle
- The cash flow timeline
- Float
- The major objectives of corporate finance and cash management
- The evolution of cash management

Outline

I. **The Overall Corporate Objective**

II. **Cash Management Objectives and the Cash Flow Timeline**
   A. Cash Management Objectives
   B. The Operating Cycle and the Cash Flow Timeline
   C. Cash Flows
   D. Cash Flow Timeline and Float
   E. Tools of Cash Management

III. **The Finance Function and Financial Decisions**
   A. The Finance Function
   B. Corporate Financial Decisions

IV. **Financial Organization**
   A. Financial Organizational Structure
   B. Key Roles and Responsibilities

V. **The Role of the Cash Manager**
   A. Cash Management
   B. Reporting Relationships
   C. Coordination with Other Internal Functions

VI. **Development of Cash Management in the United States**
   A. The 1940s and 1950s
   B. The 1960s
   C. The 1970s
   D. The 1980s
   E. The 1990s

VII. **Current Treasury Environment**
   A. Quality Management
   B. Reorganization of Treasury Operations
   C. Technology Issues
   D. Globalization

VIII. **Future Financial Trends**

I. The Overall Corporate Objective

In the classic financial management theory viewpoint, a company's primary objective is to maximize shareholder value. Shareholders invest in a company to earn a total return that exceeds that which is available from similar investment alternatives. The efficient management of a company's resources and operations will generate profits that enhance its value to shareholders. Finance and treasury departments ensure timely provision of the cash resources necessary for sustaining a company's ongoing activities. Finance and treasury activities are extremely important aspects of corporate management and are essential to the attainment of a company's overall objectives.

II. Cash Management Objectives and the Cash Flow Timeline

Managing cash is an integral part of a company's overall operations. Cash is required to sustain the operating cycle and cash managers ensure that a company's operating cycle, as shown in Exhibit 1.1, is adequately financed. Therefore, the objectives of cash management are closely related to the management of the operating cycle.

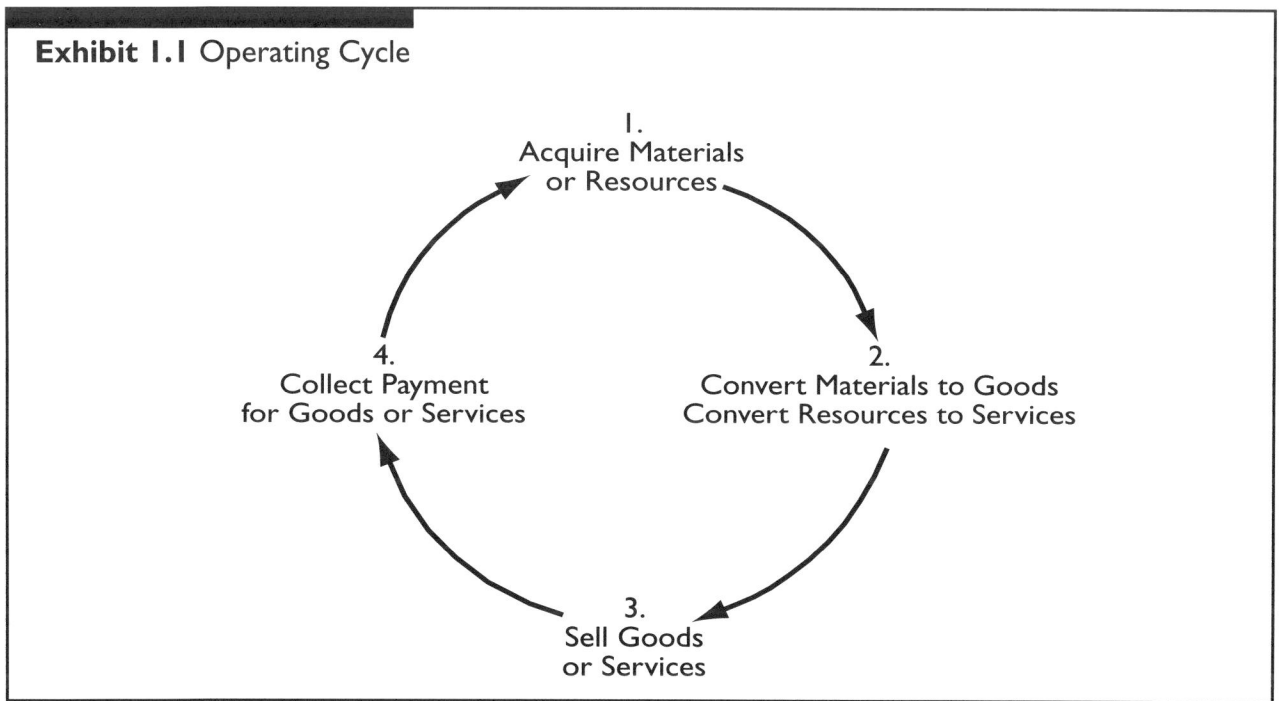

Exhibit 1.1 Operating Cycle

1. Acquire Materials or Resources
2. Convert Materials to Goods / Convert Resources to Services
3. Sell Goods or Services
4. Collect Payment for Goods or Services

A. Cash Management Objectives

The primary objective of cash management is to utilize cash as efficiently as possible in a manner consistent with a company's overall strategic objectives.

Major objectives of cash management include:

1. **Maintaining Liquidity** — Liquidity refers to a company's ability to meet current and future financial obligations in a timely and cost-effective manner.

2. **Optimizing Cash Resources** — Cash managers establish systems that reduce holdings of non-earning cash balances to minimum levels while still providing adequate liquidity. Any excess cash balances are either invested to generate additional income or used to reduce interest expense through the repayment of debt.

3. **Financing** — Cash managers assist in obtaining both short- and long-term borrowed funds in a timely manner and at an acceptable cost. These credit facilities are used to fund a company's cash shortages.

4. **Managing Risk** — Cash managers help in the monitoring and controlling of a company's exposure to interest rate, foreign exchange and other financial risks.

5. **Coordinating Financial Functions** — Cash managers help ensure that managers in other areas of the company understand and implement policies that are consistent with cash management objectives.

B. The Operating Cycle and the Cash Flow Timeline

The operating cycle consists of the day-to-day activities pertaining to the acquisition of materials and/or resources, their transformation into saleable goods, their marketing and the ensuing collection of revenues. From a cash manager's perspective, this basic operating cycle translates into a general cash flow timeline as outlined in Exhibit 1.2. The cash inflows and outflows that occur along the cash flow timeline are rarely for the same amount, nor do they occur at the same time. Given the imbalance and uncertainty of cash inflows and outflows, the challenge for cash management is to ensure that sufficient levels of cash are available at all phases of the cycle.

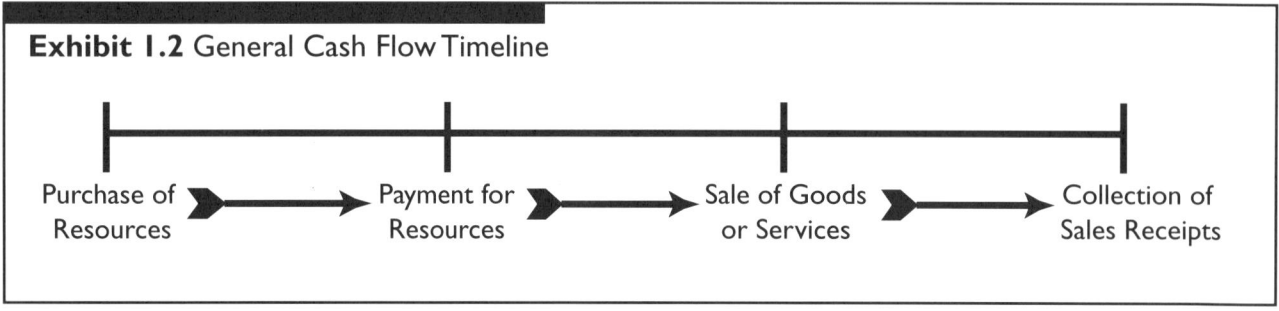

Exhibit 1.2 General Cash Flow Timeline

Purchase of Resources → Payment for Resources → Sale of Goods or Services → Collection of Sales Receipts

C. Cash Flows

There are three types of cash flows that cash managers must consider:

1. **Cash Inflows** — These are funds collected from customers, obtained from financial sources such as lenders or received from other payors.

2. **Concentration and Liquidity Management Flows** — These include internal transfers among operating units of a company and between various bank accounts owned by a company. The objective of funds concentration is to systematically create a pool (or pools) of liquid reserves held as cash or invested in cash equivalents.

3. **Cash Outflows** — These are funds disbursed from liquid reserves to vendors, employees, lenders, shareholders and other payees of the company.

D. Cash Flow Timeline and Float

The cash flow timeline comprises the total time interval from the time resources are purchased at the beginning of a company's operating cycle until the time payment is received for goods or services at the end of a company's operating cycle.

Float is a term that refers to the time interval, or delay, between the start and completion of a specific phase or process that occurs along the cash flow timeline. Despite the introduction of new technologies like the Internet and automated treasury systems, most business-to-business (B2B) transactions in the United States utilize mailed invoices and payment by a check in the mail. The delays inherent in this type of paper-based system result in many types of float that a company must manage. These are illustrated in the detailed cash flow timeline in Exhibit 1.3 on page 6.

Different float terms may refer to the same (or similar) time intervals, but their usage varies depending upon whether or not the time period covered is viewed from the perspective of the receiving party (payee) or the sending party (payor). For example, consider the terms collection float and disbursement float when a check is sent in payment of an invoice:

1. **Receiving Party's (Payee's) Perspective** — Collection float represents the delay between the time a check is mailed and the time the receiving party (payee) receives available funds in their account.

2. **Sending Party's (Payor's) Perspective** — Disbursement float represents the delay between the time the check is mailed and the time the funds are debited from the sending party's (payor's) account.

Chapter 1 • The Role of Cash Management in Corporate Finance

Exhibit 1.3 A Company's Cash Flow Timeline

The following are specific types of float that are important to the cash manager:

3. **Invoicing Float** — This represents the delay between the purchase of goods or services and the receipt of an invoice by the payor.

4. **Payment Float** — This represents the delay between the receipt of an invoice by the payor, including the credit period and the time the payor's account is debited for the funds sent in payment of the invoice.

A company typically benefits from shortening all types of float associated with cash inflows and lengthening all types of float associated with cash outflows. In principle this is true except that companies generally do not extend disbursement float to the point of jeopardizing their vendor relationships. Also, other priorities such as cost containment, customer relationships and access to required management information should be considered in addition to float optimization in developing cash management procedures.

E. Tools of Cash Management

The tools of cash management, as presented in this book, represent various techniques, products and services that enable a cash manager to manage a company's cash resources more effectively. Informed application of these tools can reduce the time and magnitude of unfavorable float that occurs along the cash flow timeline. An efficient cash management system will generally increase a company's overall liquidity. This increased liquidity not only reduces a company's risk of insolvency but will typically increase its overall profitability.

The practice of cash management is focused on resolving cash shortages or surpluses that occur along the cash flow timeline due to the unsynchronized nature of a company's cash inflows and outflows. This includes involvement in the following day-to-day operations:

- *Collection* — Collecting funds from customers or other payors
- *Concentration* — Concentrating funds where they can be most efficiently utilized
- *Disbursement* — Disbursing funds to vendors, employees, investors and other payees
- *Information Management* — Developing and maintaining appropriate information systems to gather and analyze treasury data
- *Forecasting* — Forecasting future cash flows to predict potential shortages or surpluses
- *Investment* — Investing excess cash balances
- *Borrowing* — Borrowing to meet short-term requirements
- *Managing Financial Relationships* — Managing relationships with banks and other financial service providers (FSPs)

III. The Finance Function and Financial Decisions

A company's financial policies and practices significantly influence its cash management operations.

A. The Finance Function

Finance plays a pivotal role in the achievement of a company's major objective of maximizing shareholder value. The principal roles of corporate finance include:

1. **Accounting** — The key role of the accounting function is to record and report a company's financial activity. This includes the recording of its assets, liabilities, equity, revenues, expenses and earnings. Most financial statements that are provided to third parties are prepared in accordance with generally accepted accounting principles (GAAP) as formulated by the Financial Accounting Standards Board (FASB), the organization that oversees U.S. accounting standards. A company may also develop various internal financial reports to assist management with the ongoing operation and control of its business.

    The Financial Accounting Foundation (FAF) is responsible for selecting members, providing funds and exercising general oversight for the Governmental Accounting Standards Board (GASB) and the FASB. The GASB establishes standards for state and local governments as well as state universities and other state-affiliated agencies, while the FASB establishes standards of financial accounting and reporting for all for-profit entities.

2. **Funding** — The funding function involves raising capital to finance a company's operations and capital projects.

3. **Capital Budgeting** — The capital budgeting function involves:
    - Evaluating quantitatively alternative projects in which a company could invest its capital resources. Quantitative factors include costs, profits and cash flows.
    - Estimating the economic return of projects in relation to one another and in relation to the company's cost of capital.
    - Evaluating qualitative factors of projects. Qualitative factors include such things as how a project fits into a company's core strategy and whether it is an activity in which a company would have a competitive advantage.

4. **Financial Risk Management** — The management of financial risk due to changing currency exchange, commodity prices and interest rates is a key element in the finance function of a company.

B. Corporate Financial Decisions

Important financial decisions a company must make include the following:

1. **Capital Structure** — A company must decide on a desired capital structure, including the relative proportions of debt and equity funding. The optimum mix of debt and equity financing can vary greatly from one company or industry to another.

2. **Investment Decisions** — Companies have limited financial and management resources. Therefore, they must decide what projects are appropriate and how much to invest in them. Such analysis involves estimating both the risks and returns of a given project.

   Investment decisions also encompass divestiture decisions such as the sale of a division or subsidiary, or the discontinuance of a product line because the company's capital resources can be more effectively deployed elsewhere.

3. **Financing Decisions** — A company must weigh several interrelated factors when deciding to raise additional debt or equity to finance its needs. For example, a company's capacity to raise different types of capital is influenced by its perceived risk profile, which in turn is influenced by its existing capital structure. Also, a company's projected risk profile based upon a proposed debt or equity offering can influence its ability to market such an offering.

4. **Dividend Decisions** — A company must decide how much of its earnings to distribute as cash dividends to stockholders and how much to retain and re-invest in its operations. This decision is sometimes guided by shareholder expectations, which vary widely and may be dependent on a company's industry or stage of development. Dividend decisions and payouts may also be restricted by covenants contained in a company's debt agreements.

IV. Financial Organization

The structure of a company's financial organization should facilitate the achievement of its overall objectives. Financial organizational structures vary significantly from company to company and industry to industry.

A. Financial Organizational Structure

In a large company, the treasurer and the controller typically report to the chief financial officer (CFO). Some companies have a flatter organizational structure in which all of the following functions report directly to the CFO:

- Treasury
- Accounting
- Information systems
- Audit
- Strategic planning
- Financial analysis

Exhibit 1.4 illustrates how the cash manager may fit into the financial organization of a large company.

B. Key Roles and Responsibilities

The financial function is generally divided into the following roles and responsibilities:

1. **Chief Financial Officer** — The CFO is normally a member of the executive management team, reporting to the chief executive officer (CEO). In a large company, the CFO usually oversees both domestic and international treasury and accounting functions and plays an important strategic planning role as the pivotal person in the capital budgeting and investment decision-making process. Selecting and rejecting investment projects is one of the ways a company implements its strategic plan. Final decisions on building a plant, buying or selling a subsidiary or closing down a product line are typically the responsibility of the CEO or the board of directors. However, the CFO plays a central role in presenting and quantifying decision alternatives and measuring the financial results of those decisions once they are implemented.

2. **Treasurer** — The treasurer is usually responsible for arranging external financing, managing relationships with banks and other financial institutions and overseeing day-to-day liquidity management. The international functions of treasury may be part of the treasurer's duties or may be under a separate international treasurer. Other functions for which the treasurer may be responsible include risk

Exhibit 1.4 Typical Organization of the Financial Function

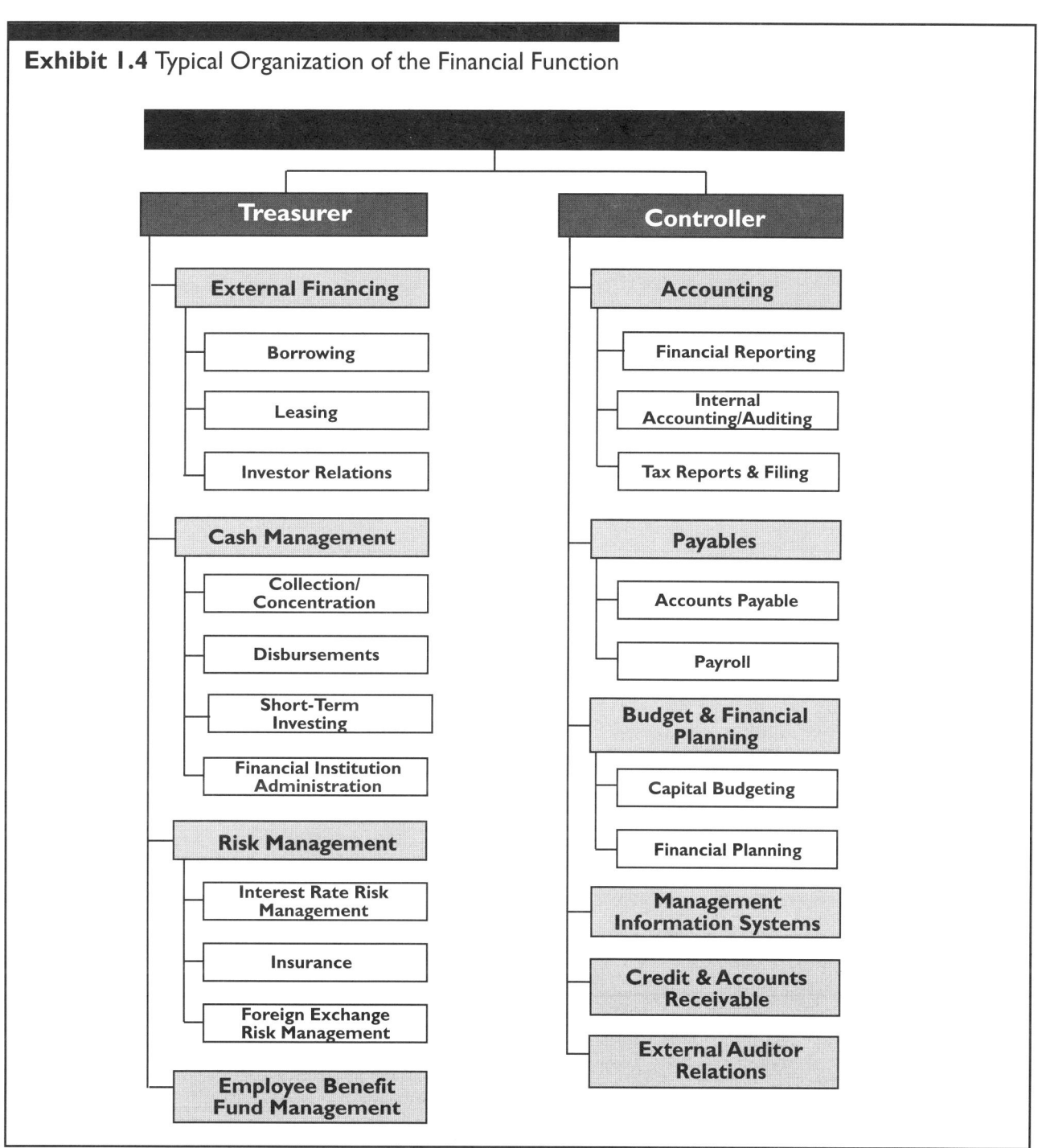

management, managing dividend disbursement, insurance and pension assets. In a large company, some of these responsibilities may be delegated to an assistant treasurer or treasury manager. As is mentioned below, the cash management function is generally part of the treasurer's oversight responsibility.

3. **Cash Manager** — The cash manager, who generally reports to the treasurer or assistant treasurer, is part of treasury and is concerned primarily with the management of day-to-day cash flows and banking relationships, as detailed in the

following section. In a smaller company, these functions may be handled by accounting personnel.

4. **Controller** — The controller is normally responsible for accounts payable, internal accounting, preparation of financial statements, internal auditing, coordination with external auditors, preparation of budgets, tax filings and monitoring budgeted capital expenditures. In some companies the Management Information Systems department and Credit department also report to the controller, whereas in other companies they report to the treasurer.

5. **Internal Auditor** — The internal auditor is responsible for determining that controls and operating procedures are in place to protect a company from losses caused by inefficiency, inaccuracy or fraud. The internal auditor typically reports directly to the board of directors, but in some companies may report to the CEO or CFO.

6. **Credit Manager** — The credit manager is responsible for preserving and collecting accounts receivable, setting corporate credit policies, approving the extension of credit terms to customers and establishing information systems to monitor accounts receivable. The credit manager generally reports to either the controller or treasurer, but in some companies may be part of the sales function.

7. **Accounts Payable Manager** — The accounts payable manager is responsible for determining the proper payments to be made to suppliers for the company. This process generally involves examining incoming invoices, matching the invoices to approved purchase orders and receiving advices and maintaining lists of authorized vendors. The results of the accounts payable process are payment vouchers that are usually sent to treasury for generation of payments. The accounts payable manager generally reports to the controller.

V. The Role of the Cash Manager

The functions and reporting relationships of cash managers typically are as follows:

A. Cash Management

The responsibilities of the cash manager within the overall treasury function will vary from company to company and may be divided among several individuals, especially in larger companies. These responsibilities generally include:

1. **Funds Management**
    - Monitoring the daily cash position
    - Controlling cash balances on deposit at financial institutions

- Moving funds from concentration accounts or other accounts to where they are needed
- Monitoring or managing foreign currencies and related accounts

2. **Banking System Administration**
   - Managing bank relationships, including compensation for banking services
   - Conducting analytical reviews and feasibility studies of banking services

3. **Liquidity Management**
   - Short-term borrowing
   - Short-term investing

4. **Forecasting**
   - Projecting future cash shortages and surpluses
   - Monitoring the accuracy of prior projections

5. **Systems Design, Implementation and Evaluation**
   - Analysis, design, implementation and ongoing evaluation of cash management systems

6. **Financial Risk Management**
   - Monitor/manage foreign exchange (FX) risk
   - Monitor/manage interest rate risk
   - Monitor/manage commodity price risk

B. Reporting Relationships

In most companies, the cash manager reports directly or indirectly to the treasurer, who, reports to the CFO. In a small company, the cash manager's job may be a responsibility of the treasurer or assistant treasurer, but in a large company a staff of several people may be devoted to cash management activities.

C. Coordination with Other Internal Functions

Cash management requires teamwork and cooperation with other internal departments of a company. The activities of other departments, such as purchasing, credit management and accounts payable, have a direct impact on the cash management function. Often these departments report to managers outside the treasury area, such as the controller. Therefore, the cash manager must often interact with these departments and assert informal influence to ensure that overall cash management objectives are met. In many companies, information from the cash management function must be integrated with the company's enterprise resource planning (ERP) system. These ERP systems provide companywide management information resources.

VI. Development of Cash Management in the United States

Cash management in the United States has been influenced by particular features of the domestic banking system, mail system and payment conventions. Although these factors are constantly evolving due to changes in legislation, financial trends and technology, the following are some of the historical characteristics that have played a key role in the development of the unique system that has become the current U.S. financial environment:

- Large numbers of banks and other financial institutions
- Limited nationwide branch banking
- Payment of most bills by check
- Extensive use of the mail for payment remittance

Cash management changed a great deal in the past 50 years. Prior to 1940, interest rates were low and corporate treasurers did not have a variety of external investment opportunities. There was more money in the banking system than there was loan demand. Banks funded their loans with interest-free demand deposit accounts (DDAs) and invested the excess in safe, low-yield government securities. Banks competed with each other far less than they do today. Interest rates were capped by law. Banks were highly selective in their corporate lending, motivating treasurers to keep large excess balances to protect credit facilities. The remainder of this section provides an overview of the historical trends that have affected cash management. Many of the topics discussed will be covered in greater detail in subsequent chapters.

A. The 1940s and 1950s

Two events in the 1940s and 1950s were notably important to cash management:

1. **The Lockbox** — A lockbox is a collection system in which a company's customers mail payments to a designated post office box. A third party collects the payments, processes the remittances and deposits the checks directly into the company's

account. RCA was one of the first companies to arrange this type of collection system in 1947. It was designed to accelerate payments from dealers who were borrowing from RCA to finance their inventory of RCA products.

2. **The Accord and the Government Securities Market** — In 1951, the Federal Reserve Board of Governors reached a historic accord with the U.S. Treasury Department. It gave the Federal Reserve (Fed) the right to pursue an independent monetary policy. The Fed subsequently adopted a policy of purchasing only short-term Treasury bills and stopped purchasing longer-term Treasury notes and bonds. The Treasury no longer had the Fed as a captive investor for notes and bonds and had to rely on a competitive market to raise funds. The Fed's removing itself from the long-term side of the Treasury market also meant that interest rates were now determined as a result of competitive market forces rather than by government action. This marked the birth of a huge market of safe, liquid securities with short-, medium- and long-term maturities for companies with excess cash.

B. The 1960s

The decade of the 1960s produced several developments that influenced the evolution of cash management.

1. **Negotiable Bank Certificates of Deposit (CDs)** — By 1960, banks needed to buy funds and compete for deposits to support their growing loan portfolios. In 1961, the Fed authorized banks to issue negotiable certificates of deposit. The introduction of CDs provided a new source of funds for banks and an investment instrument for corporations.

2. **Lockbox Models** — Bank-operated lockboxes became increasingly popular as cash managers became more aware of collection float and its related cost. In the late 1960s, a model was developed for studying mail times between one city and another. The model optimized the location of lockbox sites in relation to the disbursement banks and mail points used by payors.

3. **Diversifying Short-Term Investments** — Interest rates continued to rise in the 1960s. Treasurers diversified from low-yielding, liquid government securities into new instruments such as municipal obligations, banker's acceptances, commercial paper and repurchase agreements.

4. **Managing Bank Balances** — Treasurers managed cash resources more efficiently, reduced idle bank balances and demanded more bank services for balances on deposit. In response, banks expanded their corporate services and developed formal marketing programs.

C. The 1970s

The runaway inflation of the 1970s and high interest rates that continued from the late 1970s into the 1980s elevated the importance of cash management and prompted a great deal of financial innovation.

1. **Remote Disbursement** — Remote disbursement was designed to take advantage of the inaccessibility of certain banks. These banks, generally located in geographically isolated locations, offered significant float gains to companies that used them for check disbursement. The remoteness of these banks created difficulty in physically presenting checks drawn on them in a timely manner. The Federal Reserve was granting credit to the depositing bank before the check could be collected from the remote bank on which it was drawn. The increased use of remote disbursement throughout the 1970s, coupled with the Federal Reserve's concern over float costs and the financial health of banks used for this purpose, led to programs aimed at discouraging this practice.

2. **Controlled Disbursement** — Controlled disbursement was designed to take advantage of the Federal Reserve's presentment schedule. In a number of banks, the final presentment of checks from the Fed was sufficiently early in the day to enable a company to determine its total daily check clearings and fund this amount. The company could then make investment and/or borrowing decisions knowing there would be no additional clearings against the account that day.

3. **Funds Concentration** — The amounts deposited in local banks were reported by the depositing units to third-party service providers. The information was consolidated and relayed to the concentration bank, which created a depository transfer check (DTC) to transfer funds from the local banks into a concentration account. Today, most DTCs have been replaced by electronic depository transfers (EDTs).

4. **Bank Balance Reporting** — Banks began to offer services to gather and store bank balance and transaction information that companies could access directly. Information from multiple banks could be consolidated into a single report.

5. **Transaction Detail and Real-Time Reporting** — Customers began to get detailed transaction information on bank services. Banks offered information such as inbound wire transfer amounts with accompanying reference information during the same working day in which they were received. Methods were developed for customers to initiate funds transfers and other transactions using terminals in their offices.

6. **Electronic Payments** — Electronic payment alternatives began to be developed using the automated clearing house (ACH). The primary applications were direct deposit of payroll and collection of life insurance premiums.

7. **Commercial Paper (CP)** — Large corporations increased their borrowing by issuing short-term promissory notes, known as commercial paper. Issuing CP directly in the money markets was less expensive than borrowing from banks.

D. The 1980s

The 1980s were a decade of deregulation that continued into the 1990s and had a great impact on cash management.

1. **Depository Institutions Deregulation and Monetary Control Act (DIDMCA) (1980)** — Also known as the Monetary Control Act, this was the most comprehensive banking legislation since the 1930s. It paved the way for a number of changes that were destined to have an impact on bank services and prices for years to come. (See Chapter 3, The U.S. Financial Environment.)

2. **Noon Presentment and Payor Bank Services** — In 1983, the Fed implemented a two-step approach to reduce the use of remote disbursement services. The first step was the noon presentment, which accelerated its presentment schedule by making second presentments later in the day as part of the float-reduction program mandated by the Monetary Control Act. The second part was the establishment of payor bank services, which provided participating banks early morning electronic notification of physical presentments to be made later in the day. This allowed the bank's controlled disbursement customer to know as soon as possible all Fed presentments on their accounts.

3. **Electronic Corporate-to-Corporate Payments** — Banks began to promote corporate trade payments through ACH. Companies understood the efficiency of electronic payments, but many were reluctant to give up disbursement float.

4. **Electronic Commerce (E-Commerce) and Electronic Data Interchange (EDI)** — In its broadest context, e-commerce is the application of information and network technology to the conduct of business relationships among trading partners. E-commerce encompasses many types of formats and communications protocols, including traditional EDI and Web-based commerce. EDI is a formalized computer-to-computer communication for routine business transactions in a standard format. Financial e-commerce is e-commerce or EDI related to payments. The introduction of these new technologies caused significant changes in treasury and cash management operations.

5. **Use of Personal Computers (PCs)** — The introduction of the PC led banks and software firms to develop the treasury workstation. Software was developed to retrieve information automatically from banks and compile it into consolidated reports. The electronic spreadsheet replaced the paper spreadsheet.

6. **Integration of International Financial Markets** — Worldwide integration resulted from the global expansion of companies and banks and the development of international financial centers. Computer and communications technology played a crucial role in forging these links, in facilitating the enormous funds flows and in increasing the importance of FX management. The Eurodollar market, developed initially in the 1960s, was based on the accumulation of U.S. dollars on deposit in financial institutions outside the United States. This market broadened into the euro market, part of the worldwide offshore currency market.

7. **Financial Product Innovation** — In the early 1980s, a number of capital market innovations were introduced. These new products included interest rate and currency swaps, futures, options and asset-backed securities.

8. **Bank Creditworthiness** — Several events occurred that raised concerns about the creditworthiness of banks. The Federal Reserve became concerned about the impact that a major bank failure would have on the payments system, especially after the rash of bank and thrift institution failures in the 1980s. Banks shared this concern because of their exposure to interbank settlement risk. Treasurers, who had previously shown little interest, started to scrutinize the financial condition of their banks.

   A key factor in judging a bank's creditworthiness is its level of capital. Concerns about bank failures at the time prompted development of capital adequacy ratios that could be used on a global basis in evaluating a bank's relative financial condition.

9. **Cash Management Ethics** — In the early 1980s, the E.F. Hutton Company was involved in a widely discussed case concerning fair bank compensation. By channeling check deposits from Hutton branches through unsophisticated banks that treated ledger balances as though they were available balances, Hutton was effectively able to borrow interest-free from the banks. This case helped focus attention on the ethical application of cash management practices.

E. The 1990s

Technological and legal trends of the 1980s continued into the 1990s.

1. **Payments System Risk** — Payments system risk became a concern because of the increasing volume of money transfers through Fedwire, the clearing house interbank payments system (CHIPS) and ACH. The Federal Reserve has taken numerous steps to reduce this risk.

2. **Electronic Payment of State and Federal Taxes** — The federal government, most state governments and many local governments began requiring the elec-

tronic payment of sales, withholding, income and other taxes above a certain dollar limit. Electronic filing of tax returns and information was also offered by many government tax authorities.

3. **Interstate Banking** — Government regulations prohibiting interstate banking and branching were gradually being removed. The Interstate Banking and Branching Efficiency Act of 1994 permitted banks to operate fully integrated banking systems nationwide beginning in June 1997.

4. **Derivatives** — Advances in technology and financial theory gave rise to an astounding variety of complex financial instruments known as derivatives (securities whose value is determined by another security, index or financial value). Derivative products allowed corporate treasurers to hedge risks more precisely but may be difficult to analyze and can be extremely volatile.

5. **Technology** — Technological developments such as the Internet extended and enhanced the use of electronic commercial payment and financial information systems. In addition, the use of treasury modules of ERP systems and dedicated treasury systems significantly changed the way treasury was managed.

6. **Security Concerns** — The growing use of telecommunications equipment for transmission of financial transactions, as well as equipment that could copy documents such as checks with unprecedented clarity, necessitated development of safeguards to maintain systems security and to prevent transaction fraud. There are various technological and organizational countermeasures that companies and financial institutions can implement to prevent fraud and electronic defalcations. The development of disaster recovery plans and backup data centers also became a key security concern.

7. **Globalization** — The reduction and removal of tariffs and legal and regulatory impediments to international trade and financial activity have "globalized" finance. Agreements such as the North American Free Trade Act (NAFTA) and the Maastricht Treaty furthered the integration of the world's commercial and financial markets.

8. **Payment Cards** — The use of purchasing cards transformed the way many companies pay for their small-dollar purchases. Miniaturization of electronic components into chips that can store enormous amounts of information also led to the development of smart cards.

9. **Year 2000 (Y2K) Compliance** — Companies and financial institutions expended a tremendous amount of time and resources to ensure that their management information systems were capable of processing dates beyond December 31, 1999. Most software and many hardware systems required significant reprogramming or other modifications to enable recognition of dates in the year 2000 and beyond.

10. **European Economic Union** — The signing of the Maastricht Treaty provided a timetable for the formation of the Economic and Monetary Union (EMU). The EMU has consolidated most European countries into a single economic unit sharing a common currency called the euro.

11. **Emergence of Non-Traditional Financial Service Providers** — Though banks were still the primary source of financial services for companies, many non-bank financial service providers emerged. These include money market broker-dealers, ERP systems, dedicated treasury systems, technology systems for payments and reconciliation and third-party lockbox and payment processing centers.

VII. Current Treasury Environment

The historical factors previously mentioned have played a significant role in shaping and reshaping the corporate financial function. Treasury and cash management operations are undergoing rapid change due to various trends, outlined below.

A. Quality Management

The issue of quality has become an integral part of the overall corporate environment. Treasury departments have not been immune to this trend and are continuously challenged to produce quality results at an acceptable cost and assist other corporate departments in quality management as well.

B. Reorganization of Treasury Operations

As the treasury function has evolved, treasury professionals have continually endeavored to effectively use available resources to attain both financial and overall corporate objectives. A number of developments have prompted a re-examination of how treasury is organized, how it functions and the efficiency with which it operates. In many cases the restructuring of treasury operations has resulted in downsizing. Technological developments allow fewer people to accomplish more. Recasting treasury operations typically involves the following corporate practices:

1. **Re-engineering** — The concept of re-engineering involves a radical redesign of a particular business process with the goal of continuous process improvement. The redesign of treasury operations may include restructuring or eliminating traditional treasury processes.

2. **Benchmarking** — In the process of re-engineering the treasury function, it is valuable to seek out examples of other companies that have successfully redesigned

their operations. The best practice in a given field serves as a benchmark that can be used to compare and evaluate a company's existing process.

3. **Outsourcing** — One possible outcome of re-engineering the treasury operation may be the decision to have an outside provider perform part, or all, of a business function. This is known as outsourcing. For example, a company may decide to outsource its disbursement processing. It sends a data file containing payment information to an outside processor. The processor then initiates the specified payments on the company's behalf, using the designated method of payment (such as check, ACH or wire).

C. Technology Issues

As a result of the replacement of many legacy accounting and application systems for Y2K compliance reasons, many companies now have fully integrated management reporting or ERP systems. These new systems, along with increasing use of the Internet and browser technology for communications and linking of global operations, are transforming the way treasury operates and interacts with other parts of the company. Many companies have also developed extensive disaster recovery plans and set up duplicate remote sites for their critical systems.

D. Globalization

The trends toward globalization are continuing, especially with the establishment of unified currency (the euro) in the European region. Many companies are also establishing either regionalized or centralized global treasury management operations utilizing recently developed treasury software or treasury modules to ERP systems. The area of financial risk management is also becoming more important for both treasurers and cash managers as the number and complexity of derivative risk management vehicles increases. Finally, smaller firms are getting better information and access to FX trading via the Internet, allowing them to reduce their costs of FX and currency hedging.

VIII. Future Financial Trends

The 21st century will see a continuation of certain present trends and the development of new trends resulting from an ever-changing financial environment. Following are some of the possibilities:

- The trend towards segmented banking systems will continue, as specialized banks and financial service providers emerge to target different parts of the market. These segments will be based on size of the company, geographic region or type of industry. This segmentation/specialization trend should also drive improved quality of banks in emerging markets.

- Current legislative initiatives to allow the payment of interest on corporate demand deposits could significantly change many traditional U.S. cash management practices.

- Companies will place increased reliance on non-traditional financial service providers. Banks will continue to be needed for the actual transfer of value from one bank account to another, but many other bank services will shift to third parties.

- The increasing use of technology and communications systems will continue to be a driving force in shaping the future of treasury management in the global economy.

- An increasing number of global companies are utilizing the Internet and intranets to centralize their treasury processes but with decentralized information to/from their foreign operating divisions.

- Treasury will become more of a process management function and less of a production operation as companies increase the trend toward outsourcing.

- As a major clearing point for financial information, treasury will play a more important role in providing and monitoring data security within companies.

Test Your Understanding

These chapter questions are provided to test your understanding of the information in the text and are not examples of CCM examination questions, nor are they in the examination format.

Answers can be found at the back of the book on pages 495-497.

1. What are the major objectives of cash management?
2. Discuss the general types of cash flows that must be managed.
3. Explain the relationship between the operating cycle and the cash flow timeline.
4. What is float?
5. What is the purpose of using cash management tools?
6. Discuss the principal roles of the finance function.
7. What are the important corporate financial decisions?
8. Who are the key players (besides the cash manager) involved in the finance function?
9. Describe the cash management functions and responsibilities.
10. What major disbursement products were introduced in the 1970s?
11. What major piece of banking legislation reshaped cash management in the 1980s?
12. List and discuss the key issues in the current treasury environment.

CHAPTER 2

Financial Accounting and Related Concepts

Overview

This chapter reviews the basic principles of accounting and finance as they apply to cash management.

Learning Objectives

Upon completion of this chapter and the related study questions, the reader should know:

- How cash accounting differs from accrual accounting
- The basic financial statements — the income statement, statement of retained earnings, balance sheet and statement of cash flows
- Working capital and its components
- The basic concepts of finance: interest, the time value of money, liquidity, corporate capital structure, the cost of capital and capital budgeting
- How to calculate basic financial ratios

Key Concepts

- Cash vs. accrual accounting
- Financial statements
- Interest, discounting and the time value of money
- Capital budgeting, equity and debt financing and leverage
- Measuring liquidity, working capital and net working capital
- Basic corporate performance measurement

Outline

I. Accounting Concepts
    A. Accounting Principles
    B. Cash vs. Accrual Accounting
    C. Accounting for Cash and Float
    D. Financial Statements
    E. Auditing and Financial Statement Reliability
    F. Working Capital and Net Working Capital

II. Financial Concepts
    A. Time Value of Money
    B. Discount Rate/Opportunity Cost
    C. Financial Structure and Strategy
    D. Cost of Capital
    E. Capital Budgeting

III. Liquidity and Working Capital Measures and Ratios
    A. Why Liquidity is Needed
    B. Sources of Liquidity
    C. Levels of Liquidity
    D. Working Capital Measures and Ratios

IV. Debt Management and Coverage Ratios
    A. Times Interest Earned (TIE)
    B. Long-Term Debt to Capital
    C. Debt to Tangible Net Worth
    D. Total Liabilities to Total Assets

V. Performance Measurements
    A. Return on Common Equity
    B. Return on Sales
    C. Return on Total Assets
    D. Economic Value Added (EVA)
    E. Other Financial and Performance Measurement Concepts
    F. Use of Financial Ratios and Performance Measures

I. Accounting Concepts

This section describes the basic accounting concepts on which the system of financial reporting and record keeping used in the United States today is based.

A. Accounting Principles

Accounting provides the data necessary for measuring a company's performance and assessing its financial position. The accounting function records a company's assets, liabilities, shareholder equity, revenues and expenses and reports them according to a detailed set of rules called generally accepted accounting principles (GAAP). These principles are developed, agreed upon and published in the form of financial accounting standards (FAS) by the Financial Accounting Standards Board (FASB), an independent, self-regulating organization formed in 1973. Although not a government entity, the FASB wields great authority.

The Financial Accounting Foundation (FAF) is responsible for selecting members, providing funds and exercising general oversight for the Governmental Accounting Standards Board (GASB) and the FASB. The GASB establishes standards for state and local governments as well as state universities and other state-affiliated agencies, while the FASB establishes standards of financial accounting and reporting for all for-profit entities.

The Securities and Exchange Commission (SEC), an independent regulatory agency of the U.S. government, requires companies that issue securities to the public to file financial statements. The SEC enjoys broad powers with respect to prescribing accounting practices and standards for such reports. These are found in its financial reporting releases (FRRs), regulations S–X and decisions on cases that have come before the Commission. Much of the SEC information on specific companies can be obtained through the electronic data gathering archive research (EDGAR) database.

The SEC maintains, however, that the private sector should retain the initiative for establishing and improving accounting standards and it relies on the FASB for this purpose. Financial statements conforming to GAAP are presumed to have the SEC's support. Adherence to GAAP is important because investors, lenders and trade creditors rely on consistent financial information for decisions with regard to investing, lending and provision of credit. Companies enjoy wide latitude in keeping records for their own internal purposes. There are, however, managerial and cost accounting conventions and norms applicable to most industries and most types of commercial and non-commercial establishments.

B. Cash vs. Accrual Accounting

Some companies record their revenues, expenses and earnings strictly on the basis of when cash is received or paid out. This is known as cash accounting. In cash accounting, all accounting entries are directly related to a cash inflow or outflow. Sales are recorded as the cash is received and expenses are recorded as they are paid. Small businesses tend to use the cash accounting approach.

The other primary accounting method is accrual accounting, which recognizes revenues as they are earned and expenses as they are incurred, regardless of when the related cash flows occur. This is the fundamental difference between cash and accrual accounting. With accrual accounting, revenues may be reported but not yet collected and expenses may have been incurred but not yet paid. It is particularly important for the cash manager, who is mainly concerned with cash flows, to understand the distinction between accounting information and cash flows.

The most important accrual accounting concepts include:

1. **Income Recognition** — Revenue is recognized when sales are made. When sales are made on credit, accounts receivable are created on the balance sheet. As an asset account, accounts receivable represents revenues from sales that have been recognized but not yet collected as cash. When funds are collected from the customer, the accounts receivable balance is decreased and the cash balance is increased without any impact on income.

2. **Cost Recognition** — Product costs incurred in a time period prior to the sale are added to the inventory value. They are not treated as expenses when there is a cash expenditure. In order to match revenues and expenses, costs associated with manufacture are recognized as part of the cost of goods sold in the accounting period in which the sale takes place.

3. **Capitalized Assets** — Capitalized assets are expected to have lives greater than one accounting cycle and are not fully expensed in the period in which they are acquired. The assets are carried on the balance sheet at their acquisition cost and depreciated in subsequent periods.

4. **Depreciation and Amortization** — Accounting expense connected with a capitalized asset is recognized by depreciation in the case of fixed assets and amortization in the case of long-term intangible assets. With both depreciation and amortization, the cost of the asset is allocated over its allowable life. Neither depreciation nor amortization measures a decline in the actual value of an asset. Both are non-cash expenses; therefore, the income statement for an accounting period understates the cash flow provided by operations by the amount of depreciation expense and/or amortization taken.

5. **Deferred Taxes** — The difference between the time the applicable tax codes require companies to recognize revenues and expenses and the time they are recognized under accrual accounting results in differences between the cash disbursed for income taxes and the tax provision reported on income statements. This difference is recognized as a deferred tax and appears on the balance sheet. It is one of the reasons that net income differs from cash flow under accrual accounting.

6. **Capital and Dividends** — A number of cash flows, such as capital asset additions, retirements and dividends, are neither income nor expenses. The addition of capital to the company, through the issuance of debt or the sale of common stock, results in a cash inflow but is not income. The cash outflow for the repayment of principal on a debt obligation is not an expense. The payment of cash dividends to shareholders is a distribution of profits, not an expense.

7. **Management Discretion** — A company has some degree of latitude and must exercise judgment on the allocation of expenses and revenues. There is potential for companies to adjust the value of revenues or expenses under the accrual system. Part of the external auditor's role is to render an opinion that revenue and expense recognition conforms to GAAP. (It is permissible for a company to keep its financial records on a cash basis and adjust them to an accrual basis at the end of reporting periods. Larger corporations seldom do this, however and for reporting purposes typically use accrual-based accounting methods exclusively.) Given the leeway allowed in GAAP guidelines, some companies will make end-of-year adjustments called "window dressing" to make the annual statements look better to lenders and shareholders.

C. Accounting for Cash and Float

Cash amounts on a company's books often differ from the company's bank account balances. There are two reasons for this: 1) checks deposited by a company take time to clear (this is known as float and is reflected in the difference between ledger and collected balances at the bank) and 2) payees do not present checks issued by the company immediately.

Sometimes a company's cash account will show a negative balance. One way to avoid this is by combining the cash account with another current asset account, such as marketable securities, that may have sufficient balances to offset the cash account's deficit. As an alternative, a company can report checks issued but not yet presented for payment as a liability, such as "checks payable" or "checks not yet cleared," which will also keep the cash account balance positive. For reporting purposes, some companies reclassify these outstanding checks as liabilities instead of carrying the cash as a credit balance asset.

D. Financial Statements

GAAP requires four statements for reporting financial results: the income statement, the statement of retained earnings, the balance sheet and the statement of cash flows.

1. **Income Statement** — The income statement, or profit and loss statement, is a record of revenues and expenses, as illustrated in Exhibit 2.1. It describes the net change in the amount of shareholder equity resulting from operations over a specified period of time.

   Categories used on the income statement include:
   - *Revenues* — Revenues represent the total or gross amount derived from a company's sale of merchandise or services.
   - *Cost of Goods Sold* — The cost of goods sold represents the expense of providing goods and services for sale. It includes labor and material directly used in manufacturing the product that was sold and indirect, or allocated, manufacturing expenses.
   - *Gross Profit* — Gross profit, sometimes called gross margin, is determined by deducting costs of goods sold from revenues.
   - *Operating Expenses* — Operating expenses, such as selling or administrative expenses, represent general expenses that are incurred in the conduct of the business but are not tied directly to the production of goods and services.
   - *Depreciation* — Depreciation of fixed assets and amortization of intangible assets are typically considered operating expenses, particularly in manufacturing operations. Neither is a cash outlay.
   - *Operating Profit* — Operating profit, also known as operating income, is the profit after deducting the cost of goods sold and operating expenses from revenues. The term is often used interchangeably with earnings before interest and taxes (EBIT).
   - *Other Income/Expenses* — The income statement may include other income and expenses such as interest income and expense, or currency gains or losses. These are income and expenses that arise from non-operating activities.
   - *Net Income* — Net income is operating profit less the cost of debt financing and income taxes incurred during the accounting cycle, adjusted for other income and expenses.

2. **Statement of Retained Earnings** — The statement of retained earnings (bottom of Exhibit 2.1) shows how net income for the period was used. This statement is often included as part of a detailed income statement and includes information on preferred stock dividends, sinking fund payments, common stock dividends and the amount of retained earnings re-invested in the company.

Exhibit 2.1 Sample Year-End Income Statement

Revenues	$ 15,000,000
Less: Cost of Goods Sold	9,200,000
Gross Profit	5,800,000
Less: Operating Expenses	4,000,000
Less: Depreciation	200,000
Operating Profit/EBIT	1,600,000
Less: Interest Expense	300,000
Net Profit Before Taxes	1,300,000
Less Provision for Income Taxes	450,000
Net Income	**$ 850,000**
Earning Available for Common Shareholders	$ 850,000
Less: Common Stock Dividends Paid	250,000
Addition to Retained Earnings	$ 600,000
Earnings per Share (100,000 shares outstanding) $	8.50

Income Statement

	Current Year	Prior Year	Change
Revenue	$ 15,000,000	$ 12,500,000	$ 2,500,000
Less: Cost of Goods Sold	9,200,000	7,400,000	1,800,000
Gross Profit	5,800,000	5,100,000	700,000
Less: Operating Expenses	4,000,000	3,500,000	500,000
Less: Depreciation	200,000	150,000	50,000
Operating Profit/EBIT	1,600,000	1,450,000	150,000
Less: Interest Expense	300,000	245,000	55,000
Net Profit Before Taxes	1,300,000	1,205,000	95,000
Less Provision for Income Taxes	450,000	370,000	80,000
Net Income	$ 850,000	$ 835,000	$ 15,000

Statement of Retained Earnings

	Current Year	Prior Year	Change
Beginning Retained Earnings	$ 3,800,000	$ 3,215,000	$ 585,000
Earnings Available for Common Shareholders	850,000	835,000	15,000
Less: Common Stock Dividends Paid	250,000	250,000	–
Addition to Retained Earnings	600,000	585,000	15,000
Ending Retained Earnings	4,400,000	3,800,000	600,000
Earnings per Share (100,000 shares outstanding) $	8.50	$ 8.35	$ 0.15

3. **Balance Sheet** — A balance sheet, or statement of financial condition, is illustrated in Exhibit 2.2. It is a snapshot of a company's financial condition. It reports, as of a specific date, the following:

   • *Assets* — Assets are the items of value owned by a company. Assets are typically listed at historical cost (not present-day market value), adjusted for depreciation. Assets' depreciated value is shown as their book value. They are usually listed on the balance sheet in order of decreasing liquidity, or convertibility into cash, as follows:

- Current Assets — The basic current assets include cash, marketable securities, accounts receivable and inventories. Current assets are normally converted to cash within one year, or within the operating cycle. Current assets may also include prepaid expenses such as insurance premiums, which are paid in advance.

- Fixed Assets — Fixed assets are a company's investment in property, buildings, machinery and equipment. Fixed assets (also known as capital assets) cannot be turned into cash as readily as current assets.

- Long-Term Assets — Many companies hold long-term assets other than fixed or capital assets. These include investments in long-term debt (bonds) and equity (stocks) in other companies or in its own subsidiaries.

- Intangible Assets — Intangible assets are assets that lack physical substance. Examples are goodwill, trademarks and patents. There is often a high degree of uncertainty concerning the future benefits of intangible assets. They are amortized over their legal or useful life.

- *Liabilities* — Liabilities represent obligations of the firm. They are usually listed on the balance sheet in order of increasing maturity, as follows:

  - Current Liabilities — Current liabilities include obligations such as accounts payable, short-term loans, wages payable, taxes payable and the current portion of long-term debt (all due within one year or within the operating cycle). Accounts payable (also referred to as trade payables) are amounts due to vendors for purchased items. Short-term notes payable are typically short-term bank loans or commercial paper.

  - Long-Term Liabilities — Long-term liabilities are obligations such as term loans, mortgages and bonds due beyond one year or one operating cycle.

- *Equity* — Shareholder equity represents the owners' position in the company. It is the net book value of the company committed by and belonging to the owners in the form of shareholder capital and retained earnings. Retained earnings represent the increase in shareholder equity that can arise from retention of profits in the company.

The following equation always holds true:

Assets = Liabilities + Shareholder Equity

4. **Statement of Cash Flows** — Under accrual accounting, the reporting period when a revenue or expense item is recognized is often different from the reporting period when the corresponding cash transaction takes place. Although the income statement based on accrual accounting is a useful indication of the company's performance, lenders, creditors and investors are concerned with the company's cash flow because cash, not earnings, repays debt, pays bills and pays dividends.

CHAPTER 2 • FINANCIAL ACCOUNTING AND RELATED CONCEPTS

Exhibit 2.2 Sample Balance Sheet Current and Prior Year

ASSETS

	Current Year	Prior Year	Change
Cash	$ 1,500,000	$ 1,000,000	$ 500,000
Short-Term Investments	1,300,000	1,500,000	(200,000)
Accounts Receivable	1,700,000	1,300,000	400,000
Inventory	2,600,000	2,100,000	500,000
Pre-Paid Expenses	900,000	900,000	0
Total Current Assets	8,000,000	6,800,000	1,200,000
Property, Plant & Equipment	7,500,000	6,800,000	700,000
Total Assets	**$15,500,000**	**$13,600,000**	**$1,900,000**

LIABILITIES AND OWNERS' EQUITY

	Current Year	Prior Year	Change
Accounts Payable	$ 1,600,000	$ 1,200,000	$ 400,000
Short-Term Notes Payable	1,800,000	1,300,000	500,000
Total Current Liabilities	3,400,000	2,500,000	900,000
Long-Term Debt	3,900,000	3,500,000	400,000
Total Liabilities	7,300,000	6,000,000	1,300,000
Common Stock at Par Value	200,000	200,000	0
Paid-In Capital	3,600,000	3,600,000	0
Retained Earnings	4,400,000	3,800,000	600,000
Total Equity	8,200,000	7,600,000	600,000
Total Liabilities & Equity	**$15,500,000**	**$13,600,000**	**$1,900,000**

The statement of cash flows provides an indication of the sources of a company's cash flow and how it is being used. The statement of cash flows is divided into three sections — operating, investing and financing activities.

Exhibit 2.3 shows how a statement of cash flows can be derived from information in the income statement and balance sheet.

To calculate cash flow from operating activities, depreciation and any other non-cash charges are added to net income. Then, changes in accounts receivable and payable are added or subtracted, along with changes in other operating accruals. These items represent cash inflows and outflows to the company and must be taken into account when determining cash flows. The total is net cash provided (or used) by operating activities.

Other corporate actions that affect a company's cash flow include:

- Investing activities such as buying and selling plant and equipment and financial instruments
- Financing activities, such as issuing or retiring equity or debt

The statement of cash flows in Exhibit 2.3 shows that the company generated a cash flow from operations of $550,000. Net income provided $850,000 and depreciation was another $200,000, but net changes in balance sheet amounts absorbed $500,000, since inventory and receivables increased by $900,000, while payables increased only $400,000.

Investing activities during the period used $700,000, ($900,000 in capital expenditures offset by a $200,000 decrease in short-term investments).

During the period, the company had a net inflow of $650,000 of cash from financing activities and total cash increased by $500,000.

Exhibit 2.3 Sample Statement of Cash Flows

Cash Flows from Operating Activities		
Net Income		$ 850,000
Adjustments to Reconcile Net Income to Net Cash		
Depreciation	200,000	
Increase in Accounts Receivable	(400,000)	
Increase in Inventories	(500,000)	
Increase in Accounts Payable	400,000	
Net Cash Provided (Used) in Investing Activities		$550,000
Cash Flows from Investing Activities		
Capital Expenditures	(900,000)	
Decrease in Short-Term Investments	200,000	
Net Cash Provided (Used) in Investing Activities		($700,000)
Cash Flows from Financing Activities		
Net Borrowing — Bank Line of Credit Agreement	500,000	
Proceeds from Issuance of Long-Term Debt	400,000	
Dividends Paid	(250,000)	
Net Cash Provided (Used) by Financing Activities		$ 650,000
Net Increase (Decrease) in Cash		
Cash — Beginning of Year	$1,000,000	
Cash — End of Year	1,500,000	
Net Cash Increase (Decrease)		$ 500,000

E. Auditing and Financial Statement Reliability

Practically all businesses that borrow from banks or require credit produce some form of financial statements conforming to generally accepted formats. While the management of a company is always responsible for the financial statements it issues, not all sets of financial statements are considered equally reliable.

Typically, a company either produces its own financial statements or has a certified public accountant (CPA) or CPA firm do it.

These statements can be audited or unaudited. If the statements are audited, a CPA or CPA firm has reviewed them for compliance with GAAP using generally accepted auditing standards (GAAS) as promulgated by the Auditing Standards Board of the American Institute of Certified Public Accountants (AICPA).

Just because a CPA has helped compile a set of financial statements does not mean, however, that the statements have been audited. If audited, a set of financial statements will include an opinion letter that sets forth both the scope of the CPA's review and the extent to which the auditing CPA found that the statements are in material compliance with GAAP.

The auditor can render four types of opinions: unqualified, qualified, disclaimed or adverse.

1. **Unqualified** — In an unqualified opinion, the auditor states that the company's financial statements provide a fair description of the company's financial condition in accordance with GAAP.

2. **Qualified** — In a qualified opinion the auditor notes exceptions concerning compliance with GAAP, such as accuracy of tax liabilities, asset valuation or accounting inconsistencies.

3. **Disclaimed** — In a disclaimed opinion, the auditor states that the information management presented was insufficient to render an opinion.

4. **Adverse** — In an adverse opinion, the auditor states categorically that the financial statements do not fairly present the financial condition and/or operations of the company in conformance with GAAP.

Generally, investors and creditors give audited financial statements with an unqualified opinion more credence than those that are somehow qualified. Audited financial statements, qualified or not, are usually considered more reliable than those merely compiled by a CPA or issued by a company itself. There is also an issue of potential conflict of interest where the external auditor may also be providing consulting services to the same company.

An important item to remember is that even an unqualified audit opinion does not necessarily imply the company in question is in good financial health. The only thing an unqualified audit really says is that the financial statements provide a fair description of the company's financial condition based on information provided to the auditors. The investor or creditor must still carefully analyze the financial information. In addition, as discussed earlier, there is significant leeway in GAAP principles that could result in the statements providing a less than accurate picture of the company's true health. Also, the company's management may deliberately tamper with or withhold important information from the auditors in order to make the company appear better to investors or creditors.

F. Working Capital and Net Working Capital

Working capital refers to the funds in a company's current asset accounts — cash, accounts receivable and inventory. These are the accounts through which cash flows in a company's cash conversion cycle. Net working capital is equal to current assets minus current liabilities such as accounts payable. Net working capital represents a measure of immediate liquidity.

II. Financial Concepts

There are several key financial concepts that cash managers use on a daily basis.

A. Time Value of Money

The time value of money is a fundamental principle of finance. A dollar today is worth more than a dollar tomorrow because a dollar today can be invested to earn a return. Conversely, a dollar tomorrow is worth less than a dollar today because the opportunity to earn interest is foregone. The value of a cash flow at any point in time can be determined by using an appropriate interest rate and the number of time periods involved.

1. **Future Value** — Future value is the value in the future of a sum of money invested today.

    Future Value = Value Today x (1 + Interest Rate)$^{\text{Number of Periods}}$

    or

    $FV = PV \times (1 + i)^n$

Where:
>   FV = Future Value
>   PV = Present Value or Value Today
>   i = Interest Rate
>   n = Number of Periods

The future value of $100 for two periods at 10 percent, compounded annually, is:

$$\text{Future Value} = \$100 \times (1 + .10)^2 = \$100 \times (1 + .10) \times (1 + .10)$$
$$= \$100 \times (1.210) = \$121$$

2. **Present Value** — Present value is today's value of any sum to be received in the future. Present value can be determined by applying an appropriate discount rate to a future cash flow stream. This concept is useful for comparing alternative transactions with cash flows to be received at a future date, or dates, or to determine how much an investor would be willing to pay for an investment that provides a particular future cash flow stream.

For example, assume a company can make an investment that pays $100 at the end of three years. How much is this future payment worth if the appropriate rate of interest is 10 percent? This is determined to be $75.13, as follows:

$$\frac{100}{(1+.10)^3} = \frac{100}{[(1+.10) \times (1+.10) \times (1+.10)]} = \$75.13$$

This equation can also be expressed in the following algebraic format:

$$PV = \frac{FV}{(1+i)^n}$$

Where:
>   PV = Present Value
>   FV = Future Value
>   i = Interest Rate
>   n = Number of Periods

3. **Net Present Value (NPV)** — NPV is a calculation of the value today of cash flows at different points in the future.

The investment and costs associated with the investment are outflows, while returns on the investment are inflows. If the sum of all discounted cash flows (in and out) is positive, then the project or investment has a positive net present value. If the discounted sum is negative, then the project or investment has a negative net present value. If the company were to invest in a project with a positive net present value, then the overall value of the company would increase by the amount of the project's net present value.

Using the information from the previous example, if the company was to pay $70 to purchase the investment that paid $100 in three years, it would have a net present value of $5.13, calculated as follows:

$$\text{NPV} = \text{Present Value of Cash Inflows} - \text{Present Value of Cash Outflows}$$

$$\text{NPV} = \frac{100}{(1.10)^3} - \$70 = \$75.13 - \$70.00 = \$5.13$$

B. Discount Rate/Opportunity Cost

In determining present and future values, the interest rate is generally referred to as the discount rate. The discount rate is also known as the opportunity cost because it represents the return a company would expect to earn on alternative investment opportunities. Companies often use their cost of capital as a discount rate for evaluating their project opportunities. In riskier businesses, companies tend to have higher costs of capital and therefore usually use higher discount rates in evaluating their projects. Evaluating a given project with higher discount rates lowers its net present value because each future cash flow is discounted more deeply.

Companies may use different discount rates for different types of projects. Low-risk, short-term projects may be evaluated using a short-term opportunity cost such as the company's short-term borrowing rate or the return on its short-term investments. High-risk projects are often evaluated using a "risk-adjusted" discount rate that is greater than the company's normal opportunity cost, which factors in the additional risks these projects carry.

C. Financial Structure and Strategy

Financial structure refers to the overall mix of debt vs. equity in the financing of a company, including both short-term and long-term sources of debt. The term capital structure refers to the mix of debt and equity only on the long-term portion of the balance sheet.

1. **Debt and Equity** — Companies rely on two sources of financing:
   - Debt, which can include trade credit, bank loans and other debt instruments, such as commercial paper, notes or bonds
   - Equity, which connotes ownership

Each company must choose its own financial structure, the proportion of debt and equity it uses to finance its activities. The table in Exhibit 2.4 summarizes and compares the characteristics of both types of capital.

Exhibit 2.4 Debt vs. Equity

	Debt	Equity
Types	**Short-Term** Trade credit Bank loans Other loans Commercial paper	
	Long-Term Debentures Notes Bonds Convertible debt securities	Preferred stock Convertible preferred stock Common stock Paid-in capital Retained earnings
Characteristics	Legally binding obligation	Ownership
	No voting rights	Voting rights on common stock
	Requires repayment of principal and interest	Dividends on common stock are optional
	Interest is tax-deductible	Dividends are paid from after-tax profits
	Loan covenants can be restrictive	All cumulative preferred dividends must be paid before dividends paid on common stock

2. **Capitalizing a Company** — To a great extent, capitalizing a company is a market-driven decision. Smaller and startup companies have limited financing alternatives and often rely on the principals involved to supply equity and debt capital. Larger and more-established companies have a greater number of financing alternatives.

   Generally, equity is more expensive than debt because dividends, unlike interest, are not tax-deductible. Also, investors and financial institutions demand higher returns on equity because the risks are perceived as greater and the investor or financial institution has a subordinate claim to debt on a company's assets.

   Other factors that affect a company's debt and equity financing alternatives include industry practice, a company's financial history, earnings variability, capital intensity, barriers to competitive entry and investor predispositions toward risk and reward as demonstrated in the markets for debt and equity.

   Companies have the following incentives to finance with debt:
   - The after-tax cost of debt is typically lower than the after-tax cost of equity because interest is tax-deductible and debt is senior to equity in a company liquidation.

- Existing shareholders often prefer debt because new stock dilutes the proportion of their holdings.

However, companies capitalized through common equity tend to be considered more stable, in part because they are not required to make dividend payments and they do not have to repay debt principal at maturity.

3. **Leverage** — Leverage is the degree to which a company's use of debt or high fixed costs causes earnings to change more rapidly than revenues.

If a company is leveraged with high levels of debt or has high fixed costs (which provide operating, as opposed to financial, leverage), an increase in revenues produces a proportionately greater increase in pre-tax earnings than if the company were not leveraged. Leverage is, however, a two-edged sword. In a leveraged company, a decrease in revenue causes a proportionally greater loss of earnings. If, on the other hand, all costs are variable and the project or company is predominantly financed through equity, the impact of changes in revenues is less pronounced.

The effect of leverage when revenue increases and decreases is illustrated in the following tables in Exhibits 2.5a and 2.5b.

Exhibit 2.5a Effect of Leverage with 10% Increase in Revenue

	Leveraged Company			Unleveraged Company		
	Year 1	Year 2	% Change	Year 1	Year 2	% Change
Revenues	$100,000	$110,000	+10%	$100,000	$110,000	+10%
Fixed Costs	75,000	75,000	0%	70,000	70,000	0%
Variable Costs	5,000	5,500	+10%	10,000	11,000	+10%
EBIT	20,000	29,500		20,000	29,000	
Interest	5,000	5,000		0	0	
Pre-Tax Earnings	$15,000	$24,500	+63.3%	$20,000	$29,000	+45%

Exhibit 2.5b Effect of Leverage with 10% Decrease in Revenue

	Leveraged Company			Unleveraged Company		
	Year 1	Year 2	% Change	Year 1	Year 2	% Change
Revenues	$100,000	$90,000	−10%	$100,000	$90,000	−10%
Fixed Costs	75,000	75,000	0%	70,000	70,000	0%
Variable Costs	5,000	4,500	−10%	10,000	9,000	−10%
EBIT	20,000	10,500		20,000	11,000	
Interest	5,000	5,000		0	0	
Pre-Tax Earnings	$15,000	$5,500	−63.3%	$20,000	$11,000	−45%

D. Cost of Capital

Companies try to minimize their cost of capital, which can be calculated based on the cost of equity and after-tax cost of debt. Many companies consider their weighted average cost of capital (WACC), as expressed in the formula below, to be an appropriate discount rate for evaluating projects that have risk profiles consistent with the overall risk profile of the company.

WACC = (After-Tax Cost of Debt x % of Debt) + (Cost of Equity x % of Equity)

Assume the following:

- A company's long-term capital structure is 40% debt and 60% equity.
- The company's average cost of debt is 12%.
- The company's marginal tax rate is 34%; therefore, the after-tax cost of debt is 12% x (1 − .34) = 7.92%.
- Its cost of equity is 16%.

The WACC is calculated as follows:

$$
\begin{aligned}
\text{WACC} &= (.0792 \times .40) + (.16 \times .60) \\
&= .0317 + .0960 \\
&= .1277 = 12.77\%
\end{aligned}
$$

E. Capital Budgeting

Capital budgeting is the process companies use to evaluate alternative long-term investment projects. It uses methods such as net present value calculations and weighs other non-quantitative factors such as the company's core strategy and where it believes its competitive strengths lie. A company may compare the net present values of various projects using the WACC as the discount rate.

A company operating in several industries may use a higher assumed WACC and discount rate for its riskier businesses and a lower WACC for its less risky businesses. It may also evaluate projects by comparing their internal rates of return (IRR) to the company's WACC. The IRR is the discount rate at which the net present value is equal to zero.

III. Liquidity and Working Capital Measures and Ratios

Liquidity is the ability to turn assets into cash quickly without incurring loss. Ensuring corporate liquidity on a day-to-day basis is the responsibility of the cash manager. This ongoing task necessitates careful measurement and continual monitoring of net working capital so that the company has sufficient financial resources to pay upcoming bills and take advantage of investment opportunities that may present themselves unexpectedly.

A. Why Liquidity is Needed

There are three primary reasons a company needs to manage liquidity. These are:

1. **Transactions Requirement** — Because a company's day-to-day cash flows are unsynchronized, it must hold in reserve cash and near-cash resources to meet financial requirements.

2. **Precautionary Requirement** — Since a company's cash inflows and outflows are unpredictable, it must maintain higher levels of cash or near-cash balances to meet its expenses.

3. **Speculative Requirement** — Surplus liquid resources allow a company to take advantage of future unplanned investment opportunities that may arise.

B. Sources of Liquidity

A company's liquidity arises from:

- Cash flow from operations
- Available cash and readily marketable short-term investments
- Unused short-term borrowing capacity

C. Levels of Liquidity

Both excess and insufficient liquidity can affect a company negatively.

1. **Insufficient Liquidity** — The costs associated with not having sufficient liquidity include:
    - *Costs of Delayed Payments* — These include damage to the company's credit standing, foregone cash discounts and interest charges.

- *Cost of Lost Opportunities* — This is the opportunity cost of forgoing purchases or investments under advantageous terms and conditions.

- *Additional Interest Costs* — These are the costs that arise from unanticipated borrowing. They may be significant if interest rates are generally rising, or if the company must pay higher rates due to increased risk or a weakened financial condition.

- *Transaction Costs* — Companies can incur unnecessary brokerage and administrative costs when securities are sold or a line of credit is used to replenish a company's cash balances.

A company with inadequate liquidity may become insolvent and be forced to seek court protection by filing for bankruptcy. The liquidation that can result is expensive and the legal fees can be significant. Even if a company is allowed to continue operations, its image may be tarnished to the extent that it loses customers, creditors and shareholder confidence. It will incur higher capital costs as a result. The company will become less able to take advantage of business opportunities.

2. **Excess Liquidity** — Too much liquidity also has disadvantages. The opportunity cost of holding excess cash arises from the loss of earnings because the funds were not used more profitably.

3. **Proper Levels of Liquidity** — The dollar volume of cash inflows and outflows is a major determinant of the level of liquidity a company needs. Even slight timing differences between cash inflows and outflows can cause a large drain on cash resources. This is particularly true if individual receivables are significant in size, where only a few days' delay in a customer's payment can cause substantial problems. Also, the company's sales may fluctuate from month to month, while it incurs expenses at a steady rate. These factors require a company to maintain adequate cash reserves and make it imperative for the cash manager to continually measure, monitor and forecast liquidity.

D. Working Capital Measures and Ratios

Liquidity is measured using working capital ratios and related calculations. These standardized and widely used formulas allow a company's management to determine adequate liquidity levels, establish liquidity policy and guidelines and continually monitor liquidity. Banks, other creditors, investors, analysts and ratings agencies use the same working capital and liquidity measures to assess a company's creditworthiness and its short-term financial health. The principal methods of measuring corporate liquidity include the calculations that follow.

(The example data in the calculations refer to Exhibits 2.1 and 2.2. All dollar amounts are in thousands.)

1. **Current Ratio** — The current ratio is defined as total current assets divided by total current liabilities. This ratio measures a company's ability to meet its current obligations, or the degree to which current obligations are covered by current assets.

$$\text{Current Ratio} = \frac{\text{Total Current Assets}}{\text{Total Current Liabilities}} = \frac{\$8,000}{\$3,400} = 2.4$$

2. **Quick Ratio** — The quick ratio is defined as cash plus short-term investments and accounts receivable divided by total current liabilities. It is also known as the "acid test" ratio and is considered a more conservative measure of liquidity than the current ratio. The quick ratio measures the degree to which a company's current liabilities are covered by its most liquid current assets. (Note that inventory and prepaid expenses are not included in this ratio because they are the least liquid of the current assets.)

$$\text{Quick Ratio} = \frac{\text{Cash} + \text{Short-Term Investments} + \text{Accounts Receivable}}{\text{Total Current Liabilities}}$$

$$= \frac{\$1,500 + \$1,300 + \$1,700}{\$3,400} = 1.3$$

3. **Cash Flow-to-Total Debt Ratio** — Cash flow to total debt is defined as net income plus depreciation divided by total long-term and short-term debt. Short-term debt consists of short-term notes, commercial paper or other short-term debt obligations. A relatively low ratio indicates an inability to repay debt. Studies of failed companies have found this ratio to be accurate in predicting financial failure.

$$\text{Cash Flow-to-Total Debt Ratio} = \frac{\text{Net Income} + \text{Depreciation}}{\text{Short-Term Debt} + \text{Long-Term Debt}}$$

$$= \frac{\$850 + \$200}{\$1,800 + \$3,900} = \frac{\$1,050}{\$5,700} = 0.2$$

4. **Cash Conversion Cycle** — The cash conversion cycle measures liquidity from another perspective. It calculates the time required for a company to convert cash outflows necessary to produce goods into cash inflows through collection of accounts receivable. By adding the average age of the inventory (measured by days of inventory) and average age of accounts receivable (measured by days of receivables) and subtracting the average age of the accounts payable (measured by days of payables), it measures how efficiently a company is using its current assets and liabilities.

   - *Days' Inventory* — This item is calculated as a function of the inventory value and the cost of goods sold. The inventory value used could be ending inventory for the period or, where inventories are highly variable, an average measure of some kind. The cost of goods sold rather than sales is used in this formula because inventory is valued at its purchase cost rather than its selling price. This figure represents the average number of days it takes to convert raw materials into finished goods.

$$\text{Days' Inventory} = \frac{\text{Inventory}}{\text{Cost of Goods Sold}} \times 365 = \frac{\$2,600}{\$9,200} \times 365 = 103.2 \text{ Days}$$

- *Days' Receivables* — This item is calculated as a function of the accounts receivable value and the level of sales. Accounts receivable are valued at the full sales price that will be received when the accounts are collected. This figure is also known as average collection period or days' sales outstanding and represents the number of days it takes to convert a sale into a cash inflow.

$$\text{Days' Receivables} = \frac{\text{Accounts Receivable}}{\text{Annual Sales}} \times 365 = \frac{\$1,700}{\$15,000} \times 365 = 41.4 \text{ Days}$$

- *Days' Payables* — This item is calculated as a function of the accounts payable value and the cost of goods sold. Accounts payable are valued at the cost of goods sold, which is what is paid to suppliers for materials.

$$\text{Days' Payables} = \frac{\text{Accounts Payable}}{\text{Cost of Goods Sold}} \times 365 = \frac{\$1,600}{\$9,200} \times 365 = 63.5 \text{ Days}$$

- *Cash Conversion Cycle* — This measure uses the three time periods determined above to calculate the average number of days it takes from the beginning of the production cycle, through the sales cycle and collection cycle up to the receipt of collected funds, offset by the average number of days on the payables side. The net result is the time it takes the company to convert a cash outflow (the payment for raw materials, services and labor) into a cash inflow (collection for the items sold).

Cash Conversion Cycle = Days' Inventory + Days' Receivables − Days' Payables

= 103.2 Days + 41.4 Days − 63.5 Days = 81.1 Days

In this example, the company has cash invested in its operating cycle an average of 81.1 days.

5. **Cash Turnover** — Cash turnover is the number of cash conversion cycles through which a company goes in a year.

$$\text{Cash Turnover} = \frac{365}{\text{Cash Conversion Cycle}} = \frac{365}{81.1} = 4.5 \text{ Times}$$

The cash conversion cycle and cash turnover are measures of efficiency that can be used to compare companies in the same or similar industries.

IV. Debt Management and Coverage Ratios

Apart from liquidity ratios, there are other standard and widely used financial ratios that are used to determine a company's creditworthiness and debt coverage. No single ratio provides a complete picture of a company's financial soundness or operational efficiency, but groups of ratios considered together can reveal a great deal. Analysis of key ratios is also an integral part of the evaluation of a company by rating agencies, such as Standard and Poor's or Moody's. Rating agencies may use their own unique calculations to measure the ability of a company to meet interest payments and the overall efficiency with which it uses debt. However, most of the formulas they use are variants of the following calculations.

A. Times Interest Earned (TIE)

This is a coverage ratio that indicates how many times a company's earnings before interest and taxes exceed its interest obligations. The higher this ratio, the greater the ability of the company to pay off debt.

$$\text{TIE} = \frac{\text{Operating Profit}}{\text{Interest Expense}} = \frac{\$1{,}600}{\$300} = 5.3 \text{ Times}$$

B. Long-Term Debt to Capital

This ratio measures the percentage of long-term debt relative to all of the long-term capital used in the company's capital structure. Long-term debt includes long-term notes and bonds, term loans and capitalized lease obligations. Equity capital includes all preferred and common equity accounts. The higher this ratio, the greater the proportion of debt a company is using in its long-term capital structure and the greater the extent to which it is leveraged.

$$\text{L/T Debt to Capital} = \frac{\text{Long-Term Debt}}{\text{Long-Term Debt} + \text{Equity}} = \frac{\$3{,}900}{\$3{,}900 + \$8{,}200} = 32.2\%$$

C. Debt to Tangible Net Worth

This ratio measures a company's debt as a percentage of its tangible net worth, its total equity minus intangibles such as goodwill, patents, trademarks, etc.

$$\text{Debt to Tangible Net Worth} = \frac{\text{Total Debt}}{(\text{Total Equity} - \text{Intangible Assets})}$$

$$= \frac{\$1,800 + \$3,900}{\$8,200 - \$0} = 69.5\%$$

D. Total Liabilities to Total Assets

This ratio measures the percentage of all liabilities relative to the total asset base of the company. The higher this ratio, the more liabilities (as opposed to equity) the company uses to finance its asset base.

$$\text{Total Liabilities to Total Assets} = \frac{\text{Total Liabilities}}{\text{Total Assets}} = \frac{\$7,300}{\$15,500} = 47.1\%$$

V. Performance Measurements

These ratios measure the ability of a company to generate profits on sales or returns on assets and capital. Income statement amounts are annualized in the calculation of these ratios.

A. Return on Common Equity

This ratio measures the earnings available to common shareholders (net income less any preferred stock dividends or amortization), expressed as a percentage of the common equity. In this example, where the company has no preferred stock, the earnings available to common shareholders are equal to net income. The higher this ratio, the greater the return to the common shareholders of the company.

$$\text{Return on Equity} = \frac{\text{Earnings Available to Common Shareholders}}{\text{Common Equity}}$$

$$= \frac{\$850}{\$8,200} = 10.4\%$$

B. Return on Sales

This ratio measures the net income of a company as a percentage of its sales. The higher this ratio, the more after-tax profits the company generates on a given sales level. For this company, every $1 in revenue returns 5.7¢ in net income.

$$\text{Return on Sales} = \frac{\text{Net Income}}{\text{Revenues}} = \frac{\$850}{\$15,000} = 5.7\%$$

C. Return on Total Assets

This ratio measures the net income of a company as a percentage of its total assets. The higher this ratio, the more after-tax profits the company is generating from its asset base. For this company, every $1 in total assets generates 5.5¢ in net income.

$$\text{Return on Total Assets} = \frac{\text{Net Income}}{\text{Total Assets}} = \frac{\$850}{\$15,500} = 5.5\%$$

D. Economic Value Added (EVA)

Economic value added (EVA) is a measure of the incremental value that a company's investments add in terms of their impact on market capitalization. Put simply, it is after-tax operating profit minus an appropriate charge for the opportunity cost of all capital. Its advantage is that it is a performance measure that is tied directly to the market value of a company. In general, EVA increases under the three following scenarios:

- The rate of return earned on the existing base of capital improves.
- Additional capital is invested in projects where the return is more than the cost of new capital.
- Capital is liquidated from substandard operations.

Many companies implement EVA as a valuable management tool to provide a practical periodic performance measure for both the overall company as well as for the various divisions and operating units. When used at the divisional and operating unit level, the parent company acts as a "bank" for the individual units and EVA is determined as the difference between the unit's net operating profit and a charge for capital. Managers are rewarded for increasing EVA relative to a target and are penalized for falling short.

The general formula for EVA is as follows:

$$\text{EVA} = \text{Operating Profit} \times (1 - \text{Tax Rate}) - (\text{WACC} \times \text{Total Capital})$$
$$\text{EVA} = \$1,600,000 \times (1 - 0.34) - (0.1277 \times \$12,100,000) = (\$489,170)$$

Where:
Total Capital = Long-Term Debt + Total Equity
= $3,900,000 + $8,200,000 = $12,100,00

E. Other Financial and Performance Measurement Concepts

There are many other financial and performance measurement concepts, often related to specific industries or types of business. Two of the more commonly used performance measures are:

1. **Cash Conversion Efficiency** — This calculation measures the efficiency with which a company converts sales into cash. It is calculated by dividing cash flow from operations by sales.

$$\text{Cash Conversion Efficiency} = \frac{\text{Cash Flow From Operations}}{\text{Sales}} = \frac{\$550}{\$15,000} = 3.7\%$$

2. **Working Capital Turnover** — This ratio measures how many times per year a company converts its working capital into sales. It establishes a relationship for the amount of working capital used to support a given level of sales.

$$\text{Working Capital Turnover} = \frac{\text{Sales}}{\text{Net Working Capital}} = \frac{\$15,000}{\$8,000 - \$3,400} = 3.3 \text{ Times}$$

F. Use of Financial Ratios and Performance Measures

While financial ratios and performance measurement calculations reveal a great deal about a company's financial and operating condition, they do have certain limitations. The table in Exhibit 2.6 summarizes their advantages and disadvantages. In most companies, ratios in a given period are compared to ratio values from prior periods to analyze the changes. A table showing this analysis appears in Exhibit 2.7.

Exhibit 2.6 Use of Financial Ratios and Performance Measurements

Advantages	Disadvantages
Easily computed	Summarize accounting information and do not reflect economic value
Widely used	Express static, not dynamic, relationships
Information easily obtained	Cannot reflect qualitative value (managerial talent, intangibles)
Allow assessment of historical performance	Often miss variability of cash flows and are not necessarily indicative of future performance
Allow for comparison between companies	Use of different accounting methods or "window dressing" can distort calculations

Exhibit 2.7 Summary of Ratio Analysis

Working Capital Measures and Ratios	Current Year	Prior Year	Change
Current Ratio = $\dfrac{\text{Total Current Assets}}{\text{Total Current Liabilities}}$	2.4	2.7	(0.4)
Quick Ratio = $\dfrac{\text{Cash + Short-Term Investments + Accounts Receivable}}{\text{Total Current Liabilities}}$	1.3	1.5	(0.2)
Cash Flow-to-Total Debt Ratio = $\dfrac{\text{Net Income + Depreciation}}{\text{Short-Term Debt + Long-Term Debt}}$	0.2	0.2	(0.0)
Days Inventory = $\dfrac{\text{Inventory}}{\text{Cost of Goods Sold}} \times 365$	103.2	103.6	(0.4)
Days Receivables = $\dfrac{\text{Accounts Receivable}}{\text{Annual Sales}} \times 365$	41.4	38.0	3.4
Days Payables = $\dfrac{\text{Accounts Payable}}{\text{Cost of Goods Sold}} \times 365$	63.5	59.2	4.3
Cash Conversion Cycle = Days Inventory + Days Receivables − Days Payables	81.1	82.4	(1.3)
Cash Turnover = $\dfrac{365}{\text{Cash Conversion Cycle}}$ =	4.5	4.4	0.1
Debt Management and Coverage Ratios			
Times Interest Earned = $\dfrac{\text{Earnings Before Interest and Taxes}}{\text{Interest Expense}}$	5.3	5.9	(0.6)
L/T Debt to Capital = $\dfrac{\text{Long-Term Debt}}{\text{Long-Term Debt + Equity}}$	32.2%	31.5%	0.7%
Debt to Tangible Net Worth = $\dfrac{\text{Total Debt}}{(\text{Total Equity} - \text{Intangible Assets})}$	69.5%	63.2%	6.3%
Total Liabilities to Total Assets = $\dfrac{\text{Total Current Liabilities}}{\text{Total Current Assets}}$	47.1%	44.1%	3.0
Performance Measures			
Return on Equity = $\dfrac{\text{Earnings Available to Common Shareholders}}{\text{Common Equity}}$	10.4%	11.0%	−0.6%
Return on Sales = $\dfrac{\text{Net Income}}{\text{Revenues}}$	5.7%	6.7%	−1.0%
Return on Total Assets = $\dfrac{\text{Net Income}}{\text{Total Assets}}$	5.5%	6.1%	−0.6%
Economic Value Added = $\dfrac{\text{Earnings Before Interest and Taxes* (1-t)} -}{\text{Weighted Average Cost of Capital*TC}}$	(489,170)	(460,470)	(28,700)
Cash Conversion Efficiency = $\dfrac{\text{Cash Flow From Operations}}{\text{Sales}}$	3.7%	3.2%	0.5%
Working Capital Turnover = $\dfrac{\text{Sales}}{\text{Net Working Capital}}$	3.3	2.9	0.4
WACC			
(Assume 40% Debt and 60% Equity)	12.77%	12.77%	–
Marginal Tax Rate	34%	34%	–
Cash Flow From Operations (From Statement of Cash Flows)	500,000	400,000	150,000

Test Your Understanding

These chapter questions are provided to test your understanding of the information in the text and are not examples of CCM examination questions, nor are they in the examination format.

Answers can be found at the back of the book on pages 498-499.

1. What is GAAP?

2. Explain the difference between cash and accrual accounting.

3. Discuss the methods a company can use in its reporting of a negative cash balance.

4. What are the basic financial statements?

5. What are different types of opinions that an auditor can render for financial statements?

6. Determine the present value of $1,500 two years from now if the opportunity cost is five percent.

7. What are the primary incentives for a company to finance its capital structure with debt?

8. Discuss the impact of leverage on financial results.

9. What are the primary reasons a company needs liquidity?

10. List the common ratios used to measure working capital.

11. Discuss the cash conversion cycle.

12. Discuss the scenarios under which EVA will increase.

13. What are the disadvantages of using financial ratios?

CHAPTER 3

The U.S. Financial Environment

Overview

This chapter describes the role of the various types of financial markets and institutions in the United States, the agencies that supervise them and the legislation and regulations that impact the treasury function.

Learning Objectives

Upon completion of this chapter and the related study questions, the reader should understand:

- The workings of the primary financial markets in the United States
- The principal functions of commercial banks, investment banking firms, thrifts and other institutions
- The functions and structure of various agencies with responsibilities for chartering, regulating and/or monitoring different types of financial institutions
- How the banking system evolved through significant legislative, regulatory, legal and market developments
- How key Federal Reserve regulations affect a cash manager
- How the uniform commercial code affects a cash manager

Key Concepts

- Structure and dynamics of the U.S. financial system
- Regulatory institutional framework
- Role of the Federal Reserve
- Evolution of the U.S. financial system

Outline

I. Introduction

II. Financial Markets
- A. Different Types of Financial Markets
- B. Flotation Costs
- C. Public Offerings and Private Placements

III. Financial Institutions: Functions and Services
- A. Commercial Banks
- B. Investment Banking and Brokerage Firms
- C. Thrift Institutions
- D. Credit Unions
- E. Mutual Funds
- F. Industrial Credit and Capital Companies
- G. Factors
- H. Insurance Companies
- I. Consumer Finance Companies

IV. Regulatory Agencies
- A. Federal Reserve System (the Fed)
- B. Office of the Comptroller of the Currency (OCC)
- C. Office of Thrift Supervision (OTS)
- D. Federal Deposit Insurance Corporation (FDIC)
- E. Federal Financial Institution Examination Council (FFIEC)
- F. Office of Foreign Assets Control (OFAC)
- G. Securities and Exchange Commission (SEC)
- H. Department of Justice (DOJ)
- I. State Banking Boards and Commissions

V. Federal Legislation
- A. Federal Reserve Act
- B. Edge Act
- C. McFadden Act
- D. Glass-Steagall Act
- E. The Securities Laws of 1933, 1934 and 1940

F. Community Reinvestment Act (CRA)
   G. Electronic Funds Transfer Act (EFTA)
   H. Depository Institutions Deregulation and Monetary Control Act (DIDMCA)
   I. Garn-St. Germain Depository Institutions Act
   J. Expedited Funds Availability Act
   K. Financial Institutions Reform, Recovery and Enforcement Act (FIRREA)
   L. Federal Deposit Insurance Corporation Improvement Act (FDICIA)
   M. Interstate Banking and Branching Efficiency Act (IBBEA)
   N. Gramm-Leach-Bliley Act
   O. Electronic Signatures in Global and National Commerce Act

VI. Federal Reserve Regulations
   A. Regulation D
   B. Regulation E
   C. Regulation J
   D. Regulation Q
   E. Regulation BB
   F. Regulation CC

VII. The Uniform Commercial Code (UCC)
   A. Article 3 — Negotiable Instruments
   B. Article 4 — Bank Deposits and Collections
   C. Article 4A — Funds Transfers
   D. Article 5 — Letters of Credit

I. Introduction

To protect against a concentration of economic and political power, U.S. regulators have historically made it difficult for banks and financial institutions to consolidate and/or acquire major equity positions in industrial enterprises. The legal and regulatory framework has encouraged institutional segmentation. As a result, different entities tend to serve different functions: commercial lending and deposit taking, mortgage provision, insurance sales and securities underwriting. This makes the U.S. financial markets and system distinct from its counterparts in other developed countries, where financial institutions are less segmented and in many cases may own equity in industrial enterprises.

The current regulatory environment is fostering a liberalization of these restrictions and the continued consolidation of the financial services industry.

II. Financial Markets

Financial markets are institutions and procedures that facilitate transactions in all types of financial claims. Within the context of the corporate world, financial markets exist to bring together those companies that need money and those that have excess money. Financial intermediaries such as commercial banks and investment bankers offer their services to facilitate these transactions.

Corporations raise funds to finance future growth, often using an investment banker as the intermediary to merchandise the securities. These funds can be in the form of long-term debt or the issuance of capital stock. The investment banker will underwrite, distribute and advise the securities through private placement or public offering.

A. Different Types of Financial Markets

1. **Money Markets and Capital Markets** — The main distinction between the money market and the capital market is the maturity of the securities that are traded in them. Money market instruments are those securities that would be considered as short-term in nature, with or less than one year until maturity. Money market instruments are generally highly liquid and are issued by borrowers with high credit ratings. Capital markets are long-term, with maturities that extend beyond one year. This encompasses term loans, leases, equities and bonds. For a more detailed discussion of the money and capital markets, refer to Chapter 12, Investing.

2. **Security Exchanges and Markets** — Organized stock exchanges exist to facilitate the buying and selling of securities. There are two national organized security

exchanges, the New York Stock Exchange (NYSE) and the American Stock Exchange (AMEX), as well as the primary over-the-counter market, the National Association of Stock Dealers Automated Quotations (NASDAQ). Additionally, there are regional exchanges such as the Midwest Stock Exchange, the Pacific Stock Exchange and others.

It is important for treasury managers to understand the benefits of the stock exchanges, which are:

- Organized exchanges provide a continuous market, with frequent trading executed quickly with reduced price volatility.

- An organized exchange permits security prices to be issued by competitive forces or the law of supply and demand underlying the security.

- An organized exchange enables companies to raise capital through new offerings.

3. **Primary Markets and Secondary Markets** — New issues of debt or equities can be issued in the primary market or secondary market. Primary markets are those in which the issue is being offered for the first time to investors. These new issues represent transactions that increase the outstanding stock or indebtedness. Secondary markets represent those transactions for securities that are currently outstanding or issued. All transactions after the initial purchase occur in the secondary market and do not affect the total outstanding stock or indebtedness of a company.

B. Flotation Costs

A company raising long-term capital incurs two types of flotation costs. The underwriter's spread is the difference between the gross and net proceeds for the issue. The issue costs include the expenses incurred for the issue, such as printing and engraving, legal fees, accounting fees, trustee fees and other miscellaneous components. The underwriter's spread is larger than the issuing costs.

Flotation costs are greater for common stock issues, followed by preferred stock and finally bonds. This is based on the concept that common stock inherently has more risk than preferred stock or bonds; hence the underwriting risk is greater and flotation costs increase. Flotation costs will also decrease with the size of the issue, expressed as a percentage of gross proceeds.

C. Public Offerings and Private Placements

When a company decides to raise debt or equity capital, these funds can be raised through a private placement or public offering. In a public offering, the managing investment banker or the syndicate makes the securities available to the public. Both individual and institutional investors have the opportunity to purchase the securities. Initial public offerings are often referred to as IPOs.

In a private or direct placement, the securities are offered and sold on to a limited number of investors. The investment banker will meet with the prospective buyers and confirm the details of the offering. In a private placement, the investment banker acts as a broker, bringing the issuer and investors together. Generally a private placement is completed quicker than a public offering, offers reduced flotation costs and offers the investment banker some flexibility to meet the needs of the company. However, private placements often incur higher interest rates and may have more restrictive covenants.

III. Financial Institutions: Functions and Services

This section discusses the functions of commercial banks and other types of financial institutions as well as the services they offer.

A. Commercial Banks

Defined by law as a financial institution that accepts deposits and makes business loans, a commercial bank offers a wide range of products and services. The term commercial bank is used to describe everything from small, single-facility community banks with a few million dollars in assets to large, global institutions with numerous locations and billions in assets. According to the Federal Deposit Insurance Corporation (FDIC), in the United States, the number of commercial bank main offices held steady at around 13,000 to 14,000 from the 1930s through the mid-1980s, with the number of branches rising from around 17,000 in the 1930s to 44,000 in the mid-1980s. By 1998, however, the number of main offices had dropped to just under 9,000, while the number of branches had exploded to more than 70,000.

Most large banks are owned by bank holding companies, which may also own limited-purpose non-bank subsidiaries. Commercial banks, their holding companies and non-bank subsidiaries provide a wide range of products and services, as detailed below.

1. **Deposit Accounts** — An important function of a commercial bank is to serve as a depository for cash. There are two basic types of depository accounts: demand deposit accounts and time deposit accounts. There are also interest-bearing accounts that combine the features of demand and time deposits.

    - *Demand Deposit Accounts (DDAs)* — Commonly referred to as checking accounts, DDAs are a method by which an account holder uses a financial institution to transfer funds to a third party. The method of payment can be by check, wire transfer or automated clearing house (ACH) transfer. At the time of publication, the law prohibits payment of interest on demand deposits held by businesses. The three exceptions to this regulation are sole proprietorships, government entities and not-for-profit organizations. This regulation is currently under review and may be changed in the future. Balances are held in DDAs for the following purposes:

— *Transaction Balances* — Deposits held by companies to facilitate collection and disbursement activity.

— *Compensating Balances* — Deposits held by companies in the form of collected balances that are used to pay for bank services.

— *Correspondent Bank Balances* — Deposits from other banks held to facilitate check clearing, securities settlement, negotiation of letters of credit and other transactions.

- *Time Deposits* — Time deposits must be held at a bank, thrift or credit union for a specified period. Examples of time deposits include:

    — *Certificates of Deposit (CDs)* — Negotiable or non-negotiable obligations of a bank offered at either fixed or variable interest rates. Jumbo CDs are deposits of $100,000 or more; they are sold to individuals and companies. Maturities may range from seven days to several years.

    — *Negotiable CDs* — Generally sold in $1 million blocks to companies, money market funds and other large investors. Being negotiable, they can be sold to another investor prior to maturity. Maturities generally range from 14 days to five years, but most have maturities of 12 months or less.

    — *Retail CDs* — Non-negotiable CDs sold to individual investors in amounts that vary from institution to institution. Maturities generally range from three months to five years.

    — *Savings Accounts or Passbook Savings Accounts* — Accounts that pay interest on balances. They are mainly held by individuals and not-for-profit institutions, but companies may also hold them.

- *Other Interest-Bearing Accounts* — Accounts that have some of the features of both demand and time deposits. Some examples are the following:

    — *Money Market Deposit Accounts* — Accounts that pay an unregulated rate of interest determined by the bank and allow limited check writing transfers and electronic withdrawals. They are available to all types of businesses and individuals.

    — *Negotiable Order of Withdrawal (NOW) Accounts* — Accounts that offer unrestricted check writing and pay unregulated rates of interest. NOW accounts are limited to individuals, sole proprietorships, not-for-profit organizations and governmental entities.

2. **Credit Services** — Banks provide loans to companies of all sizes, to not-for profit organizations and to individuals. The following are examples of credit services:

- *Short-Term Loans* — Loans designed primarily for working capital purposes such as temporary or seasonal increases in inventory or accounts receivable. Short-term loans are expected to be repaid from conversion of the current assets they finance. Short-term borrowing is often under a line of credit, which allows a company to borrow up to a specified amount, repay and borrow again at any time. (See Chapter 13, Borrowing.)

- *Long-Term Loans* — Loans designed primarily for capital improvements such as plant and equipment. The source of repayment is generally expected to be earnings from the project being financed.

- *Leasing* — Leases provide an alternative to long-term loans for financing capital equipment. (See Chapter 13, Borrowing.)

- *Mortgages* — Commercial banks provide mortgage financing for commercial and residential real estate.

3. **Investment Banking Services** — Investment banking services offered by commercial banks include the following:

   - *Commercial Paper (CP)* — Commercial paper consists of unsecured, short-term promissory notes issued by companies. Banks act as agents to place the commercial paper of their customers with investors. Commercial bank holding companies also issue commercial paper. Commercial paper is rated for default risk by various rating agencies. (See Chapter 12, Investing and Chapter 13, Borrowing.)

   - *Loan Sales* — Banks structure lending facilities so that short-term loans can be sold to other banks and investors.

   - *Private Placements* — Banks work with their customers to place long-term loans with institutional investors such as insurance companies.

   - *Stock and Bonds Underwriting* — Some banks underwrite corporate stocks (equity) and bonds (debt) through investment and brokerage subsidiaries.

4. **Payment and Collection Services** — Banks assist companies by acting as clearing agents for checks and by originating and receiving wire transfers and ACH transactions. (See Chapter 4, U.S. Payments System and Chapter 6, Collections.)

5. **Trade Services** — Banks may provide the following services to facilitate payment of trade obligations, particularly with foreign trading partners (see Chapter 15, International Treasury Management):

   - *Trade or Commercial Letters of Credit (L/Cs)* — L/Cs are documents issued by a bank, guaranteeing the payment of a customer's draft up to a stated amount for a specified period provided certain conditions are met. In effect, the issuing bank substitutes its name and credit on behalf of its customer.

   - *Letters of Credit Confirmations* — L/C confirmations are issued by a bank at the request of a customer when that customer is unfamiliar with or unsure of the financial condition of the original issuing bank. In such instances, another bank may confirm (guarantee) performance under the original L/C. In the event of default, the confirming bank is responsible for the payment.

- *Documentary Collections* — A documentary collection is a payment method that processes the collection of a draft and accompanying shipping documents through international correspondent banks. Instructions regarding the specifics of the transaction are contained in a collection letter or form that accompanies the documentation. It is the responsibility of the seller (exporter) to determine the specific instructions to be used in the collection letter.

- *Banker's Acceptances (BAs)* — A BA is a negotiable short-term instrument used primarily to finance the import, export or domestic shipment of goods, or the storage of readily marketable staples. It is created when a bank accepts payment responsibility for a draft issued in connection with an L/C.

6. **Foreign Exchange (FX) Services** — Banks may offer FX services to their customers in order to facilitate international business and trade. These services allow companies to buy or sell many different currencies either for immediate use (the spot market) or for future use (the forward market). In addition, many banks offer various types of hedging contracts related to foreign currencies, which provide vital risk management services to the corporate treasurer. Many large banks, especially those that operate in multiple countries, are major dealers in the FX markets. Through these operations, they can often offer competitive rates and services to their clients. (See Chapter 15, International Treasury Management.)

7. **Credit Enhancement or Payment Guaranty** — Banks may issue standby L/Cs on behalf of their customers to ensure payment of the customers' obligations to third parties.

8. **Agent or Fiduciary Services** — An agent is a bank, bank holding company or trust institution that manages assets for which title remains with the owner. A fiduciary is an individual or institution to whom certain property is given to hold in trust according to a trust agreement. Some examples of agent or fiduciary services are the following:

    - *Trust Services* — Banks invest, manage and distribute monies as instructed in wills, trusts and estates.

    - *Investment Management* — Banks manage portfolios of investments for their customers.

    - *Corporate Pension Plans* — Banks act as agents for corporations in establishing and managing employee pension programs.

    - *Qualified Employee Benefit Plans* — Banks act as agents for qualified employee benefit plans.

- *Corporate Trustee* — Banks, as trustees for a corporate bond or preferred stock issues, monitor compliance with indenture agreements. These are formal agreements between an issuer of bonds and a bondholder.
- *Transfer Agent* — Banks serve as transfer agents by keeping records of the sale and purchase of stocks and bonds and maintaining records of the shareholders of a corporation by name, address and number of shares.
- *Registrar* — Banks serve as registrars by maintaining lists of current stockholders and bondholders for the purpose of remitting dividend and interest payments.
- *Paying Agent* — Banks receive funds from an issuer of stocks or bonds to pay dividends to stockholders and principal and interest to bondholders.
- *Custody Services* — Banks provide safekeeping for securities. Under a custody agreement, a bank buys, sells, receives and delivers securities at the customer's request.

9. **Consulting Services** — Banks provide consulting services for corporate customers in areas such as treasury management, mergers and acquisitions and corporate financial structure.

10. **Risk Management Services** — Fluctuations in exchange rates, interest rates or prices of commodities can adversely impact a company's financial performance. For example, currency movements against the U.S. dollar can impact the profitability of a company that operates in international markets. To limit these risks, banks and other financial institutions offer a variety of products such as swaps, forwards, futures and options. These instruments are known as derivatives because their value is derived from, or based on, underlying assets. (See Chapter 14, Financial Risk Management.)

11. **Broker/Dealer Services** — Banks act as brokers and dealers for certain permissible investment securities and foreign currencies and trade for their own account as an extension of that role. Recent legislation (Gramm-Leach-Bliley Act of 1999) allowed banks more leeway in underwriting activities, as well as allowing securities firms to enter areas previously reserved for bankers. This act and its impacts are outlined later in this chapter.

12. **Insurance Services** — Under the Gramm-Leach-Bliley Act of 1999, banks are allowed to engage in unlimited agency and underwriting activities through a holding company affiliate, not in the bank. Insurance companies are able to affiliate with banks.

B. Investment Banking and Brokerage Firms

Investment banking and brokerage firms provide a wide range of services. Not every firm is a full-service provider. Certain firms specialize more in investment banking, others more in brokerage; certain firms deal principally with institutional customers, others with retail customers.

1. **The Investment Banker** — An investment banker is a financial specialist who acts as an intermediary in the merchandising of securities. The investment bankers performs three basic functions:

    - *Underwriting* — Underwriting refers to the selling of a security issue at a satisfactory price that will raise the necessary external funds, but also generate a profit for the investment banker. The investment banker may choose to form a syndicate to share in these responsibilities. A syndicate is a group of investment bankers who participate in buying and reselling the security issue. The investment banker who leads the syndicate is considered the lead underwriter and will receive all fees associated with the issue.

    - *Distribution* — Once the underwriting syndicate owns the new securities, each investment banker uses its distribution system to sell or distribute the issue to their customers. The syndicate is often viewed as a security wholesaler, while the dealer organization is viewed as the security retailer.

    - *Advising* — The investment banker has the responsibility of advising the issuer with regard to the prevailing and future market conditions in an effort to raise the most funds at the least cost. Additionally, the investment banker may analyze the firm's capital structure and advise the issuer as to what source of capital best suits the organization.

2. **Stock and Bond Underwriting** — Underwriting is the principal function of investment banking. When an investment banking firm underwrites a stock or bond offering, it assures the issuer of a definite sum of money for the issue at a definite time. In purchasing the entire issue from the issuer, the underwriter assumes the risk of price and marketability. The investment banker's intermediation function is often described as having two components — origination and distribution. Underwriting is the origination function and selling the securities to investors is the distribution function.

3. **Commercial Paper** — Investment bankers have traditionally acted as underwriters and dealers for commercial paper.

4. **Institutional and Retail Brokerage** — Brokerage services involve the sale of securities to institutional and retail customers. Brokerage is the distribution side of the investment banker's intermediation function.

5. **Investment Research** — Investment banking firms have research analysts who are industry specialists and who give advice to large institutions as well as individual investors.

6. **Investment Advisory and Portfolio Management** — Investment banking firms provide investment advice and manage investment portfolios for large institutions and individuals.

7. **Risk Management** — Investment banking firms offer derivative products such as interest rate and currency swaps, forwards, options and futures. They also offer FX services.

C. Thrift Institutions

Thrift institutions have traditionally been depositories that accept consumer deposits and lend money, primarily in the form of home mortgage loans. The Depository Institutions Deregulation and Monetary Control Act of 1980 (DIDMCA) provided for a phase-out of interest rate ceilings for thrift institutions and commercial banks and allowed savings institutions to make commercial as well as consumer loans. The number of thrift institutions has fallen from a high of almost 5,000 in the 1960s to just 1,700 in 1998. The Office of Thrift Supervision (OTS) supervises and regulates all federally chartered and many state-chartered thrifts. There are two types of thrift institutions:

1. **Savings and Loan Associations** — Savings and loans (S&Ls) are federally or state chartered and owned by either shareholders or depositors. Their deposits are federally insured by the FDIC, a regulatory agency described in detail in Section III.

2. **Savings Banks or Mutual Savings Banks** — Historically, savings banks and mutual savings banks have been state chartered and owned by depositors, but the Garn-St. Germain Depository Institutions Act of 1982 allowed them to switch to a federal charter and to convert to stock ownership.

D. Credit Unions

Credit unions are not-for-profit financial corporations chartered by federal or state agencies. Membership in a credit union is restricted to people with a common bond such as an employer, association or community organization. Credit unions can provide retail financial services similar to those offered by other types of financial institutions. Members/owners often enjoy higher savings and lower lending rates. The National Credit Union Share Insurance Fund (NCUSIF) insures deposits in most credit unions.

E. Mutual Funds

Mutual funds are pooled investments that sell shares to investors, offering these investors diversification and professional portfolio management. Mutual fund providers include brokerage firms, banks and investment companies. Shares may be redeemed through the provider that insures liquidity. Share values in stock and bond funds fluctuate with the performance of the underlying securities of the fund and mutual fund shares are not insured against losses as deposits are. Money market mutual funds typically maintain a stable $1 per share net asset value and invest in short-term securities such as Treasury bills, certificates of deposit and commercial paper.

F. Industrial Credit and Capital Companies

Industrial credit and capital companies are subsidiaries of large industrial corporations that raise funds in the commercial paper market and lend to companies and individuals. A captive finance company typically finances the purchase of its own company's products. Automobile finance companies (GMAC and Ford Motor Credit Company) are common examples of these.

G. Factors

Factors provide short-term financing to companies by purchasing the companies' accounts receivable at a discount. If the factor purchases the receivables "without recourse," then they assume the responsibility and the risk for collecting them. (See Chapter 5, Credit and Accounts Receivable Management.)

H. Insurance Companies

Insurance companies are primarily long-term lenders to companies. Insurance companies have started to compete with banks for short-term and medium-term loans. They also provide mortgage funding, leasing services, guaranteed investment contracts and universal life insurance policies with long-term savings features.

I. Consumer Finance Companies

Consumer finance companies extend credit to individuals and businesses.

IV. Regulatory Agencies

The United States has a dual banking system of federally and state-chartered banks. At the federal level, bank supervision is shared primarily by three agencies: the Board of Governors of the Federal Reserve System, the FDIC and the Office of the Comptroller of the Currency (OCC). The Securities and Exchange Commission (SEC) and the Department of Justice (DOJ) have regulatory roles as well. At the state level, banks are regulated by state banking boards and commissions.

A. Federal Reserve System (the Fed)

The Fed is the central bank of the United States and is an independent agency of the U.S. government. It was founded by Congress in 1913 to provide the nation with a safer, more flexible and more stable monetary and financial system. The following is a description of the roles and structure of the Fed:

1. **Organization** — The Fed has three components: the Board of Governors, the Federal Open Market Committee (FOMC) and the 12 Federal Reserve banks and their branches.

    - *Board of Governors* — Each of the seven members is appointed to a 14-year term by the President of the United States and confirmed by the Senate. Primary functions include formulation of credit and monetary policy, as well as supervision of the Federal Reserve banks, state-chartered member banks and bank holding companies. The President appoints one governor as chairman and another as vice chairman; each serves a four-year term and may be reappointed.

        The following committees advise the Board:

        — *Federal Advisory Council* — Consists of 12 members, one member (traditionally a commercial banker) from each Federal Reserve district.

        — *Consumer Advisory Council* — Members represent the interests of consumers.

        — *Thrift Institutions Advisory Council* — Members represent the interests of savings and loan associations, mutual savings banks and credit unions.

    - *Federal Open Market Committee* — The FOMC sets and implements monetary policy, principally by conducting open market operations. There are 12 committee members, including the seven members of the Board of Governors, the president of the Federal Reserve Bank of New York and presidents of four other Federal Reserve banks. They serve on a rotating basis.

    - *Federal Reserve District Banks* — There are 12 Federal Reserve districts, with one Federal Reserve bank serving each district. The 12 reserve banks have 25 branches. Additionally, there are regional check processing centers (RCPCs). Commercial banks in the region hold the stock of the Federal Reserve banks and are represented on their boards, but do not maintain control the way stockholders normally do. The Board of Governors appoints some members of each reserve bank's board as well as its chairman. A map illustrating the Federal Reserve districts is shown in Exhibit 3.1.

2. **Roles** — The Fed has five principal roles: It acts as 1) a supervisor and regulator of certain financial institutions, 2) the manager of U.S. monetary policy, 3) a wholesaler of banking services, 4) the fiscal agent of the U.S. Treasury and 5) a consumer protection agent for financial services.

- *Supervision and Regulation* — The Fed has primary responsibility for supervising and regulating several types of banking organizations:

    — All bank holding companies, their non-bank subsidiaries and their foreign subsidiaries

Exhibit 3.1 Federal Reserve Check Processing Regions
Courtesy of the Federal Reserve

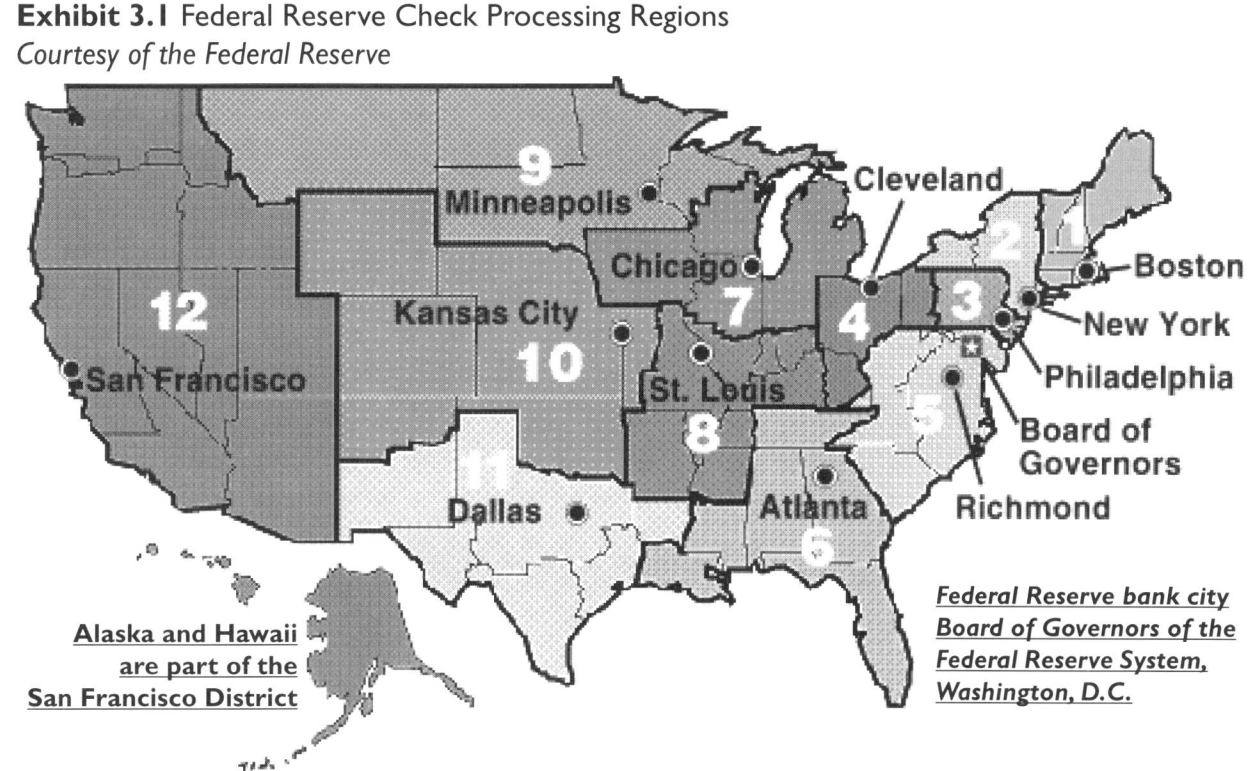

Alaska and Hawaii are part of the San Francisco District

Federal Reserve bank city
Board of Governors of the Federal Reserve System, Washington, D.C.

Region 1: Boston
RCPC — Windsor Locks, CT

Region 2: New York
Branches — Buffalo, NY
RCPC — East Rutherford Operations Center (EROC), East Rutherford, NJ

Region 3: Philadelphia

Region 4: Cleveland
Branches — Cincinnati, OH & Pittsburgh, PA
RCPC — Columbus, OH

Region 5: Richmond
Branches — Baltimore, MD & Charlotte, NC
RCPC — Charleston, WV & Columbia, SC

Region 6: Atlanta
Branches — Birmingham, AL; Jacksonville, FL; Miami, FL; Nashville, TN & New Orleans, LA
RCPC — Columbus, OH

Region 7: Chicago
Branches — Detroit, MI
RCPC — Indianapolis, IN; Milwaukee, WI; Des Moines, IA & Peoria, IL

Region 8: St. Louis
Branches — Little Rock, AR; Louisville, KY & Memphis, TN

Region 9: Minneapolis
Branches — Helena, MT

Region 10: Kansas City
Branches — Denver, CO; Oklahoma City, OK & Omaha, NE

Region 11: Dallas
Branches — El Paso, TX; Houston, TX & San Antonio, TX

Region 12: San Francisco
Branches — Los Angeles, CA; Portland, OR; Salt Lake City, UT & Seattle, WA

- State-chartered banks that are members of the Federal Reserve System (state member banks) and their foreign branches and subsidiaries

- Edge Act Agreement corporations, through which U.S. banking organizations conduct operations abroad

• *Monetary Policy* — The Federal Reserve Act directs the Fed to conduct monetary policy in such a way as to maximize employment, promote price stability and maintain moderate long-term interest rates. The Federal Reserve's monetary policies influence the demand for or supply of reserves at banks and other depository institutions. The effects of monetary policy are transmitted to the rest of the economy through the reserves market. The Board of Governors implements monetary policy primarily through open market activities (the buying and selling of securities in the financial markets). The FOMC oversees open market operations to influence money market conditions and the growth of money and credit.

• *Banking Services* — For a commercial bank, the Fed is both a regulator and a provider of services. It also oversees the payments system in the following ways:

- Check Clearing — The Fed receives check deposits from depository institutions and then clears checks back to the drawee banks.

- Wire Transfers — The Fed operates Fedwire, the domestic large-dollar same-day electronic transfer system.

- Automated Clearing House System — The Fed is the main operator of ACH, which processes and settles electronic payments in a batch mode.

• *Fiscal Agency* — The reserve banks and their branches function as the banker for the federal government. They maintain the Treasury Department's checking accounts, clear Treasury checks drawn against them, accept payments for federal taxes on behalf of the Internal Revenue Service (IRS) and act as fiscal agent for the Treasury Department to issue, redeem and transfer ownership of government securities.

• *Consumer Protection* — The Fed also issues regulations to ensure compliance with major federal laws governing consumer credit protection, such as the Truth in Lending Act, the Equal Credit Opportunity Act and the Home Mortgage Disclosure Act. Many of these regulations also apply to various lenders outside the banking industry.

B. Office of the Comptroller of the Currency (OCC)

The OCC was established by Congress in 1863 to regulate the national banking system and is a bureau in the Department of Treasury. As the administrator of nationally chartered banks, the OCC oversees the execution of laws relating to national banks and promulgates rules and regulations governing the operations of national banks. It also supervises a nationwide staff of bank examiners. Its functions include:

- Functioning as administrator of national banks and federal licensed branches and agencies of foreign banks
- Issuing rules and regulations governing national bank operations
- Approving and denying applications for new bank charters, branches, capital or other changes in corporate or banking structure
- Examining the banks for asset (loan) quality, capital adequacy, management and other key regulatory issues
- Taking supervisory action against banks that do not conform to laws and regulations or that otherwise engage in unsound banking practices

C. Office of Thrift Supervision (OTS)

The OTS is a bureau of the Department of Treasury and the primary regulator of all federal and many state-chartered thrift institutions, which include savings banks and S&Ls. The OTS is the successor to the Federal Home Loan Bank Board (FHLBB) and was established by Congress in 1989 as the primary federal regulator of all federal and state-chartered savings institutions across the nation that belong to the Savings Association Insurance Fund (SAIF). Its functions include:

- Serving as the primary regulator of all federal and state-chartered savings institutions
- Issuing federal charters for savings and loan associations and savings banks
- Adopting and enforcing regulations to ensure that both federal and state-chartered thrift institutions operate in a safe and sound manner

D. Federal Deposit Insurance Corporation (FDIC)

The FDIC is an independent agency of the federal government and its primary role is to protect depositors from losses caused by bank insolvency. FDIC responsibilities include the following:

1. **Deposit Insurance** — The FDIC insures deposits up to $100,000 per personal or corporate depositor per institution in all federally chartered banks and most state banks. The deposit insurance premium rate charged banks is set by the FDIC on the basis of a bank's risk profile. The FDIC administers two federal deposit insurance funds — the Bank Insurance Fund (BIF) and SAIF. Deposits in most commer-

cial banks and many savings banks are insured by BIF. In 1989, Congress created SAIF to succeed the Federal Savings and Loan Insurance Corporation (FSLIC) to insure deposits to specified amounts at savings associations and many savings banks. The FDIC was assigned responsibility for managing SAIF. Both the BIF and SAIF deposit insurance programs are backed by the full faith and credit of the U.S. government.

2. **Supervision** — The FDIC is the primary federal regulator of state non-member banks and, for insurance purposes, is the backup supervisor over the remaining federally insured banks and savings associations. As part of its examination, the FDIC looks for poor risk management or excessive risk taking by an institution and seeks early remedies. In addition, the FDIC examines state non-member banks to ensure their compliance with equal credit and other consumer protection laws. Two examples are the Community Reinvestment Act (CRA) and the Truth in Lending Act. The CRA encourages banks and thrifts to help meet the credit needs of their communities. The Truth in Lending Act requires accurate disclosures of interest rates and finance charges so that loan applicants can comparison-shop for mortgages or consumer loans. (See Chapter 5, Credit and Accounts Receivable Management.)

3. **Role in Bank Failures** — One of the FDIC's most important roles is in determining the course of action in the event of bank failure. The FDIC is usually appointed receiver of failed insured institutions. The agency is charged with finding a merger partner or liquidating the bank's remaining assets and paying insured depositors.

E. Federal Financial Institution Examination Council (FFIEC)

The FFIEC coordinates the activities of the Fed, the OCC, the FDIC and the OTS to ensure consistency in the implementation of regulatory policy.

F. Office of Foreign Assets Control (OFAC)

The OFAC is an office of the Treasury Department and administers and enforces economic and trade sanctions against targeted foreign countries, terrorism-sponsoring organizations and international narcotics traffickers based on U.S. foreign policy and national security goals. The OFAC has the authority to impose controls on financial transactions and freeze foreign assets under U.S. jurisdiction.

G. Securities and Exchange Commission (SEC)

The SEC is a federal agency that regulates and supervises the sale of securities to maintain a fair and orderly market for investors. Among its responsibilities are the following:

- Registering public offerings of debt or equity securities by banks or bank holding companies as well as all other corporations
- Setting financial disclosure standards for corporations that sell securities to the public
- Requiring filing of quarterly and annual financial statements by companies with publicly owned securities
- Regulating mutual funds and investment advisors

H. Department of Justice (DOJ)

The DOJ, as well as the Fed, reviews and approves proposed bank mergers and holding company acquisitions to determine their effect on competition as part of overall anti-trust supervisory responsibility.

I. State Banking Boards and Commissions

Under the dual nature of the U.S. banking system, each state has its own banking board and commission. Among the responsibilities of these state agencies are the following:

- Issuing charters for new state banks
- Supervising and examining all state-chartered banks
- Reserving the right to approve all applications of banks operating within state borders to form holding companies, to acquire affiliates or subsidiaries, or to establish branch offices
- Reserving the right to impose liquidity requirements and minimum equity capital requirements on state-chartered banks

V. Federal Legislation

The following is a summary of the key provisions of selected bank legislation that demonstrates how the U.S. banking system evolved into its current form.

A. Federal Reserve Act (1913)

- Provided the foundation for the current banking system
- Granted the Fed supervisory power over member banks (chartered national banks were required to become members and to comply with reserve requirements)

- Empowered the Fed to create a national check collection and settlement system through member banks

B. Edge Act (1918)

- Permitted U.S. banks to invest in corporations that engage in international banking and finance
- Permitted the establishment of subsidiaries to conduct international banking business such as import and export financing, foreign exchange, letters of credit and documentary collections in other cities in the United States and overseas

C. McFadden Act (1927)

- Established the state boundary as the primary limit for bank expansion by prohibiting banks from accepting deposits across state lines
- Prohibited branching across state lines unless approved by affected state governments, thereby relegating to the states the power to decide the extent of bank branching within and outside state borders

The following are two more recent legislative actions that have modified the McFadden Act:

- *The Douglas Amendment (1956)* — Allowed banks to merge across state lines if each state permitted it, but did not allow bank holding companies to acquire banks across state lines. Legislation enacted by individual states has allowed bank holding companies to acquire banks and bank holding companies in states both within and outside their regions.
- *The Interstate Banking and Branching Efficiency Act (1994)* — Phased out, over a three-year period, the state barriers against branching established by the McFadden Act.

D. Glass-Steagall Act (also known as the Banking Act of 1933)

- Prohibited commercial banks from securities underwriting except for government issues.
- Prohibited securities firms from engaging in bank-like activities such as deposit gathering.
- Required the Fed to establish interest rate ceilings on all types of accounts and prohibited the payment of interest on demand deposits. Provisions of this act are incorporated in Federal Reserve Regulation Q.

- Created the FDIC to guarantee deposits up to a stipulated maximum amount.

E. The Securities Laws of 1933, 1934 and 1940

- These laws established the SEC and govern the issuance of securities.

F. Community Reinvestment Act (CRA) (1977/1995)

- Enacted by Congress in 1977 and implemented by Regulation BB. The regulation was revised in May 1995.

- Intended to encourage depository institutions to help meet the credit needs of the communities in which they operate, including low- and moderate-income neighborhoods.

- Required that each depository institution's record in helping meet the credit needs of its entire community be evaluated periodically. That record is taken into account in considering an institution's application for deposit facilities. CRA examinations are conducted by the federal agencies that are responsible for supervising depository institutions.

G. Electronic Funds Transfer Act (EFTA) (1978)

- Defined the rights and responsibilities of individuals using electronic funds transfer (EFT) services except for wire transfers.

- Limited customer liability for unauthorized banking transactions involving automated teller machines (ATMs) and point of sale (POS) terminals, provided the customer promptly notifies the bank or other institution that issued the card. Provisions of this act are incorporated in Federal Reserve Regulation E.

H. Depository Institutions Deregulation and Monetary Control Act (DIDMCA) (1980)

- Required all deposit-taking institutions to maintain reserves at the Fed

- Made Fed services such as the discount window and check clearing available to all deposit-taking institutions

- Mandated the Fed to reduce and/or price payment system float

- Priced previously free Fed services according to the standards of a tax-paying vendor

- Provided for phasing out of Regulation Q interest rate ceilings
- Permitted banks to offer NOW accounts (check writing accounts with an unregulated interest rate for individuals, not-for-profit organizations and government entities)

I. Garn-St. Germain Depository Institutions Act (1982)

- Extended the legal lending limit of banks to 15 percent of capital and surplus for unsecured loans and 25 percent for secured loans
- Allowed the FDIC to arrange mergers of banks across state lines when suitable intrastate partners could not be found
- Allowed banks to offer accounts, known as money market deposit accounts, to compete with money market mutual funds

J. Expedited Funds Availability Act (1988)

- Defined maximum funds withdrawal time periods for deposited checks and payable through drafts
- Established return procedures for payable through drafts and checks
- Provisions of this act are incorporated in Federal Reserve Regulation CC

K. Financial Institutions Reform, Recovery and Enforcement Act (FIRREA) (1989)

- Consolidated the FSLIC resources under the FDIC
- Dismantled FHLBB and established the OTS to assume FHLBB's supervisory responsibilities
- Established the Resolution Trust Corporation (RTC) to make timely disposal of assets of failed S&Ls. (The RTC is no longer in existence.)
- Gave the FDIC increased flexibility to raise deposit insurance premiums charged to banks and S&Ls

L. Federal Deposit Insurance Corporation Improvement Act (FDICIA) (1991)

- Established numerous higher standards for financial institution safety and soundness in the wake of several bank failures during the late 1980s
- Mandated the FDIC to declare insolvent any bank or thrift that failed to maintain equity capital equal to two percent of its assets

- Required the FDIC to change its deposit insurance premiums from a flat fee basis to a risk-adjusted basis

M. Interstate Banking and Branching Efficiency Act (IBBEA) (1994)

- Also known as the Riegle-Neal Interstate Banking and Branching Act
- Permitted bank holding companies to acquire a bank located in any state effective September 1995
- Allowed banks in one state to merge with banks in another state beginning June 1997, as long as neither state took legislative action to prohibit interstate mergers between the date of enactment and May 1997
- Allowed banks to establish new branches in states where they do not maintain a branch if the host state passes a law expressly permitting such branches

N. Gramm-Leach-Bliley Act (1999)

- Eliminated many of the remaining barriers among the banking, insurance and securities businesses.
- Permitted the creation of financial holding companies (FHCs), which can engage in any activity considered "financial in nature, incidental to finance or complementary to it."
- Allowed for easier entry by foreign banks into the U.S. financial services market
- Established the Fed as the primary regulator of FHCs. FHCs will be subject to consolidated capital requirements at the parent company level and bank-style risk management at all levels.
- Barred a bank holding company from merging with an insurance or securities firm or embarking on new powers if any of its banks earned less than a "satisfactory" CRA rating in its most recent exam.
- Required financial institutions to establish privacy policies and disclose them at the start of a customer relationship and once a year thereafter. Also required banks to give customers a chance to block sharing of confidential information with third parties except in cases of marketing agreements between financial institutions. In addition, it prohibited credit card and account numbers from being shared with third-party marketers.

O. Electronic Signatures in Global and National Commerce Act (2000)

- This legislation gave digital signatures the same effect as ink signatures.
- It ensured the legal certainty of e-commerce transactions and provided a measure of confidence in the enforceability of electronic transactions.

VI. Federal Reserve Regulations

After banking legislation is passed by Congress, the law is implemented through rules and regulations imposed by the regulatory agencies. The following are examples of banking regulations affecting cash managers that are promulgated by the Federal Reserve.

A. Regulation D

- Imposes uniform reserve requirements on all depository institutions with different levels of reserves for different types of deposits. The Fed can use this regulation in controlling the supply of money.

B. Regulation E

- Establishes the rights, liabilities and responsibilities of parties to consumer-related EFTs and protects consumers using EFT systems, such as those involved in ATM, ACH and credit card transactions. Regulation E also establishes the guidelines for documentation of electronic transfers.

C. Regulation J

- Establishes procedures, duties and responsibilities for check collection and settlement through the Federal Reserve System

D. Regulation Q

- Prohibits depository institutions from paying interest on corporate demand deposit accounts. Interest rate ceilings that had been set by this regulation on all other deposit accounts were phased out in 1986 by the DIDMCA.

E. Regulation BB

- Implements the CRA and encourages banks to help meet the credit needs of their communities

F. Regulation CC

- Establishes rules designed to speed the collection and return of checks and imposes a responsibility on banks to return unpaid checks expeditiously
- Establishes endorsement standards for banks and companies to follow in depositing and clearing checks
- Imposes the same return procedures that apply to checks to payable through drafts

VII. The Uniform Commercial Code (UCC)

The UCC is a uniform set of laws governing commercial transactions enacted separately and sometimes in different forms by each state. The UCC defines the rights and duties of the parties in a commercial transaction and provides a statutory definition of commonly used business practices. The four articles (as described in the generic version of the UCC) most relevant to a treasury manager are as follows:

A. Article 3 — Negotiable Instruments

Among the provisions of Article 3 are the following:

1. **Negotiable Instruments** — Article 3 defines a negotiable instrument and the forms it may take, including a draft, a check, a certificate of deposit and a note.

2. **Accord and Satisfaction** — Originally, this section was drafted to permit a check to constitute a payment made in full (accord and satisfaction) when a message to that effect was written on the face of the check and the check was deposited. However, this allowed for the possibility of inadvertent accord and satisfaction when the customer wrote "paid in full" on a check for a disputed claim — especially if the check was collected through a lockbox. The revised section permits avoidance of inadvertent accord and satisfaction if the payee discovers the error and returns the payment to the payor within 90 days.

3. **Unauthorized Signatures** — A bank's failure to examine a forged drawer's signature is not failure to exercise ordinary care to the extent that such failure does not violate the bank's procedures and that these procedures do not unreasonably vary from general banking practices. At the same time, a bank can only charge a

customer's account for checks that are properly payable and an unauthorized signature does not pass this test. However, a company may be held liable if it does not exercise ordinary care related to check issuance and does not notify the bank of multiple forgeries by the same wrongdoer in a timely manner.

B. Article 4 — Bank Deposits and Collections

Among the provisions of Article 4 are the following:

1. **Bank Parties** — Article 4 defines the various bank parties to the deposit and collection process and their respective rights and duties.

2. **Relationship Between Payor Bank and Customer** — Article 4 defines the following:
   - When a bank may charge a customer's account
   - Bank's liability to a customer for failing to honor a good check
   - Customer's right to stop payment
   - Bank's option not to pay an item more than six months old (stale date)
   - Customer's duty to report an unauthorized signature or alteration

3. **Company Obligations** — A company has the duty to examine bank statements within a reasonable time, not to exceed 30 days after the statement has been sent and to report to the bank any unauthorized signatures or alterations. This, coupled with the ordinary care provision of UCC Article 3, makes it imperative that companies accurately reconcile their accounts on a timely basis.

C. Article 4A — Funds Transfers

Article 4A provides a legal framework that outlines the risks, rights and obligations of parties in connection with funds transfers through Fedwire, the clearing house interbank payments system (CHIPS) and ACH. Among the provisions of Article 4A are the following:

1. **Security Procedures** — The bank must make security procedures for verifying payment orders available to the customer and the bank and the customer must agree that those procedures are commercially reasonable. Some common security measures include the use of personal identification numbers (PINs), callbacks, encryption and message authentication.

2. **Consequential Damages** — Banks are not responsible for consequential damages, which are losses resulting from the action or error made by the bank beyond

the actual loss. A bank incorrectly executing a payment order remains liable for interest losses or incidental expenses. The bank is liable for consequential damages only if it agrees to assume this liability in a written agreement with the customer.

D. Article 5 — Letters of Credit

Article 5 covers commercial letters of credit requiring documentary drafts or documentary demands for payment. It does not cover standby letters of credit. Among the provisions of Article 5 are the following:

- Defines a letter of credit, a documentary draft or documentary demand for payment
- Defines the roles of the issuer of the letter of credit, the applicant for whom the credit is issued, the beneficiary of the credit, the advising bank and the confirming bank
- Defines the issuer's obligation to the applicant, including the duty to examine documents to see that they comply with the terms of the credit and to honor a demand for payment that complies with the terms of the credit

Test Your Understanding

These chapter questions are provided to test your understanding of the information in the text and are not examples of CCM examination questions, nor are they in the examination format.

Answers can be found at the back of the book on pages 500-502.

1. What is the definition of a commercial bank?

2. What are the major products and services offered by commercial banks?

3. Discuss the principal function of an investment banking firm.

4. What is an industrial credit and capital company?

5. Who charters savings banks and mutual savings banks?

6. In what ways are credit unions different from banks?

7. What are the five major roles of the Federal Reserve?

8. Who grants charters to national banks?

9. Who is the primary regulator of national S&Ls?

10. What is the FFIEC?

11. What is the OFAC?

12. What legislation permits U.S. banks to invest in corporations engaged in international banking and finance?

13. What legislation originally prohibited banks from accepting deposits across state lines and what is the current status of legislation in this area?

14. What legislation separates commercial from investment banking?

15. What legislation mandated the Federal Reserve to reduce and/or price float?

16. What legislation consolidated the two financial institution insurance funds under the FDIC?

17. Discuss the primary provisions of the Interstate Banking and Branching Efficiency Act of 1994.

18. What legislation permitted the creation of financial holding companies and what else does this legislation do?

19. What Federal Reserve regulation prohibits the payment of interest on corporate demand deposits?

20. What Federal Reserve regulation established rules for handling return of checks and payable through drafts?

21. What article of the UCC permits avoidance of inadvertent accord and satisfaction?

22. Under UCC Article 4A, is a bank responsible for consequential damages?

23. What does UCC Article 5 cover?

CHAPTER 4

U.S. Payments System

Overview

This chapter deals with the basic structure of the U.S. payments system, which processes paper-based and electronic payments. It covers the mechanics of each of its major components and instruments, the regulatory and institutional framework in which it operates and the key implications for cash management.

Learning Objectives

Upon completion of this chapter and the related study questions, the reader should understand:

- The mechanics and applications of the following principal paper instruments: checks, payable through drafts and preauthorized drafts
- The mechanics and applications of the following principal electronic payment instruments: the automated clearing house, Fedwire and the clearing house interbank payments system
- How the Federal Reserve System and the banking industry define and measure payments system risk and the actions they take to reduce it

Key Concepts

- Paper-based payment methods
- Electronic payment methods
- Check clearing
- Funds availability, balances and float
- Payments system risk

Outline

I. Overview of Payment Methods

II. Paper-Based Payments
       A. U.S. Check System Terminology
       B. Components of a Check
       C. The Check Clearing Process
       D. The Check Clearing System
       E. Funds Availability
       F. Federal Reserve Float
       G. Additional Paper Payment Instruments

III. Electronic Payments
       A. The Automated Clearing House (ACH) System
       B. Fedwire
       C. Clearing House Interbank Payments System (CHIPS)
       D. Society for Worldwide Interbank Financial Telecommunications (S.W.I.F.T.)
       E. Payments System Risk

IV. Future of the Payments System

I. Overview of Payment Methods

Checks are the most widely used method of payment in the United States today. However, while the majority of transactions are by check, the greatest volume of dollars is transferred through three electronic payment networks: Fedwire, the automated clearing house (ACH) and the clearing house interbank payments system (CHIPS).

II. Paper-Based Payments

A. U.S. Check System Terminology

A check is a demand instrument used to transfer funds from the payor to the payee. It is important for a cash manager to know the terminology associated with checks, including:

- **Payor** — The party who issues the check
- **Payee** — The party to whom the check is made payable
- **Drawee Bank** — The bank on which the check is drawn, the payor's bank
- **Depository Bank** — The bank that accepts an item for deposit for credit to a customer's account (this bank is also known as the bank of first deposit)
- **Provisional Credit** — The ledger credit a payee receives when a check is deposited, which is subject to final clearing of the check
- **Return Item** — A check the drawee bank rejects and returns to the depository bank

B. Components of a Check

All checks are similarly configured and generally contain the following elements:

1. **Signature** — A check requires the authorization, most typically the signature, of the payor. Sometimes more than one signature is required. Some companies use either mechanically generated or computer-printed facsimile signatures.

2. **Magnetic Ink Character Recognition (MICR) Line** — The information necessary to process checks by machine is contained in the MICR line, which is printed with special characters and magnetic ink on the lower portion of the check. These characters can be read by magnetic or optical scanning equipment. The information contained in the MICR line of a business check is illustrated in Exhibit 4.1.

CHAPTER 4 • U.S. PAYMENTS SYSTEM

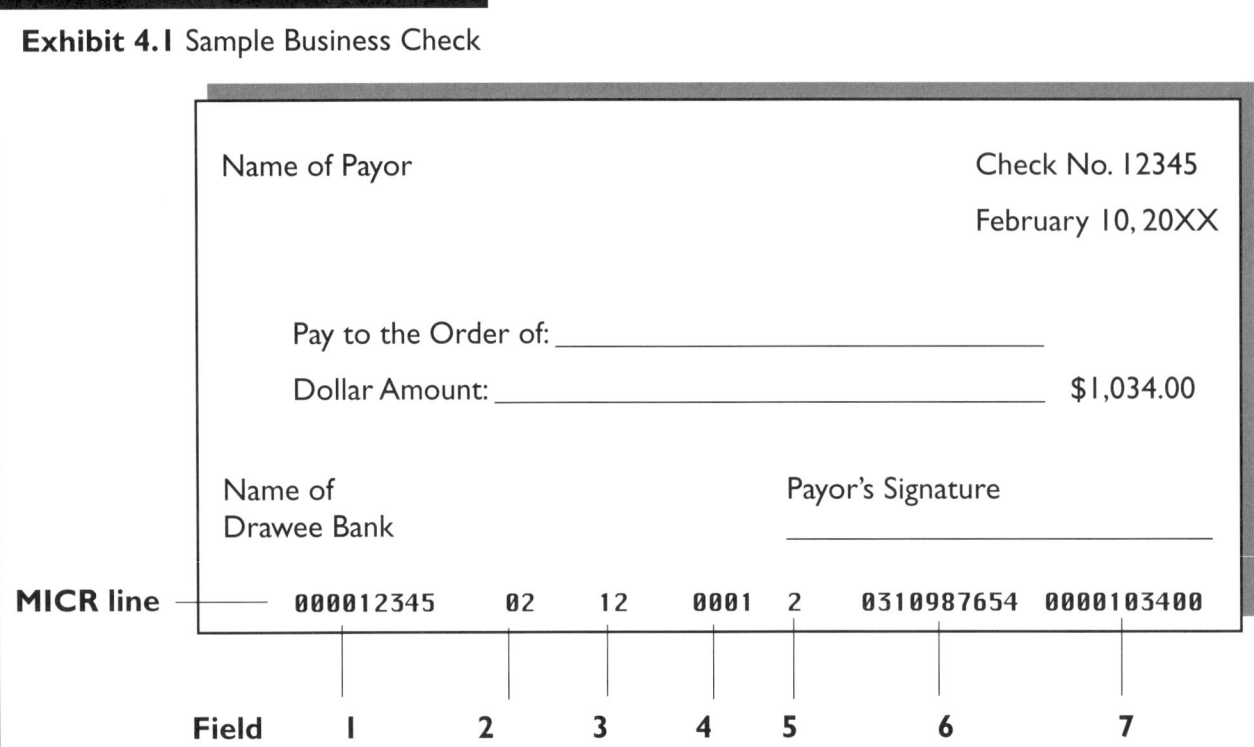

Exhibit 4.1 Sample Business Check

The **MICR** line contains information in a fixed format that allows the depository bank to route the check back to the drawee bank and the drawee bank to identify the account and amount to debit. Fields 2–5 are called the transit routing (TR) number.

1. **Serial Number** — Also called the auxiliary on-us field on a business check.
   This number is frequently the check number.
   It assists the drawee bank in providing a variety of account reconcilement services, such as sorting the cleared checks before returning them to the payor.
   It may also be used for identification codes of divisions or subsidiaries.
   It is a key to providing stop payment and positive pay services.

2. **Federal Reserve Bank Code** — Two digits (01 to 12) identify the drawee bank's Federal Reserve district. Numbers greater than 12 identify a non-bank depository institution such as a thrift.

3. **Federal Reserve Office** — The first digit identifies the Fed branch responsible for handling the drawee bank. The second digit is the availability classification.

4. **Bank Identification Number** — Four digits make up the bank's ABA identification number. That number designates the bank and location to which the item must be delivered. A number of banks have more than one identification number, which facilitates the handling of certain types of checks.

5. **Check Digit** — This digit, when combined with other numbers, enables the computer to verify the accuracy of the routing number for the benefit of the automated routing process.

6. **Payor's Account Number** — This number is assigned to the payor by the drawee bank.

7. **Encoded Amount of Check** — This number should agree with the amount placed on the check by the payor. The amount is typically encoded on the check by the depository bank.

3. **Transit Routing Number** — The MICR line on a check contains the transit routing number, which the depository bank uses to route the check back to the drawee bank.

4. **Encoded Amount of the Check** — This part of the MICR line provides the dollar amount of the check in machine-readable form. The receiving company may pre-encode incoming checks prior to depositing them or the depository bank encodes them.

C. The Check Clearing Process

To effect final settlement, a check must be presented to and accepted by the drawee bank, the institution on which it is drawn. The key event in the check clearing process is presentment — the delivery of a check to the payor's bank. At the time of presentment, value is subtracted from the bank's account with a Federal Reserve bank (the Fed), a correspondent bank or some other clearing institution. Normally, the amount is also subtracted from the payor's account on the same business day. The steps are illustrated in Exhibit 4.2.

1. **Role of the Depository Bank** — The depository bank (bank of first deposit) receives checks for credit to its customers' accounts. The bank's processing operation encodes the check amount on the MICR line. The checks are processed in batches by a reader/sorter machine, which captures and stores the information carried on each check and sorts the checks based on their transit routing numbers. The checks are then transported to the check clearing system.

2. **Role of the Drawee Bank** — In the check clearing process, the drawee bank is responsible for inspecting the check for proper signature, alterations, appropriate dating, stop payments and positive pay instructions. In practice, however, many banks do not check dates and will honor post-dated and stale-dated checks. Drawee banks also review accounts for active status, adequate funds and holds. Holds, or delays in availability, may be placed on certain checks due to their size or the location of the drawee bank. Holds placed on checks deposited by the payee into their account may reduce the amount of available funds for paying checks the payee has written.

The drawee bank has until midnight local time on the banking day following presentment to conduct a review of the check and authorize final payment. If the bank returns a check that exceeds $2,500, it must notify the depository bank of the return by 4 p.m. on the second banking day following presentment. When the depository bank receives the returned checks, they may be redeposited or charged back to the depositor's account.

Exhibit 4.2 Steps in Check Clearing System

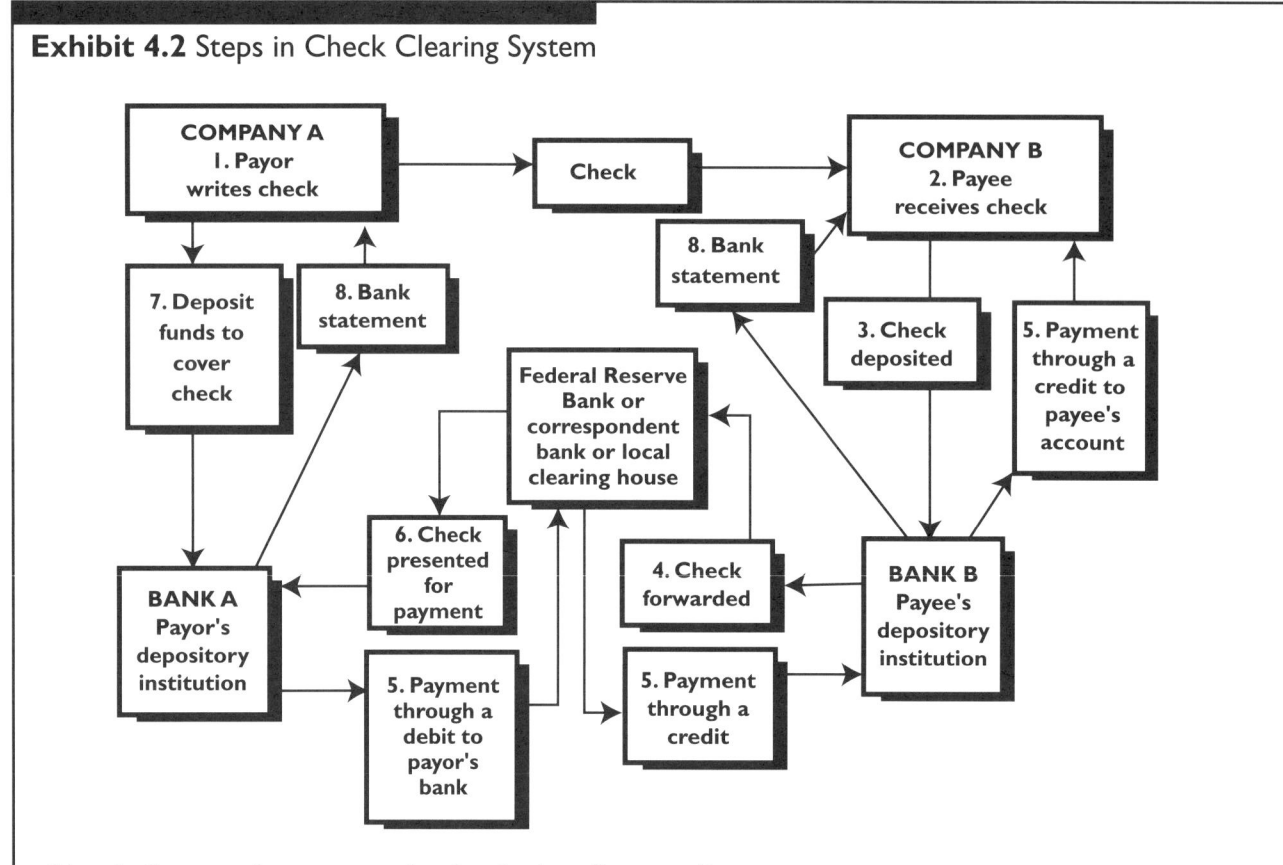

Step 1: Company A prepares and mail a check to Company B.

Step 2: Company B receives and processes the check.

Step 3: Company B deposits the check in its account at Bank B.

Step 4: Bank B processes the check and transports it to a clearing system.

Step 5: The clearing system gives value to Bank B in the amount of the check and subtracts value from Bank A for the same amount. The clearing agent (if any) can be the Federal Reserve System, a correspondent bank or local clearing house.

Step 6: The check is physically presented by the clearing agent to Bank A, where the amount is deducted from Company A's account. This step may occur simultaneously with Step 5.

Step 7: This step does not occur at a predetermined time in the cycle, but on the day of posting, Company A must have funds available in Bank A to cover the amount of the check.

Step 8: Both banks provide reports to their respective companies in the form of periodic bank statements.

D. The Check Clearing System

Banks present checks into the clearing system in in the form of cash letters, bundles of checks accompanied by lists of individual items and other control documents.

1. **Clearing Channels** — Banks use a number of channels for check clearing. Selection of a channel is a function of deposit bank processing time, geographic location and the availability schedules of clearing agents. Availability (the release of depos-

ited funds for use) is granted to the depository bank if the check reaches the endpoint (the drawee bank or location established by the clearing agent) prior to a predefined deposit deadline. Availability schedules define the number of days after deposit before funds become available for use by the depositor.

- *On-Us Check Clearing* — This channel involves a single bank and is used when the payee deposits the check in an account at the same bank on which it is drawn. The bank simultaneously debits the payor's account and credits the payee's account. This is called same-day or immediate availability.

- *Clearing Houses* — These are either formal or informal associations formed by banks in a geographic area to permit the exchange of items drawn on the member participants. Representatives from the member banks meet daily to present checks to each other. The net value is transferred by debiting and crediting correspondent accounts or through reserve accounts each bank maintains with the local Fed. The National Clearing House Association provides nationwide access to many local clearing houses across the country to its member banks.

- *Federal Reserve Bank* — The Federal Reserve bank also acts as a check clearing agent. A bank deposits checks it has received into its account at a Federal Reserve bank and the Fed credits the bank's account for the amount of the checks. The Fed then transports the checks to the drawee bank. Upon presentation at the drawee bank, the Fed subtracts the amount of the checks from the drawee bank's Fed account.

- *Correspondent Bank* — The sending bank, or depository bank, maintains a deposit account with another bank, called a correspondent bank, to which it sends checks. The correspondent bank collects the items through its local clearing house and credits the account of the sending bank with the proceeds of the checks.

2. **Direct Send** — As an alternative to using the clearing channels above, banks may make arrangements to send cash letters directly to the paying banks or to a non-local Federal Reserve bank. These arrangements enable banks to meet various deposit deadlines and achieve faster clearing times. The sending bank maintains a deposit account with the paying bank or non-local Fed, which credits the account of the sending bank with the proceeds of the checks.

3. **Drawee Endpoints** — An endpoint is the location of the drawee bank where final settlement is effected. Four general classifications of drawee endpoints are:

    - *City Items* — Checks drawn on banks located in Federal Reserve cities.

    - *Regional Check Processing Center (RCPC) Items* — Checks drawn on banks serviced by a Federal Reserve RCPC.

    - *Country Items* — Checks drawn on banks located outside the area served by a Federal Reserve city or RCPC.

- *High-Dollar Group Sort (HDGS) Items* — HDGS is a method the Fed uses to expedite the processing of high-dollar checks through the system. When the Fed identifies a bank that receives more than $10 million per day in out-of-Fed-district checks, it may choose to make a second presentment to that bank.

4. **Other Check Clearing Factors**

    - *Deposit Deadlines* — Each transit routing number has a specific deposit deadline that must be met if the clearing bank is to receive the designated availability.

    - *Same-Day Settlement* — A Federal Reserve rule requires that if a check is presented to a drawee bank by 8 a.m. local time, the drawee bank must settle in same-day funds by the close of Fedwire. No presentment fee can be charged. This rule is intended to expedite check collection services.

    - *Electronic Check Presentment (ECP)* — With ECP, the data captured by the reader/sorter, not the physical check, is electronically transmitted to the drawee bank. The drawee bank uses this information to debit the funds from the payor's demand deposit account. The actual check may be sent to the drawee bank for subsequent handling of the check or the depository bank may retain an image of the check. ECP accelerates the clearing of checks and thus the notification of checks being returned by the drawee bank.

        Banks, with the support of organizations such as the Electronic Check Clearing House Organization (ECCHO), are developing programs for the electronic exchange of check information. Electronic exchange of information enables verification of funds availability prior to physical presentment of the check to the drawee bank, affording expedited return of non-sufficient funds (NSF) checks.

    - *MICR Capture at Point-of-Sale* — Many retail outlets are implementing systems that allow customers paying by check to have their checks scanned, thus capturing the account information from the MICR line and converting the payment into an ACH debit transaction.

E. Funds Availability

The time at which funds from a check become available for use depends on several factors: the time and day the check is deposited, the drawee endpoint and the bank of deposit's ledger cutoff time and availability schedule.

1. **Ledger Cutoff Time** — A bank's ledger cutoff, set by each individual bank, is the time of day when a deposit must be received to be posted to the depositor's account. Items deposited after the ledger cutoff time are considered to have been received by the bank on the next banking day. For example, if a bank has a published ledger cutoff time of 3 p.m., a deposit made at 2 p.m. on a Friday will be credited to the

ledger balance on Friday. However, a deposit made to the same bank at 4 p.m. that day will not be credited to the ledger balance until Monday.

2. **Deposit Deadline** — A deposit deadline is the time of day, based on an item's drawee endpoint, by which an item must be at the depository bank's processing center ready for transit in order to qualify for the availability stated on that bank's availability schedule. Ledger credit must be granted prior to the deposit deadline. If a check comes into the bank processing center after the deposit deadline, the next day's deposit deadline goes into effect.

   For example, if a bank's ledger cutoff time is 3 p.m., the Wednesday banking day starts at 3:01 p.m. on Tuesday and ends at 3 p.m. on Wednesday. A Wednesday deposit deadline of 10 p.m. means the item must have been received at the processing center prior to 10 p.m. on Tuesday in order to receive the availability specified on the bank's availability schedule. If an item is deposited at 8 a.m. Wednesday, it has missed Wednesday's deposit deadline (10 p.m. Tuesday) and availability will be determined based on Thursday's deposit deadline, but ledger credit will still be granted on Wednesday. In effect, the deposit deadline specified on an availability schedule must fall between the time of deposit and the ledger cutoff time for the availability on the schedule to be granted. Exhibit 4.3 provides a detailed description of ledger and deposit deadlines.

3. **Availability Schedules** — Availability schedules specify, for each drawee endpoint, when a bank grants credit for deposited checks to the depositor's available or collected balance. The assignment of availability can be in whole or fractional banking days. Checks are generally assigned between zero and two days' availability. The Fed has availability schedules for banks, correspondent banks have availability schedules for other banks and banks have availability schedules for their customers. Many banks have multiple availability schedules depending on the customer and volume of business. Because the availability schedule impacts float balances, the schedule a bank offers to a particular customer is part of the pricing decision.

   Exhibit 4.4 illustrates a sample availabilty schedule.

CHAPTER 4 • U.S. PAYMENTS SYSTEM

Exhibit 4.3 Example of Ledger and Deposit Deadlines

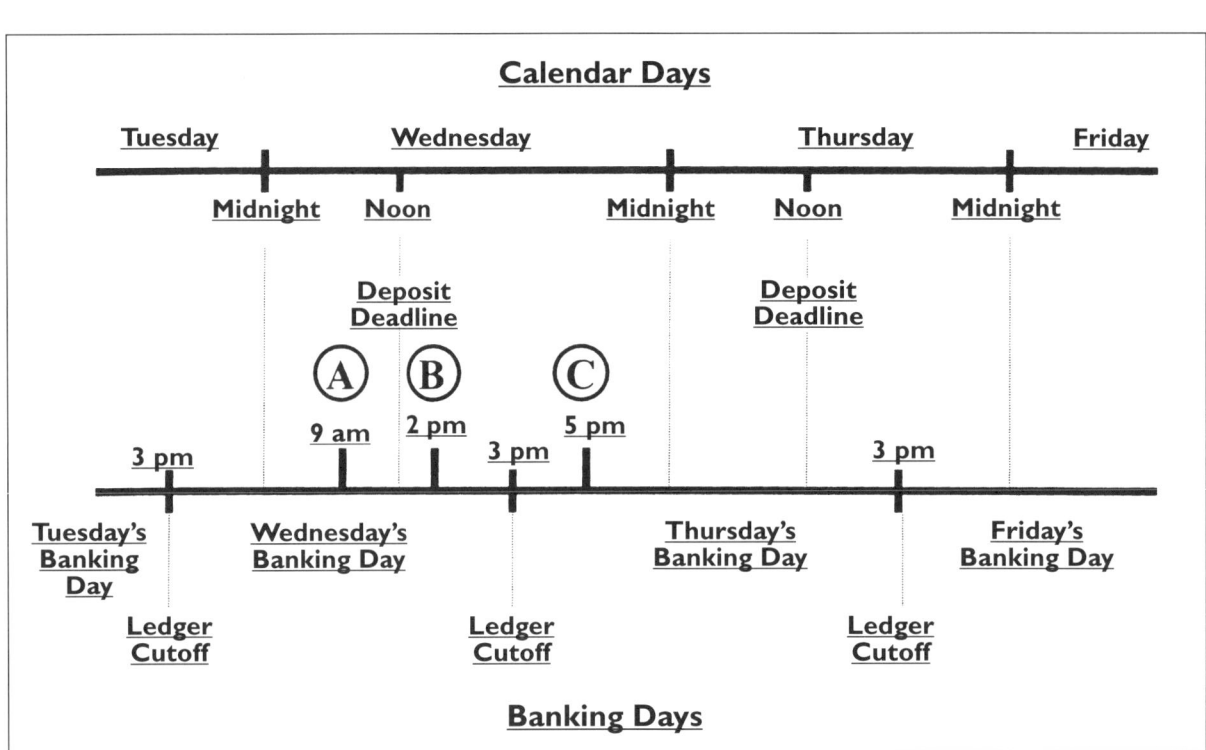

Assume a ledger cutoff time of 3 p.m. and a deposit deadline for a given item of noon. If the deposit deadline is met, the item has a one-day availability. Depositing the item at time A, B and C (as shown above) has the following results:

Time A (9 a.m. Wednesday): The deposit is made before the deposit deadline and before the ledger cutoff in Wednesday's business. The deposited item will be available on Thursday.

Time B (2 p.m. Wednesday): The deposit is made in time to meet ledger cutoff, but has missed the deposit deadline. The deposited item will be available on Friday.

Time C (5 p.m. Wednesday): The deposit has missed the ledger cutoff and is now in Thursday's business. Since the deposit was made before the Thursday deposit deadline (noon Thursday), the deposited item will be available by Friday.

4. **Balances and Float**
   - *Ledger Balances* — Ledger balances are bank balances that reflect all entries to a bank account, regardless of whether or not the deposited items have been collected and are available for withdrawal. Ledger balances are important for accounting purposes but not for funds availability or bank compensation purposes. If the ledger balance is negative, there is a ledger overdraft. There may be a service and/or interest charge for such an overdraft.
   - *Deposit Float* — Deposit float has two meanings:

Exhibit 4.4 Sample of Availability Schedule

Transit Routing	Endpoint Location	Endpoint Description	Deposit Deadline	Availability
0841-xxxx	Memphis, TN	RCPC	1 p.m.	1 day
0910-xxxx	Minneapolis, MN	City	6 p.m.	0 day
1230-xxxx	Portland, OR	City	6 p.m.	0 day
1031-xxx	Oklahoma City, OK	Country	9 a.m.	1 day
0551-xxxx	Charleston, SC	RCPC	4 p.m.	1 day
0711-xxxx	Chicago, IL	Country	11 a.m.	1 day
0220-xxxx	Buffalo, NY	City	7 a.m.	0 day

— Deposit float is the sum of the deposited items that are in the process of collection.

— Deposit float is also used to refer to the interval between the time an item is deposited and the time the funds are collected. For example, cash managers often refer to an average float of a certain number of days, meaning the average length of time they must wait for deposited funds to become available.

- *Collected Balances* — Collected balances reflect the balance in an account for which the bank of deposit has received settlement. Collected balances are the difference between ledger balances and the deposit float. If the collected balance is negative, there is a collected balance overdraft and there may be a service and/or interest charge for the overdraft.

  For example, suppose a $1,000 check deposited on Tuesday into an account with a zero balance is granted one-day availability, meaning the bank gives the customer use of the funds after a wait of one banking day. While the ledger balance increases by $1,000 on Tuesday, the collected balance does not increase until Wednesday. On Tuesday, the deposit float is equal to $1,000 and the collected balance is equal to the ledger balance of $1,000 minus the deposit float of $1,000, or $0.

- *Available Balances* — Available balances are the amount of funds available for withdrawal from an account. They are equal to the sum of: 1) the collected balances, 2) the balances that are scheduled to be collected by the end of the banking day and 3) those additional amounts for which availability must be granted under Federal Reserve Regulation CC. Assuming a ledger cutoff time of 5 p.m. and the availability schedule in Exhibit 4.4, a company would receive ledger and collected balances as shown in Exhibit 4.5 if its deposits were made on Monday at the times specified.

> **Exhibit 4.5—Application of Availability Schedule**
>
> Assuming a ledger cutoff time of 3 p.m. and the availability schedule as shown in Exhibit 4.4, a company would receive ledger and collected balances as follows if its deposits were made on Monday at noon and 5 p.m.
>
> | | Noon Deposit | | 5 p.m. Deposit | |
> | --- | --- | --- | --- | --- |
> | **Endpoint** | **Ledger Credit** | **Available** | **Ledger Credit** | **Available** |
> | Memphis | Monday | Tuesday | Tuesday | Wednesday |
> | Minneapolis | Monday | Tuesday | Tuesday | Tuesday |
> | Portland | Monday | Tuesday | Tuesday | Tuesday |
> | Oklahoma City | Monday | Wednesday | Tuesday | Wednesday |
> | Charleston | Monday | Wednesday | Tuesday | Thursday |
> | Chicago | Monday | Wednesday | Tuesday | Wednesday |
> | Buffalo | Monday | Tuesday | Tuesday | Tuesday |

5. **How Banks Assign Availability**

Most banks assign availability using the proof of deposit (POD) method. Under the POD method, availability is assigned to each check as it passes through the automated check processing equipment. Availability is assigned based on the time and day of deposit and the check's endpoint. Some banks may negotiate special availability for selected high-volume customers.

6. **Factors Determining Availability**

   - *Drawee Location* — Checks drawn on banks in geographically distant or isolated locations generally have longer availability times than those drawn on nearby banks.

   - *Time of Deposit* — Checks must reach the processing center and be ready for transit by a certain time of day in order to receive the designated availability.

   - *Day of Deposit* — Special availability considerations may apply to items deposited immediately preceding a weekend or bank holiday.

   - *Pre-Encoding* — If a customer MICR encodes the dollar amount on the checks it deposits, the customer may receive faster availability, a later cutoff time and/or reduced service charges.

   - *Reject Items* — Checks that are rejected by a bank's automated check processing equipment are likely to miss critical deposit deadlines, resulting in longer availability and additional processing fees.

- *As-Of Adjustments* — When a check takes longer to actually clear than the initial availability that was granted, the bank may add this additional time as part of the collected balance calculation. For example, if a bank originally granted one-day availability but actually cleared the check in two days, it would add one more day of float in calculating collected balances.

- *Fractional Availability* — As an alternative to as-of adjustments, a bank may grant what is known as fractional availability. For example, under normal circumstances a bank may experience an average collection interval of one day for a certain class of checks, but may miss availability deadlines five percent of the time. Rather than make as-of adjustments, it could assign a fractional availability of 1.05 days to those items.

F. Federal Reserve Float

In the process of clearing checks, banks sometimes receive availability from the Fed before the Fed can generate the offsetting debit. The difference in timing between the availability granted a clearing bank and the actual presentment of the item to the drawee bank is called Fed float. Fed float represents interest-free loans to banks and, indirectly, to companies. The 1980 Depository Institutions Deregulation and Monetary Control Act (DIDMCA) mandated both the reduction and pricing of this benefit.

Today, the Fed no longer officially carries Fed float on their books and reserve balances at the Fed are adjusted for missed presentments on an item-by-item basis. In addition, the Fed will adjust a bank's availability schedule on a monthly basis, based on the previous month's clearings.

G. Additional Paper Payment Instruments

A number of other payment instruments have check-like attributes and clear through the same channels as checks. The following are examples of these instruments:

1. **Payable Through Draft (PTD)** — A PTD is a payment instrument resembling a check that is drawn against the payor and not the bank. A draft is handled like a check through the clearing system, but the responsibility for paying the draft lies with the drawee. The primary reason companies use PTDs is to preserve the right to review the items prior to final payment. Insurance companies often use PTDs for claim reimbursement because the PTD gives them an opportunity to verify the signature and endorsements before honoring it. Some state and local governments use a form of PTD called a government warrant.

2. **Preauthorized Draft/Check** — The payor authorizes the payee to draw a draft/check against the payor's account. The payee, rather than the payor, initiates the transaction. Mortgage, insurance and other recurring payments may be made this way. Most preauthorized drafts are now done on an electronic basis via ACH debit.

3. **Money Order** — A money order is a prepaid instrument issued by parties such as companies, banks or the Post Office. The purchaser is the instrument's payor and the money order is the obligation of the issuer.

4. **Travelers Checks** — Such instruments are prepaid and similar to money orders. Two signatures typically are required by the purchaser: one at issuance and one at the time the check is used.

5. **Depository Transfer Checks (DTC)** — DTCs are checks used in moving funds from one account to another account held by the same company, usually in cash concentration systems. No signature is required, but for security there is often a payee restriction. Normally the payee can only be an account at the concentration bank. Electronic transfers (via ACH) have largely replaced paper DTCs.

6. **Sight Draft** — A sight draft is payable on demand and is usually presented in combination with other documents showing that the terms of the transaction have been met. Sight drafts are primarily used to support international trade.

7. **Time Draft** — This payment mechanism is like a sight draft but is not payable until a specified future date. Time drafts are used in international trade transactions that call for delayed payments.

8. **Cashier's Check/Certified Check** — A cashier's check, also known as an official bank check, is a check drawn by a bank on its own funds and signed by a bank officer. A certified check is drawn by a depositor on his checking account; it carries the signature of a bank officer certifying the check to be genuine and guaranteeing its payment. Due to the higher processing costs of certified checks, most banks have replaced them with cashier's checks.

III. Electronic Payments

There are three electronic funds clearing systems in the United States: ACH, Fedwire and CHIPS. This section discusses these systems as well as the Society for Worldwide Interbank Financial Telecommunications (S.W.I.F.T.) system and payments system risk.

A. The Automated Clearing House (ACH) System

The ACH system was developed by the financial industry in the early 1970s as an electronic alternative to checks. In an ACH transaction, payment information is processed and settled electronically, thereby increasing reliability, efficiency and cost effectiveness. In addition, an ACH transaction is capable of transferring more information about a payment than is possible on a check.

1. **Structure** — ACH is a network of regional associations, interbank associations and private-sector processors. These ACH associations and processors are called ACH operators. Many regional ACHs are operated by the Fed. The majority of financial institutions are members of an ACH association.

   The National Automated Clearing House Association (NACHA, or the Electronic Payments Association) is a membership organization that provides marketing and educational assistance and establishes the rules, standards and procedures that enable financial institutions to exchange ACH payments on a national basis.

2. **Processing** — The ACH system currently is a batch-process, store-and-forward system. Transactions received by the bank during the day are stored and processed later in batches. They are then forwarded in batches to the bank's ACH operator.

3. **Participants** — Exhibit 4.6 shows the parties in an ACH transaction.

4. **How ACH Transactions Differ from Checks** — The terminology and mechanics of the ACH system differ from those of the check clearing system in four ways:
   - A check is paper-based; an ACH transaction is electronic.
   - A check is limited to payment instructions; an ACH transaction can also transmit additional payment-related information.
   - The parties to a check are referred to as the payor and the payee; the parties to an ACH transaction are the originator and receiver.
   - A check can only debit a payor's account and credit a payee's account; an ACH transaction can be either a debit or a credit transaction. ACH credit transactions move funds from the originator's account to the receiver's account; ACH debit transactions move funds from the receiver's account to the originator's account.

   Exhibit 4.7, on page 99, shows the steps in a typical ACH credit transaction in

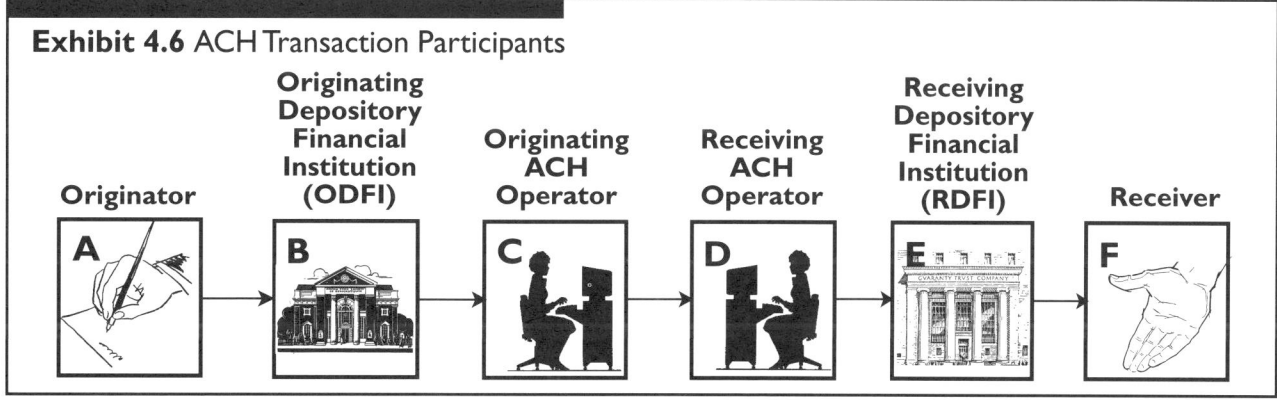

Exhibit 4.6 ACH Transaction Participants

Originator → Originating Depository Financial Institution (ODFI) → Originating ACH Operator → Receiving ACH Operator → Receiving Depository Financial Institution (RDFI) → Receiver which Company A (the originator) uses direct deposit to initiate payroll payments to its employees (the receivers).

An ACH debit transaction is identical to the credit transaction outlined in Exhibit 4.7, except that the file contains a code indicating that the account at the receiving depository financial institution (RDFI) is to be debited instead of credited and value is transferred from the receiver to the originator. An example of an ACH debit would be an insurance company using ACH debits to collect preauthorized premium payments from policyholders.

5. **ACH Risk Issues** — The increasing volume of funds being moved through the ACH system has caused regulators and system participants to become more aware of the associated risks.

    - *Credit Risk* — An originating depository financial institution (ODFI) has credit exposure as the originator of an ACH transaction. In the case of a credit origination, exposure exists from the time the ODFI releases an ACH file to the ACH operator until settlement occurs. Once a file is released to the ACH operator, it may not be recalled or reversed (reversing entries may be submitted only for correction of errors). If the originator's account has insufficient funds at the time of settlement, an overdraft occurs. If the originator filed for bankruptcy prior to settlement, the ODFI cannot settle against the originator's account. For a debit origination, the risk is that return items will be received and the funds remaining in the originator's account will not be sufficient to cover them. Electronic bill presentment and payment (EBPP) initiatives that use high levels of automated ACH debits will likely cause an increase in this type of risk. NACHA rules require ODFIs to establish and monitor exposure limits for all ACH originators.

    In addition, the Federal Reserve Payments System Risk Policy recommends that an ODFI:

    — Perform credit assessments on originators generating large-dollar volume ACH files

    — Establish intraday credit limits for originators

    — React to minimize risk if an originator's financial condition is deteriorating

    As a result, more ODFIs now require financial information, credit approval and limit monitoring, or prefunding for ACH originations.

    - *Large-Value Payment Risk* — Because ACH transactions are significantly less expensive than wire transfers, some originators have migrated large-dollar transfers to the ACH system. The technical limit for an ACH transaction is 10 characters, or $99,999,999.99. However, ACH system controls are not as extensive as wire transfer controls and credit risk to ODFIs increases with large payments. As a practical consideration, however, large-dollar

Exhibit 4.7 An ACH Credit Transaction (Direct Deposit of Payroll)

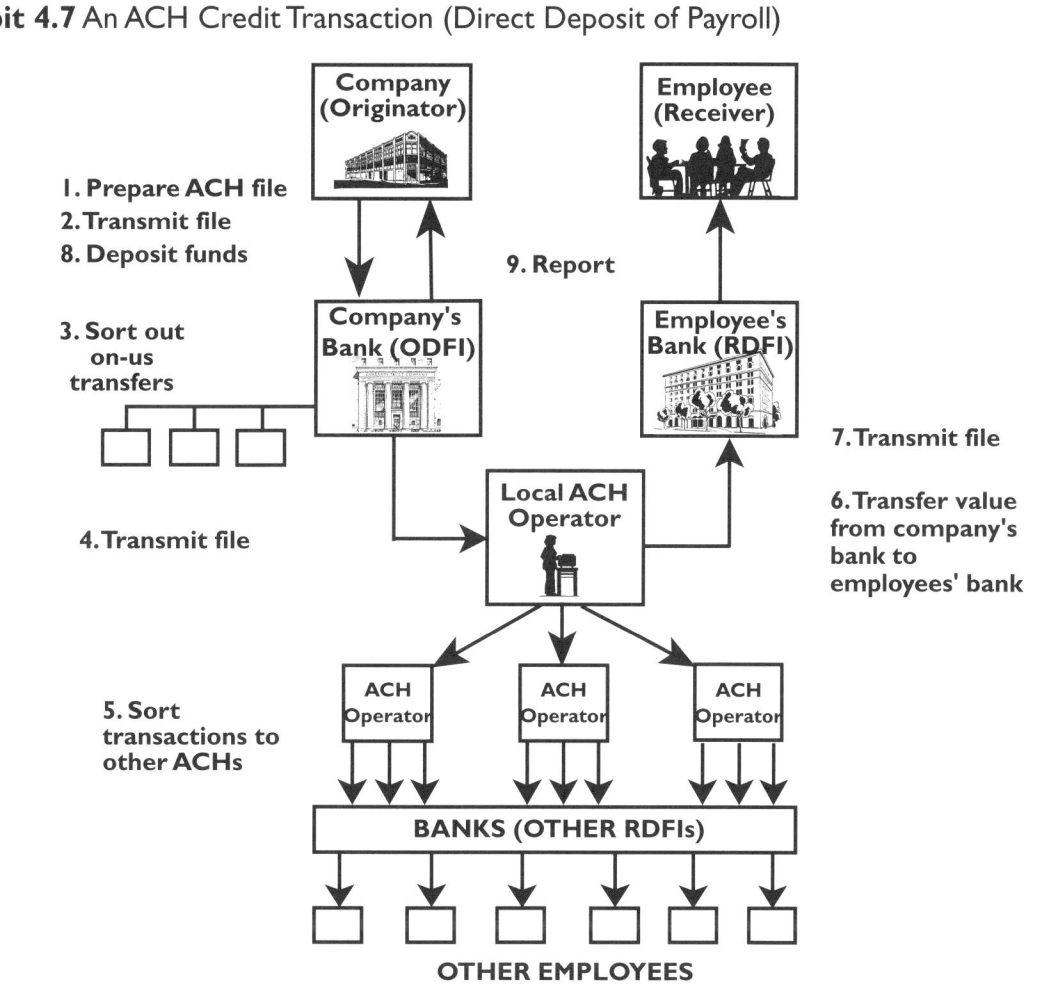

Step 1: A company prepares a file that may contain hundreds of payroll transactions. The file contains each employee's account number, the transit routing number of the employee's bank, the amount of the transfer, the transit routing number of the company's bank, the company's account number and other pertinent information.

Step 2: The company transmits the file to its bank, the originating depository financial institution (ODFI).

Step 3: The company's bank sorts out on-us transactions for employees who have accounts with the bank and credits their accounts on settlement date.

Step 4: The company's bank merges the company's transactions involving other financial institutions with transactions from other firms. A combined file is transmitted to the ACH operator servicing the originating institution.

Step 5: The local ACH operator sorts out those transactions that involve banks in its area and sends the remaining transaction to other ACH operators.

Step 6: Settlement, or transfer of value, occurs when specified in the file. For payroll this is normally after two days.

Step 7: The ACH operator presents a file to the employee's bank containing all transactions pertaining to that bank. The amount the employee receives is credited to the employee's account.

Step 8: This step does not come at a predetermined time in the cycle. On or before the day the ODFI's account is debited, the company must have funds available in the bank to cover the transactions.

Step 9: Both banks provide reports in the form of periodic bank statements and possible daily deposit and withdrawal reports.

transfers would typically move via Fedwire rather than ACH, as the money would be available one day sooner for investment purposes (this is covered in more detail in Chapter 7, Cash Concentration).

6. **ACH Payment Formats** — There are standard ACH formats for both consumer and corporate payments. All ACH payment formats move funds in essentially the same manner. The most appropriate format for a particular payment is determined by the relationship between the parties, the information exchanged and the types of ACH payment services offered by the participating banks.

The format of an ACH payment message is identified by a three-letter standard entry class in the header of the message. The basic ACH formats are as follows:

- *Prearranged Payment or Deposit (PPD)* — The PPD format is the payment application by which consumers may authorize credits or debits to their accounts by a company or financial institution. These are normally recurring payments in fixed amounts.

    — *PPD Credits* — Examples of consumer credits are payroll, expense reimbursement, dividends, social security, retirement benefits and tax refunds.

    — *PPD Debits* — Examples of consumer debits are rent and mortgage payments, subscriptions, dues and memberships, insurance premiums, installment debt payments and utility payments.

- *Cash Concentration or Disbursement (CCD)* — CCD is an electronic payment format used for concentration and disbursement of funds within or between companies. A single 94-character record contains the standard entry class indicating the type of transaction, transit routing numbers for the originating and receiving financial institutions and the originator and receiver account numbers. CCD is the only corporate ACH format that does not have space for an additional addenda record, but it does contain space for a reference number.

- *Cash Concentration or Disbursement Plus Addendum (CCD+)* — CCD+ is one of the formats used for the U.S. Treasury's Vendor Express program and for business-to-business (B2B) payments. It is useful when only a limited amount of information must be transmitted. This format is identical to CCD but with an addenda record. The addenda record is 94 characters long and includes a free-form space for up to 80 characters of descriptive data. The CCD+ addenda record is also used to report federal and state tax payment information. The data conforms to the tax payment (TXP) banking conventions.

- *Corporate Trade Exchange (CTX)* — The CTX format is designed for B2B trade payments. It consists of a standard ACH payment transaction and a variable-length message addendum designed to convey remittance information in the Accredited Standards Committee (ASC) X12 data standard. The addendum can accommodate 9,999 records of 80 characters each. CTX is useful for payments related to multiple invoices and those with substantial invoice detail.

- *Re-Presented Check Entries (RCK)* — The RCK format is utilized to transmit ACH debit entries in place of a paper check after the paper check has been returned for insufficient or uncollected funds. The general requirements are that the item be less than $2,500 and drawn on a consumer account. Originators of re-presented check entries must provide notice to the check writer, prior to receiving an item to which the re-presented check entry relates, informing the check writer that his returned check may be collected electronically if the check is returned for insufficient or uncollected funds. Originators may transmit a re-presented check entry no more than twice after the first return of a paper item and no more than once after the second return of a paper item.

The NACHA operating rules require all financial institutions participating in the ACH to accept all types of ACH entries and post the dollar amounts to the proper accounts; however, some institutions may not have the capability to process addenda records. Addenda records contain remittance details that follow the standard payment information in ACH payment messages. The Fed does sell inexpensive software that allows smaller financial institutions to extract this data and print it out for their customers.

7. **Settlement** — ACH transactions carry settlement dates that determine the availability of funds. Transactions are settled one or two business days after the file is released to the ACH operator. Both the receiver and the originator are settled on the same day, so that the float associated with checks does not exist in the ACH system. Among the conventions governing settlement are the following:

    - Credit originations are usually entered into the system at least two banking days prior to settlement.
    - Debit originations are usually entered into the system on the banking day prior to settlement.
    - Cutoff times for receipt of ACH files vary by ODFI; some ODFIs may accept files over the weekend for Monday settlement.
    - Memo posting is posting of an ACH credit or debit early in the day when the actual credit or debit will not settle until later that day.

8. **Prenotification** — Prenotifications (prenotes) are optional zero-dollar entries that are sent through the ACH system prior to live entries. Prenotes provide a verification function at the receiving bank before entries for settlement are processed. For example, when a company adds a new employee to its direct deposit of payroll program, it may use prenotification to ensure that the bank's transit routing number and the employee's personal bank account number(s) are correct. Prenotes are

optional, but are useful to ensure that all records are correct prior to transaction, especially in consumer applications. Also, while the sending of the prenote is optional, NACHA rules require the receiving financial institution to respond to them.

9. **Authorization** — Companies originating ACH transactions are required by NACHA rules to obtain prior consent from the receiver authorizing the ACH transaction. For ACH debits, this consent must be in writing. This authorization is good until terminated by either party. Once terminated or revoked, the originator must be able to produce either the original or a microfilmed copy of the authorization for a period of two years.

10. **Advantages of Using ACH** — The ACH system provides numerous advantages compared to paper-based systems. These include:
    - *Reduced Payment Costs* — An ACH transfer is less expensive than a check and much less expensive than a wire transfer.
    - *Reduced Reconciliation and Cash Application Costs* — Because payments are automated, reconciliation time is reduced. Cash application costs are generally reduced compared to paper-based systems.
    - *Faster Inflows* — The use of ACH debits accelerates cash inflow by reducing delays caused by invoicing, the mail, internal processing and bank clearing channels.
    - *Control of Payment Timing* — The use of ACH debits and credits increases control of payment initiation and funds availability.
    - *More Accurate Forecasting* — The control of payment timing increases the accuracy of cash flow forecasts.
    - *Increased Reliability* — ACH transactions reach their destination in a timely and predictable manner.
    - *Enhanced Service* — Customers and employees benefit from enhanced services such as automatic bill paying and direct deposit of payroll.
    - *Reduced Fraud* — ACH is less susceptible to fraud compared to the use of checks.

11. **Disadvantages of Using ACH** — The following are considered disadvantages of the ACH system:
    - *Reduction in Disbursement Float* — The payor may lose float benefits accruing from invoicing, mail, processing and check clearing delays. However, before switching to electronic payments, some corporate trading partners renegotiate payment terms.
    - *Loss of Control with Direct Debits* — Payors have security and liability concerns regarding direct debits. However, some banks have systems designed to prevent unauthorized debit and credit activity or amounts in excess of

preapproved limits. To comply with ACH operating rules, companies must notify their banks within 24 hours of any unauthorized ACH debit transactions posted to their accounts.

- *System Startup Costs* — There can be significant development costs, including computer software and hardware investments, training of employees and education of customers.

B. Fedwire

Fedwire is the Federal Reserve funds transfer system. It is a real-time method of transferring immediate funds and supporting information between two financial institutions, using their respective Federal Reserve accounts. The system is reliable and secure but, compared to checks and ACH transactions, relatively expensive to use.

1. **Communications and Settlement** — Fedwire is both a communications and a settlement system. Except for delays that might result from either a customer or bank temporarily reaching an overdraft limit, funds are moved almost instantaneously once a request has been received and validated by the originating bank. The transaction is final once it has been sent by the originating bank and receipt is confirmed by the Fed.

2. **Hours of Operation and Deadlines** — Fedwire hours are 12:30 a.m. to 6:30 p.m., Eastern Standard Time (ET). Banks establish earlier cutoff times for customers and other internal departments to allow time for processing.

3. **Mechanics of a Wire Transfer** — Exhibit 4.8 shows the steps in a typical wire transfer. The entire process generally takes only minutes.

4. **Payment Finality** — In the event the sending bank fails to settle, the Federal Reserve guarantees the transferred funds to the receiving bank.

5. **Fedwire Format** — The Fedwire format is designed to interface with CHIPS and the S.W.I.F.T. system. The current format includes information required by federal authorities to combat illegal money laundering activity.

6. **Types of Fedwire Funds Transfers** — Among the different classifications of Fedwire transfers are the following:

    - *Repetitive* — Repetitive transfers are used when a company makes a transfer frequently between the same debit and credit parties. The bank has a record of the debit and credit parties and receives electronic and telephonic instructions to make the transfer. A unique identifier is assigned to each instruction template. Only the date and dollar amount may be changed. This significantly decreases the risk of misdirected funds.

Exhibit 4.8 Mechanics of a Wire Transfer

Step 1: Company A initiates a request to transfer funds to Company B. This is typically done through a treasury workstation or by a telephone call. Security procedures may include the use of personal identification numbers (PINs), test key calculations or message authentication algorithms, dual authorization of the transfer or callbacks to verify instructions. Most telephone calls are recorded for security purposes and to resolve disputes.

Step 2: Bank A checks to see if Company A has sufficient funds in its account. If it does, Bank A debits Company A's account. If not, appropriate credit approval must be obtained or the transfer must wait until sufficient funds are available.

Step 3: Bank A uses Fedwire to transfer funds to Company B through the Federal Reserve System.

Step 4: The Federal Reserve (Fed) debits Bank A's reserve account and credits Bank B's reserve account.

Step 5: The Fed notifies Bank B of the transfer, including account information for Company B. If Bank B is in a different Fed district from Bank A, the information is routed through the Fed's communication network to the appropriate receiving Federal Reserve bank.

Step 6: Bank B credits Company B's account.

Step 7: Bank B notifies Company B of receipt of wire transfer.

- *Semirepetitive* — With semirepetitive transfers, the debit and credit parties remain the same, but the description may be changed, along with the date and dollar amount. Semirepetitive transfers allow some of the control of repetitive transfers and some of the flexibility of non-repetitive transfers.

- *Non-repetitive (Free-Form)* — With non-repetitive transfers, the debit and credit parties are different each time. Additional security steps are generally required for these types of transfers.

- *Drawdown* — A drawdown is a request sent by a company to a bank to initiate a wire transfer from its own or another party's account. The party being debited must preauthorize the transfer. Drawdowns are most frequently used as part of a company's concentration system.

7. **Wire Transfer Security** — Security in wire transfer is critical. Commercially reasonable security procedures are necessary in order to comply with Uniform Commercial Code Article 4A (UCC4A). Security procedures are generally outlined in a bank's wire transfer agreement. Among the types of security procedures that are commonly used are the following:

   - Physical security and limited access at both the company and the bank.
   - Passwords and personal identification numbers (PINs) to identify authorized users.
   - Test keys or codes to validate wire transfers.
   - Repetitive wires to limit where and to whom funds can be transferred.
   - Dual approval (one person enters the wire and another reviews and releases it).
   - Electronic security methods such as encryption (the scrambling of a message by the sender and the unscrambling of the message by the receiver), message authentication (a digital signature that prevents an unauthorized person from changing a wire) and digital certificates (a third-party service that ties a user's public and private encryption keys together). (See Chapter 9, Electronic Commerce for more information on electronic security.)
   - Security devices or keys to guard against misuse or fraud.

8. **Pricing** — The total price to a user of a wire transfer varies significantly. Both the sending institution and the receiving institution may impose a charge.

C. Clearing House Interbank Payments System (CHIPS)

CHIPS is an independent large-dollar funds transfer network operated by the New York Automated Clearing House. It was established in 1970 to substitute electronic payments for paper checks used in international dollar transactions between foreign and American banks. It is also used for payments under letters of credit and documentary collections and for third-party transfers. Any commercial bank with a regulated presence in the United States can become a member of CHIPS and gain access to their system. CHIPS currently has approximately 60 U.S. and international bank participants and clears more than 95 percent of the international payments made in U.S. dollars.

1. **Operation** — Transfers between member banks are received and authenticated during the day. Prior to 2001, transfers were batched and at the end of the day the

net amounts due to or from each of the settling participants were determined (an end-of-day net settlement system). These net amounts were then settled using the clearing banks or the Fed, with non-settling participants settling via correspondent banks. Transfers were executed on a same-day basis and could be unwound (reversed) only if a member bank could not honor its net debit position. In 2001, CHIPS implemented a "real-time" netting system, which offered finality of payments at the time of their release. Under this new process, each CHIPS member bank funds a special account maintained by CHIPS at the Federal Reserve Bank of New York. Throughout the day — from shortly after midnight until 5 p.m. ET — participant banks send their payments to CHIPS. The system continuously searches the database of payments and uses bilateral and multilateral netting to match and release payments. A payment is considered final when CHIPS releases it.

2. **Finality** – The new CHIPS system allows for real-time netting, with even very large payments being netted out quickly. This effectively eliminates daylight overdraft situations as well as bottlenecks that may slow down the payment process. Settlement via CHIPS is a viable alternative to Fedwire, especially for transfers between member banks. The new CHIPS settlement procedures remove the need for various risk mitigating procedures used previously, such as pledging of U.S. Treasury securities and the use of bilateral limits and debit caps.

3. **Future of CHIPS and Electronic Commerce (E-Commerce)** — Effective June 2001, CHIPS will be able to transmit significant amounts of remittance information with a payment. Up to 9,000 characters of data in either standard electronic data interchange (EDI) formats (ASC X12, UN EDIFACT [United Nations EDI for Administration, Commerce and Transportation]) or new Internet-based formats such as eXtensible Mark-up Language (XML) can flow with each CHIPS payment. Invoice numbers, discount details, rebates, bank fees and foreign exchange data will be able to move electronically from remitter to beneficiary. Fedwire does not currently offer this capability.

D. Society for Worldwide Interbank Financial Telecommunications (S.W.I.F.T.)

S.W.I.F.T. is the major international interbank telecommunications network that transmits international payment instructions as well as other financial messages. It is not a funds transfer network. Messages are transferred requesting debits and credits to correspondent accounts (in addition to other types of messages). Settlement occurs through Fedwire, CHIPS, correspondent accounts or other real-time gross settlement systems such as Bankers Automated Clearing Service (BACS) in the U.K. The formats and uses of the S.W.I.F.T. network are being enhanced to include functions such as balance reporting.

E. Payments System Risk

The growth of payment volume in recent decades and several large bank failures during the 1970s have prompted greater attention by the Federal Reserve System to reducing payments system risk.

1. **Types of Risk** — Today's payments system creates four kinds of risk for banks:
   - *Systemic Risk* — The risk that the failure of one major bank could cause other banks to fail and cause a collapse of the payments system
   - *Credit Risk* — The risk that the party funding a transaction will default on its settlement obligation
   - *Operational Risk* — The risk of processing mistakes, or system disruptions
   - *Fraud Risk* — The risk that someone might alter a transaction or enter a false item that could cause a loss for the disbursing party

2. **Daylight Overdrafts** — A daylight overdraft is an intraday exposure occurring when an account is in an overdraft position during the business day. Banks may have daylight overdrafts in their Federal Reserve bank accounts and companies may have daylight overdrafts in their accounts at commercial banks.

   Examples of transactions that often create daylight overdrafts include the following:
   - A bank may repay Fed funds borrowed for the previous night but not receive the proceeds of new borrowings until later that day.
   - A bank customer that issues commercial paper may repay funds to investors in the morning but not receive funds from investors in a replacement issue until the afternoon.

   Controlling daylight overdrafts has been one of the primary objectives of recent Federal Reserve measures to control risk among the large-dollar payment networks. The Fed has mandated that all banks using the large-dollar payment systems must have in place a sender net debit cap limiting the intraday overdraft that the bank may incur over all the large-dollar systems. The caps are determined by a Fed schedule based on the bank's self-evaluation of its overall creditworthiness as an institution, its credit policies and operational controls. The self-evaluation must be approved by a bank's board of directors.

   The Fed uses pricing as the primary method of controlling the level of daylight overdrafts. In effect, this is a market solution rather than a regulatory solution. It measures daylight overdrafts on a minute-by-minute basis and charges fees based on the magnitude and duration of the overdraft.

Daylight overdraft limits have not been a major obstacle to corporate money transfers, although there are occasional delays when companies or banks reach their limits.

In addition, the Fed has mandated that all banks must establish bilateral net credit limits that define the maximum amount of net payments the bank may receive from another bank over private networks such as CHIPS. The reason for the net credit limits is that payments on these networks may not be settled until the end of the day. A higher amount of payments received and credited to beneficiaries means a higher exposure to the sending bank's failure to settle at the end of the day.

IV. Future of the Payments System

Electronic methods for moving funds have evolved rapidly in recent years and the trend away from paper-based systems is continuing. New methods for accessing and communicating via the payments system are also evolving rapidly. Recent innovations include financial electronic data interchange (FEDI), home banking, personal computer (PC) based financial transactions, electronic bill presentment and payment and the use of the Internet for initiating payment instructions. Many companies that accept large numbers of checks are implementing new methods to convert paper-based items to electronic. Technological developments are expected to continue influencing payment methods into the foreseeable future.

Test Your Understanding

These chapter questions are provided to test your understanding of the information in the text and are not examples of CCM examination questions, nor are they in the examination format.

Answers can be found at the back of the book on pages 503-505.

1. With a check, what is the difference between the payor and the payee?
2. What is the purpose of the magnetic ink character recognition (MICR) line of a check?
3. Discuss the various methods used to clear checks.
4. Define cash letter.
5. Define direct send.
6. Define on-us item.
7. What are high-dollar group sort (HDGS) items?
8. Discuss the difference between a ledger balance and a collected balance.
9. What is deposit float?
10. List the factors that determine availability.
11. What is an availability schedule?
12. Why is a payable through draft (PTD) not a check?
13. What differentiates a time draft from a sight draft?
14. How do ACH transactions differ from checks?
15. Outline the different types of ACH formats.
16. When does settlement occur in an ACH transaction?
17. How does settlement through Fedwire differ from settlement through ACH?
18. How does a repetitive wire transfer differ from a non-repetitive transfer?
19. What are the various security procedures used to provide commercially reasonable security for wire transfers?
20. Discuss the major difference between CHIPS and S.W.I.F.T.
21. Why is the Federal Reserve concerned about daylight overdrafts and what action has it taken to address this concern?

CHAPTER 5

Credit and Accounts Receivable Management

Overview
This chapter describes how and why companies extend credit, how they manage accounts receivable and forecast income and how cash managers are involved in these and related activities.

Learning Objectives
Upon completion of this chapter and the related study questions, the reader should understand:

- The objectives of corporate credit and accounts receivable management
- How credit and accounts receivable management fit into corporate finance and treasury operations
- How companies develop credit policies
- How companies calculate the costs and benefits of credit policies
- The forms of credit extension
- The commonly used terms of sale, including credit terms
- How companies make customer credit decisions
- How companies measure and monitor accounts receivable
- How companies finance accounts receivable
- How the cash application process works
- Legislation that affects credit and collection

Key Concepts
- Rationale for credit sales
- Credit management
- Accounts receivable monitoring and control
- Aging of receivables — days' sales outstanding (DSO)
- Collection management

Outline

I. Objectives of Trade Credit and Accounts Receivable Management

II. Organization of the Credit and Accounts Receivable Management Function
    A. Responsibility
    B. Role of the Cash Manager

III. Credit Policies
    A. Reasons for Offering Trade Credit
    B. Credit Policy Constraints
    C. Financing Implications
    D. Income and Expenses

IV. Credit Standards
    A. Considerations in Credit Extension Decision Making
    B. Information Sources
    C. The Five Cs of Credit
    D. Quantitative Credit Analysis
    E. Billing and Collection Methods

V. Forms of Credit Extension
    A. Open Account
    B. Installment Credit
    C. Revolving Credit
    D. Letter of Credit (L/C)

VI. Considerations Pertaining to Terms of Sale
    A. Common Terms of Sale
    B. Common Credit Practices
    C. Offering Discounts

VII. Accounts Receivable Monitoring and Control
    A. Purpose
    B. Days' Sales Outstanding (DSO)
    C. Aging Schedule
    D. Accounts Receivable Balance Pattern

VIII. Financing Accounts Receivable
　　A. Unsecured Borrowing
　　B. Secured Borrowing
　　C. Securitization
　　D. Captive Finance Subsidiary
　　E. Third-Party Financing
　　F. Credit Cards
　　G. Factoring
　　H. Private Label Financing

IX. Cash Application
　　A. Open Item
　　B. Balance Forward

X. Legislation Affecting Credit and Collections
　　A. Pricing and Interest Charge Restrictions
　　B. Consumer and Commercial Credit Legislation
　　C. Uniform Commercial Code (UCC)
　　D. Bankruptcy and Reorganization

XI. Developments in Credit and Accounts Receivable
　　A. Electronic Commerce (E-Commerce) and Electronic Data Interchange (EDI)
　　B. Electronic Bill Presentment and Payment (EBPP)
　　C. Outsourcing of Accounts Receivable

I. Objectives of Trade Credit and Accounts Receivable Management

Accounts receivable result from a company's decision to sell goods and services on a credit basis. Accounts receivable are an asset of the company evidencing the extension of trade credit. Sales, accounting and finance personnel all become involved in credit and accounts receivable management activity. Effective credit and accounts receivable management entails the following:

- Establishing and communicating a company's credit policies
- Establishing terms of sale consistent with overall company objectives
- Evaluating customer creditworthiness and setting customer credit lines
- Ensuring prompt and accurate customer billing in conjunction with customer service or billing departments
- Creating, preserving and collecting accounts receivable
- Maintaining up-to-date records of accounts receivable
- Following up on overdue accounts and initiating collection procedures when necessary

II. Organization of the Credit and Accounts Receivable Management Function

Typically, companies break down credit and accounts receivable management along the following lines:

A. Responsibility

1. **Credit Management** — Credit managers administer credit policies that include:
    - Establishing credit-granting standards
    - Establishing terms of credit extension
    - Approving customers for credit sales
    - Setting individual and aggregate credit limits

2. **Accounts Receivable Management** — Administration of a company's accounts receivable is generally the responsibility of the credit manager, although other finance personnel may also be directly involved. Either way, receivable management entails:

- Billing and processing payments
- Monitoring payment patterns
- Collecting delinquent accounts

3. **Sales and Customer Service** — Sales and customer service departments work closely with credit managers to develop credit policies because credit is principally a tool used to facilitate sales to customers.

4. **Outsourcing Credit and Accounts Receivable Management** — Captive finance companies, or factors, may in some cases assume full or partial responsibility for credit and accounts receivable management. Additional information and recent developments in this area are provided in Section XI of this chapter.

B. Role of the Cash Manager

Working relationships with other departments and employees involved in credit management are important for a cash manager.

1. **Organizational Relationship** — Credit policy and collection of accounts receivable have a significant impact on timing of cash inflows. Typically, credit and/or accounts receivables managers, but not cash managers, are responsible for such matters.

2. **Information Links** — Credit and cash managers need strong information links and cooperative working relationships with employees in a company's other areas, such as sales, billing and accounting, in order to:

   - *Track Customer Payments* — A cash manager is responsible for establishing and maintaining the banking network. The credit management function needs to have input to and receive feedback from this network regarding customer payments when a financial institution collects accounts receivables through a lockbox or asset-based borrowing arrangement.

   - *Forecast Accurately* — The credit department provides important information used in cash forecasting. Credit policies affect the accuracy, nature and timing of cash flows.

   - *Process Collections and Apply Payments* — The cash manager may also oversee collections processing. This includes applying payments to customer accounts and generating information required for posting to the accounts receivable ledger.

III. Credit Policies

Company credit policies delineate credit standards, credit terms and collection policies. If a company is to offer credit, it must address the following matters:

- *Credit Standards* — Granting credit has two stages: 1) determining who will be granted credit and 2) determining a customer's credit limit.
- *Credit Terms* — The contract must clearly specify the terms of sale to different customers.
- *Collection Policy* — A company must establish policies and procedures to collect payment should a credit customer fail to pay according to the specified terms.

To ensure consistent application and fairness, it is important for a company to have written credit policies and procedures. After a company has established its basic credit policies, it must develop procedures and information systems necessary to monitor accounts receivable for compliance with credit terms and to detect changes in customer payment patterns.

A. Reasons for Offering Trade Credit

Credit is a sales tool. Companies consider the following factors when extending credit:

- *Market Share* — The portion of the market they are targeting
- *Competition* — The credit terms competitors offer
- *Promotional Efforts* — Credit terms necessary to attract new customers
- *Sales Facilitation* — The needs of potential customers without access to other sources of credit
- *Convenience* — The ease with which customers and potential customers can make credit purchases on an open account basis
- *Profit* — The potential profitability of charging for credit through interest income

B. Credit Policy Constraints

The following factors influence a company's credit policies:

1. **Industry Practice and Company Strategy** — The credit terms customarily offered in many industries may not change for extended periods. It may be difficult for a seller to change from customary practices unless a buyer is offered some form of incentive, such as a discount, in return.

2. **Contractual Obligations** — Changes in receivable balances can affect working capital ratios, which must be kept in compliance with any debt covenants.

3. **Legal Issues** — The Robinson-Patman Act prohibits various forms of price discrimination. State commerce and usury laws may also limit certain credit practices or forbid them outright.

C. Financing Implications

Companies offering trade credit generate accounts receivable that convert to cash when the customers pay bills in the normal course of business. A company's credit terms, together with its sales and collection patterns, determine the levels of its accounts receivable and impact a company's financing needs.

1. **Use of Funds** — Receivables are assets that must be financed. A company's ability to extend credit is directly related to its ability to finance receivables. Mismanagement of receivables can cause liquidity problems due to delayed customer payment.

2. **Source of Liquidity Collateral** — Existing accounts receivable can be used as collateral for loans. Alternatively, they can be sold for cash to third parties called factors.

D. Income and Expenses

Trade credit can increase a company's income, but there are also associated costs.

1. **Income**

    - *Increased Sales* — Offering credit terms may attract additional sales volume and may result in increased profitability.

    - *Interest Income* — Interest on installment payment arrangements can be a significant source of profit.

2. **Expense**

    The expenses involved in trade credit include:

    - *Accounts Receivable Carrying Costs* — Like any other asset on a company's balance sheet, accounts receivable have carrying costs. Typically, a company determines this cost by using its marginal cost of short-term borrowings or its weighted average cost of capital.

    - *Credit Department Costs* — These may include personnel costs, data and payments processing and other costs required to sustain a department responsible for a company's trade credit operation.

- *Credit Evaluation* — This includes the costs of obtaining and analyzing credit information.

- *Discounted Payments* — When customers take advantage of an offered discount, but sales volumes do not increase, total net revenue is reduced. This loss of revenue may be fully or partially offset by a reduction in accounts receivable carrying costs.

- *Selling, Production and Administration Costs* — A liberalized credit policy can increase sales, but also often increases administration and production costs of handling the increased volume.

- *Collection Expenses* — The cost of collecting delinquent accounts can be significant.

- *Bad-Debt Expense* – According to generally accepted accounting principles (GAAP), accounts receivable that are determined to be uncollectible must be charged off. Most companies estimate their level of losses and create a reserve account through periodic charges to bad-debt expense. The timing and volume of bad-debt expense and charge-offs are important aspects of credit policy.

- *Insurance* — Companies can reduce the impact of bad debts by purchasing various types of insurance designed to cover sales losses. Companies must include insurance premiums in the cost/benefit analysis when they assess the potential profitability of credit sales. (See Chapter 14, Financial Risk Management and Chapter 15, International Treasury Management.)

- *Discrepancies in Payments* — The cost of monitoring, investigating and resolving discrepancies between invoices and payments customers make can be high. Personnel must research discrepancies, ascertain the legitimacy of shortfalls and deductions and handle all related bookkeeping, invoicing and payment adjustment matters.

IV. Credit Standards

It is important for a company to set and maintain its credit standards, which apply both to credit extension and billing and collection policies.

A. Considerations in Credit Extension Decision Making

Companies wish to avoid two circumstances in extending trade credit:

1. **Rejection of Acceptable Credit Risks** — If a company rejects a customer who is a good risk, the company loses potential sales.

2. **Acceptance of Substandard Risks** — If a company accepts a customer who does not pay according to the specified terms, the company incurs monitoring, collection and/or bad-debt costs.

Making credit standards more stringent will generally reduce risks but will also increase the frequency of rejecting acceptable risks. In practice, the costs of these two types of considerations are difficult to quantify. However, credit is a sales tool and a zero default rate probably means that a company's credit terms are too strict.

B. Information Sources

A company must consider the type, quantity and cost of information when establishing its method of analyzing credit requests. It can gather credit information in stages from internal and external sources, at each stage weighing costs against the expected benefits.

1. **Internal Sources** — The most important sources of internally generated credit information include the following:
   - A credit application and agreement form completed by the applicant
   - The company's own records regarding actual payment history of the applicant

2. **External Sources** — A company can use a wide variety of external sources to assist in determining the creditworthiness of a credit applicant.
   - *Financial Statements* — Both audited and unaudited financial statements provide important information on corporate credit applicants. These statements and related ratios could be compared to industry averages from sources such as Robert Morris and Associates.
   - *Trade References* — Other companies are contacted to obtain their actual payment experiences regarding credit terms extended to the applicant.

- *Banks or Other Creditors* — The customer's bank or other financial creditors (commercial finance or leasing companies) can also provide valuable information about the customer's financial condition and available credit. Though banks or financial creditors may be reluctant to discuss their detailed experience with trade creditors, they will typically provide standardized credit information.

- *Agencies* — Various local and nationwide agencies collect, evaluate and report information on the credit history of most companies. Their credit reports include information such as payment history, financial information, maximum outstanding credit amounts, length of time credit has been available and any actions that have been necessary to achieve collection.

C. The Five Cs of Credit

Credit analyses depend upon the type of information available and the trade-off between costs and the benefits. The traditional factors companies consider are known as the five Cs of credit. These are:

1. **Character** — The perceived honesty or integrity of an individual applicant, or of the officers of a corporate applicant. These are seen as an indication of intent or willingness to pay, as evidenced by personal or corporate payment history.

2. **Capacity** — The current and future financial resources a company or individual can commit to pay obligations when due. This is often assessed using financial liquidity ratios and cash flow forecasts.

3. **Capital** — A customer's short- and long-term financial resources that could be called upon if the immediate cash flow is insufficient to meet payment obligations.

4. **Collateral** — The assets or guarantees available to secure an obligation in the event payment is not made as agreed.

5. **Conditions** — The general economic environment and economic conditions existing for the customer and the seller that affect the ability of the customer to pay and the willingness of the company to grant the credit.

D. Quantitative Credit Analysis

Quantitative methods for both corporate and consumer credit analysis include:

1. **Business Credit Analysis** — Quantitative analysis of credit information begins with an examination of a credit applicant's financial statements, frequently through ratio analysis, which assesses a customer's financial condition. The measures used most often include liquidity and working capital ratios (current, quick

and cash flow-to-debt ratios), debt management and coverage ratios (times interest earned, long-term debt-to-capital, debt-to-total assets and total liabilities-to-total assets ratios) and profitability measures (return on equity, return on sales and return on total assets). Ratios can provide valuable insight when evaluated in relation to industry standards published by credit rating agencies and other associations. Some commercial credit analysis can involve credit scoring, which is described below. (See Chapter 2, Financial Accounting and Related Concepts, for more information on ratio analysis.) Commercial credit can also be evaluated by purchasing credit reports from companies such as Dun and Bradstreet.

2. **Consumer Credit Analysis** — Major issuers of retail credit, such as department stores, use quantitative credit scoring models and often develop a different model for each billing region. These quantitative approaches are cost effective and can aid in complying with consumer credit legislation, which is discussed later in this chapter. Formal statistical analysis is often used to identify the factors that distinguish paying customers from non-paying customers. Credit bureaus also assess creditworthiness based on proprietary models.

3. **Credit Scoring** — One technique companies use to estimate the creditworthiness of applicants is known as credit scoring. It involves a four-step process:
   - Differentiating standard and high-risk accounts based on such data as monthly income, outstanding obligations and the employment history of the applicant
   - Weighting the characteristics of those who fit into each category to establish creditworthiness
   - Setting cutoff scores for credit approval and denial
   - Applying further analysis to applicants whose scores fall in between the cutoff points

E. Billing and Collection Methods

The major objective of a collection policy is to speed the conversion of accounts receivable into cash while minimizing collection expense and bad-debt losses. The type of credit a company offers impacts significantly the collection methods it uses.

1. **Invoicing** — The first step in collecting an account is to send prompt and correct invoices with the terms of payment clearly stated. Effective cash management involves reducing invoice float, the interval between the time goods and services are purchased and the time the customer receives an invoice. Delays in invoice preparation or errors on the invoice can extend the entire payment process by days or even weeks.

2. **Statements** — Sometimes companies send summary statements of outstanding invoices as a reminder to customers that payment is due. Retail consumer billing typically involves sending statements listing goods or services purchased over a month's period.

3. **Delayed Payments** — When payment is not received by the due date, a company has a variety of options:
   - Sending a duplicate invoice
   - Mailing a form letter or series of form letters
   - Making telephone calls, which will also determine if there is a perceived dispute or need for a duplicate invoice
   - Visiting the customer in person
   - Suspending further sales until past due items are paid
   - Negotiating with the customer for payment of past due amounts
   - Reporting the customer's delinquent account to credit bureaus
   - Claiming or realizing proceeds of any pledged collateral
   - Attempting to negotiate additional corporate or personal guarantees or trying to obtain a lien on specific assets
   - Initiating direct legal action or turning delinquent accounts over to a collection agency

V. Forms of Credit Extension

Trade credit can be extended to a customer in the following ways.

A. Open Account

This method, sometimes called open book credit, is the most common type of commercial trade credit in the United States. It works as follows:

- A seller issues an invoice, which is formal evidence of the obligation and records the sale as an account receivable.
- The customer is billed for each transaction by an invoice and/or by a monthly statement covering all invoices generated during the billing period.
- Full payment of invoiced amounts is expected within the specified credit terms unless certain discounts or deductions are made available to the customer.

- A buyer's creditworthiness is reviewed periodically, but the buyer does not need to apply for credit each time an order is placed.
- Companies usually charge fees for late payment.

B. Installment Credit

In this form of credit, a company requires a customer to make equal monthly payments, each of which contains a principal and an interest component. Installment credit is used frequently for the purchase of high-value consumer durables such as automobiles. Frequently the seller requires the buyer to sign a contract, which specifies the terms of the obligation, explains credit terms in full and discloses rates of interest and other costs.

C. Revolving Credit

Under revolving credit terms, a company grants credit without requiring specific approval of each transaction as long as the account is current. The account is usually considered current if the credit outstanding is below an established credit limit and minimum payments have been made on time. If the account is not paid in full by the monthly payment due date, an interest charge is calculated based on the average amount outstanding over the entire period. (Revolving credit also refers to a type of bank loan, which is described in Chapter 13, Borrowing.)

D. Letter of Credit (L/C)

An L/C is an instrument used to effect a payment in which a bank guarantees a seller that the bank, not the buyer, will pay for the agreed-upon purchase when the seller presents documents conforming to specified conditions pertaining to the sale and delivery of goods or services. Typically, it is the buyer who pays for opening an L/C. L/Cs are commonly used in import/export transactions.

A variant of a commercial L/C is a standby L/C, which serves as a guarantee to secure credit sales to a specific buyer. Whereas a commercial L/C is almost always drawn upon to complete the transaction, a standby L/C is only drawn upon if payment in the transaction it supports is not made. (See Chapter 15, International Treasury Management.)

VI. Considerations Pertaining to Terms of Sale

Buyers and sellers have a variety of standard terms of sale that they can choose from to conclude transactions. They are often specified in sales agreements, invoices or other legal or commercial documents.

A. Common Terms of Sale

Standard sale terms stipulate the form and timing of payment and receipt of goods or services; many involve credit. The most common credit terms include:

1. **Cash Before Delivery (CBD)** — CBD terms require the buyer to make full and final payment before shipment or receipt of goods. CBD is often used when the seller does not know the buyer or when the seller considers the buyer a greater credit risk than the seller is willing to accept.

2. **Cash on Delivery (COD)** — The seller ships the goods and the buyer pays upon receipt. If the buyer refuses to pay, the goods are returned and the seller must pay the shipping cost.

3. **Cash Terms** — The buyer generally has a week to 10 days to make payment. This method is frequently used in sales of highly perishable items.

4. **Net Terms** — The seller specifies a net due date by which the buyer must pay in full. For example, terms of net 30 require the buyer to pay within 30 days from the date of invoice, date of delivery or some other specified date.

5. **Discount Terms** — In addition to specifying a net due date, the seller may also offer a discount if payment is made prior to that date. Terms of 2/10 net 30 mean that the total amount is due within 30 days of the invoice date, but the buyer can take a two percent discount if payment is made within 10 days.

6. **Monthly Billing** — The seller issues a monthly statement covering all invoices prior to a cutoff date, typically the 25th of each month. The buyer must pay by a specified date the following month. The seller may allow the buyer to take a discount for prompt payment. For example, if the terms are 1/10, prox net 30, the buyer may take a discount of one percent if payment is made by the 10th day of the following month. The total due must be paid by the 30th day of the month.

7. **Draft/Bill of Lading** — This collection method is also known as a documentary collection. The seller collects payments through banking channels. Having shipped goods to the buyer, the seller sends shipping and title documents to the bank, which then transmits them to the buyer's bank. The buyer gains possession of the documents upon paying the bank or upon signing a draft agreeing to pay at a future date. Upon collection, the buyer's bank remits payment to the seller's bank. This method is more common to international trade than it is to domestic trade.

8. **Seasonal Dating** — The seller agrees to accept payment at the end of the buyer's selling season, when the buyer has cash. This allows manufacturers to provide short-term financing for a buyer's purchases and reduces the manufacturer's inventory costs. It is common in industries with distinct seasonality of sales such as toys, greeting cards, garden supplies, sporting goods or textbooks. The seller may offer sliding discounts to encourage the buyer to pay early.

9. **Consignment** — Under a consignment agreement, the seller ships the goods to the buyer with no obligation to pay until the goods have been sold or used. The title to the goods remains with the seller until that date.

B. Common Credit Practices

Considerations regarding credit terms are as follows:

1. **Penalty Fees** — In addition to offering credit terms, companies often assess a penalty fee for payments received after the due date. This fee is usually a percentage of the past due amount. The fee should be clearly stated at the time of the sale and shown on the invoice.

2. **Credit Limits** — In addition to the terms of each sale, companies' credit managers must also determine the aggregate amount of credit they should grant each customer. Companies usually grant new customers credit at the lowest limit. After a period of satisfactory payment performance, they raise the credit limit to the next level. Companies review credit levels periodically to determine relevance and adjust them as necessary.

3. **Eligibility for Discount** — Companies determine a benchmark date for eligibility for discounts. This can be the postmark date of the payment remittance or the date funds are received.

C. Offering Discounts

The seller, when offering cash discounts, must evaluate the cost of doing so vs. the benefits to be gained from receiving payment early. Exhibit 5.1 shows how the annualized cost of trade credit is calculated.

Standard practice provides the following alternative methods of accounting for sales discounting:

1. **Gross Method** — Gross sales revenues are recorded on the income statement and discounts are taken as an expense on the income statement.

> **Exhibit 5.1** Annualized Cost of Trade Credit
>
> $$\text{Annualized Cost of Trade Credit} = \frac{\text{Early Payment Discount}}{(1-\text{Early Payment Discount})} \times \frac{365}{(\text{Net Payment Period} - \text{Discount Payment Period})}$$
>
> **Example**
>
> Given terms 2/10 net 30, the cost of not taking the discount (i.e., paying the net amount on Day 30 rather than the discounted amount on Day 10) can be calculated as:
>
> $$\text{Cost of Trade Credit} = \frac{.02}{(1-.02)} \times \frac{365}{(30-10)} = 37.24\%$$
>
> If a buyer were able to borrow funds at a rate of less than 37.24%, then he should do so and take the discount for early payment. If borrowed funds cost more than 37.24% or if they are not available, then the buyer should delay payment until the net due date.
>
> A company with excess cash reserves must compare this annualized cost to investment rates. If alternative investment rates available to the company exceed the annualized cost of trade credit, then the discount should be delayed until the net due date.

2. **Net Method** — Amounts are entered into the receivables and revenue accounts net of the discounts. Any discounts not taken are then shown as income.

VII. Accounts Receivable Monitoring and Control

Monitoring and controlling a company's accounts receivable are important aspects of the overall credit policy. They are often the responsibility of the cash manager.

A. Purpose

Monitoring of accounts receivable should be performed at both an individual account and an aggregate level. A customer aging schedule is a useful method for tracking individual receivables and a report of days' sales outstanding is a useful measure of the collection rate for accounts receivable.

1. **Monitoring Individual Accounts** — Companies should monitor individual accounts for the following reasons:
    - There may be errors or delays in the invoicing or payment process.
    - Some customers may intentionally delay payment until follow-up is initiated.

- A change in financial condition may alter the ability of a customer to make timely payments and may require a curtailment of future credit sales.

2. **Monitoring Aggregate Accounts Receivable** — Companies should monitor aggregate accounts receivable for the following reasons:
    - Changes in accounts receivable may impact liquidity and prompt the need for additional financing.
    - A significant change in the level of overall accounts receivable may be a symptom of a change in business that could affect a company's financing needs. Management should analyze these changes to determine underlying causes and any corrective actions that need to be taken. Developments that could prompt significant changes include:
        - Variations in sales volume
        - Modifications of credit standards policy
        - Fluctuating economic conditions
        - Responding to competitors' actions
    - Accounts receivable serve as a basis for forecasting the amount and timing of future cash receipts.

B. Days' Sales Outstanding (DSO)

Another method of measuring accounts receivable is days' sales outstanding (DSO), which companies calculate by dividing accounts receivable outstanding at the end of a time interval by the average daily credit sales of the period. DSO gives a single number that can be compared to stated credit terms or to a historic trend to provide an indication of a company's overall collection efficiency. It may, however, be distorted by changing trends in sales volume or by strong seasonality in sales.

Exhibit 5.2 describes a basic method for calculating DSO. The average daily sales of $3,444.44 are computed without considering the pattern of sales for the period.

C. Aging Schedule

An aging schedule divides accounts receivable into those that are current and those that are past due in 30-day increments. Companies can analyze the aging of receivables on an aggregate or customer-by-customer basis. An aging analysis identifies past-due accounts, which become less collectible as their age increases.

An example of an aging schedule is shown in Exhibit 5.3. With credit terms of net 30, this aggregate aging schedule shows that 30 percent of the accounts receivable are past due.

Exhibit 5.2 Days' Sales Outstanding (DSO) Calculation

Assume

Outstanding receivables of $285,000 at the end of Month 3
Credit terms of net 60
DSO averaging period of 3 months (90 days)
Credit sales history:
- Month 1 = $ 90,000.00
- Month 2 = $ 105,000.00
- Month 3 = $ 115,000.00

DSO Calculation

$$\text{Average Daily Credit Sales} = \frac{(\$90,000.00 + \$105,000.00 + \$115,000.00)}{90} = \$3,444.44$$

$$\text{Days' Sales Outstanding (DSO)} = \frac{\text{Outstanding Accounts Receivable}}{\text{Average Daily Credit Sales}} = \frac{\$285,000.00}{\$3,444.44} = 82.74 \text{ Days}$$

Average Past Due Calculation

Average Past Due = DSO − Average Days of Credit Terms
= 82.74 Days − 60 Days = 22.74 Days

Exhibit 5.3 Example of an Aging Schedule

Age of Accounts	Accounts Receivable	% of Account Receivable
0 – 30 days	$1,750,000	70%
31– 60 days	375,000	15%
61–90 days	250,000	10%
91+ days	125,000	5%
Total	$2,500,000	100%

The aging schedule can be a more informative breakdown than DSO because it provides information on the distribution, not just a single average. However, an aging schedule can send the same potentially misleading signals as DSO when sales vary significantly from month to month.

D. Accounts Receivable Balance Pattern

Aging schedules are used to establish receivables balance patterns, which are useful cash forecasting tools. They specify the percentage of credit sales in a time period, usually a month, that remains outstanding in the company's accounts receivable at the end of that and each subsequent time period.

Exhibit 5.4 gives an example of a company whose sales are collected as follows:

- 5% of sales collected in the current month of sale
- 40% of sales collected in the month after sale
- 35% of sales collected two months after sale
- 20% of sales collected three months after sale

At the end of March, there will still be $50,000 of accounts receivable outstanding (uncollected) from January's sales. This can be forecast as follows:

January Sales		=	$ 250,000.00
Collected in: January	= (.05 x $250,000)	=	$ 12,500.00
Collected in: February	= (.40 x $250,000)	=	$ 100,000.00
Collected in: March	= (.35 x $250,000)	=	$ 87,500.00
Total Collections		=	$ 200,000.00
Total Outstanding Receivables from January Sales		=	$ 250,000 – $ 200,000 = $50,000

A company's collection history determines its normal balance pattern. Management can evaluate any shifts by comparing current patterns with historical norms. Furthermore, variations in sales patterns do not affect balance patterns, nor do they send misleading signals regarding future cash inflows. Companies can use balance patterns to project accounts receivable levels and collections and to forecast future cash inflows.

Exhibit 5.4 Example of a Receivables Balance Pattern

Month Sales	Sales	Remaining Accounts Receivable from Month Sales at the End of March	Remaining Accounts Receivable as a % of Month Sales
January	$250,000	$50,000	20%
February	$300,000	$165,000	55%
March	$400,000	$380,000	95%
April	$500,000		

The total outstanding accounts receivable balance at the end of March is:
$595,000 = ($50,000 + $165,000 + $380,000)

The estimate of cash inflows for April = 5% of April sales + 40% of March sales + 35% of February sales + 20% of January sales:

Estimated April inflows = (.05 x $500,000)
+ (.40 x $400,000)
+ (.35 x $300,000)
+ (.20 x $250,000)
= $340,000

VIII. Financing Accounts Receivable

Accounts receivable, which are a major component of current assets, can be financed in a variety of ways.

A. Unsecured Borrowing

A company that offers trade credit can borrow unsecured funds from a financial institution to support accounts receivable if it has sufficient available credit capacity.

B. Secured Borrowing

If a company cannot finance its accounts receivable with unsecured borrowings, it may be able to pledge its accounts receivable as collateral and borrow on a secured basis. A bank will select those accounts receivable it accepts as collateral and extend the company a loan. The company will remit the funds owed to the bank upon collection of the receivables.

C. Securitization

Large companies, particularly those with finance subsidiaries such as automobile and credit card companies, bundle their receivables and issue securities backed by them. Consumers' installment payments are used to pay off the instruments' principal and interest. Securitization allows a company to free up capital and enhances its creditworthiness. (See Chapter 12, Investing and Chapter 13, Borrowing.)

D. Captive Finance Subsidiary

A company may be able to create a wholly owned subsidiary to perform credit operations and obtain accounts receivable financing for the sale of its products. Because many companies' receivables represent a significant proportion of their assets, operating a captive finance subsidiary enhances the parent's liquidity significantly and allows the parent company to obtain capital at a lower cost than it otherwise could.

E. Third-Party Financing

A company collects the information necessary to complete a credit application from its customer and forwards it to a financial institution, which decides whether or not to grant credit. Because of the administrative costs this entails, the companies that do this tend to manufacture and market big-ticket items such as production machinery.

Although third-party financing through an institution can free up capital, companies that use it relinquish control over the type of customer they want to attract and may miss marketing opportunities. Furthermore, a company may have to discount the price of the goods sold in order to compensate the third party and thus forgo potential income.

F. Credit Cards

A third party, usually a bank or another financial institution, may offer a credit card that a merchant accepts as payment. The agreement between the seller and the financial institution specifies that the seller receives payment electronically on the day following the transaction.

1. **Advantages** — Credit cards offer the following advantages:
   - The seller bears none of the direct costs of running a credit department.
   - Depending upon the agreement, the seller has few or no funds tied up in financing accounts receivable.
   - The third party usually absorbs bad-debt losses.

2. **Disadvantages** — The disadvantages in using credit cards for customer financing are as follows:
   - The seller loses control over the determination of acceptable credit customers.
   - The seller loses the promotional aspects of having its own list of credit customers.
   - Major direct costs include fees associated with the transaction, which depend upon the method of execution (terminal, Internet, paper), the average size of the sale, the total volume, the type of card used (regular credit card vs. commercial cards) and the type of business or organization.

G. Factoring

Factoring usually involves the outright sale of receivables to a factor, which is a company specializing in the financing and management of receivables. In most factoring arrangements, the buyer of the receivables has no recourse to the seller. In other words, the factor must absorb the loss if the customer fails to pay. However, in some cases, the factoring arrangement stipulates the factor does have recourse, in which case the seller is still liable if the factor cannot collect.

Most factoring is performed on a notification basis. The company notifies the customer that the account has been sold and the payment is remitted directly to the factor.

1. **Advantages of Factoring** — Factoring has the following advantages:
   - It grows automatically with increases in sales.
   - It reduces or eliminates the cost of maintaining a credit department.
   - It reduces uncertainty in the timing of payments.
   - It extends the range of customers to whom a company can grant credit. Because the factor can share the risk, together they may be able to extend credit to customers that the company otherwise could not.
   - It may improve the credit-extension process. The factor may have access to information that enables it to extend more credit with fewer delinquencies.

2. **Disadvantages of Factoring** — Disadvantages of factoring include the following:
   - Factors may charge high fees, particularly in non-recourse agreements, which may be a problem for companies in narrow profit margin industries.
   - The seller loses control over who is granted credit and may require its own credit operation to assess those customers rejected by the factor.
   - Some companies believe that having their receivables factored conveys a sign of financial weakness; in certain industries, however, factoring is a standard practice.

H. Private Label Financing

With private label financing, a third party operates the credit function in the name of the seller rather than the seller administering its own credit program. Private label financing allows the seller to retain many of the promotional aspects of conducting its own credit function while incurring none of the costs of maintaining a credit operation or financing accounts receivable. At the same time, the seller does not receive the full face value of the sale and may lose the authority to decide which customers should receive credit. From the customer's perspective, the credit appears to be arranged through the seller.

IX. Cash Application

Cash application is the process of applying a customer's payment against outstanding invoices. There are two basic ways to accomplish this:

A. Open Item

An open item system is most commonly used in business-to-business sales. Each invoice sent to a customer is recorded in the accounts receivable file. When a payment is received, it is matched with the specific invoices being paid and any payment discrepancies (discounts, allowances, adjustments, etc.) are noted. Remittance information, which typically accompanies payments, usually details which invoices are being paid, as well as any adjustments to the payment. This application process may be manual, automated or a combination of the two.

Many companies have automated cash application programs that take the payment and remittance information and, through a series of algorithms, apply the payments by matching them to specific invoices. A high rate of successful automated applications greatly reduces the amount of manual effort required to complete the application process.

Lockbox processors may provide payment and remittance data to a company to facilitate the cash application process. One common service is to capture the data in the magnetic ink character recognition (MICR) line of the check. Elements captured include the drawee bank's transit routing number, the payor's bank account number and the check amount. The transit routing number and bank account number can be used to identify the customer using a database maintained by the receiving company. The lockbox processor may also capture additional customer information manually or automatically with pre-encoded payment stubs. Additional remittance data may include such items as:

- Invoice numbers
- Amounts paid
- Customer account numbers
- Remitter's name
- Discounts and adjustments taken
- Dates
- Other pertinent information

Some lockbox processors access a company's accounts receivable system information during lockbox processing in order to look up such things as account numbers and other pertinent information. Others match payments and invoices — to the extent possible — prior to data transmission to the company using information provided by the company or on encoded payment stubs returned with the payments. Another recent development is the increasing use of imaging to capture and transmit the remittance information. These services are designed to increase a company's automated payment application rate, thereby increasing the overall efficiency of the process.

B. Balance Forward

Balance forward systems are used most often by companies selling goods and services to individual consumers. In a balance forward system, a credit limit is established for each individual and as purchases are made or services are provided, the accounts receivable outstanding increases. When payments are made, the accounts receivable balance is reduced by the amount of the payment.

X. Legislation Affecting Credit and Collections

Many laws and regulations affect the area of credit and collections.

A. Pricing and Interest Charge Restrictions

Because the extension of credit is a benefit to the buyer, credit terms can be considered a part of the price of the product or service being sold.

1. **Robinson-Patman Act (1936)** — The Robinson-Patman Act specifically prohibits price discrimination among customers where a cost basis cannot be demonstrated as the reason for price differences. Different credit terms are acceptable if they are industry practice or in cases in which cost differences can be substantiated.

2. **Usury Laws** — Usury laws, which vary significantly from state to state, restrict the interest rates or penalty fees that companies can charge on installment credit.

B. Consumer and Commercial Credit Legislation

A number of laws regulate the statement of terms, the credit analysis and approval process and the collection practices that can be employed when selling on a credit basis to consumers. Some of the more important federal legislation and regulations are:

1. **Truth in Lending Act (1969)** — This act requires lenders to disclose the true annual interest rate and the total dollar cost on most types of loans.

2. **Fair Credit Reporting Act (1971)** — This law enables consumers to access the information in their credit files at little or no cost.

3. **Fair Credit Billing Act (1975)** — This act is an amendment to the Truth in Lending Act and protects charge account customers from billing errors by permitting them to use the same legal defenses against banks or other third-party credit card companies that they could previously use against merchants.

4. **Equal Credit Opportunity Act (1975)** — This act prohibits creditors from discriminating against credit applicants on the basis of sex, marital status, race, color, religion, national origin, age or receipt of public assistance.

5. **Fair Debt Collection Practices Act (1978)** — This act is designed to eliminate abusive and unfair debt collection practices such as threats of financial ruin, loss of job or reputation, or harassing telephone calls.

C. Uniform Commercial Code (UCC)

In general, revolving credit, installment credit and sales finance transactions are covered by provisions of the UCC, which is the model for many state laws pertaining to commerce.

D. Bankruptcy and Reorganization

Under the Federal Bankruptcy Reform Act of 1978, a company may file for liquidation under Chapter 7 or reorganization under Chapter 11. Individuals typically file for reorganization under Chapter 13. Reorganization allows a company to pay off debts gradually and operate under a court-supervised plan for returning to financial soundness. Filing of a petition protects the debtor from a list of actions by creditors. The law established a federal bankruptcy court system with exclusive jurisdiction over bankruptcy cases.

XI. Developments in Credit and Accounts Receivable

A. Electronic Commerce (E-Commerce) and Electronic Data Interchange (EDI)

Given the increased use of e-commerce and EDI, a company's accounts receivable system must be able to process electronic payments and remittance information in order to use this information to properly apply payments. Because of the increased remittance information accompanying the payment in an e-commerce/EDI environment, the cash application rate may be increased through automation of the process. (See Chapter 9, Electronic Commerce.)

B. Electronic Bill Presentment and Payment (EBPP)

Many companies and banks are implementing EBPP systems that allow them to send electronic statements to their customers and allow for the customers to pay these bills by electronic means. In most cases these applications are Web-based and usable by anyone with Internet access. The biggest issue with these systems is that they are competing with the current mail/check billing and payment system which is a "bill anybody — pay anybody system." Most of the current systems offer a limited number of billers and limited number of customers.

C. Outsourcing of Accounts Receivable

Companies outsourcing their accounts receivable function have traditionally utilized factors for this purpose. The development of new Internet-based services, however, is rapidly changing this market. Banks and other third parties are able to offer low-cost processing and management of the accounts receivable function. In addition, the increasing use of purchasing or procurement cards is helping to convert many small manually processed payments into a single large payment with automated remittance information attached.

Test Your Understanding

These chapter questions are provided to test your understanding of the information in the text and are not examples of CCM examination questions, nor are they in the examination format.

Answers can be found at the back of the book on pages 506-509.

1. Discuss the major objectives of credit management.
2. What are the elements of a credit policy?
3. List the major factors that may constrain a company's credit policy.
4. What are the major expenses involved in offering trade credit?
5. What external sources can be used to determine the creditworthiness of an applicant?
6. What are the five Cs of credit?
7. Define credit scoring.
8. Define revolving credit terms.
9. Define seasonal dating.
10. Calculate the effective cost of not taking a discount under terms of 3/20, net 60.
11. Why is it important to monitor accounts receivable at both the individual account and aggregate levels?
12. A firm has outstanding receivables of $125,000. Its credit terms are net 30. If during the past three months sales are $75,000, $100,000 and $90,000, how many days' sales are outstanding?
13. What is the accounts receivable balance pattern and what is it used for?
14. Discuss the use of factoring.
15. What are the different types of cash application processes?
16. Discuss the federal legislation that prohibits price discrimination.
17. What federal legislation requires disclosure of the true cost of a loan?
18. Define EBPP.

CHAPTER 6

Collections

Overview

This chapter discusses the objectives of a collection system, the principal methods that companies and other organizations use to collect payments and the role of the commercial banking system in the collection process.

Learning Objectives

Upon completion of this chapter and related study questions, the reader should know:
- The objectives of a corporate collection system
- The components of collection float
- How companies select processing systems
- The differences among over-the-counter, mail and electronic collection methods
- The service features of lockbox providers
- The differences between wholesale and retail lockboxes
- How to conduct a collection study
- How to calculate the cost of float and the dollar savings from a lockbox
- The functions and applications of electronic and other collection systems

Key Concepts

- Collection system purposes
- Components of collection system float
- Differences among collection methods
- Different types of lockboxes
- Collection studies
- Lockbox costs and benefits
- Other electronic collection systems

Outline

I. Objectives of a Collection System

II. Collection Float
    A. Components
    B. Measurement

III. Collection System Considerations
    A. Payment Practices
    B. Payments System
    C. Nature of the Business
    D. Payment Instrument Characteristics
    E. Float/Administrative Cost Trade-off

IV. Collection Methods and Products
    A. Over-the-Counter/Field Deposit Systems
    B. Mail Processing Systems
    C. Electronic Systems

V. Types of Lockboxes
    A. Wholesale Lockbox
    B. Retail Lockbox
    C. Hybrid Lockbox

VI. Issues Pertaining to Lockbox Selection
    A. Lockbox Cost/Benefit Analysis
    B. Collection Studies
    C. How Lockbox Service Features Vary
    D. Lockbox Networks
    E. Customized Services

VII. Image Technology

VIII. Electronic Collection Systems
    A. Wire Transfers
    B. ACH Business-to-Business Payments
    C. Preauthorized Payments

IX. Other Collection Systems
    A. Net Settlement Systems
    B. Retail Collection Systems

I. Objectives of a Collection System

A collection system is a set of arrangements and management procedures used to gather and process customer payments. The major objectives of a corporate collection system include:

1. **Mobilizing Funds** — Move funds from a customer's (payor) account into a company's (payee) account within the banking system as quickly and cost effectively as possible. To do this, a company must integrate its collection system with its cash concentration system.

2. **Accessing Information** — Provide accurate and timely information on cash flows, levels of bank balances and availability of funds in a manner that interfaces easily with other components of a company's treasury information management system.

3. **Updating Accounts Receivable** — Update accounts receivable records promptly and accurately. Mistakes or failures to update customer files can jeopardize potential sales because of credit limitations, thereby damaging customer relationships. Use linkages to update credit and treasury management systems.

4. **Providing Audit Trails** — Provide audit trails for the company's internal and external auditors.

II. Collection Float

Collection float is the interval between the time the payor mails the check and the time the payee receives available funds at its financial institution. Converting accounts receivable as quickly as possible into collected funds requires minimizing collection float.

A. Components

Collection float has three components: mail, processing and availability. Each represents a float interval along the cash flow timeline.

1. **Mail Float** — Mail float is the interval between the time a check is mailed and the date it is received by the payee or at the processing site. It usually ranges from one to five calendar days or more, depending on location, weather and other factors.

2. **Processing Float** — Processing float is the interval between the time the payee or the processing site receives the check and the time the check is deposited at a

financial institution. It can range from less than one day to three calendar days or more if there are processing delays.

3. **Availability Float** — Availability float is the interval between the time a check is deposited and the time a company's account is credited with collected funds. It typically ranges from zero to two business days and is determined by the depository institution's availability schedule. (This is the same as deposit float discussed in Chapter 4, U.S. Payments System.)

The components of collection float are illustrated in Exhibit 6.1.

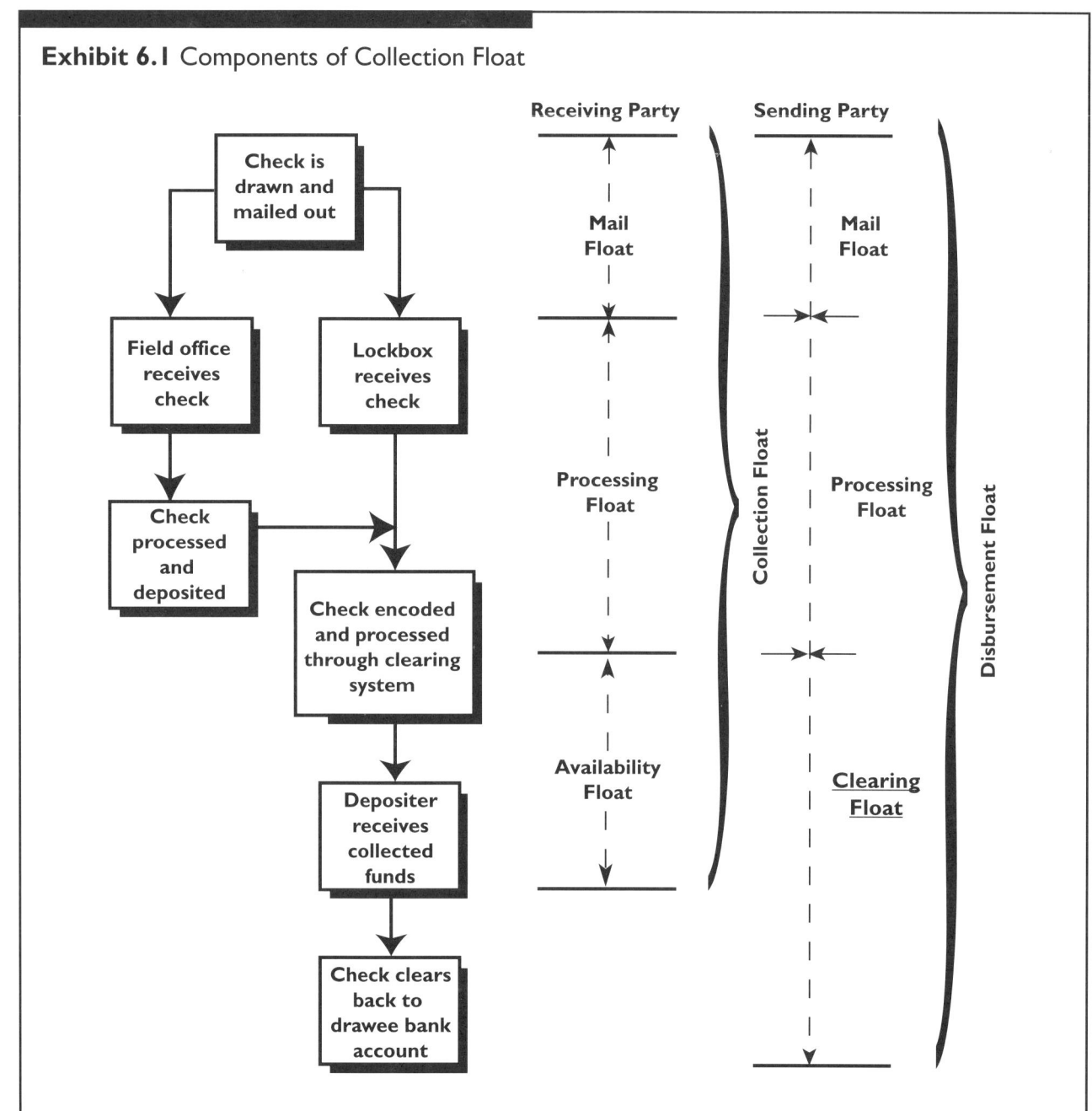

Exhibit 6.1 Components of Collection Float

B. Measurement

Collection float is usually measured in dollar-days and is a function of the transaction's dollar amount and the number of days' delay. The dollar-days of float on an individual check are calculated by multiplying the dollar amount of the check by the number of days between the time a payor mails the check and the time the receiver's bank credits collected funds into the payee's account.

Exhibit 6.2 provides a step-by-step analysis of float measurement as follows:

- Each of the three batches of checks has a different number of calendar days of float.
- The dollar-days of float are calculated for each batch and then totaled.
- The average daily float is calculated by dividing the total dollar-days of float by the number of calendar days in the period.
- The average delay, or the average number of days of float, is calculated by dividing the total dollar-days of float by the total dollar amount.
- The annual cost of float is calculated using a company's incremental opportunity cost of funds.

III. Collection System Considerations

In designing a collection system, a company must take into account the following issues:

- Commonly accepted payment practices
- The structure of the payments system
- The nature of its business (wholesale vs. retail)
- Characteristics of the payment instrument used
- The cost of float and system administration

A discussion of each of these considerations follows.

A. Payment Practices

In the United States, checks are the most frequently used payment instrument for both corporate and consumer bill paying, although the dollar volumes of electronic payments are vastly greater and the use of electronic payments is increasing. Electronic payments offer the potential for substantial cost savings for corporate payors and receivers. This is especially true if electronic payments become the predominant method of

Exhibit 6.2 Example of Float Measurement

Batch	Dollar Amount	Calendar Days of Float	Dollar-Days of Float
1	$1,500,000	× 4 =	$6,000,000
2	4,500,000	× 2 =	9,000.000
3	3,000,000	× 6 =	18,000,000
	$9,000,000		$33,000,000

Note: In this example there are 30 calendar days in the month and the opportunity cost of funds is 9%.

Average daily float = $\dfrac{\text{Total Dollar-Days of Float}}{\text{Total Calendar Days in Period}}$

Average daily receipts = $\dfrac{\text{Total Dollar Amount}}{\text{Total Calendar Days in Period}}$

Average delay = $\dfrac{\text{Total Dollar-Days of Float}}{\text{Total Dollar Amount}}$

Annual cost of float = Average Daily Float × Opportunity Cost of Funds

Average daily float = $\dfrac{\$33,000,000}{30} = \$1,100,000$

Average daily receipts = $\dfrac{\$9,000,000}{30} = \$300,000$

Average delay = $\dfrac{\$33,000,000}{9,000,000} = 3.67 \text{ days}$

Annual cost of float = $\$1,100,000 \times .09 = \$99,000$

payment and are used as an integral part of electronic data interchange (EDI) and electronic commerce (e-commerce) systems. However, in the United States, checks provide the payor with disbursement float and are an established way of doing business acceptable to most trading partners.

B. Payments System

All collection systems must be designed in light of the particular strengths and limitations of a country's payments system. Three features that distinguish the U.S. payments system from that of most other countries are:

- Checks are used in most payments. Large cash transactions are rare.
- There is a relatively large number of banks and financial institutions. The U.S. financial system is both highly evolved and very competitive.

- There are no true nationwide banks, but the extent of nationwide branch banking is becoming more common and is expected to be a more significant factor in coming years.

C. Nature of the Business

The nature of a company's business impacts the collection system it uses.

- Typically, high transaction volume retail operations such as fast food restaurants receive the majority of their payments in cash.

- Certain types of retail operations such as department or clothing stores collect a large portion of their payments by credit card and checks.

- A time-critical transaction such as a securities settlement or a real estate closing, or simply a very large dollar amount, may require a wire transfer with same-day value.

- In a business-to-business (B2B) environment, a supplier usually sends an invoice to its customer and receives a check as payment. The check is generally accompanied by remittance information about invoices paid, partial payments, discounts and deductions.

- As the use of the Internet expands, more companies are implementing electronic bill presentment and payment (EBPP) or using Web-based collection applications.

D. Payment Instrument Characteristics

Each payment instrument has different characteristics and uses. Often the instrument used is a matter of negotiation between the seller and the buyer. The most preferred method for the one might not be best for the other.

1. **Cash** — Cash is the principal means of payment in many retail businesses. Cash provides the seller with immediate funds, but until these funds are collected and deposited at the bank, they are not available for use by the company.

2. **Check** — A check is used for most corporate and consumer bill payments. Depending on when and how it is deposited and cleared, a check usually provides the seller with zero- to two-day availability from the day it is deposited.

3. **Payment Cards**
   - *Credit Cards* — The acceptance of credit cards by retailers is widespread. Increasingly, credit cards also are becoming a preferred method of payment among wholesalers.

- *Debit Cards* — Consumer use of debit cards as a method of payment is growing in acceptance. Debit cards replace cash and check transactions. The seller/merchant is provided with zero- to two-day availability.

- *Purchasing Cards* — Purchasing or procurement cards can be used to pay for supplies, inventory, equipment or services. Organizations using these cards have been able to reduce the costs of purchasing and maintain or increase control.

- *Smart Cards* — Smart cards have computer chips embedded within them. They are capable of storing important data that can be updated. The cards can be used as stored value devices, enabling cardholders to make fewer cash transactions. From the standpoint of collections, smart cards are similar to credit or debit card transactions.

4. **Automated Clearing House (ACH)** — Consumer and corporate use of ACH as a method of payment is growing in acceptance, as is the use of ACH by companies to pay trading partners. Settlement usually occurs one or two days after origination.

5. **Wire Transfer** — Wire transfer as a method of payment is primarily used by companies for large-dollar transactions or for those companies needing same-day confirmed funds, no matter what the amount. The payee is provided with immediate funds.

E. Float/Administrative Cost Trade-Off

An optimal collection system minimizes the sum of float, processing and administrative costs. For example, if a company chooses to use a lockbox system (a cash collection system in which a company's customers mail payments to a post office box, most often operated by the company's bank), it must determine the number and location of lockbox sites. Additionally, if more than one site is used, each customer must be assigned to a specific lockbox. While adding more collection points generally reduces float, it definitely increases administrative costs and may increase processing costs.

IV. Collection Methods and Products

Companies collect payments from their customers over the counter, through the mail and through electronic networks. Exhibit 6.3 provides an overview of these three systems.

A. Over-the-Counter/Field Deposit Systems

Various businesses may collect receipts over the counter at field locations. Field units include local offices and retail stores. Methods used by retail establishments to collect

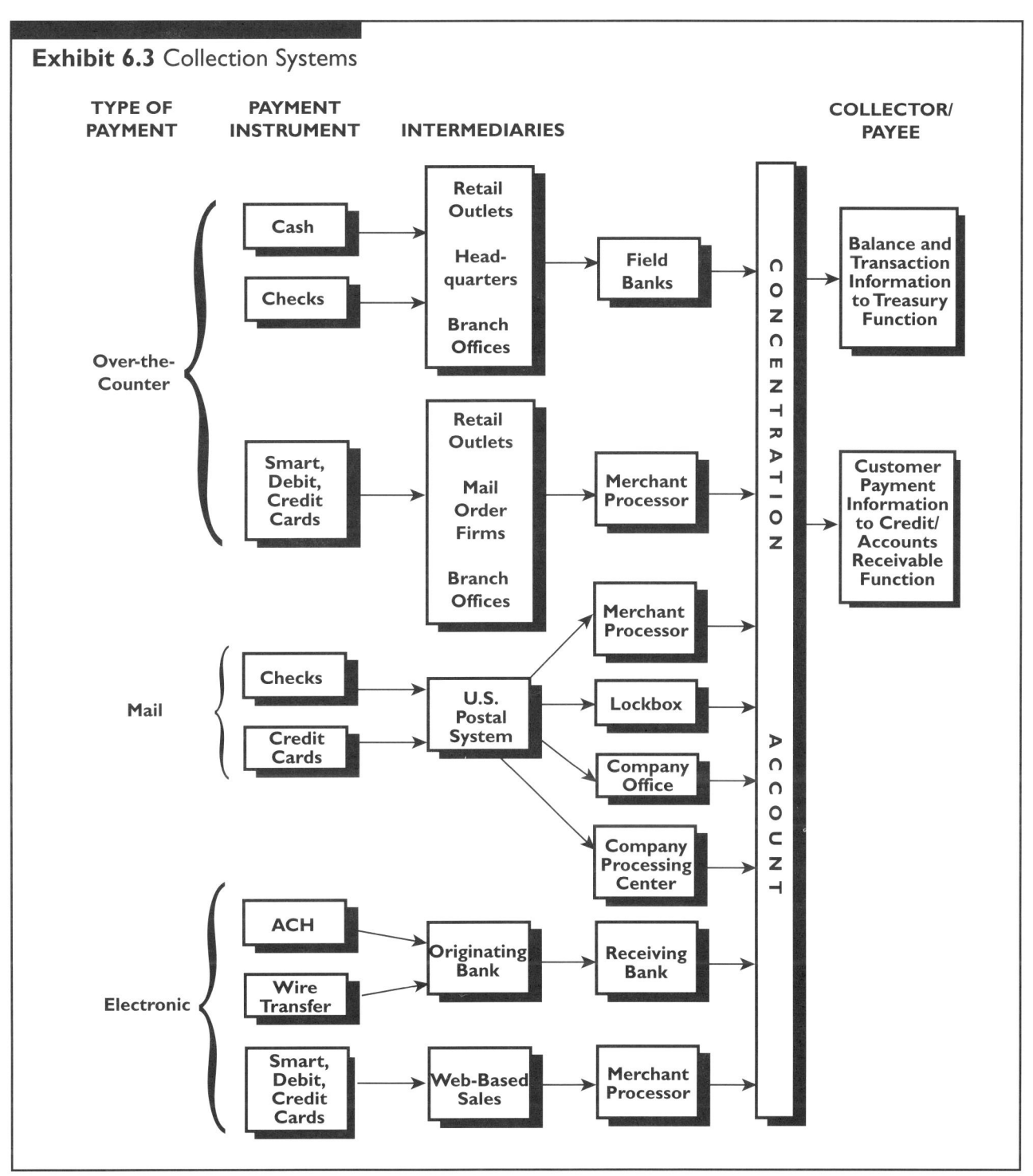

Exhibit 6.3 Collection Systems

at the point of sale include cash, checks, credit cards, debit cards and smart cards. A wholesale customer or its agent may deliver checks or cash to a vendor's office. Alternatively, a payee or its agent may pick up checks or cash from the customer when making a delivery. Companies must carefully consider various attributes when selecting deposit or collection banks, including:

1. **Location** — A deposit bank whose branches are close to the field units offers convenience and increased cash handling security for local managers.

2. **Branch Banking** — Where statewide, regional or interstate branching is available, collections may be simplified by using branches of the same bank or banks. This reduces the company's administrative and cash concentration costs. The company may, however, lose some flexibility in selecting convenient deposit bank locations and incur a risk by relying on only one bank.

3. **Compensation** — The compensation of field banks can be by fees, balances or both.

4. **Deposit Reconciliation Services** — A bank with multiple branches may offer deposit reconciliation services, also called branch consolidation services. These services enable deposits from multiple locations to be credited to a single corporate bank account. The use of magnetic ink character recognition (MICR) encoded deposit tickets allows banks to identify each company deposit location and produce reports on a daily, weekly or monthly basis.

5. **Pre-Encoded Check Deposits** — Companies that pre-encode checks to be deposited can get lower fees and/or faster availability.

6. **Cash Processing** — A company that accepts cash has two options for making cash deposits:

    - *Branch Deposits* — An employee of the company can take cash to a nearby bank or bank branch for deposit. However, because of the security risk involved, banks may refuse to accept large cash deposits at certain locations or withhold granting credit until final verification of the deposit.

    - *Centralized Cash Processing* — Centralized cash processing involves sending armored couriers to pick up cash from a company's location and deliver it to a processing site. This method is commonly used for transporting large amounts of cash because it reduces security risks. Companies may reduce fees by prepackaging cash and coins and by putting each denomination of coin in standard rolls, or by filling standard bags with loose coins of a particular denomination. If a company delivers cash in mixed denominations, the bank may charge extra for counting and verification. Banks may charge for these services in different ways, such as the amount of time required to verify the deposit, the dollar amount of the deposit or the number of bills and deposits processed.

B. Mail Processing Systems

Companies receive checks from consumers and from other companies in the mail directly or through lockboxes. For payments received in the mail, a company may use either its own processing center or a lockbox. Deciding which method to use depends primarily on the volume of checks processed and the dollar amounts of the checks.

1. **Company Processing Center** — With a company processing center, a company does its own processing and deposit preparation. It is typically used by a company with a large volume of relatively small-dollar payments.

   Advantages — The advantages of company processing centers over lockboxes may include:

   - *Control* — A company maintains total control over the operation.
   - *Flexibility* — It is easier to make changes in an internal system than it is in a lockbox processor's system.
   - *Customization* — Processing is customized to meet a company's needs rather than standardized to meet the needs of a lockbox processor.
   - *Facilitation of Updating* — Updating payor information may be faster.
   - *Reduced Cost* — With large volume and small dollars, a company may find internal processing less expensive than paying a third party for the same amount of work because a company can realize the same economies of scale as a lockbox processor.
   - *Capability Assurance* — A company is assured of future processing capability, as opposed to relying on a lockbox processor that may eliminate the service.
   - *Customer Service Quality* — The company can better monitor customer service quality in its own processing center than through a third-party provider.

   Disadvantages — The disadvantages of processing centers over lockboxes may include:

   - *Capital Investment and Ongoing Expense Requirements* — A company must staff and equip the processing center. Check volume must be sufficient for a company to have a cost-efficient operation and peak volume must be accommodated.
   - The company may be "stuck" with the sunk costs of the processing center as they move customers to EBPP and Internet billing/collection alternatives.
   - *Lack of Contingency Sites* — A company may lack a contingency site to prevent an interruption in payment processing.
   - *Reduced Processing and Efficiency* — There may be a greater time lag between processing the items and depositing the checks.
   - *Slower Delivery* — A company processing center may not receive mail through a unique ZIP code or be located where the company has operations, resulting in greater mail float.

2. **Lockbox** — A lockbox is a collection system in which a third party receives payments at a specified lockbox address, processes the remittances and deposits them in the payee's account. Lockboxes can be electronic, paper-based or a combination of the two. They are one of the most widely used cash management methods.

Advantages — Lockboxes may have the following advantages over a company processing center:

- *Reduced Float* — A lockbox reduces the three components of collection float as follows:

  — Mail Float — Mail float is usually reduced because a lockbox processor uses its own unique ZIP code to speed mail delivery. Also, a lockbox processor makes frequent mail pickups from a postal facility instead of waiting for the mail to be delivered. A lockbox may also be located close to a payor.

  — Processing Float — Processing float is usually reduced because remittances are mailed directly to the lockbox processor, eliminating a company's intermediary role in receiving, processing and delivering checks to the bank. Further, many lockbox processors operate 24 hours a day, seven days per week, with emphasis on peak periods.

  — Availability Float — Availability float is usually reduced because lockbox processors schedule work to meet critical availability deadlines. These are deadlines by which checks must reach the bank's proof and transit area.

- *Efficient Processing* — A lockbox provides efficient processing through economies of scale and potentially lower per-unit processing costs. In addition, trained personnel process the work for a particular account and others are trained to back up these specialists.

- *Greater Control and Enhanced Record-Keeping Capability* — A lockbox establishes an external audit trail for payments received and segregates check processing from other accounts receivable functions. A lockbox may be required by company auditors even when it is not economically justified based on float reduction.

- *Uninterrupted Service* — Lockboxes are less vulnerable to service interruptions and are more easily restarted following disasters (assuming the bank has better backup and contingency plans than the company).

- *Scalability* – A lockbox is generally easier to scale up or down as business volumes change.

Disadvantages — Lockboxes may have the following disadvantages relative to company processing centers:

- *Reduced Operational Control* — A company has less control over the operation than with a company processing center.

- *Greater Costs* — A company with very high transaction volume may be able to run its own processing center at a cost that is lower than that of a lockbox.

- *Harder to Customize* — A company with unique collection processing or remittance information may find it difficult to find a lockbox processor to deliver a customized system.

C. Electronic Systems

Modern telecommunications and data transmission systems linked to personal computers (PCs), along with the Internet, have transformed the way payments are remitted, transfers made and financial information disseminated. (See Chapter 9, Electronic Commerce.)

1. **Home Banking** — Home banking services are available from financial institutions or brokerage houses or can be part of software systems connecting users to third-party providers. Generally, these are PC-based services with a broad array of capabilities that may include bank or brokerage account inquiry, account transfer and transaction and bill paying services. As their use becomes more widespread, companies must adapt collection systems to accept and process payments received through these systems.

2. **Telephone Initiation** — Telephones can be used to transfer funds and make payments from accounts at financial institutions. Sometimes these transactions involve credit and other types of payment cards.

3. **Personal Computers** — When linked to the Internet and telecommunications systems, PCs can be used in a variety of financial, data transmission and analytical applications.

4. **Internet** — Organizations can use the Internet to transfer funds, receive and make payments and disseminate and acquire financial data. Web sites can be configured to provide fee-based services both related to and independent of the Internet. These utilize a number of methods for payment.

5. **Electronic Bill Presentment and Payment (EBPP)** — Many companies and banks are implementing EBPP systems that allow billers to send electronic statements to their customers and permit the customers to pay these bills by electronic means. In most cases these applications are Web-based and usable by anyone with Internet access. The biggest issue with these systems is that they are competing with the current mail/check billing and payment system which is a "bill anybody — pay anybody system." Most of the current systems offer a limited number of billers and limited number of customers.

V. Types of Lockboxes

There are three different types of lockboxes, as follows:

A. Wholesale Lockbox

Wholesale lockboxes are configured to process B2B payments, which, unlike consumer payments, are usually for large amounts and can be matched to specific invoices. Often several invoices are paid with one check. Detailed information usually is required about the invoices paid, discounts taken, returns and allowances. Wholesale collection systems emphasize float reduction and timely handling of information related to the invoices being paid. These lockbox systems:

- Process small-to-moderate numbers of large-dollar remittances for each customer.
- Minimize collection float.
- Provide accurate and timely information on payments received.
- Process partially paid invoices or one payment for several invoices.
- Adjust for discounts, returns and allowances.
- Process remittance information accompanying the payment that does not conform to a standard format or formats.
- Though some may be automated, typically remittances are processed manually.

While lockbox processes vary, the typical steps in a wholesale lockbox operation are described and illustrated in Exhibit 6.4.

- *Step 1: Mail Check* — The payor is instructed by a company to mail checks to a lockbox address.
- *Step 2: Pick Up Mail* — Mail is picked up from a postal facility according to a predetermined schedule.
- *Step 3: Sort Mail* — The processor sorts mail by lockbox number.
- *Step 4: Open Mail* — The mail is opened.
- *Step 5: Examine Checks* — Checks may be examined for postdating, restrictive legends, payee and agreement between written and numeric amounts, as agreed upon by the bank and the customer.
- *Step 6: Separate Checks and Advices* — Checks are separated from remittance advices and other contents.
- *Step 7: Capture Image of Checks* — If required, the checks are copied by means of photocopier or imaging technology. In some instances the invoices, envelope or other remittance documents may also be copied.

- *Step 8: Endorse and Encode Checks* — Checks are encoded with a dollar amount and endorsed.

- *Step 9: Prepare Deposit* — Check amounts are added and balanced and deposit tickets are prepared.

- *Step 10: Clear Checks* — Checks are sent to the proof and transit department for clearing.

- *Step 11: Send Deposit and Remittance Data* — The processor provides both deposit information (such as the amount of the deposit and its availability) and remittance information (such as invoices paid and deductions or discounts taken). This information is transmitted daily to the company or to its concentration bank.

The lockbox processor may also capture remittance data either electronically or manually from the check or remittance advice and transmit it to the company. Detailed remittance data may be captured on paper or CD-ROM and sent by courier, mail or electronically, or accessed via a Web-based browser.

B. Retail Lockbox

In retail lockbox systems, payors are generally consumers. Payments are often small-dollar amounts and frequently involve installments or recurring payments and scannable remittance documents. Because of the large number of items to be handled, processing cost is a more critical consideration than float reduction. Retail lockboxes are configured for:

- Processing large volumes of small-dollar remittances, usually from consumers

- Minimizing processing costs rather than reducing collection float

- Processing scannable, standardized remittance advices, sometimes contained on return documents, which usually accompany checks

- Using automated processes and specialized equipment that:

    - Opens envelopes

    - Reads scan lines on checks and return documents that contain information such as the payor's account number, the total amount due, the minimum amount due and the due date, using optical character recognition (OCR) and magnetic ink character recognition (MICR) techniques

    - Electronically transmits data captured to update accounts receivable

    - Automatically encodes the dollar amount of the check during the scanning process

CHAPTER 6 • COLLECTIONS

Exhibit 6.4 Example of Wholesale Lockbox Processing

Step 1: **Mail Check** — The payor is instructed by a company to mail checks to a lockbox address.

Step 2: **Pick Up Mail** — Mail is picked up from a postal facility according to a predetermined schedule.

Step 3: **Sort Mail** — The processor sorts mail by lockbox number.

Step 4: **Open Mail** — The mail is opened.

Step 5: **Examine Checks** — Checks may be examined for post-dating, restrictive legends, payee and agreement between written and numeric amounts, as agreed upon by the bank and the customer.

Step 6: **Separate Checks and Advices** — Checks are separated from remittance advices and other contents.

Step 7: **Capture Image of Checks** — If required, the checks are copied by means of photocopier or imaging technology. In some instances the invoices, envelope or other remittance documents may also be copied.

Step 8: **Endorse and Encode Checks** — Checks are encoded with a dollar amount and endorsed.

Step 9: **Prepare Deposit** — Check amounts are added and balanced and deposit tickets are prepared.

Step 10: **Clear Checks** — Checks are sent to the proof and transit department for clearing.

Step 11: **Send Deposit and Remittance Data** — The processor provides both deposit information (such as the amount of the deposit and its availability) and remittance information (such as invoices paid and deductions or discounts taken). This information is transmitted daily to the company or to its concentration bank.

C. Hybrid Lockbox

Hybrid lockboxes (sometimes referred to as automated wholesale lockboxes) combine features of both wholesale and retail lockboxes. They are configured, often on a customized basis, to process both B2B and retail payments. They are used by companies, such as utilities, whose consumer customers usually return standardized (scannable) remittance documents that can be processed automatically and whose business customers usually remit documents that require manual handling. The processor aggregates remittance data and transmits it to the company.

VI. Issues Pertaining to Lockbox Selection

Assessing the suitability of using a lockbox system or systems requires comparing the costs of paying fees to lockbox processors to internal processing costs and assessing the savings from reducing collection float.

A. Lockbox Cost/Benefit Analysis

The economic benefit of using a lockbox comprises the following elements:

1. **Float Savings** — Using a lockbox can result in float savings by reducing mail, processing and availability delays.

2. **Costs** — Lockboxes have both fixed and variable cost components. The company should compare both the fixed and the variable cost differences between a lockbox and a company processing center. Lockbox providers have many ways of charging, but the following are some basic concepts:

    - *Fixed* — Fixed monthly costs may include fees for preparing deposits, renting the post office box, sending remittance data to the company, balance reporting and account maintenance. Often several of those costs are bundled into a lockbox maintenance charge. There also may be a charge for transferring funds to a concentration bank.

    - *Variable* — Variable costs may include per-item deposit and processing charges and the charges for transmitting remittance data, photocopying, imaging and microfilming. These and other custom processing charges are often on a per-item basis. For example, some costs, such as those for deposit preparation, may be considered either fixed or variable depending on the lockbox processor.

3. **Calculation of Net Benefit** — The net benefit from a lockbox is equal to the reduction in float opportunity costs plus the reduction in internal processing costs minus lockbox processing costs. Float opportunity cost is a function of the dollar

amount of the collected items, the total collection time for items and a company's current investment or borrowing rate.

Exhibit 6.5 is an example of a lockbox cost/benefit analysis including the trade-off between the savings from float reduction and the cost of a lockbox.

B. Collection Studies

The objective of a collection study is to minimize the cost of processing and collection float. These studies use remittance data (consumer remittance envelopes, photocopies of checks and bank statements) to provide information for analysis such as:

- Location and geographic concentration of remitting customers
- Location of customers with largest payments
- Intercity mail times
- Bank availability schedules
- Difference between company and bank processing costs
- Administrative costs associated with using lockboxes

1. **Mail Time Studies** — Treasury consulting companies and some cash management banks do periodic studies to compare mail times for various combinations of cities. These services generally report mail times between central city post offices for a uniform distribution of mailings throughout the week. If necessary, adjustments can be made for non-surveyed mail points and day-of-the-week mail experience. This is especially true in areas where the post office has reduced over-the-weekend processing.

   The results of mail time studies are combined with information from banks' availability schedules to compare both city-average and banks' availability statistics. Banks or consultants use this data in conjunction with an analysis of a company's actual remittances to determine which cities or combinations of cities are the most effective collection sites.

   Computer analysis is performed to produce an optimal solution. This can be attractive for a company with many banking relationships that is willing to consider many different combinations of cities.

2. **Processing Cost** — A collection study should take into account not only collection float but the difference in processing costs between a company processing center and a lockbox and the price differences among lockbox processors.

3. **Site Selection** — In doing a study, a company will usually select a number of potential sites based on the following criteria:

Exhibit 6.5 Example of Lockbox Cost/Benefit Analysis

This exhibit shows the lockbox savings and associated costs for a company with $108,000,000 annual sales ($9,000,000 per month). Each of the items is assumed to be a batch of checks with average size of $9,000; the annual volume of checks is 12,000. The company's annual opportunity cost is 9%. The company's internal check processing cost assuming no lockbox is $.25 per item. The lockbox processor charges $10,000 per year plus a processing cost of $.50 per item.

WITHOUT LOCKBOX

Batch	Dollar Amount	Calendar Days of Collection Float Without Lockbox	Total Dollar-Days
1	$1,500,000	× 4 =	$ 6,000,000
2	4,500,000	× 2 =	9,000,000
3	3,000,000	× 6 =	18,000,000
Total Deposits	$9,000,000	Total Float Without Lockbox	$33,000,000

Divided by 30 calendar days =	$ 1,100,000
Times Opportunity Cost/Investment Rate = Annual Cost of Float (9%)	$ 99,000

WITH LOCKBOX

Batch	Dollar Amount	Calendar Days of Collection Float Without Lockbox	Total Dollar-Days
1	$1,500,000	× 3 =	$ 4,500,000
2	4,500,000	× 1 =	4,500,000
3	3,000,000	× 5 =	15,000,000
Total Deposits	$9,000,000	Total Float Without Lockbox	$ 24,000,000

Divided by 30 calendar days =	$ 800,000
Times Opportunity Cost/Investment Rate = Annual Cost of Float (9%)	$ 72,000
Annual Cost of Float Without Lockbox	$ 99,000
Annual Cost of Float With Lockbox	($ 72,000)
Lockbox Float Savings	$ 27,000
Fixed Lockbox Cost	($ 10,000)
Variable Lockbox Cost: 12,000 checks × $0.50	($ 6,000)
Saving of Internal Lockbox Processing Cost: 12,000 × $0.25	$ 3,000
Net Dollar Benefit of Lockbox	$ 14,000

- *Availability* — A lockbox in a Federal Reserve city or regional check processing center (RCPC) generally gets faster availability than one in a Federal Reserve country point.

- *Mail Center* — A lockbox is usually best located in a city with a major airport and a major postal processing center.

- *Customer Base* — A lockbox is usually best located near high concentrations of customers.

- *Service Quality* — Processors may be prescreened for service quality before they are included in a study. The overall quality of service and responsiveness to a company's inquiries are as important as mail time and availability performance. A number of processors have dedicated customer service representatives and guaranteed response times for answering inquiries. A company must evaluate the ability of a processor to serve its particular needs.

4. **Lockbox Processor Selection** — There are a number of considerations in selecting a lockbox processor:

    - *Processor Characteristics* — Among the characteristics to consider are the following:

        — *Operations*

            - Hours and days of operation
            - Return item handling capabilities
            - Costs
            - Error rates

        — *Processing*

            - Overnight mail processing capabilities
            - Payment processing capabilities
            - Check processing procedures
            - Availability schedules
            - Postal facility's mail processing capabilities
            - Discount and processing fees for credit cards

        — *Reporting*

            - Data transmission capabilities
            - Deposit and balance reporting capabilities

        — *Technical*

            - Disaster recovery capabilities

- Imaging capabilities
- Access to data via Internet
— *General*
- Expansion capabilities
- Management experience
- Length of time in business

- *City and Processor Selection* — A company may first select lockbox cities based on a lockbox study and then select processors within those cities, but there are other factors to consider that could modify the decision. Some processors may try to demonstrate features such as processing time and availability schedules that are better than the average for their cities and win customers from cities with marginally better mail times.

- *Relationship Banks* — Using lockbox services at a bank where a company has an existing relationship may allow the company to strengthen that relationship by protecting access to credit facilities and making better use of operating balances for bank compensation benefits. It may also allow the use of existing data access tools such as the Internet and balance reporting.

C. How Lockbox Service Features Vary

In selecting a lockbox processor, a cash manager should determine how the lockbox operation meets the company's particular needs. This is a more important characteristic than the technology used. The company should consider the following service features in evaluating each processor:

1. **Mail Time Performance** — Mail delivery time often varies considerably among cities. Among the reasons for this are total mail volume, post office proximity to the airport and the lockbox processor, post office processing capabilities and airline schedules. Desirable sites have post offices that process mail 24 hours per day, sort bar-coded envelopes automatically, read non-bar-coded envelopes with OCR equipment and make a unique ZIP code available to a lockbox processor.

2. **Unique ZIP Codes** — Most processors offering lockbox services have a unique ZIP code for lockbox remittances. Depending on their capabilities for fine sorting, this feature may speed processing of incoming mail and save several hours of mail and processing float daily.

3. **Deposit Deadlines** — Lockbox systems should process remittances expeditiously in order to ensure meeting deposit deadlines and achieve optimal availability. Frequent mail pickups and varying staffing levels to ensure efficient peak-time processing can help with meeting critical check clearing deadlines. As deposit

deadlines approach, some lockbox operations may identify and process large-dollar items first. The number of deposits the bank makes each day from a lockbox to a customer's account can vary according to agreed-upon terms. Each company must weigh the cost of frequent deposits vs. the benefit of improving availability.

4. **Availability** — Banks may offer several availability schedules. A company should know which availability schedule is applicable. A better availability schedule may be offered for a higher price or when merited by the overall profitability of the relationship.

   Some banks assign availability in their lockbox departments rather than in check processing. Either way, a company may receive fractional availability or bear the risk of adjustments if the bank incurs a float loss in clearing a check.

5. **Endpoint Analysis** — An endpoint analysis, in which all checks drawn on banks in selected cities are broken down by days of float, is an effective way to measure and compare different banks' availability schedules.

6. **Ledger Cutoff Time** — In evaluating a lockbox system, it is important to consider total collection time, not just availability. The bank's cutoff time for giving ledger credit on the same day can vary and must be considered in conjunction with its availability schedule. A check with one-day availability before the ledger cutoff may have two-day availability if it is processed after the ledger cutoff.

7. **Payment Media** — Some lockboxes can handle both paper and electronic payments and can capture associated remittance data.

8. **Different Ways to Access Lockbox Information** — Some lockbox facilities offer electronic accounts receivable, where the bank merges ACH, wire, EDI and lockbox information into one electronic transmission to the company. There is also increasing use of the Internet and Web-based access to lockbox and other payment information.

D. Lockbox Networks

Lockbox networks may involve several processors in different cities or a single processor with multiple locations. A network permits a company to have a number of collection points and get consolidated remittance data. Funds concentration is simplified and a company may deal with fewer processors.

E. Customized Services

Lockbox providers are beginning to include additional services such as:
- Payor address change updates
- Conversion of remittance data and payments to ACH format
- Receivables management
- Integrated collections outsourcing
- Managing databases for clients
- Creating Web-based invoices

VII. Image Technology

Image technology is used to facilitate processing of both wholesale and retail lockbox payments. This technology allows paper documents to be scanned, converted to a digital image and stored for subsequent distribution, handling and processing. The data capture process is enhanced through the use of intelligent character recognition (ICR), which reads handwritten or typed information and optical character recognition (OCR), which reads preprinted information. The documents scanned can be both checks and remittance advices. Potential benefits of applying image technology to the remittance processing function include reduced overall processing costs, increased productivity, improved accuracy and the ability to capture data for automated posting to accounts receivable.

The degree of data capture automation achievable with image technology is generally higher with retail than with wholesale payments because of the presence of a scannable return document. This facilitates posting of retail remittances.

Wholesale payments often do not contain the seller's original invoice or OCR advice. Instead, a buyer may enclose its own payment document, a check stub with limited information or nothing at all. As a result, any machine-readable data is often supplemented with manual entry data for wholesale remittances.

Imaging services allow companies to identify potential unauthorized check activity and obtain copies in a more timely fashion, allowing companies to respond quickly to customer, employee and vendor inquiries. In addition to the actual processing of items, it can be applied to the delivery and storage of remittance data output. A lockbox provider can transmit to a company images of its deposit and detailed payment information, supply this data on a CD-ROM or archive the information in electronic format for later retrieval. Companies that can benefit from this feature are those that must research payment information to respond to a high volume of customer service inquiries.

VIII. Electronic Collection Systems

A company can receive a payment via wire transfer or ACH. In recent years, there has been a proliferation of software and/or service providers that facilitate the mechanical part of this process at reasonable cost and with little strain on resources. In many cases this involves the generation of ACH files for high volumes of debits.

A. Wire Transfers

Wire transfers are used for large-dollar payments when speed and finality are important.

B. ACH Business-to-Business Payments

Electronic payments through ACH are less expensive than wire transfers, but payment instructions must be submitted to the bank one or two days prior to settlement. Vendors may issue ACH debits against customer accounts or customers may issue ACH credits to vendor accounts. Companies generally consult with their trading partners in advance to determine which payment formats are appropriate, as well as to negotiate the timing of ACH payments.

1. **Applications** — Though most bills are paid by check, companies may collect a portion of their payments by ACH. A number of companies have initiated comprehensive programs to originate payments through ACH. Examples of applications include:

    - *Manufacturer's Suppliers* — Many suppliers to manufacturing companies are receiving payments through ACH as part of a more comprehensive EDI program that includes electronic issuance of purchase orders and invoices.

    - *Dealers with Floor Plans* — A floor plan is a loan to a dealer to finance inventory that is paid back when the financed item is sold. Automobile, truck and farm equipment suppliers that provide floor plan financing have utilized the ACH network extensively to debit their dealers.

    - *Debit Programs* — Companies can also collect funds by debiting their customer's bank accounts. This is typically done in one of two ways. A supplier may notify a customer in advance of the data and the exact amount of the debit. Or a buyer can notify the supplier of the desire to make a payment. The supplier then originates an ACH debit. The latter option offers the customer greater control.

    - *Internet Merchants* — Internet merchants typically collect only via credit/debit cards or other electronic means.

2. **Advantages** — Potential benefits of ACH B2B payments for the payee include:

    - *Reduced Float* — Reduction of collection float, depending upon the terms of the trading partner agreement

    - *Lowered Cost* — Reduction of receivables processing cost; lower overall cost compared to either a check payment or wire transfer

    - *Improved Forecasting* — Improved cash flow forecasting

3. **Disadvantages** — Despite possible cost-saving opportunities in the long run, there are potential impediments to the use of ACH corporate payments. The disadvantages include:

    - *Need for Trading Partner Negotiation* — The payor (buyer) and the payee (seller) must agree to make the switch.

    - *Adjusting Float* — When a company starts to receive payments electronically, there must be agreement on when the effective use of funds is being transferred under the existing system and what the settlement date of the ACH transaction should be. The payor and the payee may negotiate a settlement time for an ACH transaction that puts each party in approximately the same economic position as when checks were used to settle invoices.

    - *Setup Costs* — Preparation to receive ACH B2B payments may require an additional investment in processing software and communications equipment.

    - *Reluctance* — In the case of remittance information accompanying ACH debits, a company may be reluctant to give someone outside the company the authority to debit its bank account.

4. **Preparation** — A company preparing to receive ACH B2B payments for the first time should take the following steps:

    - *ACH Formats* — Since many ACH payment formats are available, the format to use should be discussed and agreed upon with the payor.

    - *Bank Capabilities* — ACH receiving and translating capabilities should be discussed and agreed upon with the bank where payments will be received.

    - *Payment-Related Information* — The company should determine how to receive payment-related information. The capabilities and costs of banks and value-added networks (VANs) to transmit full details related to the payment should be compared. VANs are computer-based systems that facilitate invoicing and payment between organizations and vendors. They ensure that the systems are compatible. A company may want to consider buying translation software to enable automated receipt of ACH remittance information to update its accounts receivable system.

There is still debate about the preferable alternative. Some favor sending the payment and payment information together through a bank, while others favor sending the payment through a bank and the payment information through a VAN.

C. Preauthorized Payments

Preauthorized debits are a payment method in which the payor approves in advance the transfer of funds from the payor's bank account to the payee's bank account. These payments are often for the same dollar amount and at the same time each month, but variable dollar amounts and schedules are possible. Where there is payment variability, written notice of the withdrawal must be provided to the customer 10 days prior to the transfer of funds.

Preauthorized payments are for the most part made through ACH. Consumer payments are governed by Federal Reserve Regulation E and National Automated Clearing House Association (NACHA) rules; electronic B2B payments are governed by Article 4A of the uniform commercial code and NACHA rules.

1. **Applications** — Preauthorized payments are used by both consumers and companies. Company payments are made to pay suppliers and trading partners. Consumer payments are commonly made for applications such as:

    - Insurance payments
    - Utility, wireless and cable payments
    - Mortgage payments
    - Association or club dues
    - Loan and lease payments
    - Credit card payments

2. **Advantages** — The advantages of preauthorized payments include:

    - Possible elimination of invoicing
    - Reduction of processing float
    - Elimination of availability float because of immediate availability on settlement day
    - Fewer delinquent payments
    - Reduction of the incentive for the customer to switch vendors
    - Reduction of cash application costs
    - More timely notification of account closing

3. **Disadvantages** — The disadvantages of preauthorized payments include:
   - Additional costs and time needed to educate customers
   - Customer resistance to having their bank accounts debited by another party
   - Cost and time involved in preparing and sending billing statements to meet regulatory requirements or customer service considerations
   - Initial time and effort needed to set up each customer's standard monthly payment instructions, including the correct bank transit routing number and customer account number
   - Cost and time involved in handling returned transactions

IX. Other Collection Systems

A. Net Settlement Systems

In some industries, such as airlines, oil/gas, telecommunications and securities, companies make exchanges and buy and sell from each other. For example, Airline A accepts a ticket from Airline B in exchange for a passenger making a change in reservations. Through a clearing system, it returns the ticket and is reimbursed by the airline that originally wrote the ticket. Similarly, Airline B may accept tickets from other airlines, including Airline A. At the end of the day, all of the participants to the netting system determine the net flows required to balance out the system. These clearing systems process transaction information and allow participants to make periodic net settlements with each other.

B. Retail Collection Systems

There are a number of alternative retail collections systems that may have benefits such as improving cash flow, reducing paperwork, reducing per-item transaction costs and increasing the accuracy and timeliness of accounts receivable updating. These systems include the following:

1. **Credit Cards** — Credit cards are a frequently used payment method. They are accepted both electronically and manually. From the seller's perspective, purchasing card collections are treated as credit card transactions.
   - *Electronic Acceptance* — Using a stand-alone credit card authorization/draft capture terminal or a magnetic stripe reader integrated into the merchant's cash register system, the merchant swipes the presented card through the reader so that the magnetic stripe on the back of the card is read. This stripe

contains, among other things, the cardholder's account number and name. Once the dollar value of the sale is entered into the terminal, the transaction is routed via telephone lines to the merchant's bank/processor for authorization. If approved, a receipt is printed for the customer to sign. The terminal accumulates transaction information throughout the day and, at settlement time, transmits the accumulated transaction information to the merchant's bank/processor. Within two business days, the merchant's bank/processor credits the merchant's checking account for the total dollar amount of the accumulated transactions. Electronic acceptance has become the predominant method of processing credit card transactions.

- *Manual Acceptance* — Using a paper sales draft and a telephone, the merchant records the sales transaction information on the draft and obtains an authorization from a voice operator or an audio response unit. If approved, the merchant obtains the cardholder's signature on the draft. The merchant can mail or deliver the drafts to its bank/processor. The bank may treat these deposits as various availability items, usually one, two or three days.

- *Charges* — At the end of the month the merchant bank/processor typically deducts a fee (priced as a percentage of the sale and generally known as the merchant discount) and other charges from the merchant's checking account. Alternatively, these charges may be invoiced to the merchant. Availability and discount amounts are pricing decisions negotiated between the bank/processor and the merchant. Other charges may include terminal rental, transmission fees, authorizations and supplies.

- *Authorizations and Chargebacks* — A credit card payment is not guaranteed, even when authorized. An authorization indicates that the cardholder has available credit but it does not indicate that the right person is using the card. A merchant may receive a chargeback (a returned transaction) for as long as six months after funds have been received. When fraud occurs, the time may be even longer. Signature verification is necessary to determine if the authorized person is using the card.

2. **Debit Cards** — Debit cards work like credit cards except that the transactions post to bank deposit accounts as withdrawals rather than to credit card accounts as future amounts owed. In addition, debit card transactions are generally priced to the accepting merchant on a per-transaction basis rather than as a percentage of sale like credit cards.

Upon settlement of a transaction, money has been transferred from the purchaser's account to the merchant's account. Debit cards settle in one of the following ways:

- *Online* — A personal identification number (PIN) is required to initiate the transaction. Positive authorization is received from the cardholder's bank. The merchant receives zero- to two-day availability.

- *Offline* — There are two types of offline programs:

— National Association (VISA or MasterCard) Debit Cards — The purchaser's bank deposit account is automatically debited. Availability is usually two days.

— Proprietary Cards — Settlement for proprietary cards is through ACH. Availability is usually one day.

3. **Automated Teller Machine (ATM) Networks** — Vendors that deal with a large number of retail customers may be able to make arrangements with banks for bills to be paid at ATMs. The payment is transferred manually or electronically from the customer's account to the vendor's account at the time of sale, or when the customer initiates payment through the ATM.

4. **Telephone Banking** — Vendors can make arrangements with financial institutions that offer telephone banking services to have consumers authorize the debiting of their accounts by phone. Smart or screen telephones with added capabilities are increasingly used to facilitate this process.

5. **Bill Paying Services** — Individuals usually use these services to make payments to companies, primarily utilities and retailers. Methods for initiating bill paying services include ATMs, phones and personal computers.

6. **Home Banking** — Home banking services are offered by financial institutions or can be part of a personal financial software system that connects the user to a third-party provider. Generally, these services are PC-based products with a broad array of capabilities that may include bank account inquiry, account transfers and bill paying services. As more of these services are used by consumers, companies must adapt their collection systems to receive and process these types of payments.

7. **The Internet** — The Internet can be used to make remittances and to transfer payments and financial data. Web sites on the Internet can be configured to receive payments, either for Internet-related activity or to purchase other goods and services. Such transactions involve credit card payments or the generation of ACH debits from checking or savings accounts. The use of the Internet for financial transactions and data transfer is evolving quickly with a wide variety of banks and other providers offering a range of services in this area.

8. **Agents** — Retailers and financial institutions may act as agents for collecting monthly payments related to service providers such as cable and utility companies.

9. **Smart Cards** — Smart cards are plastic cards that have computer chips embedded within them. This is an emerging technology that is capable of storing important data, including monetary value that can be electronically replenished. The cards can be used as stored value devices that enable cardholders to make fewer cash transactions. From a collections standpoint, smart cards operate in a manner similar to credit or debit card electronic transactions.

10. **Cross-Border Collections** — For companies collecting funds across borders and/or in foreign currencies, the collections process can be expensive and time-consuming. Most global banks offer cross-border collection services to help with this process.

Test Your Understanding

These chapter questions are provided to test your understanding of the information in the text and are not examples of CCM examination questions, nor are they in the examination format.

Answers can be found at the back of the book on pages 510-512.

1. List the major objectives in establishing a collection system.

2. What elements compose collection float?

3. What determines availability float?

4. List the key considerations in designing a collection system.

5. What features distinguish the U.S. payments system from those of most other countries?

6. Describe the major collection methods.

7. What is deposit reconciliation?

8. A company has provided the following information:

Batch	Dollar Amount	Calendar Days of Float	Dollar-Days of Float
1	$100,000	3	$ 300,000
2	$350,000	4	$ 1,400,000
3	$210,000	2	$ 420,000
			$ 2,120,000

    If the company's opportunity cost is seven percent and there are 30 calendar days in the month, what is the annual cost of float?

9. What determines the selection of a mail payment processing system?

10. Discuss the major advantages of a lockbox over a company processing facility.

11. What are some of the recent developments in electronic systems?

12. Outline the differences between a wholesale and a retail lockbox.

13. The company in Question 8 is considering using a lockbox, which would reduce float as follows:

Batch	Dollar Amount	Calendar Days of Float	Dollar-Days of Float
1	$100,000	1	$ 100,000
2	$350,000	2	$ 700,000
3	$210,000	1	$ 210,000
			$ 1,010,000

    The lockbox processor will charge $1,000 per year and a processing cost of $.30 per item. The current internal processing cost is $.20 per item. The annual volume of checks is 6,000. If the annual float cost without the use of a lockbox is $4,947 (see Question 8), is a lockbox appropriate for this company?

14. Describe an over-the-counter/field deposit collection system.

15. What is a preauthorized debit?

16. Define endpoint analysis.

17. What system would benefit companies in the same industry that buy and sell from each other on a regular basis?

18. What impact does image technology have on collection systems?

19. List and discuss the advantages and disadvantages of ACH B2B payments.

20. What are the major types of retail collection systems?

CHAPTER 7

Cash Concentration

Overview

This chapter discusses why companies concentrate cash, the objectives of a cash concentration system, the principal funds concentration mechanisms and how to minimize cash concentration system costs.

Learning Objectives

Upon completion of this chapter and related study questions, the reader should understand:

- The objectives of a cash concentration system
- Factors impacting cash concentration system configuration
- The advantages and disadvantages of the principal funds transfer mechanisms used in cash concentration systems
- The cost components of a cash concentration system and how to minimize them
- How to reduce risk and increase control in a cash concentration system

Key Concepts

- Cash concentration system objectives
- Cash concentration system design determinants
- Funds transfer mechanism alternatives
- Cash concentration system cost components
- Risk and control considerations as applicable to cash concentration systems

Outline

I. Objectives of a Cash Concentration System

II. Concentration System Configuration
    A. Collection System
    B. Disbursement System
    C. Funds Transfer Alternatives
    D. Banking Network

III. Cash Concentration Cost Components
    A. Excess Bank Balances
    B. Transfer Charges
    C. Administrative Costs

IV. Techniques to Reduce Concentration System Costs
    A. Improving Transfer Timing
    B. Reducing Transfer Costs
    C. Comparing Transfer Costs

V. Risks and Controls
    A. Timely Processing
    B. Fraud
    C. Bank Overdraft
    D. Bank Failure
    E. Disaster Recovery Plans
    F. Legal Restrictions

I. Objectives of a Cash Concentration System

Cash concentration is the transfer of funds from outlying depository locations to a central bank account, commonly referred to as a concentration account, where they can be managed more efficiently. A cash concentration system should be designed to accomplish the following:

1. **Minimize Bank Balances** — Fewer accounts with balances mean fewer excess balances and more efficient cash use. Concentrating cash enables a company to reduce excess bank balances.

2. **Pool Funds** — Concentrating cash enables a company to buy larger blocks of short-term securities, thus saving on commissions and possibly boosting portfolio yield. It may also allow a company to reduce debt or take greater advantage of supplier discounts.

3. **Simplify Cash Management** — The account consolidation made possible by a cash concentration system enables cash managers to manage a company's daily liquidity more easily.

4. **Improve Control** — Separation of deposit gathering from other cash management functions, such as disbursement control, tracking and forecasting, enables cash managers to control a company's funds more easily. Cash concentration also provides a clearer audit trail for incoming deposits.

5. **Reduce Transfer Costs** — Account consolidation concentrates cash and reduces total transfer costs.

II. Concentration System Configuration

The configuration of a company's concentration system depends on the size and geographic dispersion of its collection and disbursement system, the funds transfer alternatives available to it and the capabilities of the banking network it uses.

A. Collection System

The collection system a company uses has a major impact on its cash concentration system. The two major types of collection systems are:

1. **Over-the-Counter/Field Banking Systems** — Companies with regional sales offices or widely dispersed retail outlets deposit over-the-counter cash and checks in various accessible outlying depository banks. Such systems are characterized by:

- *Multiple Collection Points* — A company with many locations needs a local depository convenient to each location.

- *Multiple Banks* — A field banking system may use various local banks if their locations are proximate to field offices.

- *Limited Provision of Cash Management Services* — Because sales and deposit information is often sent directly to company headquarters or a concentration bank by the company's field units, headquarters may require fewer deposit and balance reporting services from field banks. Generally, field offices do not use cash management services extensively, even if the field banks can provide them.

- *Deposit Availability* — Deposits consist mainly of coin, currency and local checks. Coin and currency are usually given immediate availability. Local checks may take one day to clear; on-us items may clear faster.

2. **Lockbox Systems** — These allow a company to collect payments at one or more lockbox sites that will transfer available funds to a concentration bank. A company may use several lockbox sites to optimize collection float and may also use separate lockboxes for different subsidiaries.

Though lockbox cash concentration systems vary, most have the following characteristics:

- *Limited Collection Points* — Most companies try to consolidate their lockbox systems at one or more lockbox sites.

- *Use of Regional and Money Center Banks and Third-Party Processors* — A lockbox system often uses regional or money center banks and third-party processors.

- *Provision of Corporate Services* — Lockbox systems typically offer the following capabilities and services:

    — Daily reporting of transaction details and ledger and collected balances

    — Movement of funds through wire transfer or the automated clearing house (ACH)

    — Other treasury management services

- *Deposit Availability* — Because some of the checks a lockbox processes are drawn on non-local endpoints, a portion of a company's daily deposit may not be available for one or two banking days from the day of deposit.

A typical concentration system incorporating both a field banking system and a lockbox system is illustrated in Exhibit 7.1.

Exhibit 7.1 Example of a Cash Concentration System

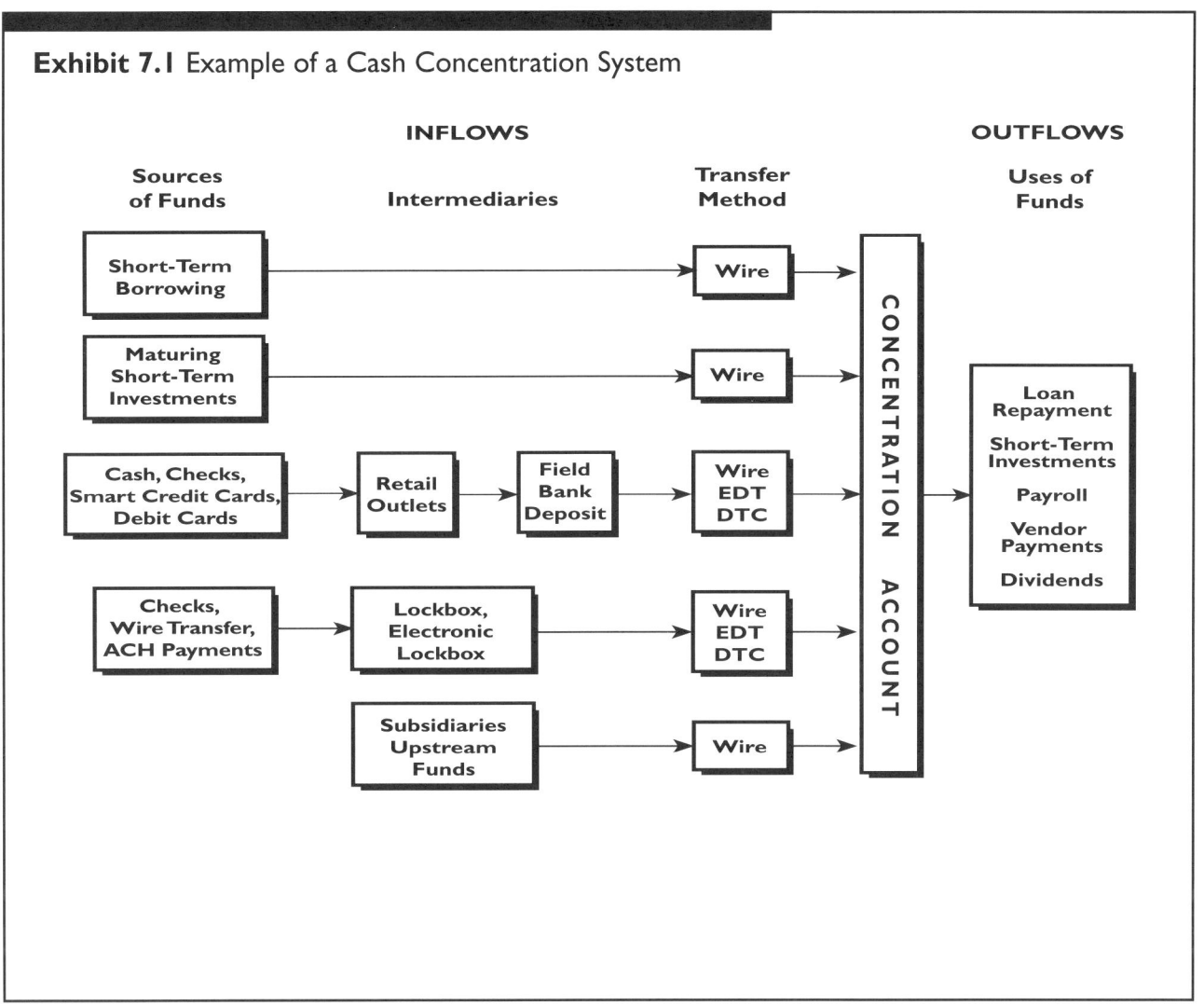

- *Electronic Lockbox* — Many cash management banks offer electronic lockboxes that allow inbound ACH and wire payments and related information to be gathered and reported on a consolidated basis. The growing use of electronic data interchange (EDI) transactions reduces, but does not eliminate, the need for multiple lockbox sites.

B. Disbursement System

The degree to which a company's disbursement system is centralized also helps determine its cash concentration system configuration. The differences, which are examined in detail in Chapter 8, Accounts Payable and Disbursements, include:

1. **Centralized Check Issuance** — In this type of system, headquarters controls disbursement accounts and is responsible for check writing and account reconciliation.

2. **Decentralized Check Issuance** — In this type of system, checks are written on local disbursement banks and account reconciliation is performed at the local level. Decentralized systems require closer monitoring of disbursement accounts by a company's headquarters.

3. **Checks Written at Local Level on a Centralized Disbursement Bank** — In this system, check issuance and check reconciliation (in some cases) are performed at the local level, but checks clear on a centralized disbursement bank. Headquarters is responsible for choosing disbursement banks and funding disbursement accounts.

C. Funds Transfer Alternatives

The most frequently used mechanisms for concentration are electronic depository transfers (EDTs) and wire transfers.

1. **Electronic Depository Transfers** — An EDT, which is an ACH transaction that concentrates cash, is the most common method of depository transfer in use today. It has virtually replaced depository transfer checks (DTCs), which are paper instruments used by companies to transfer funds from outlying depository locations to their concentration account. The diagram of EDT clearing is presented in Exhibit 7.2.

    Field offices, field banks, headquarters offices, lockbox banks and concentration banks can originate EDTs. A field office can initiate a credit transfer from the field account to the concentration account, notifying headquarters of the transfer amount. Alternatively, the field office may notify either headquarters or the concentration bank of the deposit amount and the headquarters or concentration bank then initiates a debit transfer from the field account to the concentration account.

    Some large retail networks transmit information on cash receipts from point-of-sale (POS) terminals to headquarters. Headquarters then transmits ACH debit instructions to a concentration bank. The origination of the ACH debits can be performed either by the headquarters or the field bank units/lockbox provider through several methods.

    - *Headquarters* — Field units/lockbox providers report sales and deposit data directly to headquarters. Headquarters then determines the transfer amounts and prepares an ACH debit file, which is delivered to the concentration bank. ACH files may be created by a company's own data processing, by using bank provided software or a combination of both.

    - *Third-Party Vendor* — Several third-party providers specialize in gathering deposit information from field units. Deposit data may be gathered by phone, POS terminal or computer. After gathering the deposit data the third party may:

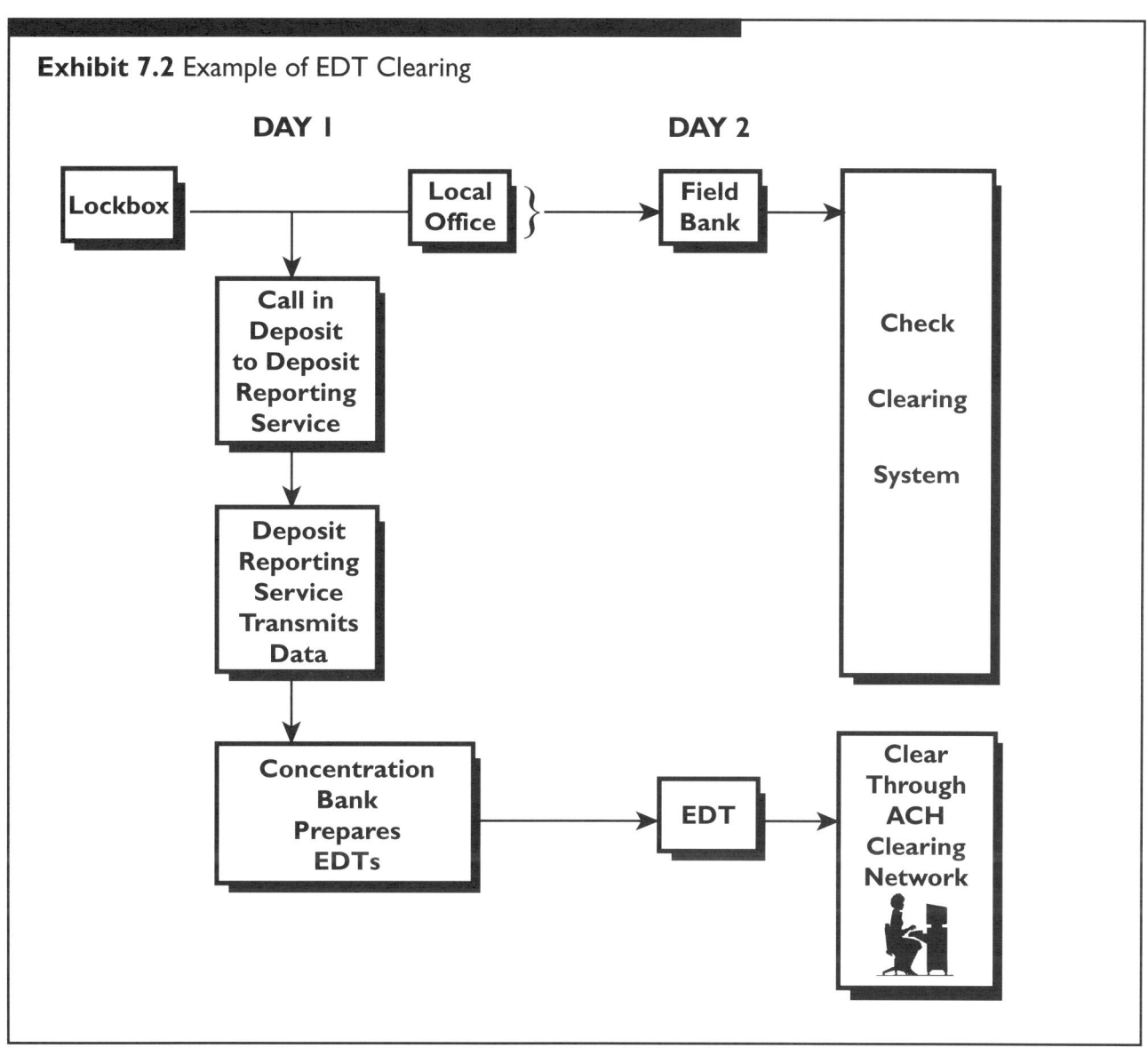

Exhibit 7.2 Example of EDT Clearing

— Create an ACH file that is sent directly to the bank for origination. Deposit data is additionally sent to headquarters for follow-up of non-reporting units and reconciliation services.

— Send deposit data to headquarters to allow them to determine the transfer amounts and prepare an ACH debit file for the EDTs, which is delivered to the concentration bank.

- *Concentration Bank* — Some banks are able to receive deposit data directly from the field units/lockbox provider, reported by phone, e-mail or other electronic communication. This data is used to create the ACH debit file that is originated without intervention by headquarters. Data is sent to headquarters for reconciliation activities. Some banks offer online access for headquarters to review deposit-reporting activity and to identify non-reporting units.

- *Cost* — EDTs are the least expensive method for transferring funds. In many cases the cost of an EDT includes both a charge for the transaction and a charge for the amount of transmission time.

- *Settlement* — One-day settlement is the industry norm.

2. **Wire Transfers** — Wire transfers, the most expensive funds transfer mechanism, are an alternative method for concentrating large-dollar amounts where same-day value and finality are critical. Typically, repetitive wires are used for this purpose.

Funds can be transferred using the following methods:

- Either the local manager or the headquarters staff may initiate a request to a depository bank to wire funds to a concentration bank.

- A field or lockbox bank may have standing instructions to transfer funds that exceed a specified balance on a periodic basis. Standing instructions specify the amount, frequency and destination of the transfer.

- Headquarters may send transfer instructions to a concentration bank to wire funds from a field or lockbox bank. This is known as a drawdown transaction.

A company gives standing instructions to a lockbox or field bank authorizing a concentration bank to initiate the wire transfers.

Deposit information that is related to the wire transfer can be sent to headquarters through deposit reports, telephone or electronic data transmission.

Wire transfers provide immediate funds and help reduce excess balances at deposit banks. They are typically used when large amounts of immediately available funds are deposited in a lockbox or a field bank.

D. Banking Network

The number of banking relationships a company has will impact the transfer and administrative costs of its concentration system. If branches of a single bank can be used, the number and costs of concentration transfers can be reduced. In addition, administrative tasks like account reconciliation are simplified. The growth in statewide and interstate branch banking will benefit companies by reducing concentration costs.

III. Cash Concentration Cost Components

The costs of cash concentration include the opportunity costs of maintaining excess balances, transfer charges and administration.

A. Excess Bank Balances

An account has an excess balance when its average collected balance is greater than either the amount that a bank requires for compensation or the target level that a company has chosen to maintain.

1. **Determining Required Balances** — Determining required balances in concentration system accounts involves the following:

    - *Account Analysis* — Many banks provide an account analysis statement showing the price of each service used, the volume of activity and the compensation required. Banks may charge clients by requiring maintenance of certain balance levels or by fees.

    - *Estimates for Field Banks* — Some field banks may not provide account analyses. In the absence of an account analysis, a company and its bank may have to decide jointly on a fair compensating balance.

    - *Average Level of Chargebacks* — The level of chargebacks (returned items) will also have an impact on the required balance. Accounts with high chargeback levels will generally require a higher balance to accommodate the returned items.

2. **How Excess Balances Arise** — Excess balances arise for the following reasons:

    - *Deposit Reporting Delays* — Deposit reports by field units may be delayed by local management or the deposit information gathering system, resulting in delayed concentration transfers and excess balances.

    - *Clearing Delays* — Concentration using EDTs can cause one or more days of delay between transfer initiation and clearing or settlement. Excess balances may be created when immediately available funds are deposited, or when checks deposited in field or lockbox banks clear before the concentration transfers clear back to the deposit account.

    - *Transfer Initiation Delays* — A company or its concentration bank may fail to prepare transfers on time. Failure to originate an EDT in time to meet the bank's deadline delays settlement an extra day.

B. Transfer Charges

Collection systems involve various transfer and service reporting costs. Typically these include:

1. **Bank Charges** — Deposit and concentration banks may charge for the following: deposits, deposited items, inbound and outbound wires, EDT clearings, deposit reports, overdrafts, negative collected balances and account maintenance.

2. **Third-Party Vendor Charges** — A company may use vendors to assist in concentration. Vendors charge for collecting deposit information from field units or lockbox providers and for transmitting data to a concentration bank and/or company.

C. Administrative Costs

The administrative costs of operating a concentration system include the following:

1. **Managing Deposit Reporting** — Receiving and monitoring daily deposit reports from local managers, lockbox providers and concentration banks are major administrative responsibilities.

2. **Scheduling Cash Transfer** — Cash transfer scheduling involves deciding when and what amounts to transfer. These are routine decisions if a company's policy is to transfer the entire amount of the daily deposit. Otherwise, there is a cost associated with deposit monitoring and decision making.

3. **Incurring Overdrafts** — Occasionally, accounts in concentration systems are overdrawn due to misdirected transfers, missed deposit deadlines or returned items. When a check deposited at a field or lockbox bank is returned after it was included in the concentration transfer, a field office may reimburse a field bank for it directly or reduce the next transfer by the amount of the check.

4. **Missing Deposit Deadlines** — Ensuring that deposits are made in field banks in time to receive same-day ledger credit accelerates the availability of funds and reduces expenses related to overdrafts.

IV. Techniques to Reduce Concentration System Costs

Companies can improve concentration system efficiency (and reduce overall costs) by improving transfer timing and reducing transfer costs. To do this, they must factor the value of accelerated funds into the calculations they use in comparing various concentration system alternatives.

A. Improving Transfer Timing

Companies can reduce excess balances by removing information delays, anticipating availability or deposits, or by using a faster transfer mechanism.

1. **Removing Information Delays** — Delays in informing a concentration bank of required transfers can extend the float interval, thereby delaying availability. The process can be expedited by:

    - *Establishing Cutoff Times* — Cutoff times can be set so that transfer reports meet a concentration bank's schedule.

    - *Requiring Timely Reports* — Monitoring both non-reporting and reporting locations enables companies to eliminate information delays.

2. **Anticipating Availability** — Anticipation involves initiation of a transfer before cash becomes available at the deposit bank. The bank initiates the transfer on the basis of projected deposit availability. Because the ledger balance is certain, there exists little risk of ledger overdraft. However, this method risks drawing on uncollected funds since potential delays in the clearing system or returned items can cause collected balances to be unpredictable.

3. **Anticipating Deposits** — This type of anticipation involves initiation of a transfer before cash is actually deposited at the deposit bank. The transfer is initiated on the basis of forecasted cash flows over a given period. Because there is a substantial risk of ledger overdraft, this is considered an aggressive cash management technique, but it is acceptable as long as 1) the transfers are based on reasonably accurate forecasts, 2) the deposit bank is notified of the practice and 3) the company and the deposit bank agree on procedures and compensation in the event of an overdraft. In terms of overall control of the concentration system, this approach actually encourages managers at the field to make sure deposits are made on a timely basis. From the perspective of headquarters, notification from a deposit bank of a ledger overdraft alerts them to problems early in the process.

4. **Using Faster Payment Mechanisms** — Wire transfers make funds available immediately, whereas EDTs become available after one day.

B. Reducing Transfer Costs

Companies can reduce the costs of operating cash concentration systems by transferring funds less frequently and by using less expensive transfer mechanisms.

1. **Transfer Timing** — Transfer costs can be reduced by altering policies and procedures governing timing of transfers as follows:

    - *End Daily Transfers* — While daily transfers are often the norm, many companies transfer less frequently if the deposit amounts do not justify the expense, particularly if daily deposits are smaller than target balances. Transferring funds once a week or less may be sufficient.

    - *Match Timing of Receipt with Timing of Transfer* — Companies that deposit receipts on certain days of the week can increase efficiency by making transfers only on those days.

    - *Balance Averaging* — Companies can time transfers to keep account balances positive and offset service charges. Banks average collected balances monthly and some days' positive balances may offset other days' negative balances for calculating earnings credit.

2. **Transfer Mechanisms** — Companies can change the transfer mechanisms they use.

    - *EDT vs. Wire Transfer* — For companies whose deposits are mostly checks with delayed availability, it is advantageous to transfer funds using an EDT on the day of deposit rather than to initiate a wire transfer on the day funds become available.

    - *Repetitive Wire and EDT Transfers* — Repetitive transfers are usually less expensive than non-repetitive transfers.

3. **Target and Threshold Concentration** — Target and threshold concentration are two methods of limiting balances. Many bank concentration systems offer headquarters the flexibility to change amounts reported by field units, thereby adjusting the amount transferred.

    - *Target Concentration* — With target concentration, a target balance is set and all funds above that balance level are transferred to the concentration bank. This system maintains balances at the desired level. It could involve transfers as frequently as daily.

    - *Threshold Concentration* — Threshold concentration minimizes the number of transfers. With threshold concentration, a company allows account balances to build to a predetermined level before transferring funds to the concentration bank. A cash manager can monitor average balances and adjust them as necessary over time.

4. Deposit Reconciliation Services — By using deposit reconciliation, a company may

deposit funds from multiple locations to its regional or central concentration account. Magnetic ink character recognition (MICR) encoded deposit tickets identify each location and enable a bank to produce daily, weekly or monthly deposit reports by location. This service reduces the number of bank accounts that must be maintained and thus the number of transfers, possibly decreasing concentration system costs. Deposit reconciliation is becoming more prevalent as statewide branch banking and interstate banking become more widespread.

C. Comparing Transfer Costs

In determining whether to use an EDT or a wire transfer to concentrate funds, it is important to establish the value of funds acceleration. By comparing this value to the costs of the alternative transfer methods, the appropriate transfer mechanism can be selected. The opportunity cost of funds is typically either the short-term investment rate earned for net investors or the short-term borrowing rate for net borrowers.

For example, assume the following:

- Total costs for an EDT are $1
- Total costs for a wire transfer are $20
- Transfer amount is $100,000.
- The opportunity cost of funds is 10%.
- A wire transfer accelerates funds one day faster than an EDT.

Funds Value = Transfer Amount × Days Accelerated × Opportunity Cost

$$= \$100,000 \times 1 \times \frac{.10}{365} = \$27.40$$

Because the funds value, $27.40, exceeds the incremental cost of a wire transfer ($20.00 − $1.00 = $19.00), it is advantageous for the company to use a wire transfer rather than an EDT.

An approach for determining the minimum wire transfer amount required to break even is as follows:

$$\text{Minimum Transfer} = \frac{\text{Wire Cost} - \text{EDT Cost}}{\text{Days Accelerated} \times \frac{\text{Opportunity Cost}}{365 \text{ Days}}}$$

$$= \frac{\$20.00 - \$1.00}{1 \text{ Day} \times \frac{.10}{365 \text{ Days}}} = \$69,350$$

As long as the wire transfer amount is larger than $69,350, the additional cost of the wire transfer is justified.

V. Risks and Controls

The operation of cash concentration systems involves a number of issues, including the following.

A. Timely Processing

The primary operational risk of a concentration system is the failure to make deposit calls and/or report deposits accurately by a concentration bank's clearing deadline. Many banks offer services that allow companies to monitor deposit reporting.

B. Fraud

A potential for fraud exists when an employee does not deposit the amount reported, or does not deposit or report the amount received. This type of fraud may go undetected for a period of time. Preventive measures include the following:

- Requiring more than one type of report from field offices, such as a sales report that allows a comparison with deposits
- Requiring these different reports to be prepared and reviewed by different staff members daily
- Conducting unscheduled audits of field offices
- Instructing field banks to return any items that can result in overdrafts and to notify headquarters of these actions
- Promptly reconciling bank accounts

C. Bank Overdraft

The potential for overdraft exists at concentration banks. Failure to make a transfer from a deposit bank to a concentration bank can cause account overdrafts at the concentration bank. Conversely, making too large a transfer or an unanticipated return item can cause an overdraft at the deposit bank.

D. Bank Failure

Field deposit systems typically have many banks and a company may be at risk if one fails. Timely concentration limits this risk. To reduce this risk further, a cash manager needs to monitor the creditworthiness of each bank in a company's concentration system.

E. Disaster Recovery Plans

All companies are vulnerable to the collapse of their concentration systems. Should a company's system or any of its components go down, it can take a long time and great expense for the company to recover. To minimize the impact of a disaster, companies should draw up comprehensive disaster recovery plans.

F. Legal Restrictions

For some types of companies dealing in real estate, oil leases or investment trusts, there are legal restrictions regarding the commingling of deposits. The concentration systems for these types of companies must accommodate these restrictions.

Test Your Understanding

These chapter questions are provided to test your understanding of the information in the text and are not examples of CCM examination questions, nor are they in the examination format.

Answers can be found at the back of the book on pages 513-514.

1. Describe the objectives of a cash concentration system.

2. Why is the pooling of funds a valuable objective of cash concentration?

3. What are some of the key considerations in designing a cash concentration system?

4. What are the characteristics of an over-the-counter/field banking concentration system?

5. Outline the characteristics of a lockbox concentration system.

6. Define EDT.

7. What is the other electronic alternative available for concentration besides EDT and when is it generally used?

8. List the major cost components of a cash concentration system.

9. What can cause excess balances?

10. Define anticipation.

11. What is threshold concentration?

12. Discuss a deposit reconciliation service.

13. A company provides the following information:
    - EDT costs total $1
    - Wire transfer costs are $22
    - A wire accelerates availability one day.
    - Opportunity cost of funds is 8%.

    What is the minimum wire transfer required to break even?

14. How can fraud be prevented in a concentration system?

CHAPTER 8

Accounts Payable and Disbursements

Overview

This chapter discusses the objectives of accounts payable and disbursements and the principal methods and products used for disbursements.

Learning Objectives

Upon completion of this chapter and the related study questions, the reader should understand:

- The objectives of accounts payable and disbursement systems
- The components of disbursement float
- How companies organize disbursement activities
- Disbursement products and their applications
- The accounts payable function
- Check reconciliation and supporting services
- Technological developments in accounts payable

Key Concepts

- Accounts payable and disbursements
- Disbursement float
- Check reconciliation and supporting services

Outline

I. Accounts Payable and Disbursement System Objectives
    A. Accounts Payable Process
    B. Disbursement Cost Reduction
    C. Disbursement Float Management
    D. Other Considerations in Disbursements

II. Disbursement System Considerations
    A. Centralization vs. Decentralization
    B. Control and Fraud Prevention
    C. Special Payment Types
    D. Interface to Accounts Payable System
    E. Other Considerations

III. Disbursement Products and Methods
    A. Zero Balance Account (ZBA)
    B. Controlled Disbursement
    C. Payable Through Draft (PTD)
    D. Multiple Drawee Check
    E. Imprest Account
    F. Electronic Disbursement Methods

IV. Account Reconciliation and Supporting Services
    A. Account Reconciliation Services
    B. Positive Pay
    C. Inquiries and Stop Payments
    D. Check Retention (Check Safekeeping)
    E. High-Order Prefix (Divisional Sort)

V. Accounts Payable Developments
    A. Integrated or Comprehensive Accounts Payable
    B. Purchasing/Procurement Cards
    C. Imaging Services
    D. Internet Applications

I. Accounts Payable and Disbursement System Objectives

The basic goal of managing an accounts payable and disbursement system is to disburse funds to vendors, suppliers, employees and other payees in a timely, accurate and cost-effective manner.

A. Accounts Payable Process

The primary responsibility of the accounts payable function is to verify incoming invoices and authorize them to be paid, a process some companies call vouchering. This process generally involves the traditional "three-way match," where the invoice is matched to both an approved purchase order and receiving information. This ensures that the items being billed to the company were indeed authorized for purchase from an approved vendor and that they were received in satisfactory condition. Once this approval process is complete, the invoice can be approved or vouchered for payment. In a typical business-to-business environment, multiple invoices are often combined into a single payment. Once the payments have been approved, they are typically forwarded to the cash manager or disbursements area where the checks or electronic payments are generated.

B. Disbursement Cost Reduction

A company's net cost of making payments and managing the disbursement process includes:

1. **Opportunity Costs**
    - The cost of excess borrowing or lost investment income when idle balances exist in disbursement accounts
    - The cost of missed or early payments, which includes:
        — The costs of paying bills late, such as lost discounts, late fees and ill will
        — The opportunity costs of paying bills early, such as interest income lost or extra interest expense incurred

2. **Disbursement Account Costs**
    - Fixed costs, such as account maintenance and balance reporting
    - Variable costs, including checks paid, account reconciliation, stop payments and zero balance transfers
    - Overdraft costs, including the monetary costs of overdrawing disbursement accounts and the cost of possible damage to the banking relationship

C. Disbursement Float Management

Disbursement float results from the delay between the time a payor mails a check and the time funds are debited from the payor's account. Since checks are the most commonly used form of payment, this type of float is a significant consideration. Disbursement float is analogous to collection float, except that it is viewed from the payor's perspective. This type of float has the following components:

1. **Mail Float** — Mail float is the interval between the time a check is mailed and the date it is received by the payee or at the processing site. It usually ranges from one to five calendar days or more, depending on location, weather and other factors.

2. **Processing Float** — Processing float is the interval between the time the payee or the processing site receives the check and the time the check is deposited at a financial institution. It can range from less than one day to three calendar days or more if there are processing delays.

3. **Clearing Float** — Clearing float is the delay between the time a check is deposited by the payee and the time the payor's account is debited. Generally, the payee's account is credited with collected funds at the same time the payor's account is debited.

The components of disbursement float are illustrated in Exhibit 8.1.

D. Other Considerations in Disbursements

1. **Information Access** — Obtaining timely and accurate information about the status of disbursement accounts and disbursement clearings enables a company to manage its cash position effectively.

2. **Fraud Prevention** — Funds should be protected from unauthorized use through written policies and internal controls, prompt bank reconciliation, and the use of quality check stock and banking services such as positive pay.

3. **Relationship Maintenance** — It is important for companies to maintain good relationships with payees such as employees, vendors, suppliers, tax agencies and shareholders and/or bondholders.

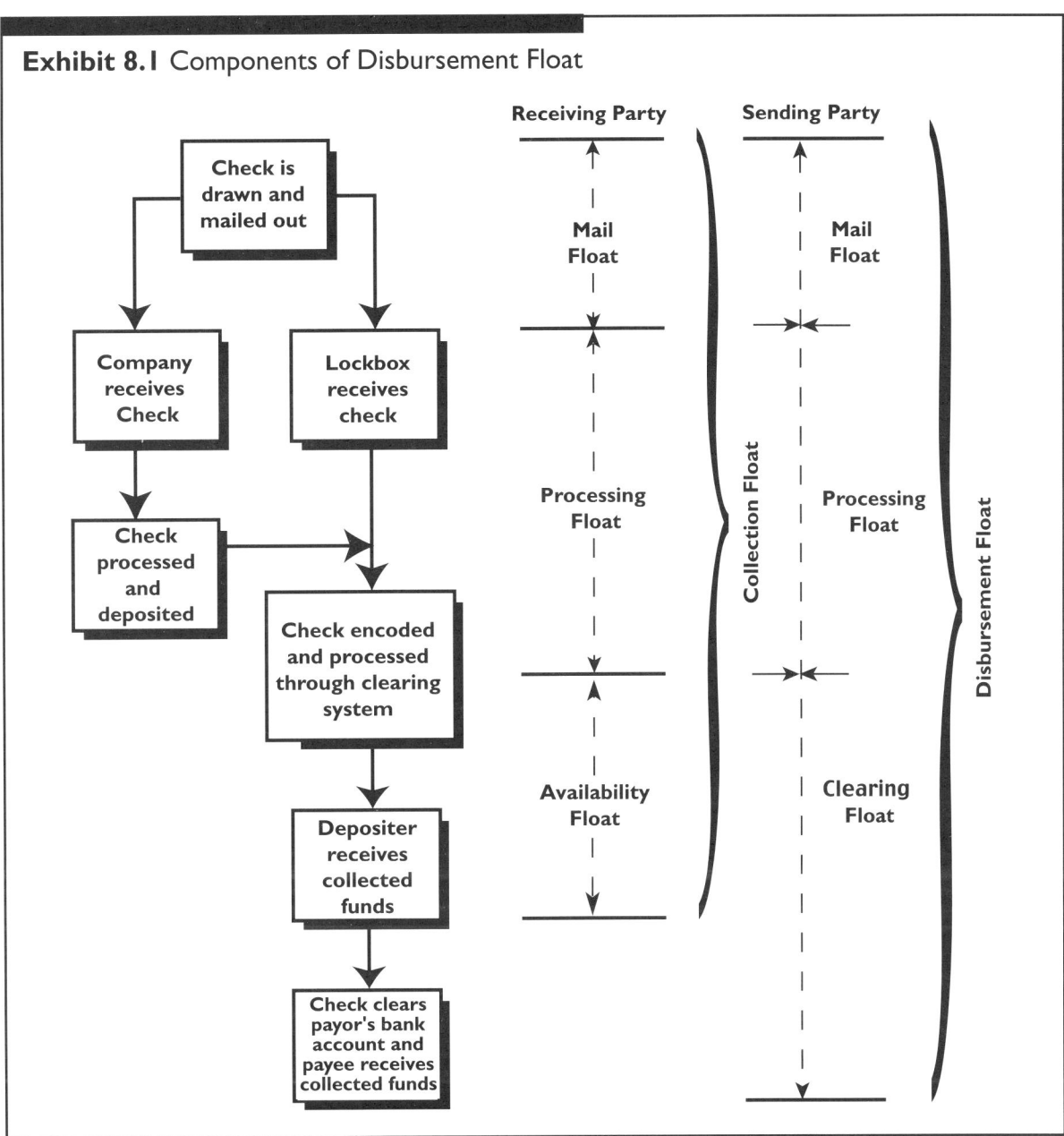

Exhibit 8.1 Components of Disbursement Float

II. Disbursement System Considerations

There are several considerations in planning and managing a disbursement system.

A. Centralization vs. Decentralization

Disbursement systems may be centralized, decentralized or a combination of both. Each system has advantages and disadvantages.

1. **Centralized Check Issuance** — In this type of system, headquarters or a centralized processing center issues checks and funds and reconciles accounts.

The advantages of centralized check issuance may include:

- Concentrated excess cash, which can be used for loan repayment or investment
- Improved access to cash position information
- Improved coordination of cash inflows and outflows
- Restricted access to the system, thus improving overall control
- Reduced transaction and administrative costs

The disadvantages of a centralized check issuance may include:

- Potential increase of disbursement float, which can damage relations with payees
- Delayed payments to suppliers, resulting in loss of discounts
- Need for coordination between headquarters and field offices to resolve problems

2. **Decentralized Check Issuance** — With this type of system, a company issues and reconciles accounts at the local level. Typically, checks are drawn on a local bank.

The advantages of decentralized check issuance may include:

- Improved relationships with vendors and other payees, since disputes may be resolved more directly
- Greater autonomy for local managers

The disadvantages of decentralized check issuance may include:

- Increased possibility of excess balances at the local level
- Increased difficulty of obtaining information about a company's day-to-day cash position
- Reduced disbursement float, if disbursement bank and payees are local
- Increased likelihood of unauthorized disbursements because of greater access to the system
- Increased transfer, reconciliation and administrative costs

3. **Checks Written at Local Level on a Centralized Disbursement Bank** — In this system, check issuance is performed at the local level, but checks clear on a centralized disbursement bank. Headquarters is responsible for choosing disbursement banks and funding disbursement accounts.

The advantages of checks written locally on a centralized disbursement bank may include:

- Reduced excess balances in field locations
- Improved access to information about a company's cash position
- Reduced number of banking relationships
- Decentralized control, which facilitates proper payment timing
- Approval of payments at the local level
- Increased opportunity for volume discounts on disbursement bank services

The disadvantages of checks written locally on a centralized disbursement bank may include:

- Reduced control by headquarters over check issuance
- Increased administrative costs due to dual nature of system
- Increased difficulty of problem resolution since a non-local bank is used for checks sent to local vendors
- Higher transaction costs if the volume discounts are not available

B. Control and Fraud Prevention

Disbursement fraud is a significant problem. Technological advances have increased the frequency, sophistication and ease of creating fraudulent checks. These advances include color copiers, high-resolution laser printers and document scanners designed for use with a personal computer. As a result, control and fraud prevention are an important responsibility of accounts payable and treasury operations. Control and fraud prevention measures include the following:

- Developing and implementing written policies and procedures for the creation and distribution of disbursement checks.
- Separating functional authority for collection and disbursement of funds.
- Separating expense approval, check-signing authority and account reconciliation responsibilities.
- Using safety paper and watermarks that are difficult to reproduce on check stock.
- Using reputable printing companies.
- Storing check stock and signature plates in separate secured areas with controlled access.
- Securing canceled checks or switching to check safekeeping with CD-ROM output.

- Using either printing processes that do not require preprinted check stock (such as laser printing of checks and magnetic ink character recognition [MICR] lines) or preprinted stock that incorporates micro-print or other safety features.

- Using positive pay, a service that matches check serial numbers and dollar amounts against the company's issue file to determine the checks to be paid.

- Setting a maximum dollar amount limit on checks issued from each type of account (checks issued above this limit are returned to the depositor as unauthorized).

- Increasing the use of electronic payment methods, utilizing appropriate security features.

- Using an electronic payment authorization service (similar to positive pay for checks) to protect against fraudulent automated clearing house (ACH) debits.

- Monitoring other types of fraud such as fraudulent endorsements and holder in due course. (These topics are discussed in greater detail later in this chapter.)

C. Special Payment Types

1. **Freight Payments** — Some banks and third parties offer a payment service in which freight payment specialists pay all of a shipper's freight bills, audit bills for possible overcharges and duplicate payments and provide reports that help a company compare costs for different routes and carriers.

2. **Tax Payments**
   - *Federal Tax Deposits* — The Electronic Federal Tax Payment System (EFTPS) is the primary method for collecting and accounting for taxes withheld by employers from individuals' salaries and wages, as well as corporate business and excise taxes. In recent years, most companies have been mandated to make these deposits electronically. The primary mechanism for making electronic tax payments is ACH. Either debits or credits may be used. Wire transfers also are allowed.
   - *State Tax Payments* — Many states require companies with tax payments above certain amounts to remit taxes electronically. This may be done with an ACH credit or debit, with some states permitting the use of a wire transfer as well. The standard payment convention for state tax payments via ACH is known as the tax payment (TXP) format, but usage and specific formats vary from state to state.

3. **Electronic Benefit Transfers** — Most states have implemented or are in the process of developing electronic benefit transfer systems for food stamps. These

systems allow recipients of government transfer payments to receive benefit payments through automated teller machines (ATMs) and point-of-sale (POS) terminals. Also, many companies with large numbers of low-income or temporary workers (who often do not have bank accounts) are experimenting with payroll cards that work in a manner similar to electronic benefit transfer systems.

4. **International and Cross-Border Payments** — Companies with large numbers of international and/or cross-border payments typically look to their banks to provide systems that allow them to either maintain multicurrency accounts or easily make electronic payments in a variety of currencies on a multinational basis.

5. **Travel Reimbursements** — Many companies either develop in-house systems or work through third-party services to manage travel and expense reimbursements for their employees. The current trend is to allow employees to file expense reports electronically and receive their reimbursements through an ACH credit to their account.

6. **Internet Payment Options** — As the use of electronic bill presentment increases, so will the use of the Internet to initiate payments. Many consumers and smaller businesses already utilize Internet-based payment services available through their banks or other third parties.

D. Interface to Accounts Payable System

There are two critical areas of interface between cash management and accounts payable related to disbursements. The first is the communication from accounts payable regarding the invoices vouchered for payment, while the second is the communication from cash management back to accounts payable regarding the reconciled payments. Companies with integrated enterprise resource planning (ERP) or accounting systems that include treasury management modules are typically able to easily integrate these functions. Many companies, however, either use separate systems for disbursement management or utilize bank-provided treasury information software that may not easily interface with the accounts payable ledger. In these cases, customized "patches" or middleware (in a client-server environment) will be required to facilitate the transfer of information between applications.

E. Other Considerations

1. **Disbursement Networks** — Disbursement networks are systems that establish check mailing locations and drawee banks based on disbursement studies. They are designed to optimize disbursement float and are not widely used. The cost and control benefits of making disbursements from just one or two banks often outweigh the float benefits of using a greater number of banks.

2. **Compliance with Trade Terms** — An accounts payable manager needs to monitor compliance with trade payment terms (for example, compliance with having paid a bill by a postmark date in order to take advantage of a trade discount opportunity or avoid late payment charges or interest penalties).

3. **Funding Disbursement Accounts** — A cash manager must ensure that disbursement accounts are adequately, but not excessively, funded.

III. Disbursement Products and Methods

There are several disbursement products or methods that cash managers can utilize to manage the disbursement process.

A. Zero Balance Account (ZBA)

ZBAs are used by many companies to help manage their disbursement processes.

1. **Description** — A ZBA is a disbursement account on which a company writes checks, even though the balance in the account is maintained at zero. A transfer of funds from a master account located in the same bank covers checks debited against a ZBA for payment.

   Funding of the ZBA is automatic and involves only an accounting entry by the bank. A ZBA can also be a depository account from which funds are debited and transferred into a master account at the end of each day. Some ZBAs are used for both collections and disbursements.

2. **How ZBAs Work** — Credits and debits to be posted are netted at the close of each business day. If there is a debit balance in the ZBA, the ZBA will be credited and a debit made to the master account. This brings the balance in the ZBA back to zero.

3. **ZBAs in Multidivision Companies** — Multi-tiered ZBAs may be used to allow companies with multiple divisions or subsidiaries to write checks on separate accounts or to segregate different types of payments such as payrolls, dividends and accounts payable. The cash manager can control the balances and funding of a master account and its associated ZBAs as if they were all one large account. This reduces excess balances and the need for multiple manual transfers.

B. Controlled Disbursement

Another method used to minimize balances in disbursement accounts is controlled disbursement.

1. **Description** — Controlled disbursement is a bank service that provides notification of the dollar amount of checks that will clear against the controlled disbursement account that day. This information is usually available by early or mid-morning. The disbursement bank must receive its final cash letter of the day from the local Federal Reserve bank (Fed) early in the morning so that the checks can be sorted and the company notified of its funding requirement for the account. The company must then provide adequate funds to the account to cover the value of the checks presented.

   Payor bank services is an information service of the Fed, which electronically notifies controlled disbursement banks early in the morning of all checks that will be physically presented later that day. There are typically two notifications: the first between 5:30 and 7:30 a.m. local Fed time and the second between 9:00 and 10:30 a.m. local Fed time. Banks process the Fed data and notify customers of their funding requirements.

   One of the principal advantages of a controlled disbursement account is that it allows a company to calculate its daily cash position early enough to take advantage of better market rates for investing or borrowing.

   Under the Fed's high-dollar group sort (HDGS) program, the local Fed automatically makes a second presentment to drawee banks with more than $10 million in daily presentments from banks outside their Fed district. This presentment delays the communication of final clearing totals until mid-morning.

2. **Discrepancies After Notification** — There are several instances where discrepancies arise between the reported disbursement clearings and the actual amount of checks presented for payment:

   - Controlled disbursement accounts must deal with same-day presentment items. These are checks drawn on the disbursement bank, which are directly presented from another bank by 8 a.m. According to Fed regulations, these checks must be paid the same day they are presented. These same-day presentment items may need to be handled by a different processing method than the rest of the controlled disbursement checks. Banks also have the option of designating the local Fed as the clearing point for same-day presentment items, thereby eliminating the challenge of combining presentment totals.

   - There is risk of presentment after the morning notification. A check missed by the Fed in the payor bank services notification but discovered the same morning will be presented that day.

   - Checks may also be presented for payment at the disbursement bank by the payee. These checks, commonly known as over-the-counter items, may also cause discrepancies in clearing totals.

- Checks may be mis-encoded or unreadable on their first pass through the system and become exception items. These items may be handled separately from other items and may come into the bank after the usual presentment times.

    Some banks offer options to prevent problems caused by late presentments. The bank guarantees that the final presentment amount will be equal to the morning notification and makes necessary adjustments to the account the next day.

3. **Funding Controlled Disbursement Accounts** — A controlled disbursement account is normally funded from a company's concentration account. Either the company or the bank can fund the account. The transfer is usually on a same-day basis. In many cases the disbursement account is set up as a ZBA, where funding is automatic.

If concentration and controlled disbursement accounts are in unrelated banks, a wire transfer or ACH can be used for funding. Credit approval may be required for ACH funding and the bank may demand that a company maintain some minimum balance in the disbursement account. The level for this balance is generally set at either one day's maximum clearings or one day's average clearings over some previous period.

4. **Credit Risk** — The fact that controlled disbursement poses credit risk (over and above the normal risk of disbursement checking accounts) for a bank has important implications for companies. There are two situations in which a bank has credit exposure:

    - With ACH funding, there is risk that an ACH funding debit may be returned by the bank on which the debit is drawn. By the time the returned ACH debit reaches the disbursement bank, it may be too late to return any disbursement checks. The disbursement bank is owed funds and becomes a creditor of the company.

    - With the use of an affiliated bank for disbursing, with funding through the parent bank, there is no problem if the affiliate bank is funded directly on a same-day basis by a wire transfer. However, if the parent bank automatically funds the affiliate with immediate funds before the parent bank receives good funds from the company, there is an intraday overdraft and a potential overdraft problem at the parent bank. Since the affiliate bank does not have an overdrawn account, it cannot legally refuse to pay the checks even though there may be an overdraft at the parent bank, unless this option is provided for in the service agreement.

    Such risks make it very likely that a bank will undertake a credit review of a company that wants to use its controlled disbursement service. In some cases, a formal credit facility may be required.

5. **How to Select a Controlled Disbursement Bank** — In addition to overall relationship considerations, companies should consider several other factors when selecting a controlled disbursement bank. While disbursement float remains important for some companies, other considerations have become more important. They include:

- *Timeliness of Reporting of Disbursement Totals* — This is important because a company wants to make investing or borrowing decisions as early as possible to take advantage of better market rates.

- *Processing Accuracy* — Processing errors can result in overfunding or underfunding of the disbursement account.

- *Volume Capacity* — Check processing capacity should be sufficient, so that reporting deadlines can be met.

- *Reporting Detail and Reconciliation Services* — Reports should contain adequate detail and be timely enough to meet a company's information needs.

- *Price* — Service pricing should reflect fair and reasonable compensation.

- *Customer Service Support* — Bank customer service staff should provide prompt and knowledgeable responses to a company's requests.

C. Payable Through Draft (PTD)

A PTD is a payment instrument resembling a check that is drawn against the payor, not the bank and for which the payor has a period of time to honor or refuse payment. Some important aspects of PTDs and their use include:

- The deadline under Federal Reserve Regulation CC for approval or rejection of a PTD is the same as for a check (one business day).

- PTDs are frequently used for insurance claims and other field office disbursements that have multiple signers and require final headquarters' approval. They give a company time to ensure that all terms have been met or expenditures authorized.

- Some PTDs may be in electronic form and are essentially ACH debits to a company's account in which the company is notified in time to pay or reject each item.

D. Multiple Drawee Check

Multiple drawee checks, also known as payable-if-desired (PID) checks, are checks that can be presented for payment at a bank other than the drawee bank. Both bank names appear on the check.

1. **Applications** — Examples include payroll in states that require employees to be paid by checks payable in the state, payroll for employees on assignments away from the company office and dividend checks.

2. **Banking Arrangements** — Companies maintain balances and/or pay a fee at an alternate payment bank to compensate it for cashing multiple drawee checks. The alternate bank will require indemnity from the paying company for any loss, including fraud, relating to those checks. Some banks are unwilling to provide this service.

E. Imprest Account

An imprest account is an account maintained at a prescribed level for a particular purpose or activity and periodically replenished to the prescribed level. For example, a field office may have an imprest account for local disbursements with a balance sufficient for one or two months' expenses. Based on an established time frame or level of imprest account balances, the office submits expenses to headquarters for approval and headquarters reimburses the imprest account.

F. Electronic Disbursement Methods

Electronic disbursements via Fedwire and ACH are used for payments from corporations to individuals, from individuals to corporations and from corporations to corporations. (See Chapter 4, U.S. Payments System.) The item volume of such payments is low compared to checks, but continues to increase as the value of float declines and the emphasis on expense control increases. The increasing use of electronic commerce will also stimulate the growth of these forms of electronic disbursements. The developments in this area are discussed in detail in Chapter 9, Electronic Commerce.

IV. Account Reconciliation and Supporting Services

Banks provide account reconciliation services to meet companies' information and control requirements. The following services are available:

A. Account Reconciliation Services

1. **Full Reconciliation** — With a full reconciliation service, a company supplies an electronic file of checks issued to its bank and the bank matches checks paid against the file. The bank supplies a listing, as a paper report and/or in electronic format, of checks paid and outstanding in check serial number order.

2. **Partial Reconciliation** — In a partial reconciliation service, a bank lists all checks paid in numerical order by check serial number, or in chronological order by date paid. For each item, the paid report generally shows the check serial number, dollar amount and date paid. The listing is available as a paper report, on CD-ROM and/or via electronic transmission.

3. **Sort Only** — In a sort only service, a bank sorts the checks by check serial number for a company.

B. Positive Pay

Positive pay is used to combat check fraud. With this service, the company transmits a file of issued check information to the bank soon after issuance. The bank matches check serial numbers and dollar amounts of checks presented for payment against the issue file and pays only those checks that match. Exceptions are conveyed to the company for disposition. Some positive pay services match against the payee field as well as the serial number and amount in an effort to detect altered payees. In most cases, banks providing positive pay services combine the service with full reconciliation.

A similar service, known as reverse positive pay, occurs when the bank transmits a file of the checks presented for payment to the company on a daily basis. The company matches this file to its list of checks issued and notifies the bank of any items it wishes to have returned. Due to the time-critical nature of this service, it is increasingly being offered via the Internet. This service, however, does not prevent fraudulent checks from being cashed at the payor bank teller line since the bank does not have access to the issue file.

It is also important to note that neither of the above services protects against certain types of fraud such as fraudulent endorsement or holder in due course. Fraudulent endorsement is where an authorized check is stolen or intercepted by a third party and then endorsed and cashed by that party. As long as the check amount and check number are not altered, the fraud will not be detected by positive pay. The holder in due course issue arises when an entity accepts or cashes a fraudulent item in good faith. An example might be where a check cashing store that regularly accepts payroll checks from a company accepts a fraudulent item that is virtually identical to the company's regular payroll checks. Positive pay would reject this item, but the company may ultimately be held liable for the item if the check cashing store is deemed a holder in due course (i.e., they took the check in good faith, with the understanding that the check was bona fide and contained no defects). In addition to these problems, some companies encounter significant problems with exception items due to repeat number checks or large numbers of manual checks.

C. Inquiries and Stop Payments

A company can initiate stop payments by voice, electronically or in writing. Written confirmation may be required by the bank for telephone instructions. Stop payments are usually good only for six months and must be renewed, if necessary.

Many banks offer information reporting systems that allow customers to electronically inquire whether a check has been paid, to place a stop payment and/or to request a copy of the paid item. (See Chapter 10, Information Management and Technology.)

D. Check Retention (Check Safekeeping)

In a check retention service, a bank retains paid checks for periods that typically range from one to six months. Microfilm or image records are maintained by the bank for seven years. Companies can receive images of the checks on microfilm, microfiche or CD-ROM. Some banks offer online retrieval of images.

E. High-Order Prefix (Divisional Sort)

The high-order prefix sorting service allows a single account to be used by a company with multiple units. Codes identifying the various units are included in the check serial number field. Reports are available showing unit subtotals. This is used when checks are drawn for multiple units on the same disbursement account.

V. Accounts Payable Developments

There are several relatively new services that have an important impact on the operation and management of the accounts payable area.

A. Integrated or Comprehensive Accounts Payable

An integrated or comprehensive accounts payable service allows a company to outsource all or part of the company's accounts payable and/or disbursements functions. Two common approaches to managing an integrated or comprehensive accounts payable service are:

- A company sends a single data file to a financial service provider (FSP) containing a list of all payments to be made. The file contains information on when to issue a disbursement and to whom, as well as instructions on the payment method to be used (check, wire, ACH, foreign drafts or foreign currency).

- Alternatively, the FSP maintains a database of a company's payees that includes detailed information such as preferred payment methods, specific remittance information and receiving financial institutions. The database is periodically updated as new payees are added or an existing payee's remittance profile changes (for example, if a payee switches to ACH instead of check for its standard payment type). In such cases, as a company makes a disbursement, it sends to the FSP only limited payment information.

With either approach, the FSP issues the payments immediately or warehouses them until a future date as instructed by the data file. A company using these types of services is outsourcing much of its disbursements function and potentially reducing the overall costs of its accounts payable operations.

B. Purchasing/Procurement Cards

Many companies are implementing the use of purchasing (or procurement) cards for the small dollar purchase of supplies, inventory, equipment and service contracts. Though companies have long used charge cards for travel and entertainment expenses, the use of charge cards for routine procurement is growing. Cards are issued to designated employees, with spending limits and types of purchases pre-specified for each employee. The advantages of a purchasing card may include:

- Cost savings by eliminating the processing of high-volume, low-dollar purchasing orders and payments
- Improved control over expenditures by applying spending parameters before purchases are made rather than through the expense reimbursement process
- Better vendor relations through earlier payments
- Improved reporting on spending with specific vendors, which may aid in the negotiation of more favorable discounts
- Ability to make spot purchases with mobility
- Earlier shipment of goods

C. Imaging Services

Imaging technology is a major component of many disbursement services. Both the front and the back of a check may be captured and converted into digital information using optical scanning. Check images (all of them or selected ones) may be transmitted to a company's computer and stored there or sent to a fax machine. The check images may also be stored in a bank database, which a company can access to view or retrieve the images. Any of these methods allows a company faster access to check information.

Imaging services are particularly useful in conjunction with positive pay services. They help a company identify potential unauthorized check activity and make critical pay/no-pay decisions on checks in a timely manner. Images of checks can be obtained in a more timely fashion than photocopies, allowing companies to respond quickly to inquiries from customers, employees and vendors.

Some financial institutions are capturing check images on CD-ROM as a substitute for microfilm or microfiche.

D. Internet Applications

The rapid expansion of Internet services over the past few years has resulted in a wide variety of accounts payable and disbursement applications on the Web for companies of all sizes. Some of these services are offered as part of a total accounting or ERP package or as stand-alone services. For larger companies trying to increase their level of automation of financial functions, the Web offers a mechanism for their smaller trading partners to send invoices via a Web page, which can then be paid via an ACH transaction with remittance information returned via the Internet. These types of applications are discussed in more detail in Chapter 9, Electronic Commerce.

Test Your Understanding

These chapter questions are provided to test your understanding of the information in the text and are not examples of CCM examination questions, nor are they in the examination format.

Answers can be found at the back of the book on pages 515-518.

1. What are the five major objectives of a disbursement system?
2. Describe the basic accounts payable process.
3. How may disbursement systems be organized?
4. What are the three components of disbursement float?
5. Discuss the various ways of preventing check fraud.
6. What is a disbursement network?
7. Explain the critical areas of interface between cash management and accounts payable.
8. Define zero balance account (ZBA).
9. What is controlled disbursement?
10. What is the Electronic Federal Tax Payment System (EFTPS)?
11. Who provides payor bank services?
12. Discuss the factors that should be examined in the selection of a controlled disbursement bank.
13. What is a multiple drawee check?
14. Define positive pay.
15. What is the difference between a partial and full reconciliation?
16. How does controlled disbursement cause credit risk for a bank?
17. Discuss common approaches to managing an integrated or comprehensive accounts payable service.

18. What are purchasing cards and what is their benefit to a company?

19. How are imaging services used in disbursements?

20. What are the recent Internet applications and developments in disbursements?

CHAPTER 9

Electronic Commerce

Overview

This chapter describes electronic commerce (e-commerce) in its various forms and how it impacts the treasury area and electronic payments systems. It discusses the costs, benefits and barriers to e-commerce, as well as the standards for sending and receiving electronic messages. It also discusses the roles of the various software and service providers and the impact of e-commerce on a company.

Learning Objectives

Upon completion of this chapter and the related study questions, the reader should understand:

- The basics of e-commerce
- The evolution of e-commerce as well as the cost, benefits and barriers to implementation
- How e-commerce standards are used
- The key terms and languages used for e-commerce on the Internet
- The security issues involved in e-commerce and their solutions
- The role of value-added networks (VANs) and banks in e-commerce
- How e-commerce can affect an organization

Key Concepts

- Different types of e-commerce
- The benefits, costs and barriers to e-commerce
- The infrastructure of electronic data interchange (EDI)
- The impact of the Internet on e-commerce
- Security issues for e-commerce
- Implementation issues for e-commerce

Chapter 9 • Electronic Commerce

Outline

I. Basics of Electronic Commerce (E-Commerce)
    A. Definitions
    B. Different Types of E-Commerce
    C. Traditional Electronic Data Interchange
    D. Use of the Internet and Web for E-Commerce and EDI

II. Evolution of E-Commerce
    A. Key Issues for Development of E-Commerce
    B. Benefits of E-Commerce
    C. Costs of E-Commerce
    D. Barriers to E-Commerce

III. Electronic Data Interchange
    A. EDI Standard Formats
    B. EDI Software
    C. Value-Added Networks
    D. Electronic Banking (E-Banking) Services
    E. Computer Hardware

IV. The Internet and E-Commerce
    A. Key Terms and Definitions
    B. The Languages of E-Commerce
    C. Security Issues

V. Credit Terms and E-Commerce Transactions
    A. Impact of E-Commerce and EFT
    B. Negotiating Shared Benefits

VI. E-Commerce Implementation
    A. Evaluated Receipts Settlement (ERS)
    B. Paid-on-Production
    C. Future of E-Commerce

I. Basics of Electronic Commerce (E-Commerce)

The majority of business documents and payments exchanged among companies in North America are paper-based and move through the check clearing and postal systems. E-commerce is an alternative to this paper-based system and companies are implementing it in various forms. E-commerce is enabling companies to form closer ties and become strategic partners with their vendors and customers.

A. Definitions

There are several important definitions related to e-commerce:

1. **Electronic Commerce** — In its broadest context, e-commerce is the application of information and network technology to the conduct of business relationships among trading partners. E-commerce encompasses many types of formats and communications protocols, including traditional electronic data interchange (EDI) and Web-based commerce.

2. **Internet** — The Internet is a worldwide collection of many computers, communications switches and computer networks linked together to form a backbone of communications pathways. The Internet is an unrestricted, worldwide network to which everyone with the appropriate hardware and software has access. Communication on the Internet is made possible by open communication standards and protocols among users operating over an Internet service connection using inexpensive and commonly available browser software.

3. **Intranet** — This is the term used for internal networks (for use within a company) that utilize browser technology to provide data and applications for users. An intranet uses the open standards of the Internet rather than proprietary software for communication among computers. This allows users to access information via commonly available browsers rather than proprietary user interfaces.

4. **Extranet** — An extranet is an external network (for use outside a company with its trading partners and/or customers) that utilizes browser technology to provide data and access to applications. In most cases, companies will place some type of security "firewall" between this system and their internal applications.
This is discussed in greater detail later in this chapter.

5. **World Wide Web (the Web)** — The Web is the most used method of accessing the Internet through the use of browser technology. The Web is a user-friendly subset of the Internet that allows users to access text and graphical links and move easily from site to site. There are millions of sites on the Web and it is growing at an astounding rate.

6. **Browser** — A browser is software that allows a user to access Web-based sites on the Internet, intranets or extranets. Advanced browsers offer a wide range of options and features that provide users a means to obtain, organize and utilize data from the Internet, intranets or extranets. Advanced browsers also incorporate built-in security features such as secured socket layer or SSL (discussed later in this chapter).

7. **Electronic Data Interchange** — EDI is a traditional form of e-commerce that utilizes structured electronic transactions in established standards to exchange data from one company's application system to another company's application system.

8. **Trading Communities/Market Places** — The environment of business consists of groups or trading communities of suppliers, customers, distribution, logistics, employees, agents, etc. They can be vertical communities such as supply chains or horizontal communities such as trade groups or associations.

9. **Electronic Funds Transfer (EFT) and Financial EDI (FEDI)** — These are subsets of EDI. The distinguishing feature that characterizes EFT is the exchange of value, which requires the involvement of financial intermediaries such as banks to send and receive electronic payments. Examples of EFT include wire transfers and automated clearing house (ACH) payments.

   FEDI is the electronic transmission of payments and payment-related information in standard formats between company trading partners and/or their banks. FEDI includes electronic format for invoices, payment initiation, lockbox deposit reports and remittance information sent either directly to a trading partner or processed through a financial institution or communications intermediary.

B. Different Types of E-Commerce

E-commerce is generally described as either business-to-consumer (B2C) or business-to-business (B2B).

1. **Business-to-Consumer E-Commerce** — Much of the initial development of Internet-based e-commerce was in the B2C area. Companies found that the Internet was a cost-effective way to advertise and sell their products and services to consumers, as well as provide enhanced customer service. In most cases, the consumer does most of the work in the process: reviewing available products and services, filling out forms and providing shipping and billing information.

2. **Business-to-Business E-Commerce** — B2B e-commerce really began with EDI, but has expanded into a wide array of formats and protocols for doing business electronically. The typical B2B applications include:

- Purchasing from suppliers
- Logistics and supply chain management
- Selling to customers
- Billing and payment
- EDI and Web EDI
- Web-based e-commerce
- Auction marketplaces

C. Traditional Electronic Data Interchange (EDI)

1. **Basics of EDI** — EDI provides a vehicle for the electronic movement of business data in a standard format from one company's application system (such as an order entry system, purchasing system, or billing system) to another company's application system. It allows senders to generate EDI messages directly from their applications and it allows receivers to bring data into their applications without the need to re-enter any of the information. Specific EDI standards may be used in multiple industries, a single industry or among selected trading partners as detailed below:

   - *Proprietary EDI* — Proprietary EDI is developed by one company for exclusive use with its trading partners.

   - *Industry Convention EDI* — Industry convention EDI is a specific format standard or a subset of the more generic cross-industry EDI standards used within a particular industry. Examples of industries that utilize these types of EDI standards include grocery, retail, automotive, electrical manufacturing and chemical production and distribution.

   - *Cross-Industry EDI* — Cross-industry EDI are format standards that address the needs of many different users in many industries. If a company sends a cross-industry EDI purchase order to another company that conforms to the same standard, the receiving company can capture the purchase order data directly without re-entering data.

2. **Relationship Between EDI, FEDI and EFT** — Exhibit 9.1 shows an example of the relationship between companies and their financial and communications intermediaries engaging in non-financial EDI, FEDI and EFT. A supplier (seller) may send an EDI invoice to a customer. The customer (buyer) sends an FEDI payment instruction to its bank. The customer's bank sends an electronic payment and associated information to the supplier's bank through the ACH system. The supplier's bank notifies the supplier of the received payment through an electronic deposit report. The payment-related information transmission is an example of FEDI. EFT involves a value transfer and typically only occurs between financial

institutions. FEDI is any EDI transaction set that either results in a value transfer (instructions to send funds via wire, ACH, etc.) or results from a value transfer (bank notifies payee that funds have been received, i.e., electronic transmission of lockbox information).

3. **Factors Influencing the Use of EDI** — The structures of companies' EDI systems vary widely, depending on the number of trading partners, the volume and type of EDI transactions used and whether the company is an originator or receiver of EDI transactions. Companies implement EDI for many reasons, including:

    - *Reaction to a Request from Customer or Supplier* — Some companies implement EDI at the request (sometimes at the mandate) of key customers. These companies are generally suppliers to a company that is already a heavy EDI user. This type of EDI implementation is often done on a small scale initially, using a PC and off-the-shelf software. Over time, the use of EDI at these companies may grow, but in the early stages, they are implementing EDI only with one or more major customers and they are referred to as EDI spokes.

    - *Cost Savings and Greater Efficiency* — Other companies implement EDI to reduce costs. They usually implement EDI after analyzing the benefits and costs, as well as surveying potential trading partners. EDI also facilitates the outsourcing of financial functions to a third-party provider.

    - *As Part of a Redesign or Re-Engineering Process* — Some companies implement EDI on a large scale to maintain, or possibly increase, their competitive edge. Historically, these companies have been large manufacturers and retailers, who stand to benefit from the cost reductions, improved productivity or decreased order lead times from EDI. Companies that encourage many of their suppliers to implement EDI are referred to as EDI hubs. Though these hubs often start as EDI originators (sending EDI purchase orders to their suppliers), they tend to become EDI recipients also as their trading partners begin to send EDI invoices in response to purchase orders. One of the major challenges for a large EDI hub is to provide the necessary support and training for the many EDI spokes with which it deals. In many cases, companies are migrating from traditional EDI into more generic forms of e-commerce in order to maintain their competitiveness.

D. Use of the Internet and Web for E-Commerce and EDI

1. **Web-Based E-Commerce** — This approach utilizes the Internet and Web technology to link business applications between trading partners. The primary difference between this type of commerce and Web-EDI is that the data transfer is in a non-EDI format. The format used may be proprietary between two users, or some more general standard used within an industry. One of the key objectives is to push data entry and other tasks toward a company's trading partners and the ultimate result is a transfer of data required to complete an electronic transaction.

Exhibit 9.1 Relationship Between EDI, FEDI and EFT

2. **Web EDI** — In this form of EDI, the Web is used by large EDI hubs to bring smaller trading partners into the EDI world. The transaction is Web-based for smaller trading partners who access a Web site to either receive information or create business documents using fill-in forms. The large hub can still utilize standard EDI transaction sets to send to or receive information from the smaller trading partners. This approach is useful for low transaction volumes within limited trading communities.

II. Evolution of E-Commerce

A. Key Issues for Development of E-Commerce

1. **Technological Deployment** — In most cases, the technology needed for e-commerce to fully develop is already available and deployed.

2. **Legislative Evolution** — Though this area is beginning to develop, much of the legal and business environment is still based on paper documents and controls. In 2000, the passage of the Electronic Signatures in Global and National Commerce Act (the "E-Sign Law") gave digital signatures the same effect as ink signatures. This legislation ensures the legal certainty of e-commerce transactions and provides a measure of confidence in the enforceability of electronic transactions.

3. **Social Acceptance** — As is shown by the rapid development of the B2C segment of e-commerce, consumers are often the first adopters of new technology, while business lags behind. Also, legislation generally lags behind the adoption of e-commerce practices by business.

4. **Future Development of B2B E-Commerce** — This will depend on the development of trading communities that emphasize the purchase of indirect materials (office supplies) and direct materials (raw materials for manufacturing). The development of the direct materials market will require greater expertise and integration with enterprise resource planning (ERP) systems and supply chain planning and execution. These ERP systems are fully integrated, companywide accounting and management information systems that utilize sophisticated database software to provide reports and information in a timely manner to management. Most modern ERP systems provide interfaces to EDI and e-commerce formats and protocols that allow for easy implementation of e-commerce practices into the organization.

B. Benefits of E-Commerce

1. **Improved Productivity** — Once data is entered at the beginning of a transaction, the same data can be moved from one application to another without manual intervention. E-commerce eliminates manual processes such as filing, matching, sorting and retrieving material as well as envelope stuffing, stamping and mailing.

2. **Reduced Cycle Time** — E-commerce transactions have no mail-time delays, involve minimal processing time and facilitate just-in-time (JIT) inventory management in many companies, lowering inventory levels.

3. **Lower Error Rates** — Since e-commerce makes data re-entry unnecessary, it reduces error rates and enables faster data processing. For example, using

e-commerce for receiving remittance information may allow for greater accuracy in the posting of payments to the accounts receivable ledger.

4. **Improved Cash Forecasting** — E-commerce eliminates mail time, thereby reducing or eliminating uncertainty in cash flow timing, enabling more accurate cash flow forecasting and improving management of working capital.

5. **Improved Communication Capabilities** — With e-commerce, it is possible to be notified that the other party has received a message. Acknowledgment that a customer has received an invoice (which is not available in a mail-based system) can help to resolve issues of payment timing between buyer and seller.

C. Costs of E-Commerce

Among the costs that need to be considered in the implementation of e-commerce are the following:

1. **Software** — Data from electronic transactions must be integrated with data from existing applications. This usually requires modification of current business software applications. In addition, data must be translated from the company's current format into a recognized e-commerce format. Commercially available software packages are capable of performing translation processes for standard e-commerce formats.

2. **Hardware** — E-commerce may require additional investments in computer equipment. If existing systems are not adequate for handling the e-commerce needs, then new or updated hardware must be added.

3. **Communications** — E-commerce data must be sent from one party to another. This communication may be done either directly (usually over telephone lines) or through a value-added network (VAN) or bank. Another option is to utilize the Internet combined with intranet and extranet systems to transmit e-commerce data. Regardless of how data is transmitted, costs must be determined. The company should include costs of communications software and hardware (modems, communications interfaces, etc.) as well as ongoing monthly fees to communications and Internet service providers in this process.

4. **Security** — Encryption and message authentication as well as security measures to ensure the integrity of the system are required in any type of e-commerce implementation. (Security issues are addressed in greater detail later in this chapter.)

5. **Education and Training** — E-commerce often requires that a company train both its internal personnel and its trading partners. For a company adding e-commerce to a major application, this can be a significant expense.

6. **Trading Partner Selling and Support** — Many of the benefits of e-commerce depend on economies of scale and accrue when a significant number of transactions are involved. Implementation often requires the company to seek trading partners who are willing to send and receive e-commerce messages. As more companies move towards Web-enabled e-commerce, even low levels of trading partner activity can be managed in a cost-effective manner.

7. **Negotiating with Trading Partners** — Implementing e-commerce may affect the timing of payments and require the renegotiation of credit terms. Negotiation can be costly and protracted, particularly if it involves legal or audit matters.

D. Barriers to E-Commerce

In addition to the readily identifiable costs of implementing e-commerce systems, there are other barriers and drawbacks to implementation, including:

1. **Convenience of Paper-Based Systems** — The U.S. Postal Service delivers to all addresses in the United States for a uniform postage fee and provides low cost delivery of paper-based correspondence and payments. Virtually all companies and individuals have access to the postal delivery system, as well as a bank or other financial intermediary, to handle the payment part of the cycle.

2. **Tradition of Paper-Based System** — Legal, audit and processing structures surrounding paper-based systems in the United States are highly evolved. Almost all of the uniform commercial code and most accounting and legal standards are based on paper-based contracts and business conventions that require signatures for reporting and control purposes. Attempts to address the regulatory, legal and audit issues involved with e-commerce are still evolving.

3. **Dual Systems May Be Required Initially** — Many companies implementing e-commerce and/or electronic payments find they must continue to use dual systems (both paper and e-commerce) after implementation.

4. **E-Commerce Capabilities of Banks** — Banks and other financial intermediaries have only recently been required to pass remittance information from the receiving bank to the receiving company. Companies trying to make electronic payments to suppliers may find that some of their suppliers' banks are not yet capable of fully complying with this mandate.

III. Electronic Data Interchange (EDI)

EDI is a traditional form of e-commerce that is based on four primary infrastructure components:

- EDI standard formats
- EDI software
- Communication networks and standards
- Computer hardware

A. EDI Standard Formats

To send information electronically, companies must agree on a specific format and structure for electronic messages and the data they contain. In the early days of EDI, some companies designed proprietary formats and communication interfaces and either encouraged or mandated trading partner participation. Proprietary data formats and technical requirements are adequate when a company deals with a small number of partners. When a company has many EDI partners, however, a common standard becomes necessary.

1. **Development of EDI Standards** — EDI standards have evolved from proprietary standards to the current cross-industry and international standards.

    - *ASC X12 Standards* — The Accredited Standards Committee (ASC) of the American National Standards Institute (ANSI) is the coordinating body that develops cross-industry EDI standards in North America. The development of the current U.S. standards for EDI began in 1968 with efforts of the transportation industry to establish standards for communications between and within railroads, ocean carriers, air carriers and motor carriers. Based on this early work, the grocery and retail industries also developed EDI standards. In 1979, ASC X12 was formed to develop general EDI standards that could be used in a variety of industries.

    - *Industry Modification of ASC X12 Standards* — Several industries (such as the automotive, chemical, communications and health care industries) have adopted ASC X12 standards. Others have adopted subsets of X12 standards. This practice is expected to continue in other industries with common requirements.

    - *UN/EDIFACT Standards* — Many countries have become involved in developing EDI standards. This has led to the development of United Nations EDI for Administration, Commerce and Transportation (UN/EDIFACT) rules, a set of internationally agreed-upon standards, directories and guidelines for the electronic interchange of structured data that relates to trade in goods and services between independent computerized information systems. UN/EDIFACT standards are widely used in Europe and some Asian countries.

- *Web-Based EDI Standards* — Web-based EDI Internet sites are being developed in XML (eXtensible Markup Language). The specifics of XML are discussed in greater detail later in this chapter. Standard EDI transaction sets are converted either into or from Web-based forms for transferring information between large EDI hubs and smaller trading partners.

2. **ASC X12 Structure** — The ASC X12 format standard consists of rules governing the translation of one or more business documents into electronic messages.

    - *Transaction Set* — A transaction set is the electronic equivalent of a paper business document or form. Specific rules govern formats for standard business documents. Examples of typical business documents that are converted to EDI transaction sets are purchase orders, shipping documents, invoices and remittance advices.

    - *Data Segments* — Related information elements, such as the line item in the purchase order, are known as data segments. Most transaction sets contain at least three data segments and usually many more.

    - *Data Element* — Data segments consist of data elements, such as price, unit of measure and quantity. Data elements are defined in a data dictionary.

3. **ASC X12 Financial Transaction Sets** — By convention, numbers and names are used to identify ASC X12 transaction sets. Some of the common EDI transaction sets used in the finance area include:

    - *810 Invoice* — This allows the user to convey invoice data, such as unit price, quantities purchased and terms of sale, from a seller to a buyer.

    - *820 Payment Order/Remittance Advice* — This transaction set has two purposes. It initiates a money transfer to a payee and/or provides the payee with information describing the purpose of the associated payment. The 820, which allows multiple invoices to be paid in a single payment, also includes the amount of discounts and other payment adjustments.

    - *821 Financial Information Reporting* — This transaction set facilitates bank-to-corporate account reporting. It provides for the reporting of multiple levels of financial information, including balances, transaction summaries and individual transactions. It can be used for balance and transaction reporting, account reconciliation and bank account statements.

    - *822 Customer Account Analysis* — This transaction set allows banks to transmit account analysis information (balances, services, volumes, service charges, etc.) to their corporate customers. The Association for Financial Professionals (AFP), formerly the Treasury Management Association, service codes are used in the 822 transaction set to identify bank balances, services and associated charges.

- *823 Lockbox Information* — This transaction set conveys lockbox check data including remittance detail (such as payors, invoices and amounts being paid), deposit totals and available funds.

- *824 Application Advice* — This transaction set accommodates acceptance, acceptance with change or rejection of data received from another transaction set. It can be used to notify a payor of changes in information received in an 820 Payment Order/Remittance Advice.

- *828 Debit Authorization* — A company can use this transaction set to provide information to a financial institution regarding electronic debits that the company has authorized against its accounts by another company. It allows the payor (buyer) greater control; it can specify certain payees (sellers), certain time periods, dollar limits and even specific debit transactions. This transaction set can also be used to convey check issue files for positive pay or reconciliation applications.

- *835 Health Care Claim Payment/Advice* — The health care industry uses this transaction set to transmit medical claim payment and remittance information.

- *997 Functional Acknowledgment* — A recipient uses this transaction set to confirm to an originator that the transmitted sets were received and that they were in compliance with ASC X12 standards.

4. **National Automated Clearing House Association (NACHA) Standard Formats for ACH Payments** — ACH transactions use various standardized formats. Formats that can be used by the treasury area include:

   - *Prearranged Payments and Deposits (PPD)* — Companies use this format to effect a transfer of funds to or from a consumer account. Applications using PPD formats include direct deposit of payroll and consumer payments.

   - *Cash Concentration or Disbursement (CCD)* — This format is used to effect transfer of funds between companies or between one company's accounts. Applications include cash concentration and corporate-to-corporate payments. In an EDI environment, a company may use its treasury information system to generate a list of required concentration transfers for electronic transmission to its financial institution. This format contains only limited space for ancillary payment information and thus has limited use for corporate-to-corporate trade payment information exchange.

   - *CCD Plus Addenda (CCD+)* — The CCD+ format combines the widely used CCD record with a 94-character addenda record, 80 characters of which can be used to specify the invoice being paid or give other reference information necessary for application of the payment. The federal government's Vendor Express program uses the CCD+ format and has been expanded to use the corporate trade exchange format.

- *Tax Payment Format (TXP)* — This format is a modification of the CCD+ format designed for the electronic payment of taxes to state and federal governments.

- *Corporate Trade Exchange (CTX)* — The CTX format combines the record structure and enveloping required by the ACH system with the flexible length standards of ASC X12. A CTX transfer is essentially an ASC X12 820 (Payment Order/Remittance Advice), 813 (Electronic Filing of Tax Return Data), 823 (Lockbox Information) or 835 (Health Care Claim Payment/ Advice) using ACH communications protocol. By utilizing up to 9,999 records of 80 characters each, it allows the remittance information contained in the ASC X12 820, 813, 823 or 835 to move through the ACH network rather than having to be separated from the payment and sent using a third-party network or through direct communication.

- *Re-Presented Check Entries (RCK)* — The RCK format is utilized to transmit ACH debit entries in place of a paper check after the paper check has been returned for insufficient or uncollected funds. The current general requirements are that the item be less than $2,500 and drawn on a consumer account. Originators of re-presented check entries must provide notice to the check writer, prior to receiving an item to which the re-presented check entry relates, informing the check writer that his returned check may be collected electronically if the check is returned for insufficient or uncollected funds. After the *first* return of a paper item, the receiver of the check may transmit a re-presented check entry no more than twice. If the RCK is not sent until after the *second* return of a paper item, then it may be used only once.

5. **Issues in Using CCD+ and CTX Formats for Business-to-Business Payments** — The key issue in using CCD+ and CTX formats for B2B payments is whether to keep the payment and remittance information together or to separate them. While using CCD+ and CTX formats keesp the "dollars and data" together, many smaller banks receiving these formats cannot process the remittance information and pass it along to their customer (the payee). Payors that follow the separate approach send payments through the ACH system, while the remittance information moves through a VAN or the Internet. The advantages of this approach are that the payment and remittance advice can be sent to almost any payee, regardless of the ability of the payee's bank to process the remittance information. The problem with the separate approach is that the payment and remittance information must be re-associated or matched up by the payee so they can complete their payment application process.

6. **Changing Standards and Recent Developments** — As information needs change and companies gain experience in EDI, the standards themselves evolve. Each year, most standards bodies publish revisions. While this process is necessary to adapt the standards to changing needs, it poses some problems for EDI users.

A company's trading partners may be using different versions of the standard, and an EDI user must often support multiple versions of the EDI standards. EDI software, VANs and banks help to rectify these problems.

B. EDI Software

EDI systems rely on specialized software or ERP systems that are able to interpret EDI messages, converting data into standard formats and transmitting it between trading partners.

1. **Functions Performed by EDI Software** — EDI software assembles information into transaction sets for electronic transmission. Transaction sets can be created by a company itself or provided by a third party. They can be provided by a single integrated software package or by several software programs exchanging information with each other. The process, illustrated in Exhibit 9.2, is for an outgoing EDI message. It is reversed for an incoming message.

   - *File Conversion* — The first step is to convert paper-based information from the company's records into an electronic file that is readable by the formatting component of the EDI software.

   - *Translation* — This stage, also known as formatting, takes the input data from the file conversion step and translates it into the desired EDI standard format. Most software is capable of formatting data into any accepted cross-industry standard or industry convention. In essence, this step creates EDI transaction sets according to required formats and protocols. Some banks perform EDI translation services for their customers.

Exhibit 9.2 Steps Performed by EDI Software

- *Communication* — This software application establishes communications either directly with the trading partner or with a VAN or bank. It sends (or receives) the EDI-formatted data to (or from) another party using mutually acceptable communication protocols. If the Internet is used as a communications channel, then this process should include software for encrypting and establishing a secure communication session for both sending and receiving parties. It should also be accompanied by using secure file transfer protocol (FTP) for file transmission.

2. **Availability of EDI Software** — EDI software packages with mapping utilities are available for most computer platforms and operating systems. In addition, most EDI software is table-driven, meaning that all of the requirements and formats for EDI transaction sets are stored in easy-to-change tables. By changing them, the software can produce any desired transaction set and can be easily updated as standards evolve.

C. Value-Added Networks

A VAN is a communication intermediary that provides various services to the users of e-commerce. VANs resolve interface problems between two companies that have different computer systems, different format needs and different protocols. Thus, VANs make it easier for companies to implement EDI and to add new EDI trading partners. VANs offer many services to their customers, including the following:

- *Communications Capacity* — VANs maintain large numbers of communication lines with many different transmission speeds and communications protocols. Companies using VANs are assured of sufficient communications capacity to meet their EDI needs.

- *Mailboxing* — This enables one trading partner to send transaction sets to the other's mailbox for storage. When the other trading partner is ready, it retrieves the transaction sets. This solves the problem of finding a time when both partners can communicate.

- *Protocol Conversion* — This enables one partner to use a communication package with one transmission protocol to communicate with a partner that uses another protocol.

- *Standards Conversion* — Some VANs offer the ability to receive a document in one format and translate it into another format before sending the information to the customer.

- *Gateway to Other VANs or Banks* — Gateways enable companies to communicate with any of their trading partners who use different VANs or banks.

- *Implementation Assistance* — This is frequently offered in the form of consulting, software and training of trading partners.

- *Security Services* — Because a VAN is essentially a private network, it can provide enhanced security for commercial transactions.

D. Electronic Banking (E-Banking) Services

Some banks provide VAN-related services for payment information. They make possible the translation of electronic payment and remittance information between trading partners that use different communication protocols. Some of these banks may also provide EDI services that are not directly related to payments or FEDI.

1. **E-Banking Payment Services** — E-banks can provide integrated payables (see Chapter 8, Accounts Payable and Disbursements) in two different ways:
   - One approach is to have a company send a single data file to the bank containing a listing of all payments to be made. The file contains information on when to issue a payment and to whom, as well as instructions on the payment method to be used (check, wire, ACH, foreign currency draft). These instructions may be in a proprietary format or in an ASC X12 820 transaction set (Payment Order/Remittance Advice).
   - Alternatively, the bank maintains a database of a company's payees that includes detailed information, such as preferred payment methods, specific remittance information and receiving financial institutions. The database is periodically updated as new payees are added or an existing payee's remittance profile changes (i.e., payee switches to ACH instead of check for its standard payment type). In such cases, a company making payments sends only limited information to the third party.

   With either approach, the bank either issues the payments immediately or warehouses them until a future date as instructed by the data file. A company utilizing these types of services is outsourcing much of its disbursement functions and potentially reducing the overall costs of its accounts payables operations.

2. **E-Banking Collection Services** — Some banks offer collection services that record the receipt of incoming payments (such as checks, ACHs and wires), reformat the data and transmit the data to the company. This service is generally referred to as an electronic lockbox and provides the information to a company in a proprietary format, a Banking Administration Institute (BAI) lockbox format or an ASC X12 format.

3. **Electronic Clearing House Services** — There are several national and regional electronic clearing house services operated by third parties or member banks that specialize in providing various types of EDI services to their members and/or customers. These clearing houses allow member banks to offer a wider range of EDI services than they could provide on their own.

E. Computer Hardware

A variety of computer systems, ranging from single-user personal computers (PCs) to large mainframes, can accommodate EDI. Some companies, particularly those new to EDI, may initially choose a PC because of low cost and ease of implementation. As EDI transaction volumes increase, companies may choose to implement EDI on their mainframes or in a client-server environment.

IV. The Internet and E-Commerce

Increasingly, companies are using the Internet as a payment and financial information channel. Because the Internet is accessible by virtually anyone with a PC almost anywhere in the world, it is attractive to many businesses as a means to reach more customers and to make it easier for customers to do business with them. However, the very openness and extent of the Internet make security a major concern for financial uses. Many Internet-based systems are proprietary intranets that have sophisticated security systems in place to ensure confidentiality of information, protect company networks and databases from unauthorized access and prevent fraud. Properly secured systems, such as these, can handle company-to-company transmissions, consumer-to-company transactions or both.

A company must trust its e-commerce partners much more than it trusts its paper trading partners because of the following factors:

- Their access to the company's own internal systems
- The speed with which errors can be made and propagated through the trading channel
- The consequences for the trading partners of security breaches of a company's system

A. Key Terms and Definitions

1. **Internet Service Provider (ISP)** — This is a communications intermediary that provides Internet service to individuals and small businesses, typically over telephone lines, cable, satellite or wireless.

2. **Application Service Providers (ASP)** — This is a company that offers individuals or organizations access over the Internet to application programs and related services that would otherwise have to be located in their own personal or organization computers.

3. **Enterprise Application Integration (EAI)** — This is the process of fully integrating Internet systems with existing business ERP and application systems.

4. **File Transfer Protocol (FTP)** — This is a standard Internet protocol that is the simplest way to exchange files between computers on the Internet.

5. **Hypertext Transfer Protocol (HTTP)** — This is a set of rules for exchanging files (text, graphic images, sound video and other multimedia files) on the Web.

6. **Uniform Resource Locator (URL)** — This is an address format utilized on the Web. For example, a typical Web address might be as follows: http://www.afponline.org/search/index.html

B. The Languages of E-Commerce

1. **Electronic Data Interchange** — A highly structured method of sending e-commerce information in standardized electronic transactions. This topic was covered in detail earlier in this chapter.

2. **Hypertext Markup Language (HTML)** — This is the language used to create Web pages on the Internet and other browser-based delivery formats. The information, text and graphic content can be presented in a consistent format, independent of the browser used to view the data.

3. **eXtensible Markup Language (XML)** — This is an extension of HTML, which allows for content as well as structure to be defined. In essence, while HTML provides a consistent format for display of the information, XML adds "tags" to the information that define specifically what the information is. For example, HTML format will make sure that the price of an item on the Web page will appear on a certain place on the page and in a specific font, size and color; XML will further define the field as the price of a specific item. Once a data element has been clearly identified, it is easy to transfer this information from the Web page to an application within the company. There are some specific considerations in the current and future use of XML:

    - XML is an open standard, but this does not imply ease of information exchange. A given variable (name, price, catalog number, etc.) can be defined a variety of ways and still meet XML standards. The users must agree on a standard format for information exchange in order to ensure proper transfer to their respective applications.

    - XML adds a great deal of overhead to a particular message. For example, a payment-related ACH transaction that might use three addenda records containing EDI information could easily take 100 or more addenda records if the message is converted into XML. Thus, short messages can balloon out of usable range. The full power of XML, however, comes into play with longer data sets needing full definition for exchange between unknown trading partners.

- XML messages include a URL that defines the tags to be used in the message.
- XML can be viewed as HTML in advanced browsers and is also human readable.
- There are tools being developed for importing data from an XML message into business application systems.
- ASC X12 has created an XML task group to address the development of standards in the use of XML in a B2B environment.

4. **Financial Services Markup Language (FSML)** — This is a language developed to implement e-checks and other secure financial documents. It is designed to include encryption and digital signatures necessary to create electronic checks. It was developed and is supported by a group of financial institutions and is *not* directly compatible with XML standards.

C. Security Issues

1. **Basics of Security** — Security is the assurance that transactions are safe from intrusion, detection and modification. There are four key factors that security must provide:

    - *Privacy* — This is the assurance that the message is readable only to the intended recipient and that data will not be used for unintended purposes.
    - *Authentication* — This is the ability to know with a reasonable amount of certainty who sent or received a message.
    - *Integrity* — This is the ability to ensure that a message was not modified in transit, which is especially important for financial transactions.
    - *Non-Repudiation* — This is the inability of the sender or receiver of a message to deny having sent or received that message.

2. **Firewalls** — Wherever external users are allowed access to internal applications or data, it is important to utilize a "firewall" to protect the internal systems. These firewalls may be software or hardware based or a combination of both and their purpose is to ensure that only authorized users are allowed to access or manipulate data and systems in the organization. Firewalls can also help to protect against viruses and other system compromises.

3. **Solving Security Issues** — The use of encryption technology with public/private keys can help to resolve many of the security issues on the Internet. Many e-commerce Web sites have already implemented a form of encryption/authentication technology known as SSL (secure sockets layer) to ensure privacy, integrity and authentication of data moving between clients and servers. SSL is built into most major browsers and part of the basic Web infrastructure.

4. **Shared-Secret Key System** — In a shared-secret key (symmetric key) system, both the sending and receiving party have a private key to encrypt/read messages. Since both parties to the message must have the same private key, key distribution and management may be difficult and complex. This type of arrangement is most often used between two regular trading partners.

5. **Public Key Infrastructure (PKI) System** — This type of key system enables e-commerce and file exchange over a public network. The encryption technology is based on ANSI X.500 and X.509 standards for public key certificates and directory services and can be used for virtually all secure EDI Web transactions. Some of the key issues in the use of PKI include:

    - It uses public/private key pairs based on RSA (named after the developers, Rivest, Shamir and Adleman) standard encryption technology.
    - The private key is held in a secret, secure file that is protected with a password or personal identification number (PIN), while the corresponding public key is freely distributed to trading partners.
    - Anyone can use public keys to encrypt a message, while only the receiver with the proper private key can open and read messages.
    - It definitely identifies a person or organization and allows for privacy.
    - It is most often used in the form of digital signatures and digital certificates.

6. **Digital Signatures** — This is an encoded message based on the sender's secret private key. The receiver can identify its source using the sender's public key. As long as the private key is never shared with anyone, it is impossible for others to forge a digital signature. A digital signature is tied to the document as well as to the signer and the signer's digital signature will be different for each document signed. Note, a digital signature is different from a "digitized signature," which is used as a facsimile signature on laser printed checks. The digital signature serves four purposes:

    - Data integrity (verifies that the message has not been altered)
    - Origin authentication (verifies where the message came from)
    - User authentication (verifies who sent the message)
    - Non-repudiation (verifies the message/transaction cannot be repudiated)

7. **Digital Certificates** — These consist of a user's public key and tie the identity of the user (private key) to the user's public key. The identification information is secured by a trusted party's digital signature on the certificate. The trusted party is known as the certificate authority.

8. **Smart Card Authentication Devices** — These devices, also known as tokens, generally look like a credit card and contain circuitry that encodes personal information and manages password protection. When the card or token is inserted into a specially equipped computer, the identity of the user can be verified.

9. **Biometric Devices** — These types of devices provide authentication through electronic recognition of personal characteristics such as fingerprints, retinal patterns, voice prints, hand or face geometry, etc. The advantage to this approach is that while passwords, encryption keys or smart cards can be lost, stolen or copied, a biometric "key" is unique to each individual and easy to use.

10. **Other Security Initiatives** — Banks and other third parties are forming partnerships with security companies, certificate authorities, software providers and other technology firms to administer the public/private key infrastructure and issue electronic certificates that serve as virtual passports to subscribers. The objectives of these types of partnerships could include:

    - To help corporations trust the identity of their digital partners through real-time authentication and validation of the transmission under legally binding contracts

    - To allow users to verify unknown buyers through a trusted financial institution

    - To establish multilateral trust through a single bilateral customer agreement

    - To store certificates in a smart card with a two-factor authentication: the smart card itself and an assigned PIN to unlock the card

V. Credit Terms and E-Commerce Transactions

Most credit terms used today assume a paper-based system involving mailed invoices and checks. These terms are being renegotiated as we move in a more electronic environment.

A. Impact of E-Commerce and EFT

E-commerce enables companies to complete processing more rapidly. EFT also removes much of the payment float due to mail, processing and availability delays. Therefore, many companies are re-examining conventional credit terms. Other things being equal, faster payments are a disadvantage to buyers and an advantage to sellers. To compensate for changes in the cash flow timeline, companies are beginning to negotiate new e-commerce-based credit terms.

Another impact is that many companies are utilizing e-commerce to negotiate single sourcing arrangements with suppliers. The manufacturer receives the benefits of e-commerce and a lower price on raw materials. The vendor receives a much larger order than they would otherwise receive. For vendors, this may also result in faster collections and a shortened cash flow cycle.

Many retailers are utilizing e-commerce/EFT initiatives such as check truncation at point-of-sale to reduce their paperwork loads and collect the large volumes of consumer checks they receive in a more timely and cost-effective manner.

B. Negotiating Shared Benefits

E-commerce can bring significant cost savings to both parties by making it possible to shift the timing and/or amount of cash flows so that both buyer and seller realize significant savings. Buyers and sellers can transfer value by changing the terms of transactions. It is important to note that some companies will negotiate terms separately with each of their trading partners, while other companies may decide to unilaterally adjust terms for all of their trading partners. Two common approaches are:

1. **Price Changes (Discount)** — The seller offers the buyer a cash discount to compensate for earlier payment. For example, a seller offers a 1.5 percent discount if a customer allows its account to be electronically debited on the day the product or service is delivered. This may compare to normal payment under the paper system of 30 days or more.

2. **Payment Timing Changes** — The buyer delays payment to take advantage of the shorter intervals of electronic payment, compared with the time required for paper checks. For example, a customer initiates an ACH payment to its supplier

three days later than a check payment would have been mailed out. This offsets or mitigates the loss of float resulting from the switch to EFT.

The amount of the discount required to renegotiate credit terms successfully in an e-commerce environment depends on the present value impact of changing the payment timing and any transaction cost savings resulting from electronic vs. paper-based payments. Companies using a discount approach will set the discount for electronic payment approximately equal to the benefits or cost reduction derived from the earlier payment.

Companies that change the timing of the payment will often determine a "float-neutral" solution to payment timing, which simply makes the electronic payment date equal to the paper payment date, plus the normal collection float. Regardless of the approach, a successful solution will be one that provides benefits to both the buyer and the seller.

VI. E-Commerce Implementation

E-commerce plays an integral part in the redesign of finance functions or processes. Two important integration techniques and primary examples of treasury re-engineering are the implementation of evaluated receipts settlement and paid-on-production.

A. Evaluated Receipts Settlement (ERS)

ERS is a payment method designed to eliminate the need for a supplier to provide an invoice to the customer. The dollar amount for ERS payments is based not on an invoice, but on a calculation of the quantity actually received by the customer multiplied by a predetermined price. The supplier does not send an invoice, but is simply paid by the customer on an agreed date after receipt of the shipment. The use of ERS allows the customer to automate its payables process and the supplier to automate the receivables and payment application process.

B. Paid-on-Production

Paid-on-production is the process by which a payment record is created for goods and/or services when they are used rather than when they are shipped or delivered. It is similar to consignment sales in retail, but is based on usage within a manufacturing environment. Typically there is only one supplier and title to the product transfers when the product is used in the manufacturing process rather than at the receiving dock as in ERS. Because of legal concerns relating to liability, potential bankruptcy and use of inventory assets for supporting loans, it is important to determine exactly when and where title to the inventory transfers from the supplier to the manufacturer.

C. Future of E-Commerce

The Internet and e-commerce have dramatically changed the face of business and will continue to impact how companies are developed and managed in the future. The ability of the Internet and the Web to provide easy access for all divisions and functional areas of a company on a global basis will cause major changes in the way information is gathered and disseminated. The latest concept in this area of distributed computing is known as peer-to-peer (P2P), where each computer linked to the Internet can be linked directly to another computer to share information. Applications being developed that do P2P computing are essentially automating the machine-to-machine communication process. As business and treasury departments look at ways to take advantage of Internet technology, the expansion of their internal network capabilities and connections with the outside world will be required. Information management will continue to be the most challenging problem facing companies in the coming years.

The other key area for e-commerce will be in the growth and maturation of application service providers. ASPs already offer such applications as accounting, contact management, time and billing and project management. Treasury-oriented ASPs are just being developed and becoming available. The advantage to using these services is not necessarily cost savings, but rather that they are much easier to get up and running in a widely dispersed operating environment and they are much easier to maintain and update.

Test Your Understanding

These chapter questions are provided to test your understanding of the information in the text and are not examples of CCM examination questions, nor are they in the examination format.

Answers can be found at the back of the book on pages 519-523.

1. What is the difference between the Internet, intranet and extranet?

2. Define the two types of electronic commerce.

3. What is the relationship between FEDI and EFT?

4. How is general Web-based e-commerce different from Web-EDI?

5. Discuss the major benefits of e-commerce.

6. What are the four primary infrastructure components of EDI?

7. List and discuss the four types of EDI standards.

8. Give a brief description of the following ASC X12 transaction sets: 820, 821, 823 and 835.

9. What is the difference between the CCD, CCD+ and TXP transaction formats?

10. Define the RCK transaction.

11. What is the key issue for using CCD+ and CTX formats for B2B payments?

12. What is a VAN and what kinds of services do VANs offer to their customers?

13. Briefly discuss the following terms: ISP, FTP, HTTP, URL, HTML and XML.

14. What are the issues in the current and future use of XML?

15. List and discuss the key factors that security must provide.

16. Define digital signature.

17. What is paid-on-production?

CHAPTER 10

Information Management and Technology

Overview

This chapter introduces information management, technology and treasury systems as used by treasury managers to perform a variety of tasks on both a daily and ongoing basis. It covers the objectives of information management, gathering information from banks and other external sources, the different types of treasury systems available and the security, database management and disaster recovery issues involved with their use, as well as the impact of the Internet on treasury management systems.

Learning Objectives

Upon completion of this chapter and the related study questions, the reader should know:

- The objectives of daily information management
- The role of information management in treasury
- The cash management perspective on processing tasks, responsibilities, time frames and data in the corporate treasury environment
- The basic choices in linking corporate treasury to their banks and financial service providers
- Examples of treasury workstations and uses of transaction initiation
- Options available in treasury management systems and software
- Use of the Internet in treasury

Key Concepts

- Daily information management
- Treasury information management
- Information exchange between financial service providers and treasury
- Treasury systems and software
- Use of the Internet in treasury

Outline

I. Objectives of Information Management and Technology

II. The Role of Information Management in Treasury
    A. General Benefits of Treasury Information Management
    B. Benefits of Treasury Information Management for a Global Company

III. Treasury Information Management — The Cash Management Perspective
    A. Cash Management Processing Tasks and Responsibilities
    B. Cash Management Processing Time Frames
    C. Cash Management Internal Data
    D. Cash Management External Data
    E. Multibank Reporting
    F. External Information Formats

IV. Information Exchange Between Financial Service Providers (FSPs) and Treasury
    A. Basic Choices in Linking Treasury to an FSP
    B. Service Level Agreements
    C. Treasury Workstations
    D. Transaction Initiation

V. Treasury Management Systems and Software
    A. History of Treasury Management Systems
    B. Basic Choices in Treasury Management Systems
    C. Treasury Management Systems Benefits and Costs
    D. Selecting a Treasury Management System
    E. Treasury Management Systems Security
    F. Accounting for Financial Risk of Derivatives

VI. Use of the Internet in Treasury
    A. Benefits of Using the Internet in Treasury
    B. Challenges of Using the Internet in Treasury

VII. Future Issues in Treasury Management Systems
    A. Changing Role of Corporate Treasury
    B. Treasury Management Systems Vendors and Solutions
    C. Role of the Internet

I. Objectives of Information Management and Technology

Information management is an integral part of treasury management. The treasury and finance area of a company is often the clearing house for a wide variety of information flows and the future of treasury depends on its ability to integrate its operations with those in other areas of the firm. In most larger companies, enterprise resource planning (ERP) systems are used to exchange data between the different areas. The areas of integration are:

- Bank reporting
- Payments
- General ledger
- Dealing (foreign exchange [FX] and investments)
- Risk management
- Pension management
- Procurement
- Supply chain management

In order to accomplish this integration, treasury must gather and manage a wide range of information flows:

- Daily banking information (balances, clearings, payments, etc.)
- Working capital
- Balance sheet management
- Risk management (financial, credit risk, operational risk)
- Capital markets
- Asset management
- Financial reporting
- Capital budgeting
- Pension administration
- Bank and financial service provider (FSP) account administration

Looking at these information flows from the more narrow perspective of cash management, the key responsibility is to prepare a company's daily cash position or statement. This task requires access to timely and accurate information on the following:

- Bank balances (ledger, collected, available)
- Cash inflows (collections and concentration)

- Cash outflows (disbursements)
- Maturity status of short-term investments
- Maturity status of short-term debt

On a daily basis, therefore, the objectives of information management are as follows:

1. **Determining Cash Requirements** — A daily cash position assists a cash manager in determining a company's cash needs. If additional cash is required to meet short-term obligations, it may be necessary to access lines of credit or sell marketable securities. If excess cash is available, it may be invested or used to pay down debt.

2. **Tracking Activity** — As part of preparing a daily cash position, a cash manager obtains information about a wide variety of individual transactions such as incoming and outgoing wire transfers, the collection of accounts receivable, the clearing of disbursement items and automated clearing house (ACH) credits and debits. This information is often used to identify exception items, resolve problems and identify potential fraud.

3. **Identifying Opportunities** — Knowing a daily cash position enables a cash manager to take advantage of investment, trade payment and debt repayment opportunities.

4. **Updating Forecasts** — A daily cash position facilitates comparison of forecasted cash flows with actual cash flows. Variances are used to update forecasts, if necessary. As part of this process, a cash manager may also adjust target or compensating balances at financial institutions.

5. **Updating Management Information** — The daily cash position is compared to financial data compiled from a wide range of sources. The cash manager and others within the company use the information to update performance measurements, long-term forecasting and budget analyses. While management information is gathered daily, it is usually reported weekly, monthly or quarterly, depending on the size and needs of the company.

Although the treasury function's use of information and technology involves more than just the preparation of a cash position, this daily compilation has been the driving force behind the development of bank/FSP-related treasury workstations.

Information management in treasury will be discussed in several contexts:

- The overall role of treasury information management
- The cash management perspective of treasury systems
- Options available in treasury software

- Treasury modules of ERP systems vs. stand-alone or customized treasury systems
- Use of the Internet in treasury

II. The Role of Information Management in Treasury

If treasury as a department is to add real value to the company, it must expand its view of information management beyond the narrow focus of daily cash position management. The benefits of an information-enhanced treasury area are numerous, especially for larger, global companies.

A. General Benefits of Treasury Information Management

For any company, domestic or global, there are several key benefits derived from developing enhanced treasury information systems.

1. **Consistent Companywide Treasury Services** — One of the primary benefits of more proactive treasury information management is the ability to provide a consistent treasury system for the entire company. This assures the application of best practices in treasury management and results in increased quality of services and better control.

2. **Integration of Treasury with the Rest of the Company** — Either through the use of treasury modules in ERP systems or links from stand-alone treasury systems to other company information systems, the goal is to eliminate redundant processes and exchange data between treasury and the rest of the company in as seamless a manner as possible. ERP systems are sophisticated management information and accounting software packages that link different areas and divisions of a company.

3. **Implementation of Scalable, Uniform Technologies** — By utilizing existing ERP and/or stand-alone treasury systems, one goal is to increase the overall productivity of existing staff and to be able to accommodate growth without having to hire additional staff.

4. **Provision of Alternatives to Outsourcing** — As companies focus more and more on their core competencies, support areas such as treasury may become candidates for outsourcing. The ability of treasury to add value to their basic core processes and control expenses may help in keeping the treasury functions in-house, rather than outsourcing them.

B. Benefits of Treasury Information Management for a Global Company

For a global company, treasury management information can help to provide a variety of additional benefits, as outlined below. The details of many of these practices, such as pooling and netting systems, are discussed in greater detail in Chapter 15, International Treasury Management.

1. **Centralization of Global Transaction Processing** — From a global perspective, enhanced treasury information management provides the ability to centralize reporting and transaction initiation on a worldwide basis. This results in increased control and knowledge as well as reduced expenses.

2. **Global or Regional Pooling** — Enhanced treasury information management is necessary to accomplish the pooling of subsidiary funds either regionally or globally. As is discussed in more detail in Chapter 15, International Treasury Management, this allows a company to maximize overall liquidity and increase control and revenues.

3. **Global Payment and Netting Systems** — These types of systems allow a global company to minimize overall FX costs, as well as float and transaction costs. This results in better overall control as well as reduced expenses.

4. **Unifying Global Treasury Systems by Electronic Banking (E-Banking)** — E-banking is the use of automated electronic formats and communication with the company's banks. By linking treasury systems to those of their banks, a global company can enhance their funds management and reduce the overall risk of the company.

III. Treasury Information Management — The Cash Management Perspective

A. Cash Management Processing Tasks and Responsibilities

Treasury acts as a clearing house for financial information. The cash manager is specifically responsible for:

- Compiling information from a wide range of internal and external sources
- Sorting, storing and analyzing this information
- Reporting information to management

On a daily basis, therefore, the cash manager is responsible for the following:

- Obtaining account balances and transaction detail from external sources
- Obtaining internal information that affects the cash flow timeline
- Consolidating the external and internal information into the cash position worksheet
- Integrating data on current-day activities
- Determining the cash position
- Initiating funds transfers
- Executing investment and/or borrowing decisions
- Updating the cash position worksheet and the short-term cash forecast

While compiling internal financial information, a cash manager must communicate with other areas of the company such as sales, purchasing, credit and accounts receivable, accounts payable, payroll and accounting. External sources of data include financial institutions and third-party information providers. Increasingly, treasury departments use electronic systems to store, edit, share and retrieve information using compatible computer systems connected through either company networks or the Internet.

B. Cash Management Processing Time Frames

The time frames for cash management reporting vary depending on the industry, the type and size of the company and the degree to which management relies on financial information for decision-making. The following are examples of different time frames and reports:

- *Daily* — Cash position
- *Weekly* — Short-term cash forecast
- *Monthly* — Account analysis summary
- *Quarterly* — Investment and debt maturity schedule
- *Annually* — Funding and investment plan

C. Cash Management Internal Data

Internal information exchanged between treasury and other areas of the company can be classified by either classes of data or uses for the data:

1. **Classes of Data**
    - *Sales Summary Reports* — Information on actual and projected weekly or monthly sales

- *Purchasing Summary Reports* — Information on actual and projected weekly or monthly purchases
- *Cash Receipts and Disbursements* — Information on actual and anticipated collections and disbursements
- *Aging Schedule* — Information on the aggregate status of accounts receivable, as well as information on large individual collection items that are outstanding
- *Investment Schedules* — Information on the sale, purchase and maturity of short-term investments
- *Debt Repayment Schedules* — Information on the issuance and repayment of short-term borrowings along with related interest payments

2. **Uses of Data**
   - *Preparation of a Cash Journal* — The recording of individual debits and credits affecting the cash account
   - *Updating the General Ledger* — The posting of transactions to their proper general ledger accounts
   - *Cash Forecasting* — The preparation of short-term cash forecasts
   - *Funds Flows Between Operating Units* — The tracking of cash flows between different operating units of a company or between different subsidiaries of a parent company
   - *Monthly Budget Analysis* — The comparison of budget to actual financial performance and the investigation of variances

D. Cash Management External Data

On a day-to-day basis, a cash manager needs information from external as well as internal sources. The primary external sources are the company's financial institutions and service vendors. Information gathered from external sources is generally categorized as either current day or prior day information.

1. **Prior Day Information**
   - *Balance and Transaction Activity* — Information on current ledger and collected balances, one-and two-day float, debit and credit detail and adjustment items, average balances and balance history
   - *Target Balance Activity* — Information on the status of actual balances compared to target balances

- *Investment and Borrowing Activity* — Information on investment purchases and sales, as well as loan drawdowns and repayments
- *International Transaction Activity* — Information on international wire transfers, drafts, letters of credit and FX transactions
- *Custody Activity* — Information on securities safekeeping and approaching maturities
- *Check Inquiry* — Information on the clearing status of individual items that have been issued
- *Stop Payment Activity* — Information on the status of stop payment requests
- *Account Analysis* — Information on account charges and services

2. **Current Day Information**
    - *Lockbox Deposits and Remittance Detail* — Information on lockbox deposits and the float breakdown of the deposits
    - *Controlled Disbursement* — Information on the amount of check clearings that need to be funded
    - *Cash Concentration Reports* — Electronic depository transfer (EDT) activity and exception reports, such as those identifying sending locations that have not reported daily deposits (may also be available on prior day reports)
    - *Wire Transfers* — Information on both incoming and outgoing wire transfers
    - *ACH Transactions* — Information on ACH debits and credits
    - *Investments* — Information on maturing investments
    - *Money Market and FX Rates* — Information on same-day market activity for purposes of investment, borrowing and foreign currency exchange
    - *Return Items* — Checks deposited into the company's account that have been returned unpaid
    - *Positive Pay Exception Item* — Checks presented for payment for which a matching issue has not been provided by the company

3. **Uses of External Data** — A company uses external data for various purposes. Examples of different uses for the same data are outlined below:
    - Lockbox Detail
        - *Primary Use:* Update accounts receivable
        - *Other Use:* Research customer inquiries
    - Concentration Bank Deposits

- *Primary Use:* Initiate transfers
- *Other Use:* Update cash scheduling
• Controlled Disbursement
    - *Primary Use:* Fund accounts
    - *Other Use:* Manage disbursement float
• Transaction Detail
    - *Primary Use:* Track individual debits and credits
    - *Other Use:* Detect internal or external fraud
• Short-Term Investments
    - *Primary Use:* Access daily market information
    - *Other Use:* Review investment strategy
• Short-Term Borrowing
    - *Primary Use:* Initiate line of credit drawdown
    - *Other Use:* Update cash forecasting
• Account Analysis
    - *Primary Use:* Monitor target balances
    - *Other Use:* Monitor bank pricing

E. Multibank Reporting

Companies that have two or more banks may establish an arrangement in which one of the company's financial institutions or a third-party reporting service gathers and consolidates the account balances and transaction activity from each of the company's financial institutions. This arrangement is commonly referred to as data exchange. Banks are also increasingly offering this kind of information via the Internet.

F. External Information Formats

The two standardized formats for transmission of external data are the Bank Administration Institute (BAI) format and the Accredited Standards Committee (ASC) X12 821 Financial Information Reporting transaction set. The BAI format is the more established and more commonly used. However, there is a migration toward ASC X12 821, which is an electronic data interchange (EDI) transaction set. (See Chapter 9, Electronic Commerce.) As more and more use is made of the Internet, other formats and languages such as XML (eXtensible Markup Language) and FSML (financial services markup language) are being used. These are discussed in greater detail in Chapter 9, Electronic Commerce.

IV. Information Exchange Between Financial Service Providers (FSPs) and Treasury

While some companies still utilize older methods such as mail, telephone and fax to exchange information with their banks or other financial service providers, there are now a wide array of electronic communication methods that can be used. When implementing electronic communications with FSPs, treasury managers must consider cost limitations, security concerns and, for global companies, the infrastructure peculiarities of different countries. How the FSP information is linked to the company's other applications or ERP system must also be considered.

A. Basic Choices in Linking Treasury to an FSP

1. **Proprietary Software** — Due to security concerns and legacy systems, this is the most common mechanism used to link to FSPs today. It is relatively inexpensive and allows a user to make connection by modem to the FSP's computer to access account information and to give a variety of treasury-related instructions. The access to the bank may be via server or personal computer (PC) based software at the company, or through terminal access to software residing at the FSP.

2. **Host-to-Host Link** — This approach is more sophisticated than that above and is a direct two-way link between the FSP and customer computers. It is generally expensive to set up and maintain, but can handle high volumes of data in an automated fashion and allows a company to use more of a bank's services.

3. **Internet** — Many FSPs already offer a wide range of services via the Internet. These include cash balance, transaction reporting and trade financing support. In addition, FSPs are also moving away from server or PC-based solutions (known as fat clients, since the application software resides on the customer's desktop computer) to Internet-based, thin client solutions (where the application software resides at a central server site, most often at the bank).

B. Service Level Agreements

When adding new FSP electronic services, it is important to clearly set expectations regarding these services. This is typically done in the form of a service level agreement. These agreements should cover the following areas:

- What electronic banking services are to be purchased
- How the services will operate relative to other services
- What the FSP is providing
- What the buyer (company) has to provide
- Responsibilities of both parties
- Service levels and fees
- Support at setup and in production
- Implementation and training
- Security issues and procedures
- Legal matters (law, jurisdiction, redress, etc.)

C. Treasury Workstations

A treasury workstation (cash management software) is typically a PC or client/server that has software that gathers information from both internal and external sources, then compiles the data for purposes of analysis and decision making. A treasury workstation can either be stand-alone or part of a company network. In addition to automating a number of manual tasks, treasury workstations enable cash managers to prepare and distribute financial information in a variety of customized spreadsheets and management reports. Treasury workstation software can either be purchased from a vendor or developed in-house. Treasury workstations generally have three primary attributes:

1. **Modularity** — Treasury workstation software is modular in design. Among the basic modules included in many systems are balance reporting, cash forecasting, investment portfolio management, payment initiation and debt scheduling. Additional modules offer the user choices such as general ledger interface, word processing, electronic mail (e-mail), FX management and letter of credit initiation capabilities. Typical treasury workstation modules and related applications are shown in Exhibit 10.1.

2. **Data Integration** — A treasury workstation is capable of integrating a wide range of information from both internal and external sources. The data may be downloaded into the computer and organized in a report format.

3. **Database Management** — Treasury workstations also provide the user with database management capabilities. This allows the user to determine how to store, retrieve and organize information. It also allows the user to produce formatted financial reports.

Exhibit 10.1 Treasury Workstation Modules

Treasury Workstation Module	Treasury Application
Account Balance Report	Monitor Ledger and Collected Balances
Target Balance Report	Manage Compensating Balances
Cash Position Worksheet	Manage Cash Position
Transaction Detail Report	Monitor Individual Debits and Credits
Investment Portfolio Management	Manage Short-Term Investments
Debt Scheduling	Monitor Debt Repayment
Letters of Credit	Issue Letters of Credit

D. Transaction Initiation

Increasingly, cash managers are using more automated methods such as treasury workstations for initiating transactions once they have compiled and analyzed data and completed the daily decision-making process. Examples of the types of transactions that cash managers can initiate include:

- Wire transfers
- ACH debits and credits
- Stop payments
- Letters of credit
- Investment purchases and sales
- Loan drawdowns and repayments
- FX transactions

V. Treasury Management Systems and Software

The treasury workstations discussed in the previous section are only one example of systems and software utilized in the treasury area. Treasury software can be any of the following:

- *Treasury Workstations* — Bank-supplied or third-party applications for balance reporting and cash management services
- *Spreadsheets* — Company or third-party developed spreadsheets to collect, manage and report data from a variety of sources

- *Templates* — Database tools used for aggregating debt and/or investment positions
- *Analytical Tools* — Typically used for forecasting and financial risk management
- *Deal Capture and Support* — Used for monitoring counterparty exposures and keeping track of competing bids
- *Middleware* — Special software designed to provide linkages between treasury systems and other company software applications

A. History of Treasury Management Systems

1. **Early Systems** — Most of the early systems in the treasury area were custom developed in the early 1980s and were designed to provide manual capture, then manipulation and analysis of data. There were few interfaces to other systems and little automation of repetitive tasks. Often these systems relied on manual entry of data from telephone, spreadsheet, fax sources and mailed bank statements.

2. **First Commercial Systems** — In the United States in the mid to late 1980s, these systems focused on cash management activities and were often bank-provided or designed to link to bank systems for information. Outside the United States, the first commercial systems tended to focus on FX and interest rate risk management. Most of these systems were stand-alone character-based or spreadsheet systems with limited external interfaces. Though there were a few non-bank providers of software, they were typically independent of the major business software providers. Many large companies developed their own proprietary solutions for their cash management needs.

3. **PC-Based and Client Servers with Windows™** — The advent of Microsoft Windows in the early 1990s allowed for the development of user-friendly interfaces to treasury workstations. Though the systems still suffered from a lack of full integration with other company systems, they were a significant improvement over earlier versions. Many banks and other third-party sources began to provide treasury applications for a wide range of hardware and company sizes.

4. **Modern Treasury Management Systems** — Today companies have a wide range of products for stand-alone cash management and risk management activities to fully integrated treasury modules for large ERP systems. Many of these systems take advantage of the Internet and browser technology to easily access and utilize data with treasury and the rest of the company.

B. Basic Choices in Treasury Management Systems

Treasury management systems can generally be classified as either a treasury module of ERP software, third-party treasury management software, or customized treasury systems developed in-house. In addition, many of these systems are beginning to utilize the Internet for communications and browser technology to provide a user-friendly interface. Each of these options is discussed in detail below.

1. **Treasury Modules of ERP Software** — Many of the large ERP software providers offer treasury modules for their systems. These ERP systems provide value to companies that implement them throughout all departments by tying information technology to corporate strategy and communicating management information on a standardized and consistent basis. Generally, however, the currently available treasury modules do not have the same level of functionality as stand-alone offerings. The advantage of ERP treasury software is that it makes the task of interfacing to other areas of the company such as accounts receivable and accounts payable much more seamless.

2. **Stand-Alone Treasury Systems** — There are a wide range of stand-alone treasury management products available for companies of all sizes. The treasury workstations and other cash management software offered by FSPs fit into this category, as well as sophisticated (and expensive) treasury management systems offered by non-FSP third parties. These systems are often tailored to specific needs of treasury departments offering support for cash management, debt/investment and risk management activities. Most of the larger systems also provide access to multibank reporting and interfaces to major ERP systems. The more sophisticated of these systems also address very treasury-specific issues such as financial risk management and support for Financial Accounting Standard 133 (FAS 133, discussed later in this chapter), which the typical ERP system does not address.

3. **Customized Treasury Systems** — Given the unique needs of some companies, it may be advantageous for such a company to develop its own customized treasury system. This solution is often best for treasury departments that have special needs (multicurrency environment, foreign tax and regulatory constraints, widely dispersed operations, etc.) that may not be addressed by off-the-shelf software. Another rationale for a customized system is where treasury has advanced models or analysis approaches that it regards as strategic.

C. Treasury Management Systems Benefits and Costs

1. **Benefits** — The benefits of implementing treasury management systems may include:
    - Improved productivity
    - Expedited data gathering, compilation and analysis

- Increased forecasting accuracy
- Reduced borrowing expenses
- Improved short-term investment returns
- Improved management reporting

2. **Costs** — The costs of implementing treasury management systems may include:
   - Hardware and software selection, purchase and installation
   - Startup and personnel training expenses
   - Administration, maintenance and overhead
   - Telecommunications charges
   - Transaction service charges
   - System security expenses

D. Selecting a Treasury Management System

In buying a treasury management system, it is critical to have a well-defined selection process with the right people and departments involved in the process. Requirements should be clearly defined with a detailed project and implementation plan. Many companies utilize a formal request for proposal (RFP) process managed by a selection/implementation team of key internal and external stakeholders.

E. Treasury Management Systems Security

1. **Database Management Issues** — Treasury data files contain information that, if improperly disseminated or misused, can leave companies vulnerable to defalcations and breaches of confidentiality. Consequently, controlling access to treasury information is vital. Proper internal control requires separation of duties pertaining to data access and use. For example, the same individual should not create, approve and send a wire transfer. Determining who should have access to information entails not only consideration of technical competency but also of appropriate designation of responsibilities within the company. A user must have a working knowledge of how to:
   - Set up a database correctly
   - Enter, edit and update data accurately
   - Protect the database's security, confidentiality and integrity at all times

2. **Security Risks** — The three most common types of risks treasury management systems involve are data loss, unauthorized user access and computer viruses, as outlined below:

   - *Data Loss* — This can be precipitated by a number of factors, including:
     - Power surges or failures
     - Computer failure
     - Telecommunications system failure
     - Software defects
     - Intentional tampering with data
     - User error
     - Misplaced or lost storage devices, such as disks, compact discs (CDs), tapes

     The degree of data loss risk depends on the nature of the information that is lost and the amount of time involved in restoring it — if it can be restored at all.

   - *Unauthorized User Access* — There are two different types of unauthorized user access:
     - Unauthorized individuals within the company are able to access information by logging on to a computer in the treasury area or by means of a company's local area network (LAN).
     - Unauthorized users outside the company access information either accidentally or intentionally.

     The risks in both cases are that the unauthorized user has access to confidential information, can intentionally or unintentionally alter or destroy data and/or may initiate unauthorized or fraudulent transactions.

   - *Computer Viruses* — A computer virus is a software program that is designed to corrupt or destroy data. Some viruses are relatively harmless and may affect only a small portion of a software program. Other viruses can sabotage an entire information system. Readily available anti-virus protection programs should be employed but are not always fail-safe.

3. **Security Safeguards** — Companies need to take steps to prevent either authorized or unauthorized users from executing fraudulent transactions. Companies can safeguard the security of treasury systems by:

   - *Creating a Security Officer/System Administrator Position* — Assigning specific responsibility for treasury system security to a designated individual is a basic safeguard. This individual should be responsible for developing, monitoring and enforcing information security policies and procedures.

- *Developing Written Policies and Procedures* — Companies should establish formal policies that spell out all procedures for approval of access levels and protection of passwords. As with all such written policies, they are only effective if they are implemented, enforced and periodically updated.

- *Periodic System Test/Audit* — To maintain ongoing integrity of the system, it should be tested on a regular basis with internal audit support to ensure that it operates as planned. Internal auditors examine the operation of the system to verify that the processes and data management are working properly.

- *Establishing Physical Security* — Physical security includes protection of both hardware and software. Actions range from simply storing computer systems and software in a secure place to restricting physical access to certain areas. The degree of physical security, as with all safeguards, depends upon many factors, including the risks involved, the costs, personnel constraints and the practicality of imposing such controls.

- *Instituting Basic Access Requirements* — Access requirements should include the use of passwords, monitoring log-on activity, limited sign-on attempts, use of smart-card and/or biometric controls and enforcing periodic password changes.

- *Establishing Different Levels of User Access* — An additional safeguard is to establish different levels of access and segregation of duties. For example, a transaction should not be transmitted by a person who entered or edited it.

- *Requiring Backup Storage* — Backup storage can be accomplished in different ways depending on the system.

- *Instituting Computer Virus Protection Methods* — Software and data should be scanned at both the system and workstation level to ensure that systems have not been compromised.

- *Using Electronic Security* — Two of the most common methods of electronic security are encryption and message authentication via the use of electronic signatures or certificates. (These are covered in greater detail in Chapter 9, Electronic Commerce)

4. **Disaster Recovery** — All treasury management systems and other electronic communications systems are vulnerable to disasters such as earthquakes, fires and power outages. Banks and corporate treasuries should have disaster recovery plans that include:

    - Identifying internal and external threats
    - Assessing business risks
    - Monitoring for corporate espionage
    - Determining what is needed to perform critical tasks
    - Developing backup or alternative systems and sites

- Obtaining management approval
- Testing at least every six months
- Keeping the plan current

F. Accounting for Financial Risk of Derivatives

FAS 133 requires that all derivatives be marked-to-market on the balance sheet. Marking-to-market means that the derivatives must be valued as of the date of the balance sheet. Given the highly volatile nature of derivatives, this means that the value of the derivative holdings may vary significantly from period to period. This is a significant difference from the off-balance-sheet approach of current practice. From a treasury manager's perspective, this requires substantial record keeping and computation to determine the value of their derivative-based hedges at any point in time. The measurement and monitoring of hedge effectiveness will be a critical part of treasury management reporting in the future and should be a consideration in evaluating treasury management systems. This topic is covered in greater detail in Chapter 14, Financial Risk Management.

I. Use of the Internet in Treasury

As treasury systems have developed over the years, they have moved from mainframe-based systems to PCs and servers, which are now migrating to an Internet and browser-based approach. For a variety of reasons, the Internet is significantly changing the treasury environment.

A. Benefits of Using the Internet in Treasury

1. **Easy Access to Services and Applications** — In an Internet/browser environment, the software typically resides on a server, rather than locally on a user's PC. This makes it possible to access a wide range of applications with greater flexibility from multiple, non-traditional locations and business units outside treasury. This easy access may also simplify bringing a system back up after a shutdown or other disaster.

2. **Easier Implementation and Version Control** — For many applications, software does not have to be installed at the user's site, thus making initial implementations and upgrades accessible from a large number of sites a much simpler process.

3. **Easy to Use** — Due to the consistent layout and navigation format of browser-based applications, it is much easier for first-time users to access the system, reducing the need for training during implementation.

4. **Less Expensive Communications** — The Internet has proved to be an extremely inexpensive communications infrastructure. This is a clear benefit to large, global companies with a widely dispersed operating base.

B. Challenges of Using the Internet in Treasury

1. **Security Issues** — General security issues have already been covered earlier in this chapter and in Chapter 9, Electronic Commerce. Though best practices such as 128-bit encryption are standard on business Internet communications, many companies have not fully implemented them on their electronic commerce (e-commerce) applications. In addition, most financial institutions are still not comfortable with the security practices and procedures relating to transaction initiation and funds transfers.

2. **Identity Problems** — One of the significant risks in using the Internet is that of counterparty risk. While the risks of trading with known suppliers and customers is minimal, the risk of trading with unknown companies and individuals is significant. This is especially the case in auction markets, where a company may be bidding to buy or sell products and services with many unknown trading partners. The same is true in a dealing environment where a company may be with working unknown dealers to buy or sell FX or financial instruments. Many companies are looking to certificate authorities or the development of closed trading communities to reduce this risk. (This topic is covered in greater detail in Chapter 9, Electronic Commerce and Chapter 14, Financial Risk Management).

VII. Future Issues in Treasury Management Systems

A. Changing Role of Corporate Treasury

In many cases, the changing role of treasury will help to drive the treasury management systems of the future. Treasury will have greater responsibility for risk management and will also have to deal with an increasing volume of more and more complex transactions moving at faster speeds. Additionally, there is the continuing trend to globalize treasury operations. The broad-based automation of treasury processes should also continue, allowing treasury to cope with the higher transaction volume and to free up resources to focus on true value-added activities such as risk management, financial analysis, effective execution of transactions and making investments.

B. Treasury Management Systems Vendors and Solutions

There has already been significant consolidation in the third-party treasury management software market as well as in the bank market. This trend will continue, as will as the trend of ERP treasury modules offering a wider range of functionality. Future solutions will likely be developed by teams of banks, ERP vendors and third-party vendors for a wide range of companies.

C. Role of the Internet

The Internet and e-commerce will continue to play an expanding role in future treasury systems. The initial focus has been on full-service, Web-based corporate banking and cash management services, expanding to dealing (FX and investments) and risk management. Within a company, browser-based applications on intranets will expand from simply delivering data to allowing full interaction with treasury and ultimately allowing any department to initiate transactions in a safe and controlled manner.

Test Your Understanding

These chapter questions are provided to test your understanding of the information in the text and are not examples of CCM examination questions, nor are they in the examination format.

Answers can be found at the back of the book on pages 524-529.

1. List the different information flows that must be collected and managed by treasury.

2. What are the objectives of information management?

3. Discuss the general benefits of treasury information management.

4. What are the specific benefits of treasury information management for a global company?

5. Treasury acts as a clearing house for financial information. For which types of information is a cash manager specifically responsible?

6. List and discuss the different classes of cash management internal data.

7. What are the different types of prior day information used by cash managers?

8. List the different types of current day information used by cash managers.

9. Define multibank reporting.

10. Discuss the basic choices in linking treasury to a financial service provider.

11. What is a treasury workstation?

12. List the primary attributes of a treasury workstation.

13. What types of transactions do cash managers typically initiate?

14. What are the basic types of treasury software?

15. List and discuss the different choices in treasury management systems.

16. What are the benefits of treasury management systems?

17. What are the costs of treasury management systems?

18. What are the basic security risks involved in treasury management systems?

19. List the security safeguards companies need to take to prevent unauthorized usage and fraudulent transactions.

20. What is FAS 133 and what does it require?

21. List the benefits of using the Internet in treasury.

22. What are the challenges of using the Internet in treasury?

CHAPTER 11

Forecasting Cash Flows

Overview

This chapter describes the objectives of forecasting. It explains forecast horizons and the principal techniques used for forecasting.

Learning Objectives

Upon completion of this chapter and the related study questions, the reader should know:

- The objectives of cash forecasting
- The distinction between short-, medium-and long-term forecasting
- The steps in the forecasting process: data selection, source selection, forecast method selection and forecast validation and implementation
- The various forecasting methods and how to apply them to forecasting cash flows

Key Concepts

- Short-, medium-and long-term forecasting
- Steps in the forecasting process
- Forecasting methods

Outline

I. Objectives of Cash Forecasting

II. The Forecasting Process
    A. Forecasting Horizons
    B. The Operating and Cash Flow Cycles
    C. Cash Flow Components
    D. Degree of Certainty
    E. Data Identification and Organization
    F. Forecast Method Selection and Validation

III. Forecasting Methods
    A. Receipts and Disbursements Forecast
    B. Distribution Forecast
    C. Pro Forma Financial Statements
    D. Statistical Forecasting

I. Objectives of Cash Forecasting

Forecasting cash flows is one of the more important tasks of cash management. The objectives of predicting cash flows include:

1. **Liquidity Management** — Forecasting a company's net cash position at different intervals is essential for scheduling investment maturities and anticipating borrowing requirements.

2. **Financial Control** — Using variance analysis to compare actual cash flows with projected cash flows can help identify problems such as unanticipated inventory changes, delays in accounts receivable collection and mistiming of payments. Early identification allows a company to initiate corrective measures.

3. **Meeting Strategic Objectives** — Cash flow forecasts are used to project future funding requirements and to support a company's strategic objectives.

4. **Capital Budgeting** — Forecasts of revenues, expenditures and funding are required for evaluating potential projects and capital budgeting.

5. **Managing Costs** — Cash forecasts can help management optimize cash usage by minimizing borrowing costs and excess bank balances and enhancing short-term investment income.

6. **Managing Currency Exposure** — Companies conducting business internationally can use various forecasting techniques to determine foreign cash flows and to assess their degree of foreign currency exposure.

II. The Forecasting Process

Development of a particular forecast depends on many factors, such as the forecast horizon, the company's size and its industry, treasury structure, the primary goal of forecasting, sources of information and forecasting tools.

A. Forecasting Horizons

The time interval over which information is to be forecast is an important consideration. Cash flow forecast horizons can range from one day to several years. The forecast horizon can be thought of as a continuum, with distinctions made between short-, medium- and long-term intervals.

1. **Short-Term Forecasting** — Short-term forecasts predict cash receipts and disbursements and the resulting balances on a daily, weekly or monthly basis.

Short-term forecasts aid in scheduling cash concentration transfers for field and lockbox accounts, funding disbursement accounts and making short-term investing and borrowing decisions. Short-term forecasting is also important in establishing and managing target balances for purposes of bank compensation.

2. **Medium-Term Forecasting** — Cash flow forecasts from one to 12 months are an integral part of cash budgeting and are referred to as medium-term forecasts. They project the inflows (collections from sales and other sources of funds) and outflows (expenses and other uses of funds) on a monthly basis. They are used to determine the company's need for short-term credit or the availability of funds for short-term investments. They can also serve as a benchmark for performance by comparing actual cash flows to projected cash flows from the cash budget.

3. **Long-Term Forecasting** — Long-term forecasts cover any period beyond one year. They take into consideration projections of long-term sales and expenditures as well as market factors. Such forecasts are of strategic importance because they relate to long-term financial planning for the company. They are also used by financial institutions and rating agencies for credit analysis and evaluation.

B. The Operating and Cash Flow Cycles

The business operating cycle determines the basic configuration of day-to-day cash flows. A company's credit, inventory and payables policies (and those of its suppliers) have an impact on cash flows as shown by the cash flow timeline. The business operating cycle and the cash flow timeline are discussed in Chapter 1, The Role of Cash Management in Corporate Finance.

C. Cash Flow Components

Proper forecasting of cash flows necessitates dividing them into their components. One approach is to divide cash flows into categories of operating, investing and financing activities. These categories can be further segregated into outflows and inflows. For example, operating cash inflows might be segregated by product line, type of customer or region, while operating cash outflows can be segregated into large-dollar vendor payments, small-dollar vendor payments, payroll and taxes.

D. Degree of Certainty

Proper forecasting of cash flow also necessitates assigning degrees of certainty to each component.

1. **Certain Flows** — For many companies, the timing and amounts of a significant number of cash flows are known in advance. Typical examples of certain cash

flows include interest, debt principal repayments, dividends, royalties and tax payments.

2. **Predictable Flows** — Cash collections from credit sales are an example of a cash flow component that can be predicted with reasonable accuracy. The cash flow on a given day depends on factors such as the recent history of credit sales. A prediction of future cash flows can then be made on the basis of past observations. Disbursements such as payroll are also predictable, based as they are on records of hours worked and projected float on payroll checks. Similarly, patterns of clearings of vendor checks can also be determined on the basis of past clearing times.

3. **Less Predictable Cash Flows** — Some cash flows, such as those related to sales of a new product, unexpected repairs pending settlement of insurance claims or the cost of settling a strike, are difficult to forecast. The experience and judgment of the forecaster are important in these instances.

E. Data Identification and Organization

The identification of suitable data to be used in the forecast is an important element of the forecasting process. Cash managers should consider the following factors:

1. **Sources** — Information should be gathered from external and internal sources, including the company's banks, field managers, sales managers and the accounts payable, accounts receivable and payroll departments. In addition, many treasury information systems or workstations provide modules to either manage forecasting data or actually do the forecast itself.

2. **Identification** — The identification of sources is affected by the degree of centralization or decentralization in the company's structure. In a decentralized company, field managers usually have the most current financial data related to their operations. A centralized company is less dependent on numerous field sources.

3. **Account Structure** — The bank account structure used by the company is also important. For example, using a single master account to collect all cash inflows and disburse all cash outflows via zero balance accounts (ZBAs) helps facilitate cash flow forecasting compared to a system of multiple stand-alone accounts.

4. **Reporting Requirements** — In order to ensure the usefulness of the data selected, it is essential that the data be precisely defined and accurately reported in a timely manner.

5. **Historical Data** — Prior period data can be useful in determining the timing and amount of future cash flows related to sales — for example, previous credit sales experience and individual customer payment histories.

F. Forecast Method Selection and Validation

The process of selecting a method of forecasting involves:

1. **Establishing Data Relationships** — Cash managers should ascertain the statistical relationship between the available data and the cash flow components to be forecast before selecting the appropriate forecasting method. This determination can come from forecaster intuition, past experience, graphical views of the data or more sophisticated quantitative statistical techniques. For example, cash disbursements can be modeled as a function of invoices received for payment and cash collections can be based on prior period credit sales.

2. **Selecting a Method** — A forecasting method is selected after the relationship is determined between the input data and the cash flow to be forecast. Forecasting models should be cost-effective. Any forecasting system or model must be maintained along with the data required to produce the forecast. Sophisticated computer-based models may require systems support and personnel to provide data input. The cost of more detailed analyses must be weighed against the expected improvement in the accuracy of forecasts.

3. **Testing and Validating Relationships** — The degree of explanatory power can be assessed in the course of model development; the higher the correlation between expected (predicted) values and actual values on which the model is based, the better it is.

   A model can be refined and validated using the following methods:
   - *In-Sample Validation* — In-sample validation tests how well the model works using the historical data from which the model was developed. Using randomly chosen data within the sample, the forecast model's predicted results are compared with actual values.
   - *Out-of-Sample Validation* — Out-of-sample validation tests the accuracy of the forecasting models using data not involved in the model's estimation. For example, if three years (36 months) of monthly data are available, the model may be estimated using the first 30 months of data. The model can then be validated by comparing the model's predictions to actual values over the remaining six months of data.
   - *Ongoing Validation* — Continuing feedback from projected vs. actual comparisons allows continuous evaluation and refinement of the model.

4. **Document the Process** — It is important to document how the forecast process works, the sources of data, contacts, etc. This allows others in the treasury area and future forecasters to better understand how the forecast was developed.

III. Forecasting Methods

The method a company uses for a given forecast depends greatly on the forecasting horizon. Many companies use short-term forecasts based on information relating to receipts and disbursements that will occur in the near future. There are a number of methods that incorporate individual cash flow details to develop accurate short-term cash projections. Two of the more important methods for short-term forecasting include receipts and disbursements forecasts and distribution forecasts. Medium-and long-term forecasting methods include generating pro forma financial statements. Statistical analytical techniques may be applied across all time horizons.

A. Receipts and Disbursements Forecast

Projecting receipts and disbursements is fundamental to short-term cash forecasting. This begins with the creation of separate schedules of cash receipts and disbursements. Both schedules are prepared on a cash basis rather than an accrual basis. This method tends to forecast cash accurately in the short-term and near medium-term, especially when accounts receivable and accounts payable data are incorporated.

1. **Receipts Schedule** — A receipts schedule consists of a projection of collections from customers (cash sales or payments on accounts receivable) and other cash inflows such as interest or dividends received from investments. A receipts schedule should also include expected non-recurring cash inflows such as the proceeds from asset sales.

2. **Disbursements Schedule** — A disbursements schedule involves forecasting the cash disbursements for purchases and other cash outflows, such as payroll, taxes, interest, dividends, rent and debt repayments.

3. **Completed Forecast** — Completing the forecast involves combining the receipts and disbursements schedules and comparing the results to a desired minimum cash balance.

In Exhibit 11.1, a company has determined its minimum cash requirements to be $50,000 to cushion it against unexpected expenses or to allow it to take advantage of unanticipated opportunities. The beginning cash balance is the ending cash balance from the prior week. The final two lines of the forecast represent the forecasted surplus or deficit cash position each week. With this information, a company can better manage its borrowing and investing activity. In this example, the forecast shows a surplus of funds in Week 1, which could be invested to earn interest. In Weeks 2 and 3, however, the forecast shows shortages of cash that would need to be managed by borrowing funds on a short-term basis or liquidating short-term investments.

Exhibit 11.1 Receipts and Disbursements Forecast

$ Amounts in $1,000	Week 1	Week 2	Week 3
Cash Receipts	$ 1,000	$ 1,000	$ 950
Cash Disbursements	(870)	(1,450)	(1,000)
Net Cash Flow	130	(350)	(50)
Beginning Cash Balance	100	230	(120)
Ending Cash Balance	230	(120)	(170)
Minimum Cash Req. (Target Balance)	(50)	(50)	(50)
Financing Needed (Deficit)		$ 170	$ 220
Investable Funds (Surplus)	$180		

B. Distribution Forecast

A distribution forecast provides estimates of the cash flow effect of a single event, on a daily basis over a specified interval based on historical patterns. It is particularly appropriate for short-term forecasts. The distribution percentages may be calculated two ways:

1. **Simple Average** — Distribution percentages can be estimated by averaging past daily cash flows related to a particular category of disbursements. For example, the cash manager may sample past clearings of payroll checks and discover that, on average, 40 percent of a certain category of payroll checks cleared on the day checks were issued, 50 percent the day after and 10 percent two days after check issuance. The problem with taking a simple average is that more factors than just the number of days after check issuance may affect the check clearing delay.

2. **Regression Analysis** — It is very likely that the day of the week the check was distributed, the day of the month of check issuance and/or the proximity of holidays may affect the distribution of check clearings. If more than one factor affects the proportion of a period's cash flow that one day represents, the method requires application of a statistical estimation technique such as regression analysis. This distribution method allows seasonality and other trends to be incorporated into forecasts. However, it requires large amounts of data and may need to be revised as business conditions change.

Exhibit 11.2 is an example of forecasting using the distribution method.

Exhibit 11.2 Forecasting Using the Distribution Method

A company has used regression analysis based on historical data to estimate the proportion of dollars that will clear on a given business day. It has determined that this proportion depends on the number of business days since the checks were distributed. The estimated proportions are given below.

Business Days Since Distribution	Percentage of Dollars Expected to Clear
1	13%
2	38%
3	28%
4	13%
5	8%
Total	100%

Therefore, if $100,000 in checks are distributed on Wednesday, May 1, the checks are estimated to clear according to the schedule below.

Date	Business Days After Distribution	Day of the Week	Percentage of Dollars Clearing	Forecast of Dollars Clearing
May 2	1	Thursday	13%	$ 13,000
May 3	2	Friday	38%	$ 38,000
May 6	3	Monday	28%	$ 28,000
May 7	4	Tuesday	13%	$ 13,000
May 8	5	Wednesday	8%	$ 8,000
		TOTAL	100%	$100,000

C. Pro Forma Financial Statements

Projected income statements and balance sheets can be used to forecast cash flows over a longer time horizon. One of the simplest procedures for constructing pro forma financial statements is based on the percentage-of-sales method, as illustrated in Exhibit 11.3.

The percentage-of-sales method involves projecting financial statements based on sales forecasts and the historical relationship between sales and certain balance sheet items such as cash, accounts receivable, inventory and accounts payable. It also considers other balance sheet and income statement items that can be forecasted based on other factors (e.g., debt repayment schedules).

The percentage-of-sales method is accomplished by:

- Forecasting the income statement and balance sheet based on the relationships mentioned above.

- Calculating the projected ending cash balance by determining the impact on cash of the forecasted income statement and balance sheet changes. It should be noted that this method measures the change in cash over the period and is not used for daily cash position setting.

> **Exhibit 11.3** Forecasting with Pro Forma Financial Statements (Percentage-of-Sales Method)
>
> Assume the following income statement and balance sheet (in thousands) represents a company's actual position as of December 31, 2001.
>
> **Income Statement**
>
> | | |
> |---|---|
> | Sales | $ 2,000 |
> | Cost of Goods Sold | (1,500) [75% of Sales] |
> | Selling & Admin. Exp. | (200) [10% of Sales] |
> | Depreciation | (100) |
> | Interest Expense | (38) |
> | Income Before Taxes | 162 |
> | Taxes | (55) [34% Tax Rate] |
> | Net Income | $ 107 |
>
> **Balance Sheet**
>
> | | | | |
> |---|---|---|---|
> | Cash | $ 100 | Payables | $ 50 |
> | Receivables | 300 | Notes (at 12%) | 150 |
> | Inventory | 200 | Bonds (at 10%) | 200 |
> | Total Assets | $ 1,000 | Total Liab. & Equity | $ 1,000 |
>
> To generate the percentage-of-sales forecast, the following assumptions are made (all numbers are in thousands):
>
> - Sales will increase by 10% to $2,200 in the year 2002.
> - Cost of goods sold, selling and administrative expenses, payables and operating current assets and liabilities (receivables, inventory and payables) are a constant percentage of sales.
> - Cash balance is derived from the cash flow statement.
> - Additional fixed assets in the amount of $100 will be purchased.
> - Depreciation will be $50.
> - Notes will be reduced to $100 at the beginning of the year.
> - Dividends will be $24.

(Continued)

- Comparing the projected ending cash balance with the company's target cash balance and adjusting the pro forma statements to fund any shortfall or apply any surplus cash

D. Statistical Forecasting

Statistical forecasts project cash flows in two ways:

- Through extrapolation, where past trends are identified and used to determine future values of cash flows

- By determining the relationship (correlation) between a predicted cash flow or cash flow component (dependent variable) and other known cash flow components (independent variables or determinants)

Statistical forecasting is particularly applicable to projections requiring analysis of extensive data and it is useful for identifying and analyzing trends.

> **Exhibit 11.3** Forecasting with Pro Forma Financial Statements (Continued)
>
> **Projected Income Statement (in thousands) — Year Ending December 31, 2002**
>
> | | | |
> |---|---|---|
> | Sales | $ 2,200 | |
> | Cost of Good Sold | (1,650) | [75% of Sales] |
> | Selling & Admin. Expense | (220) | [10% of Sales] |
> | Depreciation | (50) | |
> | Interest Expense | (32) | [.12 × 100 + .10 × 200] |
> | Income Before Taxes | 248 | |
> | Taxes | (84) | [34% Tax Rate] |
> | Net Income | $ 164 | |
> | Dividends | (24) | |
> | Retained Earnings | $ 140 | |
>
> **Projected Balance Sheet (in thousands) — Year Ending December 31, 2002**
>
> | | | | |
> |---|---|---|---|
> | Cash (From Cash Flow Statement) | $ 95 | Payables (2.5% of Sales) | $ 55 |
> | Receivables (15% of Sales) | 330 | Notes | 100 |
> | Inventory (10% of Sales) | 220 | Bonds | 200 |
> | Net Fixed Assets (NFA) (Prior NFA + New Fixed Assets – Depreciation) ($400 + $100 – $50) | 450 | Common Equity (Prior Common Equity + Retained Earnings) ($600 + $140) | 740 |
> | Total Assets | $ 1,095 | Total Lib. & Equity | $ 1,095 |
>
> All of the projected account balances except cash are calculated based upon the given assumptions. The ending cash balance is determined by evalutating the impact on cash of the income statement activity and balance sheet changes and adjusting the beginning cash balance accordingly. (This procedure is described in Chapter 2, Section 1, D, 4 "Statement of Cash Flows.")

(Continued)

Two of the more common techniques of statistical analysis are:

1. **Time Series Forecasting** — A time series model seeks to forecast a variable based on past observations of that variable. The primary types of time series forecasting applicable to cash forecasting are discussed on the next page.

    • *Simple Moving Average* — Simple moving averages base a forecast on a rolling or moving average of past historical values. A forecast prepared using a simple moving average will always lag any trend in the actual cash flow. Choice of the appropriate number of observations is important to the usefulness of this model. The longer the time period over which the moving average

> **Exhibit 11.3** Forecasting with Pro Forma Financial Statements (Continued)
>
> **Projected Statement of Cash Flows (in thousands) — Year ending December 31, 2002**
>
> | | | |
> |---|---:|---:|
> | Beginning Cash | | $100 |
> | **Cash Flows from Operating Activities** | | |
> | Net Income | $164 | |
> | Adjustments to reconcile net income to cash | | |
> | Depreciation | 50 | |
> | Increase in Accounts Receivable | (30) | |
> | Increase in Inventory | (20) | |
> | Increase in Accounts Payable | 5 | |
> | Net Cash Provided (Used) in Operating Activities | | 169 |
> | **Cash Flows from Investing Activities** | | |
> | Purchase of Fixed Assets | | (100) |
> | **Cash Flows from Financing Activities** | | |
> | Net Repayment on Debt | (50) | |
> | Dividends Paid | (24) | |
> | Net Cash Provided (Used) by Financing Activities | | (74) |
> | Ending Cash Balance | | 95 |
>
> If the projected ending cash balance is less than the company's established target balance, the shortfall must be funded through taking on additional debt, issuing equity or selling assets. Conversely, if the projected cash balance exceeds the target, the surplus may be invested in additional assets, used to reduce debt and/or distributed to shareholders. In the above example, if the target cash balance were $110, then $15 in additional cash would need to be raised. If this were accomplished through an increase in notes payable, then the December 31, 2002, balance sheet would appear as before, except that cash would be $110 and notes payable would be $115.

is calculated, the greater the smoothing of individual data point variances; the shorter the time period, the less the smoothing of individual data point variances. Exhibit 11.4 shows how to calculate a five-day moving average.

- *Exponential Smoothing* — Exponential smoothing is a variation of a simple moving average. The exponential smoothing technique uses the previous forecast value, the most recent actual value and a user-determined value known as the smoothing constant. This smoothing constant is typically designated as "α" (referred to as alpha) and may range between 0 and 1. Setting α closer to 1 will result in more weight being placed on the most recent actual value and correspondingly less weight on the forecast value for the current period, resulting in less smoothing of the series.

The forecaster must determine how much smoothing is required and choose the smoothing constant, α, accordingly. Note, α value of a can be estimated

Exhibit 11.4 Forecast with Simple Moving Averages and Exponential Smoothing

	Moving Average Forecast			Forecast with Exponential Smoothing	
Day	Actual Cash Flow (X_t)	Forecast (N = 5)	Error (α = .4)	Forecast	Error
1	$110,000				
2	120,000				
3	115,000				
4	122,000				
5	126,000				
6	124,000	$118,600	$5,400	$118,600	$5,400
7	129,000	121,400	7,600	120,760	8,240
8	133,000	123,200	9,800	124,056	8,944
9	132,000	126,800	5,200	127,634	4,366

Moving Average Forecast
Moving Average Forecast for Day 6 is:
($110,000 + 120,000 + 115,000 + 122,000 + 126,000)/5 = $118,600
Which results in a forecast error of $124,000 − 118,600 = $5,400

Exponential Smoothing Forecast
The exponential smoothing forecast begins with the Day 6 forecast of
$118,600 based on the moving average forecast.
Then, the Day 7 forecast using exponential smoothing is:
.4 [$124,000] + (1 − 0.4) [$118,600] = $120,760
This results in a forecast error of $8,240 ($129,000 − $120,760 = $8,240).

statistically from historical data. Exhibit 11.4 provides an example of exponential smoothing based on the relationships developed in the following:

Next Period Forecast = α [Current Period Actual] + (1 − α) [Current Period Forecast]

This formula can be expressed more formally as:

$$F_{t+1} = \alpha X_t + (1 - \alpha) F_t$$

Where:
- F_{t+1} = Cash flow forecast for the next period (t + 1)
- F_t = Cash flow forecast for the current period (t)
- α = Smoothing constant ($0 \leq \alpha \leq 1$)
- X_t = Actual cash flow for the current period (t)

As in the simple moving average forecast, a simple exponential smoothing forecast will lag trends in the data. To correct for this and to allow for seasonality in the forecast, more complex extensions of exponential smoothing allow the user to incorporate these factors.

2. **Regression Analysis** — Regression analysis is a statistical technique that systematically identifies the relationship between the variable being predicted (the dependent variable) and selected or appropriate explanatory or independent variables. Though there are many forms of regression analysis, the most basic is a simple linear regression model. This approach essentially determines a line that best represents the relationship between a single dependent variable and a single explanatory variable. Regression analyses (especially the more complex types) are most often done using a computer program that determines the relationship between the variables in question through a series of mathematical algorithms and that can also display the relationship in a graphic format.

Test Your Understanding

These chapter questions are provided to test your understanding of the information in the text and are not examples of CCM examination questions, nor are they in the examination format.

Answers can be found at the back of the book on pages 530-531.

1. What are the objectives of cash forecasting?

2. Describe the major steps involved in the forecasting process.

3. What are the two major short-term forecasting methods?

4. One long-term forecasting method is the use of pro-forma statements. What is the technique that is used to prepare a pro-forma statement?

5. Outline the primary types of time series forecasting.

6. The following cash flow information is provided:

Day	Cash Flow
1	$ 100
2	$ 150
3	$ 250
4	$ 210

    What is the four-day moving average forecast for Day 5?

7. What is the advantage of exponential smoothing vs. the simple moving average forecast?

8. What are the steps in selecting a forecasting method?

9. Discuss the different types of forecast validation.

10. Define regression analysis.

11. What is a distribution forecast and how can it be calculated?

12. Explain the function of "α" in the exponential smoothing forecast approach.

CHAPTER 12

Investing

Overview

This chapter explains why companies hold short-term investments and how they determine and carry out investment policies. It presents the characteristics of various short-term financial instruments — the returns they offer, their risks and the fundamentals of different short-term investment strategies. Though selected long-term investment instruments will be discussed, the primary focus of the chapter is on short-term investing.

A financial instrument or security evidences a transaction between two parties. To one party it represents an investment; to the other, an obligation or liability. This chapter discusses financial instruments from the investor's point of view (as assets). Chapter 13, Borrowing, discusses financial instruments from the borrower's perspective (as liabilities).

Learning Objectives

Upon completion of this chapter and the related study questions, the reader should know:

- Why companies hold short-term investments
- How companies assign authority and responsibility for short-term investments
- How companies typically determine investment policies
- Factors influencing short-term investment yields
- The most frequently issued short-term government, agency, municipal, bank and corporate short-term investment instruments
- How prices are quoted for short-term investment instruments and how yields are calculated according to money market, bond-equivalent and effective annual yield quoting conventions

- The basic term structure of interest rates and how yield curves can change under different market environments
- The differences between active and passive short-term investment strategies and specific strategies such as matching, riding the yield curve and dividend capture

Key Concepts

- Short-term investments
- Liquidity and marketability
- Money and capital markets
- Yield
- Term structure of interest rates
- Short-term investment strategy

Outline

I. Introduction

II. Why Companies Hold Short-Term Investments
    A. Liquidity
    B. Temporary Surplus Funds
    C. Income Generation

III. Investment Issues and Corporate Policies
    A. Short-Term Investment Objectives
    B. Responsibilities for Short-Term Investment Policies
    C. Factors that Influence Short-Term Investment Policies
    D. Instrument and Portfolio Characteristics and Attributes
    E. Investment Management
    F. Performance Measurement
    G. Safekeeping

IV. Markets for Financial Instruments
    A. Money Market (Short-Term Financial Instruments)
    B. Capital Market (Long-Term Financial Instruments)

V. Financial Instruments
    A. U.S. Treasury Securities
    B. Agency Securities
    C. Municipal Obligations
    D. Bank Financial Instruments
    E. Corporate Obligations
    F. Money Market Mutual Funds
    G. Other Types of Short-Term Investments

VI. Yield
    A. Factors that Influence Yields
    B. Basic Yield Definitions
    C. Yield Quoting Conventions
    D. Yield Calculations
    E. Duration
    F. The Yield Curve

VII. Investment Strategies
    A. Replicate an Index or Market
    B. Outsource Investment Management
    C. Match Maturities to Funds Needs
    D. Ride the Yield Curve
    E. Dividend Capture
    F. Hedge Short-Term Investments

I. Introduction

Ensuring corporate liquidity, meaning the ease with which assets can be converted into cash without material loss, is a key objective of successful cash management.

Companies need cash to meet their ongoing obligations in a timely manner. However, the opportunity cost of holding cash in checking accounts can be significant. In order to minimize foregone interest income, companies invest actively in readily marketable, interest-earning securities that have a stable market value.

A company will quickly become insolvent if it is not liquid (i.e., if it does not have sufficient resources to meet its day-to-day obligations). A company's short-term investment strategy should facilitate reducing the cost of maintaining ample liquidity while increasing interest income. Though some topics related to long-term investments will be covered in this chapter, long-term investments are not generally the concern of the cash manager.

II. Why Companies Hold Short-Term Investments

Companies generally hold short-term investments, which are defined as those that mature in a year or less, for three main reasons:

A. Liquidity

Reserve liquidity is the primary reason companies invest in short-term securities. Companies cannot always depend on sufficient cash inflows during a period to cover that period's financial obligations. A portfolio of short-term investments can help adjust working capital imbalances and it may be used in conjunction with short-term borrowing.

B. Temporary Surplus Funds

From time to time, a company may receive cash for which it has no immediate use. This can come from a variety of sources, including:

1. **Ongoing Operations** — A company may gradually accumulate excess cash from positive operating cash flow.

2. **Seasonal Performance** — A company, such as a retail outlet during the holiday season, may generate a large proportion of its cash in one period of time. It will need those funds to finance its operations over the rest of the year.

3. **Asset Sales** — A company may sell assets and have no immediate use for the proceeds.

4. **Securities Issuance** — The amount and timing of equity and debt offerings are often determined by economic factors other than a company's short-to medium-term financial requirement. The timing of such issues is determined not only by corporate need, but also by financial market conditions. When interest rates are low, it is advantageous for companies to issue debt instruments. When equity prices are considered to be high, companies are more likely to sell stock. Proceeds from securities offerings often exceed a company's immediate cash needs and may be invested in short-term securities.

C. Income Generation

Companies may also invest in short-term financial instruments to generate income as opposed to leaving the money in non-earning deposit accounts from time to time. A variety of instruments offer both safety and yield. Companies should manage their short-term investments prudently and in a manner consistent with their policies governing risks and expected investment returns. Looking at short-term investment management as a profit center is generally not viewed as good financial management for a company. In most cases, a company's long-term cost of capital (as measured by its weighted average cost of capital — see Chapter 2, Financial Accounting and Related Concepts) is much greater than the rate that can be earned on a short-term investment portfolio.

III. Investment Issues and Corporate Policies

A company failing to manage cash properly can incur high costs for working capital and forego the potential revenues that short-term securities can yield. It can lose significant amounts through making poor investment choices, assuming unnecessary risks, assigning investment responsibilities to unqualified personnel or failing to implement effective cash management practices.

To address these issues and to meet its overall short-term investment objectives, a company should implement a clearly defined and written investment policy. Such a policy should not only put forth criteria for instrument suitability and portfolio configuration, but also delineate specific individual responsibilities for making policy, implementing it on a day-to-day basis and reviewing and auditing investment performance. This is important whether the company manages its own short-term investment portfolio or outsources it to a third-party investment manager or money market mutual fund. The policy statement should also provide for its own periodic review.

In most cases, long-term investment portfolios and related policies are outside the scope of cash management. However, some cash managers are finding that the management of the pension fund assets and portfolios related to self-insurance and risk management are coming under their area of responsibility. This topic will be briefly covered later in this chapter.

A company's short-term investment policy is indicative of its tolerance for risk. An investment policy must address several key issues, including the following:

- Requirements governing security selection and portfolio configuration
- Management responsibilities and authority vìs-a-vìs short-term investment activity
- Financial controls
- Performance measurement

A. Short-Term Investment Objectives

A company conducts its short-term investment activity to meet several objectives:

1. **Preservation of Principal** — This is the guiding principle most companies follow in choosing among short-term investment alternatives. Some degree of risk is inherent in all investments. Those that offer higher returns usually carry greater risks. Ensuring against loss involves controlling risk, as follows:

    - Identifying risks to which various investment alternatives are subject
    - Determining the relationships between security risks and the financial returns they offer
    - Choosing instruments that offer both income and safety of principal

2. **Liquidity Management** — Holding a portfolio of short-term instruments is one way companies enhance liquidity. Unused borrowing capacity is another.

3. **Investment Return and Risk** — Companies seek to maximize returns from short-term investments, but the risks and returns different companies consider acceptable can vary depending on factors such as risk tolerance, earnings predictability, investment size, industry practice and resources available for selecting and monitoring their short-term investments. While longer-term investments often carry higher returns, they are likely to be more volatile than short-term financial instruments.

B. Responsibilities for Short-Term Investment Policies

Delineating responsibilities for short-term investment involves the following:

1. **Setting Policy** — A company's short-term investment policy should identify those who are ultimately responsible for such matters. In most companies, the board of directors or a designated committee of the board determines and monitors overall investment policy.

2. **Implementation** — The treasurer, cash manager, their staffs or an internal or external specialized investment manager or managers may all be involved in implementing a company's investment policy. The responsibilities of each individual or group of individuals involved must be clearly delineated.

3. **Periodic Review Process** — The short-term investment policy must be reviewed and updated on a regular basis by the board of directors or designated committee. This ensures the policies are in line with the changing needs of the company.

C. Factors that Influence Short-Term Investment Policies

Companies' short-term investment policies and decisions regarding them are influenced by factors such as:

1. **Purpose** — Different companies emphasize somewhat different objectives for short-term investments. Some stress liquidity preservation; others stress income generation.

2. **Maturity and Segmentation** — A portion of a company's short-term investment portfolio may be required at all times as a liquidity reserve, while other portions may be designated for less immediate use. The maturity profile should reflect capital spending plans and cash flow forecasts. One approach to investment management is to match the maturity of short-term investments to the need for cash.

3. **Tax Status** — A company must consider the tax implications of its investment decisions. Its effective tax rate determines the after-tax return from taxable investments and the advantage offered by tax-exempt alternatives.

4. **Resources** — Carrying out an active internally managed short-term investment program requires resources, including staff and systems. Alternatively, a company may find it more cost effective to use an outside investment management company or to utilize money market mutual funds.

5. **Investment Restrictions** — Laws, industry guidelines, internal corporate policies and covenants to loans or debt instruments can restrict short-term investment choices.

6. **Reporting Requirements** — Financial Accounting Standard 65 (FAS 65) requires that securities maturing within 90 days be listed as cash and cash equivalents on corporate balance sheets. Those investments that have maturities greater than 90 days are listed as marketable investments.

A company may report additional information on certain types of short-term investments on its balance sheet to satisfy the requirements of shareholders, creditors or industry regulators.

D. Instrument and Portfolio Characteristics and Attributes

A comprehensive investment policy must also address the types of securities or financial instruments a company considers appropriate, any limits to their use or proportion in the portfolio and requirements for the portfolio's overall diversification.

1. **Acceptable Instruments** — Typically, a company will specify the types of securities that are acceptable investments in terms of their characteristics.

    - *Maturity* — Most financial instruments other than money market funds have a maturity date on which the obligation they represent is settled. Original maturities vary from overnight to many years in the future. Interest rate movements affect the prices of all securities and the prices of fixed-income securities move inversely to changes in interest rates. The longer a security's term to maturity, the greater its price variation as interest rates change.

    - *Credit Quality* — The credit quality of the security is a measure of the default risk of the issue. Most securities other than U.S. Treasuries are rated as discussed below. Some securities are also credit enhanced by the use of a standby letter of credit or backup line of credit.

        — Rated Securities — The credit quality of many instruments can be determined by ratings assigned by credit rating agencies. There are rating systems for corporate bonds, bank issues, banks, municipal obligations, commercial paper, certain types of preferred stock and money market funds.

        — Unrated Securities — With some securities, such as unrated commercial paper or loan participations, the investor must analyze and evaluate the credit quality of the borrower.

        — Credit Enhanced Securities — If a financial intermediary provides support or credit enhancement by issuing an instrument such as a standby letter of credit to guarantee the obligation of the borrower, the obligation then assumes the credit rating of the institution providing the credit enhancement.

> **Exhibit 12.1** Selected Short-Term Credit Rating Agencies
>
> **Moody's Ratings**
> Prime-1 (P1)   Superior ability for short-term debt repayment
> Prime-2 (P2)   Strong ability for short-term debt repayment
> Prime-3 (P3)   Acceptable ability for short-term debt repayment
> Not Prime   Rated below the first three categories
>
> **Standard & Poor's Ratings**
> A-1+   Top degree of safety for short-term debt repayment
> A-1   Strong degree of safety for short-term debt repayment
> A-2   High degree of safety for short-term debt repayment
> A-3   Acceptable degree of safety for short-term debt repayment

Exhibit 12.1 contains examples of the different ratings that selected rating agencies assign to short-term financial instruments.

- *Marketability* — Securities that can be sold in large volumes quickly and without substantial price concessions are a primary source of corporate liquidity. A large, active secondary market for a security ensures its marketability. Securities for which secondary markets are not active are less liquid. To compensate investors, instruments with less liquidity often carry higher yields.

2. **Diversification** — The risk inherent in a portfolio differs from the average risk of the securities that make up the portfolio. Proper diversification reduces portfolio risk.

    Investment policies can set minimum requirements for, or limits on, various types and categories of securities. Requirements can be stated in terms of maturities or other instrument characteristics, such as issuance by a particular entity (for example, the U.S. Treasury) or by rating classification. An investment policy may express limits in dollar amounts or in terms of portfolio proportion. For example, a company's policy might limit investment in any one money market fund to $10 million and stipulate that 25 percent of its short-term investment portfolio consists of U.S. Treasury obligations maturing in three months or less.

3. **Acceptable Dealers and/or Issuers** — Accredited securities dealers such as those belonging to the National Association of Securities Dealers (NASD) or accredited banks and other financial institutions are typically less likely to buy or sell securities of questionable or indeterminate value.

4. **Investment Authority** — A policy should clearly state the size and types of transactions in which company officials can engage. For example, investment in banker's acceptances (BAs) might be limited to 40 percent of the portfolio or com-

mercial paper might be limited to $2 million per issuer with total holdings limited to 50 percent of the portfolio.

5. **Custody Requirements** — Physical securities purchased by a company are typically delivered against payment in accounts at financial institutions where the securities were purchased or other institutions selected for that purpose. The policy should specify an authorized custodian.

E. Investment Management

A company has alternatives for managing short-term investments. Whether to handle short-term investments internally or externally depends on the size of the company's investment portfolio, investment objectives and policies.

1. **Internal** — A company can manage its short-term investments using its own staff exclusively.

2. **External** — A company can hire an investment management company, a bank or a financial advisory service to manage or assist in managing its short-term investments.

F. Performance Measurement

Portfolio performance should be measured using an appropriate benchmark, or basis of comparison that allows for equitable and meaningful assessment. Typically, short-term investment portfolios are measured in comparison with the return of U.S. Treasury instruments, the Fed funds rate (the rate the Fed sets for overnight bank borrowing), an index rate for commercial paper or the London Interbank Offered Rate (LIBOR). LIBOR is the interest rate used on interbank Eurodollar borrowings and is often used as a rate basis for different types of commercial borrowing.

In any case, a portfolio's performance is typically stated in basis points (a basis point is 1/100 of one percent, or .0001) over or under the benchmark for the interval of time being measured. For example, a portfolio of short-term investments might return 20 basis points under high-grade corporate commercial paper or five basis points above three-month U.S. Treasuries over a specified time period. Benchmarks should also be used to evaluate outside portfolio managers or the performance of money market mutual funds.

G. Safekeeping

Safekeeping banks can provide the institution or organization with added expertise, without the costs of developing and maintaining an in-house investment staff. The safekeeping bank acts as an agent to hold stock certificates or bonds, tracks trades and provides periodic reports. The safekeeping bank can give the institution/organization an international presence through worldwide banking affiliates. Safekeeping banks can be an integral part of a cash management system.

IV. Markets for Financial Instruments

The market for debt and equity instruments has two major components: 1) the money market, on which short-term fixed-income or debt securities trade and 2) the capital market, which is where longer-term instruments, stocks and bonds trade. Generally, cash managers concern themselves with the money market. Cash managers have numerous resources available, including the Internet, for securities research and dealing.

A. Money Market (Short-Term Financial Instruments)

Rather than a single integrated entity or a particular exchange, the money market is a group of markets on which debt instruments that mature in a year or less are traded. Money market securities include Treasury bills, federal agency securities, municipal obligations, commercial paper, banker's acceptances, negotiable certificates of deposit, loans to securities dealers and repurchase agreements (repos).

The major direct participants in the money market are U.S. and foreign government securities dealers (some of which are large diversified financial institutions), commercial paper dealers, banker's acceptance dealers and money market brokers specializing in various short-term instruments.

B. Capital Market (Long-Term Financial Instruments)

The term capital market refers to the exchanges where long-term debt and equity instruments are bought and sold and also refers to the dealers involved. There are two types of long-term debt instruments: 1) notes, which mature in less than 10 years and 2) bonds, which mature in 10 years or more. Equity instruments are stocks, the most conventional of which are common and preferred issues. The major U.S. exchanges are the New York Stock Exchange (NYSE), the American Stock Exchange (AMEX) and the National Association of Stock Dealers Automated Quotations (NASDAQ).

While treasury managers in many companies do not invest extensively in long-term securities, treasury managers should concern themselves with the capital market for the following reasons:

1. Capital market developments may affect the money market (i.e., interest rate fluctuations).

2. Even though companies do not often invest in long-term securities, bonds maturing within a year or preferred stock may be suitable for some companies' short-term portfolios.

3. Evaluation of a company's long-term securities can help ascertain the creditworthiness of that company and the overall risk profile for all the securities it issues, including its short-term instruments.

4. There are some instances (especially in not-for-profits and government entities) where the short-term investment manager may have to match cash flow needs beyond a one-year horizon.

5. In some companies or organizations, the treasury manager must manage or oversee long-term portfolios related to pension funds or risk management.

V. Financial Instruments

Short-term securities in which companies typically invest reflect widely differing credit quality, yields, maturities and marketability. Long-term securities will be discussed only in the context that they relate to use in treasury.

Almost all short-term securities are fixed-income securities and are issued in registered form; they are typically placed in the name of the investor or held in the street name (the name of the broker/dealer through which they were purchased). Only the owner or his legal agent can collect interest and principal payments or sell the securities. Historically, short-term instruments have also been issued in bearer form. In this case, the name of the investor is not recorded upon issuance and the holder of the security is entitled to interest and/or principal payments or to sell the instrument. Bearer instruments are increasingly rare.

Many of the short-term investment instruments discussed below (primarily short-term government notes and commercial paper) are discount-type securities, meaning the investor pays less than the face value at the time of purchase and receives the full face value at maturity. These types of instruments generally do not have any interim interest or coupon payments. Many short-term bank investments such as certificates of deposit and longer-term bonds are interest-bearing securities that have a payment stream composed of both interim interest and coupon payments, along with the repayment of principal at maturity.

A. U.S. Treasury Securities

U.S. Treasury securities are instruments the U.S. government issues to finance its activities. The U.S. government issues large amounts of debt securities that appeal to a broad spectrum of investors. The market for U.S. Treasury securities is the largest and most actively traded in the world.

U.S. Treasury securities are considered risk-free with respect to default. They are virtually the only securities issued in the world to enjoy this reputation and they serve as a benchmark for other financial instruments. The interest rates as determined by the market for U.S. Treasury instruments are used as a reference point and market indicator. Many other securities (and loans) have yields established as a spread over a similar-term Treasury instrument.

Typically, U.S. Treasuries account for the safest portion of a company's portfolio of short-term financial instruments.

1. **Characteristics** — Characteristics of U.S. Treasuries and the markets on which they trade are known to all participants in financial markets worldwide. They include:

   - *Issuance Through Auctions* — Virtually all primary Treasury offerings are sold at a type of auction known as a Dutch auction. A Dutch auction is a process whereby the price of a security is lowered (yield increased) until it prompts a responsive bid, whereupon the security is sold. When a Treasury instrument is to be offered, the Treasury officially invites bids. Eligible banks, broker/dealers and other private and governmental entities tender bids for specific amounts of securities at specific yields. The securities go to the bidders offering the highest prices (i.e., lowest yield/interest cost to the Treasury).

   - *Registered Form of Issue* — Treasury securities are registered and issued in book entry form. Securities certificates do not physically move when they are traded. Book entries are made when ownership changes. Treasury securities may be held either directly with the U.S. Treasury or through the commercial book entry system where the securities are held by a financial institution, government securities broker or dealer.

   - *Marketability and Liquidity* — The secondary market for U.S. Treasury securities is enormous and has low transaction costs. Participants can readily and efficiently buy and sell significant volumes with negligible (if any) impact on market prices.

   - *Value Retention* — U.S. Treasuries are backed by the full faith and credit of the U.S. government. Because of this, they are considered to be free from default risk.

- *Partial Tax Exemption* — Interest income on Treasuries is exempt from state income tax. However, some states do charge corporations a franchise tax from which U.S. Treasury securities are not exempt.

- *Widely Regarded Yields* — Yields on U.S. Treasury securities are generally the standard against which rates and prices in the other fixed income securities markets are compared. Other investment alternatives generally trade at yields above those of government securities, reflecting their perceived relative default risk.

2. **Types of U.S. Treasury Securities** — In its financing operations, the U.S. Treasury issues the following types of securities:

    - *Treasury Bills (T-Bills)* — T-bills are the most liquid securities in the money market because of the volumes issued, their credit quality and their short maturities. They are issued each week on a discount basis in maturities of less than one year (typically 13 or 26 weeks). T-bills are available in a minimum denomination of $1,000 with additional amounts in multiples of $1,000, but are generally traded in round lots of $1,000,000. The discount rate on T-bills is quoted in annualized terms.

    - *Treasury Notes (T-Notes)* — T-notes are issued with original maturities of between one and 10 years. The minimum denomination for T-notes is $1,000 with additional amounts in multiples of $1,000. As in the case of T-bills, T-notes are usually traded in round lots of $1,000,000. T-notes are interest-bearing securities on which interest is paid semiannually. Interest is calculated on the actual number of elapsed days using a 365-day year.

    - *Treasury Bonds (T-Bonds)* — T-bonds are similar to T-notes, but with original maturities of greater than 10 years.

    - *Inflation-Indexed Securities* — The U.S. Treasury offers two kinds of notes and bonds: fixed principal and inflation indexed. Both pay interest twice a year, but the principal value of inflation-indexed securities is adjusted to reflect inflation as measured by the consumer price index (CPI). With inflation indexed notes and bonds, the semiannual interest payments and maturity payment are calculated based on the inflation-adjusted principal value of the security.

3. **Money Market Treasury Funds** — An alternate means to investing in U.S. Treasury securities is to invest in money market funds that carry the same credit quality given to obligations of the U.S. government because they are made up exclusively or principally of U.S. Treasury securities.

B. Agency Securities

Another type of investment instrument (commonly referred to as agency issues) has some degree of federal government backing, although few are issued by federal government agencies. In a few cases, such as securities issued by the Government National Mortgage Association (Ginnie Mae) and the Department of Veterans Affairs (VA), the securities are, in effect, backed by the full faith and credit of the U.S. government. In most cases, such as the mortgage-backed securities (MBSs) issued by the Federal National Mortgage Association (Fannie Mae) and Freddie Mac (formerly the Federal Home Loan Mortgage Corporation), the securities are backed by the strength of the corporation, though there is a strong implication that in a crisis the federal government would intervene to help repay investors.

1. **Characteristics**

    - *Liquidity and Yield* — Although the amount of outstanding agency issues is smaller than Treasuries, the liquidity of most agencies compares favorably with other money market instruments. Agencies usually trade at higher yields than Treasuries of the same maturity.

    - *Low Credit Risk* — While credit risk exists, the market tends to view it as minimal.

    - *Limited Tax Exposure* — Interest income on many agency issues is exempt from state and local income taxes but not state franchise taxes.

    - *Re-Investment Risk* — Mortgage-backed securities are particularly susceptible to re-investment risk. Since MBS-type investments are essentially bundles of mortgages, their payment stream is impacted by mortgages in that package being refinanced. Generally, if interest rates fall, homeowners tend to refinance their mortgages to take advantage of the lower rates. As mortgages backing an MBS are paid off due to refinancing, the proceeds are distributed to the MBS investors. The investors now have unexpected cash flows that must be re-invested, possibly at a lower than expected interest rate (remember, the falling interest rates that benefit the homeowner will hurt the investor).

2. **Issuers**

    - *Housing-Related Organizations* — Fannie Mae and Freddie Mac were originally government agencies but now are private, shareholder-owned companies often referred to as government-sponsored enterprises (GSEs). Both can borrow from the U.S. Treasury. They purchase mortgages from lenders and package them into MBSs. Ginnie Mae is part of the Department of Housing and Urban Development (HUD). It creates MBSs and other securities that it guarantees for timely payment of principal and interest with the full faith and credit of the U.S. government. The VA securitizes certain real estate loans, the "Vinnie Macs," which are also backed by the full faith and credit of the federal government.

The Federal Home Loan Bank (FHLB) System, a GSE, is the largest issuer of private debt in the world. It funds its activities through a variety of debt products called consolidated obligations (COs), which are typically AAA rated by Standard & Poor's and Moody's.

The other federal housing corporations are the Financial Assistance Corporation and the Resolution Funds Corporation.

- *Agricultural Corporations* — There are four agricultural GSEs that issue high-quality debt. The cooperatively owned Federal Farm Credit Banks Funding Corporation raises capital for the 225 lending institutions in the Farm Credit System through the sale of systemwide bonds and notes. These are insured by the Farm Credit System Insurance Corporation. The federal Farm Credit Administration is the regulator of the banks, the Funding Corporation and the Insurance Corporation.

  The CoBank (Central Bank for Cooperatives) and district Banks for Cooperatives issue debt to make funds available to agricultural cooperatives. The Federal Agricultural Mortgage Corporation (Farmer Mac) provides a secondary market for agricultural loans and rural real estate and home mortgages.

- *Sallie Mae* — Founded as a federally chartered, shareholder-owned company, Sallie Mae was reorganized in 1997 as SLM Holding Corporation (SLMHC), a private Delaware corporation. Though not considered a GSE, SLMHC still conducts most of its student loan financing activities through the Student Loan Marketing Association, a wholly owned subsidiary, which is a GSE. The GSE funds its operations through issuance of debt securities, which are considered agency securities. Sallie Mae uses the proceeds to purchase college loans that are insured by guaranty agencies and re-insured by the federal government.

- *Other Government Corporations* — There are more than 20 other government corporations, such as the Tennessee Valley Authority, that issue highly rated debt obligations.

C. Municipal Obligations

Municipal obligations are debt instruments issued by state and local governments or their agencies. State and local government agencies include school districts, housing authorities, sewer districts, municipally owned utilities and authorities running toll roads, bridges and other transportation facilities. These securities may be insured by private insurance companies, which will enhance the credit rating.

1. **Notes and Bonds** — Municipalities generally issue notes or bonds, many of which are exempt from various state and local income taxes as well as federal income tax.

    - *Notes* — Municipal notes, also known as anticipation notes, are municipal debt instruments with an original maturity of two years or less. These notes are usually issued to help overcome a temporary cash shortage in anticipation of forthcoming revenues.

- *Bonds* — Most municipal obligations are long-term bonds. State and local governments generally sell long-term bonds to finance the construction of schools, housing, pollution-control facilities, roads, bridges and other capital projects. A secondary market for municipal bonds exists but is not as active as the market for newly issued municipal bonds.

2. **Types of Securities** — Municipal securities fall into three broad categories. These are:

   - *General Obligation Securities* — General obligation securities have the full faith, credit and taxing power of the issuing entity securing the payment of principal and interest. This usually means that the securities are backed by all of the issuer's resources and its authority to levy taxes.

   - *Certificates of Participation (COPs)* — COPs are securities used by municipal issuers to finance certain equipment purchases and capital projects. In most cases, the equipment or project assets are pledged as security for the issue.

   - *Revenue Securities* — Payments of interest and principal on revenue securities are made from specific sources such as tolls, user fees or rents paid by those who use the facilities financed by the proceeds of the security issue. Sometimes they are enhanced by letters of credit or other guarantees.

D. Bank Financial Instruments

Domestic and foreign banks issue short-term certificates of deposit (CDs), time deposits and banker's acceptances. Typically they all offer higher yields than Treasuries.

1. **Certificates of Deposit**
   - *Retail CDs* — Retail CDs are interest-bearing deposits that financial institutions in the United States offer, with original maturities ranging from seven days to several years. These are also referred to as domestic CDs and generally have maturities of less than one year. They require a minimum investment of $100,000, but are usually traded in $1,000,000 units. Since most retail CDs that companies hold are negotiable, there is a secondary market for these instruments. There is a wide variety in types of CDs. The basic ones are:

     — *Fixed-Rate CDs* — The interest rate is established at the time of issue. Interest is paid periodically over the term or at maturity.

     — *Floating (Variable) Rate CDs* — Interest is adjusted periodically as rates change.

For example, on six-month floating-rate CDs, interest is paid and the rate is reset every 30 days. Floating-rate CDs with maturities of one year or longer may pay interest and reset rates every three months. The rate is expressed as a spread (percentage and/or basis points) over a widely used index rate such as the 90-day T-bill, Fed funds or LIBOR.

- *Yankee CDs* — Yankee CDs are U.S. dollar-denominated CDs issued by foreign banks through their branches in the U.S. market.

- *Eurodollar CDs* — Eurodollar CDs are U.S. dollar-denominated CDs issued by banks outside the United States Although the primary issuers are European banks, Eurodollar CDs may be issued by any bank located outside of the United States, including foreign branches of U.S. banks. Original maturities are usually less than two years, although most have maturities of six months or less. Eurodollar CDs are negotiable and there is a large secondary market. Eurodollar CDs offer marginally higher yields than domestic CDs because they are slightly less liquid and entail higher risk. The risk derives from the fact that they are not subject to U.S. banking regulations.

2. **Eurodollar Time Deposits** — Eurodollar time deposits are non-negotiable, fixed-rate time deposits issued by banks outside the United States, with maturities ranging from overnight to several years. Most have maturities in six months or less. Because they are subject to foreign risk, they offer higher yields than comparable domestic time deposits.

3. **Banker's Acceptance** — A BA is a negotiable short-term instrument used primarily to finance the import, export or domestic shipment of goods or the storage of readily marketable commodities. The debt obligation on the part of the bank is evidenced by a time draft drawn by the borrower that is then accepted by the bank on which it is drawn. By accepting the draft, the bank becomes directly obligated for payment of the draft on the maturity date. By substituting its own credit for that of the borrower, the bank creates a readily marketable instrument that can be discounted in the money market. (See Chapter 13, Borrowing and Chapter 15, International Treasury Management.)

4. **Bank Notes** — Bank notes represent unsecured or subordinated debt of the bank. Corporate cash investors buy them because they may offer yields competitive with similarly rated commercial paper, but they offer the additional advantage of being direct obligations of the bank, rather than of a bank holding company. However, they do not carry federal deposit insurance.

E. Corporate Obligations

Several types of corporate debt and equity obligations are suitable for short-term investment portfolios.

1. **Commercial Paper** — Commercial paper (CP) is an unsecured promissory note issued by a corporation for a specific amount to mature in 270 days or less.

    - CP may be interest bearing or discounted; it is usually discounted.

    - Issuers sell CP directly to investors or through dealers. Dealers include securities companies and commercial banks.

    - The issuer's obligation may be backed by a standby letter of credit, which is similar to a guarantee from a bank, or a bond issued by an insurance company with a high credit rating.

    - CP is rated by credit rating agencies based on attributes such as liquidity, cash flow potential, earning trends, position in the industry, quality of management and backup credit facilities.

    - Some dealers also sell unrated CP. These unrated issues carry substantially higher yields to compensate investors for the greater credit risk they incur.

    - Some commercial paper is also sold directly by one company to a single investor (either another corporation or to an institutional investor such as an insurance company or pension fund) and is called private placement. These private placements may have maturities up to 360 days.

2. **Preferred Stock** — Preferred stock is a type of equity instrument that has preference over common stock in its claim to a company's earnings and assets. Preferred dividends are paid before common stock dividends can be paid and, like common stock, offer a tax advantage to corporate investors. Currently, a corporate investor may exclude 70 percent of stock dividends received from current income as long as the stock is held at risk (cannot be hedged) for more than 45 days. This is called the intercorporate dividend deduction.

    Generally, preferred stock is considered a long-term investment, but there are several types of preferred stock that are designed to be suitable for short-term investors. They usually feature some type of adjustment to the stated dividend amount that is expressed as a percentage and is tied to an interest rate index in order to provide a stable price. Typically, the types of preferred stocks suitable for short-term investments are as follows:

    - *Adjustable-Rate Preferred* — Adjustable-rate preferred stock has a dividend rate that is adjusted quarterly based on current Treasury yields.

    - *Dutch Auction Preferred* — Also known as money market preferred stock, auction-rate preferred is characterized by a dividend rate that adjusts every 49 days, which is beyond the minimum holding period for the intercorporate dividend deduction. The dividend rate adjustment is based on bids from investors. Its benchmark is the 60-day, AA-rated, commercial paper composite. Securities dealers are invited by the issuer to bid in a Dutch auction every seven weeks. Typically, they act as agents for their clients. Existing holders may retain their shares and receive dividends at the new rate.

F. Money Market Mutual Funds

Money market mutual funds are commingled funds of highly liquid, diversified short-term money market instruments in which investors have an ownership interest. They are an increasingly important component of corporate short-term investment portfolios and offer an acceptable alternative to other securities, particularly under changing interest rate conditions. For example, when interest rates are falling, fund managers can extend their maturities to lock in yield. Investors in the fund thus get the greater return of longer-term instruments while enjoying the liquidity and stability of a principal comparable to investments with shorter maturities.

For many companies, using a money market mutual fund makes economic sense, especially when the costs of running and overseeing a short-term investment portfolio are considered. Using a mutual fund rather than in-house management may also free valuable treasury resources for other tasks.

Money market mutual funds are configured to report a net asset value (NAV) of $1 per share. They generate different yields and have slightly different risk thresholds. Money market mutual funds can provide a company with a professionally managed marketable securities portfolio at a low management cost. These funds can also be useful in providing a benchmark for assessing short-term investment portfolio performance. Money market mutual funds charge management fees or service charges based on the investor's balance, level of activity and services provided.

Some mutual fund companies offer a variety of funds based on differing average maturities or duration. In most cases, the longer maturity funds offer higher average returns, but also a higher risk of losing some net asset value. Unlike money market mutual funds, these funds may not be configured to maintain a stable $1 per share NAV. In using these funds, the cash manager could place some portion of short-term investment funds in a low-risk, short-maturity fund to meet near-term needs and other portions in longer-maturity funds to meet needs further in the future. This approach helps a treasury manager to more closely match investment needs with forecasted cash flows.

G. Other Types of Short-Term Investments

1. **Asset-Backed Securities** — Asset-backed securities are debt obligations issued by companies that are secured by specific assets. These can include receivables, such as the obligations that credit card holders have to credit card companies or

the installment payments that consumers pay finance subsidiaries, major retailers and automobile companies. Asset-backed securities can even be backed by inventories. Rating agencies rate many issues of asset-backed securities just as they do other types of financial instruments. Asset-backed securities enable issuing companies to free up capital the same way that they do through factoring receivables.

2. **Collateralized Mortgage Obligations (CMOs)** — A CMO refers to a type of mortgage-backed security created and backed by federal agencies such as Fannie Mae and Freddie Mac. These securities are formed from pools of mortgages divided into different instruments (tranches), each of which contains a specified portion of the principal and interest payment streams emanating from the aggregated mortgages to separate CMO securities.

   CMOs are sometimes enhanced with options and/or futures. Different CMOs have varying performance characteristics. Although many types of mortgage-backed securities are safe and generally stable investments, some may be highly volatile should interest rates change. It is important for the investor to fully understand all the ramifications of their investment choices, especially where small changes in interest rates may cause large changes in the value of the investment.

3. **International Money Market Investments** — In addition to the Eurodollar deposits discussed in the section on bank financial instruments, there are other international money market investments. Many foreign governments issue short-term bills and notes, or other fixed income securities similar to U.S. Treasuries and agencies. Similarly, many foreign-based corporations issue investments similar to commercial paper in international money markets. There are also interest-bearing deposit accounts and certificates available in many foreign currencies that are available from multinational banks. In addition to the normal credit and default risk concerns familiar to domestic investors, foreign investors must also consider foreign exchange (FX) risk and risk from potential blocked currencies. These risks are discussed in greater detail in Chapter 15, International Treasury Management.

4. **Repurchase Agreements (Repos)** — A repurchase agreement, or repo, is a type of collateralized transaction between a securities dealer or bank and an investor. For an investor, a repo involves the purchase of a security with an agreement to sell it back to the initial seller at a future date. Most repos are negotiated with U.S. Treasury or agency securities, or mortgage-backed pass-through securities and CMOs issued or guaranteed by Ginnie Mae, Fannie Mae or Freddie Mac. Repos reflect direct negotiation between the buyer and seller, with terms based on the needs of the counterparties. Interest is calculated on an actual/360-day basis. The seller of a security under a repo agreement continues to receive all interest and principal payments on the security. The purchaser receives a fixed rate of interest on a short-term investment.

Repos can be viewed as relatively safe. However, investors have incurred significant losses on repo investments because they did not exercise proper care in controlling and valuing their collateral. Repos may become unsecured transactions if the purchaser does not take the appropriate steps to perfect an interest in the collateral.

The repo market has grown because it is a relatively attractive money market instrument for investors and a comparatively inexpensive financing alternative for security owners. Repo yields are determined by the supply and demand of other money market instruments. They also depend on the type of collateral used (highest quality, most liquid collateral results in repos with the lowest yield). Since repos are negotiated directly between buyer and seller, terms are flexible. Maturities can range from overnight to more than one year. Often, transactions involve an "open repo," which is an overnight repo that rolls over automatically until terminated.

Many banks that offer overnight "sweep" accounts invest their depositors' funds in a pool of repos. In this case, the rate offered by the bank will typically reflect the bank demand for funds and internal liquidity demand. The investor must also realize that in this type of arrangement, they generally do not have any security interest in the securities underlying the pool of repos.

Some important characteristics of repos are:

- *Structure* — Typically, a securities dealer will sell a security to an investor who agrees to sell it back at a specific time, either overnight or for a specific number of days or on open contract, at a price that will result in a predetermined yield. The securities dealer collateralizes the repo with bonds. The investor is providing the dealer short-term funds, while the dealer is providing the investor short-term collateralized investments.

  The Public Securities Association repurchase agreement is considered the industry standard. In addition to repos backed by U.S. Treasuries, there are also agency-backed, corporate-backed, money-market and whole loan collateral repos.

- *Purpose* — Repos help securities dealers finance their inventory of securities, typically Treasuries. (A similar type of transaction known as a reverse repo helps dealers borrow inventory and make deliveries.)

- *Risk* — The market for repos is not as liquid as the market for many other instruments. In a repo transaction, the investor takes collateral but is still exposed to the creditworthiness and business practices of the dealer. Also, the investor must continually monitor the value of the collateral to make sure it does not drop below the value of the repo. If a dealer breaches the agreement, the investor, under its terms, has the right to the collateral.

  Investors may take collateral in the following ways in decreasing order of safety:

- In delivery vs. payment (DVP), the investor pays the custodial agent, who maintains an account for the investor.

- In a tri-party arrangement, the dealer's custodial agent maintains a custodial account for the investor. The dealer pays the fee.

- Under hold-in-custody, the dealer maintains a custodial account and monitors the collateral.

5. **Swaps and Derivatives** — In the true sense, these instruments are not really investments, but rather are intended to be used to reduce the overall risk of other investments due to changing interest rates or exchange rates. The use of swaps and derivatives is covered in detail in Chapter 14, Financial Risk Management.

6. **Securities Lending** — Securities lending results from the lending of securities from broker to broker. The borrowing broker will provide collateral to the lending broker. The collateral is generally two percent to five percent greater than the value of the borrowed securities. The collateral is marked-to-market daily to assure that its value has not diminished below the value stipulated in the contract of the participating brokers. The broker/borrower usually borrows securities to cover short sales.

VI. Yield

Yield is a measure of the gain an investor derives from a financial instrument. Typically, it is stated as an annual rate of return, expressed as a percentage.

A. Factors that Influence Yields

There are five interrelated factors that determine the investment suitability of a short-term financial instrument:

1. **Marketability** — The marketability of securities affects their yield because investors require a higher return for holding securities that are more difficult to sell.

2. **Default Risk** — Investors typically require a higher yield to compensate for the risk that the principal will not be paid under the original terms. The greater the likelihood of default, the higher the risk premium and the higher the expected yield. A risk premium is the extra yield above the yield of a risk-free security that investors require as compensation for assuming the additional risk. U.S. government securities are considered to have no default risk and other short-term securities are evaluated in comparison to them. Credit rating services attempt to quantify relative default risk through evaluation and assignment of credit ratings.

3. **Price Risk** — Price risk is the uncertainty over the price at which a security can be sold prior to maturity and is a function of interest rates. An increase in rates will cause the price of fixed income securities to fall. A decrease in interest rates will cause the price of fixed income securities to rise. Generally, securities with longer maturities are subject to more price risk than similar securities with shorter maturities.

4. **Re-Investment Risk** — This is the risk that an investor faces when cash flows from an investment must be re-invested under changing interest rates. The best example in the money market area are MBSs, where falling interest rates result in mortgages in the security pool being prepaid, causing a premature cash flow to the investor. These cash flows must then be re-invested at now lower interest rates.

5. **Tax Status** — The tax status of an investment has an impact on its yield. Tax-exempt securities provide a lower pre-tax yield than taxable securities of similar maturity and default risk. When comparing taxable and tax-exempt instruments, the tax-exempt yield is usually converted to a taxable equivalent yield as follows:

$$\text{Taxable Equivalent Yield} = \frac{\text{Tax-Exempt Yield}}{(1 - \text{Marginal Tax Rate of Investor})}$$

This taxable equivalent yield can then be used to compare the tax-exempt instrument with other taxable investments. An example of a calculation of taxable equivalent yield is shown in Exhibit 12.2.

Exhibit 12.2 Example of Taxable Equivalent Yield Calculation

Assuming a corporate investor's marginal tax rate of 34 percent, the taxable equivalent yield for an investment with a tax-exempt yield of 6 percent is determined as follows.

$$\text{Taxable Equivalent Yield} = \frac{\text{Tax-Exempt Yield}}{1 - \text{Marginal Tax Rate of Investor}}$$

$$\text{Taxable Equivalent Yield} = \frac{.06}{1 - .34} = 9.09\%$$

The interest income from obligations of the U.S. government is exempt from state income taxes (though not from state franchise taxes), while the income from obligations of state and local governments is generally exempt from federal income taxes. Securities issued by a given state are often exempt from income taxes in that state but may not be exempt from taxes in other states.

B. Basic Yield Definitions

Yield can be calculated in two different ways:

1. **Current Yield** — This is an instrument's annual interest payment divided by its price. It indicates what the instrument will return in terms of interest on an annual basis.

   For example, if a five percent note with a face, or par, value of $1,000 is bought at a market price of $900, the annual interest payment from the note is $50, but since only $900 was paid for it, the current yield is $50 divided by $900, or 5.56 percent.

2. **Yield to Maturity (YTM)** — This is a calculation of a debt instrument's total yield from a specific date to maturity. It takes into account the discount or premium on an instrument in addition to its coupon or interest payments. (When an instrument is purchased at a premium to face value, the calculation assumes an amortization to par and when it is purchased at a discount, the calculation assumes an increase in value to par.)

   Algebraically, the relationship among these factors can be expressed as:

   $$P_0 = \frac{C_1}{(1+YTM)^1} + \frac{C_2}{(1+YTM)^2} + \ldots + \frac{C_n}{(1+YTM)^n} + \frac{FV}{(1+YTM)^n}$$

   Where:
   - P_0 = Current market price
   - n = Number of periods until maturity
   - $C_{1, 2, \ldots n}$ = Dollar amount of the coupon payment in periods 1, 2, ... n
   - FV = Face value of the instrument
   - YTM = Yield to maturity

   For example, if a bond with a face value of $1,000 maturing in one year has a coupon of five percent and a price in the market of $950, its yield to maturity is 10.53 percent. The numerator is the coupon (five percent, or $50) added to the principal ($1,000). The denominator is one plus the yield to maturity, raised to the first power. That expression is equal to the current price ($950). Solving for yield to maturity results in 10.53 percent:

   $$\$950 = \frac{(\$1,000 + \$50)}{(1+YTM)^1}$$

   If n (the number of periods) is greater than one, complex algorithms are necessary to solve for YTM.

C. Yield Quoting Conventions

Not all rates quoted in the markets are easily comparable. Rates for various financial instruments are quoted and priced differently and interest payments are timed differently.

1. **Interest-Bearing Instruments** — Some instruments (for example, CDs and Eurodollar deposits) pay interest in arrears at maturity or at periodic intervals and are thus called interest-bearing instruments.

2. **Discount Instruments** — Other instruments, such as Treasury bills and banker's acceptances, are discounted; the investor pays the face value of the instrument minus the interest (the discount) and receives the face value at maturity. The discount is the face value multiplied by the discount rate, multiplied by the number of days to maturity divided by the year basis (360 or 365).

3. **Year Basis** — Most short-term instruments, commercial paper and Treasury bills, for example, pay interest calculated on a 360-day basis. Treasury bonds and Treasury notes pay interest on a 365-day basis.

4. **Nominal Yield** — The quoted yield on an annual basis for most investments is a simple annual rate, called a nominal yield and does not reflect compounding.

5. **Money Market Yield** — Money market yield (MMY) is the nominal yield quoted on a 360-day basis.

6. **Bond Equivalent Yield** — Bond equivalent yield (BEY) is the nominal yield quoted on a 365-day basis.

7. **Effective Annual Yield** — The most reliable way to compare all of these instruments is to calculate their effective annual yields. Effective annual yields assume compounding and are calculated on a 365-day basis. Because of compounding, an effective annual yield assumes that the investor always has the opportunity to re-invest funds at the same rate. For example, assume a company receives $500 in interest on an investment of $10,000 and the investment matures in 150 days. The approximate interest rate is calculated as:

$$\frac{\$500}{\$10,000} \times \frac{365}{150} = 12.2\%$$

The effective annual yield calculation is as follows:

$$EAY = \left[1 + \frac{I}{P}\right]^{\frac{365}{DM}} - 1$$

Where:
- EAY = Effective Annual Yield
- P = Principal
- I = Interest amount
- DM = Days to maturity

Solution of this equation requires the use of complex algorithms.

$$EAY = \left[1 + \frac{\$500}{\$10,000}\right]^{\frac{365}{150}} - 1 = 12.6\%$$

To compare the yields on two different investment instruments, it is often necessary to convert from one yield quoting convention to the other.

An easy way to remember the different conventions and how they relate to each other is to appreciate the logic of the sequence above: starting with the discount basis, converting to the simple, annualized (but not compounded) money market yield on a 360-day basis; moving to the still not-compounded bond-equivalent annual yield, calculated on a 365-day basis; and finally moving to the effective annual yield, both compounded and calculated on a 365-day basis. A summary of the yield quoting conventions is provided in Exhibit 12.3.

Exhibit 12.3 Summary of Yield Quoting Conventions

Yield Quoting Convention	Characteristics
Nominal Yield	Annualized Not Compounded 360- or 365-Day Basis
Money Market Yield	Annualized Not Compounded 360-Day Basis
Bond Equivalent Yield	Annualized Not Compounded 365-Day Basis
Effective Annual Yield	Annualized Compounded 365-Day Basis

D. Yield Calculations

The yield on any instrument can be determined as a function of the cash flows received from the investment, the amount paid for that investment and the maturity or holding period. One approach is to take the cash flows and determine the interest rate (discount rate) at which the present value of the cash flows is equal to the amount paid. This is, in fact, the approach used with most long-term fixed income securities, but it is difficult to apply to short-term instruments. The practice in the money market is to use algebraic approximations for the calculations, rather than the mathematically correct (and computationally more difficult) exponential approach. In most cases, the calculations of yield for money market investments can be determined by dividing the expected future cash flow by the amount paid for the investment, then adjusting for the holding period.

The following formulas and sample calculations show the relationships among the dollar discount, the discount rate, the purchase price and the discount rate for a T-bill. The calculations for determining the yield on a commercial paper issue are similar to those of a T-bill. For any discounted instrument, to determine the yield, the first step is to determine the dollar discount and purchase price. The dollar discount is a function of the discount rate, the face amount of the instrument and the days to maturity. The purchase price of the investment is then figured by subtracting the dollar discount from the face or maturity value. The price is thus the amount paid for the investment and the dollar discount is the expected future cash flow.

1. **Purchase Price for a Discounted Instrument** — The dollar discount is equal to the discount rate multiplied by the face or redemption value. This value is then multiplied by the number of days to maturity divided by the appropriate year basis. For T-bills, 360 is used as the year basis.

    $$\text{Dollar Discount} = (\text{Discount Rate} \times \text{Face Value}) \times \frac{\text{Days to Maturity}}{360}$$

    The discount rate on a period basis is equal to the dollar discount divided by the face value. To annualize that rate, divide by the number of days to maturity and multiply by 360.

    $$\text{Discount Rate} = \frac{\text{Dollar Discount}}{\text{Face Value}} \times \frac{360}{\text{Days to Maturity}}$$

    The purchase price is equal to the face value minus the dollar discount.

    $$\text{Purchase Price} = \text{Face Value} - \text{Dollar Discount}$$

Examples of the calculation of the purchase price and the discount rate for T-bills are provided in Exhibits 12.4 and 12.5.

Exhibit 12.4 Example of T-Bill Purchase Price Calculation

The purchase price of a 91-day $100,000 T-bill sold at a 7.91 percent discount rate is calculated as follows:

$$\text{Dollar Discount} = (\text{Discount Rate} \times \text{Face Value}) \times \frac{\text{Days to Maturity}}{360}$$

$$DD = (DR \times FV) \times \frac{DM}{360}$$

$$= (.0791 \times \$100,000) \times \frac{91}{360} = \$1,999.47$$

$$\text{Purchase Price} = \text{Face Value} - \text{Dollar Discount}$$

$$PP = FV - DD$$

$$= \$100,00 - \$1,999.47 = \$98,000.53$$

Exhibit 12.5 Example of T-Bill Discount Rate Calculation

The discount rate on a 182-day $100,000 T-bill that is currently selling at a price of $95,875 is calculated as follows:

$$\text{Dollar Discount} = \text{Face Value} - \text{Purchase Price}$$

$$DD = FV - PP$$

$$= \$100,000 - \$95,875 = \$4,125$$

$$\text{Discount Rate} = \frac{\text{Dollar Discount}}{\text{Face Value}} \times \frac{360}{\text{Days of Maturity}}$$

$$DR = \frac{DD}{FV} \times \frac{360}{DM}$$

$$\text{Discount Rate} = \frac{\$4,125}{\$100,000} \times \frac{360}{182} = 8.16\%$$

2. **Money Market Yield for a Discounted Instrument** — The money market yield states the annual yield of a discounted security on a short-term interest-bearing basis with a 360-day year.

$$\text{Money Market Yield} = \frac{\text{Dollar Discount}}{\text{Purchase Price}} \times \frac{360}{\text{Days to Maturity}}$$

This calculation is made in two steps. First, the dollar discount is divided by the purchase price to obtain the period yield; next, the period yield is annualized. A period yield is the effective yield for a particular period such as a week, a month or a year. A 30-day instrument with a simple annual yield of 12 percent has a period yield of one percent. An example of this calculation is provided in Exhibit 12.6.

Exhibit 12.6 Example of Money Market Yield Calculation

The money market yield of a 91-day $100,000 T-bill sold at a discount rate of 7.91 percent as presented in Exhibit 12.4 is calculated as follows:

$$\text{MMY} = \frac{\text{Dollar Discount}}{\text{Purchase Price}} \times \frac{360}{\text{Days of Maturity}}$$

$$= \frac{\text{DD}}{\text{PP}} \times \frac{360}{\text{DM}}$$

$$\text{MMY} = \frac{\$1{,}999.47}{\$98{,}000.53} \times \frac{360}{91} = 8.07\%$$

3. **Converting to Bond Equivalent Yield from a Discount Rate or Money Market Yield** — Exhibit 12.7 shows how the yield on a discounted security can be converted to the BEY (365 days). Note that there are several ways to calculate the BEY.

Exhibit 12.7 Example of Bond Equivalent Yield Calculations

The bond equivalent yield of the previous 91-day $100,000 T-bill example with a 7.91 percent discount rate is calculated as follows:

$$\text{BEY} = \frac{\text{Dollar Discount}}{\text{Purchase Price}} \times \frac{365}{\text{Days to Maturity}}$$

$$= \frac{\text{DD}}{\text{PP}} \times \frac{365}{\text{DM}}$$

$$= \frac{\$1{,}999.47}{\$98{,}000.53} \times \frac{365}{91} = 8.18\%$$

or

$$= \text{MMY} \times \frac{365}{360} = 8.07\% \times 1.0139 = 8.18\%$$

or

$$= \frac{365 \times \text{Discount Rate}}{360 - (\text{Discount Rate} \times \text{Days to Maturity})}$$

$$= \frac{365 \times .0791}{360 - (.0791 \times 91)} = 8.18\%$$

4. **Calculation of Commercial Paper Nominal Yield** — The calculation of the yield on commercial paper is similar to that of the BEY for a T-bill. Like T-bills, commercial paper is normally sold on a discount basis, but the nominal yield is calculated using a 365-day basis.

$$\text{Commercial Paper Nominal Yield} = \frac{\text{Dollar Discount}}{\text{Purchase Price}} \times \frac{365}{\text{Days to Maturity}}$$

An example of this calculation is provided in Exhibit 12.8.

5. **Algebraic Notation for Yield Equations** — All of the yield formulas presented in this chapter can also be presented in a general algebraic notation format. These formulas are shown in Exhibit 12.9 on page 304.

E. Duration

Duration actually has two basic definitions in the investment world. The first is that it is the weighted average of a security's cash flow stream, where the present values of the cash flows act as weights. An alternative definition states that duration is the future point in time at which, on average, an investor has received exactly half of the original investment in present value terms. As a theoretical model, duration formulas were developed using an assumption of continuous compounding. In practical application, most practitioners utilize a modified version of duration that takes into account the semiannual compounding used in many fixed income securities such as bonds.

A more practical way to view modified duration is as follows: A 100 basis point (one percent) change in a security's yield will reflect a price change in percentage

---

Exhibit 12.8 Example of Commercial Paper Nominal Yield Calculation

The normal yield of a 45-day, $100,000 commercial paper issue selling at a price of $98,750 is calculated as follows:

Dollar Discount	=	Face Value − Purchase Price
DD	=	FV − PP
	=	$100,000 − $98,750 = $1,250
Commercial Paper Nominal Yield	=	$\frac{\text{Dollar Discount}}{\text{Purchase Price}} \times \frac{365}{\text{Days of Maturity}}$
CPY	=	$\frac{DD}{PP} \times \frac{365}{DM}$
	=	$\frac{\$1{,}250}{\$98{,}750} \times \frac{365}{45} = 10.27\%$

Exhibit 12.9 Summary of Yield Equations

The yield equations in this chapter expressed in a general algebraic format are as follows:

$$TEY = \frac{TXY}{1 - MT}$$

$$CY = \frac{C}{P}$$

$$P_o = \frac{C_1}{(1+YTM)} + \frac{C_2}{(1+YTM)^2} \ldots \frac{C_n}{(1+YTM)^n} + \frac{FV}{(1+YTM)^n}$$

$$DD = (DR \times FV) \times \left(\frac{DM}{360}\right)$$

$$DR = \left(\frac{DD}{FV}\right) \times \left(\frac{360}{DM}\right)$$

$$PP = FV - DD$$

$$MMY = \left(\frac{DD}{PP}\right) \times \left(\frac{360}{DM}\right)$$

$$BEY = \frac{DD}{PP} \times \left(\frac{365}{DM}\right)$$

or

$$BEY = MMY \times \left(\frac{365}{360}\right)$$

$$BEY = \frac{365 \times DR}{360 - (DR \times DM)}$$

$$CPY = \left(\frac{DD}{PP}\right) \times \left(\frac{365}{DM}\right)$$

$$EAY = \left[1 + \frac{I}{P}\right]^{365/DM} - 1$$

Where:

BEY	=	Bond Equivalent Yield	MMY	=	Money Market Yield
C	=	Coupon Amount	MT	=	Marginal Tax Rate
CPY	=	Commercial Paper Nominal Yield	n	=	Number of Intervals
CY	=	Current Yield	p	=	Price
DD	=	Dollar Discount	Po	=	Current Market Price
DM	=	Days to Maturity	PP	=	Purchase Price
DR	=	Discount Rate	TEY	=	Taxable Equivalent Yield
EAY	=	Effective Annual Yield	TXY	=	Tax Exempt Yield
FV	=	Face Value (redemption value)	YTM	=	Yield to Maturity
I	=	Interest Amount			

approximately equal to the number of years measured by the modified duration statistic. For example, a duration of five years indicates an approximate five percent change in price, given a 100 basis point change in yield to maturity in either direction (i.e., the longer the maturity, the more volatile the portfolio).

In the area of short-term investment management, duration measurements are typically replaced by a simple calculation of average maturity. This is determined as a weighted average (by percentage of total portfolio value) of the maturities of the short-term securities in the portfolio.

F. The Yield Curve

How the market values a debt instrument in comparison with other similar securities that have longer or shorter maturities is revealed by the yield curve, which expresses the term structure of interest rates. A yield curve depicts the differences in yield of securities that are identical except for their dates of maturity.

The relationship between market yield and maturity is illustrated by Exhibits 12.10 and 12.11.

1. **Normal Yield Curve** — The most common shape of the yield curve is upward sloping, reflecting the greater return over time that investors require to compensate for the increased price risk.

2. **Inverted Yield Curve** — An inverted yield curve slopes downward, indicative of a market situation where short-term yields are higher than long-term yields. Yield curve inversion happens infrequently and contravenes the usual condition that securities with longer maturities must offer higher yields. One theory explaining an inverted yield curve is that short-term uncertainties, such as an anticipated recession, shift investor preferences away from short-term instruments to those carrying longer maturities, driving down long-term rates.

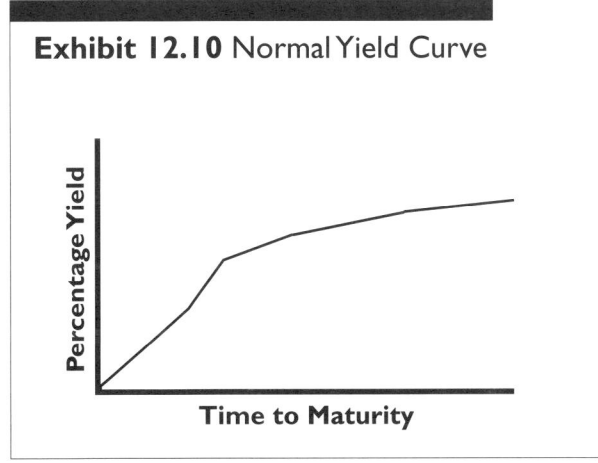

Exhibit 12.10 Normal Yield Curve

Exhibit 12.11 Inverted Yield Curve

VII. Investment Strategies

There are a variety of short-term investment strategies, depending on the company's objectives. In order to increase yield and provide certain fiduciary comfort, many companies may outsource their investment management by hiring registered investment advisors or utilizing money market mutual funds. Common investment strategies include:

A. Replicate an Index or Market

The objective of an indexed approach to short-term investment management is to replicate, on a dollar-weighted basis, performance of a market for a type of security (or securities) comparable to those in the portfolio, or a suitable market index.

B. Outsource Investment Management

A company can sweep excess funds on hand at the end of every day into an account used to purchase repos. Alternate investment options for an overnight sweep program are investments in Eurodollar time deposits, commercial paper or money market mutual funds. Such strategies entail minimal risk, time and effort and typically produce lower but extremely safe returns. Many companies of all sizes utilize the services of a money market mutual fund for their short-term investment needs. This approach frees treasury personnel to focus on more important tasks. The wide range of funds available allows a company to easily tailor its investments to risk/return objectives.

C. Match Maturities to Funds Needs

Matching involves purchasing securities that mature when funds are required to meet an expected obligation or obligations.

- Matching allows companies to invest for extended periods and potentially increase yields.

- This strategy requires careful forecasting of future cash flows and capital requirements. If cash is needed sooner than expected, the securities purchased to match a specific cash outflow may have to be sold prematurely, perhaps at a loss, due to marketability problems or changes in interest rates.

- Companies that match tend to do so judiciously, covering a portion, but not the entire amount, of the expected capital need.

D. Ride the Yield Curve

This strategy may provide returns superior to that of a matching strategy, as long as the shape of the yield curve does not change. If a company expects interest rates to rise in the future (upward sloping or normal yield curve), it can purchase securities that mature beyond the time when funds are needed. The securities are sold prior to maturity, providing a return that exceeds that of the matching strategy. The risk of this strategy is that interest rates may increase more than anticipated, reducing the value of the security at the time it is sold. If interest rates are expected to generally fall in the future (a downward sloping or inverted yield curve), then the strategy is to purchase securities for shorter than the time when funds are needed and then re-invest the funds when the first set of securities mature. The risk of this strategy is that interest rates may fall further than expected and the funds must be re-invested at a lower than planned interest rate.

E. Dividend Capture

Companies may increase the yield on their short-term investment portfolios through a dividend capture or dividend rollover program. Under this type of tax-motivated trading program, a company buys a stock just before the ex-dividend date (the first date on which a new holder of the stock does not receive the last declared dividend). The stock is held for a period long enough to receive the dividend and at least 46 days to qualify for the 70 percent intercorporate dividend deduction. This is considered suitable for a cash management investment when stocks in mature, blue-chip companies are used. This is because once the dividend is announced, it is a virtual certain cash flow. Add to that the tax-advantaged status of the investment and it is attractive to many short-term investors.

F. Hedge Short-Term Investments

Many companies utilize interest rate swaps, futures and options to hedge the risk in their short-term investment portfolios. This topic is covered in more detail in Chapter 14, Financial Risk Management.

Test Your Understanding

These chapter questions are provided to test your understanding of the information in the text and are not examples of CCM examination questions, nor are they in the examination format.

Answers can be found at the back of the book on pages 532-534.

1. What are the major purposes of having a short-term investment portfolio?
2. Discuss the factors that influence a company's investment policy.
3. What characteristics do companies specify in their investment guidelines and how are they determined?
4. What are the three major areas that influence the acceptability of a financial instrument for inclusion in the short-term investment portfolio?
5. Explain the major categories of financial markets.
6. Define the term "book entry."
7. What are the three major U.S. Treasury securities?
8. List the federal agency securities.
9. What are the broad categories of municipal securities?
10. What makes municipal securities an attractive investment?
11. Define Eurodollar CDs.
12. When are banker's acceptances used?
13. What is a repo?
14. What is the maximum time to maturity for commercial paper?
15. What is money market preferred stock?
16. Explain the factors that influence yield.
17. Discuss the concept of inverted yield curve.
18. What is the purchase price of a 182-day, $100,000 T-bill sold at a 4.53 percent discount rate?
19. What is the bond equivalent yield of the T-bill in Question 18?
20. What bank product is frequently used in an overnight investment strategy?
21. What are the major investment strategies?

CHAPTER 13

Borrowing

Overview

This chapter covers borrowing objectives and alternative strategies. It discusses the principal types of borrowing and how they are priced. It also covers the legal considerations and mechanics of borrowing. All borrowing or debt arrangements represent an asset (or security) to one party and a liability (or obligation) to another party. Chapter 12, Investing, covers debt instruments from a corporate investor's point of view. This chapter covers them from a borrower's point of view.

Learning Objectives

Upon completion of this chapter and the related study questions, the reader should understand:

- A company's borrowing objectives and strategies
- The principal features of borrowing alternatives
- How to calculate the all-in cost for lines of credit and commercial paper
- The most common provisions of loan agreements

Key Concepts

- Borrowing objectives and strategies
- Borrowing alternatives
- Calculating the costs of borrowing
- Common provisions of loan agreements

Outline

I. Corporate Borrowing Strategy and Objectives
    A. Capital Structure and Borrowing Strategy
    B. Short-Term Borrowing Objectives
    C. Long-Term Borrowing Issues
    D. Equity Financing Issues

II. Variables Affecting the Cost of Borrowing
    A. Loan Pricing
    B. Credit Risk
    C. Credit Support
    D. Term or Maturity

III. Short-Term Borrowing Alternatives
    A. Line of Credit
    B. Revolving Credit Agreement
    C. Commercial Paper (CP)
    D. Reverse Repurchase Agreement
    E. Banker's Acceptance (BA)
    F. Asset-Based Borrowing
    G. Securitization
    H. Loan Syndication and Participation
    I. Trade Credit
    J. Export Financing Programs

IV. Medium-and Long-Term Borrowing Alternatives
    A. Medium-Term Notes
    B. Bonds
    C. Special Types of Bonds
    D. Debt-Equity Hybrids
    E. Term Loan
    F. Leasing
    G. Private Placement

V. Repayment of Principal
    A. Amortization
    B. Sinking Fund

VI. Legal Aspects of Borrowing
    A. Loan Agreements and Bond Indentures
    B. Promissory Notes

I. Corporate Borrowing Strategy and Objectives

A. Capital Structure and Borrowing Strategy

For a company to realize its long-term financial objectives, it must have access to debt or equity capital. Debt represents a legal liability of the company to repay a creditor for borrowed funds. Equity represents an ownership claim in the company.

Each alternative involves a trade-off between risk and return. The cost of debt is represented by an interest rate; the value of equity is represented by either a stock price or the net value of a company's assets. Interest is a tax-deductible expense; dividends paid on equity shares are not tax-deductible. Debt financings may influence the operation of the company through loan agreement covenants; shareholders exert control through the exercise of specified voting rights.

The mix of debt and equity in a company's capital structure determines its leverage. The greater the debt, the greater the financial leverage and financial obligation. The use of debt increases earnings whenever the return on the capital investment for which the borrowed funds are used exceeds the cost of debt. The converse is also true. For these reasons, a company's borrowing program is often coordinated with its capital budgeting, the process by which a company's management decides how to make capital investments.

In formulating a borrowing strategy, management must decide how much debt to assume, for what purposes, from what sources and at what cost. To do this it must take into consideration the implications of:

- Debt vs. equity financing
- Short-vs. long-term borrowing
- Fixed-vs. floating-rate interest payments
- Secured vs. unsecured debt
- On-vs. off-balance-sheet financing

The cash manager needs to be cognizant of the impact of short-term borrowing on the financial structure of the company.

B. Short-Term Borrowing Objectives

On a day-to-day basis, a cash manager is concerned primarily with a company's short-term borrowing needs, the objectives of which include:

- Establishing adequate credit facilities to ensure liquidity through the availability of borrowed funds sufficient to meet short-term cash requirements

- Minimizing the overall cost of funds, the major component of which is interest
- Minimizing risks such as insolvency due to an excessive debt burden or default due to tightly structured covenants
- Maximizing flexibility by maintaining alternate sources of short-term borrowing

C. Long-Term Borrowing Issues

As discussed above, the long-term borrowing objectives are closely linked to the overall capital structure of the company as well as the availability of assets that can be used as security for the debt. The level of long-term debt vs. equity is often discussed in terms of a target long-term capital structure, which is determined as a function of business and financial risk, as well as access to and costs of the various capital components. The key challenge for corporate treasurers is to analyze the business opportunities for the company and to obtain the required capital at the best mix and price to meet these opportunities. It is also important to understand that the use of debt in a particular firm will change over time. As existing long-term debt is retired, the capital structure of a company will change, unless new debt of a similar type is added. The acceptable target debt levels may change over time as the perceptions of debt by financial markets change. During times of high growth, use of large amounts of debt may be more acceptable than during slow growth periods.

D. Equity Financing Issues

Once the decision regarding the use of debt vs. equity in the long-term capital structure of a company has been determined, the type of equity raised must be considered. Equity can be raised either through the use of retained earnings or by issuing new common stock. Retained earnings are not "free funds," but rather belong to the owners (stockholders) of the company. The appropriate cost for this capital component is based on the concept of opportunity cost, which states that the firm should be able to earn at least the prevailing equity rate of return for the company on any earnings retained rather than paid out in dividends. Newly issued common stock is valued at the general cost of equity plus any underwriting or issue costs. In general, the use of common stock for capital funding has some advantages and disadvantages.

1. **Advantages of Using Common Stock** — The main advantage of common stock financing is that it is does not obligate the firm to make fixed payments to investors. In addition, it has no specific maturity date. For the creditors, stock offers a cushion against losses and, if the company's future is bright, equity can often be raised at an attractive rate. Finally, if a company has sufficient equity, this may enhance its ability to issue debt.

2. **Disadvantage of Using Common Stock** — Sale of common stock may extend voting rights and control to more people. This may be a problem for smaller companies where management is the primary owner. In the event the company does well, the profits must be shared with new stockholders. The cost of underwriting common stock is considerable when compared to other sources of capital and common equity financing does not enjoy the tax shield (deductibility of interest expense) that debt financing provides, thus making it considerably more expensive than on an after-tax basis.

Another equity financing issue, especially for newer or smaller companies, is the use of venture capital. Venture capital is provided to help new, smaller companies grow quickly and develop new products or markets. In return for this venture capital, the providers are typically granted a significant equity position in the firm. The venture capitalist may also provide managerial or consulting expertise to the new company. Due to the low success rate of these types of endeavors, the risks and costs of venture capital are usually quite high.

II. Variables Affecting the Cost of Borrowing

Money, like any other commodity, has a cost associated with its use. The total cost of borrowing depends upon the following variables:

A. Loan Pricing

When a company borrows funds from a financial institution in the form of a loan, the key determinant of the cost is the interest rate. Features of interest rates include:

- An interest rate is usually quoted in terms of a base rate plus a spread. The spread includes an adjustment for perceived risk that is related to the overall creditworthiness of the borrower. The sum of the base rate and the spread is called the all-in rate. Typical base rates include:

    — *London Interbank Offered Rate (LIBOR)* — LIBOR is quoted for a full range of short-term maturities, including 30, 60, 90 and 180 days. It is the most commonly used base rate for short-term borrowing. LIBOR is set on a daily basis in London and is the wholesale rate used by multinational banks for borrowing/lending funds among themselves.

    — *Prime Rate* — Traditionally, prime was the rate at which commercial banks loaned money to their most creditworthy corporate customers. Prime rates vary by financial institution. Prime-based pricing is becoming less common for large corporate borrowers, but is widely used for small business and consumer loans.

- *Other* — The U.S. Treasury bill rate, the Fed funds rate, the banker's acceptance rate, certificate of deposit rates and a financial institution's weighted average cost of funds are examples of other base rates.

- Rates can be fixed or variable. A fixed rate remains unchanged during the term of the debt, whereas a variable rate is subject to periodic adjustments.

- The effective interest rate will be slightly higher than the stated rate if the lender uses a 360-day year basis in calculating the interest due on a loan. When a 360-day year basis is used, the interest expense is calculated based on the actual number of days in the billing period divided by 360 days times the stated annual rate. Banks typically use a 360-day year LIBOR-rate basis and a 365-day year prime-rate basis for commercial loans.

- The interest rate on a loan may be lower if the lender is being compensated in other ways, such as loan fees or compensating balance requirements, which are also considerations affecting loan pricing.

- Rate swaps are used by many companies as part of their financial risk management program. These swaps are usually in the form of either fixed vs. floating or a rate basis swap (prime vs. LIBOR). This topic is covered in greater detail in Chapter 14, Financial Risk Management.

B. Credit Risk

Whenever a company borrows from a financial institution or issues debt instruments, a major determinant of the price is the company's overall creditworthiness. For non-public debt issues, creditworthiness is assessed based on a credit analysis performed by the lender. In essence, the lender wants to determine how the borrower is going to repay the debt and what alternate sources of payment are available if the primary repayment plan does not work out.

When a company obtains financing from the capital markets in the form of corporate bonds or commercial paper, it will normally contract with one or more recognized credit rating agencies to obtain a credit rating. A credit rating is assigned based on the perceived risk of the credit issue, with higher ratings associated with lower risk. Although a credit rating applies to a specific debt issue, it can be a useful tool in assessing a company's overall creditworthiness. Two of the major credit ratings agencies are Moody's and Standard & Poor's. (See Chapter 12, Investing.)

Factors that enter into a lender's credit analysis or the determination of a rating by a credit rating agency include current earnings, leverage, future prospects of the company and the type of collateral securing the debt. As a rule, lower credit risk correlates with lower borrowing costs. In addition, many banks practice portfolio credit risk management where they choose to limit loan exposure by region, industry type and/or risk rating.

C. Credit Support

Another key variable affecting the cost of borrowing for a company issuing corporate bonds or commercial paper is credit support or enhancement. Credit support is provided when a third party with a higher credit rating than the borrower guarantees the debt obligations of the borrower. The guarantee may take the form of an indemnity bond, a standby letter of credit or insurance. A fee is charged for such support. With such support in place, the borrower's debt assumes the credit rating of the guarantor, which may reduce the borrowing cost or enhance the marketability of the debt.

Another way of enhancing or supporting a credit issue is through the use of asset backing. An asset-backed issue is typically collateralized by inventories or assets such as equipment to which instrument holders take title in case of default.

D. Term or Maturity

The life span of a debt instrument is known as its term or maturity. Debt maturities range from overnight to 100 years. Interest rates tend to increase with length of maturity, reflecting the greater risk for long-term instruments and investor demands for higher returns.

III. Short-Term Borrowing Alternatives

Short-term debt instruments mature in less than one year. They are generally used to finance current assets such as accounts receivable and inventory. Any type of loan or credit arrangement can be referred to as a credit facility.

A. Line of Credit

A line of credit is an agreement in which the lender gives the borrower access to funds up to a maximum amount over a specific period of time. A line of credit may be used to provide short-term financing, to back up commercial paper or to provide a liquidity cushion. Some companies with seasonal borrowing requirements have lines of credit in which the maximum amount available varies over the year. A significant portion of credit lines are in the form of "base borrowing" where accounts receivable are used to provide collateral for the line and the amount of the commitment will vary month to month as the base of accounts receivable change.

1. **Key Characteristics** — The key characteristics of a line of credit include:
    - *Commitment* — Lines of credit are either committed or uncommitted. A committed line usually involves a formal loan agreement that specifies the terms and conditions of the credit facility. A committed line of credit typically

requires compensation in the form of balances or fees. Under a committed facility, the lender is obligated to provide funding up to the credit limit stipulated in the agreement as long as the borrower is not in default. Money market or demand lines of credit are examples of uncommitted lines. Uncommitted lines are usually made available for a one-year period and can be canceled at any time by the lender.

- *Revolving* — Lines of credit are usually revolving, meaning the borrower may borrow, repay and reborrow funds during the commitment period.

- *Security* — Lines of credit may be unsecured or secured. Secured lines require the borrower to pledge some form of collateral.

- *Cleanup* — To assure the lender that the line is not being used as a permanent source of financing, a cleanup period of 30 to 60 days is sometimes required. No outstanding borrowings are allowed during the agreed-upon cleanup period. Typically this requirement is used only for middle market and small companies.

2. **Effective Rate for a Line of Credit** — Pricing for a line of credit is usually negotiable. The lender may take into account various aspects of the overall lender/borrower relationship in pricing the line. There are three basic pricing components for lines of credit:

    - *All-In Rate* — This rate consists of a spread that is added to a base rate such as LIBOR, prime or the Fed funds rate. This rate is normally variable and will adjust in relation to changes in the base rate.

    - *Commitment Fee* — For committed lines, the lender may charge a percentage fee based either on the total amount of the commitment or on the unused portion of the commitment. Payment is usually made quarterly. Fees vary depending on the creditworthiness of the company, the stated purpose of the line and the term of the commitment.

    - *Compensating Balances* — Some banks may also require compensating balances, which are maintained in the company's deposit accounts at the bank and do not earn interest or offset other service charges. This practice has become less common. In a compensating balance arrangement, the balance requirement can be specified as a percentage of the total commitment, the unused amount of the commitment, or the outstanding borrowings. If compensating balances are required, their effect is to reduce the amount of the borrowed funds that can be used by the borrower, thereby increasing the effective annual interest rate.

    To compute the effective borrowing rate for a line of credit, the following formula is used:

    $$\text{Effective Annual Borrowing Rate} = \frac{\text{Total Interest Paid} + \text{Total Fees Paid}}{\text{Average Usable Loan}} \times \frac{365}{\text{\# of Days Loan is Outstanding}}$$

Where:

- Total interest paid is calculated as the all-in rate times the average loan amount outstanding.
- Total fees paid include all commitment fees, placement fees and any issuance costs.
- Average usable loan is the net amount of borrowed funds available after any compensating balances are deducted.
- Number of days loan is outstanding is the effective term of the loan or the time over which the funds are borrowed.

This formula can also be represented in an algebraic format as follows:

$$i = \frac{I + F}{L} \times \frac{365}{\text{Days to Maturity}}$$

Where:

i = The effective annual borrowing rate
I = Total interest paid (in dollars)
F = Total feels paid
L = Average usable loan

An example of this calculation is provided in Exhibit 13.1 on page 318.

B. Revolving Credit Agreement

A revolving credit agreement, also known as a revolver, is a facility that allows the borrower to borrow, repay and reborrow up to a defined amount. Revolving credits are contractual commitments with loan agreements, including covenants. Usually there is a commitment fee on the unused portion, as well as a facility fee. While often used for short-term borrowing, the commitment term typically ranges from two to five years and may be followed by a period in which the principal is systematically repaid.

C. Commercial Paper (CP)

CP is an unsecured promissory note issued by a company for a specific amount, with maturities ranging from overnight to 270 days for public issues. Limiting the maturity of public issues of CP avoids the Securities and Exchange Commission (SEC) registration requirement for securities whose maturities exceed 270 days. Some privately placed commercial paper may be issued for periods greater than 270 days.

> **Exhibit 13.1** Effective Annual Borrowing Rate Calculation Example
>
> 1. Over a one-year period a company has an average loan outstanding of $1,000,000.
> 2. The commitment is $3,000,000.
> 3. The lender requires non-compensating balances.
> 4. The commitment fee is 0.25% based on the unused portion of the line.
> 5. The interest rate charged is set annually with a spread of 2% over prime. (Prime is assumed to be 8%.)
> 6. Year basis used is 365.
>
> The effective annual borrowing rate is:
>
> $$\text{Effective Annual Borrowing Rate} = \frac{(\text{Interest Rate} \times \text{Average Loan Outstanding}) + \text{Commitment Fee}}{\text{Usable Funds Borrowed}}$$
>
> $$= \left(\frac{(.10 \times \$1,000,000) + (.0025 \times \$2,000,000)}{\$1,000,000}\right) \times \left(\frac{365}{365}\right)$$
>
> $$= \left(\frac{(\$100,000 + \$5000)}{\$1,000,000}\right) \times (1) = 10.5\%$$
>
> The commitment fee in this example adds 50 basis points (1/100 of an interest point) to the interest rate of 10%. If there is a compensating balance requirement, the average amount of compensating balances is subtracted from the amount of funds in the denominator to determine the amount of the usable funds. Given the above assumptions with a compensating balance requirement equal to 10% of the commitment amount, the effective annual borrowing rate becomes 15%, calculated as follows:
>
> $$\text{Effective Annual Borrowing Rate} = \frac{(\text{Interest Rate} \times \text{Average Loan Outstanding}) + \text{Commitment Fee}}{\text{Usable Funds Borrowed}}$$
>
> $$= \left(\frac{(.10 \times \$1,000,000) + (.0025 \times \$2,000,000)}{\$1,000,000 - (3,000,000 \times .10)}\right) \times \left(\frac{365}{365}\right)$$
>
> $$= \left(\frac{\$100,000 + \$5000}{\$700,000}\right) \times (1) = .15 = 15\%$$

The key characteristics of CP include:

1. **Discount Issuance** — CP is generally issued on a discount basis similar to Treasury bills (T-bills). The actual rate paid by a company is market-based and is a function of the issuing company's credit rating, the size of the issue and general market short-term interest rates. Companies with the highest credit ratings can usually raise funds by issuing CP at a lower effective rate than borrowing under a commercial bank line of credit. When CP is issued, there are underwriting or agency fees and charges related to any credit enhancement obtained, but these are usually small relative to the size of the CP issue.

2. **Distribution** — CP is usually sold through dealers, either investment banking companies or commercial banks. Some companies sell CP directly to investors. The general process of commercial paper issuance is outlined in Exhibit 13.2.

3. **Credit Enhancement** — Some CP borrowers arrange back-up lines of credit that may be used if market conditions are not conducive to issuing or refinancing CP. Another alternative to a backup line is to obtain a bank standby letter of credit.

4. **Credit Rating** — CP of a specific issuer is generally rated by the major credit rating agencies.

5. **Effective Annual Interest Cost for Commercial Paper** — The effective annual interest cost for CP takes into account the discount rate, the dealer fee and, in some cases, the cost of a back-up line or standby letter of credit. An example of this calculation is provided in Exhibit 13.3.

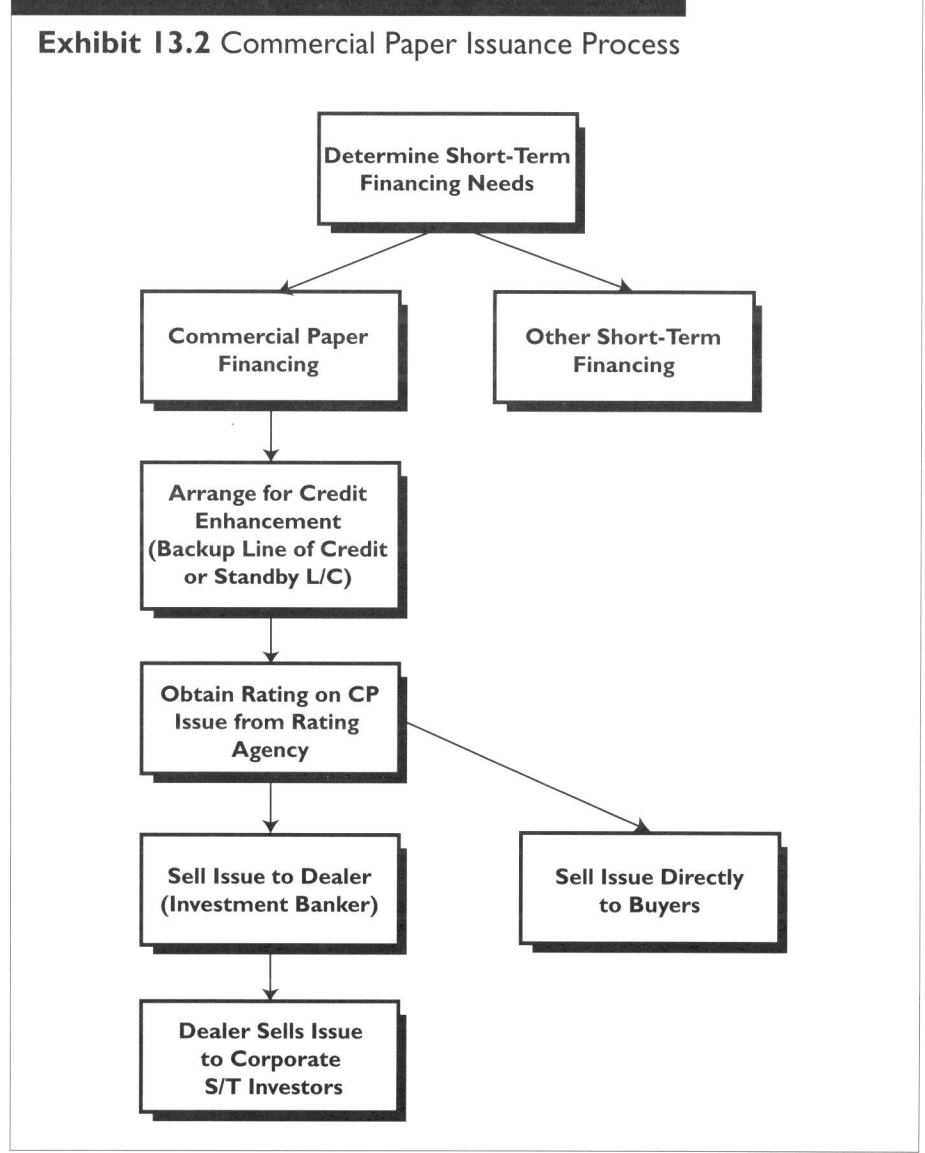

Exhibit 13.2 Commercial Paper Issuance Process

D. Reverse Repurchase Agreement

In a reverse repurchase agreement (reverse repo), sometimes known as a resale agreement, a company holding securities in its short-term portfolio sells the securities to a dealer with an agreement to buy them back at a specific price at a specific time. In effect, the company is borrowing cash from the dealer and using its securities as collateral for the loan. This is the reverse of a repurchase agreement, or repo. (See Chapter 12, Investing.)

E. Banker's Acceptance (BA)

A BA is a negotiable short-term instrument used primarily to finance the import, export or domestic shipment of goods or the storage of readily marketable staples. (See Chapter 15, International Treasury Management.) A BA has the following characteristics:

- It is a debt obligation evidenced by a time draft drawn by the borrower that is accepted by the bank on which it is drawn. By accepting the draft, the bank becomes directly obligated for payment of the draft on the maturity date.

- It is a readily marketable instrument that can be discounted in the money market. The discounted proceeds are advanced to the borrower, who is obligated to pay the full draft amount to the accepting bank at maturity. The accepting bank is, in turn, obligated to pay the investor who purchased the BA.

- The pricing compares favorably with other short-term borrowing rates. The all-in rate for acceptance financing includes the discount rate plus the BA commission paid to the accepting bank.

- Acceptance financing is often provided to a buyer or seller in connection with a letter of credit, but acceptances can be created to finance open account transactions as well.

F. Asset-Based Borrowing

Some financial institutions specialize in a form of secured lending based on the pledging of accounts receivable, inventory or equipment as collateral for a loan. The following are examples of asset-based borrowing:

1. **Collateralizing Accounts Receivable** — Accounts receivable represent the most common form of collateral for asset-based borrowing. In establishing this type of borrowing arrangement:

    - The lender evaluates the type of customers who buy from the borrower by analyzing the volume of customer purchases, delinquency rates and the level

Exhibit 13.3 Effective Cost for Commercial Paper Calculation Example

1. A company issues $20,000,000 of commercial paper with a 30-day maturity at a discount rate of 8%.
2. The paper is sold through a dealer at an annual charge of 1/8 of 1%.
3. The company has a backup line of credit in the amount of $20,000,000 and pays an annual commitment fee of 0.25% on the line.
4. Since this commercial paper is sold at a discount, the company will receive only $20,000,000 less 30 days' worth of interest at 8%.
5. A 360-day-year basis is the U.S. convention for this instrument.

The amount of usable funds is:

$$\text{Usable Funds} = \text{Face Value} \times \left[1 - \left(\text{Discount Rate} \times \frac{\text{Days to Maturity}}{360}\right)\right]$$

$$= \$20,000,000 \times \left[1 - \left(.08 \times \frac{30}{360}\right)\right] = \$19,866,667$$

The interest cost is the difference between the face value of $20,000,000 and the funds received, $19,866,667, which equals $133,333.

In addition to interest cost, the dealer charges and backup line of credit costs must be considered to determine the total issue costs.

Most commercial paper users issue new commercial paper on a fairly continuous basis, so the prorated figures for both the dealer cost and the cost of the backup credit line are the most appropriate in determining total issue costs.

$$\text{Prorated Dealer Cost} = .00125 \times \$20,000,000 \times \left(\frac{30}{360}\right) = \$2,083$$

$$\text{Prorated Backup Credit} = .0025 \times \$20,000,000 \times \left(\frac{30}{360}\right) = \$4,167$$

Total Issue Costs = Interest Cost + Prorated Dealer Cost + Prorated Backup Credit Line Costs
 = $133,333 + $2,083 + $4,167 = $139,583

The effective annual interest cost is determined by dividing the total costs by the amount of usable funds and annualizing this rate. The effective annual cost of the issue to the company is:

$$\text{Effective Annual Cost of Issue} = \left(\frac{\text{Total Issue Costs}}{\text{Usable Funds}}\right) \times \left(\frac{365}{\text{Maturity}}\right)$$

$$= \left(\frac{\$139,583}{\$19,866,667}\right) \times \left(\frac{365}{30}\right) = .0855 = 8.55\%$$

The interest cost paid by the issuer is the interest earned by an investor. The usable funds available to the issuer is the purchase price an investor must pay for the CP. Therefore, the yield to the investor is calculated as follows:

$$\text{Yield to Investor} = \left(\frac{\text{Interest Cost}}{\text{Usable Funds}}\right) \times \left(\frac{365}{30}\right)$$

$$= \left(\frac{\$133,333}{\$19,866,667}\right) \times \left(\frac{365}{30}\right) = .0817 = 8.17\%$$

of bad-debt write-offs. The lender also monitors the borrower's accounts receivable aging schedule to determine the timeliness of customer payments.

- An advance rate is determined based on this evaluation. The advance rate is stated as a percentage of accounts receivable outstanding. This percentage, when applied to the amount of pledged accounts receivable, determines the maximum amount that can be borrowed. For example, a lender may restrict a borrower's loan amount to the lesser of the commitment amount or 80 percent of its accounts receivable under 90 days of age. When used in conjunction with a line of credit, the commitment amount will vary on a monthly basis as the accounts receivable change.

- An asset-based lender normally requires the borrower's customers to remit payments directly to the lender. These payments are then applied to the outstanding loan balance.

2. **Collateralizing Inventory** — Inventory represents the other most common form of collateral for asset-based borrowing. As with accounts receivable financing, borrowing is limited by the advance rate and is calculated as a percentage of inventory. In determining the advance rate, the lender has to take into consideration the risk that the borrower will not be able to sell the inventory for reasons such as fluctuating market conditions, changes in commodity prices, spoilage or obsolescence.

    Generally, inventory lenders are more willing to advance against finished goods and raw materials than work in process. Sometimes different advance rates are determined for these different types of inventories. However, the advance rate is typically much less than it is for accounts receivable.

3. **Floor Planning** — This type of financing is frequently used to support the inventory of dealers who specialize in high-cost durable goods such as automobiles, trucks, farm equipment and major appliances. The lender advances funds to pay for specific inventory purchases. To secure the amount owed to it by the dealer, the lender retains legal title to the goods until they are sold. The proceeds from the sale are then used to repay the loan.

4. **Other Asset-Backed Borrowing** — Borrowers sometimes pledge real estate, machinery or other tangible property as collateral for loans.

5. **Factoring** — Factoring is the sale or transfer of title to accounts receivable to a third party (factor). A factor is a financing institution that discounts acceptable accounts receivable with or without recourse to the borrower. For this service, the factor charges a percentage commission on the amount of receivables depending on the quality of the receivables. The advantage of factoring is that the factor lends based on the quality of the company's clients and is not, therefore, dependent on the company's financial statements. A factoring arrangement is also able to re-

spond more quickly to changes in sales level (and thus receivables) than a typical lending facility. (This topic is covered in more detail in Chapter 5, Credit and Accounts Receivable Management.)

G. Securitization

Securitization is a financing technique by which a company issues debt securities backed by a pool of its selected receivables such as mortgages, auto loans, credit card receivables or equipment leases. Assets suitable for debt securitization usually have a predictable cash flow stream to retire the issue and a low level of historical loss experience.

Securitization is a type of off-balance-sheet financing. Neither the debt nor the assets securing the financing appear on a company's balance sheet. By removing debt financing from the balance sheet, securitization improves some companies' financial ratios.

Sometimes securitized issues are credit enhanced in order to receive a higher credit rating. Typical methods of credit enhancement include:

- Providing over-collateralization with securitized assets that have a higher present value than that of the debt issue they are backing.
- Opening a letter of credit from a financial institution.
- Establishing a spread account, which is a reserve built from excess cash flow from underlying assets beyond that required for debt service.
- Providing recourse to the issuer should the securitized assets not provide the projected cash flow to pay off the debt.
- Current accounting guidelines under Financial Accounting Standard 125 (FAS 125) require that funds from securitized issues must be segregated from other cash flows.

H. Loan Syndication and Participation

Loan syndications and participations enable a company to structure large credit facilities with a number of lenders to overcome legal or policy limitations faced by a single lender.

1. **Loan Syndication** — In a loan syndication, multiple financial institutions share a single credit facility. The syndicate, or group of lenders, is led by an agent who acts as the intermediary between the company and the syndicate for purposes of negotiating the credit terms and documentation, making advances and payments on the

loan and disseminating information. All the syndicate members share common documentation, but each lender has a promissory note, making it a direct lending relationship.

2. **Loan Participation** — With a loan participation, a financial institution purchases an interest in another lender's credit facility. This purchaser is called a participant and the seller is commonly referred to as the lead institution. The participant does not have a separate note and has only an indirect relationship with the borrower. The participation agreement specifies the rights and the obligations of both the participant and the lead institution. In the case of a blind participation, the participation is not disclosed to the borrower and the participant may not directly contact the borrower or disclose the participant's role in the credit facility.

I. Trade Credit

Trade credit is financing that is created when a seller grants credit terms on purchases made by its customers. The most common form is an open account in which the seller gives the buyer a specified period of time to pay for goods or services purchased. Trade credit can be an important part of a company's overall financing strategy. (See Chapter 5, Credit and Accounts Receivable Management.)

J. Export Financing Programs

Export and import financing is available from both commercial lenders and through various programs offered by the Export-Import Bank of the United States. (See Chapter 15, International Treasury Management.)

IV. Medium-and Long-Term Borrowing Alternatives

From an accounting perspective, anything maturing beyond one year is considered long-term. For the purposes of borrowing, however, a distinction is made between medium-and long-term debt. Medium-term debt is generally considered to mature between two and 10 years from the date of issuance. Long-term debt typically has a maturity of more than 10 years. Typically, companies borrow long-term to finance long-term needs such as capital expenditures and borrow short-term for short-term needs such as working capital.

A. Medium-Term Notes

Medium-term notes are a form of debt and are usually sold in two to 10 year maturities. Many companies are increasingly using medium-term notes to finance their needs.

B. Bonds

A bond is a form of long-term debt that may be issued at face value and bears interest over its term. It may also be issued at a discount and accrete to face value at maturity. The agreement among all the parties to a bond issue is known as an indenture. It defines details of the issue such as terms and conditions, covenants, events of default, subordination, sinking fund, property to be pledged, if any and the duties of the trustee.

Bonds have the following components or characteristics:

1. **Trustee Administration** — Bonds are administered through a trustee. The trustee is a third party who is responsible for ensuring that the bonds are authentic, ensuring that sinking fund and interest payments are properly paid and applied and administering redemption. In the event of default, the trustee represents the bondholders in legal proceedings.

2. **Ratings** — Bonds are often rated by credit rating agencies according to factors such as the financial strength and future prospects of the company and the collateral securing the bond. The ratings apply to the bonds themselves, not the company. (See Chapter 12, Investing.)

3. **Marketability** — Bonds are usually traded publicly through securities dealers and securities exchanges, but may also be sold directly to institutional investors. Changes in interest rates affect the value of a bond that is traded prior to maturity.

4. **Security** — Bonds may be either secured or unsecured. Secured bonds are collateralized by a specific asset or revenues from a specific project. Secured debt gives the investor a lien against an asset. Bonds may be secured by various assets, including

inventories, real estate or fixed (capital) assets. Unsecured bonds, called debentures, offer no collateral. Debenture holders have a general claim against a company but not against a specific asset.

5. **Ranking** — Bonds may be equal, senior, or subordinated in relation to other debt obligations. In the event of liquidation, holders of secured debt, whether senior or junior, will be paid off before holders of unsecured debt. Then senior unsecured debt holders will be paid off before the subordinated debenture holders. The more junior the debt, the greater the risk to the investor and the higher the borrowing costs to a company.

6. **Retirement Before Maturity** — A call feature on a bond allows the issuer to retire the security before maturity. Bondholders must sell the security back to the company at par (face value) or a predetermined premium over face value. A call provision is often useful for the issuer if there is a good possibility that interest rates will fall during the life of the bond. The company can call the bond and refinance with less expensive debt.

C. Special Types of Bonds

Special types of bonds include:

1. **Municipal Bonds** — Municipal bonds are bonds issued by a state or local government entity and are typically repaid out of tax revenue. Most municipal bonds enjoy special tax-exempt status for federal tax purposes. The most common type of municipal bond is a general obligation security. (See Chapter 12, Investing.)

2. **Industrial Revenue Bonds** — Industrial Revenue Bonds (IRBs) are a special classification of municipal bonds issued by a government entity, often for the purpose of financing specific projects that are either publicly or privately managed.

3. **High-Yield Bonds** — These bonds are also known as junk bonds and are high-yield, non-investment-grade securities. These bonds are typically issued by companies that are already highly leveraged.

4. **Zero Coupon Bonds** — These are bonds that require no periodic interest payments, but only a single payment of face value at maturity. Due to this single-payment feature, they are sold at deep discount from their face value.

5. **Eurobonds** — Eurobonds are bonds issued outside the country where the currency of those bonds is domiciled. For example, dollar-denominated Eurobonds are bonds issued in U.S. dollars outside the United States. They offer the U.S. issuing company access to foreign capital markets without exchange risk and offer foreign investors easy access to U.S. dollar-denominated investments.

6. **Foreign Bonds** — Foreign bonds are issued in a country's local currency by companies based outside that country (for example, a U.S.-based company that issues Swiss Franc bonds in Switzerland). Foreign bonds are typically used to finance the issuer's operations in that area.

D. Debt-Equity Hybrids

Debt-equity hybrids have both debt and equity characteristics. The following are types of debt-equity hybrids:

1. **Convertible Bonds** — Convertible bonds are bonds that are convertible into shares of a company's common stock at a defined price. They generally provide the borrower with a lower interest rate than non-convertible bonds because of the equity conversion option.

2. **Bonds with Equity Warrants** — An equity warrant is a long-term option to buy a stated number of shares of common stock at a specified (exercise) price. When a warrant is attached to a bond, the resulting combination provides the same type of hybrid as a convertible bond. However, warrants are usually detachable from the bond so that they may be exercised without having to surrender the bond.

3. **Redeemable Preferred Stock** — Redeemable preferred stock is stock that has a predetermined redemption schedule. In addition, redeemable preferred stock normally provides for the accrual or payment of a regular dividend. The dividend and redemption features are essentially the same as the interest and repayment features on bonds.

E. Term Loan

Term loans are made for a fixed period of time, typically two to 10 years, usually to support equipment purchases and more permanent capital financing. Repayment schedules vary depending on the type of loan and the nature of the project being financed. Typical amortization schedules require periodic payments of principal plus interest, but some may require periodic interest payments with repayment of principal upon maturity.

F. Leasing

Leasing, an alternative to term lending, is used extensively as a means of financing equipment. Leasing arrangements are characterized by the following:

- In a typical leasing arrangement, the lessor actually owns the equipment and leases it to the lessee.

- In leasing, typically 100 percent of the equipment's cost is financed and payment amounts can be fixed or variable.

- A leasing arrangement can be structured as either on-or off-balance-sheet. An on-balance-sheet arrangement is referred to as a capital lease; an off-balance-sheet arrangement is referred to as an operating lease. Accounting and tax issues must be evaluated to determine the proper classification of a lease.

- An operating lease offers tax advantages to both parties. The lessor realizes the benefit of depreciation and the lessee has tax-deductible operating expenses.

- End-of-term options typically allow the lessee to return, purchase or re-lease the equipment.

G. Private Placement

A private placement is typically a direct sale of securities by a company to institutional investors such as insurance companies or pension funds. Private placements have the following characteristics:

- Private placements are not registered with the SEC.

- Terms and conditions are often spelled out in an agreement called a note-purchase agreement or a private placement memorandum.

- A private placement can be arranged by an investment banking company, a commercial bank or the borrower.

- Private placements are usually less costly for the issuer to arrange than publicly issued debt and may offer longer and more flexible terms than commercial bank term loans. However, the interest rate on private placement issues may be higher than public debt of similar credit quality and maturity.

V. Repayment of Principal

Corporate debt can be structured to allow for various principal and interest payment schedules. In general, the repayment of debt should be matched to the cash flows related to the underlying asset or project being financed.

The two most common methods of debt repayment are amortization and sinking fund.

A. Amortization

Amortization is the repayment of the loan principal in installments over the life of the loan. This enables the borrower to pay off the principal gradually, rather than at one point in time. It also reduces the lender's risk by shortening the average life of the loan.

The characteristics and options of amortization schedules include:
- The schedule may be matched to the cash flows expected from the project or equipment being financed and may vary depending on the type and maturity of the loan.
- Some schedules provide for equal principal installments over the life of the loan; others, such as mortgages, have equal payments incorporating both principal and interest over the life of the loan.
- Some schedules allow a grace period whereby the repayment of principal does not begin until some specified future date. For example, an eight-year loan with a two-year grace period would mean that principal payments would not commence until the third year of the loan.
- Some schedules have balloon payments where the principal is amortized over time, but a large "balloon" payment is due at maturity. Balloon payments result when the amortization period exceeds the contractual term of the loan.
- Some loans have bullet maturities in which the entire principal is due on the final maturity date and no amortization occurs.

B. Sinking Fund

A sinking fund assures creditors that adequate funds are available to meet payments at maturity. The borrower makes periodic payments to a separate custodial account that is used to repay the debt.

VI. Legal Aspects of Borrowing

A. Loan Agreements and Bond Indentures

Loan agreements and bond indentures are legal documents that spell out the terms and conditions under which the debt is extended. The primary components of a loan agreement or bond indenture include:

1. **Representations and Warranties** — Representations and warranties are the conditions that exist at the time the loan agreement is executed as attested to by the borrower.

    They generally include:
    - Affirmation of the valid legal existence of the borrowing company, a resolution by the borrower's board of directors authorizing the borrowing and the authority of the corporate officers signing the documents
    - The company confirming its compliance with the Employee Retirement Income and Security Act (ERISA)
    - An indemnity protecting the lender from environmental liabilities

2. **Covenants** — Covenants are provisions that restrict the borrower's activities in ways that protect the lender during the term of the agreement. Examples of covenants include the following:
    - Financial Ratios
        — Maximum debt to equity ratio
        — Minimum interest coverage ratio
        — Minimum tangible net worth
        — Minimum current ratio or working capital
    - Borrower Limitations
        — Limitations on capital expenditures
        — Limitations on incurring other debt or lease obligations
        — Limitations on payment of dividends
        — Limitations on mergers and acquisitions
        — Limitations on the sale or pledge of assets
        — Limitations on stock or debt repurchases
    - Borrower Obligations

— Requirement to comply with environmental requirements for properties

— Requirement to maintain adequate insurance coverage

3. **Events of Default** — An event of default may occur if any term or condition under a debt agreement is breached or violated by the borrower. Events of default are incidences such as non-payment of interest or principal when due, a material adverse change in the condition of the borrower or violation of a specified covenant. The characteristics of events of default include the following:

- A cure period, or a period of time in which an event of default may be corrected before the lender is allowed to pursue his default remedies, is often specified in the agreement.

- Remedies available to a lender when a default occurs normally include an acceleration of all principal and interest on the debt.

- Waivers of defaults may be given at the lender's discretion.

B. Promissory Notes

A promissory note is an unconditional promise to pay a specified amount plus interest at a defined rate either on demand or on a certain date. A promissory note can be issued for each individual borrowing or for a total line amount against which multiple borrowings are made.

A master note is a type of promissory note used to simplify the paperwork connected with loans that have a multiple advance feature such as lines of credit and revolvers. A company signs one comprehensive promissory note for the total amount of the line of credit. Any loans or repayments under the note are covered by the terms of the master note.

Test Your Understanding

These chapter questions are provided to test your understanding of the information in the text and are not examples of CCM examination questions, nor are they in the examination format.

Answers can be found at the back of the book on pages 535-537.

1. What are the major objectives of a company's borrowing program?

2. What is venture capital?

3. Define LIBOR.

4. Explain the concept of credit support or enhancement.

5. What is a committed line of credit?

6. A firm has an average loan outstanding of $200,000 on a $500,000 line of credit. There is a commitment fee of 0.25 percent on the unused portion of the line and the interest rate on the borrowed funds is seven percent. If there is no compensating balance requirement, what is the effective annual borrowing rate on the loan?

7. How are lines of credit used in conjunction with commercial paper?

8. A company issues $1,000,000 of commercial paper with a 60-day maturity at a discount rate of six percent. The paper is sold through a dealer for a charge of 1/4 of one percent. There is no backup line of credit. What is the effective annual interest cost of issuing the commercial paper?

9. Explain loan participation.

10. What are two characteristics an asset should have to be suitable for securitization?

11. What is a bond indenture?

12. Discuss the difference between an operating lease and a capital lease.

13. What is a sinking fund?

14. Why will a company issue convertible bonds?

15. What may the lender do if a default occurs?

CHAPTER 14

Financial Risk Management

Overview

Uncertainty about the future course of financial prices — such as interest rates, exchange rates and commodity prices — exposes a company to financial risk. This chapter deals with the basics of financial risk and introduces the reader to the alternative methods and instruments that can be used by companies to manage this risk.

Learning Objectives

Upon completion of this chapter and the related study questions the reader should understand:

- Why there is a need for risk management
- The objectives of financial risk management
- The definition and types of financial derivatives
- How financial derivatives are used to manage risk
- The definition of interest rate exposure and how to manage it
- The definition of exchange rate exposure and how to manage it
- The definition of commodity price risk and how to manage it
- Accounting and tax issues related to financial risk management

Key Concepts

- Nature of financial risk
- Identification of risk
- Measurement of risk
- Risk management instruments
- Monitoring performance

Outline

I. What is Risk Management?

II. Overview of Financial Risk Management
    A. Risk Management Process
    B. The Risk Profile
    C. Hedging, Speculation and Arbitrage
    D. Risk Management, Cash Flow Variability and Value of the Company

III. Derivative Instruments Used as Risk Management Tools
    A. Forwards
    B. Futures
    C. Swaps
    D. Options

IV. Interest Rate Exposure
    A. Examples of Interest Rate Exposure
    B. Different Types of Interest Rate Derivatives

V. Exchange Rate Exposure
    A. Types of Foreign Exchange Exposure
    B. Currency Derivatives Used to Hedge Foreign Exchange Exposure

VI. Commodity Price Exposure
    A. Examples of Commodity Exposure
    B. Derivative Instruments Used to Hedge Commodity Exposure

VII. Accounting and Tax Issues
    A. Accounting Issues
    B. Tax Issues Related to Hedging

I. What is Risk Management

Companies face a variety of risks ranging from those that are considered operational to those that are more financial in nature. The most common risk is that of general risk from daily operations (i.e., the overall risk of being in business). One type of risk faced by all companies is that of making poor business decisions on products, services or even marketing strategy that result in losses and ultimately the demise of the company. The more traditional view of risk management is actually tied closely to determining and managing the "insurable" risks faced by a firm from losses due to accidents, natural disasters and other unforeseen events.

Companies are also exposed to various sources of financial risk. This financial risk stems from the uncertainty of the future level of interest rates, exchange rates and commodity prices. Since the late 1960s, there has been a significant increase in the volatility of interest rates, exchange rates and commodity prices. In recent years, the role of the treasury manager in determining and handling financial risk has increased significantly. Though the topics of operational and insurance risk management are important to the overall survival of a company, they are not often under the control of the treasury manager. This chapter, therefore, will focus on the area of financial risk management.

There are several examples of industries and companies that have been subjected to the pressures of financial risk.

1. **Interest Rate Risk** — The case of the savings and loan (S&L) industry in the United States during the 1980s is an example of a sector exposed to risk stemming from interest rate changes. As interest rates were rising, many S&Ls were locked into low interest rate loans on the asset side of their balance sheets, but had to offer higher and higher rates on deposits to compete with newly created money market and mutual funds. The ultimate result was that a significant number of S&Ls engaged in highly speculative real estate lending that ultimately caused a near collapse of the industry.

2. **Foreign Exchange (FX) Risk** — A classic case dealing with exchange rate risk is the story of Laker Airlines. In the late 1970s, the British pound was strong relative to the U.S. dollar. This increased the demand for air travel from Britain to the United States. Laker Airlines increased the supply of airline seats by buying five DC-10s and financing them with U.S. dollars. The company's revenues were primarily in pounds, while payment for the newly acquired aircraft was in dollars. The result was a mismatch of revenues and expenses, exposing Laker Airlines to exchange rate risk. In 1981, the pound weakened relative to the dollar, increasing the airline's expenses (Laker had to pay more pounds to make payments on its dollar debt) and reducing revenues (from a decrease in the demand for air travel to the United States because of the weaker pound). The consequence of this foreign exchange exposure was one of the factors that put Laker Airlines into bankruptcy.

3. **Commodity Price Risk** — Continental Airlines fell victim to the invasion of Kuwait by Iraq in 1990 when the price of a commodity — oil — changed unfavorably. Unable to cope with sharp increases in the price of jet fuel, the company ultimately filed for reorganization under bankruptcy laws.

It is this increased volatility of financial prices and the inability to deal with it that made the financial environment within which companies operate more risky than it had been in the past. This, in turn, created a demand for financial risk management, which sowed the seeds for financial innovation and the growth of a market for financial derivatives (such as forwards, futures, options and swaps) as instruments in the risk management process.

It is also important to note that the very nature of treasury operations makes it very vulnerable to significant financial risks. Treasury transactions are time sensitive, typically involve large sums of money and require decisions to be made in often volatile financial markets. Further complicating the risk management picture is the fact that treasury managers have access to an ever-increasing range of complex financial instruments, many of which are not even fully understood by the dealers offering them. Errors or mistakes in using these financial instruments for financial management may have an immediate cash impact and be very expensive to rectify.

II. Overview of Financial Risk Management

This section explains the process of managing financial risk. In addition, it explains how changes in a financial price variable will affect the value of the company, indicates how managing the exposure alters the company's risk profile and introduces the concepts of hedging, speculation and arbitrage.

A. Risk Management Process

The risk management process involves five steps:

1. **Determine the Company's Risk Attitude** — Different companies will take different attitudes toward taking risk. New companies in highly competitive and developing industries may be more willing to take on significant operational and financial risks as part of their strategic plan. More established companies in mature industries might be looking for much lower levels of risk. Some companies may desire to eliminate or hedge all financial risks, while others may only undertake partial hedges or manage only selective exposures. The key point for the treasury manager is to have clearly defined risk management policy directives from the highest management level possible, (the board of directors). This document should contain:

- A discussion of the company's attitude towards risk
- Objectives of treasury with respect to risk management functions
- Hierarchy of decision making and objectives
- Roles and responsibilities of key treasury individuals
- How results/performance are measured and reported

2. **Identifying the Exposure** — The interest rate changes, FX rate changes or commodity price changes to which a company is exposed will depend on its line of business. Because it may be exposed to one or more of these financial price changes, identification of the exposure in each area is necessary.

3. **Measuring the Exposure** — Once the exposure has been identified, measuring and quantifying that exposure is required. Management then needs to decide whether the company is in a position to tolerate the risk, or whether it should reduce or eliminate that exposure via an appropriate risk management strategy.

4. **Implementing an Appropriate Risk Management Strategy** — If the company needs to manage its risk, it must determine an appropriate strategy. The first step in the process is to examine the basic operating procedures and exposures to determine where balance sheet hedges can be used. A balance sheet hedge would match exposed liabilities against exposed assets. For example, the S&L industry could have created a balance sheet strategy of matching interest-sensitive assets with interest-sensitive liabilities, eliminating the exposure to interest rate changes. In many cases, it is not possible to hedge all exposures with balance sheet hedges and the mismatch can be managed using derivatives. The remainder of this chapter develops the strategy approach using derivatives.

5. **Monitoring the Exposure and Evaluating the Strategy** — Finally, the company must periodically monitor the exposure in each financial area. The time interval for monitoring the exposure is decided on an individual basis and may be shortened if volatility in the underlying asset market increases unexpectedly. In addition, the company needs to monitor the effectiveness of the strategy selected.

B. The Risk Profile

The way unexpected changes in a financial price variable such as interest rates, exchange rates or commodity prices may affect the value of a company can be demonstrated by a company's risk profile. The risk profile of a company is the relationship of how the value of the company changes as some financial price variable changes. The basic risk profile determines the sensitivity of the value of the company (typically measured by the company's equity value) as some important financial variable such as interest rates or FX rates change. The risk profile analysis needs to identify risks, classify them into clearly defined categories and quantify them with respect to their probability of occurrence and impact on the company. Following this analysis, the appropriate risk reduction measures (such as forwards, futures, swaps and options) and their impact on the final outcome must be determined.

1. **Value-at-Risk (VAR)** — One approach to determining how the value of a company is impacted by changing financial variables is called value-at-risk. This measure was actually developed in the trading rooms of financial institutions to provide an estimation of the possible loss for the entire trading operation. It was specifically designed to handle a wide range of risk factors and to summarize their impact on the operation into a single measure. In the VAR approach, risk is determined as a function of the probability and monetary impact of a particular adverse event over a certain period of time. For example, a company may determine that its foreign operations in a given country have a five percent chance of losing more than $1 million in the coming month due to exchange rate fluctuations. Typically companies will utilize historical simulations or scenario analysis to determine these VAR risk profiles. There are an increasing number of treasury system and other software providers who offer various types of VAR applications for their corporate and banking customers.

2. **Role of the Treasury Manager** — Treasury is becoming an increasingly critical participant in the determination of the risk profile for the company. As was discussed in Chapter 10, Information Management and Technology, treasury is becoming a clearing house for much of the financial information moving through the company. In addition, the development of many new types of financial derivative instruments and new requirements for disclosure of the use of these instruments make the treasury manager's role even more critical.

C. Hedging, Speculation and Arbitrage

It is critical for the treasury manager to understand the difference between hedging, speculation and arbitrage.

1. **Hedging** — Hedging is the process by which a company uses financial instruments to reduce or eliminate the risk associated with the uncertainty about the future price of the asset under consideration. The key point is that a hedging arrangement or transaction is one that reduces the company's risk.

2. **Speculation** — Speculation involves betting on the direction of the market. Speculators are those market participants who are willing to assume risk. In other words, speculators are betting that the price of the asset will either go up or go down. They have an open position in the asset and, unlike hedgers, do not have an underlying exposure they are offsetting. The key point here is that a speculation arrangement or transaction is one that increases the company's risk.

3. **Arbitrage** — Arbitrage is the process by which buying in one market and simultaneously selling in another leads to a riskless profit. Arbitrageurs do not assume

any risk, but attempt to profit from market inefficiencies. Taking advantage of such arbitrage opportunities keeps financial markets efficient. A true arbitrage arrangement or transaction should have no impact on the company's overall risk. Typically, however, it is difficult for a corporate treasury manager to take advantage of arbitrage opportunities. The market inefficiencies that cause arbitrage are extremely short-lived and small, meaning that only major players in the market with large amounts of capital can truly take advantage of them. For example, the major participants in the FX arbitrage market are the large banks and third-party dealers in the foreign currency markets.

D. Risk Management, Cash Flow Variability and Value of the Company

Risk management helps reduce the variability of a company's future cash flows, which in turn adds value to the company. As a risk management tool, hedging enables a company to smooth its cash flows over time, while the cash flows of the unhedged company tend to be more volatile.

The company with a lower variability of future cash flows as a result of hedging increases its value in several ways:

- As a result of hedging, the company is in a better position to assess its costs and revenues, which lowers the probability of financial distress.
- Shareholders attribute a higher value to companies with less volatile future cash flows.
- The hedged company with less volatile future cash flows is perceived as being less risky and has a borrowing advantage in credit markets.

III. Derivative Instruments Used as Risk Management Tools

A derivative instrument is a financial product that derives value from some underlying asset. The underlying asset could be a financial instrument, a currency or a commodity. Four basic types of derivative securities are forwards, futures, swaps and options.

A. Forwards

1. **Definition of Forwards** — A forward contract is an agreement between two parties to buy or sell a fixed amount of an asset to be delivered at a future date at a price agreed upon today. The company purchasing the forward contract is one of the parties; the other is typically referred to as the counterparty. In forward currency contracts, the counterparty is typically a bank or dealer in the FX markets.

- The asset involved is also referred to as the underlying asset. This underlying asset could be a financial instrument (such as stock index or debt instrument), currency (such as the euro or pound sterling) or a commodity (such as gold or coffee).

- The future date is also called the maturity date of the contract.

- The price is the delivery price of the contract.

  The party that has agreed to buy the asset is said to be long a forward contract, while the counterparty is short a forward contract. The long position in a forward contract gains value when the underlying asset price rises and loses value when the asset price falls. The short position gains value when the underlying asset price falls and loses value when the asset price rises. Exhibit 14.1a and Exhibit 14.1b depict the payoff profiles from a long and short position respectively in a forward contract.

2. **Basic Features of Forwards** — Some notable features of a forward contract are:
   - The forward markets are managed and supported by a group of banks, dealers and traders who act as market makers. Market makers are individuals who will quote both a bid and ask price whenever they are asked to do so. Therefore, forward contracts are private contracts between two parties.
   - These contracts are customized to each party's needs and not standardized like a futures contract. In other words, the amount of the underlying asset and the maturity date for the contract are set at the time the contract is negotiated.
   - Delivery of the underlying asset takes place at maturity.

3. **Example of Use of Forwards** — Suppose a U.S. importer needs to pay a 50,000 British pound sterling invoice in 90 days. The importer could purchase a forward contract now for sterling quoted at $1.69 per pound deliverable in 90 days. At the end of 90 days, the importer would pay $84,500 ($1.69 x £50,000) and receive £50,000 in order to pay the invoice. Thus, no matter what fluctuation occurred in the exchange rate of the 90-day time horizon, the purchase of the forward contract would lock in the exchange rate for the future time period.

B. Futures

1. **Definition of Futures** — Futures are similar to forwards in intent, but differ in execution. For example, the payoff profile from a long position in a futures contract and a short position in a futures contract looks exactly the same as the payoff from a forward contract (see Exhibit 14.1a and 14.1b). The main difference between futures and forwards is that futures are standardized contracts traded on organized exchanges.

Exhibit 14.1a Forward Contract — Long Position

Exhibit 14.1b Forward Contract — Short Position

2. **Features of Futures** — Some of the more notable features of futures contracts are:

   • Futures contracts are traded on an organized exchange. In the United States, futures contracts are traded on the Chicago Board of Trade (grains, metals, financials), the Chicago Mercantile Exchange (livestock, wood, meat) and its International Money Market (IMM) wing (which trades foreign currency futures) and the New York Mercantile Exchange (metals, petroleum, fiber), among others.

   • Futures contracts are standardized by the exchanges and have a range of delivery dates. The size of the contract and its maturity date are set by the exchange. An implication of this is that a treasurer may not be able to perfectly hedge an underlying position using a futures contract. For example, the size of a typical euro (€) contract on the Chicago Mercantile Exchange (CME) is €125,000. If the treasurer has an exposure that is not a multiple of this number, using a futures contract to hedge may exceed or fall short of the exposure.

- Futures trading requires a margin account that is marked-to-market on a daily basis. This means that the investor's/hedger's gains or losses on the position are reflected on a daily basis. If the margin account drops below a specified amount (the maintenance margin), a margin call is issued. This requires the holder of the account to replenish the account to the initial (margin) level or close out the position.

- Futures contracts are rarely settled by actual delivery and are usually closed out prior to maturity.

3. **Example of Use of Futures** — Suppose a company buys oil as an input to its chemical production process. The company is uncertain as to the future cost of oil and wishes to protect itself from fluctuations in the commodity price. In such a case the company could purchase a futures contract for oil now and hold it until it must purchase oil in the commodity market.

If the price of oil goes up, causing an increase in the company's raw material cost, the company could sell the futures contract, whose price would also rise, for a profit. The profit gained on the futures contract could then be used to offset the higher purchase cost of the commodity.

To put the above example in numerical terms, assume the futures contract allows the company to purchase oil for $35 a barrel. When the company needs to buy oil in the future, the price has risen to $40 a barrel. In this scenario, the company would buy its needed oil in the open market, paying $40 a barrel. The futures contract that it holds to buy oil at $35 a barrel has a profit of $5 per barrel. The company sells its futures contract and uses the $5 per barrel profit to offset its purchase price on the spot market, effectively achieving a net price of $35 per barrel.

If instead, the price of oil were to drop to $30 per barrel, then the company would still buy the needed oil on the open market and close its futures contract at a loss of $5 per barrel. The net cost of oil to the company would still be $35 per barrel.

C. Swaps

1. **Definition of Swaps** — A swap is an agreement between two parties to exchange (or swap) a set of cash flows at future points in time.

2. **Features of Swaps** — Some of the more notable features of swap contracts are:
    - The most common type of swap is an interest rate swap. In such an arrangement, Party X may agree to pay Party Y a stream of cash flows equal to a floating rate of interest on some mutually agreed-upon amount referred to as

a notional principal. At the same time, Party Y agrees to pay Party X a stream of cash flows equal to a fixed rate of interest on the same notional principal at the same future dates. The principal is notional because it does not exchange hands. Only the interest payments are exchanged. In other words, Party X is swapping a fixed-rate loan for a floating-rate loan, while Party Y is doing exactly the opposite.

- There are several other types of swap arrangements, with the more common ones being currency and commodity swaps. Currency swaps are where the agreement is to convert an obligation in one currency to an obligation in another currency. Commodity swaps are where a floating price for a commodity is exchanged for a fixed price.

- One of the primary risks in using swaps is that of counterparty risk. The value of the swap depends on the other party fulfilling their obligations to make the agreed-upon payment stream. If the other party (the counter-party) does not make their payments, the first company may still be liable for the original payment stream or cash flow. Using a trusted third party such as bank or FX dealer may help to mitigate these risks.

- Some bankers are requiring some of the asset-based borrowers (especially those of sub-investment grade) to swap their initially floating-rate credit facility into a fixed-rate facility so that they can better manage interest rate risk.

3. **Example of Use of Swaps** — Consider the following example. Suppose that two parties, X and Y, both wish to borrow $20 million for 10 years. Also assume that X has a better credit rating than Y and that each has been offered the borrowing rates given below:

	Fixed Rate	Floating Rate
Party X	10.00%	6-month LIBOR + 0.50%
Party Y	11.00%	6-month LIBOR + 1.00%

Assume Party X wants to borrow at a floating rate, while Party Y wants to borrow at a fixed rate due to its own particular financial strategy needs. Because Party X has a better credit rating than Party Y, it pays a lower rate in both fixed and floating markets. Even though Party Y pays more in both markets, it pays relatively less in the floating-rate market. So Party X has a comparative borrowing advantage in the fixed-rate market, while Party Y has a comparative borrowing advantage in the floating-rate market. This provides the basis for an interest rate swap.

A potential interest rate swap would be the following:

- Party X borrows at a fixed rate of 10 percent and Party Y at a floating rate of the London Interbank Offered Rate (LIBOR) plus one percent.

- They then enter into a swap agreement, by which Party X agrees to pay for funds at a floating-rate and Party Y agrees to pay for funds at a fixed rate.

- Assuming that Parties X and Y get in touch with each other directly or through a third-party dealer, they may negotiate a swap agreement as shown in Exhibit 14.2.

- The net advantage to the swap agreement is 50 basis points, which we assume for this example will be split evenly between the two parties (i.e., each will be better off by 25 basis points as a result of the swap agreement).

- Party X makes payments to a lender at a fixed rate of 10 percent. It makes payments based on LIBOR to Party Y and receives payments from Party Y at a fixed rate of 9.75 percent to offset the payments to its lender. The rate of 9.75 percent is determined by taking the 10 percent fixed rate and subtracting the 25 basis point advantage due to each party. The net effect of this arrangement for Party X is that it ends up paying LIBOR plus .25 percent, which is 25 basis points less than what it would have paid if it borrowed directly from the floating-rate market.

- On the other hand, Party Y makes payments to a lender at a fixed rate of LIBOR plus one percent. It makes payments based on a fixed rate of 9.75 percent to Party X and receives payments based on LIBOR from Party X. The net effect of this for Party Y is that it ends up paying a fixed rate of 10.75 percent, (9.75 percent to Party X and one percent on the LIBOR loan). The net fixed rate paid is 25 basis points less than what it would have paid if it borrowed directly from the fixed-rate market.

There are several other types of swap arrangements. Among the more common ones are:

- Currency swaps, where the agreement is to convert an obligation in one currency to an obligation in another currency.

- Commodity swaps, where a floating price for a commodity is exchanged for a fixed price.

D. Options

1. **Definition of Options** — An option is a contract between two parties wherein the buyer of the contract has the right (but not the obligation) to either buy or sell a fixed amount of some underlying asset at a fixed price, on or before a specified date. The party offering the option is called the writer of the option.

2. **Features of Options** — Some of the more notable features of options contracts are:

    - If the contract gives the owner the right to buy the underlying asset at a fixed price, the option is a call option.

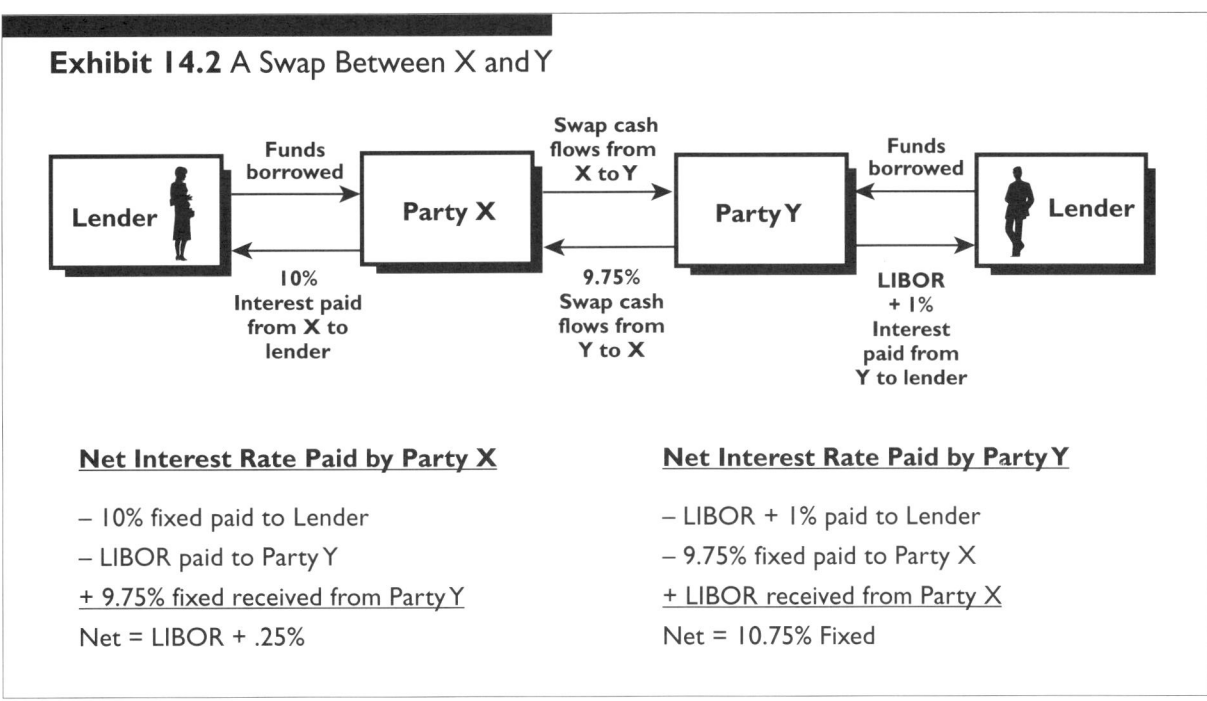

Exhibit 14.2 A Swap Between X and Y

Net Interest Rate Paid by Party X

− 10% fixed paid to Lender
− LIBOR paid to Party Y
+ 9.75% fixed received from Party Y
Net = LIBOR + .25%

Net Interest Rate Paid by Party Y

− LIBOR + 1% paid to Lender
− 9.75% fixed paid to Party X
+ LIBOR received from Party X
Net = 10.75% Fixed

- If the contract gives the owner the right to sell the underlying asset at a fixed price, the option is a put option.

- The fixed price is called the strike/exercise price of the contract and the specified date is the maturity date (or exercise date) of the contract.

- If the contract allows the buyer to exercise (buy/sell the underlying asset) the option only at maturity, then the contract is called a European option contract. If the contract allows the owner to exercise the option at any time prior to maturity, then the contract is called an American option contract. There are American calls and puts as well as European calls and puts.

- Unlike forwards and futures, options have a premium associated with them. The seller of the option (also called the writer of the contract) receives a premium from the buyer (or holder) of the contract. In return, the writer has the obligation to fulfill the contract (sell or buy the underlying asset) if the buyer chooses to exercise the contract.

- There are a variety of payoff possibilities with options:

    – An option is at-the-money if the underlying asset price is equal to the strike price of the option.

    – A call option is out-of-the-money if the asset price is less than the strike price of the option.

    – A put option is out-of-the-money if the asset price exceeds the strike price of the option.

- An important feature of using options to manage financial risk is that they allow the hedger to participate in a favorable market. Forwards and futures lock the hedger into a price independent of market changes.

- Options may also be useful for a company bidding on a project that may cause financial exposures if the bid is accepted. For example, a U.S. company bids on providing products or services priced in euros to a French company. Due to a large number of other bidders, it is uncertain if it will win the bid. If the bid is accepted, then the company will have an exposure due to the euro-denominated receivables that will result. A currency option would allow them to lock in a minimum value for the euro for a known premium. If the company does not win the bid, then they can close out the option if it has a value or let it expire if it is out-of-the-money. They are not obligated to exchange the currencies as they would with a forward or exposed to potential losses as they would with a future.

3. **Example of Use of Options** — Consider the following examples.
   - *Call Option Example* — Consider an investor who buys a three-month crude oil call option with a strike (or exercise) price of $40 per barrel and pays $2 for it. The payoff (or profit and loss) from this would look like Exhibit 14.3a. If at maturity the market price of crude oil is less than or equal to the strike price of $40, the investor does not exercise the option (because it is cheaper to buy oil at the market price than by exercising the option) and has a loss (of $2) equal to the option premium. When the market price is greater than the strike price plus the option premium ($40 + $2 = $42), the investor makes a profit.

   - *Put Option Example* — Consider an investor who buys a one-month put option on crude oil with a strike (or exercise) price of $35 per barrel and pays $1 for it. The payoff (or profit and loss) from this would look like Exhibit 14.3b. If at maturity the market price of crude oil is greater than or equal to the strike price of $35, the investor does not exercise the option (because the investor will receive more by selling oil at the market price than by exercising the option) and takes a loss (of $1) equal to the option premium. If at maturity the market price of crude oil is less than the strike price, the investor exercises the option. When the market price is less than the strike price minus the option premium ($35 − $1 = $34), the investor makes a profit.

   - As in the case of futures, the purchaser of the option would not typically take or make delivery of the underlying assets (crude oil in this example). The actual commodity transaction would take place in the spot market and the options contract would be used to offset any losses if the price were higher (call option) or lower (put option) than expected. Essentially for the call option user, they have placed a ceiling on the price they will pay for crude oil and for the put option user, they have placed a floor on the price they will receive for the oil.

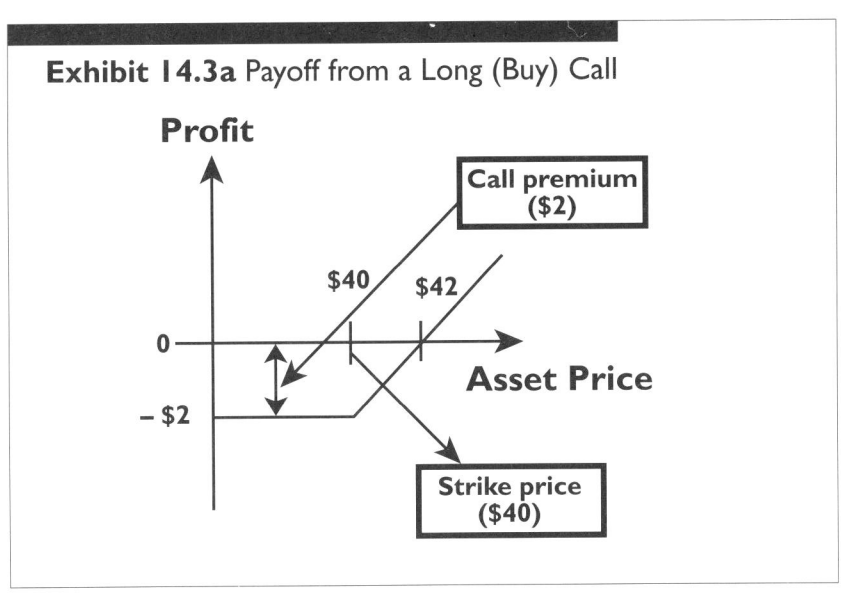

Exhibit 14.3a Payoff from a Long (Buy) Call

Exhibit 14.3b Payoff from a Long (Buy) Put

IV. Interest Rate Exposure

Many companies face financial risk due to exposure to interest rate changes. This exposure may arise from the inherent nature of their business or from their financing activities. This section outlines some examples of interest rate exposure and the types of instruments used to manage interest rate risk.

A. Examples of Interest Rate Exposure

1. **Falling Rates** — Companies with variable interest rate investments face the possibility of lower earnings when interest rates fall.

2. **Rising Rates** — Companies with debt tied to variable interest rates face higher borrowing costs when interest rates rise.

B. Different Types of Interest Rate Derivatives

There are several types of interest rate derivative instruments used by companies to manage their exposure to interest rate changes. The rest of this section defines some of the more commonly used instruments.

1. **Forward Rate Agreement (FRA)** — An FRA is a forward contract on interest rates in which two parties agree that a certain interest rate will apply to a certain principal during a specified future period of time. The notional principal amounts are agreed upon but never exchanged. If at settlement the actual rate is different from the rate agreed in the contract, then one party pays the other a cash amount equal to the present value of the difference between the interest in the contract rate and the actual rate. The majority of FRAs are based on Eurodollar rates, although others are available.

2. **Interest Rate Futures** — Interest rate futures are futures contracts on an underlying asset whose price is solely dependent on the level of interest rates. The most popular short-term (90-day) interest rate contracts are the T-bill, the Eurodollar contracts traded on the CME and bank certificates of deposit (CDs). In the T-bill futures contract, the underlying asset is the 90-day Treasury bill. In the Eurodollar futures contract, the underlying asset is a three-month Eurodollar deposit. The interest earned on a Eurodollar deposit is the three-month LIBOR. The most actively traded long-term interest rate contracts are the five-year and 10-year U.S. Treasury notes and the 30-year U.S. Treasury bonds.

3. **Interest Rate Swaps** — A common type of interest rate swap is the exchange of a fixed interest rate cash flow for a floating interest rate cash flow — both cash flows being in the same currency. If both interest rates are floating, then the exchange of the cash flows is called a basis-rate swap. An example of a basis-rate swap is the exchange of interest payments based on LIBOR for interest payments based on the commercial paper rate.

4. **Interest Rate Options** — Interest rate options are options where the payoff depends on the level of interest rates. There are three basic types of interest rate options:

    - *Interest Rate Cap* — Interest rate caps ensure that the borrower of a floating rate loan receives a ceiling rate if interest rates rise above a specified level. This level is known as the cap rate. If rates fall, the borrower is not obligated to exercise the option and can still enjoy the benefits of the lower borrowing costs. The price of this insurance is the premium paid for the cap.

    - *Interest Rate Floor* — A company with a floating-rate asset can use an interest rate floor to hedge against rates dropping below a certain level. If rates fall, the floating-rate asset is protected by this put option on interest rates. If interest rates rise, the company can still benefit, as it is not obligated to exercise the option. Again, the cost of this insurance is the premium paid for the interest rate floor.

- *Interest Rate Collar* — A combination of an interest rate cap and an interest rate floor is called an interest rate collar. A company that buys a cap and sells a floor is effectively locking in a range for its borrowing costs. The cap establishes a maximum borrowing rate, thereby protecting the company against higher interest rates, while the floor sets a minimum borrowing rate. A collar can be costless if the income received from selling the floor matches the premium paid for the cap. Costless collars are popular hedging vehicles, as they provide some interest rate protection at no cost.

Besides caps, floors and collars, there are several other types of interest rate options. As an example, an option on an interest rate swap is called a swaption, where the buyer of the option has the right to enter into an interest rate swap at a future date.

V. Exchange Rate Exposure

Companies that deal with foreign currencies are faced with different kinds of exposure. This section explains the types of currency exposure and the alternate currency derivatives that can be used to manage FX exposure.

A. Types of Foreign Exchange Exposure

Companies dealing in foreign currencies face three kinds of exposure: transaction, translation and economic exposure. Additional types of exposure due to foreign operations are covered in Chapter 15, International Treasury Management.

1. **Transaction Exposure** — If a company's balance sheet, either receivables or payables, is affected in value by changes in FX rates, then the company has a transaction exposure. Transaction exposure usually occurs if the receivables and payables are in different currencies. Adjusting the selling price for adverse changes in the exchange rate does not necessarily eliminate transaction exposure. For example, a U.S. exporter sells merchandise to a French buyer agreeing to accept payment (in euros) three months from now. The exporter records the transaction as an accounts receivable. However, the exporter is exposed to a possible loss in value if, in three months, the euro depreciates relative to the U.S. dollar (because the receivables would convert into fewer dollars).

2. **Translation Exposure** — Companies with foreign subsidiaries or foreign operations are exposed to translation exposure. Translation exposure is created when a foreign subsidiary's financial statements are converted (or translated) into the parent company's home currency to consolidate the parent's financial statement. This exposure must be reported on a quarterly basis in accordance with Financial Accounting Standard 52 (FAS 52) as discussed later in this chapter. It is difficult to

use financial instruments to hedge this type of risk due to the potential large amounts involved. One effective approach, however, is to use a balance sheet hedge (i.e., offset foreign asset exposures by borrowing funds to finance those assets in the same country and currency). This hedges the balance sheet and reduces the net exposure to the parent company.

3. **Economic Exposure** — Economic exposure is the long-term effect of exchange rate changes on the present value of future cash flows to the company. Multinational corporations that do business in several different currencies will, in the long run, always be subject to fluctuations in cash flows because of exchange rate changes. Even purely domestic companies are exposed to economic exposure. For example, a company that purchases its supplies and sells its product locally is clearly not affected by transaction exposure. However, if there is foreign competition within the local market and the local currency appreciates against the competitor's, then the company's earnings in the long run may be affected as demand shifts towards the relatively cheaper foreign competitor's product.

B. Currency Derivatives Used to Hedge Foreign Exchange Exposure

Once a company has identified and quantified its exposure to exchange rate changes, it decides whether or not to hedge that exposure. There are several instruments that a company can use if it decides to manage its exchange rate risk. The most common type of FX exposure hedged through the use of currency derivatives is that of transaction exposure. Since this type of exposure is clearly related to projected receipts and disbursements in foreign currencies, it is easy to manage using the instruments outlined below.

1. **Currency Forwards** — A currency forward is a commitment to buy or sell a specified amount of foreign currency at a future date at an exchange rate that is agreed upon today. FX forwards are traded in most major currencies with standard maturities of one, two, three, six, nine and 12 months. Since forwards are credit instruments (and entail credit risk due to mandated delivery at the end of the contract), the dealers in FX forwards are usually banks. Also, most of the documentation concerning FX forwards involves credit issues.

2. **Currency Futures** — Currency futures contracts are similar to currency forwards except that they are traded on an exchange and are therefore standardized contracts in terms of amount and maturity date. Currency futures are available for only a relatively few major currencies.

3. **Currency Swaps** — A currency swap involves the exchange of a floating-rate cash flow denominated in one currency with a fixed-rate cash flow denominated in another currency, in addition to an exchange of principal.

4. **Currency Options** — A foreign currency option gives the buyer the right to buy (call option) or sell (put option) a fixed amount of a foreign currency at a fixed exchange rate (strike price), on or before a specific future date. A foreign currency put option establishes a floor value (in terms of the domestic currency) for the foreign currency, which is the exercise price less the premium on the put. Similarly, a foreign currency call option sets a ceiling cost (in terms of the domestic currency) for the foreign currency. The ceiling cost is the strike price plus the premium paid for the call.

For example, an importer with an accounts payable due in three months in British pounds can ensure a maximum cost for the pounds by going long (buying) a call option on the pound. If at the time of payment the spot market price of the pound is less than the strike price of the call option, the importer does not exercise the option and loses only the premium. The net cost of the pounds to the importer is the spot price of the pound plus the option premium. The option acts as insurance against the spot price of the pound rising above a specific level; for this, the importer pays a premium, which is the option price.

VI. Commodity Price Exposure

Markets exist for several commodities that are either used by companies in their production process or that are sold by companies to customers. The most common commodities markets are in the areas of agricultural and meat products, oil and gas, minerals and metals. This section provides examples of commodity price exposure and the different commodity derivatives used to manage that exposure.

A. Examples of Commodity Exposure

There are two types of commodity exposure:

1. **Price Exposure** — The primary commodity price exposure faced by companies is the potential for changes in the price of that commodity. If a company utilizes commodities in the input process, rising prices create an exposure for the company (the risk profile of the company is negatively sloped). Conversely, if a company sells the product (the risk profile is positively sloped), then falling prices would create an exposure.

2. **Delivery Exposure** — For some companies (mainly energy users) regular supply of the commodity is crucial. In addition to price exposure, these companies also face delivery exposure. Entering into a long-term agreement with an energy producer can mitigate this exposure.

B. Derivative Instruments Used to Hedge Commodity Exposure

As with interest rate risk and FX risk, commodity price risk can also be managed using forwards, futures, swaps and options, or even combinations of these basic tools. The following are two examples:

- In an oil swap, the parties would agree on a notional principal that is expressed in barrels of oil (not dollars) and, similar to currency or interest rate swaps, make regular settlements on the basis of fixed and floating oil prices. The floating price used in an oil swap is usually the average price of oil over a specified period.

- To reduce the uncertainty associated with the change in a commodity price, the company may decide to use a costless collar (a combination of a cap and a floor).

VII. Accounting and Tax Issues

A. Accounting Issues

Due to the nature of the instruments used in financial risk management, there are special accounting issues that must be considered. Many of these issues are addressed by the Financial Accounting Standards Board (FASB). Some of the critical FASB pronouncements related to financial risk management include:

1. **Financial Instruments Disclosure** — The pronouncements concerning disclosure have resulted in FAS 105, which deals with the disclosure of information about the use of instruments with off-balance-sheet risk and instruments with a concentration of credit risk and FAS 107, which concerns the disclosure of the fair market value of financial instruments. Additional requirements concerning disclosure are provided in FAS 114 (Accounting by Creditors for Impairment of a Loan), FAS 115 (Accounting for Certain Investments in Debt and Equity Securities) and FAS 133 (Accounting for Derivative Instruments and Hedging Activities). FAS 133 was amended by FAS 138, which addressed some implementation concerns relative to common current hedging approaches. FAS 133 and its amendments have significant impacts for financial risk management. Some of the key considerations in FAS 133 are:

    - The fundamental difference between FAS 133 and prior practice is that FAS 133 does not recognize the principal of off-balance-sheet deferral accounting. FAS 133 requires that all derivatives be marked-to-market and placed on the balance sheet.

- FAS 133 recognizes three types of hedges:

  — Fair-Value Hedges — Hedges of exposures to the changes in value of a recognized asset or liability or an unrecognized firm commitment

  — Cash Flow Hedges — Hedges of a forecasted transaction, or the variability in the cash flow of a recognized asset or liability

  — Net Investment Hedges — Hedges of the net investment in a foreign operation

- The key issue for treasury is the impact of FAS 133 on reporting and managing intracompany (between company subsidiaries) risk exposure. For a company with a centralized treasury and risk management operation, FAS 133 allows them to hedge intracompany risk, but only if they can point to an original risk at the operating unit level. There must also be a formal agreement between the operating unit and a centralized entity to execute the hedge on its behalf.

- The process of preparing for the adoption of FAS 133 and its amendments is a difficult and complex process requiring input and coordination from many areas of the company, including accounting, treasury, risk management, legal, investments and information systems.

2. **Other Accounting Issues** — Hedge accounting is an accounting technique that is applied to the components of a hedge, so that the fair value of the hedged asset and the hedging vehicle are included in earnings for the same period. As a result of the tremendous growth in alternative hedging instruments, no standard accounting guidelines have been established for financial derivatives. Although hedge accounting has been addressed in FAS 80 (Accounting for Futures Contracts) and FAS 52 (Foreign Currency Translation), they contain certain conceptual inconsistencies. FAS 52 limits hedge accounting for currency transaction to those future transactions that are firmly committed, while FAS 80 extends hedge accounting to those anticipated future transactions that are not firmly committed, provided certain hedge criteria are met.

B. Tax Issues Related to Hedging

Since the U.S. tax system differentiates between ordinary income and capital gains, the main issue for tax treatment here is whether the gains/losses on a hedge should be treated as ordinary gains/losses or capital gains/losses. As of October 1993, the temporary regulations on hedging transactions of the Internal Revenue Service (IRS) consider the gains/losses on "most business" hedges as ordinary gains/losses. If the loss on the hedge is treated as a capital loss, then the company can deduct the loss only to the extent that it offsets other capital gains in the business. If the gains are not sufficient, then there can be a situation in which the loss on the hedge cannot be deducted against income.

Test Your Understanding

These chapter questions are provided to test your understanding of the information in the text and are not examples of CCM examination questions, nor are they in the examination format.

Answers can be found at the back of the book on pages 538-539.

1. What is financial risk management, where does it stem from and why is it important?

2. Outline the steps involved in the financial risk management process.

3. What is the risk profile? How does it differ between a firm that hedges and a firm that does not hedge?

4. How can risk management increase the value of a firm?

5. What is the difference between hedging, speculation and arbitrage?

6. List the basic types of contracts or instruments used in financial risk management.

7. What is a derivative instrument?

8. Explain the differences between a forward contract and a futures contract.

9. What are the primary types of interest rate exposure?

10. Define caps, floors and collars.

11. What is the difference between transaction exposure and translation exposure?

12. Explain how a firm wishing to invest in floating-rate investments can use a swap to manage its interest rate exposure.

13. Explain how a company selling oil in the spot market can use futures contracts to hedge the future selling price of its product.

14. What are the two types of commodity exposure?

15. Explain the accounting issues related to hedging.

16. What are the tax issues related to hedging transactions?

CHAPTER 15

International Treasury Management

Overview

This chapter describes the principal methods of international treasury management, including the application of cash management principles to the business environment of other countries and techniques specific to cross-border cash management. It describes the principal international trade payment methods such as letters of credit and documentary collections and introduces export financing and insurance.

Learning Objectives

Upon completion of this chapter and the related study questions, the reader should know:

- The importance of international treasury management
- The objectives of international treasury management
- The basics of foreign exchange rates and markets
- The differences between various countries' payment and banking systems
- How cross-border check payments and wire transfers are made
- The techniques used to help manage international cash flows
- The types and uses of letters of credit and documentary collections
- The principal methods of export financing and credit management
- The tax considerations of international treasury management

Key Concepts

- Objectives of international treasury management
- Differences between various countries' payment and banking systems
- Cross-border check payments and wire transfers
- Managing international cash flows
- Letters of credit and documentary collections
- International tax implications

Outline

I. Introduction to International Treasury Management
A. Increased Globalization of Business
B. Increased Competition in the Domestic Marketplace
C. Need for Cash Management Services on a Global Basis

II. Objectives of International Treasury Management
A. International Treasury Management Issues
B. Foreign Exchange
C. International Treasury Management Organization
D. Shared Service Center (SSC)
E. In-House Banking

III. Characteristics of International Banking Systems
A. Bank Regulations and Operations
B. Characteristics of Banks and Banking Systems in Some Other Countries

IV. Characteristics of International Payments Systems
A. Paper-Based Payments Systems
B. Electronic Payments Systems

V. International Trade Financing Methods
A. Open Account
B. Documentary Collection
C. Letter of Credit
D. Other Trade Payment Methods
E. Banker's Acceptance (BA)
F. Trade Acceptance

VI. International Treasury Management Issues and Techniques
A. Credit and Accounts Receivable Management
B. Pooling
C. Netting
D. Leading and Lagging
E. Re-Invoicing
F. Internal Factoring
G. Multicurrency Accounts
H. Electronic Banking Services

VII. International Financing, Taxation and Other Considerations
A. Export Financing
B. Financing International Operations
C. Tax Considerations
D. Legal and Ethical Issues
E. Sovereign Risk

I. Introduction to International Treasury Management

International treasury management is becoming increasingly important as companies expand their presence in the global marketplace. This global marketplace, however, is a constantly changing and complex environment in which to do business. Each country operates under different sets of laws, business practices and banking systems. The U.S. banking and payments system is significantly different from those used elsewhere in the world.

A. Increased Globalization of Business

Almost every company in the United States is affected by events on a global basis. Even small, localized companies use supplies with some foreign content or sell goods that compete with imported products. Organizations such as the World Trade Organization (WTO) and agreements such as the North American Free Trade Agreement (NAFTA) have facilitated trade between countries, increasing the level of international business activity.

B. Increased Competition in the Domestic Marketplace

Increased competition in the domestic marketplace has caused many companies to look internationally for sources of additional revenue, either through export sales or expansion into foreign markets. The same competitive forces and costs have also caused many companies to seek non-domestic suppliers for their product or raw material needs.

C. Need for Cash Management Services on a Global Basis

Companies expanding abroad have a need for the same kinds of cash management services they have in the United States. Companies operating multinationally have many of the same concerns related to collection, concentration, disbursement and information management they have in the United States, but these issues may have to be dealt with in a very different manner. The selection of financial service providers to assist a company in its international operations is a critical part of the international treasury management process.

II. Objectives of International Treasury Management

The objectives of international treasury management are similar to those for U.S. cash management. The main objective is the efficient utilization of a company's global cash resources in a manner consistent with its strategic goals. International treasury management is the application of basic functions such as collection, concentration, disbursement, investment, borrowing and information management to each international environment. International treasury management is also concerned with cross-border funds movement, foreign exchange and cash management practices within countries outside the United States.

A. International Treasury Management Issues

International treasury management involves many of the same issues as domestic cash management, with several additional challenges:

1. **Cash Flow Complexity** — A multinational company must deal with cash flows from subsidiaries, suppliers and customers in each of the countries in which it operates. As a result of widely differing regulations, banking systems and information availability, companies operating internationally must manage a complex series of cash flows that are typically in different currencies and that often cross national boundaries.

2. **Foreign Exchange (FX) Exposure** — International companies dealing in various foreign currencies are exposed to FX rate risk. A company must assess the types and levels of its exposure to FX rate fluctuations and volatility for the specific currencies in which it operates. (See Chapter 14, Financial Risk Management.)

3. **Political Issues** — Multinational companies are exposed to varying degrees of political risk as they become corporate citizens of different sovereign nations. Companies with operations in foreign countries must be knowledgeable about the laws, regulations, taxes and customs that will govern their business activities. They should also be aware of the overall political and social dynamics of the various countries in which they have invested their capital.

B. Foreign Exchange

International treasury management requires a basic understanding of FX rates and markets.

1. **Foreign Exchange Rates** — FX rates are quoted in several ways, depending on the currencies and the markets involved.

- *Rate Quoting Conventions* — An FX rate is the equivalent number of units of one currency per unit of a different currency. From a U.S. perspective, there are two ways to quote FX rates: the U.S. dollar equivalent of a unit of the foreign currency, or the amount of the foreign currency per U.S. dollar. The following example shows those quotation formats for selected foreign currencies.

Currency	U.S. $ Equivalent	Currency per U.S. $
British Pound (£)	1.4235	0.7025
Euro (€)	0.9356	1.0688
Japanese Yen (¥)	0.009058	110.40

    Using this information, some examples can be determined:

    £250,000 would be equivalent to $355,875 (£250,000 x 1.4235)

    €250,000 would be equivalent to $233,900 (€250,000 x 0.9356)

    ¥250,000 would be equivalent to $2,264.50 (¥250,000 / 110.40)

- *Bid-Offer Spreads* — Banks and other dealers quote both bid and offer rates for foreign currency. The bid rate is the rate at which a dealer is willing to purchase currency. The offer rate is the rate at which a dealer is willing to sell currency. The spread between the bid rate and the offer rate provides income for the dealer.

    For example, assume a dealer provides a bid-offer quote of ¥110.30 – 110.50/$. This means the dealer is willing to buy (bid) one U.S. $ at ¥110.30 and sell (offer) one U.S. $ at ¥110.50.

    - If a U.S. cash manager wanted to sell a dealer $50,000 in exchange for ¥, the dealer would buy (bid) the $50,000 from the cash manager for ¥ 5,515,000. This is calculated as $50,000 x 110.30.

    - However, if the same U.S. cash manager turned around and sold back the ¥5,515,000 to the dealer in exchange $, the dealer would sell (offer) the cash manager only $49,910, calculated as ¥5,515,000 / 110.50.

    - The difference of $90 ($50,000 – $49,910) illustrates the dealer's spread on this transaction.

2. **FX Markets** — For FX, there are two basic markets: the spot market and the forward market.

    - *Spot Market* — A rate quoted in the spot market for currency is called a spot FX rate (spot rate). These rates are generally quoted for delivery one or two business days from the date of the trade. Faster delivery may be possible, but at the expense of a rate higher than the quoted spot rate.

    - *Forward Market* — The forward FX market is one in which an exchange rate for a future delivery of currencies can be fixed today.

— A forward FX rate (forward rate) is an exchange rate established today for a currency transaction with delivery occurring beyond two days in the future.

— Deliveries under most forward FX contracts occur within a year from the trade date. However, delivery dates beyond one year are available for actively traded currencies.

— Forward exchange rates are based on the spot exchange rate and the difference in interest rates between two countries. The terms par, discount and premium describe the relationship between spot and forward exchange rates. The interest rate differential between two countries will determine if their respective currencies will trade at par, at a discount, or at a premium in the forward market.

— If the spot rate and forward exchange rate are the same, then the forward rate is at par to the spot rate. In theory, this would imply that the interest rate structure between the two countries is exactly the same. As this is rarely the case, currencies will generally trade at a discount or premium.

— A currency is at a discount if it is worth less in the forward market than in the spot market. The currency with the higher interest rate will sell at a discount in the forward market against a currency with the lower interest rate.

— A currency is at a premium if it is worth more in the forward market than in the spot market. The currency with the lower interest rate will sell at a premium in the forward market against a currency with the higher interest rate.

- *Interest Rate Parity* — The relationship between the spot, forward and money markets is known as interest rate parity. As long as FX and interest rate markets are efficient, it is not possible to take money from one country, invest in another country's money market, return it back to original country and make a higher rate of return than could have been earned in the original country's money market. Thus, the differences observed between the spot and forward markets are not necessarily a prediction of the future movement of the spot rate, but rather just an adjustment for the differential interest rates between the two countries in question.

C. International Treasury Management Organization

The organization of the international treasury management function may be centralized, decentralized or a combination of both.

1. **Centralized Control** — Centralized control over international treasury management gives relatively little autonomy to field office personnel. A company that operates overseas sales offices with limited personnel will typically centralize

control of its treasury functions at its head office. A centralized function can result in economies of scale for services and lower a company's operating costs.

2. **Decentralized Control** — A company with relatively autonomous international subsidiaries is more likely to have a decentralized treasury structure. Field personnel are responsible for delegated treasury functions and are typically required to submit management reports summarizing bank balances, loans, investments and other indicators of performance. Headquarters personnel may make periodic visits to international offices to audit and train treasury staff.

3. **Combined (Regional)** — Some large multinational companies have combined some of the features from both of the above structures and operate regional treasury centers. These regional centers are responsible for providing treasury services to specific subsidiaries within a designated geographic area.

D. Shared Service Center (SSC)

Many large global companies and multinational banks are utilizing a structure called shared service centers (SSCs). The formal SSC was developed to establish, measure and maintain the cost and contribution of back-office business processes and operations. SSCs have been set up in a wide range of areas such as accounting functions, receivables and payables, human resources, payroll, benefits management, legal/tax and treasury. Much of the recent interest in SSCs in the treasury area has been as a result of the Internet and browser technology enabling the recentralization of database management and maintenance. Many global treasury back-office operations do not necessarily benefit from local management and could be profitably centralized into an SSC. The development of treasury management systems (as discussed in Chapter 10, Information Management and Technology) has provided standardization of information and processes, which further enhances the benefits of SSCs. The Economic and Monetary Union (EMU) and the euro have forced both European and U.S. treasury managers to look at SSCs as a response to the consolidation of European banking structures.

There are several key issues to be considered in establishing an SSC:
- Determining the economic contribution of treasury back-office processes
- Comparing an SSC structure to outsourcing of the processes
- Selecting the location for the SSC
- Choosing and implementing the technology for the SSC
- Setting up a compensation system for rewarding SSC staff and managers

E. In-House Banking

Many large global companies have established their own "in-house banks" in their centralized treasury departments. In these types of arrangements, treasury becomes the main provider of banking service for all of the company's operating entities. Treasury then contracts with financial institutions to clear transactions and provide services on a bulk basis. The primary benefit is a reduction in overall banking costs by aggregating many small transactions into fewer, larger transactions. The in-house bank can also provide many of the international treasury management services such netting, pooling and re-invoicing, which are covered later in this chapter. Finally, the overall risk management of the company can be enhanced through centralized management of FX exposure.

III. Characteristics of International Banking Systems

Each country's banking system is structured differently and has different regulations and capabilities and offers different services.

A. Bank Regulations and Operations

1. **Central Bank** — The central bank or monetary authority of a country usually establishes the conditions under which both domestic and foreign banks can operate. Changes in these conditions and restrictions are occurring rapidly in many countries. In general, recent changes have tended to create more competition and to have a positive impact on the efficiency of all financial institutions operating within the country.

    Many central banks perform functions similar to those of the U.S. Federal Reserve System, which operates the payments system, regulates banks, acts as lender of last resort and controls the money supply. In many foreign countries, one or a small group of large banks operates the payments system, rather than the central bank. In addition, many foreign central banks act as issuers of government debt, which is a function performed by the Treasury Department in the United States.

2. **Bank and Company Relationships** — In many countries, banks are permitted to own minor or controlling ownership positions in corporations through equity investments. In the United States, commercial banks are, by law, precluded from such corporate stock ownership.

3. **Number of Banks** — Foreign banking systems are often less fragmented than the U.S. system. In the United States, there are thousands of independent financial institutions, ranging from those with extensive branch networks to those with a

single location. In most other countries, the banking system is characterized by fewer banks, operating on a nationwide basis.

4. **Restrictions on Corporate Demand Deposit Accounts** — In the United States, legislation prevents payment of interest on corporate demand deposit accounts offered by banks (there are current legislative initiatives that could change or lift this restriction). In many other countries, banks pay interest on corporate demand deposit accounts with positive balances. This makes many of the cash management services offered by U.S. banks, such as zero balance and sweep accounts, unnecessary for domestic purposes in other countries. These techniques are, however, used extensively for cross-border liquidity management.

5. **Overdrafts on Corporate Demand Deposit Accounts** — Running overdrafts (negative balances) is allowed by the banking regulations of many countries outside the United States. The use of overdrafts provides a convenient, if somewhat expensive, source of short-term funds. Outside the United States, most corporations can hold demand deposit accounts that pay interest on positive balances and charge interest on negative balances, thus significantly simplifying the task of daily cash position management.

6. **Value Dating** — Outside the United States, banks typically use value dating as compensation for services provided to their customers. Under a value dating system, the bank sets the dates upon which it grants credit for deposits or it debits the account for checks or electronic payments from the account.

    - The forward value date is the date in the future upon which the firm will be granted credit for deposited items. This practice is similar to the concept of determining availability for deposited items in the U.S. banking system.

    - The back value date is the prior date upon which checks or electronic transactions from an account are debited from that account. For example, if a check is back valued, the date of the debit reflected on a customer's account will be earlier than the date the item was presented. Back value dating can also be applied to other services that result in a debit to a customer's account, such as outgoing wires or other electronic transfers.

    - Value dating policies may be negotiable depending upon the bank and the country.

B. Characteristics of Banks and Banking Systems in Some Other Countries

Banks and banking systems vary widely from country to country and generally are different from the U.S. banking system. Following are general overviews of the financial systems that exist in countries that are the major trading partners of the United States.

1. **Canada** — Canada is the largest U.S. trading partner. It is joined with the United States and Mexico in NAFTA. The characteristics of the Canadian banking system and other financial institutions include:

    - The major financial institutions provide nationwide banking through their branches.

    - The Canadian Payments Association (CPA) developed and operates the national clearing and settlement system. Typically, all deposits receive same-day availability. The CPA is spearheading the introduction of the large value transfer system, an electronic mechanism to handle large or time-sensitive national and international payments.

    - Cross-border settlement between U.S. and Canadian banks is available via the automated clearing house (ACH).

    - Lockboxes are used less frequently in Canada. They are used primarily to reduce mail and processing float or for reductions in processing costs. Lockboxes have no impact on availability float, since all deposits receive same-day availability.

    - Canadian financial institutions offer a variety of electronic services, including support for electronic data interchange (EDI).

    - Many Canadian financial institutions offer support for cross-border transactions such as U.S.-dollar check settlements via U.S.-dollar accounts in Canada or via U.S. Federal Reserve (Fed) banks or branches.

2. **Mexico** — In recent years, the Mexican banking system has undergone significant turmoil with many smaller banks failing, some opening of the financial industry to foreign financial institutions and FX controls lifted after a major peso devaluation. Banking in Mexico is still dominated by a few large banks, but foreign banks are increasing their presence, in some cases having part ownership of the traditional larger banks. Although electronic banking capabilities are growing rapidly, many Mexican companies still pay invoices in person at the vendor's bank. Some Mexican banks offer a bill presentment system, where a company sends details of its invoices sorted by creditor to its bank. Due to high levels of check fraud in the system, many banks are offering a version of positive pay to ensure that only proper checks are paid. NAFTA has had some impact in opening up the Mexican system, but not as much as had initially been predicted (i.e., NAFTA did *not* allow for U.S. or Canadian banks to establish branches in Mexico). Also, while the National Automated Clearing House Association (NACHA) initiatives for cross-border ACH transfers have worked out well between the United States and Canada, cross-border ACH to Mexico has not been as successful. Given the recent change in the Mexican government and the ongoing financial uncertainties, treasury and banking operations in Mexico should be monitored very closely.

3. **United Kingdom (U.K.)** — There are many similarities between the U.K. and U.S. banking and payment systems. Among these similarities are the following:

- The U.K. has a highly developed banking system that provides a full spectrum of financial and transactional services to customers in wholesale and retail markets.

- London, like New York, is one of the major financial centers of the world and it features one of the largest international real-time, high-value clearing and settlement systems of the world: the clearing house automated payment system (CHAPS). CHAPS-euro is the major clearing system for the euro in the U.K., enabling payments to be made both between parties within the U.K. and cross-border through its link to the Trans-European Automated Real-Time Gross Settlement Express Transfer System (TARGET). (See the information on the euro in the next section.)

- Payments systems in the U.K. parallel those in the United States. Checks are the primary method of payment. However, there is increasing use of a wide range of electronic banking services by consumers, such as telephone banking, home banking and an ACH-like system called the Bankers Automated Clearing Service (BACS).

There also are several aspects of the U.K. banking and payments system that appear similar to those in the United States but have some subtle differences. Among them are the following:

- The Bank of England performs a regulatory and supervisory role similar to that of the Federal Reserve, but unlike the Fed, the Bank of England does not operate the clearing system. Also, in its monetary role, the Bank of England was recently granted authority to establish interest rates.

- Both the corporate and consumer banking systems are dominated by a few major U.K. banks that operate the clearing system for England, Scotland, Wales and Northern Ireland. Recently, a series of mergers among building societies, the U.K. equivalent of the U.S. mutual savings banks, have begun to challenge the dominant status of these major U.K. clearing banks.

4. **Europe** — Northern European banks generally are efficient and offer a full array of electronic services. However, banking systems in such countries as Italy, Portugal and Greece tend to be somewhat less efficient. Banking in Eastern Europe continues to evolve in conjunction with political reform efforts and the general trend toward market-driven economies. Traditional U.S. cash management services are typically unavailable in Eastern Europe or are in the early stages of development.

The banking systems and financial markets will be dramatically affected by growing economic integration within Europe. In early May 1998, the Council of the European Union finalized the launch of the Economic and Monetary Union (EMU). The 11 nations that joined the union and adopted irrevocable conversion rates for the euro in January 1999 included Austria, Belgium, Finland, France, Germany, Ireland, Italy, Luxembourg, the Netherlands, Portugal and Spain. The chief aims of the EMU were the introduction of the euro and linkage of economic policies for all member countries.

The European Central Bank (ECB), which was established in July 1998, oversees a single monetary policy for all EMU members. The euro was initially used primarily in capital markets by the central banks, commercial banks and corporations. Smaller companies and consumers converted to the euro over a three-year period. Euro banknotes and coins are scheduled to be released on January 1, 2002. The national currencies of participating countries will cease to be legal tender within six months after the introduction of euro banknotes and coins.

To encourage acceptance and use of the euro, new government-issued debt will be denominated in euros, as will operation of interbank, monetary, capital and exchange markets. The effects of a transition to the euro include:

- Elimination of currency exposures between the EMU countries
- Reduced transfer and FX transaction costs
- Consolidation of banking relationships
- Simplification of certain international treasury management techniques such as pooling and netting. (These techniques are presented later in this chapter.)
- Reduced FX exposure, resulting in simplified exchange risk management

There are four primary mechanisms for the settlement of euro payments and transfers:

- Beginning in January 1999, TARGET provided real-time settlement for cross-border payments, similar to Fedwire in the United States. The system is used primarily for urgent, high-value payments. An important function of TARGET is to enable central banks to mobilize liquidity around Europe in order to manage monetary policy objectives as determined by the ECB.
- Correspondent banking, the traditional clearing method, currently remains the most common method of cross-border payment for many banks, primarily for low-value, bulk payments.
- European network banks continue to use their own networks and access local clearing systems directly.
- The Euro Bankers Association (EBA), an association of major clearing banks, currently operates a net settlement system similar to the clearing house interbank payments system (CHIPS) settlement procedure in the United States, but it is used primarily for financial, rather than commercial, transactions. This system was converted to euro-denominated transactions in January 1999.

5. **Japan** — The Japanese banking system is highly developed, with many banks having extensive international operations or alliances throughout the world. The following are some characteristics of the Japanese financial system:

- The Bank of Japan (BOJ) is Japan's central bank and performs many of the same activities as the Fed in the United States. The BOJ is responsible for implementing monetary policy, examining financial institutions and serving as the lender of last resort. It also provides payment settlement through direct entries to the deposit accounts maintained by financial institutions.

- The nucleus of the banking system comprises approximately 140 city and regional commercial banks. In addition, the Japanese post offices provide some financial services, similar to giros in Europe (see discussion of giros later in this chapter), including the receipt of funds for postal savings, insurance and pension accounts.

- Clearing of paper-based items in Japan is handled through local and regional clearing houses. The largest is the Tokyo Clearing House, which also facilitates operation of an automated clearing house system. Unlike the ACH system in the United States, this system currently handles only credit transfers.

- The Zengin Data Telecommunications System (Zengin System) is the online network through which most domestic funds transfers are initiated. In 1990, the Zengin System went to a real-time basis and established a cap on intraday net debit positions for each participating institution. Nichigin Net is the interbank settlement system operated by the BOJ. Financial institutions that maintain accounts with the BOJ are provided online access to initiate settlement transfers between accounts.

- The banking and financial markets are highly regulated, with both the Ministry of Finance and the BOJ playing major roles. There are efforts under way to deregulate certain aspects of the financial marketplace, but involvement of foreign financial institutions remains somewhat limited.

IV. Characteristics of International Payments Systems

When describing international payments systems, there are two important considerations to keep in mind. Different systems or methods are used for intracountry payments vs. cross-border payments. Payments may be denominated in a country's local currency or the currency of another country. These issues have a significant impact on settlement procedures.

A. Paper-Based Payments Systems

International paper-based systems involve payment and clearing of checks, also referred to as drafts, within and between countries. There are several key issues in international check clearing. They include:

1. The check clearing process within a country varies significantly from country to country. Some countries have nationwide clearing; others do not. The clearing of checks may be accomplished by the central bank (as the Fed does in the United States), by several of the major banks acting as clearing agents or by correspondent relationships between different banks.

2. The clearing of checks between countries (cross-border clearing) is often a slow and complicated process. Intercountry checks generally clear as collection items that must be presented back to the bank in the country where they are drawn. Settlement is typically accomplished through correspondent bank accounts. For smaller-value items the drawee bank may replace the original check for one that can be cleared in the payee's country. This check is then returned to the payee's bank for deposit.

3. Some financial institutions offer specialized international check clearing services that speed up the process of collecting cross-border payments.

B. Electronic Payments Systems

Many countries offer different types of electronic systems for both corporate and consumer payments.

1. **Business-to-Business (B2B) Electronic Payments Systems** — Electronic payment of company obligations is more common in some areas of the world than it is in the United States. The actual structure and operation of these payments systems vary from country to country, but they also have some common characteristics:

- *Credit-Based Transactions* — Most B2B electronic payments are credit transactions, where the payor initiates a transfer of funds to the payee. In this sense, these payments are similar to ACH credits or Fedwire transactions in the United States. The method by which a company accesses its bank to initiate payment varies widely by country, bank and company. Generally, the payment initiation systems are provided by the banks to their customers on a proprietary basis.

- *Transactions Cleared Through Correspondent Balances* — The majority of electronic payments systems outside the United States. are cleared through correspondent balances of the banks involved in the transfers. Between countries, this clearing is usually done bank-to-bank on a bilateral basis. Within a country, the clearing may be done on a bilateral basis, or through a netting system run by a few clearing banks. These systems are different from the Fedwire system in the United States, where value is transferred by debits and credits to bank reserve balances at the Federal Reserve.

- *Role of the Society for Worldwide Interbank Financial Telecommunications (S.W.I.F.T.)* — S.W.I.F.T. is an interbank telecommunications network that enables banks to send authenticated electronic messages in standard formats. It was established in the 1970s and has more than 4,000 member banks. The communications, initiated and received by member banks, cover a wide variety of international banking services and are known as S.W.I.F.T. messages. A company can request its bank to initiate a balance transfer or foreign payment through S.W.I.F.T. It should be noted that S.W.I.F.T. communications contain payment-related information but do not transfer value. The actual clearing and settlement of S.W.I.F.T. messages regarding the transfer of funds are accomplished through correspondent bank balances. Standardized S.W.I.F.T. messages have also been developed for other international service needs including balance reporting, letters of credit, FX transactions and documentary collections.

2. **Consumer Electronic Payments Systems** — The use of electronic payments systems by consumers is more common in many areas of the world than in the United States. These types of payments include those from consumers to companies and governments, as well as consumer-to-consumer payments. As in the case of B2B payments, the structure and operation of the payment systems vary from country to country. Some of the most common systems and applications are as follows:

    - *Use of Giros* — Many European countries have giro systems that operate through their postal or banking systems. Giro systems allow payments from one giro account to another using direct debits and credits. Payments from consumers to companies and to governments (for taxes) represent the bulk of payment volumes in these systems. Consumers use the giro system in place of checks for payment of their monthly bills and statements. In some countries, consumers access these systems via personal computers (PCs), terminals or telephone. Though these systems are primarily used for consumer-initiated payments, there is experimental use of giros for B2B and business-to-consumer payments in some countries.

- *Debit Cards* — Debit cards outside the United States operate similarly to U.S. cards. As consumers use these cards for purchases, the funds are debited from their bank or giro account and credited to the seller's account.

- *Smart Cards* — These cards are similar to debit cards but contain a microchip with additional information and security protection. Smart cards may be used for prepaid value transactions, where the consumer prepays the bank, giro, or company issuing the card. The card then keeps track of purchases and any remaining balance.

V. International Trade Financing Methods

In the United States, it is customary for a seller to check the credit standing of a buyer prior to selling on open account. Invoices are often sent with each shipment and included in a statement of amounts due at the end of the month. Exporting goods to a non-domestic buyer necessitates more credit risk protection, particularly for a new business relationship.

The most frequently used international trade payment mechanisms — open account, documentary collection and letter of credit (L/C) — can be explained in terms of increasing levels of protection, complexity and cost. Open account terms are the simplest and the least costly, but they offer the least protection. Documentary collections are more complex and costly and offer more protection to both parties. L/Cs are the most complex, costly and secure vehicles for international trade. Exhibit 15.1 shows the hierarchy of trade payment mechanisms.

Exhibit 15.1 Hierarchy of International Trade Payment Methods

Regardless of the method of trade payment, the currency to be used must be agreed upon by the buyer and seller. Payment is generally specified in either the buyer's currency or the seller's currency, but it may be in a third currency if mutually acceptable to both parties. The majority of world trade is denominated in a third-party currency, the U.S. dollar.

A. Open Account

Under the open account method, the seller ships the merchandise and sends an invoice to the buyer. The buyer is then responsible for initiating payment to the seller in accordance with any agreed-upon credit terms. The open account is the most frequently used method of payment for well-established relationships.

B. Documentary Collection

Documentary collections are another method of payment used in international trade. The characteristics and uses of this method follow:

1. **Definition** — A documentary collection is a payment method that processes the collection of a draft and accompanying shipping documents through international correspondent banks. Instructions regarding the specifics of the transaction are contained in a collection letter or form that accompanies the documentation. It is the responsibility of the exporter to determine the specific instructions to be used in the collection letter.

2. **Role of Banks** — The banks involved in a documentary collection act only as collecting and paying agents and, unlike an L/C, assume no direct obligation for ensuring that payment will be made. Banks involved in these transactions may play the following roles:

    - *Remitting Bank* — The remitting bank is the seller's (exporter's) bank that prepares the collection letter and forwards documents to a correspondent bank in the buyer's (importer's) country.

    - *Collecting Bank* — The collecting bank is the remitting bank's correspondent and is responsible for contacting the buyer (importer), collecting the amount due and releasing the documents as instructed.

3. **Collection Letter** — A collection letter specifies the exact procedures to be followed before shipping documents are released to the importer. The importer usually requires physical possession of the shipping documents in order to obtain the merchandise. Documents are typically released either against payment or acceptance as follows:

- Documents against payment use a sight draft, which is a draft payable on demand and require that the collecting bank receive full and final payment of the amount owed prior to releasing the documents.

- Documents against acceptance use a time draft, which is a draft payable on a specified future date that must be accepted by the importer before the collecting bank may release documents. Upon maturity of the time draft, it is presented to the importer for payment.

4. **Payment** — Once full and final payment is received, the collecting bank transfers the funds to the remitting bank, as instructed, for payment to the exporter.

5. **Non-Payment or Non-Acceptance** — In the event of non-payment or non-acceptance, the exporter bears the risk and cost of remarketing the goods to another buyer or, possibly, returning the merchandise. The exporter may have the collecting bank initiate formal action against the importer for non-performance. Exhibit 15.2 illustrates a documentary collection.

C. Letter of Credit

An L/C is a document issued by a bank, guaranteeing the payment of a customer's draft up to a stated amount for a specified period provided certain conditions are met. An L/C substitutes a bank's credit for that of the buyer, virtually eliminating the seller's credit risk. L/Cs are a widely used method of payment for import and export shipments. L/Cs can also be used as a financing vehicle for international trade transactions.

1. **Commercial L/C** — A commercial L/C is issued by a bank in relation to a trade transaction involving the domestic or international shipment of merchandise. It is the intended mechanism of payment and typically requires presentment of a draft, commercial invoice and related shipping documents.

2. **Documentary Nature of L/C** — It is important to realize that an L/C is documentary in nature. This means that a bank's role in an L/C transaction is the examination of documents, not the underlying merchandise. Since a bank deals solely with documents, it is the responsibility of the importer (buyer) to specify the documentation required for payment that will reasonably ensure their receipt of the exact merchandise ordered.

3. **Role of Banks** — Banks may have the following roles in L/C transactions:
    - *Issuing Bank* — The issuing bank is the buyer's (importer's) bank that issues the L/C in favor of the beneficiary (seller/exporter).
    - *Advising Bank* — The advising bank advises the beneficiary of an L/C in its favor.

Exhibit 15.2 Illustration of a Documentary Collection

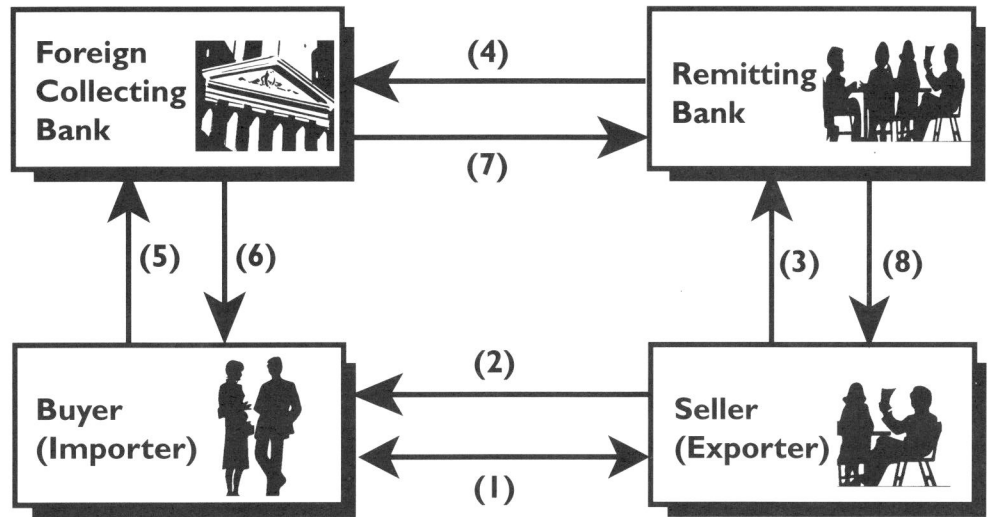

Step 1. Buyer and seller agree to a sales contract requiring the use of a documentary collection.

Step 2. The seller/exporter ships merchandise to the buyer/importer.

Step 3. The seller/exporter delivers the draft and documents to the remitting bank.

Step 4. The remitting bank forwards the documents and collection letter to the buyer/importer's bank, the foreign collecting bank.

Step 5. The buyer/importer makes payment to the foreign collecting bank in the case of a sight draft, or accepts a time draft.

Step 6. The foreign collecting bank releases the documents so that the buyer/importer may take delivery of the merchandise.

Step 7. The foreign collecting bank transfers funds to the remitting bank.

Step 8. The remitting bank pays the seller/exporter.

- *Negotiating Bank* — The negotiating bank examines the documents presented by the beneficiary, receives payment from the issuing bank and pays the beneficiary. The advising and negotiating bank is often the same bank.

- *Confirming Bank* — If requested, the advising bank may add its confirmation to an L/C. In doing so, the confirming bank commits to the beneficiary that payment will be made if documents meet the terms and conditions of the L/C, regardless of the issuing bank's ability to pay. If an L/C is confirmed, the confirming bank will also be the negotiating bank.

Exhibit 15.3 illustrates a typical international commercial letter of credit transaction.

4. **Commitment** — Most L/Cs are irrevocable, meaning that the L/C cannot be canceled or amended without the agreement of all parties to the transaction. The parties that must agree are the buyer, beneficiary (seller), issuing bank and, if the L/C is confirmed, the confirming bank.

5. **Payment Timing** — Once conforming documentation has been presented, the L/C may provide for either immediate or deferred payment to the beneficiary (seller/exporter).

    • When the advising/negotiating bank has confirmed the L/C and the L/C requires the presentment of a sight draft (payable on demand) the confirming bank pays the seller immediately and is reimbursed by the issuing bank.

Exhibit 15.3 Illustration of a Letter of Credit Transaction (Time Draft)

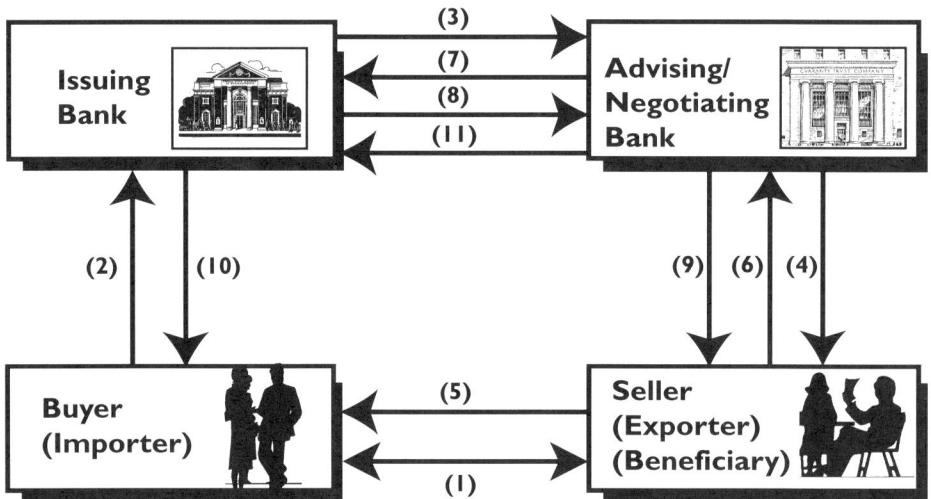

Step 1. The buyer and the seller agree to a sales contract in which the buyer is required to open an L/C in favor of the seller.
Step 2. The buyer chooses a bank in its country and opens an L/C in favor of the seller.
Step 3. The issuing (buyer's) bank sends the L/C to a bank in the seller's country. The latter bank becomes the advising bank.
Step 4. The advising bank sends details of the credit to the seller, who is the beneficiary of the credit.
Step 5. The seller ships the merchandise to the buyer.
Step 6. The seller presents the draft and documents to the advising/negotiating bank.
Step 7. The advising/negotiating bank examines the documents and sends them to the issuing bank.
Step 8. The issuing bank examines the documents, and if everything is in order, accepts the time draft that draws on the L/C. This accepted draft now becomes a banker's acceptance (BA). The BA is returned to the advising/negotiating bank. At this point, the seller may ask their bank to sell the BA at discount so they can receive immediate funds or hold the BA until maturity and receive the full amount at that time.
Step 9. The seller receives either full payment at the maturity of the BA or a discounted amount immediately.
Step 10. The issuing bank notifies the buyer it has the documents and, after payment terms are settled, releases the documents to the buyer. With the documents (primarily the bill of lading, which is title to the goods), the buyer is able to claim the merchandise.
Step 11. At the maturity date of the BA, the holder presents it to the issuing bank, which honors the BA for the face value.

- The L/C may require presentment of a time draft, which provides for payment at a future date. The use of a time draft is a way for the seller to provide credit terms to the buyer. The seller may be able to receive payment prior to maturity by discounting (selling for its discounted value) the time draft to a local bank.

- A deferred payment L/C provides for presentation of one or more sight drafts at specified dates in the future and this sometimes extends over several years. When medium-term financing is provided for the export of capital goods, a deferred payment L/C may be used in conjunction with a term loan agreement.

6. **Standby Letter of Credit** — A standby L/C is a variant of a commercial L/C. Standby L/Cs are issued primarily by U.S. banks, which are legally prohibited from issuing formal guarantees. Once issued, the standby L/C serves as a vehicle to ensure the financial performance of a bank's customer to a third-party beneficiary. Standby L/Cs typically require presentation of a sight draft and documentation that supports the beneficiary's claim of non-performance on the part of the issuing bank's customer. Standby L/Cs are frequently used as credit enhancement for commercial paper programs or to guarantee a bid tender or financial performance on a contract.

D. Other Trade Payment Methods

Other less frequently used international trade payment mechanisms include the following:

1. **Cash Before Delivery (CBD)** — CBD is when the seller requires the total protection of receiving payment before shipment of goods.

2. **Consignment** — Consignment involves the shipment of goods to a foreign agent where the exporter (seller) retains legal title to the goods. When the goods are sold by the agent, payment is due to the exporter and title transfers to the buyer. Regaining possession of unsold goods may be difficult and costly.

3. **Barter** — Barter involves the direct exchange of goods or services between two end users without using money. It is most frequently used when funds cannot be repatriated.

4. **Countertrade** — Countertrade is a method of payment used by companies that do not have access to sufficient hard currencies (internationally traded currencies) to pay for imports from other countries. For example, a U.S. exporter ships merchandise to the countertrading country and takes in exchange merchandise that can be sold elsewhere in the world for U.S. dollars or any other convertible currency.

5. **Trading Companies** — Trading companies are used when an exporter (seller) can also sell its products at a discount to an export trading company, which, in turn, resells the products internationally.

E. Banker's Acceptance (BA)

BA is most often used to finance the import, export or domestic shipment of goods, but it can also be used to finance storage of properly titled goods. BAs are commonly, but not necessarily, used in conjunction with L/Cs requiring a time draft drawn on a bank.

A BA is a time draft on the face of which the drawee bank has written the word "accepted" over its signature. The drawee bank is the bank which has issued the L/C and upon which the draft is drawn (or payable). The date and place payable are also indicated. The bank accepting and agreeing unconditionally to pay the draft at a particular time and place is known as the acceptor.

By accepting the draft, the bank creates a BA, indicating its commitment to pay the face amount of the draft at maturity. Through its acceptance of the payment risk, the bank creates a short-term negotiable instrument. Therefore, a bank can fund a BA transaction by selling it to an investor or by holding the BA in its own portfolio.

1. **Cost** — The cost of acceptance financing has two components: the discount rate (the rate earned by the investor) and the bank's acceptance commission.

2. **Eligibility** — Most acceptance financing is done with eligible acceptances. An eligible BA is an acceptance that may be discounted at the Federal Reserve. To be eligible for discount, the acceptance may not have a maturity of more than 180 days. Eligible underlying transactions include the following:
   - Import or export of goods
   - Domestic storage transactions with documents conveying title attached
   - Storage of readily marketable staples secured by warehouse receipts

F. Trade Acceptance

A trade acceptance is another instrument that may be used in international transactions. It is similar to a BA except that it is typically drawn on and accepted by a company, usually the buyer (importer). It can be used to evidence a buyer's obligation to pay for purchased merchandise where the seller (exporter) is satisfied with the credit risk.

VI. International Treasury Management Issues and Techniques

A. Credit and Accounts Receivable Management

Managing and evaluating credit can be more difficult in foreign countries where unsecured consumer credit is less prevalent and where rating agencies and credit information systems are less evolved. Whenever this is the case, companies generally require stricter credit terms. Similarly, companies typically are more careful about managing accounts receivable in foreign countries because defaulted receivables there are more difficult to collect than those in the United States.

B. Pooling

Companies concentrate cash internationally for the same reason they do domestically: to utilize cash more efficiently. In the U.S. cash management environment, concentration of funds typically involves physical movement of funds from depository banks into a concentration bank. Outside the United States, this physical concentration is usually referred to as "sweeping" the funds (not to be confused with "sweep accounts" used for overnight investments). Outside the United States, in countries where banks are allowed to pay interest on positive demand deposit balances and to charge interest on negative balances, the typical method of concentration is known as pooling.

In the most popular form of pooling as practiced in the European cash management market, any excess funds in the accounts of a company or its subsidiaries may be used to offset any deficits in other accounts of the parent or its subsidiaries. This type of pooling arrangement typically is offered for a variety of currencies.

- Pooling requires a company and all its subsidiaries to maintain their accounts at the same bank.

- Positive and negative balances may be aggregated each day for the calculation of interest earned or due. Normally, funds are not actually transferred; they are merely totaled for the purpose of calculating interest. This practice is known as notional pooling.

- Credit facilities of some kind are usually required by the bank to support any negative balances in the pool.

- Most pooling is single-currency/one-country pooling, where a company's subsidiaries within a given country are allowed to pool their balances in that country's currency. As the euro becomes accepted across Europe, the instance of single-currency/cross-border pooling will become more prevalent. In this case a company's subsidiaries throughout Europe can pool their euro-denominated funds, even though they may be in different countries.

C. Netting

Netting is an internal company system designed to reduce the number of cross-border payments among units of a company through the elimination or consolidation of individual funds flows denominated in different currencies. Many countries impose restrictions on the use of netting systems and formal approval may be required.

1. **Bilateral Netting** — In a bilateral netting system, purchases between two subsidiaries of the same company are netted against each other so that periodically — typically once a month — only the net difference is transferred. If the payments to be netted are in different currencies, the total due each subsidiary is converted to a common reference currency to determine the net amount due.

   For example, subsidiaries of a multinational company, one located in France and another in the U.K., hold payments until one or two regularly scheduled times during the month. Prior to the settlement date, the payments in both directions are totaled, the net due one of the subsidiaries determined and a single transfer is scheduled.

2. **Multilateral Netting** — This system is similar to bilateral netting but with more than two subsidiaries. Each subsidiary informs a central treasury management center of all planned cross-border payments. To determine netting transactions, the payments between all subsidiaries are converted into a common, reference currency. Payments are combined into fewer, but larger, transactions and each unit is informed prior to the settlement date of the net amount to pay or to be received in its own currency. The netting center makes the necessary FX conversions. Although multilateral netting is used primarily for intracompany transactions, some companies include third-party payments or receipts in their systems.

   The mechanics of multilateral netting are illustrated in Exhibit 15.4.

3. **Benefits** — The benefits of netting include:
   - Reduction of the number of FX transactions and cross-border wire transfers
   - Availability of more favorable FX rates for the larger FX trades resulting from consolidation
   - Improved cash forecasting for both the subsidiary and the parent as a result of the ability to preplan cross-border payments

4. **Costs** — There are setup and maintenance costs that must be considered when starting and operating a netting system.

Exhibit 15.4 Illustration of Multilateral Netting

D. Leading and Lagging

Netting systems may be used to implement leading and lagging. Leading and lagging involve making cross-border payments between subsidiaries either ahead of schedule (leading) or behind schedule (lagging). Liquidity is moved from one subsidiary to another. Leading can be helpful when a currency is expected to depreciate, while lagging will be used when the currency is expected to appreciate relative to the parent's home currency.

E. Re-Invoicing

Re-invoicing is a method of centralizing the responsibility for monitoring and collecting international accounts receivable and more effectively managing the related FX exposure. A re-invoicing center is a company-owned subsidiary that buys the goods from an exporting subsidiary and resells the goods to an importing subsidiary. The exporting unit invoices and receives funds from the re-invoicing subsidiary in its own currency, while the importing unit is invoiced and pays funds to the re-invoicing subsidiary in its own currency. Although title to the goods passes through the re-invoicing center, usually the actual goods are shipped directly from the exporting subsidiary to the importing subsidiary. Establishing a re-invoicing center requires local government approval and negotiation on how the subsidiary will be taxed.

1. **Benefits** — The benefits of a re-invoicing center include:
    - Centralization of FX exposure in the re-invoicing center where it can be more effectively managed.
    - Improvement in a company's worldwide short-term liquidity management by providing flexibility in intersubsidiary payments. For instance, re-invoicing enables leading and lagging arrangements to be implemented easily, improves export trade financing and collections, reduces bank costs and improves FX rates by enabling larger trades. It is particularly beneficial for the ability to set worldwide/international pricing, but may be heavily regulated by foreign monetary authorities.

2. **Costs** — Re-invoicing center expenses include physical location and administration costs as well as costs specifically associated with netting centers.

    Re-invoicing is illustrated in Exhibit 15.5.

F. Internal Factoring

The purpose of an internal factoring center is similar to that of re-invoicing. Rather than taking actual title to the goods as with re-invoicing, the internal factoring unit buys accounts receivable from the exporting unit and collects from the importing unit. The benefits of internal factoring are the same as they are for re-invoicing. Most internal factoring is done on a recourse basis, where the factor can come back to the company (or subsidiary) if the account cannot be collected.

G. Multicurrency Accounts

Multicurrency accounts are a special arrangement between a bank and its corporate customer whereby the bank allows the customer to receive or make international payments in a range of currencies from a single account or multiple subsidiary accounts.

The agreement generally specifies the following:

- The base currency in which the account will be denominated
- The portfolio of currencies that will be accepted
- The spread or margin over the spot rate that will be used for purposes of exchanging each currency back to the base currency
- The value date that will be applied to debits and credits for each transaction type and currency

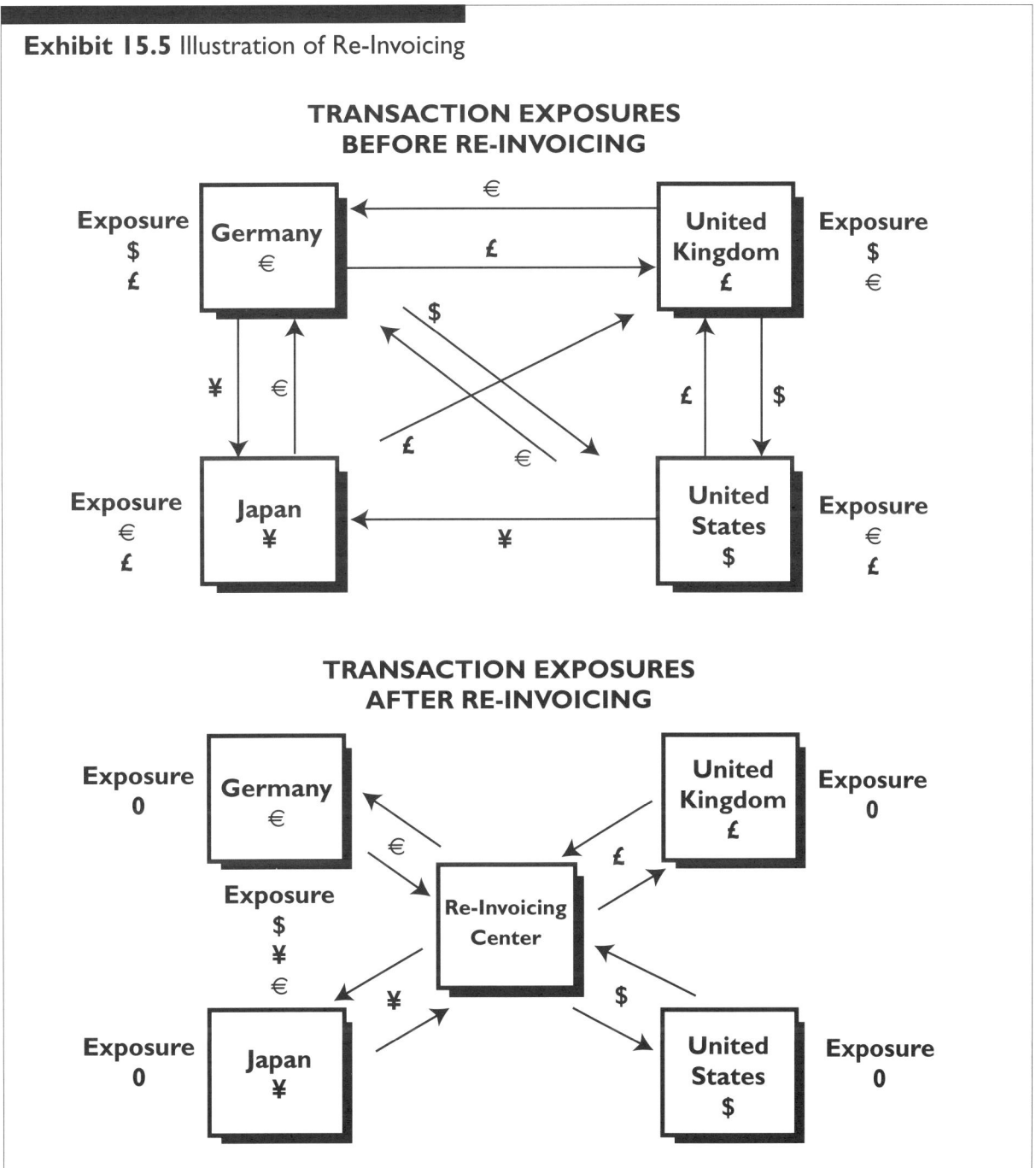

Exhibit 15.5 Illustration of Re-Invoicing

H. Electronic Banking Services

Major banks in Europe and Asia offer a wide range of electronic banking services. One of the most popular are reporting services that provide information on balances and previous day transaction detail. Such reporting services allow both local and international access. For example, the balances and debit and credit details for a Dutch subsidiary of a U.S. company can be reported to local management in the Netherlands as well as to the parent. Major international banks and third-party service providers can consolidate reporting by a company's banking network, both foreign and domestic operations, into a single daily report. The major global banks also offer a range of electronic transaction initiation services. These services typically allow companies to initiate international wires and other global electronic transactions in a variety of foreign currencies. The general topic of electronic banking services is covered in more detail in Chapter 10, Information Management and Technology.

VII. International Financing, Taxation and Other Considerations

Export financing, export credit insurance, offshore financing alternatives and tax implications are important considerations for a multinational company.

A. Export Financing

A critical issue for many companies selling internationally is how to finance their sales to foreign buyers. For U.S.-based companies, the primary sources of financing are commercial banks and the Export-Import Bank of the United States (Eximbank).

1. **Commercial Banks** — Some commercial banks in the United States specialize in providing direct financing to the foreign buyers of U.S. exports.

2. **Export-Import Bank of the United States** — The Eximbank is an independent agency of the U.S. government established to finance and guarantee payment for U.S. exports. The Eximbank is directed by its corporate charter to:
   - Develop export financing programs that are competitive with those offered by other countries
   - Ensure that financing or repayment guarantees are made to borrowers with a reasonable capacity to repay
   - Enhance or supplement financing offered by private commercial banks

3. **Export Credit Insurance** — A common method of insuring payment of foreign accounts receivables is through the purchase of export credit insurance. This insurance is provided by the Eximbank and by certain private insurers. Export insurance can cover both political (sovereign) risk and commercial risk. Insurance coverage is available for shipments to almost every country with which the United States has diplomatic relations. The insurance obtained through the Eximbank is backed by the U.S. government.

The Eximbank's programs also include a working capital program aimed at small businesses, a loan guarantee program to encourage private-sector loans and a direct loan program used in situations in which foreign competitors receive government subsidized financing.

B. Financing International Operations

Offshore financing involves raising funds outside a company's home country. Companies may finance outside their country for the following reasons:

1. **Diversification of Funding** — A company may want to diversify its funding sources rather than depend on one market for several reasons:

    - Too much debt in a particular market may saturate investors' desire for a company's debt and therefore raise the cost of borrowing additional amounts.

    - In times of tight credit, it is helpful to have relationships with a number of different lenders.

2. **Hedging in Foreign Currencies** — Liabilities in a foreign currency can hedge a similar term asset in the same currency. For example, if a U.S. company had accounts receivable denominated in British pounds, it may consider short-term debt denominated in pounds. In this case, if foreign currency-denominated assets depreciate, liabilities denominated in the same foreign currency depreciate as well, thereby minimizing FX translation exposure. This is also known as a balance sheet hedge. (See Chapter 14, Financial Risk Management.)

3. **Lower Borrowing Rates for Parent Company** — A U.S. parent company may be able to borrow in a foreign currency at a lower borrowing rate than its U.S. borrowing rate, even after hedging.

4. **Lower Borrowing Rate for Foreign Subsidiaries** — An international subsidiary may be able to borrow in its local market from one of its local banks at lower rates than it can through its parent company.

5. **Tax Advantages** — There may be tax advantages available in the subsidiary's home country.

Companies may also establish offshore financing subsidiaries to obtain funding and benefit from favorable tax regulations. A company may fund the needs of a number of subsidiaries in different countries through its offshore finance company, thus taking advantage of lower rates by borrowing in large amounts. Companies can also invest in short-term foreign financial instruments through offshore subsidiaries.

C. Tax Considerations

Multinational companies must deal with tax codes in all the countries in which they have operations or sales. Some of the more important considerations include:

1. **Foreign Tax Credits** — A U.S. company's income derived from its foreign operations is typically included in its tax return to determine the amount of the U.S. income tax due. If this foreign source income has already been subject to foreign income taxes, the same income is being taxed twice.

   To relieve the effect of this double taxation, the U.S. tax law allows a U.S. company a tax credit against its total U.S. income tax liability for those foreign income taxes paid by the parent and its subsidiaries. This credit is called the foreign tax credit. It is allowed only for those foreign taxes that are income taxes and do not exceed U.S. tax rates.

2. **Foreign Tax Planning** — The complexity of the law regarding the taxation of non-domestic income makes it important for treasury personnel to work with tax experts.

3. **Tax-Advantaged Business Centers** — To attract multinational businesses and related employment opportunities, a number of countries offer tax incentives for subsidiaries that perform certain administrative and financial functions.

D. Legal and Ethical Issues

In many countries, "commissions" or "fees," which would be considered bribes in the United States, are deeply ingrained in the commercial culture. However, the Foreign Corrupt Practices Act forbids U.S. companies to engage in such practices. Another consideration is whether a company's foreign activities may come under the jurisdiction of the Office of Foreign Assets Control (OFAC). The OFAC is an office of the Treasury Department and administers and enforces economic and trade sanctions against targeted foreign countries, terrorism-sponsoring organizations and international narcotics traffickers based on U.S. foreign policy and national security goals. The OFAC has the authority to impose controls on financial transactions and freeze foreign assets under U.S. jurisdiction.

E. Sovereign Risk

One type of risk that must be considered is known as sovereign risk. This is the risk that a company's operations in a foreign country may be expropriated or nationalized by the government of that country. Other types of less severe sovereign risk include: 1) blocked currencies, where profits cannot be converted from the local currency into a major trading currency; 2) forced re-investment, where funds cannot be transferred out of the country in any form; or 3) required majority ownership by local residents of the country.

Test Your Understanding

These chapter questions are provided to test your understanding of the information in the text and are not examples of CCM examination questions, nor are they in the examination format.

Answers can be found at the back of the book on pages 540-541.

1. Why is international treasury management becoming increasingly important for companies?

2. What are some of the key characteristics in which international banking systems differ?

3. Explain the concept of value dating.

4. What must a payee do if it receives a check drawn in a different country?

5. How do payment practices vary outside the United States?

6. What is pooling, as applied in non-U.S. banking systems?

7. Describe a multicurrency account.

8. List and discuss the major benefits of using a netting system.

9. What is a re-invoicing center and how does it differ from internal factoring?

10. What risk is eliminated by the use of a letter of credit?

11. Describe an irrevocable letter of credit.

12. What is a standby letter of credit?

13. Discuss the major difference in the role of the banks under a documentary collection as opposed to a letter of credit.

14. Explain the concept of countertrade.

15. What is the maximum maturity for a banker's acceptance to remain eligible for discount at the Federal Reserve?

16. What is the Eximbank?

17. Why do companies use offshore financing?

CHAPTER 16

Relationship Management

Overview

This chapter describes the objectives of relationship management. It explains the various issues involved in selecting financial service providers. It explains the role of account analysis in financial institution compensation and the different methods of compensating financial institutions.

Learning Objectives

Upon completion of this chapter the reader should know:

- The objectives of relationship management
- How companies select and evaluate financial institutions and other financial service providers
- What an account analysis statement is and how it is used in relationship management
- How to perform collected balance and earnings credit calculations
- The options for compensating financial institutions

Key Concepts

- Objectives of relationship management
- Selection and evaluation of financial institutions
- Account analysis statement
- Collected balance and earnings credit calculation
- Financial institution compensation

Chapter 16 • Relationship Management

Outline

I. Objectives of Relationship Management

II. Service Provider Selection
    A. Selection Process
    B. Selection Criteria
    C. RFP/RFI Etiquette

III. Issues in Financial Institution Relationship Management
    A. Creditworthiness of Financial Institution
    B. Number of Relationships
    C. Negotiation and Pricing
    D. Relationship Documentation
    E. Audit and Control
    F. Performance Measurement and Evaluation

IV. Financial Institution Compensation and Account Analysis
    A. Relationship Approach
    B. Account Analysis
    C. Financial Institution Compensation Practices
    D. Comparing Service Charges
    E. Fee vs. Balance Compensation

I. Objectives of Relationship Management

The objectives of relationship management generally include:

1. **Access to Credit** — A company requires access to credit facilities to meet short-term working capital needs and longer-term financing requirements.

2. **Access to Non-Credit Services** — A company requires access to services such as cash management, investments, trust, international services and risk management.

3. **Management of Costs and Quality** — A company selects and monitors financial institutions and other service providers to ensure that the relationship is cost-effective and that services provided are consistent with agreed-upon standards.

4. **Monitoring Risks** — A company monitors the risk of a disruption in a financial institution relationship arising from changes in management policy, merger, acquisition or failure.

5. **Development of a Partnership Approach** — A partnership approach means that the relationship is mutually beneficial.

II. Service Provider Selection

Consolidation and specialization among financial institutions and other financial service providers (FSPs) have made the selection process critical for many companies. Consolidation reduces the number of providers in certain product areas. Specialization raises the importance of matching a given company's needs with a particular provider's strengths.

A. Selection Process

1. **Informal** — Selecting a financial institution or FSP does not always involve a formal process. Sometimes a company may already have established a relationship with a particular service provider or financial institution or may have targeted specific candidates. In such cases, the selection process does not involve a formal written proposal.

2. **Request for Information** — In some cases, a request for information (RFI) may be used in the selection process. An RFI is often used by a company simply to confirm that use of a current provider of a service is justified, or to narrow the field of potential providers before issuing a request for proposal (RFP). An RFI is also used

to solicit ideas from service providers on how to solve a particular business or operational problem.

3. **A Request for Proposal** — An RFP is a formal document prepared by a company outlining its objectives and service requirements. An RFP can be used to obtain bids for everything ranging from one particular service to a company's entire relationship. By law, some government entities are required to prepare RFPs on a periodic basis, usually every three to five years, to ensure that they are receiving comparable services at competitive prices. Many private sector companies also periodically prepare RFPs for similar reasons. Outside consultants are sometimes used to assist in the preparation of RFPs and evaluation of responses. There are now standard formats that allow for electronic submission and comparison of proposals. The Association for Financial Professionals (AFP) and the Bank Administration Institute (BAI) have published standard RFP formats for common banking services.

A typical RFP requests the following:
- Background information on the provider
- Objectives to be met
- Summary of the proposed solution
- Service descriptions
- Service features and benefits
- The provider's commitment to support and enhance services
- A price schedule and a cost/benefit analysis
- Pro forma account analysis statement (financial institutions only)
- Sample service commitments or agreements
- Timetable for service implementation
- Customer references

B. Selection Criteria

Selecting service providers involves assessing capabilities based on the following criteria:
- Knowledge of a specific industry or business
- Responsiveness to questions asked in the selection process and understanding of the company's needs and objectives
- Quality of customer service
- Pricing of services

- Willingness to provide credit on flexible terms and at competitive rates
- Ability to provide financial advice or consulting services
- Financial strength of service provider
- Commitment to a company, industry or service
- Quality and expertise of relationship managers and technical specialists
- Ability to customize services and develop new services
- Geographic and other convenience considerations
- Ability to meet future needs of the company

In recent years, some companies have started to send out technical RFPs that stress the level and quality of services rather than the pricing. This trend will likely continue as companies look to banks and other vendors to provide mission-critical services for the treasury department on an outsourced basis.

C. RFP/RFI Etiquette

One of the dangers in the RFP process for both treasury managers and FSPs in the RFP process is that the creation of the RFP and the response to the RFP could become so standardized and automated that neither party really benefits from the process. The RFP/RFI process can lead to a true exchange of new ideas and fresh concepts as companies prompt FSPs for new services and FSPs develop innovative ideas for their customers. Many bankers will respond to RFPs that they know they have little chance of winning just to increase the prospects for future business and to establish their credibility and expertise. Another problem area in RFP etiquette is companies that use frequent RFPs to try to drive down the prices of services. This process can lead to turning key cash management services into commodities, which benefits neither the customer nor the FSP.

III. Issues in Financial Institution Relationship Management

When assessing the suitability of a financial institution, companies consider the following factors:

A. Creditworthiness of Financial Institution

The creditworthiness of financial institutions is a concern of treasurers and cash managers — particularly since the 1980s when some financial institutions failed or were acquired in lieu of being liquidated. Failures and acquisitions affect access to credit and other services that are crucial to a company's business operations.

The ratings that agencies give financial institutions have become increasingly important. Ratings are a proxy for creditworthiness and a number of agencies offer ratings services. Some offer ratings only, while others also offer detailed backup reports that provide both quantitative financial analyses and qualitative assessments of management.

Among the most common methods of rating depository financial institution strength is the CAMELS rating, a system widely used by regulators. CAMELS is the acronym for Capital adequacy, Asset quality, Management capability, Earnings, Liquidity and Sensitivity to market risk. Although banks are prohibited from disclosing their CAMELS ratings, rating agencies such as Standard & Poor's, Moody's and Bankwatch evaluate the same factors in their assessment processes.

1. **Capital Adequacy** — A financial institution is expected to maintain capital commensurate with the nature and extent of its risks and the ability of management to identify, measure, monitor and control these risks.

2. **Asset Quality** — The asset quality rating reflects the existing and potential credit risk associated with the loan and investment portfolio, other assets and off-balance-sheet items.

3. **Management Capability** — This rating reflects the capability of the board of directors and management, in their respective roles, to identify, measure, monitor and control the risks of an institution's activities and to ensure the institution's safe, sound and efficient operation in compliance with applicable laws and regulations.

4. **Earnings** — This rating indicates the level of earnings, earning trends and sustainability. A bank's profitability, asset quality and credit risk management can affect its earnings ratings.

5. **Liquidity** — This aspect of the rating pertains to current and future levels of liquidity in comparison with funding needs. It also indicates the adequacy of funds management practices relative to an institution's size, complexity and risk profile.

6. **Sensitivity to Market Risk** — This is the degree to which changes in interest rates, foreign exchange rates, commodities prices or equities prices can adversely affect a financial institution's earnings or capital.

B. Number of Relationships

Typically, the number and nature of financial institution relationships a company maintains depends upon the following considerations:

1. **Credit Accessibility/Adequacy** — Many companies establish multiple relationships to ensure that they have adequate credit facilities or to diversify service providers.

2. **Costs** — There are internal and external costs for each financial institution relationship, resulting in an incentive to optimize the number of relationships. There has been a trend among large companies toward fewer financial institution relationships.

3. **Collection/Concentration System** — Companies in the United States with a nationwide over-the-counter/field bank collection and concentration system (see Chapter 6, Collections and Chapter 7, Cash Concentration) often find themselves dealing with hundreds of small banks. This is unique to the U.S. banking market, where there is a lack of true nationwide banking.

4. **Global Banking** — Companies operating on a global basis may need a wider number of banking relationships to provide coverage in all the countries where they have a presence.

5. **Strategic Implications** — Each institution should serve a purpose in the company's business strategy. Because of increasing financial institution consolidation and specialization, there is a trend toward establishing and maintaining relationships based on a particular need.

6. **Relative Strength and Capabilities** — When a company has multiple financial institution relationships, often one is designated a lead institution. There may be different lead institutions for credit and other services.

7. **Services Provided** — The types, sophistication and geographic location of services needed by a company may require multiple relationships. This is especially true with services such as trust, safekeeping, imprest accounts, payable-if-desired accounts and automated billing/invoicing.

C. Negotiation and Pricing

Negotiation plays an important part in managing relations with financial institutions, particularly since financial institutions have developed more sophisticated methods for measuring relationship profitability.

For example, pricing of loans is often based on interdependent factors such as the cost of funds, risk, total loans committed and outstanding, service fees, deposit balances and the range of other services used. Likewise, pricing of services is often based on such factors as business strategy, volume, customization, exception handling requirements, costs of providing the service, deposit balances, operational overhead and other services used.

D. Relationship Documentation

The important documents associated with the establishment of a financial institution relationship include:

1. **Account Resolution** — This document is the basic account authorization and is usually a board of directors' resolution. It specifies:
    - What functions can be performed by specific individuals or job titles, authorized signers on the account and the liability of each party.
    - The scope and limitations of the relationship. It may be general or specific regarding actions that the financial institution may take on behalf of the company.

   The resolution can be a standard one used by all commercial customers of a given financial institution, or it can be customized for a given company. Some companies have developed their own standard resolutions that they use for all their financial institution relationships and their banks' use of the company standard is a matter of negotiation.

2. **Signature Cards** — Financial institutions require companies to furnish signatures of authorized signers or specimens of facsimile or computerized signatures.

3. **Terms and Conditions** — Financial institutions may provide terms and conditions to companies when depository accounts are established. This document will detail the responsibilities of the bank and the account holders in the maintenance of accounts. Some of the important areas contained in the document may include information on funds availability, time frames during which errors must be reported and the bank's right of offset against accounts related to fees owed. These terms are amended from time to time and notice is generally mailed out with account statements.

4. **Service Agreements** — Financial institutions or companies may require service agreements. The agreements may be standardized or customized. The elements of a service agreement can include:
    - Operational policies and procedures, including the detailed processing requirements for the service, information needs and people who are authorized to make changes

- Performance standards that define agreed-upon levels of service performance and quality
- Compensation policies, including pricing, method of payment, payment frequency, excess/deficit balance arrangements, contract length and adjustments
- Liability clauses defining responsibilities for specified risks
- Terms and conditions

E. Audit and Control

The audit and control issues facing a company in managing its relationships with financial institutions include the following:

- Establishing and updating policies and procedures for opening accounts that cover such matters as:
  - Approval required for opening accounts
  - Corporate resolution(s)
  - Individuals authorized to open accounts or contract for services
  - Individuals authorized as signatories
- Timely reconciliation of accounts and timely reporting of problems and exceptions. Under Article 4 of the uniform commercial code (UCC), a company has 30 days to report any unauthorized activities. This time frame can be extended by agreement between both parties.
- A clear separation of transaction initiation, accounting and reconciliation duties.
- Maintenance of account documentation and record keeping, including corporate resolutions, contracts for services and signatories on accounts.
- Tracking of unresolved discrepancies.

F. Performance Measurement and Evaluation

Service quality is a very important aspect of relationships with financial institutions. An important task for a company is to determine exactly what quality standards it wants and what error rates are reasonable for the various services. The company's performance expectations should be based on the service levels stipulated in its agreements with the bank. Two of the most common types of performance measurement techniques are report cards and relationship reviews.

1. **Report Cards** — A report card is a tool companies use to obtain a quantitative rating of a bank's level of service and responsiveness to problems. Criteria commonly found in report cards include:

    - Number of errors by service
    - Reporting times for information services
    - Responsiveness to questions
    - Timeliness of error resolution
    - Effectiveness of personnel

    Companies prepare report cards monthly, quarterly or annually. Some companies that deal with many financial institutions and other service providers rank them by their ability to meet the companies' quality criteria on a service-by-service basis.

2. **Relationship Review** — A relationship review is another procedure companies use to qualitatively assess the service levels and personnel responsiveness. Reviews can be either formal or informal. Formal reviews typically involve a quarterly, semiannual or annual meeting of the senior management representatives of both parties. Informal reviews typically involve weekly or monthly contacts by individuals who are responsible for the day-to-day management of the relationship.

    Financial institutions also initiate relationship reviews by preparing summaries of services, fees, error rates and other relationship information. Relationship reviews also enable financial institutions and companies to discuss future strategies and needs.

    The BAI has developed calculations that can measure performance quality in cash management services.

IV. Financial Institution Compensation and Account Analysis

A. Relationship Approach

Mutual success in every long-term relationship involves the accommodation of both parties. The factors that increase the mutual benefit and profitability of the relationship include:

- Open and frequent two-way communications
- Regular and timely feedback

- Clear expectations as established by agreements and legal contracts
- Fair compensation of the financial institution by the company and fair pricing of services by the financial institution
- Complete disclosure by both parties of information essential to the success and ethical basis of the relationship

B. Account Analysis

The account analysis statement is a paper or electronic report a bank provides to its commercial customers specifying services provided, volumes processed and charges assessed. It is essentially an invoice for services provided along with detailed information on balances and credit earned for those balances. However, banks often use varying terminology in describing these services. Services and fees can be detailed and itemized, bundled into a single line item or some combination of the two. Fee structures are varied and complex, as are the account analysis formats banks use to report them.

1. **AFP (formerly TMA) Account Analysis Standard** — In 1987, AFP (formerly known as the Treasury Management Association or TMA) developed a standard format for account analysis that included a standard set of service codes. A revised version of the account analysis standard was published in 1998.

    The current AFP standard account analysis consists of sections that provide:
    - Customer information
    - Balance and compensation information
    - Rate information
    - Service information
    - Adjustment detail
    - Summary of accounts
    - Optional historic balance and compensation information

2. **AFP (formerly TMA) Service Codes** — The six-character alphanumeric AFP service codes provide standard, uniform references and terms for identifying, describing and reporting bank services and associated charges. By simplifying and organizing the varied and complex terminology often used to identify bank services, the codes also help resolve errors in volume and pricing. Examples of the AFP service code product families (indicated by the first two characters of the service code) are:
    - *Lockbox Services (05)* — This product family includes services associated with wholesale and retail lockbox processing and covers document handling, data capture and programming as well as lockbox deposit reporting and information delivery.

- *Depository Services (10)* — This product family includes services associated with the processing of coin and currency, encoded and unencoded check deposits, branch and vault deposits, supplies of coin and currency and services related to domestic collections and return item processing. It also includes deposit reconciliation services, reports and software.

- *Paper Disbursement Services (15)* — This product family includes services associated with the issuance, control and processing of checks and drafts paid against an account; controlled disbursement; positive pay; and payable through draft services. It also includes check inquiries and stop payments, returned checks, teller services, check sorting, microfilming and retention and disbursement information reporting and software.

- *General ACH Services (25)* — This product family includes services associated with the origination and receipt of ACH transactions, ACH input processing, ACH activity reporting, master file maintenance, ACH returns and exception processing and ACH software.

3. **ASC X12 822 Account Analysis Format** — The Accredited Standards Committee (ASC) of the American National Standards Institute (ANSI) has developed a standardized format (Transaction Set 822 — Account Analysis) for financial institutions to use in sending account analysis statements to companies electronically. The ASC X12 822 transaction set can accommodate the AFP standard account analysis format and service codes. The AFP Guide To Account Analysis includes a detailed transaction set 822 implementation guide.

4. **Account Analysis Terminology** — Common terms used in account analysis statements include:

    - *Service Charges* — The explicit fees or prices charged for services provided by a financial institution. Service charges are usually expressed in the form of a per-item or per-unit price. The unit price is multiplied by the volume.

    - *Earnings Credit* — The total credit that can be used to offset service charges incurred during the period. It is calculated by multiplying the collected balances (adjusted for the reserve requirement) by the earnings credit rate for the period.

    - *Average Ledger Balance* — The sum of the daily ending ledger balances (both positive and negative) divided by the number of days in the analysis period. Balances are net of current period adjustments (e.g., misposted wire transfers, deposits with missed deadlines or items with encoding errors).

    - *Average Deposit Float* — The sum of the daily dollar amount of items in the process of collection divided by the number of days in the analysis period.

    - *Reserve Requirement Balances* — Non-interest-bearing deposits that must, by law, be maintained by financial institutions at the Federal Reserve. The reserve requirement is one of the key components of U.S. monetary policy. (See Chapter 3, The U.S. Financial Environment.) For compensation purposes, a financial institution may use a reserve percentage other than that which is required by the Federal Reserve.

- *Earnings Credit Rate (ECR)* — The rate used to calculate the earnings credit. While the method of determining this rate varies by financial institution, the most commonly used measure is the 90-day Treasury bill (T-bill) rate. If a bank utilizes a reserve-adjusted ECR, the impact of the reserve requirement is included in the ECR calculation. (The examples in this book do not use reserve-adjusted ECR.)

- *Average Collected Balance* — The sum of the daily ending collected balances (both positive and negative) divided by the number of days in the analysis period. In many account analysis statements this item is calculated as the average ledger balance minus the deposit float.

- *Investable Balance* — The balance on which the ECR is applied. This value can be either positive or negative. A negative balance indicates a shortage of investable funds. Some banks calculate the investable balance as the average collected balance reduced by the reserve requirement balance. Other banks reduce the ECR by the reserve requirement (a reserve-adjusted ECR) and, in this case, the average collected balance is used as the investable balance. (The examples in this book do not use reserve-adjusted ECR.)

5. **Earnings Credit Calculation** — The formula for converting collected balances into the earnings credit is:

$$\text{Earnings Credit} = \text{Collected Balances} \times (1 - \text{Reserve Requirement}) \times \left(\text{Earnings Credit Rate} \times \frac{\text{Days in Month}}{365} \right)$$

$$EC = CB \times (1 - RR) \times \left(ECR \times \frac{D}{365} \right)$$

Where:

EC	=	Earnings Credit
CB	=	Actual Collected Balance
RR	=	Reserve Requirement
ECR	=	Earnings Credit Rate
D	=	Number of Days in the Month

Note: Some banks use the earnings credit rate divided by 12 instead of using the actual number of days to determine this monthly calculation.

An example of the earnings credit calculation is provided in Exhibit 16.1.

CHAPTER 16 • RELATIONSHIP MANAGEMENT

> **Exhibit 16.1** Earning Credit Average Calculation Example
>
> **Assumptions:**
>
> | | |
> |---|---|
> | Average ledger balance | $ 250,000 |
> | Deposit Float | $ 30,000 |
> | Reserve requirement | 10% |
> | Earnings Credit rate | 5% |
> | Service charges for the month | $ 1,000 |
> | Days in month | 30 |
>
> **Average Collected Balance Calculation:**
>
> | | |
> |---|---|
> | Average ledger balance | $ 250,000 |
> | Less: deposit float | ($ 30,000) |
> | Equals: average collected balance | $ 220,000 |
>
> $$\text{Earnings Credit} = \text{Collected Balances} \times (1 - \text{Reserve Requirement}) \times \left(\text{Earnings Credit Rate} \times \frac{\text{Days in Month}}{365} \right)$$
>
> $$EC = CB \times (1 - RR) \times \left(ECR \times \frac{D}{365} \right)$$
>
> $$= \$220{,}000 \times (1 - .10) \times \left(.05 \times \frac{30}{365} \right) = \$220{,}000 \times .90 \times .0041 = \$811.80$$
>
> The answer above assumes that intermediate calculations are rounded as shown.
>
> If the current service charges are $1,000, but the amount of earnings credit is only $811.80, the company did not keep sufficient collected balances on deposit to cover the cost of services over the period. In effect, the company has a companion deficit of $188.20, which is owed to the financial institution.

$$\text{Collected Balances Required} = \frac{\text{Monthly Service Charges}}{\left(\text{Earnings Credit Rate} \times \frac{\text{Days in Month}}{365} \right) \times (1 - \text{Reserve Requirement})}$$

$$CB = \frac{SC}{\left(ECR \times \frac{D}{365} \right) \times (1 - RR)}$$

6. **Calculation of the Collected Balances Required** — The collected balances required is the daily average balance needed to offset service charges for the current analysis period. The formula for this computation is:

   Where:
   - CB = Collected Balances Required for Services
   - SC = Service Charges
   - ECR = Earnings Credit Rate
   - RR = Reserve Requirement
   - D = Number of Days in the Month

Exhibit 16.2 Collected Balances Required Calculation

A company uses services with charges that total $10,000 per month. The earnings credit rate is 5%. The reserve requirement is 10%. Assuming a 30-day month, the average collected balances required to compensate the financial institution for the services used is as follows:

$$\text{Collected Balances Required} = \frac{\text{Monthly Service Charges, Fees or Costs}}{\left(\text{Earnings Credit Rate} \times \frac{\text{Days in Month}}{365}\right) \times (1 - \text{Reserve Requirement})}$$

$$CB = \frac{SC}{\left(ECR \times \frac{D}{365}\right) \times (1 - RR)}$$

$$= \frac{\$10,000}{\left(.05 \times \frac{30}{365}\right) \times (1 - .10)} = \frac{\$10,000}{(.0041 \times .90)} = \frac{\$10,000}{.0037} = \$2,702,703$$

The answer above assumes that intermediate calculations are rounded as shown.

Note: If $1.00 is used as the service charge in the above formula, the balance multiplier is calculated. This number, 270.27, multiplied by the service charges, gives the collected balances required to pay for services.

Note: Some banks use the earnings credit rate divided by 12 instead of using the actual number of days to determine this monthly calculation.

An example of the collected balances required calculation is provided in Exhibit 16.2.

C. Financial Institution Compensation Practices

Compensation practices vary among financial institutions. Some of the principal features include:

- *Compensation for Excess Collected Balances* — If a company has collected balances in excess of the amount required for compensation, interest cannot be paid on the balances according to Regulation Q. (See Chapter 4, U.S. Payments System, for a discussion of Regulation Q.) Policies vary on how financial institutions treat the excess. Institutions may or may not allow these excesses to be carried forward to future periods.

- *Collection of Deficit Service Charges* — Deficit service charge amounts are collected by the financial institution either by direct debit of a customer's account or by invoicing the customer.

- *Calculation of Earnings Credit* — Most financial institutions calculate the earnings credit on collected balances net of reserve requirements (net collected balances). Some apply the ECR to the monthly average collected balance. Others apply it to the daily collected balance. If it is applied to the daily amount, this may result in a borrowing rate being charged on days when there is a negative net collected balance.

- *Basis for Compensation* — Accounts may be considered individually or on a combined basis for compensation. If accounts are combined, all balances are averaged together. This approach is helpful for a company that has excess balances in some accounts but deficit balances in others. By combining the balances for purposes of compensation, overall service charges can be reduced.

- *Analysis Consolidation* — A company that has multistate locations may use a financial institution that has facilities in each of the states. In some cases, the financial institution will prepare a combined account analysis for all of the company's accounts in all states. The practice of preparing a combined account analysis statement may become more common as interstate branching increases.

D. Comparing Service Charges

Companies compare financial institution service charges both during the initial selection process and during periodic relationship reviews. There is software available from a variety of vendors that can aid in comparing service charges from multiple banks. Service charge comparisons are difficult to make for the following reasons:

- Financial institutions have different pricing strategies.

- Service charges may be bundled or unbundled. Bundling is the practice of charging for a group of related services. Unbundling is charging individually for each service used. For example, with controlled disbursement, one provider may have all charges combined in a single per-item price. Another provider may have a charge for each check paid, one for account reconciliation services, another for reporting the amount of checks clearing each day and another for funding the account. As a result, to make valid comparisons between providers, it is necessary to know all the service charge components that make up a service. Some companies rebundle unbundled prices in order to facilitate comparison of total charges.

- Prices may vary depending on the level of service provided to a company. Some services or agreement provisions can influence bank compensation in ways that do not show up on a schedule of service charges. These include earnings credit for balances, deficient balance charges and availability schedules.

E. Fee vs. Balance Compensation

Financial institutions allow companies to pay for services in fees, collected balances or by a combination of both. The advantages and disadvantages of each method vary depending on whether they are viewed from a company or a financial institution perspective. Some financial institutions may encourage their customers to utilize one type of compensation because of their business strategy or desire for deposits or fees. In practice, most companies compensate their banks with a mix of fees and balances, leaving necessary transaction balances for partial compensation purposes, then paying for the remainder of services in fees.

1. **Fee Compensation: Company Perspective** — Among the reasons companies favor fee compensation are:

    - *Opportunity Cost* — A company can generally earn more interest on its investments than it can obtain in earnings credit on collected balances. The primary reasons for this are the deduction for the reserve requirement when balance compensation is calculated and the fact that the ECR is typically tied to short-term investment instruments with lower rates. This is an even more compelling reason where the company can use the funds to pay off short-term debt, which has a significantly higher opportunity cost than the ECR.

    - *Explicit Cost Control* — Fees can be budgeted and compared with other costs, while balances are not as directly comparable.

2. **Fee Compensation: Financial Institution Perspective** — Financial institutions often favor fee compensation for the following reasons:

    - *Capital Requirements* — Because deposit balances increase the liabilities on a financial institution's balance sheet, they can lead to a need for additional capital to meet regulatory or other requirements.

    - *Annuity Factor* — Compared to interest income from loans, fees from services are a recurring — and generally lower risk — source of earnings for a financial institution.

3. **Balance Compensation: Company Perspective** — Factors favoring balance compensation for a company include:

    - *Transaction Balance Levels* — Daily transaction requirements or unanticipated deposits often result in some collected balances in deposit accounts. If a company's concentration system does not mobilize all of these funds, the collected balances can be used for compensation.

    - *Relationship Considerations* — Some financial institutions price loans and other services more favorably if collected balances are maintained.

    - *Soft Dollar Budgeting* — Balance compensation is not as visible as fees for budgeting purposes.

- *Differential Charges for Fee Compensation* — Some financial institutions' preference for deposit balances is so strong that they charge less if services are paid in balances rather than fees.

4. **Balance Compensation: Financial Institution Perspective** — The factors prompting financial institutions to favor balance compensation include:

    - *Funding Strategies* — Some financial institutions' strategy involves attracting deposits to fund their loans and investments.

    - *Potential Investment Returns* — Because of the spread between the ECR it pays and the investment rates earned, services may be more profitable to a financial institution when paid in balances rather than fees.

5. **Compensation by Both Fees and Balances** — If collected balances can be used as the compensation base with any deficiencies paid in fees, a company can maximize the value of transaction balances and may reduce its overall service costs.

Test Your Understanding

These chapter questions are provided to test your understanding of the information in the text and are not examples of CCM examination questions, nor are they in the examination format.

Answers can be found at the back of the book on pages 542-545.

1. List the major objectives of relationship management.

2. What are some of the criteria for selecting service providers?

3. Discuss the primary components commonly used to measure a depository financial institution's strength.

4. Why does a company seek to optimize the number of financial institutions with whom it has relationships?

5. What are the major documents associated with the establishment of a relationship with a financial institution?

6. Explain the major audit and control issues regarding managing financial institution relationships.

7. What types of performance are commonly graded on a service provider report card?

8. List and discuss the key factors in ensuring a successful relationship between a company and its financial institutions.

9. Define account analysis.

10. What are some of the basic product families of AFP service codes for account analysis?

11. A company uses services with charges that total $4,000 per month. The bank's earnings credit rate is six percent and the reserve requirement is 10 percent. Assuming a 30-day month, what is the average collected balance required to compensate the bank for services used?

12. The following information is provided:

Average ledger balance	$100,000
Deposit float	19,000
Reserve requirement	10%
Earnings credit rate	6%
Service charges for the month	$650
Days in the month	30

Is the earnings credit sufficient to cover the service charges?

13. What is bundling of service charges?

14. How may financial institutions be compensated?

15. Explain the major factors favoring fee compensation to a financial institution from the company perspective.

Glossary

Accord and Satisfaction: Originally, this section of the uniform commercial code (UCC) was drafted to permit a check to constitute a payment made in full (accord and satisfaction) when a message to that effect was written on the face of the check and the check was deposited. However, this allowed for the possibility of inadvertent accord and satisfaction when the customer wrote "paid in full" on a check for a disputed claim — especially if the check was collected through a lockbox. The revised section permits avoidance of inadvertent accord and satisfaction if the payee discovers the error and returns the payment to the payor within 90 days.

Account Analysis Statement: The account analysis statement is a paper or electronic report a bank provides to its commercial customers specifying services provided, volumes processed and charges assessed. It is essentially an invoice for services provided along with detailed information on balances and credit earned for those balances. However, banks often use varying terminology in describing these services. Services and fees can be detailed and itemized, bundled into a single line item or some combination of the two. Fee structures are varied and complex, as are the account analysis formats banks use to report them.

Account Reconciliation Service: Banks provide account reconciliation services to meet companies' information and control requirements. The following services are available: 1) full reconciliation, 2) partial reconciliation and 3) sort only.

Account Resolution: This document is the basic account authorization and is usually a board of directors' resolution. It specifies: 1) what functions can be performed by specific individuals or job titles, authorized signers on the account and the liability of each party and 2) the scope and limitations of the relationship. It may be general or specific regarding actions that the financial institution may take on behalf of the company.

Accounts Payable (A/P): Accounts payable is a liability balance sheet account that represents the amounts owed by the company to its vendors and suppliers. The primary responsibility of the accounts payable function is to verify incoming invoices and authorize them to be paid.

Accounts Receivable: Accounts receivable result from a company's decision to sell goods and services on a credit basis. Accounts receivable are an asset of the company evidencing the extension of trade credit. Sales, accounting and finance personnel all become involved in credit and accounts receivable management activity.

GLOSSARY

Accounts Receivable Balance Pattern: Aging schedules are used to establish receivables balance patterns, which are useful cash forecasting tools. They specify the percentage of credit sales in a time period, usually a month, that remains outstanding in the company's accounts receivable at the end of that and each subsequent time period.

Accredited Standards Committee (ASC): The Accredited Standards Committee of the American National Standards Institute (ANSI) is the coordinating body that develops cross-industry electronic data interchange (EDI) standards in North America. The development of the current U.S. standards for EDI began in 1968 with efforts of the transportation industry to establish standards for communications between and within railroads, ocean carriers, air carriers and motor carriers. Based on this early work, the grocery and retail industries also developed EDI standards. In 1979, ASC X12 was formed to develop general EDI standards that could be used in a variety of industries.

Accrual Accounting: This form of accounting recognizes revenues as they are earned and expenses as they are incurred, regardless of when the related cash flows occur. This is the fundamental difference between cash and accrual accounting. With accrual accounting, revenues may be reported but not yet collected and expenses may have been incurred but not yet paid.

Adjustable-Rate Preferred: Adjustable-rate preferred stock has a dividend rate that is adjusted quarterly based on current Treasury yields.

Adverse Opinion: In an adverse auditing opinion, the auditor states categorically that the financial statements do not fairly present the financial condition and/or operations of the company in conformance with generally accepted accounting principles (GAAP).

Advising Bank: In a letter of credit transaction, the advising bank advises the beneficiary of a letter of credit in its favor.

AFP Service Codes: (AFP [formerly TMA] Account Analysis Standard): In 1987, the Association for Financial Professionals (AFP, formerly known as the Treasury Management Association or TMA) developed a standard format for account analysis that included a standard set of service codes. A revised version of the account analysis standard was published in 1998.

After-Tax Cost of Debt: This is the cost of debt adjusted for the tax-deductibility of the interest payments. It is typically calculated by multiplying the before-tax cost of debt (D_{bt}) by 1 minus the marginal tax rate (t) or: After-Tax Cost of Debt = D_{bt} x (1 – t)

Agency Security: Federal agency securities are debt instruments issued by agencies with some degree of backing by the U.S. government. Agencies act as financial intermediaries in certain credit markets. For example, the Federal National Mortgage Association (Fannie Mae) helps provide liquidity to the mortgage market.

Agent and Fiduciary Services: An agent is a bank, bank holding company or trust institution that manages assets whose title remains with the owner. A fiduciary is an individual or institution to whom certain property is given to hold in trust according to a trust agreement.

Aging Schedule: An aging schedule divides accounts receivable into those that are current and those that are past due in 30-day increments. Companies can analyze the aging of receivables on an aggregate or customer-by-customer basis. An aging analysis identifies past-due accounts, which become less collectible as their age increases.

All-In-Rate: An interest rate is usually quoted in terms of a base rate plus a spread. The spread includes an adjustment for perceived risk that is related to the overall creditworthiness of the borrower. The sum of the base rate and the spread is called the all-in rate.

Alpha (α): This is the smoothing constant used in exponential smoothing, which is a variation of a simple moving average. See Exponential Smoothing.

American Institute of Certified Public Accountants (AICPA): The Auditing Standards Board of this accounting industry group develops and promulgates generally accepted accounting standards (GAAS).

American National Standards Institute (ANSI): This group develops and coordinates standards in a wide range of industries and disciplines.

American Option: If an option contract allows the owner to exercise the option at any time prior to maturity, then the contract is called an American option contract.

Amortization (Accounting): Accounting expense connected with long-term intangible assets. With amortization, the cost of the asset is allocated over its allowable life, but the decline in the actual value of an asset is not measured. It is a non-cash expense; therefore, the income statement for an accounting period understates the cash flow provided by operations by the amount of amortization taken.

Amortization (Debt Service): Amortization is the repayment of the loan principal in installments over the life of the loan. This enables the borrower to pay off the principal gradually, rather than at one point in time. It also reduces the lender's risk by shortening the average life of the loan.

Annualized Cost of Trade Credit: This is the cost to the buyer of not paying within the discount period and thus losing the cash discount. It is a function of the discount amount and the number of additional days of trade credit taken beyond the discount period.

Application Advice (ASC 824): This transaction set accommodates acceptance, acceptance with change or rejection of data received from another transaction set. It can be used to notify a payor of changes in information received in an 820 Payment Order/Remittance Advice.

Application Service Provider (ASP): This is a company that offers individuals or organizations access over the Internet to application programs and related services that would otherwise have to be located in their own personal computers or their organization's computers.

Arbitrage: Arbitrage is the process by which buying in one market and simultaneously selling in another leads to a riskless profit. Arbitrageurs do not assume any risk, but attempt to profit from market inefficiencies. Taking advantage of such arbitrage opportunities keeps financial markets efficient.

ASC X12 Standards: See Accredited Standards Committee.

As-Of Adjustment: When a check takes longer to actually clear than the initial availability that was granted, the bank may add this additional time as part of the collected balance calculation. For example, if a bank originally granted one-day availability but actually cleared the check in two days, it would add one more day of float in calculating collected balances.

Asset-Backed Security: Asset-backed securities are debt obligations that companies issue that are secured by specific assets. These can include receivables, such as the obligations that credit card holders have to credit card companies or the installment payments that consumers pay finance subsidiaries, major retailers and automobile companies. Asset-backed securities can even be backed by inventories. Rating agencies rate many issues of asset-backed securities just as they do other types of financial instruments. Asset-backed securities enable issuing companies to free up capital the same way that they do through factoring receivables.

Asset-Based Borrowing: Some financial institutions specialize in a form of secured lending based on the pledging of accounts receivable, inventory or equipment as collateral for a loan.

Assets: Assets are the items of value owned by a company. Assets are typically listed at historical cost (not present-day market value) adjusted for depreciation. Assets' depreciated value is shown as their book value. They are usually listed on the balance sheet in order of decreasing liquidity or convertibility into cash.

Authentication: This is the ability to know with a reasonable amount of certainty who sent or received a message via the Internet. Authentication is used as a security measure in electronic data interchange and electronic commerce.

Automated Clearing House (ACH) System: The ACH system was developed by the financial industry in the early 1970s as an electronic alternative to checks. In an ACH transaction, payment information is processed and settled electronically, thereby increasing reliability, efficiency and cost-effectiveness. In addition, an ACH transaction is capable of transferring more information about a payment than is possible on a check. In the United States, the Federal Reserve is the main operator of the ACH system.

Automated Teller Machine (ATM): These machines, which are available virtually everywhere, are linked to a banking network that allows depositors to access their accounts, check balances, transfer funds and obtain cash.

Availability Float: Availability float is the interval between the time a check is deposited and the time a company's account is credited with collected funds. It typically ranges from zero to two business days and is determined by the depository institution's availability schedule.

Availability Schedule: Availability schedules specify, for each drawee endpoint, when a bank grants credit for deposited checks to the depositor's available or collected balance. The assignment of availability can be in whole or fractional banking days.

Available Balance: Available balances are the amount of funds available for withdrawal from an account. They are equal to the sum of: (1) the collected balances, (2) the balances that are scheduled to be collected by the end of the banking day and (3) those additional amounts for which availability must be granted under Federal Reserve Regulation CC.

Average Collected Balance: The sum of the daily ending collected balances (both positive and negative) divided by the number of days in the analysis period. In many account analysis statements this item is calculated as the average ledger balance minus the deposit float.

Average Deposit Float: The sum of the daily dollar amount of items in the process of collection divided by the number of days in the analysis period.

Back Value Date: The back value date is the prior date upon which checks or electronic transactions from an account are debited from that account. For example, if a check is back valued, the date of the debit reflected on a customer's account will be earlier than the date the item was presented. Back value dating can also be applied to other services that result in a debit to a customer's account, such as outgoing wires or other electronic transfers.

Bad-Debt Expense: According to generally accepted accounting principles (GAAP), accounts receivable that are determined to be uncollectible must be charged off. Most companies estimate their level of losses and create a reserve account through periodic charges to bad-debt expense. The timing and volume of bad-debt expense and charge-offs are important aspects of credit policy.

Balance Forward Invoicing Method: Balance forward systems are used most often by companies selling goods and services to individual consumers. In a balance forward system, a credit limit is established for each individual and as purchases are made or services are provided, the accounts receivable outstanding increases. When payments are made, the accounts receivable balance is reduced by the amount of the payment.

Glossary

Balance Sheet: A balance sheet or statement of financial condition, is a snapshot of a company's financial condition. It reports, as of a specific date, the value of a company's assets, liabilities and equity accounts.

Balance Sheet Hedge: This is a hedging process where a company offsets foreign asset exposures by borrowing funds to finance those assets in the same country and currency. This hedges the balance sheet and reduces the net exposure to the parent company.

Bank Administration Institute (BAI): The two standardized formats for transmission of external data are the Bank Administration Institute (BAI) format and the Accredited Standards Committee (ASC) X12 821 Financial Information Reporting transaction set. The BAI format is the more established and more commonly used. However, there is a migration toward ASC X12 821, which is an electronic data interchange (EDI) transaction set.

Bank Insurance Fund: The Federal Deposit Insurance Corporation (FDIC) insures deposits up to $100,000 per personal or corporate depositor per institution in all federally chartered banks and most state banks. The deposit insurance premium rate charged banks is set by the FDIC on the basis of a bank's risk profile. The FDIC administers two federal deposit insurance funds — the Bank Insurance Fund (BIF) and the Savings Association Insurance Fund (SAIF). Deposits in most commercial banks and many savings banks are insured by the BIF.

Bank Note: Bank notes represent unsecured or subordinated debt of the bank. Corporate cash investors buy them because they may offer yields competitive with similarly rated commercial paper, but they offer the additional advantage of being direct obligations of the bank, rather than of a bank holding company. However, they do not carry federal deposit insurance.

Banker's Acceptance (BA): A BA is a negotiable short-term instrument used primarily to finance the import, export or domestic shipment of goods or the storage of readily marketable commodities. The debt obligation on the part of the bank is evidenced by a time draft drawn by the borrower that is then accepted by the bank on which it is drawn. By accepting the draft, the bank becomes directly obligated for payment of the draft on the maturity date. By substituting its own credit for that of the borrower, the bank creates a readily marketable instrument that can be discounted in the money market.

Banker's Acceptance Rate: This is a base rate used in some lending arrangements. It is based on the average rate for banker's acceptances and is similar to a certificate of deposit (CD) rate.

Bankers Automated Clearing Service (BACS): This is a U.K.-based payment system similar to the automated clearing house system in the United States. It is primarily used for non-urgent small-value payments.

Bankruptcy: Under the Federal Bankruptcy Reform Act of 1978, a company may file for liquidation under Chapter 7 or reorganization under Chapter 11. Individuals typically file for reorganization under Chapter 13. Reorganization allows a company to pay off debts gradually and operate under a court-supervised plan for returning to financial soundness. Filing of a petition protects the debtor from a list of actions by creditors. The law established a federal bankruptcy court system with exclusive jurisdiction over bankruptcy cases.

Banks for Cooperatives: The CoBank (Central Bank for Cooperatives) and district banks for cooperatives issue debt to make funds available to agricultural cooperatives. The Federal Agricultural Mortgage Corporation (Farmer Mac) provides a secondary market for agricultural loans and rural real estate and home mortgages.

Barter: Barter involves the direct exchange of goods or services between two end users without using money. It is most frequently used when funds cannot be repatriated.

Base Rate: An interest rate is usually quoted in terms of a base rate plus a spread. The spread includes an adjustment for perceived risk that is related to the overall creditworthiness of the borrower. The sum of the base rate and the spread is called the all-in rate.

Basis Point: A basis point is 1/100 of one percent or .0001, (there are 100 basis points in a percentage point).

Bearer Instrument: Historically, short-term instruments have also been issued in bearer form. In this case, the name of the investor is not recorded upon issuance and the holder of the security is entitled to interest and/or principal payments or to sell the instrument. Bearer instruments are increasingly rare.

Benchmarking: In the process of re-engineering the treasury function, it is valuable to seek out examples of other companies that have successfully redesigned their operations. Benchmarking is the identification of best practices in a given field that can be used to compare and evaluate a company's existing process.

Bid-Offer Spread: Banks and other dealers quote both bid and offer rates for foreign currency. The bid rate is the rate at which a dealer is willing to purchase currency. The offer rate is the rate at which a dealer is willing to sell currency. The spread between the bid rate and the offer rate provides income for the dealer.

Bilateral Netting: In a bilateral netting system, purchases between two subsidiaries of the same company are netted against each other so that periodically — typically once a month — only the net difference is transferred. If the payments to be netted are in different currencies, the total due each subsidiary is converted to a common reference currency to determine the net amount due.

Bond: A bond is a form of long-term debt that may be issued at face value and bears interest over its term. It may also be issued at a discount and accrete to face value at maturity. The agreement among all the parties to a bond issue is known as an indenture. It defines details of the issue such as terms and conditions, covenants, events of default, subordination, sinking fund, property to be pledged, if any and the duties of the trustee.

Bond Equivalent Yield (BEY): Bond equivalent yield is the nominal yield quoted on a 365-day basis. It can be used to compare discounted securities (like Treasury bills) to interest-bearing investments (like certificates of deposit).

Bond Indenture: Loan agreements and bond indentures are legal documents that spell out the terms and conditions under which the debt is extended.

Bond with Equity Warrants: An equity warrant is a long-term option to buy a stated number of shares of common stock at a specified (exercise) price. When a warrant is attached to a bond, the resulting combination provides the same type of hybrid as a convertible bond. However, warrants are usually detachable from the bond so that they may be exercised without having to surrender the bond.

Branch Banking: Where statewide, regional or interstate branching is available, collections may be simplified by using branches of the same bank or banks. This reduces the company's administrative and cash concentration costs. The company may, however, lose some flexibility in selecting convenient deposit bank locations and incur a risk by relying on only one bank.

Branch Deposit: An employee of the company can take cash to a nearby bank or bank branch for deposit. However, because of the security risk involved, banks may refuse to accept large cash deposits at certain locations or withhold granting credit until final verification of the deposit.

Broker/Dealer Services: Banks act as brokers and dealers for certain permissible investment securities and foreign currencies and trade for their own account as an extension of that role. Recent legislation (Gramm-Leach-Bliley Act of 1999) allowed banks more leeway in underwriting activities, as well as allowing securities firms to enter areas previously reserved for bankers.

Browser: A browser is software that allows a user to access Web-based sites on the Internet, intranets or extranets. Advanced browsers offer a wide range of options and features that provide users with a means to obtain organize and utilize data from the Internet, intranets or extranets. Advanced browsers also incorporate built-in security features such as secured socket layer (SSL).

Business-to-Business (B2B): B2B electronic commerce (e-commerce) really began with electronic data interchange (EDI), but has expanded into a wide array of formats and protocols for doing business electronically. The typical B2B applications include purchasing from suppliers, logistics and supply chain management, selling to customers, billing and payment, EDI and Web-EDI, Web-based e-commerce and auction marketplaces.

Business-to-Consumer (B2C): Much of the initial development of Internet-based electronic commerce (e-commerce) was in the B2C area. Companies found that the Internet was a cost-effective way to advertise and sell their products and services to consumers, as well as provide enhanced customer service. In most cases, the consumer does most of the work in the process — reviewing available products and services, filling out forms and providing shipping and billing information.

Call Option: A call option gives the owner the right to buy the underlying asset at a fixed price.

CAMELS Rating: The six components commonly used to measure a depository financial institution's strength are referred to as a CAMELS rating. CAMELS is an acronym for Capital adequacy, Asset quality, Management capability, Earnings, Liquidity and Sensitivity to market risk.

Canadian Payments Association (CPA): The Canadian Payments Association developed and operates the national clearing and settlement system. Typically, all deposits receive same-day availability. The CPA is spearheading the introduction of the large value transfer system, an electronic mechanism to handle large or time-sensitive national and international payments.

Capital Adequacy: A financial institution is expected to maintain capital commensurate with the nature and extent of its risks and the ability of management to identify, measure, monitor and control these risks.

Capital Budgeting: Capital budgeting is the process companies use to evaluate alternative long-term investment projects. It uses methods such as net present value calculations and weighs other non-quantitative factors such as the company's core strategy and where it believes its competitive strengths lie. A company may compare the net present values of various projects using the weighted average cost of capital (WACC) as the discount rate. The capital budgeting function involves 1) evaluating quantitatively alternative projects in which a company could invest its capital resources, 2) estimating the economic return of projects in relation to one another and in relation to the company's cost of capital and 3) evaluating qualitative factors of projects.

Capital Market: Capital markets are long-term, with maturities that extend beyond one year. This encompasses term loans, leases, equities and bonds.

Capital Structure: Capital structure refers to the relative proportions of long-term debt and equity (or capital) used in funding a company. The optimum mix of debt and equity financing can vary greatly from one company or industry to another. The mix of debt and equity in a company's capital structure determines its leverage. The greater the debt, the greater the financial leverage and financial obligation. The use of debt increases earnings whenever the return on the capital investment for which the borrowed funds are used exceeds the cost of debt. The converse is also true. For these reasons, a company's borrowing program is often coordinated with its capital budgeting, the process by which a company's management decides how to make capital investments.

Capitalized Assets: Capitalized assets are expected to have lives greater than one accounting cycle and are not fully expensed in the period in which they are acquired. The assets are carried on the balance sheet at their acquisition cost and depreciated in subsequent periods.

Captive Finance Subsidiary: A company may be able to create a wholly owned subsidiary to perform credit operations and obtain accounts receivable financing for the sale of its products. Because many companies' receivables represent a significant proportion of their assets, operating a captive finance subsidiary enhances the parent's liquidity significantly and allows it to obtain capital at a lower cost than it otherwise could.

Carrying Costs: Like any other asset on a company's balance sheet, accounts receivable have carrying costs. Typically, a company determines this cost by using its marginal cost of short-term borrowings or its weighted average cost of capital.

Cash Accounting: In cash accounting, all accounting entries are directly related to a cash inflow or outflow. In accrual accounting, revenues are recognized as they are earned and expenses as they are incurred, regardless of when the related cash flows occur.

Cash Application: Cash application is the process of applying a customer's payment against outstanding invoices. There are two basic ways to accomplish this: the balance forward approach and the open item approach.

Cash Before Delivery (CBD): CBD terms require the buyer to make full and final payment before shipment or receipt of goods. CBD is often used when the seller does not know the buyer or when the seller considers the buyer a greater credit risk than the seller is willing to accept.

Cash Concentration: Cash concentration is the transfer of funds from outlying depository locations to a central bank account, commonly referred to as a concentration account, where they can be managed more efficiently.

Cash Concentration or Disbursement (CCD): CCD is an electronic payment format used for concentration and disbursement of funds within or between companies. A single 94-character record contains the standard entry class indicating the type of transaction, transit routing numbers for the originating and receiving financial institutions and the originator and receiver account numbers. CCD is the only corporate automated clearing house format that does not have space for an additional addenda record, but it does contain space for a reference number.

Cash Concentration or Disbursement Plus Addendum (CCD+): CCD+ is one of the formats used for the U.S. Treasury vendor express program and for business-to-business (B2B) payments. It is useful when only a limited amount of information must be transmitted. This format is identical to CCD but with an addenda record. The addenda record is 94 characters long and includes a free-form space for up to 80 characters of descriptive data. The CCD+ addenda record is also used to report federal and state tax payment information. The data conforms to the tax payment (TXP) banking conventions.

Cash Conversion Cycle: The cash conversion cycle measures the time it takes a company to convert a cash outflow (for payment of inventory purchases) into a cash inflow (collection of accounts receivable). This measure uses the average age of the inventory, the average days of accounts receivable and the average age of the accounts payable to indicate how efficiently a company is using its current assets and liabilities.

Cash Conversion Efficiency: This calculation measures the efficiency with which a company converts sales into cash. It is calculated by dividing cash flow from operations by sales.

Cash Flow Hedge: A cash flow hedge is a hedge of a forecasted transaction or the variability in the cash flow of a recognized asset or liability.

Cash Flow Timeline: The cash flow timeline comprises the total time interval from the time resources are purchased at the beginning of a company's operating cycle until the time payment is received for goods or services at the end of a company's operating cycle.

Cash Flow-to-Total Debt Ratio: Cash flow to total debt is defined as net income plus depreciation divided by total long-term and short-term debt. Short-term debt consists of short-term notes, commercial paper or other short-term debt obligations. A relatively low ratio indicates an inability to repay debt. Studies of failed companies have found this ratio to be accurate in predicting financial failure.

Cash Journal: The recording of individual debits and credits affecting the cash account.

Cash Letter: A cash letter is a bundle of checks accompanied by a list of individual items and other control documents.

Cash Management: The primary objective of cash management is to utilize cash as efficiently as possible in a manner consistent with a company's overall strategic objectives. Basically, cash management includes maintaining liquidity, optimizing cash resources, financing, managing risk and coordinating financial functions.

Cash Manager: The cash manager, who generally reports to the treasurer or assistant treasurer, is part of treasury and is concerned primarily with the management of day-to-day cash flows and banking relationships. In a smaller company, accounting personnel may handle these functions.

Cash on Delivery (COD): The seller ships the goods and the buyer pays upon receipt. If the buyer refuses to pay, the goods are returned and the seller must pay the shipping

GLOSSARY

cost.

Cash Position Worksheet: A worksheet prepared on a daily basis to determine the balances in all of the company's cash, checking and investment accounts.

Cash Receipts and Disbursements: This is information on actual and anticipated collections and disbursements of funds in the company.

Cash Terms: The buyer generally has a week to 10 days to make payment. This method is frequently used in sales of highly perishable items.

Cash Turnover: Cash turnover is the number of cash conversion cycles through which a company goes in a year. It is calculated by dividing 365 by the cash conversion cycle.

Cashier's Check: A cashier's check, also known as an official bank check, is a check drawn by a bank on its own funds and signed by a bank officer.

Central Bank: The central bank or monetary authority of a country usually establishes the conditions under which both domestic and foreign banks can operate. Changes in these conditions and restrictions are occurring rapidly in many countries. In general, recent changes have tended to create more competition and to have a positive impact on the efficiency of all financial institutions operating within the country.

Centralized Check Issuance: In this type of system, headquarters controls disbursement accounts and is responsible for check writing and account reconciliation.

Centralized Control: Centralized control over international treasury management gives relatively little autonomy to field office personnel. A company that operates overseas sales offices with limited personnel will typically centralize control of its treasury functions at its head office. A centralized function can result in economies of scale for services and lower a company's operating costs.

Centralized Disbursement System: In this type of system, headquarters or a centralized processing center issues checks and funds and reconciles accounts.

Certificate Authority: A trusted third-party who maintains a secure database of public/private key information. See Digital Certificate.

Certificate of Deposit (CD): Negotiable or non-negotiable obligations of a bank offered at either fixed or variable interest rates. Jumbo CDs are deposits of $100,000 or more; they are sold to individuals and companies. Maturities may range from seven days to several years.

Certificate of Participation (COP): Certificates of participation are securities used by municipal issuers to finance certain equipment purchases and capital projects.

Certified Check: A certified check is drawn by a depositor on his checking account; it carries the signature of a bank officer certifying the check to be genuine and guaranteeing its payment. Due to the higher processing costs of certified checks, most banks have replaced them with cashier's checks.

Chargeback: A credit card payment is not guaranteed, even when authorized. An authorization indicates that the cardholder has available credit, but it does not indicate that the right person is using the card. A merchant may receive a chargeback (a returned transaction) for as long as six months after funds have been received. When fraud occurs, the time may be even longer. Signature verification is necessary to determine if the authorized person is using the card.

Check: A check, also called a draft, is a demand instrument used to transfer funds from the payor to the payee.

Check Retention: In a check retention (or check safekeeping service), a bank retains paid checks for periods that typically range from one to six months. Microfilm or image records are maintained by the bank for seven years. Companies can receive images of the checks on microfilm, microfiche or CD-ROM. Some banks offer online retrieval of images.

Check Safekeeping: See Check Retention.

Chicago Board of Trade: This is an organized exchange where futures contracts on grains, metals and financials contracts are traded.

Chicago Mercantile Exchange (CME): This is an organized exchange where futures contracts on livestock, wood and meat are traded.

Chief Financial Officer (CFO): The CFO is normally a member of the executive management team, reporting to the chief executive officer (CEO). In a large company, the CFO usually oversees both domestic and international treasury and accounting functions and plays an important strategic planning role as the pivotal person in the capital budgeting and investment decision-making process.

City Item: Checks drawn on banks located in Federal Reserve cities.

Cleanup Period: To assure the lender that the line is not being used as a permanent source of financing, a cleanup period of 30 to 60 days is sometimes required. No outstanding borrowings are allowed during the agreed-upon cleanup period. Typically this requirement is used only for middle market and small companies.

Clearing Channels: Banks use a number of channels for check clearing. Selection of a channel is a function of deposit bank processing time, geographic location and the availability schedules of clearing agents. Availability (the release of deposited funds for use) is granted to the depository bank if the check reaches the endpoint (the drawee bank or location established by the clearing agent) prior to a predefined deposit deadline. Availability schedules define the number of days after deposit before funds become

Glossary

available for use by the depositor.

Clearing Float: Clearing float is the delay between the time a check is deposited by the payee and the time the payor's account is debited. Generally, the payee's account is credited with collected funds at the same time the payor's account is debited.

Clearing House: These are either formal or informal associations formed by banks in a geographic area to permit the exchange of items drawn on the member participants. Representatives from the member banks meet daily to present checks to each other. The net value is transferred by debiting and crediting correspondent accounts or through reserve accounts each bank maintains with the local Federal Reserve. The National Clearing House Association provides nationwide access to many local clearing houses across the country to its member banks.

Clearing House Automated Payment System (CHAPS): London, like New York, is one of the major financial centers of the world and it features one of the largest international real-time, high-value clearing and settlement systems of the world — the clearing house automated payment system (CHAPS). CHAPS-euro is the major clearing system for the euro in the U.K., enabling payments to be made both between parties within the U.K. and cross-border through its link to the Trans-European Automated Real-Time Gross Settlement Express Transfer System (TARGET).

Clearing House for Interbank Payment System (CHIPS): CHIPS is an independent large-dollar funds transfer network operated by the New York Automated Clearing House. It was established in 1970 to substitute electronic payments for paper checks used in international dollar transactions between foreign and American banks. It is also used for payments under letters of credit and documentary collections and for third-party transfers. Any commercial bank with a regulated presence in the United States can become a member of CHIPS and gain access to their system. CHIPS currently has approximately 60 U.S. and international bank participants and clears more than 95 percent of the international payments made in U.S. dollars.

CoBank: See Banks for Cooperatives.

Collateral: Collateral is some type of asset (or assets) used to secure a borrowing arrangement. Accounts receivable and inventory are often used as collateral for bank lines of credit.

Collateralized Mortgage Obligation (CMO): A CMO refers to a type of mortgage-backed security created and backed by federal agencies such as Fannie Mae and Freddie Mac. These securities are formed from pools of mortgages divided into different instruments (tranches), each of which contains a specified portion of the principal and interest payment streams emanating from the aggregated mortgages to separate CMO securities.

Collected Balances: Collected balances reflect the balance in an account for which the bank of deposit has received settlement. Collected balances are the difference between ledger balances and the deposit float. If the collected balance is negative, there is a collected balance overdraft and there may be a service and/or interest charge for the overdraft.

Collecting Bank: In a documentary collections transaction, the collecting bank is the remitting bank's correspondent and is responsible for contacting the buyer (importer), collecting the amount due and releasing the documents as instructed.

Collection: Collecting funds from customers or other payors.

Collection Float: Collection float is the interval between the time the payor mails the check and the time the payee receives available funds at its financial institution. Converting accounts receivable as quickly as possible into collected funds requires minimizing collection float.

Collection Letter: In a documentary collections transaction, the collection letter specifies the exact procedures to be followed before shipping documents are released to the importer. The importer usually requires physical possession of the shipping documents in order to obtain the merchandise.

Collection Policy: A company must establish policies and procedures to collect payment should a credit customer fail to pay according to the specified terms. The major objective of a collection policy is to speed the conversion of accounts receivable into cash while minimizing collection expense and bad-debt losses. The type of credit a company offers impacts significantly the collection methods it uses.

Commercial Bank: A commercial bank is defined by law as a financial institution that accepts deposits and makes business loans, offering a wide range of products and services. The term commercial bank is used to describe everything from small, single-facility community banks with a few million dollars in assets to large, global institutions with numerous locations and billions in assets.

Commercial Letter of Credit (L/C): A commercial L/C is an instrument used to effect a payment in which a bank guarantees a seller that the bank, not the buyer, will pay for the agreed-upon purchase when the seller presents documents conforming to specified conditions pertaining to the sale and delivery of goods or services. Typically, it is the buyer who pays for opening an L/C. L/Cs are commonly used in import/export transactions.

Commercial Loans: These are loans or lines of credit from a commercial bank.

Commercial Paper (CP): Commercial paper is an unsecured promissory note issued by a corporation for a specific amount to mature in 270 days or less. It is typically sold on a discount basis and can be sold either directly to investors or through dealers (securities companies and commercial banks). The issuer's obligation may be backed by a standby letter of credit, which is similar to a guarantee from a bank or a bond issued by an insurance company with a high credit rating. Some commercial paper is also sold directly by one company to a single investor (either another corporation or to an institutional investor such as an insurance company or pension fund) and is called private placement. These private placements may have maturities up to 360 days.

Commercial Paper Nominal Yield: The calculation of the yield on commercial paper is similar to that of the bond equivalent yield for a Treasury-bill (T-bill). Like T-bills, commercial paper is normally sold on a discount basis, but the nominal yield is calculated using a 365-day basis.

Commitment Fee: For committed lines, the lender may charge a percentage fee based either on the total amount of the commitment or on the unused portion of the commitment. Payment is usually made quarterly. Fees vary depending on the creditworthiness of the company, the stated purpose of the line and the term of the commitment.

Commodity Price Risk: This is financial risk related to the future level of and uncertainty in commodity prices (oil, power, agricultural products, metals, etc.).

Community Reinvestment Act (CRA): This was enacted by Congress in 1977 and implemented by Regulation BB. The regulation was revised in May 1995. It was intended to encourage depository institutions to help meet the credit needs of the communities in which they operate, including low- and moderate-income neighborhoods. The act requires that each depository institution's record in helping meet the credit needs of its entire community be evaluated periodically. That record is taken into account in considering an institution's application for deposit facilities. CRA examinations are conducted by the federal agencies that are responsible for supervising depository institutions.

Compensating Balance: Some banks may also require compensating balances, which are maintained in the company's deposit accounts at the bank and do not earn interest or offset other service charges. This practice has become less common. In a compensating balance arrangement, the balance requirement can be specified as a percentage of the total commitment, the unused amount of the commitment or the outstanding borrowings. If compensating balances are required, their effect is to reduce the amount of the borrowed funds that can be used by the borrower, thereby increasing the effective annual interest rate.

Comprehensive Accounts Payable: An integrated or comprehensive accounts payable service allows a company to outsource all or part of the company's accounts payable and/or disbursements functions.

Computer Virus: A computer virus is a software program that is designed to corrupt or destroy data. Some viruses are relatively harmless and may affect only a small portion of a software program. Other viruses can sabotage an entire information system. Readily available anti-virus protection programs should be employed but are not always fail-safe.

Concentration: Concentrating funds where they can be most efficiently utilized.

Concentration and Liquidity Management Flows: Concentrated funds are those that are systematically transferred to create a centralized inventory of liquid reserves held as cash or invested in cash equivalents. Concentration funds include internal transfers among operating units of a company and between various bank accounts owned by a company.

Confirming Bank: In a letter of credit transaction, the advising bank may add its confirmation to a letter of credit. In doing so, the confirming bank commits to the beneficiary that payment will be made if documents meet the terms and conditions of the L/C, regardless of the issuing bank's ability to pay. If an L/C is confirmed, the confirming bank will also be the negotiating bank.

Consequential Damages: Banks are not responsible for consequential damages, which are losses resulting from the action or error made by the bank beyond the actual loss. A bank incorrectly executing a payment order remains liable for interest losses or incidental expenses. The bank is liable for consequential damages only if it agrees to assume this liability in a written agreement with the customer.

Consignment: Consignment involves the shipment of goods to a foreign agent where the exporter (seller) retains legal title to the goods. When the goods are sold by the agent, payment is due to the exporter and title transfers to the buyer. Regaining possession of unsold goods may be difficult and costly.

Consolidated Obligation (CO): The Federal Home Loan Bank (FHLB) System, a government-sponsored enterprise, is the largest issuer of private debt in the world. It funds its activities through a variety of debt products called consolidated obligations, which are typically AAA rated by Standard & Poor's and Moody's.

Controlled Disbursement: Controlled disbursement is a bank service that provides notification of the dollar amount of checks that will clear against the controlled disbursement account that day. This information is usually available by early or midmorning. The disbursement bank must receive its final cash letter of the day from the local Federal Reserve early in the morning so that the checks can be sorted and the company notified of its funding requirement. Payor bank services are often used to aid in this process.

Controller: The controller is normally responsible for accounts payable, internal accounting, preparation of financial statements, internal auditing, coordination with external auditors, preparation of budgets, tax filings and monitoring budgeted capital expenditures. In some companies the Management Information Systems department and Credit department also report to the controller, whereas in other companies they report to the treasurer.

Convertible Bonds: Convertible bonds are bonds that are convertible into shares of a company's common stock at a defined price. They generally provide the borrower with a lower interest rate than non-convertible bonds because of the equity conversion option.

Corporate Trade Exchange (CTX): The CTX format combines the record structure and enveloping required by the automated clearing house (ACH) system with the flexible length standards of Accredited Standards Committee (ASC) X12. A CTX transfer is essentially an ASC X12 820 (Payment Order/Remittance Advice), 813 (Electronic Filing of Tax Return Data), 823 (Lockbox Information) or 835 (Health Care Claim Payment/Advice) using ACH communications protocol. By utilizing up to 9,999 records of 80 characters each, it allows the remittance information contained in the ASC X12 820, 813, 823 or 835 to move through the ACH network rather than having to be separated from the payment and sent using a third-party network or through direct communication.

Correspondent Account: An account held by one bank at another bank, typically used for clearing items or transferring funds between the two banks.

Correspondent Balances: Deposits from other banks held to facilitate check clearing, securities settlement, negotiation of letters of credit and other transactions. The majority of electronic payments systems outside the United States are cleared through correspondent balances of the banks involved in the transfers. Between countries, this clearing is usually done bank-to-bank on a bilateral basis. Within a country, the clearing may be done on a bilateral basis, or through a netting system run by a few clearing banks. These systems are different from the Fedwire system in the United States, where value is transferred by debits and credits to bank reserve balances at the Federal Reserve.

Correspondent Bank: In clearing checks and other items, the sending bank or depository bank, maintains a deposit account with another bank, called a correspondent bank, to which it sends checks. The correspondent bank collects the items through its local clearing house and credits the account of the sending bank with the proceeds of the checks.

Costs of Goods Sold: The direct costs related to producing products for sale. It generally includes variable costs for raw materials and production labor.

Counterparty: The other party to any business or financial transaction. One of the significant risks in using the Internet is that of counterparty risk. While the risks of trading with known suppliers and customers is minimal, the risk of trading with unknown companies and individuals is significant. This is especially the case in auction markets, where a company may be bidding to buy or sell products and services with many unknown trading partners. The same is true in a dealing environment where a company may be working with unknown dealers to buy or sell FX or financial instruments.

Countertrade: Countertrade is a method of payment used by companies that do not have access to sufficient hard currencies (internationally traded currencies) to pay for imports from other countries. For example, a U.S. exporter ships merchandise to the countertrading country and takes in exchange merchandise that can be sold elsewhere in the world for U.S. dollars or any other convertible currency.

Country Item: Checks drawn on banks located outside the area served by a Federal Reserve city or regional check processing center (RCPC).

Covenants: Covenants are provisions that restrict the borrower's activities in ways that protect the lender during the term of the agreement. Examples of covenants include financial ratios, borrower limitations and borrower obligations.

Credit Accessibility: Many companies establish multiple relationships to ensure that they have adequate credit facilities or to diversify service providers.

Credit Card: This is a type of payment card that is accepted on a widespread basis by most retailers and many wholesalers. It is used by both consumers and businesses and typically involves a monthly statement of the charges over the period.

Credit Enhancement or Payment Guaranty: Banks may issue standby letters of credit on behalf of their customers to ensure payment of the customers' obligations to third parties. Some commercial paper borrowers arrange back-up lines of credit that may be used if market conditions are not conducive to issuing or refinancing commercial paper. Another alternative to a back-up line is to obtain a bank standby letter of credit.

Credit Evaluation Costs: These include the costs of obtaining and analyzing credit information.

Credit Facility: Short-term debt instruments mature in less than one year. They are generally used to finance current assets such as accounts receivable and inventory. Any type of loan or credit arrangement can be referred to as a credit facility.

Credit Management: Credit management includes establishing credit-granting standards, establishing terms of credit extension, approving customers for credit sales and setting individual and aggregate credit limits.

Credit Manager: The credit manager is responsible for preserving and collecting accounts receivable, setting corporate credit policies, approving the extension of credit terms to customers and establishing information systems to monitor accounts receivable. The credit manager generally reports to either the controller or treasurer, but in some companies may be part of the sales function.

Credit Policy: A credit policy consists of setting credit standards, specifying credit terms and establishing a collection policy.

Credit Rating Agencies: When a company obtains financing from the capital markets in the form of corporate bonds or commercial paper, it will normally contract with one or more recognized credit rating agencies to obtain a credit rating. A credit rating is assigned based on the perceived risk of the credit issue, with higher ratings associated with lower risk. Although a credit rating applies to a specific debt issue, it can be a useful tool in assessing a company's overall creditworthiness. Two of the major credit ratings agencies are Moody's and Standard & Poor's.

Credit Risk (In ACH Transactions): An originating depository financial institution (ODFI) has credit exposure as the originator of an automated clearing house (ACH) transaction. In the case of a credit origination, exposure exists from the time the ODFI releases an ACH file to the ACH operator until settlement occurs. Once a file is released to the ACH operator, it may not be recalled or reversed (reversing entries may be submitted only for correction of errors). If the originator's account has insufficient funds at the time of settlement, an overdraft occurs. If the originator filed for bankruptcy prior to settlement, the ODFI cannot settle against the originator's account. For a debit origination, the risk is that return items will be received and the funds remaining in the originator's account will not be sufficient to cover them.

Credit Risk (In Borrowing): Whenever a company borrows from a financial institution or issues debt instruments, a major determinant of the price is the company's overall creditworthiness. For non-public debt issues, creditworthiness is assessed based on a credit analysis performed by the lender. In essence, the lender wants to determine how the borrower is going to repay the debt and what alternate sources of payment are available if the primary repayment plan does not work out.

Credit Risk (In Controlled Disbursements): The fact that controlled disbursement poses credit risk (over and above the normal risk of disbursement checking accounts) for a bank has important implications for companies. There are two situations in which a bank has credit exposure. The first is with automated clearing house (ACH) funding, where there is risk that an ACH funding debit may be returned by the bank on which the debit is drawn. By the time the returned ACH debit reaches the disbursement bank, it may be too late to return any disbursement checks. The disbursement bank is owed funds and becomes a creditor of the company. The second instance is where an affiliated bank is used for disbursing, with funding through the parent bank. There is no problem if the affiliate bank is funded directly on a same-day basis by a wire transfer. However, if the parent bank automatically funds the affiliate with immediate funds before the parent bank receives good funds from the company, there is an intraday overdraft and a potential overdraft problem at the parent bank. Since the affiliate bank does not have an overdrawn account, it cannot legally refuse to pay the checks even though there may be an overdraft at the parent bank, unless this option is provided for in the service agreement.

Credit Scoring: Credit scoring is a technique used to estimate creditworthiness of credit applicants based on statistical profiles of prior credit applicants.

Credit Services: Any financial institution services related to the provision of credit (lines of credit, letters of credit, credit guarantees, etc.) are considered credit services. Banks provide loans to companies of all sizes, to not-for profit organizations and to individuals. Typical examples of credit services are short-term loans, long-term loans, leasing and mortgages.

Credit Standards: Credit standards involve determining how credit is granted. Granting credit has two stages: determining who will be granted credit and determining a customer's credit limit.

Credit Support: A key variable affecting the cost of borrowing for a company issuing corporate bonds or commercial paper is credit support or enhancement. Credit support is provided when a third party with a higher credit rating than the borrower guarantees the debt obligations of the borrower. The guarantee may take the form of an indemnity bond, a standby letter of credit or insurance. A fee is charged for such support. With such support in place, the borrower's debt assumes the credit rating of the guarantor, which may reduce the borrowing cost or enhance the marketability of the debt. Another way of enhancing or supporting a credit issue is through the use of asset backing. An asset-backed issue is typically collateralized by inventories or assets such as equipment to which instrument holders take title in case of default.

Credit Terms: Standard sale terms stipulate the form and timing of payment and receipt of goods or services; many involve credit.

Credit Union: Credit unions are not-for-profit financial corporations chartered by federal or state agencies. Membership in a credit union is restricted to people with a common bond, such as an employer, association or community organization. Credit unions can provide retail financial services similar to those offered by other types of financial institutions. Members/owners often enjoy higher savings and lower lending rates. The National Credit Union Share Insurance Fund (NCUSIF) insures deposits in most credit unions.

Creditworthiness: This is a measure of a company's ability to pay its bills or repay its debts. It can be measured both quantitatively and qualitatively.

Cross-Border Payments: Companies with large numbers of international and/or cross border payments typically look to their banks to provide systems that allow them either to maintain multicurrency accounts or easily make electronic payments in a variety of currencies on a multinational basis.

Cross-Industry Electronic Data Interchange (EDI): Cross-industry EDI consists of format standards that address the needs of many different users in many industries. If a company sends a cross-industry EDI purchase order to another company that conforms to the same standard, the receiving company can capture the purchase order data directly without re-entering data.

Currency Exposure: Companies conducting business internationally can use various forecasting techniques to determine foreign cash flows and to assess their degree of foreign currency exposure.

Currency Forward: A currency forward is a commitment to buy or sell a specified amount of foreign currency at a future date at an exchange rate that is agreed upon today. Foreign exchange (FX) forwards are traded in most major currencies with standard maturities of 1, 2, 3, 6, 9 and 12 months. Since forwards are credit instruments (and entail credit risk due to mandated delivery at the end of the contract), the dealers in FX forwards are usually banks. Also, most of the documentation concerning FX forwards involves credit issues.

Currency Future: Currency futures contracts are similar to currency forwards except that they are traded on an exchange and are therefore standardized contracts in terms of amount and maturity date. Currency futures are available for only a relatively few major currencies.

Currency Option: A foreign currency option gives the buyer the right to buy (call option) or sell (put option) a fixed amount of a foreign currency at a fixed exchange rate (strike price), on or before a specific future date. A foreign currency put option establishes a floor value (in terms of the domestic currency) for the foreign currency, which is the exercise price less the premium on the put. Similarly, a foreign currency call option sets a ceiling cost (in terms of the domestic currency) for the foreign currency. The ceiling cost is the strike price plus the premium paid for the call.

Currency Swap: A currency swap involves the exchange of a floating-rate cash flow denominated in one currency with a fixed-rate cash flow denominated in another currency, in addition to an exchange of principal.

Current Assets: The basic current assets include cash, marketable securities, accounts receivable and inventories. Current assets are normally converted to cash within one year or within the operating cycle. Current assets may also include prepaid expenses such as insurance premiums, which are paid in advance.

Current Liabilities: Current liabilities include obligations such as accounts payable, short-term loans, wages payable, taxes payable and the current portion of long-term debt (all due within one year or within the operating cycle). Accounts payable (also referred to as trade payables) are amounts due to vendors for purchased items. Short-term notes payable are typically short-term bank loans or commercial paper.

Current Ratio: The current ratio is defined as total current assets divided by total current liabilities. This ratio measures a company's ability to meet its current obligations or the degree to which current obligations are covered by current assets.

Current Yield: This is an instrument's annual interest payment divided by its price. It indicates what the instrument will return in terms of interest on an annual basis.

Custody Requirement: Physical securities purchased by a company are typically delivered against payment in accounts at financial institutions where the securities were purchased or other institutions selected for that purpose. The policy should specify an authorized custodian.

Custody Service: Banks provide safekeeping for securities. Under a custody agreement, a bank buys, sells, receives and delivers securities at the customer's request.

Customer Account Analysis (ASC 822): This transaction set allows banks to transmit account analysis information (balances, services, volumes, service charges, etc.) to their corporate customers. The Association for Financial Professionals (AFP, formerly TMA) service codes are used in the 822 transaction set to identify bank balances, services and associated charges.

Cycle Time: The total time taken from the beginning to the end of a particular business process.

Data Element: Data segments consist of data elements, such as price, unit of measure and quantity. Data elements are defined in a data dictionary.

Data Segment: Related information elements, such as the line item in the purchase order, are known as data segments. Most transaction sets contain at least three data segments and usually many more.

Daylight Overdraft: A daylight overdraft is an intraday exposure occurring when an account is in an overdraft position during the business day. Banks may have daylight overdrafts in their Federal Reserve bank accounts and companies may have daylight overdrafts in their accounts at commercial banks.

Days' Inventory: This item is calculated as a function of the inventory value and the cost of goods sold. The inventory value used could be ending inventory for the period or, where inventories are highly variable, an average measure of some kind. The cost of goods sold rather than sales is used in this formula because inventory is valued at its purchase cost rather than its selling price. This figure represents the average number of days it takes to convert raw materials into finished goods.

Days' Payables: This item is calculated as a function of the accounts payable value and the cost of goods sold. Accounts payable are valued at the cost of goods sold, which is what is paid to suppliers for materials.

Days' Receivables: This item is calculated as a function of the accounts receivable value and the level of sales. Accounts receivable are valued at the full sales price that will be received when the accounts are collected. This figure is also known at average collection period or days' sales outstanding and represents the number of days it takes to convert a sale into a cash inflow.

Days' Sales Outstanding (DSO): This is a method of measuring accounts receivable that companies calculate by dividing accounts receivable outstanding at the end of a time interval by the average daily credit sales of the period. DSO gives a single number that can be compared to stated credit terms or to a historic trend to provide an indication of a company's overall collection efficiency. It may, however, be distorted by changing trends in sales volume or by strong seasonality in sales.

Days to Maturity: The number of days until an investment matures. This figure is used in calculating yields and prices on financial securities.

Dealing: The transaction of foreign exchange and investment trades. This action is increasingly being done on the Internet.

Debit Authorization (ASC 828): A company can use this transaction set to provide information to a financial institution regarding electronic debits that the company has authorized against its accounts by another company. It allows the payor (buyer) greater control; it can specify certain payees (sellers), certain time periods, dollar limits and even specific debit transactions. This transaction set can also be used to convey check issue files for positive pay or reconciliation applications.

Debit Card: Consumer use of debit cards as a method of payment is growing in acceptance. Debit cards replace cash and check transactions. The seller/merchant is provided with zero- to two-day availability.

Debt: Debt represents funds borrowed to finance the company. It can include trade credit, bank loans and other debt instruments, such as commercial paper, notes or bonds.

Debt-to-Tangible Net Worth Ratio: This ratio measures a company's debt as a percentage of its tangible net worth, its total equity minus intangibles such as goodwill, patents, trademarks, etc.

Decentralized Check Issuance: In this type of system, checks are written on local disbursement banks and account reconciliation is performed at the local level. Decentralized systems require closer monitoring of disbursement accounts by a company's headquarters.

Decentralized Control: A company with relatively autonomous international subsidiaries is more likely to have a decentralized treasury structure. Field personnel are responsible for delegated treasury functions and are typically required to submit management reports summarizing bank balances, loans, investments and other indicators of performance. Headquarters personnel may make periodic visits to international offices to audit and train treasury staff.

Decentralized Disbursement System: With this type of system, a company issues and reconciles accounts at the local level. Typically, checks are drawn on a local bank.

Default Risk: Investors typically require a higher yield to compensate for the risk that the principal will not be paid under the original terms. The greater the likelihood of default, the higher the risk premium and the higher the expected yield. A risk premium is the extra yield above the yield of a risk-free security that investors require as compensation for assuming the additional risk. U.S. government securities are considered to have no default risk and other short-term securities are evaluated in comparison to them. Credit rating services attempt to quantify relative default risk through evaluation and assignment of credit ratings.

Deferred Taxes: The difference between the time the applicable tax codes require companies to recognize revenues and expenses and the time they are recognized under accrual accounting results in differences between the cash disbursed for income taxes and the tax provision reported on income statements. This difference is recognized as a deferred tax and appears on the balance sheet. It is one of the reasons that net income differs from cash flow under accrual accounting.

GLOSSARY

Delivery Exposure: For some companies (mainly energy users) regular supply of the commodity is crucial. In addition to price exposure, these companies also face delivery exposure. Entering into a long-term agreement with an energy producer can mitigate this exposure.

Delivery vs. Payment (DVP): In delivery vs. payment, the investor pays the custodial agent who maintains an account for the investor.

Demand Deposit Account (DDA): Commonly referred to as checking accounts, DDAs are a method by which an account holder uses a financial institution to transfer funds to a third party. The method of payment can be by check, wire transfer or automated clearing house transfer. At the time of publication, the law prohibits payment of interest on demand deposits held by businesses. The three exceptions to this regulation are sole proprietorships, government entities and not-for-profit organizations. This regulation is currently under review and may be changed in the future.

Department of Justice (DOJ): The Department of Justice, as well as the Federal Reserve, reviews and approves proposed bank mergers and holding company acquisitions to determine their effect on competition as part of overall antitrust supervisory responsibility.

Deposit Availability: Deposits consist mainly of coin, currency and local checks. Coin and currency are usually given immediate availability. Local checks may take one day to clear; on-us items may clear faster.

Deposit Deadline: A deposit deadline is the time of day, based on an item's drawee endpoint, by which an item must be at the depository bank's processing center ready for transit in order to qualify for the availability stated on that bank's availability schedule. Ledger credit must be granted prior to the deposit deadline. If a check comes into the bank processing center after the deposit deadline, the next day's deposit deadline goes into effect.

Deposit Float: Deposit float has two meanings: 1) the sum of the deposited items that are in the process of collection or 2) the interval between the time an item is deposited and the time the funds are collected. For example, cash managers often refer to an average float of a certain number of days, meaning the average length of time they must wait for deposited funds to become available.

Deposit Reconciliation Service: Deposit reconciliation services, also called branch consolidation services, may be offered by banks with multiple branches. These services enable deposits from multiple locations to be credited to a single corporate bank account. The use of magnetic ink character recognition (MICR) encoded deposit tickets allows banks to identify each company deposit location and produce reports on a daily, weekly or monthly basis.

Depository Bank: The bank that accepts an item for deposit for credit to a customer's account (this bank is also known as the bank of first deposit).

Depository Institutions Deregulation and Monetary Control Act (DIDMCA): This act, passed in 1980, required all deposit-taking institutions to maintain reserves at the Federal Reserve (the Fed) and made Fed services such as the discount window and check clearing available to all deposit-taking institutions, It also mandated the Fed to reduce and/or price payment system float and to price previously free Fed services according to the standards of a tax-paying vendor. Finally, it provided for phasing out of Regulation Q interest rate ceilings and permitted banks to offer negotiable order of withdrawal (NOW) accounts, check writing accounts with an unregulated interest rate for individuals, not-for-profit organizations and government entities.

Depository Transfer Check (DTC): DTCs are checks used in moving funds from one account to another account held by the same company, usually in cash concentration systems. No signature is required, but for security there is often a payee restriction. Normally the payee can only be an account at the concentration bank. Electronic transfers (automated clearing house or ACH) have largely replaced paper DTCs.

Depreciation: Accounting expense connected with a capitalized asset is recognized by depreciation. With depreciation, the cost of the asset is allocated over its allowable life, but the decline in the actual value of an asset is not measured. It is a non-cash expense; therefore, the income statement for an accounting period understates the cash flow provided by operations by the amount of depreciation expense.

Derivative: A complex financial instrument whose value is determined by another asset, security, index or financial value. The underlying asset could be a financial instrument, a currency or a commodity. Four basic types of derivative securities are forwards, futures, swaps and options. Derivative products allow corporate treasurers to hedge risks more precisely but may be difficult to analyze and can be extremely volatile.

Digital Certificates: These consist of a user's public key and tie the identity of the user (private key) to the user's public key. The identification information is secured by a trusted party's digital signature on the certificate. The trusted party is known as the certificate authority.

Digital Signature: This is an encoded message based on the sender's secret private key. The receiver can identify its source using the sender's public key. As long as the private key is never shared with anyone, it is impossible for others to forge a digital signature. A digital signature is tied to the document as well as to the signer and the signer's digital signature will be different for each document signed. Note, a digital signature is different from a "digitized signature," which is used as a facsimile signature on laser-printed checks.

Direct Send: A direct send is a cash letter that bypasses the local Federal Reserve. A bank sends it directly to the paying bank or a non-local Federal Reserve Bank.

Disaster Recovery: All treasury management systems and other electronic communications systems are vulnerable to disasters such as earthquakes, fires and power outages. Banks and corporate treasuries should have disaster recovery plans that include: 1) identifying internal and external threats, 2) assessing business risks, 3) monitoring for corporate espionage, 4) determining what is needed to perform critical tasks, 5) developing backup or alternative systems and sites, 6) obtaining management approval, 7) testing at least every six months and, 8) keeping the plan current.

Disbursement: Disbursing funds to vendors, employees, investors and other payees.

Disbursement Account: This is a specialized bank account used for the purpose of disbursing funds to payees of the company. These payees include vendors, suppliers, government entities, shareholders, bondholders and employees.

Disbursement Float: Disbursement float results from the delay between the time a payor mails a check and the time funds are debited from the payor's account. Since checks are the most commonly used form of payment, this type of float is a significant consideration. Disbursement float is analogous to collection float, except that it is viewed from the payor's perspective.

Disbursement Fraud: Disbursement fraud is a significant problem. Technological advances have increased the frequency, sophistication and ease of creating fraudulent checks. These advances include color copiers, high-resolution laser printers and document scanners designed for use with a personal computer. As a result, control and fraud prevention are an important responsibility of accounts payable and treasury operations.

Disbursement Networks: Disbursement networks are systems that establish check mailing locations and drawee banks based on disbursement studies. They are designed to optimize disbursement float and are not widely used. The cost and control benefits of making disbursements from just one or two banks often outweigh the float benefits of using a greater number of banks.

Disbursements Schedule: A disbursements schedule involves forecasting the cash disbursements for purchases and other cash outflows, such as payroll, taxes, interest, dividends, rent and debt repayments.

Disclaimed Opinion: In this type of auditing opinion, the auditor states that the information management presented was insufficient to render an opinion.

Discount Instrument: Investments such as Treasury bills and banker's acceptances are discounted, meaning the investor pays the face value of the instrument minus the interest (the discount) and receives the face value at maturity. The discount is the face value multiplied by the discount rate, multiplied by the number of days to maturity divided by the year basis (360 or 365).

Discount Rate (Discounted Instruments): For a discount instrument, the discount rate on a period basis is equal to the dollar discount divided by the face value. To annualize that rate, divide by the number of days to maturity and multiply by 360.

Discount Rate (Present Value): In determining present and future values, the interest rate is generally referred to as the discount rate. The discount rate is also known as the opportunity cost because it presents the return a company would expect to earn on alternative investment opportunities. Companies often use their cost of capital as a discount rate for evaluating their project opportunities. In riskier businesses, companies tend to have higher costs of capital and therefore usually use higher discount rates in evaluating their projects. Evaluating a given project with higher discount rates lowers its net present value because each future cash flow is discounted more deeply.

Discount Terms: In addition to specifying a net due date, the seller may also offer a discount if payment is made prior to that date. Terms of 2/10 net 30 mean that the total amount is due within 30 days of the invoice date, but the buyer can take a two percent discount if payment is made within 10 days.

Discount-Type Security: See Discount Instrument.

Distribution Forecast: A distribution forecast provides estimates of the cash flow effect of a single event, on a daily basis, over a specified interval based on historical patterns. It is particularly appropriate for short-term forecasts.

Diversification: This refers to holding a wide range of different investments in a portfolio. The risk inherent in a portfolio differs from the average risk of the securities that make up the portfolio. Proper diversification reduces portfolio risk.

Dividend: Payments made to the equity shareholders of a corporation. These payments generally take the form of either preferred stock dividends (usually at a fixed rate and paid first) or common stock dividends (paid after preferred dividends and variable).

Dividend Capture: Companies may increase the yield on their short-term investment portfolios through a dividend capture or dividend rollover program. Under this type of tax-motivated trading program, a company buys a stock just before the ex-dividend date (the first date on which a new holder of the stock does not receive the last declared dividend). The stock is held for a period long enough to receive the dividend and at least 46 days to qualify for the 70 percent intercorporate dividend deduction. This is considered suitable for a cash management investment when stocks in mature, blue-chip companies are used. This is because once the dividend is announced, it is a virtual certain cash flow. Add to that the tax-advantaged status of the investment and it is attractive to many short-term investors.

Documentary Collections: A documentary collection is a payment method that processes the collection of a draft and accompanying shipping documents through international correspondent banks. Instructions regarding the specifics of the transaction are contained in a collection letter or form that accompanies the documentation. It is the responsibility of the exporter to determine the specific instructions to be used in the collection letter.

Dollar-Days: Collection float is usually measured in dollar-days and is a function of the transaction's dollar amount and the number of days' delay. The dollar-days of float on an individual check are calculated by multiplying the dollar amount of the check by the number of days between the time a payor mails the check and receiver's bank credits collected funds into the payee's account.

Dollar Discount: The dollar discount is a function of the discount rate, the face amount of the instrument and the days to maturity. The purchase price of the investment is then figured by subtracting the dollar discount from the face or maturity value. The price is thus the amount paid for the investment and the dollar discount is the expected future cash flow.

Douglas Amendment: This 1956 amendment to the McFadden Act allowed banks to merge across state lines if each state permitted it, but did not allow bank holding companies to acquire banks across state lines. Legislation enacted by individual states has allowed bank holding companies to acquire banks and bank holding companies in states both within and outside their regions.

Draft/Bill of Lading: This collection method is also known as a documentary collection. The seller collects payments through banking channels. Having shipped goods to the buyer, the seller sends shipping and title documents to the bank, which then transmits them to the buyer's bank. The buyer gains possession of the documents upon paying the bank or upon signing a draft agreeing to pay at a future date. Upon collection, the buyer's bank remits payment to the seller's bank. This method is more common to international trade than it is to domestic trade.

Drafts: International paper-based systems involve payment and clearing of checks, also referred to as drafts, within and between countries.

Drawdown Wires: A drawdown is a request sent by a company to a bank to initiate a wire transfer from its own or another party's account. The party being debited must preauthorize the transfer. Drawdowns are most frequently used as part of a company's concentration system.

Drawee Bank: The bank on which the check is drawn; the payor's bank.

Drawee Endpoint: An endpoint is the location of the drawee bank where final settlement is effected. Four general classifications of drawee endpoints are city items, regional check processing center items, country items and high-dollar group sort items.

Drawee Location: Checks drawn on banks in geographically distant or isolated locations generally have longer availability times than those drawn on nearby banks.

Duration: Duration actually has two basic definitions in the investment world. The first is that it is the weighted average of a security's cash flow stream, where the present values of the cash flows act as weights. An alternative definition states that duration is the future point in time at which, on average, an investor has received exactly half of the original investment in present value terms. As a theoretical model, duration formulas were developed using an assumption of continuous compounding. In practical application, most practitioners utilize a modified version of duration that takes into account the semi-annual compounding used in many fixed-income securities such as bonds.

Dutch Auction: A Dutch auction is a process whereby the price of a security is lowered (yield increased) until it prompts a responsive bid, whereupon the security is sold. When a Treasury instrument is to be offered, the Treasury officially invites bids. Eligible banks, broker/dealers and other private and governmental entities tender bids for specific amounts of securities at specific yields. The securities go to the bidders offering the highest prices (i.e., lowest yield/interest cost to the Treasury).

Dutch Auction Preferred: Also known as money market preferred stock, auction-rate preferred is characterized by a dividend rate that adjusts every 49 days, which is beyond the minimum holding period for the intercorporate dividend deduction. The dividend rate adjustment is based on bids from investors. Its benchmark is the 60-day, AA-rated, commercial paper composite. Securities dealers are invited by the issuer to bid in a Dutch auction every seven weeks. Typically, they act as agents for their clients. Existing holders may retain their shares and receive dividends at the new rate.

Earnings Credit: The total credit that can be used to offset service charges incurred during the period. It is calculated by multiplying the collected balances (adjusted for the reserve requirement) by the earnings credit rate for the period.

Earnings Credit Rate (ECR): The rate used to calculate the earnings credit. While the method of determining this rate varies by financial institution, the most commonly used measure is the 90-day Treasury bill rate. If a bank utilizes a reserve-adjusted ECR, the impact of the reserve requirement is included in the ECR calculation. (The examples in this book do not use reserve-adjusted ECR.)

Economic and Monetary Union (EMU): In early May 1998, the Council of the European Union finalized the launch of the Economic and Monetary Union. The 11 nations that joined the union and adopted irrevocable conversion rates for the euro in January 1999 included Austria, Belgium, Finland, France, Germany, Ireland, Italy, Luxembourg, the Netherlands, Portugal and Spain. The chief aims of the EMU were the introduction of the euro and linkage of economic policies for all member countries.

Economic Exposure: Economic exposure is the long-term effect of exchange rate changes on the present value of future cash flows to the company. Multinational corporations that do business in several different currencies will, in the long run, always be subject to fluctuations in cash flows because of exchange rate changes. Even purely domestic companies are exposed to economic exposure. For example, a company that purchases its supplies and sells its product locally is clearly not affected by transaction exposure. However, if there is foreign competition within the local market and the local currency appreciates against the competitor's, then the company's earnings in the long run may be affected as demand shifts towards the relatively cheaper foreign competitor's product.

Economic Value Added (EVA): EVA is a measure of the incremental value that a company's investments add in terms of their impact on market capitalization. Put simply, it is after-tax operating profit minus an appropriate charge for the opportunity cost of all capital. Its advantage is that it is a performance measure that is tied directly to the market value of a company.

Edge Act Agreement Corporation: The Edge Act allows U.S. banks to invest in corporations engaged in international banking.

EDI Hub: Some companies implement electronic data interchange (EDI) on a large scale to maintain or possibly increase, their competitive edge. Historically, these companies have been large manufacturers and retailers, who stand to benefit from the cost reductions, improved productivity or decreased order lead times from EDI. Companies that encourage many of their suppliers to implement EDI are referred to as EDI hubs.

Effective Annual Borrowing Rate: This is the effective rate paid on a commercial loan, including the impact of the interest rate, commitment fees, the time the money is used and compensating balances.

Effective Annual Yield: The most reliable way to compare all of these instruments is to calculate their effective annual yields. Effective annual yields assume compounding and are calculated on a 365-day basis. Because of compounding, an effective annual yield assumes that the investor always has the opportunity to re-invest funds at the same rate.

Electronic Banking (E-Banking): E-banking is the use of automated electronic formats and communication with the company's banks. By linking treasury systems to those of their banks, a global company can enhance their funds management and reduce the overall risk of the company.

Electronic Benefit Transfers: Most states have implemented or are in the process of developing electronic benefit transfer systems for food stamps. These systems allow recipients of government transfer payments to receive benefit payments through automated teller machines (ATMs) and point-of-sale (POS) terminals. Also, many companies with large numbers of low-income or temporary workers (who often do not have bank accounts) are experimenting with payroll cards that work in a manner similar to electronic benefit transfer systems.

Electronic Bill Presentment and Payment (EBPP): Many companies and banks are implementing EBPP systems that allow them to send electronic statements to their customers and for the customers to pay these bills by electronic means. In most cases these applications are Web-based and usable by anyone with Internet access. The biggest issue with these systems is that they are competing with the current mail/ check billing and payment system which is a "bill anybody — pay anybody system."

Most of the current systems offer a limited number of billers and limited number of customers.

Electronic Check Presentment (ECP): With ECP, the data captured by the reader/sorter, not the physical check, is electronically transmitted to the drawee bank. The drawee bank uses this information to debit the funds from the payor's demand deposit account. The actual check may be sent to the drawee bank for subsequent handling of the check or the depository bank may retain an image of the check. ECP accelerates the clearing of checks and thus the notification of checks being returned by the drawee bank.

Electronic Commerce (E-Commerce): In its broadest context, e-commerce is the application of information and network technology to the conduct of business relationships among trading partners. E-commerce encompasses many types of formats and communications protocols, including traditional electronic data interchange (EDI) and Web-based commerce.

Electronic Data Interchange (EDI): EDI is a formalized computer-to-computer communication for routine business transactions in a standard format. Financial electronic commerce (e-commerce) is e-commerce or EDI related to payments.

Electronic Depository Transfer (EDT): An EDT, which is an automated clearing house transaction that concentrates cash, is the most common method of depository transfer in use today. It has virtually replaced depository transfer checks (DTCs), which are paper instruments used by companies to transfer funds from outlying depository locations to their concentration account.

Electronic Federal Tax Payment System (EFTPS): EFTPS is the primary method for collecting and accounting for taxes withheld by employers from individuals' salaries and wages, as well as corporate business and excise taxes. Most companies have been mandated to make these deposits electronically.

Electronic Funds Transfer (EFT): The distinguishing feature that characterizes EFT is the exchange of value, which requires the involvement of financial intermediaries, such as banks, to send and receive electronic payments. Examples of EFT include wire transfers and automated clearing house (ACH) payments.

Electronic Funds Transfer Act (EFTA): This act defined the rights and responsibilities of individuals using EFT services except for wire transfers. It also limited customer liability for unauthorized banking transactions involving automated teller machines (ATMs) and point-of-sale (POS) terminals, provided the customer promptly notifies the bank or other institution that issued the card. Provisions of this act are incorporated in Federal Reserve Regulation E.

Electronic Lockbox: Many cash management banks offer electronic lockboxes that allow inbound automated clearing house and wire payments and related information to be gathered and reported on a consolidated basis. The growing use of electronic data interchange (EDI) transactions reduces, but does not eliminate, the need for multiple lockbox sites.

Electronic Payment: A payment or value transfer done in an electronic format. In the United States, the primary electronic payment methods are the automated clearing house (ACH) or FedWire.

Electronic Signatures in Global and National Commerce Act: In 2000, the passage of this act (also known as the "E-Sign Law") gave digital signatures the same effect as ink signatures. This legislation ensures the legal certainty of e-commerce transactions and provides a measure of confidence in the enforceability of electronic transactions.

Endpoint Analysis: An endpoint analysis, in which all checks drawn on banks in selected cities are broken down by days of float, is an effective way to measure and compare different banks' availability schedules.

Enterprise Application Integration (EAI): This is the process of fully integrating Internet systems with existing business enterprise resource planning and application systems.

Enterprise Resource Planning (ERP): ERP systems are fully integrated, company-wide accounting and management information systems that utilize sophisticated database software to provide reports and information in a timely manner to management. Most modern ERP systems provide interfaces to electronic data interchange and electronic commerce (e-commerce) formats and protocols that allow for easy implementation of e-commerce practices into the organization.

Equal Credit Opportunity Act: This 1975 act prohibits creditors from discriminating against credit applicants on the basis of sex, marital status, race, color, religion, national origin, age or receipt of public assistance.

Equity: Shareholder equity represents the owners' position in the company. It is the net book value of the company committed by and belonging to the owners in the form of shareholder capital and retained earnings. Retained earnings represent the increase in shareholder equity that can arise from retention of profits in the company. Equity instruments are stocks, the most conventional of which are common and preferred issues. The major U.S. exchanges are the New York Stock Exchange, the American Stock Exchange and the National Association of Stock Dealers Automated Quotations (NASDAQ).

Euro: The euro is the common currency created and adopted by 11 nations of the Economic and Monetary Union. The countries that joined the union and adopted irrevocable conversion rates for the euro in January 1999 included Austria, Belgium, Finland, France, Germany, Ireland, Italy, Luxembourg, the Netherlands, Portugal and Spain.

Glossary

Euro Bankers Association (EBA): The Euro Bankers Association, an association of major clearing banks, currently operates a net settlement system similar to the clearing house for interbank payment system (CHIPS) settlement procedure in the United States, but it is used primarily for financial, rather than commercial, transactions. This system was converted to euro-denominated transactions in January 1999.

Eurobonds: Eurobonds are bonds issued outside the country where the currency of those bonds is domiciled. For example, dollar-denominated Eurobonds are bonds issued in U.S. dollars outside the United States. They offer the U.S. issuing company access to foreign capital markets without exchange risk and offer foreign investors easy access to U.S. dollar-denominated investments.

Eurodollar Certificate of Deposit (CD): Eurodollar CDs are U.S. dollar-denominated CDs issued by banks outside the United States. Although the primary issuers are European banks, Eurodollar CDs may be issued by any bank located outside of the United States, including foreign branches of U.S. banks. Original maturities are usually less than two years, although most have maturities of six months or less. Eurodollar CDs are negotiable and there is a large secondary market. Eurodollar CDs offer marginally higher yields than domestic CDs because they are slightly less liquid and entail higher risk. The risk derives from the fact that they are not subject to U.S. banking regulations.

Eurodollar Time Deposit: Eurodollar time deposits are non-negotiable, fixed-rate time deposits issued by banks outside the United States, with maturities ranging from overnight to several years. Most have maturities of six months or less. Because they are subject to foreign risk, they offer higher yields than comparable domestic time deposits.

European Central Bank (ECB): The European Central Bank, which was established in July 1998, oversees a single monetary policy for all Economic and Monetary Union members. The euro was initially used primarily in capital markets by the central banks, commercial banks and corporations. Smaller companies and consumers converted to the euro over a three-year period. Euro banknotes and coins are scheduled to be released on January 1, 2002. The national currencies of participating countries will cease to be legal tender within six months after the introduction of euro banknotes and coins.

European Option: If an options contract allows the buyer to exercise (buy/sell the underlying asset) the option only at maturity, then the contract is called a European option contract.

Evaluated Receipts Settlement (ERS): ERS is a payment method designed to eliminate the need for a supplier to provide an invoice to the customer. The dollar amount for ERS payments is based not on an invoice, but on a calculation of the quantity actually received by the customer multiplied by a predetermined price. The supplier does not send an invoice, but is simply paid by the customer on an agreed date after receipt of the shipment. The use of ERS allows the customer to automate its payables process and the supplier to automate the receivables and payment application process.

Excess Balances: Excess balances are balances held in a bank that are greater than the amount needed to compensate the bank for services provided. They typically arise through delays in deposit reporting, clearing or the initiation of transfers.

Exchange Rate Exposure: Companies dealing in foreign currencies face exposure due to potential changes in the exchange rates between the currencies. There are three basic kinds of exchange rate exposure: transaction, translation and economic exposure.

Ex-Dividend Date: The first date on which a new holder of the stock does not receive the last declared dividend.

Exercise Date/Price: The fixed price is called the strike/exercise price of the contract and the specified date is the maturity date (or exercise date) of the contract.

Expedited Funds Availability Act: This 1988 act defined maximum funds withdrawal time periods for deposited checks and payable through drafts. It also established return procedures for payable through drafts and checks. Provisions of this act are incorporated in Federal Reserve Regulation CC.

Exponential Smoothing: Exponential smoothing is a variation of a simple moving average. The exponential smoothing technique uses the previous forecast value, the most recent actual value and a user-determined value known as the smoothing constant. This smoothing constant is typically designated as "α" (referred to as alpha) and may range between 0 and 1. Setting α closer to 1 will result in more weight being placed on the most recent actual value and correspondingly less weight on the forecast value for the current period, resulting in less smoothing of the series. The forecaster must determine how much smoothing is required and choose the smoothing constant, α, accordingly.

Export Credit Insurance: A common method of insuring payment of foreign accounts receivables is through the purchase of export credit insurance. For U.S. companies, this insurance is provided by the Export-Import Bank of the United States (Eximbank) and by certain private insurers. Export insurance can cover both political (sovereign) risk and commercial risk. Insurance coverage is available for shipments to almost every country with which the United States has diplomatic relations. The insurance obtained through the Eximbank is backed by the U.S. government.

Export Financing: This refers to financing programs for support of export activities. Many governments provide support for export financing in order to stimulate exports from their country.

Export-Import Bank of the United States (Eximbank): The Export-Import Bank of the U.S. (Eximbank) is an independent agency of the U.S. government established to finance and guarantee payment for U.S. exports. The Eximbank is directed by its corporate charter to: 1) develop export financing programs that are competitive with those offered by other countries, 2) ensure that financing or repayment guarantees are made to borrowers with a reasonable capacity to repay and 3) enhance or supplement financing offered by private commercial banks.

Glossary

eXtensible Markup Language (XML): This is an extension of hypertext markup language (HTML), which allows for content as well as structure to be defined. In essence, while HTML provides a consistent format for display of the information, XML adds "tags" to the information that define specifically what the information is. For example, HTML format will make sure that the price of an item on a Web page will appear on a certain place on the page and in a specific font, size and color; XML will further define the field as the price of a specific item. Once a data element has been clearly identified, it is easy to transfer this information from the Web page to an application within the company.

Extranet: An extranet is an external network (for use outside a company with its trading partners and/or customers) that utilizes browser technology to provide data and access to applications. In most cases, companies will place some type of security "firewall" between this system and their internal applications.

Extrapolation: This is a forecasting technique where past trends are identified and used to determine future values of cash flows.

Factoring: Factoring is the sale or transfer of title of an accounts receivable to a factoring company. This sale may be done with recourse (where the factor has the right to come back to the seller with any uncollectible accounts) or without recourse (where the factor must absorb all losses). The primary advantage is the financing and management of the credit granting function, while the primary disadvantages are the cost and loss of control.

Factors: Factors provide short-term financing to companies by purchasing the companies accounts receivable at a discount. If the factor purchases the receivables "without recourse," then they assume the responsibility and the risk for collecting them.

Fair Credit Billing Act: This 1975 act is an amendment to the Truth in Lending Act and protects charge account customers from billing errors by permitting them to use the same legal defenses against banks or other third-party credit card companies that they could previously use against merchants.

Fair Credit Reporting Act: This 1971 law enables consumers to access the information in their credit files at little or no cost.

Fair Debt Collection Practices: This 1978 act is designed to eliminate abusive and unfair debt collection practices such as threats of financial ruin, loss of job or reputation or harassing telephone calls.

Fair-Value Hedge: The purpose of this arrangement is to hedge exposure to the changes in value of a recognized asset or liability or an unrecognized firm commitment.

Fannie Mae: Federal agency securities are debt instruments issued by agencies with some degree of backing by the U.S. government. Agencies act as financial intermediaries in certain credit markets. For example, the Federal National Mortgage Association (Fannie Mae) helps provide liquidity to the mortgage market.

Farm Credit Banks Funding: There are four agricultural government-sponsored enterprises that issue high-quality debt. The cooperatively owned Federal Farm Credit Banks Funding Corporation raises capital for the 225 lending institutions in the Farm Credit System through the sale of systemwide bonds and notes. These are insured by the Farm Credit System Insurance Corporation. The federal Farm Credit Administration is the regulator of the banks, the Funding Corporation and the Insurance Corporation.

Farm Credit System Insurance Corporation: See Farm Credit Banks Funding.

FAS 65: Financial Accounting Standard (FAS) 65 requires that securities maturing within 90 days be listed as cash and cash equivalents on corporate balance sheets. Those investments that have maturities greater than 90 days are listed as marketable investments.

FAS 133: Financial Accounting Standard (FAS) 133 requires that all derivatives be marked-to-market on the balance sheet. Marking-to-market means that the derivatives must be valued as of the date of the balance sheet. Given the highly volatile nature of derivatives, this means that the value of the derivative holdings may vary significantly from period to period. This is a significant difference from the off-balance-sheet approach of current practice. From a treasury manager's perspective, this requires substantial record keeping and computation to determine the value of their derivative-based hedges at any point in time. The measurement and monitoring of hedge effectiveness will be a critical part of treasury management reporting in the future and should be a consideration in evaluating treasury management systems.

Fat Client: When a financial service provider offers application software that resides on the customer's desktop computer, they refer to this as a fat client solution.

Fed Funds: Funds deposited by commercial banks at Federal Reserve banks, including funds in excess of reserve requirements. Banks may lend federal funds to each other on an overnight basis at the Fed funds rate to help the borrowing bank satisfy its reserve requirements or liquidity needs.

Fed Funds Rate: This is the interest rate used by banks exchanging Federal Reserve funds.

Federal Agricultural Mortgage Corporation (Farmer Mac): Farmer Mac provides a secondary market for agricultural loans and rural real estate and home mortgages.

Federal Deposit Insurance Corporation (FDIC): The FDIC is an independent agency of the federal government and its primary role is to protect depositors from losses caused by bank insolvency. FDIC responsibilities include deposit insurance, supervision of banks and determining the course of action in the event of bank failure. The FDIC is usually appointed receiver of failed insured institutions. The agency is charged with finding a merger partner or liquidating the bank's remaining assets and paying insured depositors.

Glossary

Federal Deposit Insurance Corporation Improvement Act (FDICIA): This 1991 act established numerous higher standards for financial institution safety and soundness in the wake of several bank failures during the late 1980s. In also mandated the FDIC to declare insolvent any bank or thrift that failed to maintain equity capital equal to two percent of its assets and required the FDIC to change its deposit insurance premiums from a flat-fee basis to a risk-adjusted basis.

Federal Farm Credit Administration: The federal Farm Credit Administration is the regulator of the farm credit banks, the Federal Farm Credit Banks Funding Corporation and the Farm Credit System Insurance Corporation.

Federal Financial Institution Examination Council (FFIEC): FFIEC coordinates the activities of the Federal Reserve, the Office of the Comptroller of the Currency, the Federal Deposit Insurance Corporation and the Office of Thrift Supervision to ensure consistency in the implementation of regulatory policy.

Federal Home Loan Bank (FHLB): The Federal Home Loan Bank (FHLB) System, a government-sponsored enterprise, is the largest issuer of private debt in the world. It funds its activities through a variety of debt products called consolidated obligations, which are typically AAA rated by Standard & Poor's and Moody's.

Federal Open Market Committee (FOMC): The FOMC sets and implements monetary policy, principally by conducting open market operations. There are 12 committee members, including the seven members of the Board of Governors, the president of the Federal Reserve Bank of New York and presidents of four other Federal Reserve banks. They serve on a rotating basis.

Federal Reserve (the Fed): The Fed is the central bank of the United States and is an independent agency of the U.S. government. It was founded by Congress in 1913 to provide the nation with a safer, more flexible and more stable monetary and financial system. The Fed has five principal roles: It acts as 1) a supervisor and regulator of certain financial institutions, 2) the manager of U.S. monetary policy, 3) a wholesaler of banking services, 4) the fiscal agent of the U.S. Treasury and 5) a consumer protection agent for financial services.

Federal Reserve Act: The Federal Reserve Act of 1913 provided the foundation for the current banking system. It granted the Fed supervisory power over member banks (chartered national banks were required to become members and to comply with reserve requirements) and empowered the Fed to create a national check collection and settlement system through member banks.

Federal Reserve Float: In the process of clearing checks, banks sometimes receive availability from the Federal Reserve (the Fed) before the Fed can generate the offsetting debit. The difference in timing between the availability granted a clearing bank and the actual presentment of the item to the drawee bank is called Fed float. Fed float represents interest-free loans to banks and, indirectly, to companies. The 1980 Depository Institutions Deregulation and Monetary Control Act (DIDMCA) mandated both the reduction and pricing of this benefit. Today, the Fed no longer officially carries Fed float on their books and reserve balances at the Fed are adjusted for missed presentments on an item-by-item basis. In addition, the Fed will adjust a bank's availability schedule on a monthly basis, based on the previous month's clearings.

Federal Tax Deposits: The Electronic Federal Tax Payment System (EFTPS) is the primary method for collecting and accounting for taxes withheld by employers from individuals' salaries and wages, as well as corporate business and excise taxes. In recent years, most companies have been mandated to make these deposits electronically. The primary mechanism for making electronic tax payments is the automated clearing house. Either debits or credits may be used. Wire transfers also are allowed.

Fedwire: The Fedwire is the Federal Reserve funds transfer system. It is a real-time method of transferring immediate funds and supporting information between two financial institutions, using their respective Federal Reserve accounts. The system is reliable and secure but, compared to checks and automated clearing house transactions, relatively expensive to use.

File Conversion: The first step in file conversion is to convert paper-based information from the company's records into an electronic file that is readable by the formatting component of the electronic data interchange software.

File Transfer Protocol (FTP): This is a standard Internet protocol that is the simplest way to exchange files between computers on the Internet.

Financial Accounting Standards (FAS): The accounting function records a company's assets, liabilities, shareholder equity, revenues and expenses and reports them according to a detailed set of rules called generally accepted accounting principles (GAAP). These principles are developed, agreed upon and published in the form of financial accounting standards by the Financial Accounting Standards Board (FASB), an independent, self-regulating organization formed in 1973.

Financial Electronic Data Interchange (FEDI): FEDI is any EDI transaction set that either results in a value transfer (instructions to send funds via wire, ACH, etc.) or results from a value transfer (bank notifies payee that funds have been received, i.e. electronic transmission of lockbox information).

Financial Holding Companies (FHCs): The 1999 Gramm-Leach-Bliley ACT permitted the creation of financial holding companies, which can engage in any activity considered "financial in nature, incidental to finance or complementary to it."

Financial Information Reporting (ASC 821): This transaction set facilitates bank-to-corporate account reporting. It provides for the reporting of multiple levels of financial information, including balances, transaction summaries and individual transactions. It can be used for balance and transaction reporting, account reconciliation and bank account statements.

Financial Institutions Reform, Recovery and Enforcement Act (FIRREA): This 1989 act consolidated the Federal Savings and Loan Insurance Corporation (FSLIC) resources under the Federal Deposit Insurance Corporation (FDIC), dismantled the Federal Home Loan Bank Board (FHLBB) and established the Office of Thrift Supervision to assume FHLBB's supervisory responsibilities. It also established the Resolution Trust Corporation (RTC) to make timely disposal of assets of failed savings and loan associations (S&Ls) and gave the FDIC increased flexibility to raise deposit insurance premiums charged to banks and S&Ls.

Financial Management: Managing the finance function of a company. The finance function plays a pivotal role in the achievement of a company's major objective of maximizing shareholder value. The principal roles of corporate finance include accounting, funding, capital budgeting and financial risk management.

Financial Reporting Releases (FRRs): The Securities and Exchange Commission (SEC), an independent regulatory agency of the U.S. government, requires companies that issue securities to the public to file financial statements. The SEC enjoys broad powers with respect to prescribing accounting practices and standards for such reports. These are found in its financial reporting releases, regulations S–X and decisions on cases that have come before the Commission.

Financial Risk Management: The management of financial risk due to changing currency exchange, commodity prices and interest rates is a key element in the finance function of a company.

Financial Service Provider (FSP): Banks and other non-bank providers of financial services to businesses.

Financial Services Markup Language (FSML): This is a language developed to implement electronic checks (e-checks) and other secure financial documents. It is designed to include encryption and digital signatures necessary to create e-checks. It was developed and is supported by a group of financial institutions and is *not* directly compatible with extensible markup language (XML) standards.

Firewall: Wherever external users are allowed access to internal applications or data, it is important to utilize a "firewall" to protect the internal systems. These firewalls may be software or hardware based or a combination of both and their purpose is to ensure that only authorized users are allowed to access or manipulate data and systems in the organization. Firewalls can also help to protect against viruses and other system compromises.

Fiscal Agency: The reserve banks and their branches function as the banker for the federal government. They maintain the Treasury Department's checking accounts, clear Treasury checks drawn against them, accept payments for federal taxes on behalf of the Internal Revenue Service (IRS) and act as fiscal agent for the Treasury Department to issue, redeem and transfer ownership of government securities.

Fixed Assets: Fixed assets are a company's investment in property, buildings, machinery and equipment. Fixed assets (also known as capital assets) cannot be turned into cash as readily as current assets.

Fixed-Income Security: These types of securities pay a fixed rate of interest either on a coupon basis or at maturity.

Fixed-Rate Certificate of Deposit (CD): The interest rate on these CDs is established at the time of issue. Interest is paid periodically over the term or at maturity.

Float: Float is the time interval or delay, between the start and completion of a specific phase or process occurring along the cash flow timeline.

Floating (Variable) Rate Certificate of Deposit (CD): The interest rate on these CDs is adjusted periodically as rates change.

Floor Plan: A floor plan is a loan to a dealer to finance inventory that is paid back when the financed item is sold. Automobile, truck and farm equipment suppliers that provide floor plan financing have utilized the automated clearing house network extensively to debit their dealers.

Floor Planning: This type of financing is frequently used to support the inventory of dealers who specialize in high-cost durable goods such as automobiles, trucks, farm equipment and major appliances. The lender advances funds to pay for specific inventory purchases. To secure the amount owed to it by the dealer, the lender retains legal title to the goods until they are sold. The proceeds from the sale are then used to repay the loan.

Forecast Horizon: The time interval over which information is to be forecast is an important consideration. Cash flow forecast horizons can range from one day to several years. The forecast horizon can be thought of as a continuum, with distinctions made between short-, medium- and long-term intervals.

Forecast Validation: In this stage of forecast development, the model is tested to ensure that it is a valid predictor of future values. The degree of explanatory power can be assessed in the course of model development; the higher the correlation between expected (predicted) values and actual values on which the model is based, the better it is.

Foreign Bonds: Foreign bonds are issued in a country's local currency by companies based outside that country — for example, a U.S.-based company that issues Swiss Franc bonds in Switzerland. Foreign bonds are typically used to finance the issuer's operations in that area.

Foreign Exchange (FX) Exposure: International companies dealing in various foreign currencies are exposed to FX rate risk. A company must assess the types and levels of its exposure to FX rate fluctuations and volatility for the specific currencies in which it operates.

GLOSSARY

Foreign Exchange (FX) Rate: FX rates are quoted in several ways, depending on the currencies and the markets involved. An FX rate is the equivalent number of units of one currency per unit of a different currency. From a U.S. perspective, there are two ways to quote FX rates: the U.S. dollar equivalent of a unit of the foreign currency or the amount of the foreign currency per U.S. dollar.

Foreign Exchange (FX) Risk: See Exchange Rate Risk.

Foreign Exchange (FX) Services: Banks may offer FX services to their customers in order to facilitate international business and trade. These services allow companies to buy or sell many different currencies either for immediate use (the spot market) or for future use (the forward market). In addition, many banks offer various types of hedging contracts related to foreign currencies, which provide vital risk management services to the corporate treasurer. Many large banks, especially those that operate in multiple countries, are major dealers in the FX markets. Through these operations, they can often offer competitive rates and services to their clients.

Foreign Tax Credit: A U.S. company's income derived from its foreign operations is typically included in its tax return to determine the amount of the U.S. income tax due. If this foreign source income has already been subject to foreign income taxes, the same income is being taxed twice. To relieve the effect of this double taxation, the U.S. tax law allows a U.S. company a tax credit against its total U.S. income tax liability for those foreign income taxes paid by the parent and its subsidiaries. This credit is called the foreign tax credit. It is allowed only for those foreign taxes that are income taxes and do not exceed U.S. tax rates.

Forward: A forward contract is an agreement between two parties to buy or sell a fixed amount of an asset to be delivered at a future date at a price agreed upon today. The company purchasing the forward contract is one of the parties; the other is typically referred to as the counterparty. In forward currency contracts, the counterparty is typically a bank or dealer in the foreign exchange markets.

Forward Market: The forward foreign exchange (FX) market is one in which an exchange rate for a future delivery of currencies can be fixed today. A forward FX rate (forward rate) is an exchange rate established today for a currency transaction with delivery occurring beyond two days in the future. Deliveries under most forward FX contracts occur within a year from the trade date. However, delivery dates beyond one year are available for actively traded currencies.

Forward Rate: See Forward Market.

Forward Rate Agreement (FRA): An FRA is a forward contract on interest rates in which two parties agree that a certain interest rate will apply to a certain principal during a specified future period of time. The notional principal amounts are agreed upon but never exchanged. If at settlement the actual rate is different from the rate agreed upon in the contract, then one party pays the other a cash amount equal to the present value of the difference between the interest in the contract rate and the actual rate. The majority of FRAs are based on Eurodollar rates, although others are available.

Forward Value Date: In value dating, the forward value date is the date in the future upon which the firm will be granted credit for deposited items. This practice is similar to the concept of determining availability for deposited items in the U.S. banking system.

Fractional Availability: As an alternative to as-of adjustments, a bank may grant what is known as fractional availability. For example, under normal circumstances a bank may experience an average collection interval of one day for a certain class of checks, but may miss availability deadlines five percent of the time. Rather than make as-of adjustments, it could assign fractional availability of 1.05 days those items.

Freddie Mac: Freddie Mac (formerly the Federal Home Loan Mortgage Corporation) issued mortgage-backed securities that are also secured by the strength of the corporation, not the full faith and credit of the U.S. government. However, there is a strong implication that, in a crisis, the federal government would intervene to help repay investors.

Free-Form Wires: This type of Fedwire transfer, also known as a non-repetitive transfer, allows any of the fields (including the debit and credit parties) to be changed with each transfer. It is less secure than repetitive wires and, as such, additional security steps may be required.

Functional Acknowledgement (ASC 997): A recipient uses this transaction set to confirm to an originator that the transmitted sets were received and that they were in compliance with ASC X12 standards.

Future Value: Future value is the value in the future of a sum of money invested today.

Futures Contract: Futures are similar to forwards in intent, but differ in execution. For example, the payoff profile from a long position in a futures contract and a short position in a futures contract looks exactly the same as the payoff from a forward contract. The main difference between futures and forwards is that futures are standardized contracts traded on organized exchanges.

Garn-St. Germain Depository Institutions Act: This 1982 act extended the legal lending limit of banks to 15 percent of capital and surplus for unsecured loans and 25 percent for secured loans. It also allowed the Federal Deposit Insurance Corporation to arrange mergers of banks across state lines when suitable intrastate partners could not be found and allowed banks to offer accounts, known as money market deposit accounts, to compete with money market mutual funds.

General Obligation Security: General obligation securities have the full faith, credit and taxing power of the issuing entity securing the payment of principal and interest. This usually means that the securities are backed by all of the issuer's resources and its authority to levy taxes.

Generally Accepted Accounting Principles (GAAP): Accounting provides the data necessary for measuring a company's performance and assessing its financial position. The accounting function records a company's assets, liabilities, shareholder equity, revenues and expenses and reports them according to a detailed set of rules called generally accepted accounting principles.

Giros: Many European countries have giro systems that operate through their postal or banking systems. Giro systems allow payments from one giro account to another using direct debits and credits. Payments from consumers to companies and to governments (for taxes) represent the bulk of payment volumes in these systems. Consumers use the giro system in place of checks for payment of their monthly bills and statements. In some countries, consumers access these systems via PCs, terminals or telephone. Though these systems are primarily used for consumer-initiated payments, there is experimental use of giros for business-to business and business-to-consumer payments in some countries.

Glass-Steagall Act: This act, also known as the Banking Act of 1933), prohibited commercial banks from securities underwriting except for government issues and prohibited securities firms from engaging in bank-like activities such as deposit gathering. It also required the Federal Reserve to establish interest rate ceilings on all types of accounts and prohibited the payment of interest on demand deposits. Provisions of this Act are incorporated in Federal Reserve Regulation Q. Finally, it created the Federal Deposit Insurance Corporation to guarantee deposits up to a stipulated maximum amount.

Government Accounting Standards Board (GASB): The GASB establishes standards for state and local governments as well as state universities and other state-affiliated agencies, while the Financial Accounting Standards Board (FASB) establishes standards of financial accounting and reporting for all for-profit entities.

Government-Sponsored Enterprise (GSE): Fannie Mae and Freddie Mac were originally government agencies but now are private, shareholder-owned companies often referred to as government-sponsored enterprises. Both can borrow from the U.S. Treasury. They purchase mortgages from lenders and package them into mortgage-backed securities (MBSs). Ginnie Mae is part of the Department of Housing and Urban Development. It creates MBSs and other securities that it guarantees for timely payment of principal and interest with the full faith and credit of the U.S. government. The Department of Veterans Affairs securitizes certain real estate loans, the "Vinnie Macs," which are backed by the full faith and credit of the federal government.

Gramm-Leach-Bliley Act: This 1999 act eliminated many of the remaining barriers among the banking, insurance and securities businesses and permitted the creation of financial holding companies (FHCs), which can engage in any activity considered "financial in nature, incidental to finance or complementary to it." It also allowed for easier entry by foreign banks into the U.S. financial services market and established the Federal Reserve as the primary regulator of financial holding companies. FHCs are subject to consolidated capital requirements at the parent company level and bank-style risk management at all levels. In addition, the Act barred any bank holding company from merging with an insurance or securities firm or embarking on new powers if any of its banks earned less than a "satisfactory" Community Reinvestment Act rating in its most recent exam. Finally, it required financial institutions to establish privacy policies and disclose them at the start of a customer relationship and once a year thereafter. It also required banks to give customers a chance to block sharing of confidential information with third parties except in cases of marketing agreements between financial institutions. In addition, it prohibited credit card and account numbers from being shared with third-party marketers.

Health Care Claim Payment/Advice (ASC 835): The health care industry uses this transaction set to transmit medical claim payment and remittance information.

Hedging: Hedging is the process by which a company uses financial instruments to reduce or eliminate the risk associated with the uncertainty about the future price of the asset under consideration. The key point is that a hedging arrangement or transaction is one that *reduces* the company's risk.

High-Dollar Group Sort (HDGS): HDGS is a method the Federal Reserve (the Fed) uses to expedite the processing of high-dollar checks through the system. When the Fed identifies a bank that receives more than $10 million per day in out-of-Fed-district checks, it may choose to make a second presentment to that bank.

Holder in Due Course: The holder in due course issue arises when an entity accepts or cashes a fraudulent item in good faith.

Hold-in-Custody Arrangement: Under hold-in-custody, the dealer maintains a custodial account and monitors the collateral.

Home Banking: Home banking services are offered by financial institutions or can be part of a personal financial software system that connects the user to a third-party provider. Generally, these services are PC-based products with a broad array of capabilities that may include bank account inquiry, account transfers and bill paying services.

Host-to-Host Link: In a host-to-host link, the company's computers and the financial service provider's computers are linked directly via a dedicated two-way link. This is generally expensive to set up and maintain, but can handle high volumes of data in an automated fashion.

Hybrid Lockbox: Hybrid lockboxes (sometimes referred to as automated wholesale lockboxes) combine features of both wholesale and retail lockboxes. They are configured, often on a customized basis, to process both business-to-business and retail payments. They are used by companies, such as utilities, whose consumer customers usually return standardized (scannable) remittance documents that can be processed automatically and whose business customers usually remit documents that require manual handling. The processor aggregates remittance data and transmits it to the company.

Hypertext Markup Language (HTML): This is the language used to create Web pages on the Internet and other browser-based delivery formats. The information, text and graphic content can be presented in a consistent format, independent of the browser used to view the data.

Hypertext Transfer Protocol (HTTP): This is a set of rules for exchanging files (text, graphic images, sound video and other multimedia files) on the World Wide Web.

Imaging Services: Imaging technology is a major component of many disbursement services. Both the front and the back of a check may be captured and converted into digital information using optical scanning. Check images (all of them or selected ones) may be transmitted to a company's computer and stored there or sent to a fax machine. The check images may also be stored in a bank database, which a company can access to view or retrieve the images. Any of these methods allows a company faster access to check information.

Imprest Account: An imprest account is an account maintained at a prescribed level for a particular purpose or activity and periodically replenished to the prescribed level. For example, a field office may have an imprest account for local disbursements with a balance sufficient for one or two months' expenses. Based on an established time frame or level of imprest account balances, the office submits expenses to headquarters for approval and headquarters reimburses the imprest account.

Income Statement: The income statement or profit and loss statement, is a record of revenues and expenses. It describes the net change in the amount of shareholder equity resulting from operations over a specified period of time.

Industrial Credit and Capital Companies: These are subsidiaries of large industrial corporations that raise funds in the commercial paper market and lend to companies and individuals. A captive finance company typically finances the purchase of its own company's products. Automobile finance companies (GMAC and Ford Motor Credit Company) are common examples of these.

Industrial Revenue Bonds (IRBs): IRBs are a special classification of municipal bonds issued by a government entity, often for the purpose of financing specific projects that are either publicly or privately managed.

Industry Convention Electronic Data Interchange (EDI): Industry convention EDI is a specific format standard or a subset of the more generic cross-industry EDI standards used within a particular industry. Examples of industries that utilize these types of EDI standards include grocery, retail, automotive, electrical manufacturing and chemical production and distribution.

In-House Banking: Many large global companies have established their own "in-house banks" in their centralized treasury departments. In these types of arrangements, treasury becomes the main provider of banking service for all of the company's operating entities. Treasury then contracts with financial institutions to clear transactions and provide services on a bulk basis. The primary benefit is a reduction in overall banking costs by aggregating many small transactions into fewer, larger transactions. The in-house bank can also provide many of the international treasury management services such netting, pooling and re-invoicing. Finally, the overall risk management of the company can be enhanced through centralized management of FX exposure.

Installment Credit: In this form of credit, a company requires a customer to make equal monthly payments, each of which contains a principal and an interest component. Installment credit is used frequently for the purchase of high-value consumer durables such as automobiles. Frequently the seller requires the buyer to sign a contract, which specifies the terms of the obligation, explains credit terms in full and discloses rates of interest and other costs.

Institutional and Retail Brokerage: Brokerage services involve the sale of securities to institutional and retail customers. It is the distribution side of the investment banker's intermediation function.

Intangible Assets: Intangible assets are assets that lack physical substance. Examples are goodwill, trademarks and patents. There is often a high degree of uncertainty concerning the future benefits of intangible assets. They are amortized over their legal or useful life.

Integrated Accounts Payable: See Comprehensive Accounts Payable.

Intelligent Character Recognition (ICR): This a form of image technology used to facilitate processing of both wholesale and retail lockbox payments. This technology allows paper documents to be scanned, converted to a digital image and stored for subsequent distribution, handling and processing. ICR reads handwritten or typed information.

Interest-Bearing Instrument: Some instruments (for example, certificates of deposit [CDs] and Eurodollar deposits) pay interest in arrears at maturity or at periodic intervals and are thus called interest-bearing instruments.

Interest Rate Cap: Interest rate caps ensure that the borrower of a floating-rate loan receives a ceiling rate if interest rates rise above a specified level. This level is known as the cap rate. If rates fall, the borrower is not obligated to exercise the option and can still enjoy the benefits of the lower borrowing costs. The price of this insurance is the premium paid for the cap.

Interest Rate Collar: A combination of an interest rate cap and an interest rate floor is called an interest rate collar. A company that buys a cap and sells a floor is effectively locking in a range for its borrowing costs. The cap establishes a maximum borrowing rate, thereby protecting the company against higher interest rates, while the floor sets a minimum borrowing rate. A collar can be costless if the income received from selling the floor matches the premium paid for the cap. Costless collars are popular hedging vehicles, as they provide some interest rate protection at no cost.

Interest Rate Exposure: This refers to the exposure a company faces due to changing interest rates over time.

Interest Rate Floor: A company with a floating-rate asset can use an interest rate floor to hedge against rates dropping below a certain level. If rates fall, the floating-rate asset is protected by this put option on interest rates. If interest rates rise, the company can still benefit, as it is not obligated to exercise the option. Again, the cost of this insurance is the premium paid for the interest rate floor.

Interest Rate Future: Interest rate futures are futures contracts on an underlying asset whose price is solely dependent on the level of interest rates. The most popular short-term (90-day) interest rate contracts are the Treasury-bill (T-bill), the Eurodollar contracts traded on the Chicago Mercantile Exchange (CME) and bank certificates of deposit (CDs). In the T-bill futures contract, the underlying asset is the 90-day T-bill. In the Eurodollar futures contract, the underlying asset is a three-month Eurodollar deposit. The interest earned on a Eurodollar deposit is the three-month London Interbank Offered Rate (LIBOR). The most actively traded long-term interest rate contracts are the five-year and 10-year U.S. Treasury notes and the 30-year U.S. Treasury bonds.

Interest Rate Option: Interest rate options are options where the payoff depends on the level of interest rates. There are three basic types of interest rate options: caps, collars and floors.

Interest Rate Parity: The relationship between the spot, forward and money markets is known as interest rate parity. As long as foreign exchange and interest rate markets are efficient, it is not possible to take money from one country, invest in another country's money market, return it back to original country and make a higher rate of return than could have been earned in the original country's money market. Thus, the differences observed between the spot and forward markets are not necessarily a prediction of the future movement of the spot rate, but rather just an adjustment for the differential interest rates between the two countries in question.

Interest Rate Risk: See Interest Rate Exposure.

Interest Rate Swap: A common type of interest rate swap is the exchange of a fixed interest rate cash flow for a floating interest rate cash flow — both cash flows being in the same currency. If both interest rates are floating, then the exchange of the cash flows is called a basis-rate swap. An example of a basis-rate swap is the exchange of interest payments based on the London Interbank Offered Rate (LIBOR) for interest payments based on the commercial paper rate.

Internal Auditor: The internal auditor is responsible for determining that controls and operating procedures are in place to protect a company from losses caused by inefficiency, inaccuracy or fraud. The internal auditor typically reports directly to the board of directors, but in some companies may report to the chief executive officer or chief financial officer.

Internal Factoring: The purpose of an internal factoring center is similar to that of re-invoicing. Rather than taking actual title to the goods as with re-invoicing, the internal factoring unit buys accounts receivable from the exporting unit and collects from the importing unit. The benefits of internal factoring are the same as they are for re-invoicing. Most internal factoring is done on a recourse basis, where the factor can come back to the company (or subsidiary) if the account cannot be collected.

Internal Rate of Return (IRR): The IRR is the discount rate at which the net present value is equal to zero.

International Money Market (IMM): This organized exchange is part of the Chicago Mercantile Exchange and trades foreign currency futures.

International Money Market Investments: In addition to the Eurodollar deposits discussed in the section on bank financial instruments, there are other international money market investments. Many foreign governments issue short-term bills and notes or other fixed-income securities similar to U.S. Treasuries and agencies. Similarly, many foreign-based corporations issue investments similar to commercial paper in international money markets. There are also interest-bearing deposit accounts and certificates available in many foreign currencies that are available from multinational banks. In addition to the normal credit and default risk concerns familiar to domestic investors, foreign investors must also consider foreign exchange risk and risk from potential blocked currencies.

Internet: The Internet is a worldwide collection of many computers, communications switches and computer networks linked together to form a backbone of communications pathways.

Internet Service Provider (ISP): This is a communications intermediary that provides Internet service to individuals and small businesses, typically over telephone lines or cable.

Interstate Banking: The Interstate Banking and Branching Efficiency Act of 1994 permitted banks to operate fully integrated banking systems nationwide beginning in June 1997.

Interstate Banking and Branching Efficiency Act (IBBEA): This 1994 act (also known as the Riegle-Neal Interstate Banking and Branching Act) permitted bank holding companies to acquire a bank located in any state effective September 1995 and allowed banks in one state to merge with banks in another state beginning June 1997, as long as neither state took legislative action to prohibit interstate mergers between the date of enactment and May 1997. It also allowed banks to establish new branches in states where they do not maintain a branch if the host state passes a law expressly permitting such branches.

Intranet: An intranet is an internal network (for use within a company) that utilizes browser technology to provide data and applications for users. It uses the open standards of the Internet rather than proprietary software for communication among computers.

Inverted Yield Curve: An inverted yield curve slopes downward, indicative of a market situation where short-term yields are higher than long-term yields. Yield curve inversion happens infrequently and contravenes the usual condition that securities with longer maturities must offer higher yields. One theory explaining an inverted yield curve is that short-term uncertainties, such as an anticipated recession, shift investor preferences away from short-term instruments to those carrying longer maturities, driving down long-term rates.

Investable Balance: This is the balance on which the earnings credit rate (ECR) is applied. This value can be either positive or negative. A negative balance indicates a shortage of investable funds. Some banks calculate the investable balance as the average collected balance reduced by the reserve requirement balance. Other banks reduce the ECR by the reserve requirement (a reserve-adjusted ECR) and, in this case, the average collected balance is used as the investable balance.

Investment Banker: An investment banker is a financial specialist who acts as an intermediary in the merchandising of securities. The investment bankers performs three basic functions: 1) underwriting, which refers to the selling of a security issue at a satisfactory price that will raise the necessary external funds, but also generate a profit for the investment banker, 2) distribution, where the investment banker uses its distribution system to sell or distribute the issue to their customers and 3) advising, where the investment banker has the responsibility of advising the issuer with regards to the prevailing and future market conditions in an effort to raise the most funds at the least cost. Additionally, the investment banker may analyze the firm's capital structure and advise the issuer as to what source of capital best suits the organization.

Investment Management: A company has alternatives for managing short-term investments. Whether to handle short-term investments internally or externally depends on the size of the company's investment portfolio, investment objectives and policies.

Investment Objective: A company conducts its short-term investment activity to meet several objectives: preservation of principal, liquidity management and investment return and risk.

Investment Policy: A company's short-term investment policy should identify those who are ultimately responsible for such matters. In most companies, the board of directors or a designated committee of the board determines and monitors overall investment policy.

Investment Schedule: This schedule contains information on the sale, purchase and maturity of short-term investments.

Invoice (ASC 810): This transaction set allows the user to convey invoice data, such as unit price, quantities purchased and terms of sale, from a seller to a buyer.

Invoicing Float: This represents the delay between the purchase of goods or services and the receipt of an invoice by the payor.

Issuing Bank: In a letter of credit transaction, the issuing bank is the buyer's (importer's) bank that issues the letter of credit in favor of the beneficiary (seller/exporter).

Junk Bonds: These bonds are also known as high-yield bonds and are high-yield, non-investment grade securities. These bonds are typically issued by companies that are already highly leveraged.

Just-In-Time (JIT) Inventory: An approach to inventory management where materials are supplied to the production line on an as-needed basis. The company maintains minimal inventory of both raw materials and work-in-process items.

Large-Value Payment Risk: Because automated clearing house (ACH) transactions are significantly less expensive than wire transfers, some originators have migrated large-dollar transfers to the ACH system. The technical limit for an ACH transaction is 10 characters or $99,999,999.99. However, ACH system controls are not as extensive as wire transfer controls and credit risk to originating depository financial institutions (ODFIs) increases with large payments. As a practical consideration, however, large-dollar transfers would typically move via Fedwire rather than ACH, as the money would be available one day sooner for investment purposes.

Leading and Lagging: Netting systems may be used to implement leading and lagging. Leading and lagging involve making cross-border payments between subsidiaries either ahead of schedule (leading) or behind schedule (lagging). Liquidity is moved from one subsidiary to another. Leading can be helpful when a currency is expected to depreciate, while lagging will be used when the currency is expected to appreciate relative to the parent's home currency.

Lease: Leasing, an alternative to term lending, is used extensively as a means of financing equipment. In a typical leasing arrangement, the lessor actually owns the equipment and leases it to the lessee. Typically, 100 percent of the equipment's cost is financed and payment amounts can be fixed or variable. A leasing arrangement can be structured as either on- or off-balance sheet. An on-balance-sheet arrangement is referred to as a capital lease; an off-balance-sheet arrangement is referred to as an operating lease. Accounting and tax issues must be evaluated to determine the proper classification of a lease. An operating lease offers tax advantages to both parties. The lessor realizes the benefit of depreciation and the lessee has tax-deductible operating expenses. End-of-term options typically allow the lessee to return, purchase or re-lease the equipment.

Ledger Cutoff Time: A bank's ledger cutoff, set by each individual bank, is the time of day when a deposit must be received to be posted to the depositor's account. Items deposited after the ledger cutoff time are considered to have been received by the bank on the next banking day. In evaluating a lockbox system, it is important to consider total collection time, not just availability. The bank's cutoff time for giving ledger credit on the same day can vary and must be considered in conjunction with its availability schedule. A check with one-day availability before the ledger cutoff may have two-day availability if it is processed after the ledger cutoff.

Letters of Credit (L/C) Confirmations: L/C confirmations are issued by a bank at the request of a customer when that customer is unfamiliar with or unsure of the financial condition of the original issuing bank. In such instances, another bank may confirm (guarantee) performance under the original L/C. In the event of default, the confirming bank is responsible for the payment.

Leverage: Leverage is the degree to which a company's use of debt or high fixed costs causes earnings to change more rapidly than revenues.

Liabilities: Liabilities represent obligations of the firm. They consist of current or short-term liabilities that mature in one year or less and long-term liabilities that are due in more than a year.

Line of Credit: A line of credit is an agreement in which the lender gives the borrower access to funds up to a maximum amount over a specific period of time. A line of credit may be used to provide short-term financing, to back up commercial paper or to provide a liquidity cushion. Some companies with seasonal borrowing requirements have lines of credit in which the maximum amount available varies over the year. A significant portion of credit lines are in the form of "base borrowing," where accounts receivable are used to provide collateral for the line and the amount of the commitment will vary month to month as the base of accounts receivable change.

Liquidity: Liquidity is the ability to turn assets into cash quickly without incurring loss. Ensuring corporate liquidity on a day-to-day basis is the responsibility of the cash manager. This ongoing task necessitates careful measurement and continual monitoring of net working capital, so that the company has sufficient financial resources to pay upcoming bills and take advantage of investment opportunities that may present themselves unexpectedly.

Liquidity (As Part of CAMELS Rating): This aspect of the CAMELS rating pertains to current and future levels of liquidity in comparison with funding needs. It also indicates the adequacy of funds management practices relative to an institution's size, complexity and risk profile.

Loan Agreement: Loan agreements and bond indentures are legal documents that spell out the terms and conditions under which the debt is extended.

Loan Participation: A loan participation is an arrangement whereby a bank purchases an interest in another lender's credit facility. The participant does not have a separate note and has only an indirect relationship with the borrower.

Loan Syndication: In a loan syndication, multiple financial institutions share a single credit facility. The syndicate or group of lenders, is led by an agent who acts as the intermediary between the company and the syndicate for purposes of negotiating the credit terms and documentation, making advances and payments on the loan and disseminating information. All the syndicate members share common documentation, but each lender has a promissory note making it a direct lending relationship.

Lockbox: A lockbox is a collection system in which a company's customers mail payments to a designated post office box. A third party collects the payments, processes the remittances and deposits the checks directly into the company's account.

Lockbox Information (ASC 823): This transaction set conveys lockbox check data including remittance detail (such as payors, invoices and amounts being paid), deposit totals and available funds.

Lockbox Networks: Lockbox networks may involve several processors in different cities or a single processor with multiple locations. A network permits a company to have a number of collection points and get consolidated remittance data. Funds concentration is simplified and a company may deal with fewer processors.

Lockbox System: These allow a company to collect payments at one or more lockbox sites that will transfer available funds to a concentration bank. A company may use several lockbox sites to optimize collection float and may also use separate lockboxes for different subsidiaries.

London Interbank Offered Rate (LIBOR): LIBOR is set on a daily basis in London and is the borrowing/lending rate for dollars used between multinational banks. It is also the most commonly used base rate for short-term borrowing.

Long-Term Debt-to-Capital Ratio: This ratio measures the percentage of long-term debt relative to all of the long-term capital used in the company's capital structure. Long-term debt includes long-term notes and bonds, term loans and capitalized lease obligations. Equity capital includes all preferred and common equity accounts. The higher this ratio, the greater the proportion of debt a company is using in its long-term capital structure and the greater the extent to which it is leveraged.

Long-Term Liabilities: Long-term liabilities are obligations such as term loans, mortgages and bonds due beyond one year or one operating cycle.

GLOSSARY

Maastricht Treaty: The signing of the Maastricht Treaty provided a timetable for the formation of the Economic and Monetary Union (EMU).

Magnetic Ink Character Recognition (MICR) Line: The information necessary to process checks by machine is contained in the MICR line, which is printed with special characters and magnetic ink on the lower portion of the check. These characters can be read by magnetic or optical scanning equipment.

Mail Float: Mail float is the interval between the time a check is mailed and the date it is received by the payee or at the processing site. It usually ranges from one to five calendar days or more, depending on location, weather and other factors.

Matching: Matching involves purchasing securities that mature when funds are required to meet an expected obligation or obligations.

Maturity: The life span of a debt instrument is known as its term or maturity. Debt maturities range from overnight to 100 years. Interest rates tend to increase with length of maturity, reflecting the greater risk for long-term instruments and investor demands for higher returns.

McFadden Act: This 1927 act established the state boundary as the primary limit for bank expansion by prohibiting banks from accepting deposits across state lines and prohibited branching across state lines unless approved by affected state governments, thereby relegating to the states the power to decide the extent of bank branching within and outside state borders.

Middleware: This is special software designed to provide linkages between treasury systems and other company software applications.

Modified Duration: In practical application, most practitioners utilize a modified version of duration that takes into account the semiannual compounding used in many fixed-income securities such as bonds. See Duration.

Monetary Policy: The Federal Reserve Act directs the Federal Reserve to conduct monetary policy in such a way as to maximize employment, promote price stability and maintain moderate long-term interest rates. The Federal Reserve's monetary policies influence the demand for or supply of reserves at banks and other depository institutions. The effects of monetary policy are transmitted to the rest of the economy through the reserves market. The Board of Governors implements monetary policy primarily through open market activities (the buying and selling of securities in the financial markets). The Federal Open Market Committee (FOMC) oversees open market operations to influence money market conditions and the growth of money and credit.

Money Market: Rather than a single integrated entity or a particular exchange, the money market is a group of markets on which debt instruments that mature in a year or less are traded. Money market securities include Treasury bills, federal agency securities, municipal obligations, commercial paper, banker's acceptances, negotiable certificates of deposit, loans to securities dealers and repurchase agreements (repos). The major direct participants in the money market are U.S. and foreign government securities dealers (some of which are large, diversified financial institutions), commercial paper dealers, banker's acceptance dealers and money market brokers specializing in various short-term instruments.

Money Market Deposit Account: Accounts that pay an unregulated rate of interest determined by the bank and allow limited check writing and electronic withdrawals. They are available to all types of businesses and individuals.

Money Market Instruments: Money market instruments are those securities that would be considered as short-term in nature or less than one year until maturity. Money market instruments are generally highly liquid and are issued by borrowers with high credit ratings.

Money Market Mutual Funds: Money market mutual funds are commingled funds of highly liquid, diversified short-term money market instruments in which investors have an ownership interest. They are an increasingly important component of corporate short-term investment portfolios and offer an acceptable alternative to other securities, particularly under changing interest rate conditions. For many companies, using a money market mutual fund makes economic sense, especially when the costs of running and overseeing a short-term investment portfolio are considered. Using a mutual fund rather than in-house management may also free valuable treasury resources for other tasks. Money market mutual funds are configured to report a net asset value (NAV) of $1/share. They generate different yields and have slightly different risk thresholds. Money market mutual funds can provide a company with a professionally managed marketable securities portfolio at a low management cost. These funds can also be useful in providing a benchmark for assessing short-term investment portfolio performance. Money market mutual funds charge management fees or service charges based on the investor's balance, level of activity and services provided.

Money Market Treasury Fund: An alternate means to investing in U.S. Treasury securities is to invest in money market funds that carry the same credit quality given to obligations of the U.S. government because they are made up exclusively or principally of U.S. Treasury securities.

Money Market Yield (MMY): Money market yield is the nominal yield quoted on a 360-day basis.

Money Order: A money order is a prepaid instrument issued by parties such as companies, banks or the Post Office. The purchaser is the instrument's payor and the money order is the obligation of the issuer.

Mortgage-Backed Security (MBS): Mortgage-backed securities are essentially bundles of mortgages that are packaged and resold to investors. Many of these securities are issued by government and quasi-government agencies and provide both liquidity to the mortgage market and a government-backed fixed income investment for investors.

GLOSSARY

Multibank Reporting: Multibank reporting is where companies that have two or more banks establish an arrangement in which one of the company's financial institutions or a third-party reporting service gathers and consolidates the account balances and transaction activity from each of the company's financial institutions. This arrangement is commonly referred to as data exchange. Banks are also increasingly offering this kind of information via the Internet.

Multicurrency Account: Multicurrency accounts are a special arrangement between a bank and its corporate customer whereby the bank allows the customer to receive or make international payments in a range of currencies from a single account or multiple subsidiary accounts.

Multilateral Netting: This system is similar to bilateral netting but with more than two subsidiaries. Each subsidiary informs a central treasury management center of all planned cross-border payments. To determine netting transactions, the payments between all subsidiaries are converted into a common, reference currency. Payments are combined into fewer, but larger, transactions and each unit is informed prior to the settlement date of the net amount to pay or to be received in its own currency. The netting center makes the necessary foreign exchange conversions. Although multilateral netting is used primarily for intracompany transactions, some companies include third-party payments or receipts in their systems.

Multiple Drawee Checks: Multiple drawee checks, also known as payable-if-desired (PID) checks, are checks that can be presented for payment at a bank other than the drawee bank. Both bank names appear on the check.

Municipal Bonds: Municipal bonds are bonds issued by a state or local government entity and are typically repaid out of tax revenue. Most municipal bonds enjoy special tax-exempt status for federal tax purposes. The most common type of municipal bond is a general obligation security.

Mutual Fund: Mutual funds are pooled investments that sell shares to investors, offering these investors diversification and professional portfolio management. Mutual fund providers include brokerage firms, banks and investment companies. Shares may be redeemed through the provider that insures liquidity. Share values fluctuate with the performance of the underlying securities of the fund and mutual fund shares are not insured against losses as deposits are. Money market mutual funds invest in short-term securities such as Treasury bills, certificates of deposit and commercial paper.

Mutual Savings Bank: This is a form of thrift institution, also known as a savings bank. Historically, savings banks and mutual savings banks have been state chartered and owned by depositors, but the Garn-St. Germain Depository Institutions Act of 1982 allowed them to switch to a federal charter and to convert to stock ownership.

National Automated Clearing House Association (NACHA or the Electronic Payments Association): A membership organization that provides marketing and educational assistance and establishes the rules, standards and procedures that enable financial institutions to exchange ACH payments on a national basis.

National Credit Union Share Insurance Fund (NCUSIF): NCUSIF insures deposits in most credit unions.

Negotiable Bank Certificates of Deposit (CDs): These CDs are in large denominations and have an active secondary market where they can be traded. They are a source of funds for banks and an investment instrument for corporations.

Negotiable Certificates of Deposit (CDs): These CDs are generally sold in $1 million blocks to companies, money market funds and other large investors. Being negotiable, they can be sold to another investor prior to maturity. Maturities generally range from 14 days to five years, but most have maturities of 12 months or less.

Negotiable Instruments: Article 3 of the uniform commercial code defines a negotiable instrument and the forms it may take, including a draft, a check, a certificate of deposit and a note.

Negotiable Order of Withdrawal (NOW): These accounts offer unrestricted check writing and pay unregulated rates of interest. NOW accounts are limited to individuals, sole proprietorships, not-for-profit organizations and governmental entities.

Negotiating Bank: In a letter of credit transaction, the negotiating bank examines the documents presented by the beneficiary, receives payment from the issuing bank and pays the beneficiary. The advising and negotiating bank is often the same bank.

Net Asset Value (NAV): This term is typically used for mutual funds to describe the value of a share of the fund. Money market mutual funds are generally configured to report a constant net asset value of $1/share. Other types of mutual funds may have share values that vary on a daily basis, depending on the performance of the investments in that fund.

Net Income: Net income is operating profit less the cost of debt financing and income taxes incurred during the accounting cycle, adjusted for other income and expenses.

Net Investment Hedge: This is a hedge of the net investment in a foreign operation.

Net Ledger Balance: The sum of the daily ending ledger balances (both positive and negative) divided by the number of days in the analysis period. Balances are net of current period adjustments (e.g., misposted wire transfers, deposits with missed deadlines or items with encoding errors).

Net Method of Accounting for Discounts: In this method, amounts are entered into the receivables and revenue accounts net of the discounts. Any discounts not taken are then shown as income.

Net Present Value (NPV): Net present value is a calculation of the value today of cash flows at different points in the future. The investment and costs associated with the investment are outflows, while returns on the investment are inflows. If the sum of all discounted cash flows (in and out) is positive, then the project or investment has a positive net present value. If the discounted sum is negative, then the project or investment has a negative net present value. If the company were to invest in a project with a positive net present value, then the overall value of the company would increase by the amount of the project's net present value.

Net Settlement System: In some industries (airlines, oil/gas, telecommunications, securities), companies make exchanges and buy and sell from each other. At the end of the day, all of the participants to the netting system determine the net flows required to balance out the system. These clearing systems process transaction information and allow participants to make periodic net settlements with each other.

Net Terms: The seller specifies a net due date by which the buyer must pay in full. For example, terms of net 30 require the buyer to pay within 30 days from the date of invoice, date of delivery or some other specified date.

Net Working Capital: Net working capital is equal to current assets minus current liabilities, such as accounts payable. Net working capital represents a measure of immediate liquidity.

Netting: Netting is an internal company system designed to reduce the number of cross-border payments among units of a company through the elimination or consolidation of individual funds flows denominated in different currencies. Many countries impose restrictions on the use of netting systems and formal approval may be required.

New York Mercantile Exchange: This is an organized exchange that trades in futures on metals, petroleum and fiber.

Nichigin Net: Nichigin Net is the interbank settlement system operated by the Bank of Japan. Financial institutions that maintain accounts with the Bank of Japan are provided online access to initiate settlement transfers between accounts.

Nominal Yield: The quoted yield on an annual basis for most investments is a simple annual rate, called a nominal yield and does not reflect compounding.

Non-Credit Services: These are financial institution services that are not related to the granting or guarantee of credit. They may include such services as cash management, investments, trust, international services and risk management.

Non-Repetitive Wires: See Free-Form Wires.

Non-Repudiation: This is the inability of the sender or receiver of a message to deny having sent or received that message.

Noon Presentment: This Federal Reserve practice accelerates its presentment schedule by making second presentments later in the day as part of the float-reduction program mandated by the Depository Institutions Deregulation and Monetary Control Act.

Normal Yield Curve: The most common shape of the yield curve is upward sloping, reflecting the greater return over time that investors require to compensate for the increased price risk.

Off-Balance-Sheet Financing: A leasing arrangement can be structured as either on- or off-balance sheet. An on-balance-sheet arrangement is referred to as a capital lease; an off-balance-sheet arrangement is referred to as an operating lease. Accounting and tax issues must be evaluated to determine the proper classification of a lease. Securitization is another type of off-balance-sheet financing. See Securitization.

Office of Foreign Assets Control (OFAC): The OFAC is an office of the Treasury Department and administers and enforces economic and trade sanctions against targeted foreign countries, terrorism-sponsoring organizations and international narcotics traffickers based on U.S. foreign policy and national security goals. The OFAC has the authority to impose controls on financial transactions and freeze foreign assets under U.S. jurisdiction.

Office of the Comptroller of the Currency (OCC): The OCC was established by Congress in 1863 to regulate the national banking system and is a bureau in the Department of Treasury. As the administrator of nationally chartered banks, the OCC oversees the execution of laws relating to national banks and promulgates rules and regulations governing the operations of national banks. It also supervises a nationwide staff of bank examiners.

Office of Thrift Supervision (OTS): The OTS is a bureau of the Department of Treasury and the primary regulator of all federal and many state-chartered thrift institutions, which include savings banks and savings and loan (S&L) associations. The OTS is the successor to the Federal Home Loan Bank Board and was established by Congress in 1989 as the primary federal regulator of all federal and state-chartered savings institutions across the nation that belong to the Savings Association Insurance Fund (SAIF).

On-Us Item: An on-us item is a check deposited in the same bank on which it is drawn.

Open Account: This method, sometimes called open book credit, is the most common type of commercial trade credit in the United States. The following steps occur: 1) a seller issues an invoice, which is formal evidence of the obligation and records the sale as an account receivable, 2) the customer is billed for each transaction by an invoice and/or by a monthly statement covering all invoices generated during the billing period, 3) full payment of invoiced amounts is expected within the specified credit terms unless certain discounts or deductions are made available to the customer, 4) a buyer's creditworthiness is reviewed periodically, but the buyer does not need to apply for credit each time an order is placed and 5) companies usually charge fees for late payment.

Open Book Credit: See Open Account.

Open Item: An open item system is most commonly used in business-to-business sales. Each invoice sent to a customer is recorded in the accounts receivable file. When a payment is received, it is matched with the specific invoices being paid and any payment discrepancies (discounts, allowances, adjustments, etc.) are noted. Remittance information, which typically accompanies payments, usually details which invoices are being paid, as well as any adjustments to the payment. This application process may be manual or automated or a combination of the two.

Operating Cycle: The operating cycle consists of the day-to-day activities pertaining to the acquisition of materials and/or resources, their transformation into saleable goods, their marketing and the ensuing collection of revenues. From a cash managers' perspective, this operating cycle translates into a general cash flow timeline.

Operating Expenses: Operating expenses, such as selling or administrative expenses, represent general expenses incurred in the conduct of the business, but which are not tied directly to the production of goods and services.

Operating Profit: Operating profit, also known as operating income, is the profit after deducting the cost of goods sold and operating expenses from revenues. The term is often used interchangeably with earnings before interest and taxes (EBIT).

Operational Risk: A type of payment system risk that refers to the risk of processing mistakes or system disruptions.

Opportunity Cost: In determining present and future values, the interest rate is generally referred to as the discount rate. The discount rate is also known as the opportunity cost because it presents the return a company would expect to earn on alternative investment opportunities. Companies often use their cost of capital as a discount rate for evaluating their project opportunities. In riskier businesses, companies tend to have higher costs of capital and therefore usually use higher discount rates in evaluating their projects. Evaluating a given project with higher discount rates lowers its net present value because each future cash flow is discounted more deeply.

Optical Character Recognition (OCR): This form of image technology is used to facilitate processing of both wholesale and retail lockbox payments. It allows paper documents to be scanned, converted to a digital image and stored for subsequent distribution, handling and processing. The data capture process is enhanced through the use of OCR, which reads information printed in special type fonts.

Option: An option is a contract between two parties wherein the buyer of the contract has the right (but not the obligation) to either buy or sell a fixed amount of some underlying asset at a fixed price, on or before a specified date. The party offering the option is called the writer of the option.

Option Writer: See Option.

Originating Depository Financial Institution (ODFI): The financial institution that originates an automated clearing house credit or debit transaction is referred to as the ODFI.

Outsourcing: Outsourcing is when a company uses an outside provider to perform part or all, of a business function.

Overdrafts: Overdrafts occur when there are insufficient funds in a checking account to cover items presented on the account. Occasionally, accounts in concentration systems are overdrawn due to misdirected transfers, missed deposit deadlines or returned items.

Overnight Sweep Account: Banks provide overnight sweep accounts, which automatically transfer excess balances into an interest-earning account.

Over-the-Counter/Field Banking System: Companies with regional sales offices or widely dispersed retail outlets deposit over-the-counter cash and checks in various accessible outlying depository banks. Such systems are characterized by: 1) multiple collection points, 2) multiple banks, 3) limited provision of cash management services and 4) deposit availability.

Over-the-Counter/Field Deposit System: An over-the-counter field deposit system is a collection system in which funds are received and deposited by local operating units of the company such as division offices or retail stores.

Paid-on-Production: Paid-on-production is the process by which a payment record is created for goods and/or services when they are used rather than when they are shipped or delivered. It is similar to consignment sales in retail, but is based on usage within a manufacturing environment. Typically there is only one supplier and title to the product transfers when the product is used in the manufacturing process rather than at the receiving dock, as in evaluated receipts settlement (ERS). Because of legal concerns relating to liability, potential bankruptcy and use of inventory assets for supporting loans, it is important to determine exactly when and where title to the inventory transfers from the supplier to the manufacturer.

Passbook Savings Accounts: These are depository accounts that pay interest on balances. They are mainly held by individuals and not-for-profit institutions, but companies may also hold them.

Payable-If-Desired (PID) Check: See Multiple Drawee Checks.

GLOSSARY

Payable Through Draft (PTD): A PTD is a payment instrument resembling a check that is drawn against the payor and not the bank. A draft is handled like a check through the clearing system, but the responsibility for paying the draft lies with the drawee. The primary reason companies use PTDs is to preserve the right to review the items prior to final payment. Insurance companies often use PTDs for claim reimbursement because the PTD gives them an opportunity to verify the signature and endorsements before honoring it. Some state and local governments use a form of PTD called a government warrant.

Payee: The party to whom the check is made payable.

Paying Agent: Banks receive funds from an issuer of stocks or bonds to pay dividends to stockholders and principal and interest to bondholders.

Payment and Collection Services: Banks assist companies by acting as clearing agents for checks and by originating and receiving wire transfers and automated clearing house transactions.

Payment Float: This represents the delay between the receipt of an invoice by the payor, including the credit period and the time the payor's account is debited for the funds sent in payment of the invoice.

Payment Order/Remittance Advice (ASC 820): This transaction set has two purposes. It initiates a money transfer to a payee and/or provides the payee with information describing the purpose of the associated payment. The 820, which allows multiple invoices to be paid in a single payment, also includes the amount of discounts and other payment adjustments.

Payor: The party who issues the check.

Payor Bank Services: This Federal Reserve (Fed) service provides participating banks early morning electronic notification of physical presentments to be made later in the day. This allows the bank's controlled disbursement customer to know as soon as possible all Fed presentments on their accounts.

Peer-to-Peer (P2P): This approach to distributed computing is where each computer linked to the Internet can be linked directly to another computer to share information. Applications being developed that do P2P computing are essentially automating the machine-to-machine communication process.

Penalty Fees: In addition to offering credit terms, companies often assess a penalty fee for payments received after the due date. This fee is usually a percentage of the past due amount. The fee should be clearly stated at the time of the sale and shown on the invoice.

Percentage-of-Sales: The percentage-of-sales method involves projecting financial statements (pro forma statements) based on sales forecasts and the historical relationship between sales and certain balance sheet items such as cash, accounts receivable, inventory and accounts payable. It also considers other balance sheet and income statement items that can be forecasted based on other factors (e.g., debt repayment schedules).

Personal Identification Number (PIN): This is a security procedure used to identify authorized users. PINs are typically used with automated teller machine (ATM) or debit cards to verify the cardholder before processing the transaction.

Point-of-Sale (POS) Terminal: These terminals are cash registers used in retail environments that capture and store information on items sold, money collected, credit cards processed, etc. The information can be sent on a real-time or periodic basis to the company headquarters for reporting purposes.

Pooling: Companies concentrate cash internationally for the same reason they do domestically: to utilize cash more efficiently. In the U.S. cash management environment, concentration of funds typically involves physical movement of funds from depository banks into a concentration bank. Outside of the United States, this physical concentration is usually referred to as "sweeping" the funds (not to be confused with "sweep accounts" used for overnight investments). Outside of the United States, in countries where banks are allowed to pay interest on positive demand deposit balances and to charge interest on negative balances, the typical method of concentration is known as pooling.

Portfolio: A portfolio is a grouping of investments for a particular investor. In most cases, holding a wide range of investments in a portfolio helps to provide diversification for the investor.

Positive Pay: Positive pay is a service used for fraud control. The company transmits a file of checks issued to its bank. The bank matches serial numbers and dollar amounts and pays only those checks that match.

Prearranged Payment or Deposit (PPD): The PPD format is the payment application by which consumers may authorize credits or debits to their accounts by a company or financial institution. These are normally recurring payments in fixed amounts.

Preauthorized Draft/Check: With this, the payor authorizes the payee to draw a draft/check against the payor's account. The payee, rather than the payor, initiates the transaction. Mortgage, insurance and other recurring payments may be made this way. Most preauthorized drafts are now done on an electronic basis via automated clearing house debit.

Precautionary Requirement: Since a company's cash inflows and outflows are unpredictable, it must maintain higher levels of cash or near-cash balances to meet its expenses.

Pre-Encoded Check Deposit: Companies that pre-encode checks to be deposited can get lower fees and/or faster availability.

Pre-Encoded Items: If a customer pre-MICR encodes the dollar amount on the checks it deposits using magnetic ink character recognition, the customer may receive faster availability, a later cutoff time and/or reduced service charges.

Preferred Stock: Preferred stock is a type of equity instrument that has preference over common stock in its claim to a company's earnings and assets. Preferred dividends are paid before common stock dividends can be paid and, like common stock, offer a tax advantage to corporate investors. Currently, a corporate investor may exclude 70 percent of stock dividends received from current income as long as the stock is held at risk (cannot be hedged) for more than 45 days. This is called the intercorporate dividend deduction.

Prenotification: These items (also known as prenotes) are optional zero-dollar entries that are sent through the automated clearing house system prior to live entries. Prenotes provide a verification function at the receiving bank before entries for settlement are processed. For example, when a company adds a new employee to its direct deposit of payroll program, it may use prenotification to ensure that the bank's transit routing number and the employee's personal bank account number(s) are correct. Prenotes are optional, but are useful to ensure that all records are correct prior to transaction, especially in consumer applications. Also, while the sending of the prenote is optional, National Automated Clearing House Association rules require the receiving financial institution to respond to them.

Present Value: Present value is today's value of any sum to be received in the future. Present value can be determined by applying an appropriate discount rate to a future cash flow stream. This concept is useful for comparing alternative transactions with cash flows to be received at a future date or dates or to determine how much an investor would be willing to pay for an investment that provides a particular future cash flow stream.

Preservation of Principal: This is the guiding principle most companies follow in choosing among short-term investment alternatives. Some degree of risk is inherent in all investments. Those that offer higher returns usually carry greater risks. Ensuring against loss involves controlling risk, as follows: 1) identifying risks to which various investment alternatives are subject, 2) determining the relationships between security risks and the financial returns they offer and 3) choosing instruments that offer both income and safety of principal.

Price Risk: Price risk is the uncertainty over the price at which a security can be sold prior to maturity and is a function of interest rates. An increase in rates will cause the price of fixed income securities to fall. A decrease in interest rates will cause the price of fixed income securities to rise. Generally, securities with longer maturities are subject to more price risk than similar securities with shorter maturities.

Prime Rate: Traditionally, prime was the rate at which commercial banks loaned money to their most creditworthy corporate customers. Prime rates vary by financial institution. Prime-based pricing is becoming less common for large corporate borrowers, but is widely used for small business and consumer loans.

Private Label Financing: With private label financing, a third party operates the credit function in the name of the seller rather than the seller administering its own credit program. Private label financing allows the seller to retain many of the promotional aspects of conducting its own credit function while incurring none of the costs of maintaining a credit operation or financing accounts receivable. At the same time, the seller does not receive the full face value of the sale and may lose the authority to decide which customers should receive credit. From the customer's perspective, the credit appears to be arranged through the seller.

Private Placements: In a private or direct placement, the securities are offered and sold on to a limited number of investors. The investment banker will meet with the prospective buyers and confirm the details of the offering. In a private placement, the investment banker acts as a broker, bringing the issuer and investors together. Generally, a private placement is completed quicker than a public offering, offers reduced flotation costs and offers the investment banker some flexibility to meet the needs of the company. However, private placements often incur higher interest rates and have more restrictive covenants.

Pro Forma Statements: See Percentage of Sales.

Processing Float: Processing float is the interval between the time the payee or the processing site receives the check and the time the check is deposited at a financial institution. It can range from less than one day to three calendar days or more if there are processing delays.

Promissory Note: A promissory note is an unconditional promise to pay a specified amount plus interest at a defined rate either on demand or on a certain date. A promissory note can be issued for each individual borrowing or for a total line amount against which multiple borrowings are made.

Proof of Deposit (POD): Most banks assign availability using the proof of deposit method. Under the POD method, availability is assigned to each check as it passes through the automated check processing equipment. Availability is assigned based on the time and day of deposit and the check's endpoint. Some banks may negotiate special availability for selected high-volume customers.

Proprietary Electronic Data Interchange (EDI): Proprietary EDI is developed by one company for exclusive use with its trading partners.

Proprietary Software: Proprietary software is the most common mechanism used today to link to financial service providers. The user makes a direct connection to the bank's computer to access account information and to give a variety of banking instructions.

Glossary

Provisional Credit: This is the ledger credit a payee receives when a check is deposited, which is subject to final clearing of the check.

Public Key Infrastructure (PKI): This type of key system enables electronic commerce (e-commerce) and file exchange over a public network. The encryption technology is based on American National Standards Institute (ANSI) X.500 and X.509 standards for public key certificates and directory services and can be used for virtually all secure electronic data interchange (EDI) Web transactions.

Purchasing Card: Purchasing or procurement cards can be used to pay for supplies, inventory, equipment or services. Organizations using these cards have been able to reduce the costs of purchasing and maintain or increase control.

Put Option: If an option contract gives the owner the right to sell the underlying asset at a fixed price, the option is a put option.

Qualified Opinion: A type of auditing opinion in which the auditor notes exceptions concerning compliance with GAAP, such as accuracy of tax liabilities, asset valuation or accounting inconsistencies.

Quantitative Credit Analysis: This type of credit analysis relies on analysis of numerical data to determine the creditworthiness of a buyer or borrower. It can be used for both business and consumers. For business credit analysis, the first step is typically an examination of a credit applicant's financial statements, frequently through ratio analysis, which assesses a customer's financial condition. Ratios can provide valuable insight when evaluated in relation to industry standards published by credit rating agencies and other associations. Some commercial credit analysis can involve credit scoring or purchasing credit reports from companies such as Dun and Bradstreet. On the consumer side, major issuers of retail credit, such as department stores, use quantitative credit scoring models and often develop a different model for each billing region. These quantitative approaches are cost effective and can aid in complying with consumer credit legislation. Formal statistical analysis is often used to identify the factors that distinguish paying customers from non-paying customers. Credit bureaus also assess creditworthiness based on proprietary models.

Quick Ratio: The quick ratio is defined as cash plus short-term investments and accounts receivable divided by total current liabilities. It is also known as the "acid test" ratio and is considered a more conservative measure of liquidity than the current ratio. The quick ratio measures the degree to which a company's current liabilities are covered by its most liquid current assets. (Note that inventory and prepaid expenses are not included in this ratio because they are the least liquid of the current assets.)

Rating Agency: This is an independent company that provides ratings for debt issues by companies and government entities. The primary rating agencies are Moody's and Standard & Poor's.

Real Time Gross Settlement (RTGS) System: In an RTGS system, the value transfer takes place on a real-time basis, with the paying bank being debited and the receiving bank being credited. Each transaction results in an immediate settlement and value transfer, as opposed to a net settlement system where a number of transactions are combined on a periodic basis and only the net amount of the transactions is settled with a value transfer. In the United States, the primary RTGS is the Federal Reserve's Fedwire wire system; in the U.K., it is the Clearing House Automated Payments System (CHAPS).

Receipts and Disbursements Forecast: Many companies use short-term forecasts based on information relating to receipts and disbursements that will occur in the near future. Projecting receipts and disbursements is fundamental to short-term cash forecasting. This begins with the creation of separate schedules of cash receipts and disbursements. Both schedules are prepared on a cash basis rather than an accrual basis. This method tends to forecast cash accurately in the short-term and near medium-term, especially when accounts receivable and accounts payable data are incorporated.

Receipts Schedule: A receipts schedule consists of a projection of collections from customers (cash sales or payments on accounts receivable) and other cash inflows such as interest or dividends received from investments. A receipts schedule should also include expected non-recurring cash inflows such as the proceeds from asset sales.

Receiving Depository Financial Institution (RDFI): The financial institution that receives an automated clearing house credit or debit transaction is referred to as the RDFI.

Redeemable Preferred Stock: Redeemable preferred stock is stock that has a predetermined redemption schedule. In addition, redeemable preferred stock normally provides for the accrual or payment of a regular dividend. The dividend and redemption features are essentially the same as the interest and repayment features on bonds.

Re-Engineering: The concept of re-engineering involves a radical redesign of a particular business process with the goal of continuous process improvement. The redesign of treasury operations may include restructuring or eliminating traditional treasury processes.

Regional Check Processing Centers (RCPC): An RCPC is a Federal Reserve center that performs check processing services for the region in which it is located. RCPCs are located in areas with high check volumes that are not served by a Federal Reserve district of branch bank.

Regional Check Processing Center (RCPC) Items: Checks drawn on banks serviced by a Federal Reserve regional check processing center.

Regional Treasury Center: These regional centers combine both centralized and decentralized treasury functions and are responsible for providing treasury services to specific subsidiaries within a designated geographic area.

GLOSSARY

Registered Form: Almost all short-term securities are fixed-income securities and are issued in registered form; they are typically placed in the name of the investor or held in the street name (the name of the broker/dealer through which they were purchased). Only the owner or his legal agent can collect interest and principal payments or sell the securities.

Registrar: Banks serve as registrars by maintaining lists of current stockholders and bondholders for the purpose of remitting dividend and interest payments.

Regression Analysis: Regression analysis is a statistical technique that systematically identifies the relationship between the variable being predicted (the dependent variable) and selected or appropriate explanatory or independent variables. Though there are many forms of regression analysis, the most basic is a simple linear regression model. This approach essentially determines a line that best represents the relationship between a single dependent variable and a single explanatory variable.

Re-Investment Risk: This is the risk that an investor faces when cash flows from an investment must be re-invested under changing interest rates. The best example in the money market area are mortgage-backed securities, where falling interest rates result in mortgages in the security pool being prepaid, causing a premature cash flow to the investor. These cash flows must then be re-invested at now lower interest rates.

Re-Invoicing Center: Re-invoicing is a method of centralizing the responsibility for monitoring and collecting international accounts receivable and more effectively managing the related foreign exchange exposure. A re-invoicing center is a company-owned subsidiary that buys the goods from an exporting subsidiary and resells the goods to an importing subsidiary. The exporting unit invoices and receives funds from the re-invoicing subsidiary in its own currency, while the importing unit is invoiced and pays funds to the re-invoicing subsidiary in its own currency. Although title to the goods passes through the re-invoicing center, usually the actual goods are shipped directly from the exporting subsidiary to the importing subsidiary. Establishing a re-invoicing center requires local government approval and negotiation on how the subsidiary will be taxed.

Reject Items: Checks that are rejected by a bank's automated check processing equipment are likely to miss critical deposit deadlines, resulting in longer availability and additional processing fees.

Relationship Bank: Using lockbox services at a bank where a company has an existing relationship may allow the company to strengthen that relationship by protecting access to credit facilities and making better use of operating balances for bank compensation benefits. It may also allow the use of existing data access tools such as the Internet and balance reporting.

Relationship Review: A relationship review is another procedure companies use to qualitatively assess the service levels and personnel responsiveness. Reviews can be either formal or informal. Formal reviews typically involve a quarterly, semiannual, or annual meeting of the senior management representatives of both parties. Informal reviews typically involve weekly or monthly contacts by individuals who are responsible for the day-to-day management of the relationship.

Remittance Information: This is the additional information that typically accompanies the payment. It may include information on invoices paid, discounts or deductions taken. This information allows the payee to determine what they have been paid for and to complete the payment application process.

Remitting Bank: In a documentary collections transaction, the remitting bank is the seller's (exporter's) bank that prepares the collection letter and forwards documents to a correspondent bank in the buyer's (importer's) country.

Remote Disbursement: Remote disbursement was designed to take advantage of the inaccessibility of certain geographically remote banks. The objective was to increase disbursement float as much as possible. Federal Reserve policies discourage the use of this practice.

Repetitive Wires: Repetitive transfers are used when a company makes a transfer frequently between the same debit and credit parties. The bank has a record of the debit and credit parties and receives electronic and telephonic instructions to make the transfer. A unique identifier is assigned to each instruction template. Only the date and dollar amount may be changed.

Report Cards: A report card is a tool companies use to obtain a quantitative rating of a bank's level of service and responsiveness to problems. Criteria commonly found in report cards include number of errors by service, reporting times for information services, responsiveness to questions, timeliness of error resolution and effectiveness of personnel.

Representations and Warranties: Representations and warranties are the conditions that exist at the time the loan agreement is executed as attested to by the borrower. They include: 1) affirmation of the valid legal existence of the borrowing company, a resolution by the borrower's board of directors authorizing the borrowing and the authority of the corporate officers signing the documents, 2) the company confirming its compliance with the Employee Retirement Income and Security Act (ERISA) and 3) an indemnity protecting the lender from environmental liabilities.

Re-Presented Check Entries (RCK): The RCK format is utilized to transmit automated clearing house debit entries in place of a paper check after the paper check has been returned for insufficient or uncollected funds. The general requirements are that the item be less than $2,500 and drawn on a consumer account. Originators of re-presented check entries must provide notice to the check writer, prior to receiving an item to which the re-presented check entry relates, informing the check writer that the returned check may be collected electronically if the check is returned for insufficient or uncollected funds. Originators may transmit a re-presented check entry no more than twice after the first return of a paper item and no more than once after the second return of a paper item.

Glossary

Repurchase Agreement (Repo): A repurchase agreement or repo is a type of collateralized transaction between a securities dealer or bank and an investor. For an investor, a repo involves the purchase of a security with an agreement to sell it back to the initial seller at a future date. Most repos are negotiated with U.S. Treasury or agency securities or mortgage-backed pass-through securities and collateralized mortgage obligations (CMOs) issued or guaranteed by Ginnie Mae, Fannie Mae or Freddie Mac. Repos reflect direct negotiation between the buyer and seller, with terms based on the needs of the counterparties. Interest is calculated on an actual/360-day basis. The seller of a security under a repo agreement continues to receive all interest and principal payments on the security. The purchaser receives a fixed rate of interest on a short-term investment.

Request for Information (RFI): An RFI is often used by a company simply to confirm that use of a current provider of a service is justified or to narrow the field of potential providers before issuing a request for proposal (RFP). An RFI is also used to solicit ideas from service providers on how to solve a particular business or operational problem.

Request for Proposal (RFP): An RFP is a formal document prepared by a company that outlines its objectives and service requirements. An RFP can be used to obtain bids for everything ranging from one particular service to a company's entire relationship. By law, some government entities are required to prepare RFPs on a periodic basis, usually every three to five years, to ensure that they are receiving comparable services at competitive prices. Many private sector companies also periodically prepare RFPs for similar reasons. Outside consultants are sometimes used to assist in the preparation of RFPs and evaluation of responses. There are now standard formats that allow for electronic submission and comparison of proposals. The Association for Financial Professionals (AFP) and the Bank Administration Institute (BAI) have published standard RFP formats for common banking services.

Reserve Liquidity: Reserve liquidity is the primary reason companies invest in short-term securities. Companies cannot always depend on sufficient cash inflows during a period to cover that period's financial obligations. A portfolio of short-term investments can help adjust working capital imbalances and it may be used in conjunction with short-term borrowing.

Reserve Requirement: These are non-interest-bearing deposits that must, by law, be maintained by financial institutions at the Federal Reserve. The reserve requirement is one of the key components of U.S. monetary policy. For compensation purposes, a financial institution may use a reserve percentage other than that which is required by the Federal Reserve.

Resolution Trust Corporation (RTC): The RTC was formed under FIRREA in 1989 to make timely disposal of assets of failed savings and loan associations. The RTC was dissolved when it completed this function.

Retail Certificates of Deposit (CDs): Non-negotiable CDs sold to individual investors in amounts that vary from institution to institution. Maturities generally range from three months to five years.

Retail Collection System: There are a number of alternative retail collections systems that may have benefits such as improving cash flow, reducing paperwork, reducing per-item transaction costs and increasing the accuracy and timeliness of accounts receivable updating. These systems include the following: credit cards, debit cards, ATM networks, telephone banking, bill paying services, home banking, the Internet, agents, smart cards and cross-border collections.

Retail Lockbox: In retail lockbox systems, payors are generally consumers. Payments are often small-dollar amounts and frequently involve installments or recurring payments and scannable remittance documents. Because of the large number of items to be handled, processing cost is a more critical consideration than float reduction.

Return Item: A check the drawee bank rejects and returns to the depository bank.

Return on Common Equity: This ratio measures the earnings available to common shareholders (net income less any preferred stock dividends or amortization), expressed as a percentage of the common equity. The higher this ratio, the greater the return to the common shareholders of the company.

Return on Sales: This ratio measures the net income of a company as a percentage of its sales. The higher this ratio, the more after-tax profits the company generates on a given sales level.

Return on Total Assets: This ratio measures the net income of a company as a percentage of its total assets. The higher this ratio, the more after-tax profits the company is generating from its asset base.

Revenue Security: Municipal securities classified as revenue securities pay their principal and interest from proceeds of a specific project.

Reverse Positive Pay: Reverse positive pay (similar to positive pay) occurs when the bank transmits a file of the checks presented for payment to the company on a daily basis. The company matches this file to its list of checks issued and notifies the bank of any items it wishes to have returned. Due to the time-critical nature of this service, it is increasingly being offered via the Internet. This service, however, does not prevent fraudulent checks from being cashed at the payor bank teller line since the bank does not have access to the issue file.

Reverse Repurchase Agreement (Reverse Repo): In a reverse repo, sometimes known as a resale agreement, a company holding securities in its short-term portfolio sells the securities to a dealer with an agreement to buy them back at a specific price at a specific time. In effect, the company is borrowing cash from the dealer and using its securities as collateral for the loan. This is the reverse of a repurchase agreement or repo.

Revolving Credit: Under revolving credit terms, a company grants credit without requiring specific approval of each transaction, as long as the account is current. The account is usually considered current if the credit outstanding is below an established credit limit and minimum payments have been made on time. If the account is not paid in full by the monthly payment due date, an interest charge is calculated based on the average amount outstanding over the entire period.

Revolving Credit Agreement: A revolving credit agreement, also known as a revolver, is a facility that allows the borrower to borrow, repay and reborrow up to a defined amount. Revolving credits are contractual commitments with loan agreements, including covenants. Usually there is a commitment fee on the unused portion, as well as a facility fee. While often used for short-term borrowing, the commitment term typically ranges from two to five years and may be followed by a period in which the principal is systematically repaid.

Riding the Yield Curve: The investment strategy of riding the yield curve may provide returns superior to that of a matching strategy, as long as the shape of the yield curve does not change. If a company expects interest rates to rise in the future (upward sloping or normal yield curve), it can purchase securities that mature beyond the time when funds are needed. The securities are sold prior to maturity, providing a return that exceeds that of the matching strategy. The risk of this strategy is that interest rates may increase more than anticipated, reducing the value of the security at the time it is sold. If interest rates are expected to generally fall in the future (a downward sloping or inverted yield curve), then the strategy is to purchase securities for shorter than the time when funds are needed and then re-invest the funds when the first set of securities mature. The risk of this strategy is that interest rates may fall further than expected and the funds must be re-invested at a lower-than-planned interest rate.

Risk Management Services: Fluctuations in exchange rates, interest rates or prices of commodities can adversely impact a company's financial performance. For example, currency movements against the U.S. dollar can impact the profitability of a company that operates in international markets. To limit these risks, banks and other financial institutions offer a variety of products such as swaps, forwards, futures and options. These instruments are known as derivatives because their value is derived from or based on, underlying assets.

Risk Profile: The risk profile of a company demonstrates graphically how the value of the company is impacted by unexpected changes in a financial price variable such as interest rates, exchange rates or commodity prices. The risk profile of a company that does not hedge is either positively sloped or negatively sloped. The risk profile of a hedged company is horizontal.

Robinson-Patman Act: This 1936 act specifically prohibits price discrimination among customers where a cost basis cannot be demonstrated as the reason for price differences. Different credit terms are acceptable if they are industry practice or in cases in which cost differences can be substantiated.

Glossary

Safekeeping: Safekeeping banks can provide the institution or organization with added expertise, without the costs of developing and maintaining an in-house investment staff. The safekeeping bank acts as an agent to hold stock certificates or bonds, tracks trades and provides periodic reports. The safekeeping bank can give the institution/organization an international presence through worldwide banking affiliates. Safekeeping banks can be an integral part of a cash management system.

Sallie Mae: Founded as a federally chartered, shareholder-owned company, Sallie Mae was reorganized in 1997 as SLM Holding Corporation (SLMHC), a private Delaware corporation. Though not considered a government-sponsored enterprise (GSE), SLMHC still conducts most of its student loan financing activities through the Student Loan Marketing Association, a wholly owned subsidiary, which is a GSE. The GSE funds its operations through issuance of debt securities, which are considered agency securities. Sallie Mae uses the proceeds to purchase college loans that are insured by guaranty agencies and re-insured by the federal government.

Same-Day Settlement: A Federal Reserve rule requires that if a check is presented to a drawee bank by 8 a.m. local time, the drawee bank must settle in same-day funds by the close of Fedwire. No presentment fee can be charged. This rule is intended to expedite check collection services.

Savings and Loan (S&L): Savings and loans are federally or state chartered and owned by either shareholders or depositors. Their deposits are federally insured by the Federal Deposit Insurance Corporation (FDIC).

Savings Association Insurance Fund (SAIF): The FDIC administers two federal deposit insurance funds — the Bank Insurance Fund (BIF) and the SAIF. Deposits in most commercial banks and many savings banks are insured by the BIF. In 1989, Congress created the SAIF to succeed the Federal Savings and Loan Insurance Corporation (FSLIC) to insure deposits to specified amounts at savings associations and many savings banks. The FDIC was assigned responsibility for managing the SAIF. Both the BIF and SAIF deposit insurance programs are backed by the full faith and credit of the U.S. government.

Seasonal Borrowing: Some companies with seasonal borrowing requirements have lines of credit in which the maximum amount available varies over the year. A significant portion of credit lines are in the form of "base borrowing" where accounts receivable are used to provide collateral for the line and the amount of the commitment will vary month to month as the base of accounts receivable change.

Seasonal Dating: Seasonal dating is a special credit term used in industries with highly seasonal sales. Payment is due near the end of the buyer's selling season, although sliding discounts may be offered to encourage early payment.

Seasonal Performance: A company, such as a retail outlet during the holiday season, may generate a large proportion of its cash in one period of time. It will need those funds to finance its operations over the rest of the year.

Secondary Market: This term refers to the ability to resell a particular security after the initial purchase from the issuer or another holder. Securities with active secondary markets are more liquid because they can be easily sold if necessary.

Secured Borrowing: If a company cannot finance its accounts receivable with unsecured borrowings, it may be able to pledge its accounts receivable as collateral and borrow on a secured basis. A bank will select those accounts receivable it accepts as collateral and extend the company a loan. The company will remit the funds owed to the bank upon collection of the receivables.

Secured Debt: Bonds may be either secured or unsecured. Secured bonds are collateralized by a specific asset or revenues from a specific project. Secured debt gives the investor a lien against an asset. Bonds may be secured by various assets including inventories, real estate or fixed (capital) assets. Unsecured bonds, called debentures, offer no collateral. Debenture holders have a general claim against a company but not against a specific asset.

Secured Socket Layer (SSL): Many electronic commerce (e-commerce) Web sites use a form of encryption and authentication technology known as SSL to ensure privacy, integrity and authentication of data moving between clients and servers. SSL is built into most major browsers and part of the basic Web infrastructure.

Securities and Exchange Commission (SEC): The SEC is a federal agency that regulates and supervises the sale of securities to maintain a fair and orderly market for investors. Among its responsibilities are: 1) registering public offerings of debt or equity securities by banks or bank holding companies as well as all other corporations, 2) setting financial disclosure standards for corporations that sell securities to the public, 3) requiring filing of quarterly and annual financial statements by companies with publicly owned securities and 4) regulating mutual funds and investment advisors.

Securities Issuance: The amount and timing of equity and debt offerings are often determined by economic factors other than a company's short- to medium-term financial requirement. The timing of such issues is determined not only by corporate need, but also by financial market conditions. When interest rates are low, it is advantageous for companies to issue debt instruments. When equity prices are considered to be high, companies are more likely to sell stock. Proceeds from securities offerings often exceed a company's immediate cash needs and may be invested in short-term securities.

Securities Lending: Securities lending results from the lending of securities from broker to broker. The borrowing broker will provide collateral to the lending broker. The collateral is generally 102–105 percent greater than the value of the borrowed securities. The collateral is marked-to-market daily to assure that its value has not diminished below the value stipulated in the contract of the participating brokers. The broker/borrower usually borrows securities to cover short sales.

Securitization: Securitization is a financing technique by which a company issues debt securities backed by a pool of its selected receivables such as mortgages, auto loans, credit card receivables or equipment leases. Assets suitable for debt securitization usually have a predictable cash flow stream to retire the issue and a low level of historical loss experience. Securitization is a type of off-balance-sheet financing. Neither the debt nor the assets securing the financing appear on a company's balance sheet. By removing debt financing from the balance sheet, securitization improves some companies' financial ratios. Sometimes securitized issues are credit enhanced in order to receive a higher credit rating.

Semirepetitive Wires: With semirepetitive transfers, the debit and credit parties remain the same but the description may be changed along with the date and dollar amount. Semi-repetitive transfers allow some of the control of repetitive transfers and some of the flexibility of non-repetitive transfers.

Sender Net Debit Cap: Controlling daylight overdrafts has been one of the primary objectives of recent Federal Reserve measures to control risk among the large-dollar payment networks. The Federal Reserve (the Fed) has mandated that all banks using the large-dollar payment systems must have in place a sender net debit cap limiting the intraday overdraft that the bank may incur over all the large-dollar systems. The caps are determined by a Fed schedule based on the bank's self-evaluation of its overall creditworthiness as an institution, its credit policies and operational controls. The self-evaluation must be approved by a bank's board of directors.

Service Agreements: Financial institutions or companies may require service agreements. The agreements may be standardized or customized. The elements of a service agreement can include 1) operational policies and procedures, including the detailed processing requirements for the service, information needs and people who are authorized to make changes, 2) performance standards that define agreed-upon levels of service performance and quality, 3) compensation policies, including pricing, method of payment, payment frequency, excess/deficit balance arrangements, contract length and adjustments, 4) liability clauses defining, 5) responsibilities for specified risks and 6) terms and conditions.

Service Level Agreement: When adding a new financial service provider's (FSP's) electronic services, it is important to clearly set expectations regarding these services. This is typically done in the form of a service level agreement. These agreements should cover the following areas: 1) what electronic banking services are to be purchased, 2) how the services will operate relative to other services, 3) what the FSP is providing, 4) what the buyer (company) has to provide, 5) responsibilities of both parties, 6) service levels and fees, 7) support at setup and in production, 8) implementation and training, 9) security issues and procedures and 10) legal matters (law, jurisdiction, redress, etc.).

Shared-Secret Key System: In a shared-secret key (symmetric key) system both the sending and receiving party have a private key to encrypt/read messages. Since both parties to the message must have the same private key, key distribution and management may be difficult and complex. This type of arrangement is most often used between two regular trading partners.

Glossary

Shared Service Center (SSC): Many large global companies and multinational banks are utilizing a structure called shared service centers. The formal SSC was developed to establish, measure and maintain the cost and contribution of back-office business processes and operations. SSCs have been set up in a wide range of areas such as accounting functions, receivables and payables, human resources, payroll, benefits management, legal/tax and treasury. Much of the recent interest in SSCs in the treasury area has been as a result of the Internet and browser technology enabling the recentralization of database management and maintenance. Many global treasury back-office operations do not necessarily benefit from local management and could be profitably centralized into an SSC. The development of treasury management systems has provided standardization of information and processes, which further enhances the benefits of SSCs. The Economic and Monetary Union and the euro have forced both European and U.S. treasury managers to look at SSCs as a response to the consolidation of European banking structures.

Shareholder Wealth: This refers to the value of the equity ownership of a corporation. Traditional financial theory holds that management should endeavor to maximize the wealth of the common shareholders.

Sight Draft: A sight draft is payable on demand and is usually presented in combination with other documents showing that the terms of the transaction have been met. Sight drafts are primarily used to support international trade.

Signature Card: Financial institutions require companies to furnish signatures of authorized signers or specimens of facsimile or computerized signatures.

Simple Average: Distribution percentages can be estimated by averaging past daily cash flows related to a particular category of disbursements.

Simple Moving Average: Simple moving averages base a forecast on a rolling or moving average of past historical values. A forecast prepared using a simple moving average will always lag any trend in the actual cash flow. Choice of the appropriate number of observations is important to the usefulness of this model. The longer the time period over which the moving average is calculated, the greater the smoothing of individual data point variances; the shorter the time period, the less the smoothing of individual data point variances.

Sinking Fund: A sinking fund assures creditors that adequate funds are available to meet payments at maturity. The borrower makes periodic payments to a separate custodial account that is used to repay the debt.

Smart Card: These cards are similar to debit cards but contain a microchip with additional information and security protection. Smart cards may be used for prepaid value transactions, where the consumer prepays the bank, giro or company issuing the card. The card then keeps track of purchases and any remaining balance.

Society for Worldwide Interbank Financial Telecommunications (S.W.I.F.T.): S.W.I.F.T. is an interbank telecommunications network that enables banks to send authenticated electronic messages in standard formats. It was established in the 1970s and has more than 4,000 member banks. The communications, initiated and received by member banks, cover a wide variety of international banking services and are known as S.W.I.F.T. messages. A company can request its bank to initiate a balance transfer or foreign payment through S.W.I.F.T. It should be noted that S.W.I.F.T. communications contain payment-related information but do not transfer value. The actual clearing and settlement of S.W.I.F.T. messages regarding the transfer of funds are accomplished through correspondent bank balances. Standardized S.W.I.F.T. messages have also been developed for other international service needs including balance reporting, letters of credit, foreign exchange transactions and documentary collections.

Sovereign Risk: One type of risk that must be considered is known as sovereign risk. This is the risk that a company's operations in a foreign country may be expropriated or nationalized by the government of that country. Other types of less severe sovereign risk include: 1) blocked currencies, where profits cannot be converted from the local currency into a major trading currency 2) forced re-investment, where funds cannot be transferred out of the country in any form or 3) required majority ownership by local residents of the country.

Speculation: Speculation involves betting on the direction of the market. Speculators are those market participants who are willing to assume risk. In other words, speculators are betting that the price of the asset will either go up or go down. They have an open position in the asset and, unlike hedgers, do not have an underlying exposure they are offsetting. The key point here is that a speculation arrangement or transaction is one that *increases* the company's risk.

Speculative Requirement: Surplus liquid resources allow a company to take advantage of future unplanned investment opportunities that may arise.

Spot Market: A rate quoted in the spot market for currency is called a spot foreign exchange rate (spot rate). These rates are generally quoted for delivery one or two business days from the date of the trade. Faster delivery may be possible, but at the expense of a rate higher than the quoted spot rate.

Spot Rate: See Spot Market.

Spread Account: This is a form of credit enhancing a securitization and is a reserve built from excess cash flow from underlying assets beyond that required for debt service.

Standby Letter of Credit (L/C): A standby L/C is a variant of a commercial L/C. They are issued primarily by U.S. banks, which are legally prohibited from issuing formal guarantees. Once issued, the standby L/C serves as a vehicle to ensure the financial performance of a bank's customer to a third-party beneficiary. Standby L/Cs typically require presentation of a sight draft and documentation that supports the beneficiary's claim of non-performance on the part of the issuing bank's customer.

Standby L/Cs are frequently used as credit enhancement for commercial paper programs or to guarantee a bid tender or financial performance on a contract.

Statement of Cash Flows: The statement of cash flows provides an indication of the sources of a company's cash flow and how it is being used. The statement of cash flows is divided into three sections — operating, investing and financing activities.

Statistical Forecasting: Statistical forecasts project cash flows in two ways: 1) through extrapolation, where past trends are identified and used to determine future values of cash flows or 2) by determining the relationship (correlation) between a predicted cash flow or cash flow component (dependent variable) and other known cash flow components (independent variables or determinants). Statistical forecasting is particularly applicable to projections requiring analysis of extensive data and it is useful for identifying and analyzing trends.

Stop Payment: A company can initiate stop payments by voice, electronically or in writing. Written confirmation may be required by the bank for telephone instructions. Stop payments are usually good only for six months and must be renewed, if necessary.

Strike Price: See Exercise Price.

Student Loan Marketing Association: Founded as a federally chartered, shareholder-owned company, Sallie Mae was reorganized in 1997 as SLM Holding Corporation (SLMHC), a private Delaware corporation. Though not considered a government-sponsored enterprise (GSE), SLMHC still conducts most of its student loan financing activities through the Student Loan Marketing Association, a wholly owned subsidiary, which is a GSE. The GSE funds its operations through issuance of debt securities, which are considered agency securities. Sallie Mae uses the proceeds to purchase college loans that are insured by guaranty agencies and reinsured by the federal government.

Swap: A swap is an agreement between two parties to exchange (or swap) a set of cash flows at future points in time.

Swaption: An option on an interest rate swap is called a swaption, where the buyer of the option has the right to enter into an interest rate swap at a future date.

Sweep Accounts: See Overnight Sweep Account.

Systemic Risk: This type of payment system risk relates to the possibility that the failure of one major bank could cause other banks to fail and cause a collapse of the payments system.

Target Concentration: With target concentration, a target balance is set and all funds above that balance level are transferred to the concentration bank. This system maintains balances at the desired level. It could involve transfers as frequently as daily.

Tax-Exempt Yield: See Tax Status.

Tax Payment (TXP) Convention: This is a special form of the cash concentration or disbursement plus addendum (CCD+) automated clearing house (ACH) transaction set that is used to report state and federal tax information and payments.

Tax Status: The tax status of an investment has an impact on its yield. Tax-exempt securities provide a lower pre-tax yield than taxable securities of similar maturity and default risk. When comparing taxable and tax-exempt instruments, the tax-exempt yield is usually converted to a taxable equivalent yield.

Taxable Equivalent Yield: See Tax Status.

Term Loan: Term loans are made for a fixed period of time, typically two to 10 years, usually to support equipment purchases and more permanent capital financing. Repayment schedules vary depending on the type of loan and the nature of the project being financed. Typical amortization schedules require periodic payments of principal plus interest, but some may require periodic interest payments with repayment of principal upon maturity.

Thin Client: When a financial service provider offers application software that is Internet-based and resides at a central server site, this is called a thin client solution. In the case of treasury management systems, this central site is generally a bank or other financial service provider.

Third-Party Financing: A company collects the information necessary to complete a credit application from its customer and forwards it to a financial institution, which decides whether or not to grant credit. Because of the administrative costs this entails, the companies that do this tend to manufacture and market big-ticket items such as production machinery. Although third-party financing through an institution can free up capital, companies that use it relinquish control over the type of customer they want to attract and may miss marketing opportunities. Furthermore, a company may have to discount the price of the goods sold in order to compensate the third party and thus forgo potential income.

Threshold Concentration: Threshold concentration is a method of limiting balances by minimizing the number of transfers, thus reducing a company's costs of operating a cash concentration system. With threshold concentration, a company allows account balances to build to a predetermined level before transferring funds to the concentration bank. A cash manager can monitor average balances and adjust them as necessary over time.

Thrift Institution: Thrift institutions have traditionally been depositories that accept consumer deposits and lend money, primarily in the form of home mortgage loans. The Depository Institutions Deregulation and Monetary Control Act of 1980 (DIDMCA) provided for a phase-out of interest rate ceilings for thrift institutions and commercial banks and allowed savings institutions to make commercial as well as consumer loans. The number of thrift institutions has fallen from a high of almost 5,000 in the 1960s to just 1,700 in 1998. The Office of Thrift Supervision (OTS) supervises and regulates all federally chartered and many state-chartered thrifts. There are two types of thrift institutions — savings and loan associations and savings or mutual savings banks.

Time Deposit Account: Time deposits must be held at a bank, thrift or credit union for a specified period. Examples of time deposits include certificates of deposit (CDs) and savings accounts.

Time Draft: This payment mechanism is like a sight draft but is not payable until a specified future date. Time drafts are used in international trade transactions that call for delayed payments.

Time Series Forecasting: A time series model seeks to forecast a variable based on past observations of that variable.

Time Value of Money: The time value of money is a fundamental principle of finance. A dollar today is worth more than a dollar tomorrow because a dollar today can be invested to earn a return. Conversely, a dollar tomorrow is worth less than a dollar today because the opportunity to earn interest is foregone. The value of a cash flow at any point in time can be determined by using an appropriate interest rate and the number of time periods involved.

Times Interest Earned (TIE): This is a coverage ratio that indicates how many times a company's earnings before interest and taxes (EBIT) exceed its interest obligations. The higher this ratio, the greater the ability of the company to pay off debt.

Total Liabilities-to-Total Assets Ratio: This ratio measures the percentage of all liabilities relative to the total asset base of the company. The higher this ratio, the more liabilities (as opposed to equity) the company uses to finance its asset base.

Trade Acceptance: A trade acceptance is another instrument that may be used in international transactions. It is similar to a banker's acceptance except that it is typically drawn on and accepted by a company, usually the buyer (importer). It can be used to evidence a buyer's obligation to pay for purchased merchandise where the seller (exporter) is satisfied with the credit risk.

Trade Credit: This is credit offered by a company to its customers to help them purchase the company's products. Companies offering trade credit generate accounts receivable that convert to cash when the customers pay bills in the normal course of business. A company's credit terms, together with its sales and collection patterns, determine the levels of its accounts receivable and impact a company's financing needs.

Trade or Commercial Letters of Credit (L/Cs): L/Cs are documents issued by a bank, guaranteeing the payment of a customer's draft up to a stated amount for a specified period provided certain conditions are met. In effect, the issuing bank substitutes its name and credit on behalf of its customer.

Trade Services: Banks provide a variety of services to facilitate payment of trade obligations, particularly with foreign trading partners. These include letters of credit, documentary collections and banker's acceptances.

Trading Community: The environment of business consists of groups or trading communities of suppliers, customers, distribution, logistics, employees, agents, etc. They could be vertical communities such as supply chains or horizontal communities such as trade groups or associations.

Trading Company: Trading companies are used when an exporter (seller) can also sell its products at a discount to an export trading company, which, in turn, resells the products internationally.

Transaction Balances: These are deposits held by companies to facilitate collection and disbursement activity.

Transaction Exposure: If a company's balance sheet, either receivables or payables, is affected in value by changes in foreign exchange rates, then the company has a transaction exposure. Transaction exposure usually occurs if the receivables and payables are in different currencies. Adjusting the selling price for adverse changes in the exchange rate does not necessarily eliminate transaction exposure. For example, a U.S. exporter sells merchandise to a French buyer agreeing to accept payment (in euros) three months from now. The exporter records the transaction as an accounts receivable. However, the exporter is exposed to a possible loss in value if, in three months, the euro depreciates relative to the U.S. dollar (because the receivables would convert into fewer dollars).

Transaction Set: A transaction set is the electronic equivalent of a paper business document or form. Specific rules govern formats for standard business documents. Examples of typical business documents that are converted to electronic data interchange (EDI) transaction sets are purchase orders, shipping documents, invoices and remittance advices.

Transactions Requirement: Because a company's day-to-day cash flows are unsynchronized, it must hold in reserve cash and near-cash resources to meet financial requirements.

Trans-European Automated Real-Time Gross Settlement Express Transfer System (TARGET): Beginning in January 1999, TARGET provided real-time settlement for cross-border payments, similar to the Fedwire in the United States. The system is used primarily for urgent, high-value payments. An important function of TARGET is to enable central banks to mobilize liquidity around Europe in order to manage monetary policy objectives as determined by the European Central Bank.

Transfer Agent: Banks serve as transfer agents by keeping records of the sale and purchase of stocks and bonds and maintaining records of the shareholders of a corporation by name, address and number of shares.

Glossary

Transit Routing Number: The magnetic ink character recognition (MICR) line on a check contains the transit routing number, which the depository bank uses to route the check back to the drawee bank.

Translation Exposure: Companies with foreign subsidiaries or foreign operations are exposed to translation exposure. Translation exposure is created when a foreign subsidiary's financial statements are converted (or translated) into the parent company's home currency to consolidate the parent's financial statement. This exposure must be reported on a quarterly basis in accordance with financial accounting standard (FAS) 52. It is difficult to use financial instruments to hedge this type of risk due to the potential large amounts involved. One effective approach, however, is to use a balance sheet hedge (i.e., offset foreign asset exposures by borrowing funds to finance those assets in the same country and currency). This hedges the balance sheet and reduces the net exposure to the parent company.

Travelers Checks: These instruments are prepaid and similar to money orders. Two signatures typically are required by the purchaser: one at issuance and one at the time the check is used.

Treasurer: The treasurer is usually responsible for arranging external financing, managing relationships with banks and other financial institutions and overseeing day-to-day liquidity management. The international functions of treasury may be part of the treasurer's duties or may be under a separate international treasurer. Other functions for which the treasurer may be responsible include risk management, managing dividend disbursement, insurance and pension assets. In a large company, some of these responsibilities may be delegated to an assistant treasurer or treasury manager. As is mentioned below, the cash management function is generally part of the treasurer's oversight responsibility.

Treasury Bill (T-Bill): T-bills are the most liquid securities in the money market because of the volumes issued, their credit quality and their short maturities. They are issued each week on a discount basis in maturities of less than one year (typically 13 or 26 weeks). T-bills are available in a minimum denomination of $1,000 with additional amounts in multiples of $1,000, but are generally traded in round lots of $1,000,000. The discount rate on T-bills is quoted in annualized terms.

Treasury Bond (T-Bond): T-bonds are similar to T-notes, but with original maturities of greater than 10 years.

Treasury Management: Treasury management is the management of all treasury-related activities in a company. These include the following functions: cash management, risk management, dividend disbursements, insurance and management of pension assets.

Treasury Note (T-Note): T-notes are issued with original maturities of between one and 10 years. The minimum denomination for T-notes is $1,000 with additional amounts in multiples of $1,000. As in the case of T-bills, T-notes are usually traded in round lots of $1,000,000. T-notes are interest-bearing securities on which interest is paid semiannually. Interest is calculated on the actual number of elapsed days using a 365-day year.

Treasury System: There are a wide range of stand-alone treasury management products available for companies of all sizes. The treasury workstations and other cash management software offered by financial service providers fit into this category, as well as sophisticated (and expensive) treasury management systems offered by non-FSP third parties. These systems are often tailored to specific needs of treasury departments, offering support for cash management, debt/investment and risk management activities. Most of the larger systems also provide access to multibank reporting and interfaces to major enterprise resource planning (ERP) systems. The more sophisticated of these systems also address treasury-specific issues such as financial risk management and support for financial accounting standard (FAS) 133, which the typical ERP system does not address.

Treasury Workstation: A treasury workstation (cash management software) is typically a PC or client/server, which has software that gathers information from both internal and external sources, then compiles the data for purposes of analysis and decision making. A treasury workstation can either be stand-alone or part of a company network. In addition to automating a number of manual tasks, treasury workstations enable cash managers to prepare and distribute financial information in a variety of customized spreadsheets and management reports. Treasury workstation software can either be purchased from a vendor or developed in-house.

Tri-Party Arrangement: In a tri-party arrangement, the dealer's custodial agent maintains a custodial account for the investor. The dealer pays the fee.

Trust Services: Banks invest, manage and distribute monies as instructed in wills, trusts and estates.

Truth in Lending Act: This 1969 act requires lenders to disclose the true annual interest rate and the total dollar cost on most types of loans.

Uniform Commercial Code (UCC): The UCC is a uniform set of laws governing commercial transactions enacted separately and sometimes in different forms by each state. The UCC defines the rights and duties of the parties in a commercial transaction and provides a statutory definition of commonly used business practices.

Uniform Resource Locator (URL): This is an address format utilized on the Web. For example, a typical Web address might be as follows:
http://www.afponline.org/search/index.html

Unique ZIP Code: Most processors offering lockbox services have a unique ZIP code for lockbox remittances. Depending on their capabilities for fine sorting, this feature may speed processing of incoming mail and save several hours of mail and processing float daily.

GLOSSARY

United Nations EDI for Administration, Commerce and Transportation (UN/EDIFACT): Many countries have become involved in developing electronic data interchange (EDI) standards. This has led to the development of UN/EDIFACT rules, a set of internationally agreed-upon standards, directories and guidelines for the electronic interchange of structured data that relates to trade in goods and services between independent computerized information systems. UN/EDIFACT standards are widely used in Europe and some Asian countries.

Unqualified Opinion: This is a type of auditing opinion in which the auditor states that the company's financial statements provide a fair description of the company's financial condition in accordance with generally accepted accounting principles.

Unsecured Borrowing: A company that offers trade credit can borrow unsecured funds from a financial institution to support accounts receivable if it has sufficient available credit capacity.

Unsecured Debt: A debt or borrowing arrangement that does not have any security or collateral backing it.

U.S. Treasury Security: U.S. Treasury securities are instruments the U.S. government issues to finance its activities. The U.S. government issues large amounts of debt securities that appeal to a broad spectrum of investors. The market for U.S. Treasury securities is the largest and most actively traded in the world. U.S. Treasury securities are considered risk-free with respect to default. They are virtually the only securities issued in the world to enjoy this reputation and they serve as a benchmark for other financial instruments. The interest rates as determined by the market for U.S. Treasury instruments are used as a reference point and market indicator. Many other securities (and loans) have yields established as a spread over a similar-term Treasury instrument.

Usury Laws: Usury laws, which vary significantly from state to state, restrict the interest rates or penalty fees that companies can charge on installment credit.

Value-Added Network (VAN): A VAN is a communication intermediary that provides various services to the users of electronic commerce (e-commerce). VANs resolve interface problems between two companies that have different computer systems, different format needs and different protocols. Thus, VANs make it easier for companies to implement electronic data interchange (EDI) and to add new EDI trading partners.

Value-At-Risk (VAR): One approach to determining how the value of a company is impacted by changing financial variables is called value-at-risk (VAR). This measure was actually developed in the trading rooms of financial institutions to provide an estimation of the possible loss for the entire trading operation. It was specifically designed to handle a wide range of risk factors and to summarize their impact on the operation into a single measure. In the VAR approach, risk is determined as a function of the probability and monetary impact of a particular adverse event over a certain period of time.

Value Dating: Outside of the United States, banks typically use value dating as compensation for services provided to their customers. Under a value dating system, the bank sets the dates upon which it grants credit for deposits (forward value date) or it debits the account for checks or electronic payments from the account (back value date).

Vinnie Mac: These are mortgage-backed securities created by the Department of Veterans Affairs and backed by the full faith and credit of the federal government.

Voucher: The primary responsibility of the accounts payable function is to verify incoming invoices and authorize them to be paid, a process some companies call vouchering. This process generally involves the traditional "three-way match," where the invoice is matched to both an approved purchase order and receiving information. This ensures that the items being billed to the company were indeed authorized for purchase from an approved vendor and that they were received in satisfactory condition. Once this approval process is complete, the invoice can be approved or vouchered for payment. In a typical business-to-business environment, multiple invoices are often combined into a single payment.

Web-EDI: In this form of electronic data interchange (EDI), the Web is used by large EDI hubs to bring smaller trading partners into the EDI world. The transaction is Web-based for smaller trading partners who access a Web site to either receive information or create business documents using fill-in forms. The large hub can still utilize standard EDI transaction sets to send to or receive information from the smaller trading partners. This approach is useful for low transaction volumes within limited trading communities.

Weighted Average Cost of Capital (WACC): The WACC is calculated as an average of the after-tax cost of debt and the cost of equity, each weighted by the proportion of each source of capital in the firm's capital structure.

Weighted Average Cost of Funds: Some financial institutions use a weighted average of cost of funds as a base rate for borrowing arrangements. This average may be based on the institution's cost of funds or some cross-institution cost of funds.

Wholesale Lockbox: Wholesale lockboxes are configured to process business-to-business payments, which, unlike consumer payments, are usually for large amounts and can be matched to specific invoices. Often several invoices are paid with one check. Detailed information usually is required about the invoices paid, discounts taken, returns and allowances. Wholesale collection systems emphasize float reduction and timely handling of information related to the invoices being paid.

Window Dressing: This is the practice of adjusting certain accounts just prior to the end of the accounting period to make financial statements look better.

Working Capital: Working capital refers to the funds in a company's current asset accounts — cash, accounts receivable and inventory. These are the accounts through which cash flows in a company's cash conversion cycle.

Working Capital Turnover: This ratio measures how many times per year a company converts its working capital into sales. It establishes a relationship for the amount of working capital used to support a given level of sales.

World Wide Web (the Web): The World Wide Web is the most-used method of accessing the Internet through the use of browser technology. The Web is a user-friendly subset of the Internet that allows users to access text and graphical links and move easily from site to site. There are millions of sites on the Web and it is growing at an astounding rate.

Yankee Certificate of Deposit (CD): Yankee CDs are U.S. dollar-denominated CDs issued by foreign banks through their branches in the U.S. market.

Year Basis: Most short-term instruments — commercial paper and Treasury bills, for example — pay interest calculated on a 360-day basis. Treasury bonds and Treasury notes pay interest on a 365-day basis.

Yield: Yield is a measure of the gain an investor derives from a financial instrument. Typically, it is stated as an annual rate of return, expressed as a percentage.

Yield Curve: How the market values a debt instrument in comparison with other similar securities that have longer or shorter maturities is revealed by the yield curve, which expresses the term structure of interest rates. A yield curve depicts the differences in yield of securities that are identical except for their dates of maturity.

Yield to Maturity (YTM): This is a calculation of a debt instrument's total yield from a specific date to maturity. It takes into account the discount or premium on an instrument in addition to its coupon or interest payments. (When an instrument is purchased at a premium to face value, the calculation assumes an amortization to par and when it is purchased at a discount, the calculation assumes an increase in value to par.)

Zengin Data Telecommunications System (Zengin System): The Zengin Data Telecommunications System (Zengin System) is the online network through which most domestic funds transfers are initiated. In 1990, the Zengin System went to a real-time basis and established a cap on intraday net debit positions for each participating institution. Nichigin Net is the interbank settlement system operated by the Bank of Japan. Financial institutions that maintain accounts with the Bank of Japan are provided online access to initiate settlement transfers between accounts.

Zero Balance Account (ZBA): A ZBA is a disbursement account on which a company writes checks, even though the balance in the account is maintained at zero. A transfer of funds from a master account located in the same bank covers checks debited against a ZBA for payment. Funding of the ZBA is automatic and involves only an accounting entry by the bank. A ZBA can also be a depository account from which funds are debited and transferred into a master account at the end of each day. Some ZBAs are used for both collections and disbursements.

Zero Coupon Bonds: These are bonds that require no periodic interest payments, but only a single payment of face value at maturity. Due to this single payment feature, they are sold at deep discount from their face value.

Answers

CHAPTER 1:
The Role of Cash Management in Corporate Finance

1. The major objectives of cash management are:
   - Maintaining liquidity
   - Optimizing cash resources
   - Obtaining short- and long-term financing
   - Monitoring and controlling financial risk exposure
   - Coordinating decision making with other departments in the firm

2. The general types of cash flows are as follows:
   - *Cash Inflows* — These are funds collected from customers, obtained from financial sources or received from other payors.
   - *Concentration and Liquidity Management Flows* — Concentrated funds are those that are systematically transferred to create a centralized inventory of liquid reserves held as cash or invested in cash equivalents. Concentration funds include internal transfers among operating units of a company and between various bank accounts owned by a company.
   - *Cash Outflows* — These funds are disbursed from liquid reserves to vendors, employees, lenders, shareholders and other payees of the company.

3. The cash flow timeline comprises the total time interval from the time resources are purchased at the beginning of a company's operating cycle until the time payment is received for goods or services at the end of a company's operating cycle.

4. Float is the time interval or delay, between the start and completion of a specific phase or process occurring along the cash flow timeline.

5. The tools of cash management are designed to synchronize a company's cash flows, thereby promoting the efficient operation of the cash flow timeline. Products used in the collection, concentration and disbursement of funds reduce unfavorable float that occurs along the cash flow timeline.

6. The principal roles of the finance function are:
   - *Accounting* — Reporting and record-keeping function
   - *Funding* — Raising capital to finance projects
   - *Capital Budgeting* — Determining the projects in which to invest
   - *Financial Risk Management* — Monitoring and managing the financial risk of the company

7. The major decision areas are:
   - Capital structure
   - Investment decisions
   - Financing decisions
   - Dividend decisions

8. The key players in the finance function (other than the cash manager) are:
   - Chief financial officer (CFO)
   - Treasurer
   - Controller
   - Internal auditor
   - Credit manager
   - Accounts payable manager

9. The typical cash management functions and responsibilities include:
   - Funds management
   - Banking systems administration
   - Liquidity management
   - Forecasting
   - Systems design, implementation and evaluation
   - Financial risk management

10. The 1970s saw the introduction of remote disbursement and controlled disbursement. Remote disbursement was designed to take advantage of the inaccessibility of certain geographically remote banks. The objective was to increase disbursement float as much as possible. Federal Reserve policies discourage the use of this practice. In contrast, controlled disbursement was designed to utilize the Federal Reserve's presentment schedule, providing early notification to payors of checks to

be presented to their accounts on a daily basis. This allows cash managers to fund their disbursement accounts earlier in the day and have a better opportunity to invest excess funds.

11. The Depository Institutions Deregulation and Monetary Control Act of 1980 had a major impact on bank services and prices.

12. The key issues in the current treasury environment are:

    - *Quality Concerns* — Treasury departments are being challenged to provide a high level of quality results at an acceptable cost.

    - *Reorganization of Treasury Operations* — Many companies have restructured their treasury operations using such tools as: re-engineering, benchmarking and outsourcing.

CHAPTER 2:
Financial Accounting and Related Concepts

1. GAAP (generally accepted accounting principles) are the detailed rules, developed by the Financial Accounting Standards Board, that govern financial reporting and record keeping in the United States.

2. In cash accounting, all accounting entries are directly related to a cash inflow or outflow. In accrual accounting, revenues are recognized as they are earned and expenses as they are incurred, regardless of when the related cash flows occur.

3. A company may avoid reporting a negative cash balance by combining cash and marketable securities on its balance sheet or by reporting checks written but not yet presented as a current liability.

4. The three basic financial statements are the balance sheet, the income statement and the statement of cash flows.

5. The auditor can render four types of opinion: unqualified, qualified, disclaimed or adverse.

6. The present value of $1,500 two years from now at an opportunity cost of five percent can be computed as follows:

$$\text{Present Value} = \frac{\text{Future Value}}{(1 + \text{Interest Rate})^{\text{Number of Periods}}}$$

$$= \frac{\$1,500}{(1 + .05)^2} = \$1,500 \times (1 + .05)^{-2}$$

$$= \frac{\$1,500}{(1.1025)} = \$1,500 \times (.9070) = \$1,360.5$$

7. Companies use debt for two basic reasons: 1) debt is less expensive due to its tax-deductibility and 2) the use of debt does not dilute the equity position of the shareholders.

8. If a company is leveraged with high levels of debt or other fixed costs, earnings will change at a more rapid rate than revenues.

9. A company needs liquidity for transaction requirements, precautionary requirements and speculative requirements.

10. The ratios typically used to measure liquidity are the current ratio, quick ratio, cash flow-to-total debt ratio, cash conversion cycle and cash turnover.

11. The cash conversion cycle measures the time it takes a company to convert a cash outflow (for payment of inventory purchases) into a cash inflow (collection of accounts receivable). This measure uses the average age of the inventory, the average days of accounts receivable and the average age of the accounts payable to indicate how efficiently a company is using its current assets and liabilities.

12. In general, EVA increases under the three following scenarios:
    - The rate of return earned on the existing base of capital improves.
    - Additional capital is invested in projects that return more than the cost of new capital.
    - Capital is liquidated from substandard operations.

13. Among the disadvantages of traditional ratio measures are the following:
    - Traditional ratio measures usually reflect accounting rather than economic values.
    - Ratios express static relationships that do not take the variability of cash flows into account except to the extent that the ratios themselves may vary.
    - Financial ratios provide indications but not answers. The evaluation of the company's worth is a matter of judgment.
    - Ratios are affected by differing methods of depreciation and by window dressing, the practice of adjusting certain accounts just prior to the end of the accounting period to make financial statements look better.

CHAPTER 3:
The U.S. Financial Environment

1. A commercial bank is defined by law as a financial institution that accepts deposits and makes business loans, offering a wide range of products and services. The term commercial bank is used to describe everything from small, single-facility community banks with a few million dollars in assets to large, global institutions with numerous locations and billions in assets.

2. The major products of commercial banks are:
   - Deposit accounts
   - Credit services
   - Investment banking services
   - Payments and collections
   - Trade services
   - Credit enhancement or payment guaranty
   - Acting as agent or fiduciary
   - Consulting services
   - Risk management services
   - Broker/dealer services

3. Underwriting is the principal function of an investment banking firm. It ensures the issuer of stock or bonds of a definite sum of money for the issue at a definite time. The investment banker assumes the risk of price and marketability.

4. Industrial credit and capital companies are subsidiaries of large industrial corporations that raise funds in the commercial paper market and lend to companies and individuals. A captive finance company typically finances the purchase of its own company's products. Automobile finance companies (GMAC and Ford Motor Credit Company) are common examples of these.

5. Savings and mutual savings banks have traditionally been state chartered. The Garn-St. Germain Act of 1982 allows mutual savings banks to switch to a federal charter.

6. Unlike banks, credit unions are not-for-profit financial institutions with restricted membership.

7. The five major roles of the Federal Reserve are:
   - Supervising and regulating banks
   - Conducting monetary policy
   - Providing services for banks
   - Acting as the fiscal agent for the U.S. Treasury
   - Acting as a consumer protection agency

8. National bank charters are granted by the Office of the Comptroller of the Currency.

9. The Office of Thrift Supervision is the primary regulator of nationally chartered S&Ls.

10. FFIEC stands for Federal Financial Institution Examination Council. It coordinates the activities of the Fed, the OCC, the FDIC and the OTS to ensure consistency in the implementation of regulatory policy.

11. OFAC stands for Office of Foreign Assets Control, which is an office of the Treasury Department and administers and enforces economic and trade sanctions against targeted foreign countries, terrorism-sponsoring organizations and international narcotics traffickers based on U.S. foreign policy and national security goals. The OFAC has the authority to impose controls on financial transactions and freeze foreign assets under U.S. jurisdiction.

12. The Edge Act allows U.S. banks to invest in corporations engaged in international banking.

13. The McFadden Act originally prohibited banks from accepting deposits across state lines. The Douglas Amendment allowed banks to merge across state lines if each state permitted it, but did not allow bank holding companies to acquire banks across state lines. The Interstate Banking and Branching Efficiency Act (1994) phased out, over a three-year period, the state barriers against branching established by the McFadden Act.

14. The Glass-Steagall Act separates commercial banking from investment banking.

15. The Depository Institutions Deregulation and Monetary Control Act of 1980 included mandates that the Federal Reserve reduce and/or price float.

16. The Financial Institutions Reform Recovery and Enforcement Act consolidated the two financial institution insurance funds under the FDIC.

17. The Interstate Bank and Branching Efficiency Act of 1994 has the following primary provisions:

- Permitted bank holding companies to acquire a bank located in any state effective September 1995
- Allowed banks in one state to merge with banks in another state beginning June 1997, as long as neither state had taken legislative action to prohibit interstate mergers between the date of enactment and the end of May 1997
- Allowed banks to establish new branches in states where they do not maintain a branch if the host state passed a law expressly permitting such branches

18. Financial holding companies (FHCs) are permitted by the Gramm-Leach-Bliley Act of 1999. The Act has the following provisions:
    - Eliminated many of the remaining barriers among the banking, insurance and securities businesses
    - Permitted the creation of FHCs, which can engage in any activity considered "financial in nature, incidental to finance or complementary to it"
    - Allowed for easier entry by foreign banks into the U.S. financial services market
    - Established the Fed as the primary regulator of financial holding companies
    - Barred a bank holding company from merging with an insurance or securities firm or embarking on new powers if any of its banks earned less than a "satisfactory" CRA rating in its most recent exam
    - Required financial institutions to establish privacy policies and disclose them at the start of a customer relationship and once a year thereafter

19. The payment of interest on corporate demand deposits is prohibited by Regulation Q.

20. Federal Reserve Regulation CC established rules for handling return of checks and payable through drafts.

21. Article 3 of the UCC permits avoidance of inadvertent accord and satisfaction.

22. Under UCC Article 4A, banks are not responsible for consequential damages, which are losses resulting from the action or error made by the bank beyond the simple loss of funds. A bank incorrectly executing a payment order remains liable for interest losses or incidental expenses. The bank is liable for consequential damages only if it agrees to assume this liability in a written agreement with the customer.

23. UCC Article 5 covers commercial letters of credit requiring documentary drafts or documentary demands for payment. It does not cover standby letters of credit.

CHAPTER 4:
U.S. Payments System

1. The payee is the receiver of a check and the party to whom a payment is made. The payor is the party who writes or draws the check to remit funds.

2. The purpose of the magnetic ink character recognition (MICR) line is to clear checks back to the bank on which the check is drawn and, when received by the drawee bank, to debit the payor's account.

3. Checks can be cleared through the following channels:
   - On-us clearing
   - Clearing house
   - Federal Reserve bank
   - Correspondent bank

4. A cash letter is a bundle of checks accompanied by a list of individual items and other control documents.

5. A direct send is a cash letter that bypasses the local Federal Reserve. A bank sends it directly to the paying bank or a non-local Federal Reserve bank.

6. An on-us item is a check deposited in the same bank on which it is drawn.

7. High-dollar group sort (HDGS) is the Fed's program to expedite the processing of high-dollar checks through the system. The HDGS program automatically involves making a second presentment to banks with more than $10 million of checks presented daily from outside their Fed districts. HDGS items are checks that meet this criteria.

8. A ledger balance reflects accounting entries to a bank account, while a collected balance reflects the balance in an account for which the bank of deposit has received settlement.

9. Deposit float has two meanings: 1) Deposit float is the sum of the deposited items that are in the process of collection; 2) Deposit float is also used to refer to the interval between the time an item is deposited and the time the funds are collected. For example, cash managers often refer to an average float of a certain number of days, meaning the average length of time they must wait for deposited funds to become available.

10. Factors that determine availability include:
    - Drawee's location
    - Time of deposit
    - Day of deposit
    - Pre-encoding by the customer
    - Checks rejected during processing
    - As-of adjustments
    - Fractional availability

11. Availability schedules specify, for each drawee endpoint, when a bank grants credit for deposited checks to the depositor's available or collected balance. The assignment of availability can be in whole or fractional banking days.

12. A PTD is drawn against the payor and not a bank.

13. A sight draft is payable when presented, while a time draft is payable at a specified future date.

14. The terminology and mechanics of the ACH system differ from those of the check clearing system in four ways:
    - A check is paper-based; an ACH transaction is electronic.
    - A check is limited to payment instructions; an ACH transaction can also transmit additional payment-related information.
    - The parties to a check are referred to as the payor and the payee; the parties to an ACH transaction are the originator and receiver.
    - A check can only debit a payor's account and credit a payee's account; an ACH transaction can be either a debit or a credit transaction. ACH credit transactions move funds from the originator's account to the receiver's account; ACH debit transactions move funds from the receiver's account to the originator's account.

15. The basic types of ACH formats are:
    - Prearranged payment or deposit (PPD) used for consumer transactions
    - Cash concentration and disbursement (CCD) used to move funds within or between companies
    - Cash concentration and disbursement plus addendum (CCD+) used for the U.S. Treasury Department's vendor express program and corporate-to-corporate payments
    - Corporate trade exchange (CTX) used for corporate-to-corporate payments

- Re-presented check entries (RCK) used to transmit ACH debit entries in place of a paper check after the check has been returned for insufficient or uncollected funds.

16. In an ACH transaction, settlement occurs one or two days after transmission of the payment information to the ACH operator, with the debit and credit occurring simultaneously.

17. Settlement through Fedwire is immediate rather than on a one- or two-day cycle like ACH.

18. A repetitive wire transfer is used when a company makes frequent transfers between the same debit and credit parties. A unique identifier is used to identify each transfer with only the date and dollar amount allowed to be changed. A non-repetitive wire transfer requires that all information for a wire transfer be given when making the wire transfer.

19. Some examples of the types of security procedures that are commonly used are the following:
    - Physical security and limited access at both the company and the bank
    - Passwords and personal identification numbers (PINs) to identify authorized users
    - Test keys or codes to validate wire transfers
    - Repetitive wires to limit where funds can be transferred
    - Dual approval (one person enters the wire and another reviews and releases it)
    - Electronic security methods such as encryption (the scrambling of a message by the sender and the unscrambling of the message by the receiver), message authentication (a digital signature that prevents an unauthorized person from changing a wire) and digital certificates (a third-party service that ties a user's public and private encryption keys together)
    - Security devices or keys to guard against misuse or fraud

20. CHIPS is both a message and settlement system, while S.W.I.F.T. is only a messaging system. S.W.I.F.T. sends payment instructions, while settlement occurs through another means like Fedwire, CHIPS or a correspondent bank account.

21. A daylight overdraft is an intraday exposure that occurs when an account is overdrawn during a business day. Because the Federal Reserve is guarantor of a wire transfer to the receiving bank, it could be forced to make good a wire transfer initiated by a bank that subsequently fails. The Federal Reserve has set a cap on the daylight overdraft allowed for each financial institution to lesson the risk.

CHAPTER 5:
Credit and Accounts Receivable Management

1. The major objectives of credit management are:
   - Establishing and communicating a company's credit policies
   - Establishing terms of sale consistent with overall company objectives
   - Evaluating customer creditworthiness and setting customer credit lines
   - Ensuring prompt and accurate customer billing in conjunction with the customer service or billing departments
   - Creating, preserving and collecting accounts receivable
   - Maintaining up-to-date records of accounts receivable
   - Following up on overdue accounts and initiating collection procedures when necessary

2. A credit policy consists of:
   - Setting credit standards
   - Specifying credit terms
   - Establishing a collection policy

3. The following factors may constrain a company's credit policy:
   - Industry practice and company strategy
   - Contractual obligations
   - Legal issues

4. The expenses involved in trade credit include:
   - Accounts receivable carrying costs
   - Credit department costs
   - Credit evaluation
   - Discounted payments
   - Selling, production and administration costs
   - Collection expenses
   - Bad-debt expense

- Insurance
- Discrepancies in payments

5. A company can use the following external sources to assist in determining the creditworthiness of a credit applicant:
   - Financial statements
   - Trade references
   - Banks or other creditors
   - Agencies

6. The five Cs of credit are:
   - *Character* — Willingness to pay
   - *Capacity* — Ability to pay
   - *Capital* — Financial strength
   - *Collateral* — Protection for the lender
   - *Conditions* — Economic environment

7. Credit scoring is a technique used to estimate creditworthiness of credit applicants based on statistical profiles of prior credit applicants. It involves a four-step process:
   - Differentiating standard and high-risk accounts based on such data as monthly income, outstanding obligations and the employment history of the applicant
   - Weighting the characteristics of those who fit into each category to establish creditworthiness
   - Setting cutoff scores for credit approval and denial
   - Applying further analysis to applicants whose scores fall in between the cutoff points

8. Revolving credit terms involve the granting of credit without requiring specific approval of each transaction, as long as the credit limit is not exceeded and required minimum payments are made on time.

9. Seasonal dating is a special credit term used in industries with highly seasonal sales. Payment is due near the end of the buyer's selling season, although sliding discounts may be offered to encourage early payment.

ANSWERS • CHAPTER 5

10. The formula for calculating the effective cost of not taking a discount is as follows:

$$\text{Annualized Cost of Trade Credit} = \frac{\text{Early Payment Discount}}{(1-\text{Early Payment Discount})} \times \frac{365}{(\text{Net Payment Period}-\text{Discount Payment Period})}$$

Given terms of 3/20, net 60, the cost of not taking the discount (paying the net amount on Day 60, rather than the discounted amount on Day 20) can be calculated as:

$$\text{Cost of Trade Credit} = \frac{.03}{(1-.03)} \times \frac{365}{(60-20)} = 28.22\%$$

11. Companies should monitor individual accounts for the following reasons:
    - There may be errors or delays in the invoicing or payment process.
    - Some customers may intentionally delay payment until follow-up is initiated.
    - A change in financial condition may alter the ability of a customer to make timely payments and may require a curtailment of future credit sales.

    Companies should monitor aggregate accounts receivable for the following reasons:
    - Changes in accounts receivable may impact liquidity and prompt the need for additional financing.
    - A significant change in the level of overall accounts receivable may be a symptom of a change in business that could affect a company's financing needs.
    - Accounts receivable serve as a basis for forecasting the amount and timing of future cash receipts.

12. Days' sales outstanding (DSO) in this question is determined as follows:

$$\text{Average Daily Credit Sales} = \frac{(\$75,000 + \$100,000 + \$90,000)}{90} = \$2,944.44$$

$$\text{DSO} = \frac{\text{Outstanding Accounts Receivable}}{\text{Average Daily Credit Sales}} = \frac{\$125,000.00}{\$2,944.44} = 42.45 \text{ Days}$$

13. A company's collection history will determine its normal accounts receivable balance pattern. Management can evaluate any shifts by comparing current patterns with historical norms. Furthermore, variations in sales patterns do not affect balance patterns, nor do they send misleading signals regarding future cash inflows. Companies can use balance patterns to project accounts receivable levels and collections and to forecast future cash inflows.

14. Factoring is the sale or transfer of title of an accounts receivable to a factoring company. This sale may be done with recourse, where the factor has the right to come back to the seller with any uncollectible accounts or without recourse, where the factor must absorb all losses. The primary advantage is the financing and management of the credit granting function, while the primary disadvantages are the cost and loss of control.

15. Cash application is the process of applying a customer's payment against outstanding invoices. This can be accomplished by either an open item or balance forward system. An open item system is most commonly used in business-to-business sales. Each invoice sent to a customer is recorded in the accounts receivable file. When a payment is received, it is matched with the specific invoices being paid and any payment discrepancies (discounts, allowances, adjustments, etc.) are noted. Balance forward systems are used most often by companies selling goods and services to individual consumers. In a balance forward system, a credit limit is established for each individual and as purchases are made or services are provided, the accounts receivable outstanding increases. When payments are made, the accounts receivable balance is reduced by the amount of the payment.

16. The Robinson-Patman Act is federal legislation that prohibits price discrimination.

17. The Truth in Lending Act is federal legislation that requires disclosure of the true cost of a loan.

18. EBPP or electronic bill presentment and payment, systems allow banks or companies to send electronic statements to their customers and allow for the customers to pay these bills by electronic means. In most cases these applications are Web-based and usable by anyone with Internet access.

ANSWERS • CHAPTER 6

CHAPTER 6:
Collections

1. The major objectives of a collection system are to mobilize funds, provide timely and accurate information, update accounts receivable and support audit trails for both internal and external auditors.

2. Collection float is composed of mail float, processing float and availability float.

3. Availability float is determined by the depository bank's availability schedule.

4. In designing a collection system, a company must take into consideration the following issues:

    - Commonly accepted payment practices
    - The nature of the payments system
    - The nature of its own business
    - Characteristics of the payment instrument used
    - The cost of float and system administration
    - The differences between wholesale and retail businesses

5. Three features that distinguish the U.S. payments system from those of most other countries are:

    - Checks are used in most payments. Large cash transactions are rare.
    - There is a relatively large number of banks and financial institutions. The U.S. financial system is both highly evolved and very competitive.
    - The extent of nationwide branch banking is becoming more common and is expected to be a more significant factor in coming years.

6. Companies may collect through the following methods:

    - Through an over-the-counter/field deposit system
    - By mail payments to the company or to a lockbox
    - Electronically via a wire transfer or through the ACH system

7. Deposit reconciliation services, also called branch consolidation services, may be offered by banks with multiple branches. These services enable deposits from multiple locations to be credited to a single corporate bank account. The use of MICR-encoded deposit tickets allows banks to identify each company deposit location and produce reports on a daily, weekly or monthly basis.

8. The average daily cost of float and the annual cost of float are determined as follows:

    - Average daily float = $2,120,000 / 30 = $70,667
    - Annual cost of float = $70,667 x .07 = $4,947

9. The selection of either a company processing center or a lockbox is a function of the volume of checks processed and the dollar size of the checks. For example, a low volume of checks with large-dollar amounts usually supports the use of a lockbox system.

10. A lockbox system reduces mail, processing and availability float; provides economies of scale in processing; and establishes an audit trail outside the company.

11. Modern telecommunications and data transmission systems linked to PCs, along with the Internet, have transformed the way payments are remitted, transfers made and financial information disseminated. Some of the recent developments are:

    - Home banking
    - Telephone initiation
    - Personal computers
    - Internet
    - Electronic bill presentment and payment (EBPP)

12. A wholesale lockbox is used primarily for corporate-to-corporate payments where large-dollar remittances are involved. A retail lockbox is used for large-volume, small-dollar remittance payments with scannable documents, such as consumer payments.

13. The determination of the net benefit of the lockbox is as follows:

Average float with lockbox = $1,010,000 / 30	= $ 33,667
Annual cost of float with lockbox = $33,667 x .07	= 2,357
Float savings with lockbox = $4,947 – 2,357	= 2,590
Fixed lockbox cost	= (1,000)
Variable lockbox cost = (6,000 x .30)	= (1,800)
Savings of internal processing cost = (6,000 x .20)	= 1,200
Net benefit of lockbox	= $ 990

    - A lockbox is profitable in this situation.

14. An over-the-counter/field deposit system is a collection system in which funds are received and deposited by local operating units of the company such as division offices or retail stores.

15. A preauthorized debit involves the advance approval of a payor for the payee to transfer funds from the payor's account. An example of this application is the automatic withdrawal of insurance premiums from a policyholder's account.

16. In an endpoint analysis, all checks drawn on banks in selected cities are broken down by days of float. It is an effective way to measure and compare different banks' availability schedules.

17. Net settlement systems benefit companies in the same industry that buy and sell from each other on a regular basis by requiring only periodic transfers of the net amount due to other companies.

18. Image technology is used to facilitate processing of both wholesale and retail payments. This technology allows paper documents to be scanned, converted to a digital image and stored for subsequent handling and processing. The documents scanned can be both checks and remittance advices. Potential benefits of applying image technology to the remittance processing function include reduced overall processing costs, increased productivity, improved accuracy and the ability to capture data for automated posting to accounts receivable.

19. The potential benefits of ACH B2B payments for the payee include reduced float, lowered cost and improved cash flow forecasting. For the payee, the disadvantages include the need for trading partner negotiation, float adjustments, setup costs and the reluctance of the payor to allow debits for payment.

20. The major types of retail collection systems include credit cards, debit cards, ATM networks, telephone banking, bill paying services, home banking, agents and smart cards.

CHAPTER 7:
Cash Concentration

1. The objectives of a cash concentration system include:
   - Simplifying cash management
   - Improving control of funds
   - Pooling funds for investment or debt reduction
   - Minimizing excess balances
   - Reducing transfer expenses

2. Pooling funds is a valuable objective of cash concentration because it permits a company to buy larger blocks of short-term securities, which tend to earn higher yields. Alternatively, pooled funds can be used to reduce debt or take advantage of supplier discount opportunities.

3. Among a company's concentration system considerations are its collection system, disbursement system, funds transfer alternatives and banking network.

4. Over-the-counter/field banking systems are characterized by:
   - Multiple collection points
   - Multiple banks
   - Limited provision of cash management services
   - Deposit availability of zero to one day (cash and local checks)

5. Lockbox cash concentration systems generally have the following characteristics:
   - Limited collection points
   - Use of regional and money center banks and third-party processors
   - Provision of treasury services such as daily reporting of transaction details and ledger and collected balances, movement of funds through wire transfer or ACH and other treasury management services
   - Deposit availability of one to two days with some checks drawn on non-local endpoints

6. EDT stands for electronic depository transfer, which is an ACH transaction used to concentrate funds.

7. Wire transfers may also be used for concentration. They are generally used when the amounts are large enough to justify their cost.

ANSWERS • CHAPTER 7

8. The major cost components of a cash concentration system are excess balances in the company's banks, costs to transfer funds and the administrative costs of operating the concentration system.

9. Excess balances may arise through delays in deposit reporting, clearing or the initiation of transfers.

10. Anticipation is the initiation of a transfer before funds become available at the deposit bank. Availability anticipation initiates the transfers on the basis of actual deposit information, while deposit anticipation is done on the basis of unreported, expected deposits.

11. Threshold concentration allows bank balances to build to a predetermined level and then a transfer is initiated to the concentration bank.

12. In a deposit reconciliation service, a company deposits funds from multiple locations to its regional or central concentration account. MICR-encoded deposit tickets identify each location and enable a bank to produce daily, weekly or monthly deposit reports by location. This service reduces the number of bank accounts that must be maintained and thus the number of transfers, possibly decreasing concentration system costs.

13. The minimum wire transfer required to break even is determined as follows:

$$\text{Minimum Transfer} = \frac{\text{Wire Cost} - \text{EDT Cost}}{\text{Days Accelerated} \times \dfrac{\text{Opportunity Cost}}{365 \text{ Days}}}$$

$$= \frac{\$22.00 - \$1.00}{1 \text{ Day} \times \dfrac{.08}{365 \text{ Days}}} = \$95,813$$

14. Fraud may be prevented by having different reports prepared by different people, by conducting surprise audits, by requiring daily reporting and by instructing banks to allow no overdrafts.

CHAPTER 8:
Accounts Payable and Disbursements

1. The five major objectives of a disbursement system are:

    - Cost reduction
    - Disbursement float management
    - Information access
    - Fraud prevention
    - Relationship maintenance

2. The primary responsibility of the accounts payable function is to verify incoming invoices and voucher them for payment. This process generally involves the traditional "three-way match," where the invoice is matched to both an approved purchase order and receiving information. This ensures that the items being billed to the company were indeed authorized for purchase from an approved vendor and that they were received in satisfactory condition. Once this approval process is complete, the invoice can be vouchered for payment. In a typical business-to-business environment, multiple invoices are often combined into a single payment voucher. Once the payments have been vouchered, they are typically forwarded to the cash manager or disbursements area where the checks or electronic payments are generated.

3. Disbursement systems may be centralized, decentralized or a combination of both. In a centralized system check writing and account reconciliation are controlled from headquarters, while in a decentralized system checks are drawn on a local bank and account reconciliation is performed at the local level. It is also possible for check issuance and account reconciliation to be performed at the local level but drawn on a centralized disbursement account.

4. Disbursement float is composed of mail float, processing float and clearing float.

5. Control and fraud prevention measures include the following:

    - Developing and implementing written policies and procedures for the creation and distribution of disbursement checks
    - Separating functional authority for collection and disbursement of funds
    - Separating expense approval, check-signing authority and account reconciliation responsibilities
    - Using safety paper and watermarks that are difficult to reproduce on check stock
    - Using reputable printing companies

- Storing checks and signature plates in separate secure areas with controlled access

- Using printing processes that do not require preprinted check stock (laser printing of checks and MICR lines)

- Using positive pay, a service that matches check serial numbers and dollar amounts against the company's issue file to determine the checks to be paid

- Setting a specific amount limit on checks issued from each type of account; checks issued above this limit are returned to the depositor as unauthorized

- Increasing the use of electronic payment methods and utilizing appropriate security features

- Using an electronic payment authorization service (similar to positive pay for checks) to protect against fraudulent ACH debits

6. Disbursement networks are systems that establish check mailing locations and drawee banks based on disbursement studies. They are designed to optimize disbursement float, but are not widely used. The cost and control benefits of making disbursements from just one or two banks often outweigh the float benefits of using a greater number of banks.

7. There are two critical areas of interface between cash management and accounts payable related to disbursements. The first is the communication from accounts payable regarding the invoices vouchered for payment, while the second is the communication from cash management back to accounts payable regarding the reconciled payments. Companies with integrated ERP or accounting systems that include treasury management modules are typically able to easily integrate these functions. Many companies, however, either use separate systems for disbursement management or utilize bank-provided treasury information software that may not easily interface with the accounts payable ledger. In these cases, customized "patches" or middleware (in a client-server environment) will be required to facilitate the transfer of information between applications.

8. A zero balance account is an account on which a company writes checks, even though the balance in the account is maintained at zero. The checks are covered by a transfer of funds from the company's master account in that bank.

9. Controlled disbursement is a bank service that provides notification of the dollar amount of checks that will clear against the controlled disbursement account that day. This information is usually available by early or mid-morning. The disbursement bank must receive its final cash letter of the day from the local Fed early in the morning so that the checks can be sorted and the company notified of its funding requirement. Payor bank services are often used to aid in this process.

10. EFTPS is the primary method for collecting and accounting for taxes withheld by employers from individuals' salaries and wages, as well as corporate business and

excise taxes. Most companies have been mandated to make these deposits electronically.

11. Payor bank services is an information service of the Fed that electronically notifies controlled disbursement banks early in the morning of all checks that will be physically presented later that day.

12. A controlled disbursement bank should be evaluated on the following criteria:
    - Timeliness of reporting of disbursement banks
    - Processing accuracy
    - Volume capacity
    - Reporting detail and reconciliation services
    - Price
    - Customer service support

13. Multiple drawee checks, also known as payable-if-desired (PID) checks, are checks that can be presented for payment at a bank other than the drawee bank. Both bank names appear on the check.

14. Positive pay is a service used for fraud control. The company transmits a file of checks issued to its bank. The bank matches serial numbers and dollar amounts and pays only those checks that match.

15. In a partial reconciliation service, a bank lists all checks paid in numerical order by check serial number or in chronological order by date paid. For each item, the paid report generally shows the check serial number, dollar amount and date paid. The listing is available as a paper report, on CD-ROM and/or via electronic form. With a full reconciliation service, a company supplies an electronic file of checks issued to its bank and the bank matches checks paid against the file. The bank supplies a listing, as a paper report and/or in an electronic format, of checks paid and outstanding in check serial number order.

16. There are two situations in which a bank has credit exposure. These are:
    - With delayed funding, there is risk that an ACH debit may be returned by the bank on which it is drawn. By the time the returned debit reaches the disbursement bank, it may be too late to return any disbursement checks being funded by the ACH debit. The disbursement bank is owed funds and becomes a creditor of the company.
    - With the use of an affiliated bank for disbursing with funding through the parent bank, there is no problem if the affiliate bank is funded directly on a same-day basis by a wire transfer. However, if the company funds the parent bank and the parent bank automatically funds the affiliate with immediate funds, there is a potential overdraft problem at the parent bank. Since the

affiliate bank does not have an overdrawn account, it cannot legally refuse to pay the checks even though there may be an overdraft at the parent bank, unless this option is provided for in the service agreement.

17. The two basic approaches to managing an integrated or comprehensive accounts payable service are:

    - A company sends a single data file to a third-party service provider containing a list of all its payments to be made. The file contains information on when to issue a disbursement and to whom, as well as instructions on the payment method to be used (check, wire or ACH).

    - Alternatively, the third-party provider maintains a database of a company's payees that includes detailed information such as preferred payment methods, specific remittance information and receiving financial institutions. The database is periodically updated as new payees are added or an existing payee's remittance profile changes (for example, if a payee switches to ACH instead of check for its standard payment type). In such cases, as a company makes a disbursement, it sends to the third party only limited payment information.

18. Purchasing cards are charge cards used by a company for the small-dollar purchase of supplies, inventory, equipment and service contracts. Advantages of a purchasing card include:

    - Cost savings
    - Improved control
    - Better vendor relations
    - Improved reporting

19. Image technology is a major component of many disbursement services. Both the front and the back of a check may be captured and converted into digital information using optical scanning. Check images (all of them or selected ones) may be transmitted to a company's computer and stored there or sent to a fax machine. The check images may also be stored in a bank database, which a company can access to view or retrieve the images. Any of these methods allows a company faster access to check information. Imaging services are particularly useful in conjunction with positive pay services.

20. The rapid expansion of Internet services over the past few years has resulted in a wide variety of accounts payable and disbursement applications on the Web for companies of all sizes. Some of these services are offered as part of a total accounting or ERP package or as stand-alone services. For larger companies trying to increase their level of automation of financial functions, the Web offers a mechanism for their smaller trading partners to send invoices via a Web page, which can then be paid via an ACH transaction with remittance information returned via the Internet.

CHAPTER 9:
Electronic Commerce

1. The Internet is a worldwide collection of many computers, communications switches and computer networks linked together to form a backbone of communications pathways. An intranet is an internal network (for use within a company) that utilizes browser technology to provide data and applications for users. It uses the open standards of the Internet rather than proprietary software for communication among computers. An extranet is an external network (for use outside a company with its trading partners and/or customers) that utilizes browser technology to provide data and access to applications. In most cases, companies will place some type of security "firewall" between this system and their internal applications.

2. E-commerce is generally described as either business-to-consumer (B2C) or business-to-business (B2B).

3. EFT involves a value transfer and typically only occurs between financial institutions. FEDI is any EDI transaction set that either results in a value transfer (instructions to send funds via wire, ACH, etc.) or results from a value transfer (bank notifies payee that funds have been received, i.e., electronic transmission of lockbox information).

4. Web-based e-commerce utilizes the Internet and Web technology to link business applications between trading partners. The primary difference between this type of commerce and Web-EDI is that the data transfer is in a non-EDI format. The format used may be proprietary between two users or some more general standard used within an industry. In Web-EDI, the Web is used by large EDI hubs to bring smaller trading partners into the EDI world. The transaction is Web-based for smaller trading partners, who access a Web site to either receive information or create business documents using fill-in forms. The large hub can still utilize standard EDI transaction sets to send to or receive information from the smaller trading partners. This approach is useful for low transaction volumes within limited trading communities.

5. The benefits of e-commerce are as follows:
   - Improved productivity
   - Reduced cycle time
   - Lower error rates
   - Improved cash forecasting
   - Improved communication capabilities

Answers • Chapter 9

6. EDI is a traditional form of e-commerce that is based on four primary infrastructure components:

    - EDI standard formats
    - EDI software
    - Communication networks and standards
    - Computer hardware

7. The four types of EDI standards are: 1) ASC X12 standards, 2) industry modifications of ASC X12 standards, 3) UN/EDIFACT standards and 4) Web-based EDI standards.

    - *ASC X12 Standards* — The Accredited Standards Committee (ASC) of the American National Standards Institute (ANSI) is the coordinating body that develops cross-industry EDI standards in North America. The development of the current U.S. standards for EDI began in 1968 with efforts of the transportation industry to establish standards for communications between and within railroads, ocean carriers, air carriers and motor carriers. Based on this early work, the grocery and retail industries also developed EDI standards. In 1979, ASC X12 was formed to develop general EDI standards that could be used in a variety of industries.

    - *Industry Modification of ASC X12 Standards* — Several industries (such as the automotive, chemical, communications and health care industries) have adopted ASC X12 standards. Others have adopted subsets of X12 standards. This practice is expected to continue in other industries with common requirements.

    - *UN/EDIFACT Standards* — Many countries have become involved in developing EDI standards. This has led to the development of United Nations EDI for Administration, Commerce and Transportation (UN/EDIFACT) rules, a set of internationally agreed-upon standards, directories and guidelines for the electronic interchange of structured data that relates to trade in goods and services between independent computerized information systems. UN/EDIFACT standards are widely used in Europe and some Asian countries.

    - *Web-Based EDI Standards* — Web-based EDI Internet sites are being developed in XML (eXtensible Markup Language). Standard EDI transaction sets are converted either into or from Web-based forms for transferring information between large EDI hubs and smaller trading partners.

8. Description of ASC X12 transaction sets:

    - *820 Payment Order/Remittance Advice* — This transaction set has two purposes. It initiates a money transfer to a payee and/or provides the payee with information describing the purpose of the associated payment. The 820, which allows multiple invoices to be paid in a single payment, also includes the amount of discounts and other payment adjustments.

- *821 Financial Information Reporting* — This transaction set facilitates bank-to-corporate account reporting. It provides for the reporting of multiple levels of financial information, including balances, transaction summaries and individual transactions. It can be used for balance and transaction reporting, account reconciliation and bank account statements.

- *823 Lockbox Information* — This transaction set conveys lockbox check data including remittance detail (such as payors, invoices and amounts being paid), deposit totals and available funds.

- *835 Health Care Claim Payment/Advice* — The health care industry uses this transaction set to transmit medical claim payment and remittance information.

9. All three formats are used to initiate a transfer of value between two parties and contain basic information on payor, payee and their respective bank accounts. The difference between them is in the amount and format of additional information that accompanies the payment. The CCD format is primarily just an electronic check that contains only limited space for ancillary payment information. It is used for concentration of funds within a company. The CCD+ format combines the CCD format with a 94-character addenda record, 80 characters of which can be used to specify the invoice being paid or give other reference information necessary for application of the payment. The TXP format is a modification of the CCD+ format designed for the electronic payment of taxes to state and federal governments.

10. The RCK format is utilized to transmit ACH debit entries in place of a paper check after the paper check has been returned for insufficient or uncollected funds. The current general requirements are that the item be less than $2,500 and drawn on a consumer account. Originators of re-presented check entries must provide notice to the check writer, prior to receiving an item to which the re-presented check entry relates, informing the check writer that his returned check may be collected electronically if the check is returned for insufficient or uncollected funds. After the *first* return of a paper item, the receiver of the check may transmit a re-presented check entry no more than twice. If the RCK is not sent until after the *second* return of a paper item, then it may be used only once.

11. The key issue in using CCD+ and CTX formats for B2B payments is whether to keep the payment and remittance information together or to separate them. While using CCD+ and CTX formats keeps the "dollars and data" together, many smaller banks receiving these formats cannot process the remittance information and pass it along to their customer (the payee). Payors that follow the separate approach send payments through the ACH system, while the remittance information moves through a VAN or the Internet. The advantages of this approach are that the payment and remittance advice can be sent to almost any payee, regardless of the ability of the payee's bank to process the remittance information. The problem with the separate approach is that the payment and remittance information must be reassociated or matched up by the payee so they can complete their payment application process.

12. A VAN is a communication intermediary that provides various services to the users of e-commerce. VANs resolve interface problems between two companies that have different computer systems, different format needs and different protocols. Thus, VANs make it easier for companies to implement EDI and to add new EDI trading partners. VANs offer many services to their customers, including the following:

    - Communications capacity
    - Mailboxing
    - Protocol conversion
    - Standards conversion
    - Gateway to other VANs or banks
    - Implementation assistance
    - Security services

13. The terms are defined as follows:

    - *ISP* — Internet Service Provider: This is a communications intermediary that provides Internet service to individuals and small businesses, typically over telephone lines or cable.

    - *FTP* — File Transfer Protocol: This is a standard Internet protocol that is the simplest way to exchange files between computers on the Internet.

    - *HTTP* — Hypertext Transfer Protocol: This is a set of rules for exchanging files (text, graphic images, sound video and other multimedia files) on the Web.

    - *URL* — Uniform Resource Locator: This is an address format utilized on the Web. For example, a typical Web address might be as follows: *http//www.afponline.org/search/index.html*

    - *HTML* — Hypertext Markup Language: This is the language used to create Web pages on the Internet and other browser-based delivery formats. The information, text and graphic content can be presented in a consistent format, independent of the browser used to view the data.

    - *XML* — eXtensible Markup Language: This is an extension of HTML, which allows for content as well as structure to be defined. In essence, while HTML provides a consistent format for display of the information, XML adds "tags" to the information that define specifically what the information is. For example, HTML format will make sure that the price of an item on the Web page will appear on a certain place on the page and in a specific font, size and color; XML will further define the field as the price of a specific item. Once a data element has been clearly identified, it is easy to transfer this information from the Web page to an application within the company.

14. The issues involved in the use of XML are as follows:
    - XML is a highly variable open standard. Users must agree on a standard format for information exchange in order to ensure proper transfer to their respective applications.
    - XML adds a great deal of overhead in the form of additional addenda records to a particular message.
    - XML messages include a URL that defines the tags to be used in the message.
    - XML can be viewed as HTML in advanced browsers and is also human readable.
    - There are tools being developed for importing data from an XML message into business application systems.
    - ASC X12 has created an XML task group to address the development of standards in the use of XML in a business-to-business environment.

15. Security is the assurance that transactions are safe from intrusion, detection and modification. There are four key factors that security must provide:
    - *Privacy* — This is the assurance that the message is readable only to the intended recipient and that data will not be used for unintended purposes.
    - *Authentication* — This is the ability to know with a reasonable amount of certainty who sent or received a message.
    - *Integrity* — This is the ability to ensure that a message was not modified in transit, which is especially important for financial transactions.
    - *Non-Repudiation* — This is the inability of the sender or receiver of a message to deny having sent or received that message.

16. A digital signature is an encoded message based on the sender's secret private key. The receiver can identify its source using the sender's public key. As long as the private key is never shared with anyone, it is impossible for others to forge a digital signature. A digital signature is tied to the document as well as to the signer and the signer's digital signature will be different for each document signed.

17. Paid-on-production is the process by which a payment record is created for goods and/or services when they are used rather than when they are shipped or delivered. It is similar to consignment sales in retail, but is based on usage within a manufacturing environment. Typically there is only one supplier and title to the product transfers when the product is used in the manufacturing process rather than at the receiving dock as in ERS. Because of legal concerns relating to liability, potential bankruptcy and use of inventory assets for supporting loans, it is important to determine exactly when and where title to the inventory transfers from the supplier to the manufacturer.

CHAPTER 10:
Information and Technology Management

1. Treasury must collect and manage a wide range of information flows:
    - Daily banking information (balances, clearings, payments, etc.)
    - Working capital
    - Balance sheet management
    - Risk management (financial, credit risk, operational risk)
    - Capital markets
    - Asset management
    - Financial reporting
    - Capital budgeting
    - Pension administration
    - Bank and financial service provider (FSP) account administration

2. The objectives of information management are as follows:
    - Determining cash requirements
    - Tracking activity
    - Identifying opportunities
    - Updating forecasts
    - Updating management information

3. The general benefits of treasury information management include:
    - Consistent companywide treasury services
    - Integration of treasury with the rest of the company
    - Implementation of scalable, uniform technologies
    - Provision of alternatives to outsourcing

4. The specific benefits or treasury information management for global companies include:
    - Centralization of global transaction processing
    - Global or regional pooling
    - Global payment and netting systems
    - Unifying global treasury systems by e-banking

5. Treasury acts as a clearing house for financial information. The cash manager is specifically responsible for:
   - Compiling information from a wide range of internal and external sources
   - Sorting, storing and analyzing this information
   - Reporting information to management

6. The classes of cash management internal data include:
   - *Sales Summary Reports* — Information on actual and projected weekly or monthly sales
   - *Purchasing Summary Reports* — Information on actual and projected weekly or monthly purchases
   - *Cash Receipts and Disbursements* — Information on actual and anticipated collections and disbursements
   - *Aging Schedule* — Information on the aggregate status of accounts receivable, as well as information on large individual collection items that are outstanding
   - *Investment Schedules* — Information on the sale, purchase and maturity of short-term investments
   - *Debt Repayment Schedules* — Information on the issuance and repayment of short-term borrowings along with related interest payments

7. Prior day information used by cash managers includes:
   - Balance and transaction activity
   - Target balance activity
   - Investment and borrowing activity
   - International transaction activity
   - Custody activity
   - Check inquiry
   - Stop payment activity
   - Account analysis

8. Current day information used by cash managers includes:
   - Lockbox deposits and remittance detail
   - Controlled disbursement
   - Cash concentration reports

- Wire transfers
- ACH transactions
- Investments
- Money market and FX rates
- Return items
- Positive pay exception items

9. Multibank reporting is where companies that have two or more banks establish an arrangement in which one of the company's financial institutions or a third-party reporting service gathers and consolidates the account balances and transaction activity from each of the company's financial institutions. This arrangement is commonly referred to as data exchange. Banks are also increasingly offering this kind of information via the Internet.

10. The basic choices in linking a treasury system to an FSP are proprietary software, host-to-host link or the Internet. Proprietary software is the most common mechanism used today to link to FSPs. The user makes a direct connection to a bank's computer to access account information and to give a variety of banking instructions. In a host-to-host link, the company and FSP computers are linked directly via a dedicated two-way link. This is generally expensive to set up and maintain, but can handle high volumes of data in an automated fashion. Many FSPs are using the Internet as a cost-effective communication format for exchange of data. Much of the Internet communication is in the form of thin-client solutions, where the application software resides at a central server site, most often at the FSP.

11. A treasury workstation (cash management software) is typically a PC or client/server that has software that gathers information from both internal and external sources, then compiles the data for purposes of analysis and decision making. A treasury workstation can either be stand-alone or part of a company network. In addition to automating a number of manual tasks, treasury workstations enable cash managers to prepare and distribute financial information in a variety of customized spreadsheets and management reports. Treasury workstation software can either be purchased from a vendor or developed in-house.

12. Treasury workstations generally have three primary attributes: modularity, data integration and database management.

13. Examples of the types of transactions that cash managers can initiate include:
    - Wire transfers
    - ACH debits and credits
    - Stop payments

- Letters of credit
- Investment purchases and sales
- Loan drawdowns and repayments
- Positive pay administration
- FX transactions

14. Treasury software is generally classified as one of the following:
    - Treasury workstations
    - Spreadsheets
    - Templates
    - Analytical tools
    - Deal capture and support
    - Middleware

15. The basic choices in treasury management systems include the following:
    - *Treasury Modules of ERP Software* — Many of the large ERP software providers offer treasury modules for their systems. These ERP systems provide value to companies that implement them throughout all departments by tying information technology to corporate strategy and communicating management information on a standardized and consistent basis. Generally, however, the currently available treasury modules do not have the same level of functionality as stand-alone offerings. The advantage of ERP treasury software is that it makes the task of interfacing to other areas of the company such as accounts receivable and accounts payable much more seamless.
    - *Stand-Alone Treasury Systems* — There are a wide range of stand-alone treasury management products available for companies of all sizes. The treasury workstations and other cash management software offered by FSPs fit into this category, as well as sophisticated (and expensive) treasury management systems offered by non-FSP third parties. These systems are often tailored to specific needs of treasury departments offering support for cash management, debt/investment and risk management activities. Most of the larger systems also provide access to multibank reporting and interfaces to major ERP systems. The more sophisticated of these systems also address very treasury-specific issues such as financial risk management and support for FAS 133, which the typical ERP system does not address.
    - *Customized Treasury Systems* — Given the unique needs of some companies, it may be advantageous for such a company to develop its own customized treasury system. This solution is often best for treasury departments that have special needs (multicurrency environment, foreign tax and regulatory

constraints, widely dispersed operations, etc.) that may not be addressed by off-the-shelf software. Another rationale for a customized system is where treasury has advanced models or analysis approaches that it regards as strategic.

16. The benefits of implementing treasury management systems may include:
    - Improved productivity
    - Expedited data gathering, compilation and analysis
    - Increased forecasting accuracy
    - Reduced borrowing expenses
    - Improved short-term investment returns
    - Improved management reporting

17. The costs of implementing treasury management systems may include:
    - Hardware and software selection, purchase and installation
    - Startup and personnel training expenses
    - Administration, maintenance and overhead
    - Telecommunications charges
    - Transaction service charges
    - System security expenses

18. The three most common types of risks treasury management systems involve are data loss, unauthorized user access and computer viruses.

19. Companies need to take steps to prevent either authorized or unauthorized users from executing fraudulent transactions. Companies can safeguard the security of treasury systems by:
    - Creating a security officer/system administrator
    - Developing written policies and procedures
    - Conducting periodic system tests/audits
    - Establishing physical security
    - Instituting basic access requirements
    - Establishing different levels of user access
    - Requiring backup storage
    - Instituting computer virus protection methods
    - Using electronic security

20. Financial Accounting Standard 133 (FAS 133) requires that all derivatives be marked-to-market on the balance sheet. Marking-to-market means that the derivatives must be valued as of the date of the balance sheet. Given the highly volatile nature of derivatives, this means that the value of the derivative holdings may vary significantly from period to period. This is a significant difference from the off-balance-sheet approach of current practice. From a treasury manager's perspective, this requires substantial record keeping and computation to determine the value of their derivative-based hedges at any point in time. The measurement and monitoring of hedge effectiveness will be a critical part of treasury management reporting in the future and should be a consideration in evaluating treasury management systems.

21. The benefits of using the Internet in treasury include:
    - Easy access to services and applications
    - Easier implementation and version control
    - Easy to use
    - Less expensive communications

22. The challenges of using the Internet in treasury are security issues and identity problems.

CHAPTER 11:
Forecasting Cash Flows

1. The objectives of cash forecasting are:
    - Liquidity management
    - Financial control
    - Meeting strategic objectives
    - Capital budgeting
    - Managing costs
    - Managing currency exposure

2. The steps in the forecasting process include the following:
    - Determine the forecast horizons.
    - Understand the company's cash flow cycle.
    - Divide the cash flows into their major components.
    - Categorize the cash flows by their degree of certainty.
    - Identify and organize the data to be used in the forecast.
    - Select a forecast method and validate the forecast.

3. Short-term forecasts can be prepared using either the receipts and disbursements method or the distribution method.

4. A pro forma statement is prepared using the percentage-of-sales method. This presumes the next financial statement period will retain the same relationship between sales and other income statement and balance sheet items as it did in the prior period and also recognizes other known cash flows that will occur during the period.

5. The primary types of time series forecasting are simple moving average and exponential smoothing.

6. The moving average forecast is: ($100 + $150 + $250 + $210) / 4 = $177.5.

7. Exponential smoothing is a variation on the simple moving average that weights each observation with more recent observations given heavier weights. This enables trends and seasonality to be captured in the forecast.

8. The steps in selecting a forecasting method are as follows:

    - Establish data relationships.
    - Select a method.
    - Test and validate the relationship.

9. The three types of forecast validation are in-sample validation, out-of-sample validation and ongoing validation.

10. Regression analysis is a statistical technique that systematically identifies the relationship between a variable to be predicted (the dependent variable) and other data that may be available (explanatory or independent variables).

11. A distribution forecast provides estimates of cash flows on a daily basis over a specified interval based on historical patterns. It is particularly appropriate for short-term forecasts. The distribution percentages may be calculated by using either a simple average of past cash flows related to a particular category of disbursements or by using a regression analysis of the past data to determine those percentages.

12. Exponential smoothing is a variation of a simple moving average. The exponential smoothing technique uses the forecast for the current period, the most recent actual value and a user-determined value known as the smoothing constant. This smoothing constant is typically designated as "α" (referred to as alpha) and may range between 0 and 1. Setting α closer to 1 will result in more weight being placed on the most recent actual value and correspondingly less weight on the forecast value for the current period, resulting in less smoothing of the series.

CHAPTER 12:
Investing

1. A firm has a short-term investment portfolio in order to hold temporary surplus funds, maintain a liquidity reserve and generate income with an acceptable degree of risk.

2. A company's investment policy is influenced by:
   - Purpose and objectives for short-term investments
   - Maturity and segmentation
   - Tax status of the company
   - Staffing
   - Legal or internal restrictions
   - Financial reporting requirements

3. The development, implementation and periodic review of investment guidelines are critical factors in the management of short-term investments and are generally determined by the board of directors. The important considerations are acceptable instruments, diversification, acceptable dealers/issuers, investment authority and custody requirements.

4. A company will examine the time to maturity, credit quality and marketability of a financial instrument in order to determine its fit with the company's short-term investment portfolio.

5. Financial markets may be divided into long-term or capital markets, with instruments that mature in more than one year and the money market, which consists of short-term debt instruments maturing in one year or less.

6. In a book entry transaction, the physical securities do not move when traded. Treasury securities, for example, remain in a vault at the Federal Reserve Bank of New York and book entries are made when ownership changes.

7. The U.S. Treasury issues T-bills with maturities of three months to one year, T-notes with maturities from two to 10 years and T-bonds with maturities of 10 to 30 years.

8. Federal agency securities are debt instruments issued by agencies with some degree of backing by the U.S. government. Agencies act as financial intermediaries in certain credit markets. For example, the Federal National Mortgage Association (Fannie Mae) helps provide liquidity to the mortgage market.

9. Municipal securities are classified as general obligation securities, certificates of participation or revenue securities. General obligation securities are backed by the taxing power of the issuing entity, certificates of participation are securities used by municipal issuers to finance certain equipment purchases and capital projects and revenue securities pay their principal and interest from proceeds of a specific project.

10. The income from municipal obligations is exempt from federal income tax and is often exempt from taxes in the state in which they are issued.

11. Eurodollar CDs are U.S. dollar-denominated certificates of deposit issued by banks, including branches of U.S. banks, outside the United States.

12. Banker's acceptances are short-term obligations of a bank created in financing an international or domestic trade transaction.

13. Repo is an abbreviation for a repurchase agreement, which is a transaction between a securities dealer and an investor in which the dealer sells securities to the investor with an agreement to repurchase them at a specific time and price to produce a predetermined yield to the investor.

14. Commercial paper is an unsecured promissory note that matures in 270 days or less.

15. Money market preferred stock is preferred stock in which the dividend rate is adjusted every 49 days on the basis of current Treasury yields.

16. Yield is influenced by:
    - *Marketability* — Securities without an active secondary market tend to have higher yields.
    - *Default Risk* — The lower the credit rating of the instrument, the higher its yield.
    - *Price Risk* — A reduction in a security's price increases its yield; normally the shorter the time to maturity, the lower the yield.
    - *Re-Investment Risk* — Securities that have interim cash flows, especially unexpected ones such as with MBSs, run the risk that these cash flows will have to be re-invested at a lower than anticipated rate.
    - *Tax Status* — Tax-exempt securities, like municipal securities, will have a lower pre-tax yield than a taxable instrument of similar risk.

17. An inverted yield curve means that yields on long-term securities are not as high as those of short-term securities. This is due to investor expectations of falling interest rates.

18. The purchase price of a 182-day, $100,000 T-bill sold at a 4.53 percent discount rate is calculated as follows:

$$\text{Dollar Discount} = (\text{Discount Rate} \times \text{Face Value}) \times \frac{\text{Days to Maturity}}{360}$$

$$= (.0453 \times \$100,000) \times \frac{182}{360} = \$2,290.17$$

$$\text{Purchase Price} = \text{Face Value} - \text{Dollar Discount}$$

$$= \$100,000 - \$2,290.17 = \$97,709.83$$

19. The bond equivalent yield of the T-bill in Question 18 is calculated as follows:

$$\text{Bond Equivalent Yield (BEY)} = \frac{\text{Dollar Discount}}{\text{Purchase Price}} \times \frac{365}{\text{Days to Maturity}}$$

$$= \frac{\$2,290.17}{\$97,709.83} \times \frac{365}{182} = 4.70\%$$

20. Banks provide overnight sweep accounts, which automatically transfer excess balances into an interest-earning account.

21. The basic investment strategies are as follows:
    - Replicate an index or market
    - Outsource short-term investment management
    - Match maturities to funds needs
    - Ride the yield curve
    - Dividend capture
    - Hedge short-term investments

CHAPTER 13:
Borrowing

1. The objectives of a company's borrowing program include:

    - Maintaining availability of credit
    - Minimizing the cost of funds
    - Minimizing risk
    - Maintaining flexibility

2. Venture capital is provided to help new, smaller companies grow quickly and develop new products or markets. In return for this venture capital, the providers are typically granted a significant equity position in the firm. The venture capitalist may also provide managerial or consulting expertise to new company. Due to the low success rate of these types of endeavors, the risks and costs of venture capital are usually quite high.

3. The London Interbank Offered Rate (LIBOR) is set on a daily basis in London and is the borrowing/lending rate used between multinational banks. It is also the most commonly used base rate for short-term borrowing.

4. Credit support or enhancement is a process in which a bank or an insurance company guarantees the debt obligation of the borrower using an indemnity bond or letter of credit. The borrower's debt is traded at a level that reflects the credit rating of the guarantor.

5. A committed line of credit usually involves a formal loan agreement and obligates the bank to provide funding up to the established credit limit, provided the agreement is not in default.

6. The effective annual borrowing rate (interest cost) of the loan can be determined as follows:

$$\text{Effective Annual Borrowing Rate} = \frac{(.07 \times \$200{,}000) + (.0025 \times \$300{,}000)}{\$200{,}000} \times \frac{365}{365}$$

$$= \frac{\$14{,}000 + \$750}{\$200{,}000} \times (1) = 7.38\%$$

7. Some commercial paper issuers have lines of credit to be used if market conditions are not conducive to issuing commercial paper.

8. The effective annual interest cost of issuing the commercial paper can be determined as follows:

$$\text{Usable Funds} = \text{Face Value} \times \left(1 - \left(\text{Discount Rate} \times \frac{\text{Days to Maturity}}{360}\right)\right)$$

$$= \$1{,}000{,}000 \times \left(1 - \left(.06 \times \frac{60}{360}\right)\right) = \$990{,}000$$

Interest Cost = Face Value − Usable Funds = $1,000,000 − $990,000 = $10,000

$$\text{Pro-Rated Dealer Cost} = (\text{Annual Dealer Charge} \times \text{Face Value}) \times \left(\frac{\text{Days to Maturity}}{360}\right)$$

$$= (.0025 \times \$1{,}000{,}000) \times \left(\frac{60}{360}\right) = \$417$$

Total Issue Costs = Interest Cost + Pro-Rated Dealer Cost = $10,000 + $417 = $10,417

$$\text{Effective Annual Cost of Issue} = \left(\frac{\text{Total Issue Costs}}{\text{Usable Funds}}\right) \times \left(\frac{365}{\text{Days to Maturity}}\right)$$

$$= \left(\frac{\$10{,}417}{\$990{,}000}\right) \times \left(\frac{365}{60}\right) = 6.40\%$$

9. A loan participation is an arrangement whereby a bank purchases an interest in another lender's credit facility. The participant does not have a separate note and has only an indirect relationship with the borrower.

10. An asset suitable for securitization should have a predictable, steady cash flow and a low level of historical loss experience.

11. A bond indenture is the formal agreement among all parties to a bond issue defining the details of the issue, such as the collateral, if any and the duties of the trustee.

12. A leasing arrangement can be structured as either on- or off-balance-sheet. On-balance-sheet is referred to as a capital lease; off-balance-sheet is referred to as an operating lease. Accounting and tax issues must be evaluated to determine a lease's proper classification.

13. A sinking fund is used to ensure that adequate funds are available to pay a bond issue at its maturity. Periodic payments are accumulated in a separate custodial account that is used to redeem the securities.

14. A company may issue convertible bonds to obtain a lower interest rate.

15. If a default occurs, the lender may demand repayment of the debt prior to maturity.

CHAPTER 14:
Financial Risk Management

1. Financial risk management involves the identification, measurement, hedging and monitoring of risk stemming from changing interest rates, FX rates and/or commodity prices. Management of financial risk is important because it impacts the value of the company.

2. The four steps of financial risk management involve: 1) identifying the exposure, 2) measuring the exposure, 3) implementing an appropriate risk management strategy and 4) monitoring the exposure and evaluating the strategy.

3. The risk profile of a company demonstrates graphically how the value of the company is impacted by unexpected changes in a financial price variable such as interest rates, exchange rates or commodity prices. The risk profile of a company that does not hedge is either positively sloped or negatively sloped. The risk profile of a hedged company is horizontal.

4. Risk management helps reduce the variability of a company's future cash flows, which in turn adds value to the company.

5. Hedging is typically defined as utilizing financial instruments or contracts to reduce or eliminate the risk from future changes in rates or prices. The purpose of speculation, in contrast, is to profit from a change in a future rate or price. Arbitrage is the process of buying in one market and simultaneously selling in another in order to earn a riskless profit.

6. The four basic types of contracts or instruments used in financial risk management are forwards, futures, swaps and options.

7. A derivative is a financial product that derives value from some underlying asset.

8. Though futures are similar in purpose to forwards, there are several important differences:

    - Futures are based on standardized contracts, with standard underlying assets.

    - Futures are normally bought and traded on organized exchanges and require both margin accounts and instant adjustment of the value of the future to the market.

    - The existence of margin accounts on futures allows investors in the market to benefit from leverage on their holding of futures.

    - Futures are rarely settled by actual delivery of the underlying assets and normally are closed out prior to their maturity

9. The primary types of interest rate exposure are from falling rates and rising rates.

10. Caps, floors and collars are option-like instruments that allow companies to benefit from the low cost of adjustable-rate financing while protecting themselves against interest rate movements.

11. Transaction exposure is the exposure of balance sheet accounts such as accounts receivable, accounts payable or loans to a change in FX rates between the time a transaction is recorded and the time it is paid. Companies with foreign subsidiaries are exposed to translation exposure when the subsidiary's financial statements are converted (translated) into the parent company's home currency for consolidation purposes.

12. In using an interest rate swap, a company desiring a floating-rate investment but with a comparative advantage in the fixed-rate market can invest in a fixed-rate investment and contract with a counterparty to pay the counterparty a fixed-rate return in exchange for a floating-rate return.

13. In using a futures contract, a company selling oil may wish to hedge the futures price by selling a futures contract. The company can deliver the oil at the price the contract was sold for if the expiration date of the contract matches the delivery date of the oil. If not, the contract can be bought back prior to expiration and then the oil sold at the prevailing market price. If the commodity price has decreased, the price of the futures contract will have also decreased and a profit will be made on the futures contract transaction. This profit can be used to offset the price decline in the commodity market.

14. The two basic types of commodity exposure are price exposure and delivery exposure.

15. The primary accounting issues related to hedging deal with disclosure of information about the use of derivatives. In addition, hedge accounting is a technique that is applied to the components of a hedge so that the fair value of the hedged asset and the hedging vehicle are included in earnings for the same period.

16. The primary tax issues related to hedging transactions deal with whether the gains/losses on a hedge should be treated as ordinary gains/losses or capital gains/losses.

CHAPTER 15:
International Treasury Management

1. International treasury management is becoming increasingly important due to the increased globalization of business, increased competition in the domestic marketplace and the need for cash management services on a global basis.

2. The key characteristics in which international banking systems differ are the following:
   - Central bank operations
   - Bank and company relationships
   - Number of banks and branching
   - Restrictions on corporate demand deposit accounts
   - Value dating
   - Overdrafts on corporate demand deposits

3. In most countries other than the United States, banks use value dating as compensation for services provided to their customers. Under a value dating system, the bank sets the dates upon which it grants credit for deposits or it debits the account for checks written.

4. A payee receiving a check from a foreign country must get the check back to the bank upon which it is drawn. This process of clearing of checks between countries is often a slow, complicated and expensive process. Intercountry checks generally clear as collection items that must be presented back to the bank in the country where they were drawn.

5. Check clearing processes vary significantly from country to country. Some countries have nationwide clearing; others do not. The clearing of checks may be accomplished by the central bank (as the Fed does in the United States), by several of the major banks acting as clearing agents or by correspondent relationships between different banks. Other differences include the significant use of electronic payments for both corporate and consumer payments.

6. Pooling is the practice of allowing excess balances in the accounts of some subsidiaries to be used to offset deficits in the accounts of other subsidiaries.

7. Multicurrency accounts are a special arrangement between a bank and its corporate customer whereby the bank allows the customer to receive or make international payments in a range of currencies from a single account.

8. A netting system reduces the number of FX transactions and therefore lowers the transaction cost. There is favorable pricing for larger FX transactions and cash forecasting is improved. Netting can eliminate float and result in greater certainty regarding value dating.

9. A re-invoicing center is a company-owned subsidiary that buys goods from the exporter and sells goods to the importer. Each party conducts the transaction in its own currency. Unlike a re-invoicing center, internal factoring does not involve a title transfer of goods. Internal factoring involves the purchase and collection of accounts receivables between subsidiaries.

10. A letter of credit substitutes a bank's credit for that of the buyer. Consequently, it eliminates the risk of non-payment to the seller.

11. An irrevocable letter of credit requires the issuing bank to honor all drafts presented by the seller as long as all necessary documentation is provided.

12. A standby letter of credit states that a bank will pay the beneficiary upon presentation of a signed statement by the beneficiary that the bank's customer has not fulfilled the terms of the contract.

13. Banks under a documentary collection do not assume credit risk but act only as agents in the collection process.

14. Countertrade is a method of payment in which a purchaser in a country with an insufficient amount of hard currency agrees to exchange merchandise that can be sold elsewhere by the seller to obtain payment in the required hard currency.

15. To be eligible for discount at the Federal Reserve, a banker's acceptance may not have a maturity of more than 180 days.

16. The Export-Import Bank of the United States (Eximbank) is an independent agency of the U.S. government established to finance and guarantee U.S. export loans.

17. A company may seek offshore financing in order to:
    - Diversify its funding sources
    - Hedge foreign currency assets, thereby reducing translation exposure
    - Lower borrowing rates for its parent company
    - Lower borrowing rates for foreign subsidiaries
    - Gain tax advantages

CHAPTER 16:
Relationship Management

1. The major objectives of relationship management include:
   - Access to credit
   - Access to non-credit services
   - Managing costs and quality
   - Monitoring financial institution risk
   - Development of a partnership approach

2. The criteria for selecting service providers include:
   - Knowledge of a specific industry or business
   - Responsiveness to questions asked in the selection process and understanding of the company's needs and objectives
   - Quality of customer service
   - Pricing of services
   - Willingness to provide credit on flexible terms and at competitive rates
   - Ability to provide financial advice or consulting services
   - Financial strength of service provider
   - Commitment to a company, industry or service
   - Quality and expertise of relationship managers and technical specialists
   - Ability to customize services and develop new services
   - Geographic and other convenience considerations
   - Ability to meet future needs of the company

3. The six components commonly used to measure a depository financial institution's strength are referred to as a CAMELS rating. CAMELS is an acronym for Capital adequacy, Asset quality, Management capability, Earnings, Liquidity and Sensitivity to market risk.

4. A company will want to optimize the number of financial institutions with which it has a relationship because there are internal and external costs for each relationship. As a result, there is an incentive to avoid having more relationships than are necessary.

5. Among the major documents associated with a financial institution relationship are the account resolution, signature cards, terms and conditions and service agreements.

6. Among the audit and control issues facing a company in managing its financial institution relationships are the following:

    - Establishing and updating policies and procedures for opening accounts that cover such matters as:
        — Approval required for opening accounts
        — Corporate resolution(s)
        — Individuals authorized to open accounts or contract for services
        — Individuals authorized as signatories
    - Timely reconciliation of accounts and timely reporting of problems and exceptions. Under UCC Article 4, a company has 30 days to report any unauthorized activities. This time frame can be extended by agreement between both parties.
    - A clear separation of transaction initiation, accounting and reconciliation duties
    - Maintenance of account documentation and record keeping, including corporate resolutions, contracts for services and signatories on accounts
    - Tracking of unresolved discrepancies

7. A service provider report card often includes the following items:
    - Number of errors by service
    - Reporting times for information services
    - Responsiveness to questions
    - Timeliness of error resolution
    - Effectiveness of personnel

8. Among the factors that increase the success and profitability of a relationship for both parties are the following:
    - Open and frequent two-way communications, both formal and informal
    - Regular and timely feedback, both formal and informal
    - Clear expectations as established by letters of agreement and legal contracts
    - Fair compensation of the financial institution by the company and fair pric-

ing of services by the financial institution

- Complete disclosure by both parties of information that is essential to the success and ethical basis of the relationship

9. The account analysis statement is a bank's paper or electronic report to its commercial customers of services provided, volumes processed and charges assessed. It is essentially an invoice. Services and charges can be detailed and itemized bundled into a single line term or some combination of the two.

10. The basic product families of AFP service codes for account analysis include the following:

    - Lockbox Services (05)
    - Depository Services (10)
    - Paper Disbursement Services (15)
    - General ACH Services (25)

11. The average collected balance required to compensate the bank for services used is computed as follows:

$$\text{Collected Balances Required} = \frac{\text{Monthly Service Charges}}{\left(\text{Earnings Credit Rate} \times \frac{\text{Days in Month}}{365}\right) \times (1 - \text{Reserve Requirement})}$$

$$= \frac{\$4,000}{\left(.06 \times \frac{30}{365}\right) \times (1 - .10)} = \frac{\$4,000}{.0044383} = \$901,246$$

12. Given the information in this problem, the earnings credit can be calculated as follows:

$$\text{Earnings Credit} = \text{Collected Balances} \times (1 - \text{Reserve Requirement}) \times \left(\text{Earnings Credit Rate} \times \frac{\text{Days in Month}}{365}\right)$$

$$= (\$100,000 - \$19,000) \times (1 - .10) \times \left(.06 \times \frac{30}{365}\right) = \$81,000 \times .90 \times (.0049315) = \$359.50$$

In this example, the earnings credit of $359.50 is not sufficient to cover the $650 of bank services for the month. The company will owe the bank $290.50.

13. Service charges may be bundled or unbundled. Bundling is the practice of charging for a group of related services. Unbundling is charging individually for each service used.

14. Financial institutions may allow companies to pay for services in fees, balances or a combination of both.

15. The major factors favoring fee compensation from the company perspective are the following:

    - A company can generally earn more interest on its investments than a financial institution pays on collected balances.

    - Fees can be budgeted and compared with other costs, while balances are not as directly comparable.

Index

Index